BRIT GUIDE

NEW YORK

2011

NEW YORK

2011

Amanda Statham

foulsham
LONDON • NEW YORK • TORONTO • SYDNEY

foulsham

The Oriel, Thames Valley Court, 183–187 Bath Road, Slough,
Berkshire, SL1 4AA, England

Foulsham books can be found in all good bookshops and direct from
www.foulsham.com

ISBN: 978-0-572-03598-3

Copyright © 2011 W. Foulsham & Co. Ltd

Cover photographs © Getty Images

Maps by PC Graphics (UK) Limited

A CIP record for this book is available from the British Library

The moral right of the author has been asserted

While every effort has been made to ensure the accuracy of all the
information contained within this book, neither the author nor the
publisher can be liable for any errors. In particular, since prices, times
and any hotel, holiday or venue details tend to change frequently, it is
vital that each individual checks relevant information for him or herself.

Look out for the latest editions in this series:
Brit Guide to Orlando and Walt Disney World, Simon and Susan Veness
Brit Guide to Disneyland Resort Paris, Simon and Susan Veness
Brit Guide to Las Vegas, Karen Marchbank with Jane Anderson
Brit Guide Which Ski Resort? – Europe

Printed in Italy by L.E.G.O. SpA.

Contents

Acknowledgements

With grateful thanks for all their help to Anna Catchpole at Hillsbalfour Synergy PR, which represents NYC & Co in the UK. All at NYC Visit.com, Niagara Falls Convention and Visitors Bureau and the New York State Department of Economic Development.

Thanks also to the Lower East Side Tenement Museum, the Metropolitan Museum of Art, Ellis Island Immigration Museum, the Museum of Modern Art, the Museum of Jewish Heritage, the Whitney Museum of American Art, Intrepid Sea-Air-Space Museum, the Frick Collection, the Skyscraper Museum, the National Museum of the American Indian, the Children's Museum of Manhattan, the Empire State Building, the American Museum of Natural History, the New York Stock Exchange, the Brooklyn Museum of Art, NY Waterways, the Sex And The City Tour, Harlem Spirituals, the Big Apple Greeters, David Watkins and Ponycabs, the Queens Jazz Trail, Gangland Tours, Big Onion Walking Tours, Rabbi Beryl Epstein and the Hassidic Discovery Center, former NYPD cop Gary Gorman, Gray Line, Food Tours of Greenwich, The Ritz-Carlton at Battery Park, The Warwick, The Mark, Waldorf Astoria, Le Parker Meridien, The Marriott Marquis, The Wellington, The Doral, Le Cirque, The Bull & Bear, The View at the Marriot Marquis, American Park at the Battery, Serafina Fabulous Grill, The Boathouse, Picholine, Sylvia's Restaurant, The River Café, The Water Club, World Yacht Dining Cruise, Europa Grill, The 21 Club, Tavern on the Green, Zoe's Restaurant and ONE c.p.s.

Photograph Acknowledgements

5 Ninth 173 top; 60 Thompson 237; A Voce 172; Acappella 190; Adour 177; Agnés b 136; Alvim Gimarino 2, 92, 143; Amore Pacific 147; Armani Exchange 139; Arriba Arriba! 261; Asia Society 102; Avenue Q 216; Babbo 166 top; Barbetta 183 top; Battery Gardens 160; broadway.com 219, 220; Bronx Zoo 288; Browne House 291; Bryant Park Hotel 207; buddy don 123, 132, 216; C S Helsinki 258; Café Habana 185; Chassidic Discovery Center 88; Chatwal Hotel 252; Chelsea Savoy 254; Christopher Martin Hobson 8, 9, 10, 11, 12, 14, 15, 18, 19, 25, 30, 31, 32, 44, 47, 64, 65, 67, 68, 70, 73, 76, 77, 78, 80, 82, 83, 84, 85, 89, 97, 116, 125, 126, 141, 144, 161, 180, 202, 217, 224, 239, 243, 245, 256, 266, 269, 270, 271, 274, 275, 278, 290, 299, 300; Colin Bainbridge, (pbase.com) 37 bottom; Cooper-Hewitt National Design Museum 105; Cubby Hole 259 top; Dan Brekke 149; Daniel Boulud 175 top; David (picasaweb.com) 156; David Steinberg 121 top; eater.com 170; eatthisnewyork.com 183 bottom; El Malecon II 194; End Point Corporation 41; Fatty Crab 198 top; Four Seasons 180; fr.academia. ru 121 bottom; Gabrielle Taaffe 26, 91, 96; Gansevoort Park 229, 236; Garage Restaurant 262; gettingbydreamingbig.com 34; Gotham Hall 23; Greenwich Hotel 232 bottom; Heather Cross (about. com) 145 bottom; Hotel on Rivington 235; Hotel Wolcott 255; Hudson Cafeteria 188; Inn at Irving Place 233 bottom; Jacques Marchais Museum 295 top; Jake Dobkin (www.bluejake.com) 263; Joan Marcus 222 bottom; John Mariani 166 bottom; Joey Miller 210; joshandjosh.type (pad.com) 152; Kathryn Yu 164; Kitano Hotel 241; L'Atelier de Joel Robuchon 176; Le Bernadin 184 bottom; Le Cirque 180; Le Parker Meridien 177; Leonardo.com 226, 231, 238, 240, 246; Lindsey Cox and Lucy Zehme 155; Lois DeSocio (219mag.com) 203; London NYC 175; Lucky Strike 187; Macy's 139 top; Mama Mexico 181 top; Manhattan Oriental Hotel Group 208; Mario Burger (flickr.com) 24, 58, 86, 127, 276, 280; Mark Thomas 95; Mars 2112 189; meetnowlive.com 204; Metrony.com 260; Mick Hales/Metropolitan Museum of Art 104; MTA 64; Museum of American Finance 112; Museum of Jewish Heritage 114; Museum of Modern Art 115; Museum of the City of New York 113; museum. com 35; museumplanet.com 94; New Museum of Contemporary Art 117; New York Aquarium 287; New York Botanical Garden 289; New York City Ballet 265 bottom; New York City Transit Museum/ David Shankbone 286; New York Hall of Science 118; New York Palace 234; newyorkcitynails.com 145 top; NYC & Company Inc. 13, 16, 61, 66, 72, 79, 106, 109, 111, 159, 199, 205, 211, 221 top, 225, 259, 264, 265 top, 272 bottom, 277, 279, 283 top, 293 top, 294, 295 bottom; NYC & Company Inc./Darren McGee 110; NYC & Company Inc./Jeff Greenberg 21, 29, 37 top, 49, 62, 139 bottom, 146, 153, 186, 218, 221 bottom, 267; NYC & Company Inc./Jordon Gary 151; NYC & Company Inc./Ken Howard 98; nyc-architecture.com 40, 43; nyparks.org 99; Oasis Day Spa 148; officeoftourism.us 39; Orient Express/ Mark Moloy 173; Oyster Bar 181 bottom; Papomena 133; Peter Aaron/Esto for the Jewish Museum 108; Petrossian 198; Prospect Park 285; Queens County Farm Museum 293; rationalphilosphy.net 63; Red Cat 163; Ritz-Carlton Hotel 230; Rob Maurizi (flickr.com) 7, 90, 272 top; Rocco's Pastry Shop 87; Rosewood Hotels and Resorts 228 top; Russian Tea Room 178; Saks 5th Avenue 128; Sapphire Lounge 215; Schomberg Center 119; Serafina Fabulous Grill 193; Simon Ho (simonho.org) 227, 279; Sofia Orlando 93; Sofitel 242; SoHo Grand 232 top; sothebyshomes.com 27; Staten Island Botanical Park 296; Steve Brickles 131, 134, 138, 140, 142, 150, 167, 168, 171, 174, 191, 206, 209, 257; Stitch 200; swellcityguide.com 195 bottom; Tribeca Grand 233 top; Union Square Wines and Spirits 154; Vega Transportation 17; Waldorf Towers 228; Webster Hall 213; Wellington Hotel 244; Whitney Museum 122; wikipedia.com 253; World Yacht 184 top; Yaffa Café 165; z.about.com 129, 137

Introduction

Welcome to the 2011 edition of the *Brit Guide to New York*, the guidebook that aims to be your very own personal tour guide to this amazing city.

We hope the guide will inspire you to want to visit the Big Apple again and again, for this is a city that really does capture the heart. Very few people visit once and don't return, simply because they're always left with the feeling that there's so much more to see and do. Once you've ticked the major sights off your list – such as the Empire State Building, Statue of Liberty and Central Park – you can start investigating the cosmopolitan neighbourhoods of the likes of SoHo, Greenwich Village and Chelsea and, in each new place you venture into, you'll discover a veritable treasure of shops, cafés, hotels and bars and witness the 'zoo' of residents going about their daily business.

45.6 million visitors from around the world visited the city in 2009, a major step towards New York City's Mayor Bloomberg's goal of attracting 50 million tourists by 2015. Of the visitors, 9.8 million hailed from overseas, with the UK as the Big Apple's biggest market. So what is it that makes us love this city so much?

One of the reasons is that we see it so often on television programmes and films like *Sex & The City 2*, that it already feels familiar to us. When you consider that there are around 40,000 location shoots per year in the city, including 100-plus TV shows and more than 250 feature films, it's little wonder that we feel an affinity with New York.

Another reason for its magnetism is that it is a relatively new city that is in a constant process of renewal, regeneration and regrowth. Quite simply, there's always something new to see and do. This year there is set to be a dizzying array of new hotel rooms, global cuisine, blockbuster Broadway shows, exceptional exhibitions and incomparable shopping. The record number of visitors flocking to the city proves that the insatiable demand for all things New York continues to climb, despite the recent recession.

CBS Building

THE NEW YORK STATE OF MIND

While New York is undoubtedly a melting pot of cultures and religions (Italians, Chinese, Jews, Africans, Irish and French to name but a few) there is one thing that unites everyone living in this cosmopolitan city: attitude. Resident New Yorkers are a breed unto themselves, unlike other American states where you're constantly instructed to 'have a nice day', they're not prone to saccharine sweetness. Here's how to spot a genuine New Yorker: on face value, they tend to have a sort of totally cheesed-off-with-the-world, don't-mess-with-me look. They also speak incredibly quickly as if they were eating their own words, so it can be hard to understand them.

Scratch the surface, though, and you just have your ordinary, everyday kind of person with the same kind of worries, fears and doubts as the rest of us. We've discovered two things that work a treat: firstly, smiling like mad and being genuinely polite; secondly, the British accent. You can see them looking at you askance when you smile (smile? Who on earth does that in New York?), but then deciding that you must be one of those British eccentrics they've heard about. It does the trick, though, because more often than not they'll respond in a helpful way.

And don't go thinking that all New Yorkers will tell you to f*** off if you ask for directions. Many are happy to help and we've even had people stop to help us work out where we're going when they've spotted us studying a map. This heady mix of rudeness and helpfulness is no better demonstrated than in the following anecdote from New York author Douglas Kennedy:

'On a crosstown bus I noticed two visitors from Japan having difficulty with the exact change for the fare,' he recounts. 'The driver, an overweight guy with a scowl, started giving them a hard time. "Like can't you read English or what?" he said loudly. "It says a buck-fifty. Surely they teach you how to count in Japan."

'The Japanese looked as if they wanted to commit hara-kiri on the spot until an elegantly dressed woman in her late sixties seated opposite the door came to their defence. Out of nowhere she turned to the driver and said: "Hey asshole, be polite."'

BRITTIP
If you do want to pay your respects at Ground Zero, this is also an ideal place from which to visit Wall Street and the Statue of Liberty, so give yourself time to explore Lower Manhattan.

Trump Tower

It's typical of the spirit of this vibrant, beautiful city that it has come back stronger than ever before; foreign visitors from all over the world continue to pour into the Big Apple, trade is booming and it's brimming with life and excitement whichever neighbourhood you venture into. Last year, the city became the number one destination in terms of tourism spending in the United States, with more than $30 billion spent.

PLANNING YOUR HOLIDAY

One of New York's greatest charms is its cosmopolitan nature, its hugely diverse ethnic mix. In this city you will find any type of cuisine, often available at any time of the day or night. Where music is concerned, everything from jazz and R&B to techno and rap is out there on any night of the week and the many nightclubs are among the hottest and most stylish of any in the world.

BRITTIP
If you really want to get an insight into how a New Yorker thinks, log on to *The New York Times* website nytimes.com, and read the Metropolitan Diaries, stories of city life supplied by the locals.

The drawback is that it may seem a bit overwhelming and it doesn't help that everyone gives the impression of being in the biggest hurry. But beneath their ice-cool veneer, you'll find people willing to answer questions or offer help.

In this book, we hope not only to provide all the information you need about the sights, sounds and attractions, but also to give an insight into what makes the city tick and how to get the most out of it. The book is filled with tips and insider information, but we are always happy to receive new suggestions by email at amandastatham@natmags.co.uk.

Once you have decided to go to New York, you need to work out what you want to do there, otherwise you could end up wasting a lot of valuable time. The city is so big and diverse and everyone's tastes are so different that each visit to New York is a unique experience. Are you a museum buff? Want to see a great Broadway show and some of the outstanding sights of the city? Your priorities will reflect not only your tastes, but also whether it is your first visit to the Big Apple, or whether you are becoming an old friend, as well as the time you have available. Whatever the case, the key to making the most of your time is in the planning.

The thing we emphasise most is the importance of location. When you fly into New York, seeing all the skyscrapers from your lofty perch makes Manhattan look pretty small, but do not be fooled by this. It is a narrow island, but it's longer than it looks from the air – 21km/13mls in fact – so don't be duped into believing it is easy to walk from Downtown to the Upper East Side. Nothing could be further from the truth.

It's also the case that the city's subway is

The Statue of Liberty

HOW TO USE YOUR GUIDEBOOK

We've tried to help you with your choices in as many ways as possible.

- The top sights and museums are listed in alphabetical order so you can go straight to the ones you will most likely want to see.

- In each case the area they are in has been specified – again to help you plan your day.

- Look out for our 'Top 5s', which are scattered throughout the chapters. They give you instant snippets of information – for example, the best restaurants with an outside garden area, or the 5 best shops for accessories – and provide you with some insider knowledge.

- The same is true for our Brit Tips – facts and advice that you probably won't find elsewhere.

- Plus, enjoy our New Yorker In The Know tips. I've asked people living and working in the city to share their favourite spots with us, which has uncovered some real gems. Look out for these as they're scattered throughout the book and if you want to feel like a true New Yorker, hunt them out while you're there.

- The self-guide walks in Chapter 4 have proved popular. If you try them, do let us know what you think and whether you'd like longer ones, plus some walking guides into the Outer Boroughs, too.

- If you are short of time, look out for One Day in New York on page 95 – which suggests my ideas on the best choices for a 24-hour trip.

- The chapters are designed around what most tourists want to do: take in a Broadway show (see page 217); choose from an eclectic range of excellent restaurants from our alphabetical area guide (see page 159); find their way around the different neighbourhoods and get the most out of what each one offers (see page 25).

- Since location is so vital, we recommend choosing your hotel in the area of the city in which you plan to spend most of your time. That way you can reduce the time and money you spend on getting around. Unless, of course, the hotel is the reason you're travelling to the city; for some people the experience of staying in exclusive accommodation such as The Waldorf is worth a visit to NYC before they've even thought about sightseeing.

We've tried to include everything we believe the average Brit will be interested in visiting in New York, but if you come across a sight, museum, shop, gallery, coffee shop, club, hotel or restaurant not in this book that you think is worth including, email us at amanda@mrhoppy. freeserve.co.uk.

Finally, we'd just like to wish you a wonderful trip to one of the greatest cities in the world.

The Woolworth Building

nowhere near as fast as our much-maligned London underground, nor is it that good for getting from east to west or vice versa. That means using buses is often the better option and they, like taxis, can get stuck in heavy traffic. So, when planning your activities for the day, it is a good idea to stick to one particular area so that walking everywhere – the best way to see the city – won't be so tiring.

Most New York trips are for between two and seven days. For the former, it's like dipping your toes in the water; for the latter it's a big commitment to getting to know the city. Regardless of how many days you have, though, you won't be able to see everything, so you'll need to be selective.

CHAPTER 1

Knowing New York

So what is New York all about? Due to the vast number of movies set in different periods of the city's history, many of the key people in its history, sights and areas are familiar to us Brits, though you may be a little hazy as to their whereabouts or true influence.

A BRIEF HISTORY OF NEW YORK

The great story of New York started in 1524 when Florentine Giovanni da Verrazano arrived on the island now known as Manhattan. It was a mixture of marshes, woodland, rivers and meadows, and was home to the Algonquin and Iroquois tribes of Native Americans.

No one settled on the island, though, until British explorer Henry Hudson arrived in 1609. Working for the Dutch West India Company, he discovered Indians who were happy to trade in furs, skins, birds and fruit. In 1613, a trading post was set up at Fort Nassau, and by 1624 the Dutch West India Company was given the right to govern the area by the Dutch government.

Dutch settlers soon began to arrive; Manhattan was named New Amsterdam and governor Peter Minuit bought the island for $24-worth of trinkets and blankets. Peaceful relations between the Europeans and Native Americans were disturbed by the settlers' insistence on taking over the land, and a costly and bloody war ensued, lasting two and a half years. Finally, Peter Stuyvesant was hired by the Dutch West India Company to restore peace.

Stuyvesant was an experienced colonialist and went about establishing a strong community with a proper infrastructure. One of the first things he did was to order the building of a defensive wall and ditch along what we know today as Wall Street. The new settlement prospered and even doubled in size, but Governor Stuyvesant was not well liked. He introduced new taxes, persecuted Jews and Quakers, and even limited the amount of alcohol people could drink. Trouble followed, and the locals became less and less inclined to obey him. By the time four British warships sailed into the harbour in late 1664, he had no alternative but to surrender to Colonel Richard Nichols without a shot being fired. The colony was immediately renamed New York in honour of the Duke of York, brother to the English king, and thereafter remained mostly in the hands of the British until the end of the American Revolution.

Top of the Rock Observation Deck

WHAT'S IN A NAME?

The Big Apple has become synonymous with New York City, but came into being during the 1920s when horse-racing writer John Fitzgerald popularised the term. On assignment in New Orleans for *The Morning Telegraph*, he overheard stablehands refer to New York City racing tracks as The Big Apple and decided to call his column on New York's racing scene 'Around the Big Apple'.

A decade later, jazz musicians adopted the term to refer to New York City. The favourite story of Big Onion tour guides is related to Small's Big Apple jazz club in Harlem. The story goes that when the musicians from the club went on tour around America they'd say to each other: "I'll see you in the Big Apple". But the term was still relatively unknown until it was adopted by the New York Convention and Visitors' Bureau in 1971, when they launched The Big Apple campaign.

Many New Yorkers also like to call the city Gotham – taken from the Batman stories that are based in Gotham City and believed by many to be a thinly veiled reference to New York. The name Manhattan is derived from Mannahatta, or 'land of many hills', the name given to the island by its first inhabitants, the Algonquin Indians.

By 1700, the population had reached 20,000 and it was already the rich melting-pot of cultures and religions that it remains today. In 1764, following the Seven Years War between the British and French, the Brits passed a number of laws, including the Stamp Act, allowing them to raise taxes in the colony. In response, Americans from all over the country banded together and rescinded Britain's right to collect taxes from them. In 1774, the Americans set up the Continental Congress, made up of representatives from each of the colonies. Later that year, those representatives urged all Americans to stop paying their taxes, and just two years later the Declaration of Independence was drawn up, largely by Jefferson.

During the War of Independence that inevitably followed, New York was considered strategically vital, as it stood between the New England colonies and those in the south. In 1776, British commander Lord Howe sailed 500 ships into the harbour and occupied the city. George Washington's army was defeated and forced to leave. The peace process began in 1779 and led to a treaty in 1783. The Brits, who had remained in New York since the end of the war, left just before George Washington returned to claim victory.

New York then became the country's first capital and George Washington its first president, taking his oath of office in 1789. The city was capital for just one year, but business boomed. The New York Stock Exchange, established under a tree on Wall Street by Alexander Hamilton in 1792, positively buzzed with activity as new companies were set up, bought and sold.

As the city grew, it became clear that a proper infrastructure and sanitation system was needed, so the governors introduced a grid system throughout the entire island.

North of 14th Street, it abandoned all the existing roads except for Broadway, which followed an old Indian trail, and set up wide avenues that ran south to north and streets that ran between the rivers.

THE RICH GET RICHER...

By 1818, reliable shipping services between New York and other American cities and Europe were well established and trade was booming. It was boosted further by the opening of the Erie Canal in 1825, which, together with the new railroads, opened trade routes to the Midwest. With so much spare cash to play with, businessmen started to build large summer estates and mansions along 5th Avenue up to Madison Square. At the same time, many charities and philanthropic institutions were set up and great libraries were built, as education was seen as being very important.

But the divide between rich and poor was getting wider. While water supplies, indoor plumbing and central heating were being installed in the 5th Avenue mansions, thousands of immigrant families – particularly from Ireland – had no choice but to live in the appalling tenement buildings that were being erected on the Lower East Side of Manhattan.

The impending Civil War over the question of slavery became a major issue for the poor of New York, who couldn't afford to buy their way out of conscription. Uppermost in their minds was the concern that freed slaves would be going after their jobs. The fear reached fever pitch and led to America's worst-ever riot, a four-day-long affair in which over 100 people died and thousands, mostly blacks, were injured. By 1865, however, the abolitionists won the war, finally freeing 4 million black people from the plight of slavery.

TOP 5 BOOKS ON NEW YORK HISTORY

Herbert Asbury: *The Gangs of New York; An Informal History of the Underworld*, Arrow Books (2003)

Sanna Feirstein: *Naming New York, Manhattan Places and How They Got Their Names*, New York University Press (2000)

Kenneth T Jackson: *The Encyclopedia of New York City*, Yale University Press (1995)

Mike Wallace and Edwin G Burrows: *Gotham: A History of New York City to 1898*, Oxford University Press Inc. USA (1999)

Shaun O'Connell: *Remarkable, Unspeakable New York*, Beacon Press (1997)

At the same time, New York and Boston were being hit by great tidal waves of immigrants. In the 1840s and 1850s it was the Irish fleeing famine; in the 1860s it was the Germans fleeing persecution; and in the 1870s it was the Chinese, brought into America specifically to build the railroads. In the 1880s it was the turn of the Russians, along with 1.5 million Eastern European Jews. Over 8 million immigrants went through Castle Clinton in Battery Park between 1855 and 1890. Then the Ellis Island centre was built in 1892 and handled double that number. Between 1880 and 1910, 17 million immigrants passed through the city and, by 1900, the population had reached 3.4 million.

Most of the new arrivals who chose to stay in New York ended up in the crowded tenements of the Lower East Side. Finally, in 1879, after the terrible conditions were brought to light, the city passed new housing laws requiring landlords to increase water supplies and toilets, install fire escapes and build air shafts between buildings to let in air and light. The introduction of streetcars and elevated railways also helped to alleviate the transport problem.

THE GILDED AGE

Meanwhile, the wealthy were enjoying the Gilded Age, as Mark Twain dubbed it. Central Park opened in 1858 and more and more mansions were built on 5th Avenue for the likes of the Whitneys, Vanderbilts and Astors. Row houses were also being built on the Upper West Side for wealthy European immigrants. Henry Frick, who made his fortune in steel and the railroads, built a mansion (now a museum) on the east side of the park at 70th Street, just 10 blocks from the new Metropolitan Museum of Art. Luxury hotels such as the original Waldorf Astoria and the Plaza opened, as did the original Metropolitan Opera House. The Statue of Liberty, St Patrick's Cathedral, the Brooklyn Bridge and Carnegie Hall were all built at this time.

Those were the days of the people whose names we associate with New York but don't necessarily know why: like Cornelius Vanderbilt, a shipping and railroad magnate; Andrew Carnegie, a steel and railroad baron; and John D Rockefeller, who made his millions in oil. The names of many of these millionaires live on in the gifts they gave back to the city: they provided concert halls, libraries and art museums, and donated entire collections to put in them. Carnegie built and donated Carnegie Hall to the city, Rockefeller was one of three major backers behind the opening of the Museum of Modern Art, and the Whitneys created a museum containing their own collection of modern American works of art.

The turn of the century also saw the birth of another phenomenon – the skyscraper. First to be built was the Flatiron Building in 1902, which was constructed using the new technology for the mass production of cast iron. Frank Woolworth's Gothic structure followed in 1913. The beautiful Chrysler Building went up in 1929 and the Empire State Building was completed in 1931.

PROHIBITION ARRIVES

The Volstead Act of 1919 banned the sale of alcohol at the start of the Roaring Twenties. Fuelled by lively speakeasies, illegal booze, gangsters, the Charleston and jazz, this was the real heyday of famous venues like Harlem's Cotton Club and the Apollo Theater. After several glittering years, the fun and frolics came to an abrupt end with the

Solomon R Guggenheim Museum

USEFUL WEBSITES

All website addresses are preceded by 'www'.

cityguideny.com The online site of the weekly City Guide that is provided to hotels, with all the latest events, activities, etc.

newyork.citysearch.com Packed with information on New York, events and what's happening.

clubplanet.com Complete list of what's cool, where and why; the final word on nightlife.

manhattanusersguide.com The insider's guide to what's going on where.

downtownny.com Directory of places to visit in Downtown.

nyc.gov Comprehensive information about the city's services.

nyctourist.com An official tourism site for the city.

nycgo.com The New York Convention and Visitors' Bureau's comprehensive listing includes suggested itineraries for where to stay and shop and what to do.

nymag.com The latest information on city news, politics, restaurants, bars, clubs and entertainment.

nytab.com The New York Travel Advisory Bureau's site is helpful for trip planning and gives information on major savings.

newyorkology.com Everything from arrivology to technology!

nytimes.com The *New York Times* website.

villagevoice.com The *Village Voice* website.

collapse of the Wall Street stock market on 29 October 1929. It destroyed most small investors and led to huge unemployment and poverty across the whole of America. Things started to improve only after President Franklin D Roosevelt introduced the New Deal, employing people to build new roads, houses and parks.

Washington Memorial Arch

In New York, Fiorello LaGuardia (pronounced La-gwar-dia), was elected mayor and set up his austerity programme to enable the city to claw its way back to financial security. During his 12 years in office, LaGuardia worked hard at fighting corruption and organised crime, and introduced a massive public housing project.

◀▷ BRITTIP

One of the most famous speakeasies during Prohibition was Jack & Charlies 21. You can visit it today as the rather more respectable 21 Club at 21 West 52nd Street (Tel 212-582 7200, 21club.com).

These were also the days of a great literary and artistic scene in the city. Giants of the spoken and written word, including Dorothy Parker and George Kaufman, would meet at the famous Round Table of the Algonquin Hotel, where they were joined by stage and screen legends Tallulah Bankhead, Douglas Fairbanks and the Marx Brothers.

The Second World War was another watershed for New York, as people fled war-ravaged Europe and headed for the metropolis. Both during and after the war, huge new waves of immigrants arrived, fleeing first the Nazis and then the Communists. New York was as affected by McCarthy's hunt for 'reds' among the

BEAT IT

The 1950s Beat Movement was a partly social, partly literary phenomenon with three centres – Greenwich Village in New York, the North Beach district of San Francisco, and Venice West in Los Angeles. Socially, the movement was all about rejecting middle-class values and commercialism and embracing poverty, individualism and release through jazz, sexual experience and drugs. The term 'beat' conveys not only the American connotations of being worn-out and exhausted, but also suggests 'beatitude' or 'blessedness'. The chief spokesmen were Allen Ginsberg, Jack Kerouac, whose most famous novel is *On The Road*, Gregory Corso, William S. Burroughs, Lawrence Ferlinghetti and Gary Snyder.

cultural and intellectual elite as was the rest of the country, but it bounced back when a new building boom followed the election of President Harry S Truman, whose policies were aimed specifically at helping the poor.

The Port Authority Bus Terminal was finished in 1950, the mammoth United Nations Headquarters was completed in 1953, and in 1959 work started on the huge Lincoln Center complex – built on the slums of the San Juan district that were the setting for *West Side Story*.

By the 1950s, a new period of affluence had started for the middle classes of New York. The descendants of the earlier Irish, Italian and Jewish immigrants moved out to the new towns outside Manhattan, leaving space for a new wave of immigrants from Puerto Rico and the southern US. It was also the decade of the Beat generation, epitomised by Jack Kerouac and Allen Ginsberg, which evolved into the 1960s hippy culture. This was when Greenwich Village became the centre of a new wave of artists extolling the virtues of equality for all.

By the 1970s, however, this laissez-faire attitude, coupled with New York's position as a major gateway for illegal drug importation and the general demoralisation of the working classes and ethnic groups, led to an escalation in crime. Muggings and murder were rampant, and the city was brought to the brink of bankruptcy.

Chaos was averted only by the introduction of austerity measures, which unfortunately primarily affected the poor. But new mayor Ed Koch implemented major tax incentives to rejuvenate New York's business community. A boom followed, reflected in the erection of a series of mammoth new skyscrapers, including the World Trade Center and Trump Tower.

The transformation was completed in the 1990s with Mayor Giuliani's clean-up operation. This was unpopular with the more liberal New Yorkers, but many believe it was his policies that turned New York into a city fit for the new millennium.

15

The UN Building from the Circle Line Ferry

AT-A-GLANCE HISTORY

1524	Giovanni da Verrazano arrives on Manhattan
1613	Trading post is set up at Fort Nassau
1624	Dutch West India Company establishes rule of New Amsterdam
1626	Peter Minuit buys Manhattan for trinkets worth $24
1664	Dutch surrender to the British and New Amsterdam is renamed New York
1776	War of Independence and battle for New York begins
1785	New York becomes the nation's capital
1792	New York Stock Exchange is founded
1811	Grid plan for Manhattan is introduced
1827	Slavery is officially abolished in New York
1858	Work on Central Park begins
1883	Brooklyn Bridge opens
1886	Statue of Liberty is built
1892	Ellis Island opens
1902	The Fuller (Flatiron) Building becomes the world's first skyscraper
1904	New York's first subway line opens
1919	Prohibition Act sees alcohol sales banned in New York
1923	Yankee Stadium opens
1929	New York stock market crashes
1931	Empire State Building opens
1950	United Nations building completed
1970	First New York City Marathon
1993	A terrorist bomb in the World Trade Center kills six and injures 1,000
1994	Rudy Giuliani appointed mayor and brings crime to an all-time low
2001	World Trade Center Twin Towers attacked by terrorists, killing 3,000

Most recently, the city has been known around the world for the dark day of 11 September 2001, when terrorists in two hijacked planes destroyed the twin towers of the World Trade Center and killed nearly 3,000 people. It's typical of the spirit of this vibrant city that it has come back even stronger than before. After all, from the time of the earliest immigrants, New York has represented a gateway to a new life: the American dream offered a future filled with happiness and success. And nowadays New York still draws in people in their thousands. After all, as the Sinatra song goes, 'If you can make it there, you'll make it anywhere.'

Brooklyn brownstone houses

THE BEST TIMES TO GO

Jan to Mar, and July and Aug are best for accommodation and good for flights. Just bear in mind that July and Aug are the hottest months, though it is not as bad as you might expect because all the shops and cabs have air-conditioning and you get blasts of cool air from the shops as you pass.

✠ BRITTIP

Log on to weather.gov for a 4-day prediction to make sure you've got the right clothes in your suitcase.

SEASONAL WEATHER

Month	Temp	Rainfall
Jan	-3–3°C (27–38°F)	8cm (3in)
Feb	-3–5°C (27–40°F)	8cm (3in)
Mar	1–9°C (34–49°F)	11cm (4¼in)
Apr	7–16°C (44–61°F)	10cm (4in)
May	12–22°C (53–72°F)	10cm (4in)
June	17–27°C (63–80°F)	8cm (3in)
July	20–29°C (68–85°F)	10cm (4in)
Aug	19–29°C (67–85°F)	10cm (4in)
Sep	16–25°C (60–77°F)	9cm (3½in)
Oct	10–19°C (50–66°F)	9cm (3½in)
Nov	5–12°C (41–54°F)	11cm (4¼in)
Dec	-1–6°C (31–42°F)	10cm (4in)

WHAT TO PACK

Layers are the key to comfortable clothes in New York, whatever time of year you go.

In summer the air-con in buildings can get pretty cold, while outside it is stiflingly hot. If you take a lightweight, rainproof jacket, you'll be covered for all eventualities. Natural fibres, like silk or cotton, in light shades are good for humidity and, of course, sun screen is essential.

In winter it is the other way round – warm buildings and cold streets – so it's best to have an overcoat of some sort, but nothing too heavy unless you're planning to be out of doors a lot. Also make sure you have a hat, scarf and gloves in your bag for times of emergency. At any time of the year, the skyscrapers of the city act as a kind of wind tunnel and unless you're in the sun it can get nippy pretty quickly – another reason to make sure you have a cardigan or lightweight jacket in the summer.

BRITTIP

To inspire kids aged 8 to 12 about their trip, get a copy of *Melanie in Manhattan* by Carol Weston (melaniemartin.com), a novel about a girl and her family travelling in the Big Apple. Or buy a copy of Disney's *Eloise at the Plaza* DVD.

NEW YORK FOR FAMILIES

New York is a great place to go with the family. Towering skyscrapers, mammoth bridges, vast parks, circuses and shows, bright lights and rows of shops packed with enticing kid-friendly products are enough on their own to keep children entertained. But there are plenty of other attractions to hunt out that can make a stay in NYC for the under 16s even more exciting. Central Park, for example, has a wealth of entertainment year-round, while some of the museums offer some real hands-on, fun activities. A word of warning: visiting any of the incredible children's stores with a real-life child in tow is likely to lead to credit card meltdown!

TOP 5 ATTRACTIONS FOR KIDS

Circle Line Sightseeing Cruise (page 85)

Statue of Liberty (page 67)

Empire State Building (page 69)

Times Square (page 48)

Central Park (pages 273–275)

DISABLED TRAVELLERS

New York is one of the easier destinations to tackle for disabled travellers – and certainly puts Britain to shame. Most of the road corners, for instance, have kerbs that dip to the ground, making it a lot easier to wheel yourself about the city. Again, for the wheelchair-bound, bus platforms can be lowered to the same level as the pavement to allow easy access and, where possible, some of the subway stations have had elevators installed. To find out which 59 stations are accessible to wheelchair passengers, check the MTA site mta.info. For up-to-date information on the accessibility status of lifts and escalators, call 718-596 8585/8273 (TTY) daily 6am–10pm. Access-A-Ride (AAR) is a 24-hour door-to-door shared ride service offered by them to people who are unable to use the subway or bus (877-337 2017 toll free or 718-393 4999/4259 (TTY) 7am–5pm for information and to reserve a trip). Proof of disability is needed. **Able-Ride** is a shared ride kerb-to-kerb bus service in New York State that disabled visitors can apply for (516-228 4000). Full details on both can be found at the MTA site.

If you'd like to travel in style, Vega Transportation (888-507 0500, vegatransportation.com) offers the luxury of a chauffeur-driven car for those in a wheelchair. You can rent a wheelchair on arrival (7-day, 24-hour service) from ScootAround (888-441 7575, scootaround.com). To make your life as easy as possible, here are the main organisations that deal with different aspects of travel for the disabled.

RESOURCES FOR THE DISABLED

Note: TDD or TTY = Telecommunications devices for the deaf.

Accessible NYC: 1-718 507 0500, accessiblenyc.org is a coalition of New York City businesses who work togeher to cater to travellers with disabilities.

Vega Transportation

Big Apple Greeter Access Coordinator:
1 Center Street, Room 2035, New York,
NY 10007, 212-669 8159, bigapplegreeter.
org. Has been running a disability Access
Programme since 1993. Will provide a free
tour guide for anyone with a disability.
Reserve 3–4 weeks ahead.

Hands On: Suite 7F, 159-00 Riverside Drive
West, 212-740 3087/TTY use relay 711, http://
handson.org. Provides accessibility to arts
and cultural events for the hard of hearing
through sign-interpreted performances and
a monthly cultural calendar of accessible
events.

Hospital Audiences Inc (HAI): 3rd Floor, 548
Broadway, 212-575 7676, hospaud.org has an
online access-for-all database that provides
comprehensive information on venue access,
toilet facilities and water fountains at a whole
range of cultural centres from theatres to
museums.

Their audio description service, Describe,
for people who are blind or visually impaired
includes Program Notes, which describe all
aspects of a show and staging on a CD you
can listen to before the performance. Also,
during a pause in the dialogue it transmits a
live audio description to audience members
who have a small receiver. Reservations for
both the tickets, which have to be bought
either through HAI or the theatre, and
receivers, which are provided free of charge,
must be made through HAI. Call Describe on
212-575 7676.

Lighthouse International: 111 East 59th
Street, 212-821 9200 (voice) or 212-821 9713
(TTY), lighthouse.org. Help and advice for blind
people living in or visiting the city.

New York Society for the Deaf: 817
Broadway at 12th Street, 212-777 3900,
fegs.org. Provides advice and information on
facilities for the deaf.

**Society for Accessible Travel and
Hospitality:** 347 5th Avenue, Suite 605,
NY10016, 212=447 7284, sath.org has been
a leader in this field for decades, raising
awareness of the needs of disabled travellers.

BRITTIP
Download more access
information from http://www.
nyc.gov/html/mopd/downloads/
pdf/access_ny_review_2006.pdf.

The Theater Access Program: TAP is
specifically for Broadway shows and is run
by the Theater Development Fund. Apply
online at tdf.org or email access@tdf.org.

Wall Street

Reservations for free infrared headsets or
neckloops for Broadway shows can be made
by calling Sound Associates. 424 West 45th
Street, 212-757 5679, soundassociates.com.

COMMUNICATIONS

The American ring tone is long and the
engaged tone is very short and high-pitched,
almost like a beep. Public phone booths can
be found all over the city. These booths are
coin or card operated, with prepaid cards
bought from drugstores, news-stands and
'candy stores' for international calls, ranging
from $5 to $100. To save you the bother,
many phones take credit cards. Toll-free calls
for booking lines or attractions when in New
York save on costs and are mentioned when
available. These start with the codes 800, 888,
866 and 877.

PHONES

To call New York from abroad: Dial 001
and the prefix – for instance, the main prefix
for Manhattan is 212 – then dial the 7-digit
number. The code for Brooklyn, Queens, The

BRITTIP
Make sure your mobile
phone has Tri-Band and that
you've told your phone operator;
otherwise it may not operate in the
US. Also, make sure your mobile
call plan covers calls and texts from
foreign countries; otherwise you'll be
charged a fortune!

Bronx and Staten Island are 718 and 347. Mobile phones usually use the 917 prefix.

To call abroad from New York: Dial 011 + country code + area code (dropping the first 0) + local number. The code for Britain is 44.

To call any number in New York from New York: Dial 1 + the area code + the number.

Useful numbers

Operator: 0

Directory enquiries: 411 (free from payphones)

Long-distance directory enquiries: 1 + area code + 555 1212

Free numbers directory: 1 + 800 + 555 1212 (no charge)

POST

You can buy stamps (first class stamps are 41c each) in shops – the Duane Reade chain of chemists has machines – but there is a mark-up. If you don't want to pay over the odds for the convenience of these stamps, then go to one of the many post offices dotted around the city (800-275 877, usps.com).

The main post office on 34th Street at 8th Avenue is a huge and beautiful Beaux Arts building. If the queues are long, you can buy stamps from the vending machines.

Post boxes are square, dark blue metal boxes about 1.2m/4ft tall with a rounded top that has a pull-down handle. They have a sign saying US Mail and a striking big American eagle logo on the side and can be found on street corners.

THE INTERNET

The internet revolution now means you can use your own laptop or BlackBerry all over the city, plus have access online in cafés, libraries and even bars. In fact, there are now thousands of WiFi spots in Manhattan including 178 in cafés, so you're going to be able to surf whenever you like!

WiFi Cafés

Abingdon Guest House/Brewbar Coffee: 327 West 11th Street between Greenwich and Washington Streets, 212-675-7365, abingdonguesthouse.com/brewbar.shtml.

Ace Bar: 531 East 5th Street between Avenue A and Avenue B, 212-979 8476, acebar.com.

Café 28: 245 5th Avenue New York, 212-686 7300. Subway 28th Street.

Housing Works Used Book Cafe: 126 Crosby Street between Houston and Prince Streets, 212-334 3324, housingworks.org/usedbookcafe.

Starbucks: 450 7th Avenue, 212-279 1122, starbucks.com. Subway L to 8th Avenue.

Libraries/shops with free internet access

Apple Store: 767 5th Avenue, 212-336 1440, apple.com. Free WiFi, workshops and demos.

Mid-Manhattan Library: 455 5th Avenue at 40th Street, 212-340 0849, nypl.org. Subway A, C, B, D, F, V to 42nd Street.

40 Lincoln Center Plaza: 212-870 1630, lincolncenter.org. Subway D, B, A, C to Columbus Circle 59th Street.

Internet cafés

easyEverything: 234 West 42nd Street between 7th and 8th Avenues, 212-398 0724, easyinternetcafe.com. Subway A, C, E, 1, 2, 3, 7, 9, N, R, S, B, D, F, Q to Port Authority/42nd Street/Times Square. Area: Theater District. Open 24 hours, the world's largest internet café, in the *Guinness Book of Records*, has 648 computers, plus scanners. Prices start at just $1 and it is open 7 days a week, 7am–1am.

Cybercafé: 250 West 49th Street between Broadway and 8th Avenue, 212-333 4109, cyber-cafe.com. Subway N, R, 1, 9, to 49th Street, A, C, E to 50th Street. Open 8.30am–11pm Mon–Fri and 11am–11pm Sat–Sun and costs $6.40 for half an hour on the internet.

Metropolitan Life Insurance Company

AMERICAN-SPEAK

It has often been said that the Brits and Americans are two races divided by a common language, and when you make an unexpected faux pas you'll certainly learn how true this is. So to help you on your way, here is a guide to American-speak.

General

English	American
Air hostess	Flight attendant
Anti-clockwise	Counterclockwise
At weekends	On weekends
Autumn	Fall
Behind	In back of
Camp bed	Cot
Cinema	Movie theatre
City/town centre	Downtown (not Lower Manhattan)
Coach	Bus
Cot	Crib
Diary (appointments)	Calendar
Diary (records)	Journal
Football	Soccer
From... to...	Through
Lift	Elevator
Long-distance call	Trunk call
Nappy	Diaper
Ordinary	Regular, normal
Paddling pool	Wading pool
Plaster	Band Aid
Post, postbox	Mail, mailbox
Pram, pushchair	Stroller
Receptionist	Desk clerk
Tap	Faucet
Toilet	Restroom (public) or bathroom (private)

BRITTIP
There are no ground floors in America; what we call the ground floor, they call the first floor. It may seem a silly point, but it can cause confusion!

Money

English	American
Banknote	Bill
Bill	Check or tab
Cashpoint/cash machine	ATM
Cheque	Check
1 dollar	Single
25 cents	Quarter
10 cents	Dime
5 cents	Nickel
1 cent	Penny

Food and drink

One of the biggest disappointments we had on our first trip to America was to order our breakfast eggs 'sunny-side up', only to end up with what seemed like a half-cooked egg! The Americans don't flick fat over the top of the egg when frying it, but turn it over to cook on both sides. So for eggs cooked on both sides but soft, order eggs 'over easy' and if you like yours well done, then ask for eggs 'over hard'.

There are plenty of other anomalies. Many standard American dishes come with a biscuit – which is a corn scone to us. Breakfast may also include grits, a porridge-like dish of ground, boiled corn, and hash browns – grated, fried potatoes. You'll find foods and food terms that are specific to New York on page 187.

English	American
Aubergine	Eggplant
Biscuit (savoury)	Cracker
Biscuit (sweet)	Cookie
Chick pea	Garbanzo bean
Chips	(French) fries
Choux bun	Cream puff
Clingfilm	Plastic wrap
Cornflour	Cornstarch
Courgette	Zucchini
Crayfish	Crawfish
Crisps	Chips
Crystallised	Candied
Cutlery	Silverware or place-setting
Demerara sugar	Light-brown sugar
Desiccated coconut	Shredded coconut
Digestive biscuit	Graham cracker
Double cream	Heavy cream
Essence (e.g. vanilla)	Extract or flavouring
Filled baguette	Sub or hero
Fillet (of meat/fish)	Filet
Fizzy drink	Soda
Golden syrup	Corn syrup
Grated, fried potatoes	Hash browns
Grilled	Broiled
Icing sugar	Powdered/confectioners' sugar
Jam	Jelly/conserve
Jelly	Jello
Ketchup	Catsup
King prawn	Shrimp
Main course	Entrée
Measure	Shot
Mince	Ground meat
Off-licence	Liquor store
Pastry case	Pie shell
Pips	Seeds (in fruit)
Plain/dark chocolate	Semi-sweet or unsweetened chocolate
Pumpkin	Squash

Scone	Biscuit
Shortcrust pastry	Pie dough
Single cream	Light cream
Soda water	Seltzer
Sorbet	Sherbet
Soya	Soy
Spirits	Liquor
Sponge fingers	Lady fingers
Spring onion	Scallion
Starter	Appetiser
Stoned (cherries, etc.)	Pitted
Sultanas	Golden raisins
Sweet shop	Candy store
Takeaway	To go
Tomato purée	Tomato paste
Water biscuit	Cracker

BRITTIP

New Yorkers may consider themselves broad-minded, but the average American might be shocked if you ask where the toilet is. Ask for the restroom in a public place and the bathroom if you're in someone's house!

Shopping

English	American
Braces	Suspenders
Bumbag	Fanny pack
Chemist	Drug store
Flip-flops	Thongs
Ground floor	First floor
Handbag	Purse
High street	Main street
Jumper	Sweater
Knickers	Panties
Muslin	Cheesecloth
Queue	Line, line up
Suspenders	Garters
Tights	Pantyhose
Till	Check-out
Trainers	Sneakers
Trousers	Pants
Underpants	Shorts, underwear
Vest	Undershirt
Waistcoat	Vest

Travelling around

English	American
Aerial	Antenna
Articulated truck	Semi
Bonnet	Hood
Boot	Trunk
Caravan	House trailer
Car park	Parking lot
Carriage (on a train)	Car
Crossroads/junction	Intersection
Dipswitch	Dimmer
Dual carriageway	Four-lane (or divided) highway

Flyover	Overpass
Give way	Yield
Jump lead	Jumper cables
Layby	Pull-off
Lorry	Truck
Manual transmission	Stickshift
Motorway	Highway, freeway, expressway
Pavement	Sidewalk
Request stop	Flag stop
Ring road	Beltway
Roundabout	Traffic circle
Slip road	Ramp
Subway	Pedestrian underpass
Turning	Turnoff
Underground	Subway
Walk	Hike
Wheel clamp	Denver boot
Windscreen	Windshield
Wing	Fender
Zebra crossing	Cross walk

BRITTIP

While you're at the NYC visitor centre, pick up a copy of the *NYC Guide*. It has up-to-date listings of Broadway shows, plus money-off coupons.

TOURIST INFORMATION

NYC & COMPANY CONVENTION & VISITORS' BUREAU

nycgo.com

London: 020 7367 0900 (line open Mon–Fri 9.30am–5.30pm).
New York City's official tourism agency – call to discuss any queries you have with the information officers or ask them to send you a Visitors' Guide.

New York: 810 7th Avenue at 53rd Street, 212-484 1222. Mon–Fri 8.30am–6pm; Sat and Sun 8.30am–5pm. Subway N, R, S, Q to 57th Street, B, D, E to 7th Avenue/53rd Street or 1, 9 to 50th Street/Rockefeller Center.

NYC&Co. Visitor Information Kiosk

NEW YORK TALK

Of course, in addition to the differences between American and Brit-speak, the locals have a dialect and phraseology all of their own, or slanguage as it's also known, and often talk so quickly that words run into each other. Here are just a few examples that you may well come across:

All right already: Stop it, that's enough!

Big one: A $1,000 bill

Bloomies: Bloomingdale's

Capeesh: Pronunciation of *capisce*, Italian for 'understand'

Cattle call: A theatre casting call

Dead soldier: Empty beer can or bottle

Do me a solid: Do me a favour

Don't jerk my chain: Don't fool with me

DPh: Damned fool, based on transposing PhD

Eighth Wonder of the World: Brooklyn Bridge

Finger: Pickpocket (also mechanic, dip, cannon, goniff or moll buzzer)

Fuggedaboduid: No way

Go to Jersey: An insult

Guppies: Gay yuppies

How awe ya? Typical greeting

In line: Stand in a queue

JAPs: Jewish American princesses

Jocks: Sporty types, after their straps

Mazuma: Slang for money

Meet me between the lions: A favourite meeting place: the lion statues at the New York Public Library

Met: The Metropolitan Opera House or the Metropolitan Museum

No problem: You're welcome

Nudnik or nudge: A persistently dull and boring person

On account: Because

Out in left field: Weird, unorthodox

Ozone: Very fresh, pure air

Shoot the works: Gamble or risk everything

Straphanger: Subway commuter

Suit: Businessman

Yard: Back garden

A state-of-the-art visitors' information centre in Midtown with touchscreen kiosks that provide up-to-date information on the city's attractions and events accompanied by a detailed map. There is also a cashpoint and a souvenir shop, plus an incredible range of brochures covering hotels, shops, museums, sights, tours and Broadway shows. There are also visitors' centres in Downtown, Chinatown, Harlem and the Financial District.

BRITTIP

Sign up for the NYC&Co newsletter, which is packed with great deals, recommendations and the latest events and is sent straight to your email inbox.

NEW YORK TRAVEL ADVISORY BUREAU

nytab.com

An independently run tourism agency, which is most famous for its own pocket guide to New York, the *NYPages*, and the NYCard, which gives discounts to hotels, museums and attractions – check the website for the latest update on all their available discounts. It also has downloadable walking maps and up-to-the-minute top picks.

LOST YOUR PASSPORT?

If you lose your passport or have any big problems, call the emergency number at the New York British Consulate on 212-745 0200 option 2, ukinusa.fco.gov.uk/en.

CURRENCY

The world is slowly emerging out of the global recession, which thankfully means the pound is getting stronger against the dollar (at the time of going to press) so we'll get a little more for our money. The exchange rate for the US dollar at the time of writing is around $1/£0.65, but this is fluctuating constantly (check xe.com for exchange rates before you go). UK banks' and travel agencies' rates vary, so shop around to find the best. Also check the commission – some will charge for both selling and buying back, but many will only charge once, so you can return unused dollars you bought from them free of charge. Travel agencies tend to compete with each other on rates and don't charge commission. The Post Office and Marks & Spencer do not charge commission.

BRITTIP

For a quick currency converter go to xe.com/ucc/, which also offers the latest exchange rates.

Some people use travellers' cheques, but it is often a real palaver to cash them, especially at banks in New York. Many banks simply won't take them, and if they do they'll need

TIPS ON TIPPING

You won't get a lunch, drink, ride or even a taxi door being opened for you without a tip being involved in America and it can add quite a lot to your overall expenses when you're on holiday. It's something that doesn't come naturally to us Brits, but you need to get used to it quickly.

Bartender: $1 a round.

Hotel doormen: $2–5 for hailing a cab.

Maid service: Around $5–10 per day when you leave your accommodation.

Porters: $2–5 per bag.

Taxi drivers: 15%, and if you travel by private car or limousine they'll automatically add 20% to the bill.

Waiters: General rule of thumb is 15–20%. The best way to work it out is to double the sales tax, which will come to 17%, and add a little more if you are very impressed.

Just remember, at a posh restaurant the tip alone can come to more than the price of a decent meal!

photo ID so you'll have to carry your passport around with you. Chase Bank, Manhattan has more than 400 branches and doesn't charge a fee for exchanging currencies. Visit chase. com to find a branch with full contact details, including phone numbers.

The alternative is to exchange a reasonable amount of cash in one hit to use for tips, buses and in cafés, then use your credit card as much as possible (the exchange rate is generally reasonable). If you need extra cash, make sure you know your PIN number for your credit card and you'll be able to use any of the many cashpoints (ATMs) around the city, for which there is usually a fee.

BRITTIP

You must have plenty of change and singles ($1 notes) as you'll be tipping everyone for everything, and you'll also need change for the buses.

DISCOUNT DIVAS

NYC & Co (nycvisit.com) in its Deals & Promotions section runs various money-off campaigns that cover restaurants, hotels, theatres and sightseeing tours. A good one is NYC Sunday Stays, where you can get up to 20–30% off room rates at some lovely hotels on a Sun night, plus upgrades and money off in restaurants plus complimentary breakfast.

Each year, the popular Summer Restaurant Week takes place for 2 weeks from mid-July when you can get 3-course meals at more than 150 of the city's top restaurants for around $25 (excluding tip, tax and drinks). Many restaurants also continue serving their prix-fixe lunches to the end of Aug. Establishments include Nobu, Union Square Café, Spice Market, 66, Blue Water Grill and Vento. For further information visit nycvisit.

com/restaurant week or phone either 1-800 NYC VISIT (toll-free within America) or 212-484 1222.

BRITTIP

Smoking is not allowed in taxis, buses or subways and banned in most indoor places. If you're gasping, there's a list of smoker-friendly restaurants, clubs and bars on http://newyork.citysearch.com.

TYING THE KNOT IN NEW YORK

If you're thinking about getting married in the city, then you've picked a top spot, because the Big Apple is one of the most popular places for Brits to marry abroad thanks to an abundance of romantic venues.

WHERE TO WED

There's no shortage of exceptional places to marry in New York, but it's best to get it all booked before you go. Most upmarket hotels will accommodate weddings, so be sure to contact the ones we've listed in our accommodation section (Chapter 10) for some of the best in town.

Grand Ballroom at Gotham Hall

BRITTIP

To get a better grasp of all the great NYC wedding venues check out the Great Places Directory, greatplacesdirectory.com, for ceremony and reception locations.

As well as hotels, other places you may want to investigate include Gotham Hall (1356 Broadway at 36th Street, 212-244 4300, gothamhallevents.com), a historic landmark in Midtown Manhattan that is a great venue for occasions such as weddings, holding from 25 to over 1,000 guests. There's also The Lighthouse and Pier Sixty at Chelsea Piers (23rd Street at 12th Avenue, 212-336 6144, piersixty.com) for an intimate affair to remember. Or how about New York Aquarium (610 Surf Avenue at West 8th Street, Coney Island, Brooklyn, 718-265 FISH, nyaquarium. com) for a more unusual spot?

For an outdoor ceremony, the obvious place is Central Park, and it's not difficult to organise. The Central Park Conservancy (212-310 6600, centralparknyc.org) grants the permits for wedding ceremonies and photography in venues throughout the park, including the lovely Conservatory Garden and Shakespeare Garden.

TOP 5 PLACES TO PROPOSE

Just in case you haven't got down on one knee yet, here are some of the most idyllic spots to ask for her (or his) hand:

- Top of the Empire State Building before sunset (page 69)
- By the boating lake in Central Park (page 273)
- In a helicopter flying over the city (page 82)
- The penthouse suite of the Four Seasons (page 232)
- A $10,000 Martini at the Algonquin Hotel (page 247) – it's a mix of vodka, vermouth, olive and ice, except that the ice is a sparkling diamond from the hotel's jeweller!

THE KNOW-HOW

For all the legal aspects of a wedding in New York, such as the minimum age, documentation and costs, contact the NYC Marriage Bureau (City Clerk of New York in Manhattan), Municipal Building, 1 Center Street, 2nd Floor South, NY 10007, 212-639 9675, cityclerk.nyc.gov.

The Boating Lake, Central Park

CHAPTER 2

New York Neighbourhoods

It's worth getting to know the neighbourhoods of Manhattan, as each one has a distinct flavour and is filled with its own unique sights and sounds. From the historic Downtown area of the Financial District to the charming cobbled streets of Greenwich Village and the vibrancy of Times Square, every one is well worth visiting in its own right.

Here's an outline of what you'll find in each neighbourhood, what makes them so special and how to make the most of your time there. They are placed in alphabetical order for ease of reference and each one has an at-a-glance table so you can coordinate your planning in districts.

34TH STREET

You'll have 2 major reasons for coming to this part of New York (Map 3) – the divine **Empire State Building** (page 69) and the shopping. **Macy's** is here (page 125), as well as a range of chains and most importantly a lot of retail outlets for the nearby Garment District. This was once a pretty seedy area, but thanks to the efforts of the 34th Street Business Improvement District Partnership (BID), it has been transformed.

Now the streets are constantly maintained, clean and lined with pretty flower tubs and green benches. The BID has even installed some smart green telephones with a semi-enclosure to block out some of the street noise. The kiosk at Herald Square is in matching green, as is the city's first automatic pay toilet next door. It's pretty swanky and, most importantly, it's clean! The size of the average New York bedroom, it's big enough to swing a cat in, should you wish to, and only costs 50 cents a visit!

If you plan to do the Empire State Building, make it your first port of call before the crowds and queues build up. Take the B, D, F, N, Q, R, V, W to 34th Street and walk one block east to 5th Avenue where you'll find the beautiful Art Deco entrance.

Once you've come back down to earth, take a cheap coffee break at the little-known Graduate Center (gc.cuny.edu/) at 365 5th Avenue on the corner of 34th Street, diagonally opposite the Empire State Building. Here you can buy filtered coffee or a luscious latte with a croissant and sit in relative peace at any time of the day before 4pm, which is when the graduates start pouring in. The building used to be a department store, which

View from the Empire State Building

is why there are ribbons and ties sculpted into the exterior columns. Now it is used as a research centre for students and holds free concerts. Anyone can sign up to use a computer here for up to 2 hours for free.

HERALD SQUARE

Herald Square, which is named after the now defunct newspaper, is home to the famous **Macy's** (macys.com), one of the world's largest retail outlets (the best subways for East 34th Street are the B, D, F, N, Q, R, V, W to 34th Street/Herald Square). Prior to Macy's opening in 1901, the area was down-at-heel, with lots of bordellos and seedy clubs. The opening of the department store was a fashion moment and improved the entire district.

The store's top-sellers among the Brits are the extremely well-priced Levi's and beauty products, while the 7th floor is dedicated to children's goods and it even has a McDonald's – the only department store in town to make such a proud boast.

For the grown-ups there is the wonderful **Cucina & Co.** (page 156) in the basement. A combination of buffet foods to eat in and take away, a grill restaurant and a coffee shop, it also has a sandwich station, pasta station and take-aways at incredible prices. Bearing in mind the average New Yorker spends $10 for a sandwich-style lunch and drink, Cucina's lunches are amazing value, as are their meal specials.

But don't expect it to look cheap; this is a wonderful space filled with fabulously fresh food in an indoor-market setting. Adjacent to it is **Macy's Cellar Bar & Grill**, where a complete dinner for two costs $24.95.

LITTLE KOREA

This tiny neighbourhood isn't one of New York's most famous boroughs, but it's expanding rapidly and is a great place to visit for lunch or dinner, thanks to the many excellent restaurants that are packed into West 31st and West 32nd Streets.

Situated in the Herald Square area, next to the Garment District and Chelsea in the

west, Little Korea is part of the melting pot of nationalities that have made New York their home. In the 1980s more than a million immigrants, a large percentage from Asia, arrived and took over corners of the city. Bordered by some of New York's major landmarks, this small area lies in the shadow of the Empire State Building, and is only a couple of blocks away from Macy's department store on 6th Avenue and Penn Station.

As well as the mouth-watering restaurants, such as **Gam Mee OK** at 43 West 32nd Street and **Han Bat** at 53 West 35th Street (which is open 24 hours Mon–Sun), there are also Korean bookshops, beauty salons and a great supermarket selling all sorts of exotic produce until 2am.

SHOPPERS' PARADISE

Between 5th and 8th Avenues on 34th Street is a shopper's paradise and one of the highlights is the **Sephora** beauty emporium, which has branches all over the city (page 140). With its sparkling floor-to-ceiling windows and stylish displays, this is a pristine shrine to beauty products and fragrances.

Other great shops in the area include **Old Navy**, the high-value end of the **Banana Republic** chain, **Kids R Us**, **Daffy's** and its amazingly cheap designer selection, plus **HMV**, **H&M** and **Kmart**.

PENN STATION

One block south on 33rd Street and 7th Avenue is the entrance to **Penn Station**, short for Pennsylvania Station (subways 1, 2, 3, 9 to 34th Street–Penn Station). Before you enter you'll see a **Lindy's** pastry shop. The original Lindy's in the theatre area was famous for its cheesecake, and this and the other branch (in Times Square), trade off the name but they're pricey and not unique.

BRITTIP

If you're on the west side of Penn Station, you're just a stone's throw from the block-long B&H Photo & Video store (bhphotovideo.com) on 9th Avenue from 33rd to 34th Street (page 155). It has 625 staff over its 4 floors selling thousands of items to both amateurs and professionals.

As you enter Penn Station, you'll see a handy Duane Reade (think Boots the Chemist) on the left. Walk down to the round area that sits under the **Madison Square Garden** building and on your left you'll see the information booth for the **34th Street BID Partnership**. All around are coffee shops,

Little Korea

34th Street at a glance: Empire State Building and shopping

Nightlife	Live music	209
Parks	Herald Square	26
Shopping	Department stores	125
	Electronics	155
	Food and drink	156
	Macy's	125
Sights	Empire State Building	69–70
	Madison Square Garden	77
	Penn Station	26

bakeries and a sit-down restaurant called **Kabooz**. None of them is a patch on Cucina & Co. or the Graduate Center, though. The restrooms are terrible; they have running water, but it just happens to be all over the floor! A good alternative is to head for the **Hotel Pennsylvania** on 7th Avenue opposite Penn Station, where you'll find clean WCs situated on the ground floor.

◀▮▶ BRITTIP
The main taxi ranks for Penn Station are on 7th Avenue opposite the Pennsylvania Hotel and on 8th Avenue opposite the majestic Beaux Arts General Post Office building. If you want a taxi from here, it's best to walk a block north as the queues can get quite long, or use the A, C, E, 1, 2, 3, 9 subways at 34th Street–Penn Station.

CHELSEA

This neighbourhood is only likely to be on your list of places to see if you like art galleries, want to go clubbing or if you're gay. However, it's actually worth a visit if you want to see an up-and-coming area in the process of gentrification. Originally farmland in 1750, by the late 1800s it was a commercial area filled with slaughterhouses, warehouses and the working classes. The mixture of sought-after brownstone townhouses and warehouses have made it a perfect target for artists priced out of SoHo, and although it's still rough around the edges, many of the quaint streets and buildings have been restored.

It is bounded by 6th Avenue (Avenue of the Americas) in the east, the Hudson River in the west, 16th Street in the south and 29th Street in the north. If you get off the A, C, E line at 14th Street and walk north on **8th Avenue**, you'll see the main drag of restaurants, shops, bars and gyms. Along the way you'll notice an abundance of Chippendale-type male bodies – the neighbourhood's gay boys, who love to flaunt their pecs in the local nightclubs.

At the corner of 19th stands the **Joyce Theater** (joyce.org), famous for dance and its fancy Art Deco building. Just a little further north and you're not only in the **Chelsea Historic District** – the blocks around 9th and 10th Avenues at 20th, 21st and 22nd Streets – but at the heart of the new gallery community that lies between 10th and 12th Avenues.

First port of call should be the **Dia Center for the Arts** (diacenter.org), a 4-storey, 3,700sq m/40,000sq ft warehouse, which opened in 1987 and still plays a pivotal role in the art world. Other great galleries nearby include **LFL, Leslie Tonkonow, Max Protetch Gallery, 303 Gallery** and the **D'Amelio Terras Gallery**. Two blocks north on 24th Street is the 1,950sq m/21,000sq ft **Gagosian Gallery, Barbara Gladstone Gallery** and the **Andrea Rosen Gallery**. Photographer Annie Leibovitz's studio is on 26th. Appropriately enough, given the area's new-found propensity for art, it now has its first art museum, the Chelsea Art Museum (page 103), which can be found on West 22nd Street at 11th Avenue.

Dia Center for the Arts

Chelsea at a glance: art galleries, clubbing and gay NY

Accommodation	Excellent value	246
	Medium-priced gems	242
	Theme hotels	238
Gay		254, 256–257, 260
Museums and galleries	Dia Center for the Arts	
	Chelsea Art Museum	103
	New Museum of Contemporary Art	117
Nightlife	Bars, lounges and pubs	199–200
	Comedy clubs	205
	Nightclubs	212–213
Restaurants		162–163
Shopping	Antiques and markets	149
	Beauty	145
	Books	151
	Electronics	154
	Fashion	128
	Food and drink	153, 155
	Homeware	156
	Speciality	157
Tours	Adirondark, Classic Harbor Line	84
	Bateaux New York	85
	Liberty Helicopter Tours	82
	Joyce Gold History Tours of New York	92

CHELSEA HOTEL

One of the most infamous of New York's hotels, the Chelsea Hotel (or Hotel Chelsea as it is officially known, hotelchelsea.com, page 246) is not only still going strong, but is also in the midst of a great revival. Before Sex Pistols front man Sid Vicious moved in with his girlfriend Nancy Spungen and allegedly killed her, back in the 1970s, famous inhabitants included Mark Twain, Dylan Thomas, William S Burroughs, Arthur Miller and Arthur C Clarke.

Built in 1883 and named a historic landmark in 1966, its lobby walls are covered with plaques commemorating venerated guests and their artworks, while the Spanish El Quijote restaurant is famous for its lobster.

CHINATOWN AND FIVE POINTS

The sprawling mass that is Chinatown (Map 1) has spread its wings north into the remnants of Little Italy, east into the Lower East Side and south in the Civic Center area. It is also home to the infamous Five Points area, once the most dangerous part of New York city.

Until recently, only history books and tour guides referred to Five Points. The name is derived from the five streets that intersect next to Columbus Park. Originally called Orange, Mulberry, Anthony, Little Water and Cross Streets, they are now known as Bayard, Park, Worth, Mulberry and Baxter.

In the 1820s, a pond graced a lovely area where the rich had their country homes, but they started sub-letting to tanners, who polluted the lake. Attempts to get rid of the dreadful smells from the lake by building a canal down Canal Street failed, and in the end only the poorest came to live in the area, which included freed slaves and immigrant blacks.

◀️🇬🇧 BRITTIP

Have a game plan when visiting Chinatown – it's so crowded that it's easy to feel daunted by all the hustle and bustle.

Irish immigrants arrived in the 1850s, then Italians and Eastern Europeans in the 1880s. Poverty was rife, and gangs flourished to such an extent that the streets were too unsafe for the police to patrol, and at least one person was killed each night. For almost 100 years, Five Points was considered the worst slum in the world and even shocked Charles Dickens. During that time the gangs were schools for criminals and politicians such as Johnny Torrio, Charles 'Lucky' Luciano, Al Capone and Frankie Yale. Paul Kelly set up boxing gyms to teach them how to be gangsters, use guns and extort money. Amazingly, the gangs even produced flyers with their 'services': $100 for the big job (murder), $50 for a slash on the face or $15 for an ear chewed off.

BRITTIP

Take advantage of Big Onion's (bigonion.com) Chinatown walking tour, which takes in the Church of Transfiguration, outdoor markets and Confucius statue (pages 91–92).

The appalling violence, corruption and history of this era has been genuinely brought to life by Martin Scorsese's movie *Gangs of New York*, which starred Leonardo DiCaprio and Daniel Day-Lewis.

Fortunately, Chinatown is now a very different place. Many of the overcrowded tenements were pulled down at the turn of the 20th century to build a park. Since then, the Criminal Court Building has also been built nearby, retaining a contact with the area's violent past!

The original Chinese immigrants in the 1850s huddled around Pell Street. Sadly, it was not long before the Tongs, with their extortion rackets, illegal gambling and opium dens, gave the area a new reputation for violence. As a result, the US Government passed the Exclusion Act in 1882, which banned Chinese from entering America.

That all changed in 1965 with the new Immigration Act and a new wave of Chinese immigrants arrived. Very quickly the women in particular were snapped up for poorly paid work in the garment industry, which gradually moved from its old Garment District above 34th Street into Chinatown. In more recent years, there have been more changes, as a new wave of immigrants from the Fujian province of China has once again changed the face of the area. Now many of the well-off Cantonese have moved to Queens and the Mandarin-speaking Fujinese have the upper hand.

The best way to get to Chinatown by subway is to take the A, C, E, J, M, N, Q, R, W, Z, 6 to Canal Street.

BRITTIP

You'll have a hard time getting a taxi on Canal Street – they just don't make it into Chinatown that often. Head toward The Bowery and try to hail a taxi as it comes off the Manhattan Bridge, or use the subway stations at Canal and Broadway.

At 277 Canal Street at Broadway and up some rickety old stairs you will find Pearl River Mart, Chinatown's idea of a department store, stocking everything from crockery to Buddhas, pretty lacquered paper umbrellas, clothes, shoes and slippers.

Back on the street again, you could be forgiven for feeling a little overwhelmed by the licensed and unlicensed street traders of Chinatown, who sell anything from fake watches to jewellery and handbags. It's often impossible to walk on the pavements, but also dangerous to step too far into the incredibly busy Canal Street!

Further down the road, you can get another real insight into the local lifestyle by visiting the **Kam Man** grocery store at 200 Canal Street. It offers a wide range from plucked ducks to squid. Try a bag of Konja, which is filled with deliciously refreshing bite-sized pots of lychee jelly.

Mott Street is the main thoroughfare of Chinatown. Here, along with Canal, Pell, Bayard, Doyers and The Bowery, is a host of restaurants plus tea and rice shops.

South towards Doyers Street you'll find the **Church of the Transfiguration** – one of two so named in New York – which perfectly portrays the changing nature of the immigrant population here. The oldest Catholic church building in New York, it was built in the early 19th century and Padre Felix Varela Morales, a Cuban priest who helped form the Ancient Hibernian Order, preached here. But between 1881 and 1943, no Chinese were allowed into it, apart from some wealthy merchants. It was first used by the Irish immigrants, then the Italians, but is now, finally, used by the Chinese and has services in Chinese. Also worth checking is the Wall of Democracy on Baynard Street, which is festooned with posters and newspaper cuttings that document the changing situation in China.

BRITTIP

It's pointless arriving at Chinatown before 10am as only the local McDonald's will be open.

Canal Street, Chinatown

Chinatown and Five Points at a glance: Chinese restaurants and markets		
Accommodation	Excellent value	246
Museums and galleries	Museum of Chinese in the Americas	112
Nightlife	Nightclubs	213
Restaurants		163–164
Shopping	Food and drink	155
Sights	Church of the Transfiguration	29
Tours	Enthusiastic Gourmet	87
	New York Helicopter Tours	82

May May restaurant at 35 Pell Street serves up fabulous dim sum. The chicken and shrimp combo is delicious. Dim sum, incidentally, means the 'little delicacy that will lighten up your heart' – and it certainly does when it's good! Next door is the **Chinese Gourmet Bakery** and **Vegetarian Food Center**, from where you can buy enough ingredients to make your own picnic to eat sitting in the nearby **Confucius Plaza**.

You should try to visit the beautiful **Bowery Savings Bank** on Bowery Street at Grand. When it was built in the 1890s, people liked to save locally and so the bankers tried to create the feeling that their building was a safe place for people to leave their money by making their banks stunningly beautiful inside. The Neo-Classical exterior is an incongruous sight here in Chinatown but it's worth having a peek at it.

DOWNTOWN
including Financial District and Battery Park

This is where the history of New York started and where some of the most important financial sites in the world were founded. The Downtown area covers the whole of the Financial District and the Civic Center, stretching from river to river and north to the Brooklyn Bridge/Chambers Street (Map 1).

New York Stock Exchange

Today, the winding, narrow streets of the true Downtown – a square mile south of Chambers Street from City Hall to the Battery – are a dizzying juxtaposition of colonial-era buildings and towering temples of capitalism. They were the location of some of the most important events in American history. This is where the Bill of Rights was signed, where George Washington was inaugurated as the first president and where millions arrived to begin their search for the American Dream.

BRITTIP

To find out what's new, what to see and do and info on free events in Downtown New York, log on to downtownny.com before you go.

THE WALL STREET SHUFFLE

The Dutch were the first to arrive and it was Peter Stuyvesant, New York's first governor, who ordered the building of a wooden wall at the northern edge of what was then New Amsterdam to protect the colonialists from possible attacks from Indians and the British. The name stuck and today it is known as **Wall Street**. This aspect of New York's history is presented in an exhibition in the Ionic-looking **Federal Hall National Memorial** (26 Wall Street, 212-825 6888, nps.gov/feha/), built on the site of New York's original City Hall. Cross the road into Broad Street and you're at the Neo-Classical entrance to the **New York Stock Exchange** (page 78).

Other fascinating landmarks include the **Federal Reserve Bank** in Liberty Street at Maiden Lane, which stores one-quarter of the world's gold bullion, and the Neo-Gothic **Trinity Church**, where Alexander Hamilton, the country's first secretary of the treasury, was buried after losing a duel. There has been a church on this site since the end of the 17th century and, for the first 50 years after it was built, Trinity was actually the tallest structure in New York.

BRITTIP
The Bowling Green end of Broadway is lined with coffee shops, cafés and pizza parlours. A freshly cooked slice eaten in or taken to go makes a perfect pit stop.

Just off Wall Street at 25 Broadway is probably one of the poshest post office buildings in the world. Known as the old **Cunard Building**, it was once home to the booking offices of the steamship company and the interior walls of the building are still lined with marble. There are other signs of its former use, with murals of ships and nautical mythology around the ceiling.

And it seems only fitting that the former headquarters of John D Rockefeller's Standard Oil Company at 28 Broadway should now be the home of one of New York's newest museums, the **Museum of American Finance** (page 112).

The best subway lines are the 2, 3, 4, 5 to Wall Street.

BOWLING GREEN

Blink and you'll miss this oval of greenery at the end of Broadway. You know you're there by the presence of the Greek revival-style US Customs House, which is now the **National Museum of the American Indian** (page 116) and has the world's largest collection devoted to North, Central and South American Indian cultures. Bowling Green was the site of the infamous business deal between the Dutch colony of New Amsterdam and the Indians, who were conned into selling Manhattan for a bucket of trinkets.

In the 18th century, the tiny turfed area was used for the game of bowls by colonial Brits on a lease of 'one peppercorn per year'. The iron fence that encloses it now is the original and was built in 1771, though, ironically, the once-proud statue of King George III was melted into musket balls for use in the American Revolution.

The Wall Street Bull

Here you'll also find the 3,175kg/7,000lb life-sized bronze bull. A symbol of the Financial District's stock market, it appeared overnight outside the New York Stock Exchange in 1989. Now it is a tradition to rub him for good luck!

The nearest subways to take you to Bowling Green are the 4, 5 line to Bowling Green or R, W to Whitehall.

BATTERY PARK AND CASTLE CLINTON

Thanks to hundreds of years of landfill, the whole Downtown area is quite different to how it once was. Years ago, State Street houses looked over Upper New York Bay, and Water and Pearl Streets were named because they were at or near the water's edge. The excavation works required to build the deep foundations for the World Trade Center in the 1960s, destroyed by terrorists on 11 September 2001, created enough granite blocks of earth to form 9 hectares (23 acres) of new land, which then became home to Battery Park City and the World Financial Center.

In the Battery Park area, **Castle Clinton** originally stood on an island. Built in 1811 as one of several forts that defended New York harbour, it is now part of Manhattan. It has been an opera house, an aquarium and the original immigration sorting office, dealing with 8 million immigrants before the opening of Ellis Island. It is now used as the ferry ticket office.

The opening of a plethora of new shops and cafés and the remodelling of the Battery Park public spaces has given the area a whole new lease of life.

The best subways to take here are the 1, 9 to South Ferry or 4, 5 to Bowling Green.

BATTERY PARK CITY

North-west of Battery Park, you'll find a relatively new area of land known as **Battery Park City**, which is actually the area created by landfill. It's still pretty much a quiet district, though there has been plenty of development. This is home to 2 of New York's newer museums. The **Museum of Jewish Heritage** (pages 114–115) has been so successful, it already has plans for an extension.

BRITTIP
For more fantastic views of Dame Liberty and the harbour, treat yourself to a drink in the chic bar, Rise, on the 14th floor of the Ritz-Carlton Hotel in West Street (page 230).

Downtown including Financial District and Battery Park at a glance: the Wall Street area

Accommodation	Boutique chic	235
	Excellent value	246
	Medium-priced gems	242
	Modern luxury	230
Museums and galleries	Ellis Island Immigration Museum	67–69
	Forbes Magazine Galleries	106
	Fraunces Tavern Museum	106
	Museum of American Finance	112
	Museum of Jewish Heritage	113
	National Museum of the American Indian	116
	New York City Police Museum	117–118
	Skyscraper Museum	120
	South Street Seaport Museum	120–121
	Sports Museum of America	121
Restaurants	Battery Park	160
	Financial District and South Street Seaport	165–166
Shopping	Music	157
	South Street Seaport	72
	Winter Garden	79
Sights	Battery Park and Castle Clinton	30, 274
	Brooklyn Bridge	73
	Federal Reserve Bank	76
	Ground Zero	70–71
	New York Stock Exchange	78
	Staten Island Ferry	72–73
	Statue of Liberty	67–68
	Wall Street	78
	Woolworth Building	79
Tours	Alliance for Downtown New York	90
	New York Waterway	85

At 39 Battery Place is the **Skyscraper Museum** (page 120), which tells the fascinating story of the creation of all those famous buildings. On the southern tip of the 'City' is the recently landscaped **Robert Wagner Junior Park** with a café, some WCs and street vendors selling food and drink – it is a wonderful place to sit and gaze out at the harbour.

To the north is the **World Financial Center**, which has four tower blocks and a full calendar of fairs and festivals. It's worth coming here for the **Winter Garden** (page 79), a huge, glass-ceilinged public plaza decorated by massive palm trees. From here you can see the fancy private boats docked in **North Cove**.

The nearest subways are the A, C, 1, 2, 3, 9 to Chambers Street (for the World Financial Center) or the 1, 9 to South Ferry (for the museums and park).

EAST OF BATTERY PARK

To see what life was like in 18th-century Manhattan, head for the **Fraunces Tavern Block Historic District**, which has 11 early 19th-century buildings that escaped the fire of 1835. The three-storey Georgian brick house that is home to the **Fraunces Tavern Museum** (page 106) on the corner of Pearl and Broad Streets was built in 1904 and houses an exhibition on the site's history.

A little further north-east along Water Street to the Old Slip, you'll see the tiny **First Precinct Police Station**, which was modelled on an Italian mansion and which has been used for exterior shots for both *Kojak* and *The French Connection*. Fittingly, this is now the permanent home of the **New York City Police Museum** (pages 117–118).

Just off Water Street at 70 Pine Street is the incredibly beautiful Art Deco wedding-cake-shaped **American International Building**. It has one of the most beautiful

Art Deco-designed lobbies in New York and visitors are welcome to come inside to have a look.

A little further north at piers 16, 17 and 18, you find yourself in the heart of the **South Street Seaport** (page 72), which has a museum, a shopping and restaurant complex and the 150-year-old **Fulton Fish Market**, open midnight–8am daily.

Best subways to the area are the R, W to Whitehall Street, J, M, Z to Broad Street or the 2, 3 to Wall Street.

◀▦▶ BRITTIP
Don't miss the free outdoor concerts at the South Street Seaport Museum (page 117), held almost nightly throughout the summer.

CITY HALL PARK AND THE CIVIC CENTER

City Hall Park is right opposite the entrance to Brooklyn Bridge and is also the dividing point between the Financial District and Chinatown. From here you can stroll across the **Brooklyn Bridge** or visit the Neo-Gothic **Woolworth Building** (page 79) on Broadway at Barclay Street, which is likely to be your main reason for swinging by. Check out the lobby's vaulted ceilings and its magnificent mosaics and mail boxes. When it was first built it was the tallest structure in New York and Mr Woolworth paid cash for it!

◀▦▶ BRITTIP
There is a farmers' market each Tues and Fri (April–Dec, 8am–6pm) in the City Hall Park where you can buy fresh fruits, vegetables and bread – a great way to create a picnic.

Back in the 1930s, when Prosecutor Dewey decided to target organised crime, he made the Woolworth Building his base and during that time he locked up 15 prostitutes in the building for 4 months. In the end, he worked out that the prostitutes were controlled by Lucky Luciano and successfully prosecuted him for white slavery. 'Lucky' got 32 years in prison, but lived up to his name by serving just 10 before he was pardoned for his efforts on behalf of the American government during the Second World War. Just north of City Hall Park are the **Police Plaza**, **US Courthouse**, **New York County Courthouse** and **Criminal Court Building**.

It's useful to note that there is a Lower Manhattan information kiosk in City Hall Park where you can find information on attractions and upcoming events plus maps and directions.

The best subways to take are the R, W to City Hall or the 4, 5, 6 to Brooklyn Bridge/ City Hall.

The Winter Garden

EAST VILLAGE

Forget the picturesque cobbled streets of Greenwich and the West Villages. Once you cross The Bowery (otherwise known as Skid Row) and head up to St Mark's Place you are in the heart of the **East Village** (Map 2) and an area more reminiscent of the Lower East Side than a village and currently back in vogue as one of the coolest neighbourhoods in Manhattan. No matter where you are in New York, it's easy to spot an East Villager – they have long hair and more metal in their face than a jewellery shop window display. You also know when you've entered the neighbourhood by the many tattoo studios, along with boutiques selling punk and leather outfits.

Where Greenwich Village has become upper middle class, the East Village retains its roots as a Bohemian enclave of free-thinkers and non-conformists, though the tramps are gradually being replaced by a more genteel set attracted by newly built apartment blocks and the comparatively reasonable, though not low, rents.

This was once the home of Beat Generation writer Allen Ginsberg (on East 7th Street) and was frequented by Jack Kerouac and other radical thinkers of the 1950s. One of the area's oldest clubs, **CBGB** on The Bowery closed in 2006 after more than 30 years. The punk-rock club is famous for hosting Blondie, the Ramones, Talking Heads and the Police. There are apparently plans for it to reopen, but no date has yet been announced.

Now the area is most well known for its second-hand shops, which can be found all along 7th Street and 2nd and 3rd Avenues. There's a tiny Little India on 6th Street, where you'll find a row of curry houses, but the most famous eating outlet is the **Yaffa Café** (page 165) on St Mark's Place heading towards Tompkins Square Park.

East 7th Street is home to what is claimed to be New York's oldest pub, McSorley's Old Ale House, which dates back to 1854 and still serves its own beer, while a line of Harley Davidson's on 3rd Street between 1st and 2nd Avenues is evidence of the base of the New York chapter of the Hell's Angels.

Alphabet City, which lies between Avenues A to D towards the East River, is also part of East Village. Once considered a no-go area for tourists, it was predominantly filled with a working class Latino community and had a reputation as the drug-dealing area of the city. These days, the drug problems are largely a thing of the past, and an influx of young professionals has given the area a lift. Its major historical attractions are two churches, San Isidero y San Leandro and Iglesia Pentecostal Camino Damasco, built in an elaborate Spanish-colonial style.

The best subways are the L, N, Q, R, W, 4, 5, 6 to 14th Street/Union Square and the L to 3rd Avenue and 1st Avenue.

Merchant's House Museum

East Village at a glance: Bohemian cafés and shops

Gay		257, 260–261
Museums and galleries	Merchant's House Museum	109
Nightlife	Bars, lounges and pubs	200
	Nightclubs	213
Restaurants		164–165
Shopping	Antiques and markets	150
	Books	151
	Fashion	128–129, 138
	Food and drink	153
	Music	157
Tours	Rock 'n' Roll Walking Tour	89

Garment District at a glance: sample sales and designers		
Nightlife	Bars, lounges and pubs	200
	Live music	209
	Nightclubs	214
Shopping	Antiques and markets	147

Gramercy Park at a glance: beautiful architecture		
Accommodation	Medium-priced gems	243
	Modern luxury	231
	Traditional luxury	233
Gay		255
Restaurants		166

GARMENT DISTRICT

From 34th Street to 42nd Street between 6th and 8th Avenues, you'll find the **Garment District** of New York (Map 3). Having shrunk a little in the past – a lot of work disappeared overseas or moved to the cheap labour available in Chinatown – the area is once again up-and-coming, as designers are now choosing to have their clothes manufactured in New York. If you wander around this area – and you may well if you're in search of sample sales – you'll see racks of clothes being pushed around the streets. Some are going to showrooms and warehouses, but as no one manufacturer makes an entire piece of clothing, many of the garments are being shunted from company to company to have different bits sewn on at each place!

BRITTIP
Check out the sales section of New York's *Time Out* magazine, or online at newyork.timeout. com, for up-to-date information on designer sample sales in the Garment District.

GRAMERCY PARK

Two blocks south and two blocks east of the Flatiron Building on East 20th and 21st at **Irving Place** (Map 3) is one of the prettiest squares in New York City (the nearest subway is the 6 to 23rd Street). The park itself was once a swamp but has now been beautifully laid out, though you won't be able to go in unless you are staying with a resident of the surrounding square or at the **Gramercy Park Hotel**.

The most famous building in the neighbourhood is **The Players** at 16 Gramercy Park, a private club created for actors and theatrical types by actor Edwin Booth when Gramercy Park was the centre of the theatre scene. Booth was the greatest actor in America in the 1870s and 1880s and opened the Gothic revival-style house as a club in 1888 so that actors and literary types could meet in private to interact. One tragic event overshadowed the end of Booth's life – his brother John Wilkes Booth assassinated Abraham Lincoln.

GREENWICH VILLAGE

This is one of the prettiest areas of New York and, although the radical free-thinkers have gone, its quaint cobbled and tree-lined streets, shops and Federal and Greek-style buildings are well worth a visit.

Greenwich Village proper (Map 2) is bounded in the north by 14th Street, in the south by Houston (pronounced 'Howston'), in the east by Broadway and in the west by 7th, where it becomes the West Village, which stretches west to the Hudson River.

The Players

When the Dutch first arrived in Manhattan, 'the Village' as it is known in New York, was mostly woodland, but was turned into a tobacco plantation by the Dutch West India Company. Then in the early 1800s people started fleeing from a series of cholera and yellow fever epidemics in the unhygienic Downtown.

However, when the wealthy moved into their 5th Avenue mansions at the end of the 19th century, rents came down and a whole new breed of artists, radicals and intellectual rebels moved in, creating a kind of Parisian Left Bank feel to the neighbourhood. Over the years it has been home to such literary lions as Mark Twain, Edgar Allen Poe, Dylan Thomas, Eugene O'Neill and Jack Kerouac.

Now the writers and artists have largely been forced out by the soaring rents – a tiny two-bed apartment costs at least $2,500 a month and to buy a shoebox of a studio is at least $275,000 – and in their place have come upper middle-class Americans for whom making money is the abiding principle. Yet there is still the sense of a community spirit, many restaurants cater mostly to locals rather than tourists (in New York, only Village restaurants seem filled with people who are in no particular rush) and a great variety of off-Broadway shows and other cultural events can be seen in this neighbourhood.

WASHINGTON SQUARE PARK

If you take the A, B, C, E, F or V subway to West 4th Street and Washington Square, you'll find yourself in what many people consider to be the heart of the Village – and in one of the very few genuine squares in Manhattan. The first thing you'll notice

GREAT TOURS OF THE VILLAGE

If eating's your thing, then you'll love the **Foods of New York** tour (pages 87–88) of Greenwich Village and West Village, which not only shows you the sights, food shops, restaurants and architectural secrets of the area, but will also give you a chance to taste the foods that are unique to this corner of New York.

Other great tours are the **Literary Pub Crawl** (page 92), which takes you to the watering holes once frequented by literary giants, and **Haunted Greenwich Village** (page 90), which shows you places with a legendary past.

is the Stanford White-designed marble square **Triumphal Arch** at the bottom of 5th Avenue, built in 1892 to commemorate George Washington's inauguration as the first US president.

BRITTIP

Tomoe Sushi on Thompson Street (page 169) looks pretty unappealing from the outside, but has incredible queues. Why? You can get the best sushi in New York here for about a tenth of what it would cost you at Nobu.

You may also become aware of how dingy it all looks and you may be even a little concerned about the 'grungy' nature of many of the people there, but this area is considered 'alternative' rather than dodgy. It's full of locals skating, playing chess and just hanging out, plus students from the nearby **New York**

Greenwich Village at a glance: brownstone houses, restaurants and boutiques		
Accommodation	Excellent value	247
	Total bargains	249
Museums and galleries	Forbes Magazine Galleries	106
Nightlife	Bars, lounges and pubs	201
	Hotel bars	206–207
	Live music	209–210
	Nightclubs	214
Restaurants		167–169
Shopping	Antiques and markets	150
	Books	151
	Department stores	124
	Fashion	129, 138
	Food and drink	155
	Homeware	156
	Music	157
Tours	Foods of New York	87–88

Bleecker Street and 7th

University. It used to be a place where a lot of people took drugs, but that problem is largely in the past.

A little-known fact is that the park was once used by City officials to conduct public hangings until they were moved to Sing Sing penitentiary. Apart from the arch and the people, the other main point of interest in the park is the **Dog Run**. A uniquely New York phenomenon, the idea is that instead of taking your dog for a walk along the roads, you bring them to dog runs where they can literally run around off the lead. It's rather like a parent taking their child to the swings – hilarious and has to be seen to be believed!

North from the park on 6th Avenue between Waverly Place and 9th Street is **Bigelow's Pharmacy**, the oldest traditional chemist in America. Across the street is the beautiful **Jefferson Market Courthouse**, which is now used as a library, and just off 10th Street is one of the most famous rows of mews houses in the Village – **Patchin Place**, which has been home not only to many a writer, including e e cummings and John Reed, but also to Marlon Brando. Also of note on the square is the **Forbes Magazine Galleries** (page 106), a museum filled with antique toys as well as a signed copy of Lincoln's Gettysburg Address, while the **Church of the Ascension** is an English Gothic Revival church built in 1840 with a mural of the Ascension above the altar by John La Farge.

BLEECKER STREET

Effectively the main drag of the Village, this is one of the best places to be in New York, filled as it is with sidewalk cafés, shops, restaurants and clubs. The corner of Cornelia and Bleecker Streets gives you access to some of the finest food shops and restaurants in Manhattan. To get here, take the 6 to Bleecker Street or B, D, F, V to Broadway/Lafayette Street.

At 259 Bleecker is **Zito's** old-fashioned Italian bread shop, which still uses the ovens that were built here in the 1860s and were once used by the whole community. They are particularly famous for focaccia with different toppings, such as onions and olive oil and rosemary, and their prosciutto bread is unique to them.

Next door is **Murray's Cheese Shop** (page 155), with more than 350 cheeses from around the world. Nothing is pre-cut and they have great names such as Wabash Cannonball, Crocodile Tears, Mutton Buttons and Cardinal Sin, a British cows'-milk cheese. They also have 15 different types of olives and sell chorizos, pâtés and breads. Opposite at 260 Bleecker is **Faicco's** (page 155), a landmark shop that has been here since 1900. Its famous range of sausages is made every morning and sold not only to local residents but also to many of the local restaurants. It also sells home-cooked, ready-made meals and offers a huge deli selection.

Around the corner is Cornelia Street, home to four of the best restaurants in the Village. The **Cornelia Street Café** (pages 167–168 and 212) hosts jazz, readings and other events (from $6 to $11), while **Home Restaurant** specialises in American comfort food with a gourmet twist, **Le Gigot** is a traditional country French restaurant and **Little Havana** offers great Cuban food.

Bleecker Street has two more incredible bakeries with their own seating areas. **Pasticceria Bruno** is run by popular chef Biagio. He produces an amazing range of tarts and mousses for $2 to $3 with names like Kiss Cream, Wildberries, Green Apple and Apricot. The café itself has a lot of atmosphere and old world charm. Next door is **Rocco's Pastry Shop & Espresso Café** (pages 155–156), run by Rocco, who used to be a head pastry chef at Bruno's until 1972 when he opened his own place here. An entire Italian cheesecake made of ricotta cheese costs just $12.50. The interior is much more modern, with steel-framed chairs, mirrors and more seats than Bruno's.

Murray's Cheese Shop

HARLEM

Harlem is a huge area that covers a substantial part of the northern reaches of Manhattan above Central Park, though it has various subsections. What we refer to when we use the name Harlem is actually the African-American area, which stretches from 8th Avenue in the west to 5th Avenue in the east and goes north to the East River (Map 6). The area from East 96th Street east of 5th Avenue going up to the East River is **Spanish Harlem**, known as El Barrio and populated largely by Puerto Ricans.

Named after the Dutch town of Haarlem, the area received its first Dutch settlers in the mid-19th century, when it was used as farmland and as an escape from the dust and traffic of Midtown. Better-off immigrant families started moving here following the arrival of the railroad link and the building of attractive brownstone townhouses. Then property speculators, eager to take advantage of the new subway heading for Harlem, started building good-quality homes for the upper middle classes in the early 1900s. But they'd got a little ahead of themselves. A couple of mini depressions and Harlem's distance from Midtown Manhattan put the dampers on hopes of a major middle-class movement into the area.

BRITTIP
Many avenues and streets in Harlem have 2 names that reflect both historical and more modern influences. For instance, Lenox Avenue is known as Malcolm X Boulevard and 7th Avenue is known as Adam Clayton Powell Junior Boulevard, both named after major African-American activists.

The African-American estate agents spotted a golden opportunity, bought up a whole batch of empty homes cheaply and started renting them out to blacks eager to escape the gang warfare of the West 40s and 50s in Hell's Kitchen and Clinton. This was the beginning of Harlem as the capital of the black world and when African-Americans started migrating from America's southern states, they headed straight here.

And it's no wonder really. Brits are frequently shocked to discover that the blacks may have been freed from slavery by the end of the 19th century, but there was still segregation until the 1960s. Black people were not allowed to sit on the same benches as whites, they had to drink at different water fountains and in church they were forced to wait until after the whites for Communion. When great black musicians such as **Duke Ellington** and **Louis Armstrong** went on tour, they had to stay at black-only hotels and eat at black-only restaurants.

BRITTIP
Instead of going to the somewhat touristy Sylvia's Restaurant on 125th, try the M&G Soul Food Diner on West 125th at Morningside Avenue for a truly traditional southern meal to the background sounds of great soul singers.

Back in Harlem, at least, there was some semblance of belonging and thanks to the influx of political activists, professionals and artists to the area following the opening of the subway lines between 1904 and 1906, many African-American organisations had sprung up by the early 1920s. They included the **National Urban League**, which helped people who were moving into the area to get training for jobs, and the **White Rose Mission**, which helped African-American female migrants coming to New York from the South. They were followed by the political **Universal Negro Improvement Association** and the **Union Brotherhood of Sleeping Porters**, whose leader Phillip Randolph was at one time considered by the government to be the most dangerous black in America.

BRITTIP
To experience the life and times of Harlem, pick up a copy of *Harlem's Culture: Guide to Great Events*, available at cultural centres such as the Schomburg.

THE GLORY DAYS OF HARLEM

The 1920s and 1930s were a great time for the neighbourhood, filled as it was with poets, writers, artists, actors and political activists. The combination of prohibition and great jazz musicians such as **Count Basie, Duke Ellington** and **Cab Calloway** made famous nightspots like the **Cotton Club** attractive to the upper middle classes who came in their droves to enjoy Harlem's speakeasies.

But all this was hardly doing anything for the lot of the average African-American who lived in the area. The speakeasies were strictly for whites only and even **W C Handy**, who co-wrote a song with Duke Ellington, was not allowed into the Cotton Club to hear it being played for the first time. Then there was the matter of the racism on **125th**

Street – Harlem's very centre – which runs from Frederick Douglas Boulevard to Malcolm X Boulevard. The white-owned shops and hotels here, which were used by the African-Americans, were staffed by whites and it was impossible for blacks to get anything but the most menial jobs.

In 1934, Adam Clayton Powell Junior, preacher at the Abyssinian Baptist Church, organised a boycott of these businesses, entitled 'Don't Buy Where You Can't Work'. The campaign was successful and the shops started hiring blacks. You can still see the remnants of those businesses along 125th.

You can start your experience of Harlem with a tour round the **Apollo Theater** on 125th (page 91), which was the focal point for African-American entertainment between the 1930s and 1970s. Known for its legendary **Amateur Night**, which is now broadcast on TV, it has launched the careers of Ella Fitzgerald, Marvin Gaye, James Brown and even The Jackson Five.

At the corner of 7th Avenue stands the former **Theresa Hotel**, now an office block, but which was once considered to be the Waldorf of Harlem. Back in the days of segregation **Josephine Baker** stayed in the penthouse with its vaulted ceiling and views of both rivers. Malcolm X's Unity organisation was based here in the 1950s and 1960s and, in a show of support for African-Americans, Fidel Castro moved his entire entourage to the Theresa when he came to New York in 1960 for a United Nations conference.

BRITTIP
For soul food, try Miss Maude's Spoonbread, Malcom X Boulevard (Lenox Avenue) at 137th Street or visit Manna's Too at 134th Street (or Manna's at 8th Avenue and West 125th Street) for a great selection of well-priced fresh food and drinks.

A little further down the street is **Blumsteins**, once the largest department store in Harlem. With its dilapidated frontage and peeling paintwork, it's now hard to imagine this as once being the Macy's of the area.

Another major location in Harlem is up on 135th to 137th Streets between Powell Boulevard and Malcolm X Boulevard. You can either walk from 125th Street or take the 2, 3 subway to 135th Street station. Once there you'll find yourself right outside the **Schomburg Center**, which chronicles the history of black people in North America,

South America and the Caribbean. Opposite is the **Harlem Hospital Center** where Martin Luther King was operated on after being shot. It was the first hospital in New York to be integrated.

BRITTIP
To experience a gospel choir in action, go to the Abyssinian Church on 138th Street, but you'll need to arrive early because it gets packed. Another great place is the Second Canaan Baptist Church on 110th Street and Lenox Avenue.

A couple of blocks north and you'll find the famous **Abyssinian Baptist Church** at 132 West 138th Street. It was originally founded in 1808, and as the blacks moved from the Lower East Side to Greenwich Village, then up to the West 50s and 60s before finally finding a home in Harlem, the church moved with them. This church was built in 1923 and, with Adam Clayton Powell Junior as its preacher for many years before he became a senator, it was a centre of political activity, particularly in the 1920s.

One block west on 138th and 139th Streets between Powell and Frederick Douglas Boulevards are the four rows of Stanford White houses built in 1891 and known as **Striver's Row** because this is where the middle and upper classes strove to live. The houses were filled by doctors, lawyers, nurses from Harlem Hospital, jazz musicians and politicians such as Malcolm X. Boxer Harry Wills, known as the Brown Panther, lived here. He was paid $50,000 not to fight Jack Dempsey when the mayor banned the fight because he thought a black boxer fighting a white man would lead to riots.

Harlem

Harlem at a glance: jazz and African-American culture

Museums and galleries	El Museo del Barrio	105
	Julia de Burgos Latino Cultural Center	108
	Morris-Jumel Mansion	78
	Schomberg Center for Research in Black Culture	119–120
	Studio Museum in Harlem	121
	The Cloisters	104–105
Nightlife	Live music	210
Restaurants		169
Sights	Apollo Theater	91

BRITTIP

A terrific variety of tours of Harlem are available from Harlem Heritage Tours (tel 212-280 7888, harlemheritagetours.com).

The alleys at the back of these buildings were originally created for parking horses and carriages. Houses were usually built back to back so the alleys are a rarity, but a boon for the current occupants to park their BMWs. You can still see the signs that say 'Walk your horses' or 'Park your carriages'.

BRITTIP

If you're concerned about wandering the streets of Harlem by yourself, try either a Big Onion walking tour (page 91) or a Harlem Spirituals bus tour (page 87).

DECLINE AND FALL

Sadly, the good times didn't last long and, from the 1940s to the 1960s, Harlem declined into an urban no-man's land as a result of a lack of government support and racial conflict. The once-fine apartment blocks grew shabbier as landlords were either too unscrupulous or unable to afford to maintain them on the cheap rental income.

Eventually City Hall and certain businesses started investing in the area. In 1976 the city began reclaiming properties abandoned by

Abyssinian Baptist Church

landlords who couldn't afford to pay their taxes. You can still buy one of these blocks for $1 if you have the $2m needed to renovate it. Fortunately, many have already been refurbished and, with the influx of banks and even a Starbucks improvements continue.

For some time, the brownstones of Hamilton Heights and other local neighbourhoods have been targeted by those trying to escape the substantial rents elsewhere in Manhattan. There have been other developments, too. Former president Bill Clinton has his offices on 125th Street between Lenox and 5th (the one with the huge Gap advert down the side). He's always been a favourite with African-Americans because he did a lot for racial equality and he was invited to move his offices to Harlem from Carnegie Hall. Former baseball star Magic Johnson has also been doing much to encourage a sense of community pride.

RENAISSANCE

Fast-rising house prices in other parts of the city forced the upwardly mobile to flock to a neighbourhood where previously they would never have dared to tread. Toned white women jog down streets previously used to conduct heroin deals and students stroll out of Starbucks. Old nightspots once frequented exclusively by the African-Americans have also been bought up and are being earmarked for renovation, including the Renaissance Ballroom, once a neighbourhood institution. Everyone would watch the Harlem Rennies basketball team early in the evening, then clean up to hit the nightclub. It was shut in the 1940s, but is now owned by the Abyssinian Church.

Another major venue was **Small's Big Apple** jazz club. Its sister establishment, **Small's Paradise**, was a restaurant in the 1930s and 1940s. It was so popular and the dance floor so small that it was said people had to dance on a dime here. It enjoyed a revival from the 1960s and was where Professor du Bois, who once ran the National Association for Advancement of Coloured

People, held a birthday party in the 1980s. It closed in the same decade, but is now owned by the Abyssinian Church and there's a chance it may reopen as a tourist centre.

HAMILTON HEIGHTS

The Hamilton Heights neighbourhood (Map 6) is up on the high ground north of Morningside Heights and is effectively the middle-class enclave of Harlem. It takes its name from **Alexander Hamilton**, the first secretary of the treasury to the newly formed United States of America. He lived here from 1802 until he was killed in a duel in 1804.

The area is now the home of **City College**, one of the senior colleges in the New York university system. It was founded in the 19th century to educate the children of the working classes and immigrants and used to be known as the poor man's Columbia. It used to be free, but now it charges $3,200 a year, though that is still a lot cheaper than private universities in America, which charge an average of $27,400 per year.

Further north on West 145th Street off Amsterdam is the area known as **Sugar Hill**, which was made famous in the Duke Ellington song 'Take the A Train [to Sugar Hill]'. Now a conservation area, it is filled with beautiful brownstone townhouses, and was dubbed Sugar Hill because life here was considered to be so sweet.

LITTLE ITALY

With its strong ties to Naples and a history of Mafia connections, Little Italy is still seen as a glamorous area of the city by many. The best subway to Little Italy (Map 1) is the N, R, Q, W, 6 to Canal and then walk east to Mulberry, or take the 6 to Spring and walk south. Head along Grand Street towards Mott and Mulberry Streets to **Di Palo's** (page 156), which marks the beginnings of what is left of Little Italy. Di Palo's shop at 210 Grand Street was founded 80 years ago and is still famous for its mozzarella, Italian sausages and salamis. It has its own cheese-ageing room and gets very crowded. A little further on is **Ferrara's** (page 170), the oldest and most popular pastry café in Little Italy.

Although much smaller now than it was in the 1970s due to a dwindling population,

◄║► BRITTIP

Ferrara's in Grand Street, near Mulberry, is a perfect spot for a coffee and pastry break, and you'll find the restrooms on the 1st floor. You'll also get a real slice of the Italian lifestyle.

it is still a pleasant few blocks to wander around, particularly for food-lovers, as the delis, packed full of homemade breads, pastas, sausages and cheeses, are legendary. To stop it dwindling further, the Italians struck a deal with the Chinese community to retain Mulberry Street between Hester and Kenmare Streets. It was formerly home to Italians from the Naples area of Italy and has taken St Gennaro, the patron saint of Naples, as its own saint. Every year in the 3rd week of September, Italians flock to celebrate the Feast of St Gennaro. Food carts line Mulberry Street and there is much laughing, dancing and drinking until the early hours.

◄║► BRITTIP

Little Italy is at its finest at the weekend in warm weather when the restaurants put their tables outdoors. Arrive around noon or late afternoon to get a seat outside.

Little Italy's best feature is its wonderful restaurants with outdoor seating where you can watch the world go by while tucking into some great dishes. The restaurants have a reputation for being on the pricey side, but plenty have pasta and pizza specials for a more economical $10.

Mulberry Street

Little Italy at a glance: Mediterranean food		
Museums and galleries	Children's Museum of the Arts	103–104
Nightlife	Bars, lounges and pubs	201–202
Restaurants		169–171
Shopping	Food and drink	156

Just a little bit of gruesome history for you: Da Gennaro on the corner of Mulberry and Hester Streets was the original home of **Umberto's Clam House** (which is now further south on Mulberry). This was a favoured haunt of gangster Crazy Joey Gallo and where he was murdered in 1972 while celebrating his birthday.

Further north at 247 Mulberry between Spring and Kenmare Streets is the former home of the **Ravenlight Club** and Mafia headquarters for John Gotti. He was once known as the Teflon Don because no charges could be made to stick, and this was where he made the policemen and judges on his payroll come to pay their respects.

The FBI were so determined to put him away they bugged not only the Ravenlight but also all the parking meters around the streets – but still they got nowhere. Then Gotti's underboss, Sammy Gravano, became a supergrass. He got away with 19 murders because he did a deal with the FBI that helped it put Gotti away.

LOWER EAST SIDE

One of the seedier parts of town that's becoming cool again, the Lower East Side has a fascinating history but is now known for its trendy nightclubs and bargain shopping. The Lower East Side stretches from the East River ostensibly to Chrystie Street (though Chinatown is encroaching) and south from Canal Street to East Houston in the north, while Delancey is its main thoroughfare (Map 2).

The best way to get there by subway is by taking the J, M, Z, F trains to Delancey or Essex Streets.

In many respects, the history of the Lower East Side is the history of America's immigration, which in turn has played a pivotal role in the country's development.

◀▶ BRITTIP

The Lower East Side Business Improvement District (866-224 0406, lowereastsideny.com) offers L.E.S is more, Explore! Podtour, a free walking tour you can download from their website to your MP3 player. There's also a free 2-hour weekly tour, Sun Apr–Dec at 11am in front of Katz's Delicatessen (page 171).

At one time this was the most densely populated area in the world, with 1,000 inhabitants crammed into 2.6 sq km/1 sq ml: but more of that later. Almost from the word go, the Lower East Side was a settlement for new arrivals to New York because of its cheap housing and its proximity to where people disembarked. Once these immigrants had established themselves they moved on, leaving space for a new wave of arrivals. Street names such as Essex, Suffolk and Norfolk point to the origins of their first tenants. Since then streets have been named anything from a Kleine Deutschland to a Little Italy or Ireland.

◀▶ BRITTIP

While you're in the neighbourhood, don't miss Katz's Deli (page 171) on East Houston Street at Ludlow Street. It's a real institution.

With each new wave of immigrants came friction between new and old arrivals, which often led to violence. The Protestant English were angry, for instance, when the Roman Catholic Irish built St Mary's on Grand Street in 1828 and burned it down. That led to the formation of the **Ancient Order of Hibernians** in 1830 – the organisation that started the St Patrick's Day parade. The Hibernians rebuilt the church and put walls around the outside. It is still in existence, but now runs a kosher soup service for local Jewish people.

Check out lowereastsideny.com for information on events and discounts.

SWEATSHOPS AND TENEMENTS

Other tenants of the early 1800s were relatively well-off Jews from Germany, who eventually moved further north. This was a pattern that was to be repeated again and again with each new wave of immigrants. But perhaps the saddest were the incredibly poor Jewish immigrants who started arriving from Eastern Europe in the 1860s and 70s. They were forced to eke out a miserly existence in sweatshops and live in tenement buildings. Whole families were crowded into 1.8m/6ft square rooms with no heating or running water and often little light. Visit the **Lower East Side Tenement Museum** (pages 108–109) in Orchard Street for their full story.

During this period, **Hester Street** was the main thoroughfare and it was filled with shops and pedlars selling their wares – meat, fruit and vegetables. The pedlars did very well, as they paid no tax and had no overheads such as rent. Often they made more than three times as much as teachers did. But the shopkeepers were unhappy with the unfair competition and by the 1930s the city had banned pedlars and created the Essex Market. Famous for its fresh meats, produce and

Lower East Side at a glance: nightlife and bargain shopping

Accommodation	Boutique chic	235
	Total bargains	249
Gay		259
Museums and galleries	Edwynn Houk Gallery	105
	Lower East Side Tenement Museum	108–109
Nightlife	Bars, lounges and pubs	198–200
	Live music	210
	Nightclubs	214–215
Restaurants		171
Shopping	Fashion	129, 138
	Food and drink	156

other products, the market has recently been renovated at a cost of $1.5m. It is open Mon–Fri, 8am–6pm.

BRITTIP
The Lower East Side was once known as a mugger's paradise. It's no longer so bad but, as in any city, you still need to be careful.

A NEW DAWN

The main language in Hester Street between the 1880s and 1920s was Yiddish – a mixture of Hebrew, German and Slavic. The local newspaper, *Forward*, was published in Yiddish and each edition sold 200,000 copies. Now the area is very quiet. There are still many Jews left, but the new waves of immigrants include Puerto Ricans and Latinos from the Dominican Republic.

If you want to see some real action, you need to go to **Delancey** and the big shopping area around Orchard and Ludlow Streets. Here you'll find bargain basement products and cutting-edge designer fashions – many young designers have started in the Lower East Side before moving uptown. **Orchard** and **Ludlow** between Delancey and East Houston Streets are also the main drags for the new bars and clubs that have been opening in the area. The best day to experience the Lower East Side is Sun, when the market is open and the whole area is buzzing with people. A large chunk of it is still closed on Sat to mark the Jewish Sabbath, but that is gradually changing due to the arrival of the Latinos.

BRITTIP
For excellently priced and clean accommodation in Lower East Side, stay at the Howard Johnson Express Inn (page 249) on East Houston.

An outstanding sight on Delancey is **Ratner's Dairy Restaurant** at 138 Delancey near Essex Street. Although it's still a dairy restaurant, it's now also home to **Lansky Lounge**, the chic nightspot that celebrates the place where mob boss Meyer Lansky used to hold court. The entrance is at 104 Norfolk Street.

MADISON SQUARE

It's a weird but true fact that the ugly Madison Square Garden building, constructed above Penn Station on 33rd Street (pages 77, 209 and 278), is the latest (and probably least attractive) of the four Madison Square Gardens that have been built in New York. But only the first two were, in fact, located at Madison Square (Map 3), which is where Madison Avenue begins and is the site of the recently renovated **Madison Square Park**. Facing the square is Cass Gilbert's **New York Life Building**, which was erected in 1928. In its shadow is **The Little Church Around the Corner** just off 5th Avenue at 29th Street. Its real name is the **Episcopal Church of the Transfiguration** and its stained glass windows commemorate famous actors such as Edwin Booth, who frequented the church at a time when being an actor was not considered to be a very honourable profession. The nearest subways are the N, R, W, 6 to 28th Street.

The Little Church Around the Corner

Madison Square at a glance: the Garden

Accommodation	Total bargains	249
Restaurants		172
Shopping	Antiques and markets	150
	Electronics	155
Tours	Madison Square Garden	43
Sights	New York Life Building	43
	The Little Church Around the Corner	43

Meatpacking District at a glance: fashion boutiques, bars and restaurants

Accommodation	Boutique chic	236
Nightlife	Bars, lounges and pubs	201
	Nightclubs	212
Restaurants		172–173
Shopping	Beauty	144
	Fashion	130

MEATPACKING DISTRICT

The Meatpacking District is to be found in the north-western corner of the West Village, south of West 14th Street to West 12th Street and from West Street to Hudson Street on the east side (Map 2). The nearest subway is the A, C, E to 14th Street. As the name suggests, the area was originally home to butchers and slaughterhouses for cattle in the 1930s. A handful of warehouses are still used for storing and cutting carcases to be distributed from wholesale markets around the city, but the majority have been abandoned over time and snapped up by eager young entrepreneurs who have used the loft-like spaces for everything from nightclubs to achingly trendy restaurants.

There are some fun hang-outs around this area, such as **Hogs & Heifers** (page 202), which is frequented by a mix of motorcycle groups and celebrities. Many women leave their bras on the ceiling as a memento! **Tortilla Flats** in Washington Street on the corner of West 12th Street is a cool, grungy café.

Until recently the area was very edgy and still a hang-out for transvestite prostitutes

– as depicted in *Sex And The City* when the man-eating Samantha moved here from the Upper East Side. Now, however, the dark, badly lit cobbled streets and alleyways have improved and lots of gentrification has taken place, so its edgy vibe is disappearing. This is also the area that Brit exports have gravitated towards. The last couple of years have seen the opening of über-cool designer shops from the Brit fashion pack, including Stella McCartney and Alexander McQueen, and the arrival of Soho House, the New York branch of London's coolest private members' club.

Not that this area is only about the new. There are some historic spots to hunt out, too, including the White Horse Tavern on Hudson Street at 11th Street, where poet Dylan Thomas allegedly went on his last drinking binge before his death in 1953. Also, take a trip to Chumley's at 86 Bedford Street, an unmarked speakeasy where John Steinbeck propped up the bar during prohibition era.

MIDTOWN

including Central Park

Technically, Midtown starts at 34th Street, but for the purposes of this area guide, we're starting at the more realistic 42nd Street (Map 3). From this point up to about 59th Street are some of the most beautiful and famous shops, hotels and buildings in the world, both to the east and west and on 5th Avenue itself (page 124). At the northern end of the area, 5th Avenue is lined with marvellous institutions such as **Saks, Bergdorf Goodman**, **Tiffany's** (our favourite jeweller) and **Trump Tower** (pages 78–79).

Fifth Avenue

BRITTIP

Weird but true, there are few coffee shops or coffee carts on 5th Avenue. If you want a coffee, your best bet is to try one of the side streets leading off to 6th Avenue.

Fabulous hotels in Midtown include the media den of the **Royalton** (pages 231–232) and the famous **Algonquin** (page 247). Opposite **St Patrick's Cathedral** (pages 81–82) on 5th Avenue is the main entrance into the **Rockefeller Center** complex of 19 statuesque buildings with the famous ice-skating rink in the middle of its central plaza (pages 71–72). There's so much to do here, from browsing in the shops to checking out the architecture or visiting the beautifully restored Art Deco **Radio City Music Hall** (page 67). Further north on 57th Street is **Carnegie Hall** (page 208).

Midtown including Central Park at a glance: 5th Avenue shopping and the Rockefeller Center

MIDTOWN EAST

The area between 5th Avenue and East River, **Midtown East** (Map 3) has its fair share of New York landmarks. No visit to the city would be complete without seeing the magnificent, marble **Grand Central Station** (pages 76–77) at 42nd Street, which has been restored to its former glory. It may be overshadowed by the **MetLife Building** from the outside, but nothing can detract from its gorgeous interior. The ceiling has been painted to show the sky as seen by God from above.

◄┃► BRITTIP

The area along East 45th Street between Vanderbilt and Lexington Avenues is packed with food carts selling everything from steak sandwiches to baked potatoes.

To the east is the stunning **Chrysler Building** (pages 74–76) and down by the river is the monolithic **United Nations Building** (page 79); and no visit to Park Avenue would be complete without a drink at the **Waldorf-Astoria** (page 227). Out of its many cocktail bars, the lobby bar is best for people-watching with a drink.

MURRAY HILL

It's a testimony to man's desire to tame his environment that the majority of Manhattan is flat. This is a result of the zoning plans created in the early 19th century, when the streets and avenues were laid out north of Downtown, except for the Village. At the same time, the City flattened the majority of Manhattan except for what is now Morningside Heights and Harlem, as nobody believed anyone would live up there! The only other area that has kept its contours is **Murray Hill** (Map 3), a largely residential neighbourhood for New York's gentry that lies between 5th and 3rd Avenues and 32nd and 40th Streets.

The most famous resident of the area was the multi-millionaire J P Morgan. His son lived in a brownstone on the corner of 37th Street and Madison Avenue, which is now the headquarters of the **Lutheran Church**. J P Morgan lived in a house next door until he had it knocked down to make way for an expansion of his library. Now known as the **Morgan Library** (pages 111–112), it has a unique collection of manuscripts, paintings, prints and furniture, which the financier collected on his trips to Europe. The nearest subways are the 6 to 33rd Street or the 4, 5, 6, 7, S to Grand Central/42nd Street.

Midtown East at a glance: the Chrysler and UN buildings		
Accommodation	Boutique chic	237
	Landmark hotels	227–228
	Medium-priced gems	243–244
	Modern luxury	232
	Total bargains	250
	Traditional luxury	234
	Upmarket	241
Gay		258, 261
Museums and galleries	Asia Society	102–103
	Frick Collection	106–107
	Japan Society	107
	Morgan Library	111–112
Nightlife	Hotel bars	207–208
	Nightclubs	215
Restaurants		179–182
Shopping	Beauty	140
	Books	151–152
	Antiques and markets	150
	Food and drink	154
Sights	Chrysler Building	74, 76
	Grand Central Station	76–77
	UN Building	79

including Times Square, Theater District
and Hell's Kitchen

TIMES SQUARE AND
THE THEATER DISTRICT

If you arrive at **Times Square** (Map 3) by
day when all the lights and motion are less
distracting, you may actually notice the lack
of a square. Like Greeley and Herald Squares,
Times Square is no more than a junction
where Broadway crosses 7th Avenue. The
Theater District starts on the boundary
with the Garment District at 41st Street, goes
north to 53rd Street and is bounded by 6th
and 8th Avenues. The best way to get there is
to take the 1, 2, 3, 7, 9, N, Q, R, S, W to Times
Square/42nd Street.

BRITTIP

Broadway isn't called The
Great White Way for nothing.
At night, it's at its magnificent
best around Times Square, but the
best way to see it is from a few
blocks north, where you really can
appreciate the glittering beauty of all
those neon signs.

The Theater District came into being at
the end of the 19th century – previously the
theatres were in the Union Square area and
then Chelsea – when Oscar Hammerstein I
(father of the great lyricist) built his opulent
but long-gone Olympia Theater on Broadway
between 44th and 45th Streets. Until then,
it had been an unfashionable area known as
Long Acre Square, housing the city's stables
and blacksmiths.

In 1904, when *The New York Times* set
up shop in what is now 1 Times Square, the
area was renamed in its honour (it's since
moved offices to around the corner). That
same year a massive fireworks display on
New Year's Eve became the precursor to the
now famous annual countdown watched by
millions of people. The surrounding Theater
District, home to the Ziegfeld Follies at the
New Amsterdam Theater, **Minsky's** and
Gypsy Rose Lee, blossomed in the 1920s. In
fact, so many theatres burst on to the scene
that even though many were converted into
cinemas in the 1940s, during a clean-up of
the burlesque shows by Mayor LaGuardia, 30
theatres still remain.

BAD TIMES COME

Sadly, by the 1960s, Times Square had lost
its shine and the economic problems of the
1970s and 1980s compounded the situation.
If you've seen Martin Scorsese's film *Taxi*

Driver, you'll have some idea of the level of
drugs, prostitution and seedy strip joints that
crowded the area. Crime rose dramatically
and until fairly recently it was not a safe place
to be.

Things started to change in the early
1990s, helped by the establishment of the
**Times Square Business Improvement
District**, which worked hard to clean things
up and pay for security guards, and the
discovery of an age-old law that prevents
sex shops from operating within a certain
distance of schools or churches. Since then
crime in the area has dropped by 60% and
many New Yorkers have even complained
of its relative cleanliness. The arrival of
the Disney company, which spent millions
renovating the New Amsterdam Theater to
put on *The Lion King* (page 220), was the last
nail in the coffin.

In all honesty, these dirt purists shouldn't
fret too much – there is still definitely an
edgy vibe to the neighbourhood, while the
constant stream of traffic and the grunginess
of many visitors stops Times Square from
being what some people think of as a
squeaky-clean environment.

All the same, it's safe enough for the
most part, attracts tenants who pay the
same rents as on more elegant 5th and
Madison Avenues, and has plenty to offer
everyone. New hotels have sprung up and
corporate companies have moved into the
neighbourhood, including media giants
Viacom, MTV, VH-1 studios, ABC TV's Good
Morning America, Condé Nast Publications
and Reuters news service.

BRITTIP

For dining after the show with
a good chance to spot celebs,
book into Angus McIndoe, 258
West 44th Street. Tel: 212-221 9222,
angusmcindoe.com.

Times Square

Midtown West including Times Square, Theater District and Hell's Kitchen at a glance: Broadway

There's the huge new **ESPN Zone**, a 3,900sq m/42,000sq ft sports, dining and entertainment complex, **Nasdaq MarketSite** with its massive sign – the largest video screen in the world – and **Madame Tussaud's** (page 71). In between are the Coco Chanel-style beauty emporium of **Sephora** (page 142) and the **World Wrestling Federation** entertainment and dining complex, which includes a restaurant and hot nightclub. Oh, and of course, there are the 30 theatres and nearly 50 cinema screens...

HELL'S KITCHEN/CLINTON

Running up the west side of Midtown from 34th Street to 57th from around 8th Avenue to the river is an area known as **Hell's Kitchen**. In the latter part of the 19th century, many poor Irish immigrants settled here, creating a ghetto. They were later joined by blacks, Italians and Latinos and inevitably gangs formed. The big employers were the docks (see *On the Waterfront* starring Marlon Brando for an insight into the lifestyle; although set in Brooklyn, it is equally true of all the dock areas), but when container ships came into play many lost their jobs. Other local industries included slaughterhouses and glue and soap factories.

A lot of the gangs were put out of business by the police in 1910, but it remained a scary area until fairly recently. It was renamed Clinton in 1959 to hide its violent past –

which is long before Bill came on the scene, so there's no link to the former president. Now a lot of people living there work in the Theater District and it's moving up in the world. 9th and 10th Avenues are full of restaurants, the **Intrepid Sea-Air-Space Museum** (page 107) is on the river and, on the whole, the area is pretty safe until around 11pm.

BRITTIP

If you have an evening out on the World Yacht (pages 86 and 184), you'll find yourself walking through Hell's Kitchen/Clinton in search of a taxi. Adopt 'the New York walk' (walk quickly and confidently) and head east to 7th or 6th Avenues where it's easiest to pick up a cab.

MORNINGSIDE HEIGHTS

Further north, the terrain gets hilly as you reach **Morningside Heights** (Map 6) home to the **Cathedral of St John the Divine** (pages 80–81) and **Columbia University**, one of the most exclusive universities in America where a year's tuition fees, room and board will set you back around $40,000. Even so, it has 20,000 students, of whom 4,000 are undergraduates. This is a beautiful area, which is bounded by 8th Avenue to the east and West 125th Street to the north.

NOHO

Wedged between Greenwich Village and the East Village is a small section of streets now known as NoHo – North of Houston Street (Map 2). Bounded by Broadway to the west, Bowery to the east, Astor Place to the north and East Houston Street to the south, it's a tiny triangular-shaped area cut off from both of the villages, yet teeming with bars, cafés and shops. The boutiques here are a match for nearby SoHo and some are just as pricey, but for innovative and unique designs they're streets ahead of many areas, with the exception of NoLiTa.

Get here via the 6 subway to Astor Place or Bleecker Street or the F, V, S to Broadway/ Lafayette Street.

NOLITA

NoLiTa stands for North of Little Italy and stretches from Kenmare Street in the south, to Houston in the north and from Crosby Street in the west to Elizabeth Street in the east (Map 2). The best subways to take are the 6 to Spring Street, the F, V, S to Broadway Lafayette Street and the F, V to 2nd Avenue.

A fairly new part of town, it's filled with funky coffee shops, bars and restaurants. In a very short space of time Elizabeth, Mott and

Mulberry Streets have seen a rapid growth in up-and-coming designers. This area was widely regarded as part of Little Italy until recent decades when it started to lose its Italian identity, following the relocation of Italian-Americans to outer boroughs.

Thanks to reasonable rents and vacant property, the latter half of the 1990s saw an influx of young urban professionals and it's now acknowledged as a neighbourhood in its own right. Due to the recent regeneration, the area is filled with cosmopolitan cafés, bars and restaurants. There's also a fashionable, edgy vibe, which is why it's become a magnet for unique boutiques selling products by up-and-coming designers.

The neighbourhood's most notable historic building is **St Patrick's Old Cathedral,** at the corner of Mott and Prince streets, which was erected in 1815 and rebuilt after a fire in 1868. It was Manhattan's main Catholic cathedral for years until a new St Patrick's

St Patrick's Old Cathedral

Noho at a glance: boutiques, bars and restaurants		
Restaurants		185
Shopping	Fashion	132

Nolita at a glance: cafés and boutiques		
Gay		261
Restaurants		185–186
Shopping	Books	152
	Fashion	132, 138
Sights	St Patrick's Old Cathedral	above

SoHo at a glance: shopping, fashion and contemporary art

Accommodation	Boutique chic	237–238
	Modern luxury	232
Gay		261
Museums and galleries	Artists' Space	102
	New Museum of Contemporary Art	117
	New York City Fire Museum	117
Nightlife	Bars, lounges and pubs	203–204
	Nightclubs	215
Restaurants		186–187
Shopping	Antiques and markets	150
	Beauty	140–142, 143–144, 146–149
	Fashion	133–135, 139
	Food and drink	154, 156
	Homeware	156
Tours	Hub Station/Pony Pedicab	83–84

was opened in 5th Avenue in Midtown in 1879. The original St Patrick's Old Cathedral is now used as a parish church and visitors are welcome to take a look around. Another landmark is the **Puck Building** on the corner of Houston and Lafayette streets. The ornate structure, built in 1885, was the original headquarters of the now defunct *Puck* magazine.

SOHO

SoHo means south of Houston, bounded by Lafayette Street at its eastern border, 6th Avenue to the west and Canal Street to the south (Map 2). The best subways are 6, C, E to Spring Street and N, R to Prince Street.

The main drag is on **West Broadway**, though Spring and Prince Streets are major shopping havens, too, and the whole area is reminiscent of Hampstead Village in London. OK, so there are no hills and the roads are wider, but it has the same picturesque, funky design-conscious element.

BRITTIP

If you're looking for a delicious latte and snack in SoHo, try Space Untitled in Green Street between Houston and Prince Streets.

It's hard to imagine the totally trendy and oh-so-expensive SoHo as a slum, yet just over 30 years ago this was the case. Despite the arrival of cutting-edge artists in the 1940s, who'd spotted the great potential of the massive loft spaces once used by manufacturers and wholesalers, the whole area was run down and shabby.

Then, in the 1960s, those same artists were forced to fight for their homes when the city decided to pull down all the buildings because they were only supposed to be used for light industry and not for living in. The artists successfully argued that the architecture of the cast-iron buildings was too valuable and the whole of SoHo was declared a historic district.

BRITTIP

For a cheap but tasty hamburger and fries, pop into Fanelli's Café on Prince Street at Mercer Street. It's one of the oldest eateries in the neighbourhood.

In the 1970s, art galleries first started moving into the area and the art boom of the 1980s truly transformed it. In 1992, the Guggenheim opened a downtown site on Broadway at Prince Street. These events coincided with a kind of bubble-bursting feeling for the more cutting-edge artists, especially those who could no longer afford SoHo's sky-rocketing rents. Many have now moved on to Chelsea and TriBeCa, and SoHo has become a wealthy residential neighbourhood occupied by anyone rich enough to afford large loft spaces.

However, there are still plenty of art galleries – certainly a higher density than most areas of Manhattan – but the nature of the area has changed quite substantially (and we think for the better). Designers, clothes boutiques and dedicated beauty shops have arrived en masse, though the emphasis still lies heavily on style and art in terms of presentation and decor. The Guggenheim has shut up shop to be replaced by **Prada's** stunning flagship store (page 135), but a formidable sense of style remains and can be seen daily at the fashionistas' **SoHo Grand Hotel** haunt (page 232). Coffee shops, bars and restaurants that normal mortals can afford are now in better supply and the beauty boutiques with their wooden flooring, high ceilings and gleaming displays are wonderful places to get cheap, expert beauty advice.

BRITTIP

For a well-priced, delicious lunch al fresco, head to the Gourmet Garage on the corner of Broome and Mercer Streets. It has a wonderful deli with ready-made salads to take away.

SoHo also has several historic and architectural places of interest too. While MoMA's **New Museum of Contemporary Art** (page 117) is the only remaining art museum in the area, visitors can also get an art fix by hunting out **The Broken Kilometer** at 393 West Broadway, an installation by Walter De Maria that uses 500 brass rods to play tricks on the viewer's perspective.

Another notable SoHo landmark is **Hunt the Singer Building** at 561 Broadway, a beautiful building that was constructed in 1904 for the sewing machine company. The 12-storey façade is wonderfully ornate, with wrought-iron balconies and graceful arches.

You might also want to check out the New York City Fire Museum at 278 Spring Street, which houses a fascinating collection of Manhattan fire-fighting equipment and memorabilia from the 18th to 20th centuries. Children will love the upstairs that houses rows of original fire engines.

TRIBECA

TriBeCa (Map 1) like other acronyms is a shortening of the area's location. In this case it means the triangle below Canal Street. It is bounded by Canal to the north, Murray to the south, West Broadway to the east and the Hudson River. To get here on the subway, use the 1, 9 to Canal or Franklin Streets or the 1, 2, 3, 9 to Chambers Street.

TriBeCa provides a good idea of what SoHo looked like 20 years ago. With the increasing pressure to find affordable housing, the empty warehouses of TriBeCa were ripe for the gentrification process that has been happening all over New York, including SoHo, the East Village and even the Lower East Side to a certain extent, and the area certainly has its fair share of pretty cast-iron buildings and quaint cobbled streets. Along **Harrison Street** is a row of well-preserved Federal-style townhouses and the area around White Street is particularly picturesque.

In the late 1970s, the former industrial buildings were targeted by estate agents for residential dwellings, but it was not really until the late 1980s that the area became a favourite with artists priced out of SoHo. Now TriBeCa is home to a variety of media and artistic businesses, such as galleries, recording studios and graphic companies.

Its most famous film company, the **TriBeCa Film Center** at 375 Greenwich Street, which is part-owned by Robert De Niro, has production offices and screening rooms and is used by visiting film-makers. They, of course, frequent De Niro's extremely expensive **TriBeCa Grill** on the ground floor of the building. Visiting film-makers have also been given a boost by the opening of the triangular-shaped **TriBeCa Grand Hotel**, which has its own private screening room.

Now the area is deemed quite hip – being home to Harvey Keitel and Naomi Campbell among others – it has attracted a lot of upper middle-class families, while restaurants and nightclubs are frequented by residents from the nearby Battery Park City. It is also home to the **TriBeCa Film Festival**, which showcases independent movies during the second week of May.

Tribeca at a glance: urban gentrification and film

Accommodation	Excellent value	248
	Modern luxury	232–233
Gay		261
Nightlife	Bars, lounges and pubs	203–204
	Hotel bars	209
	Nightclubs	216
Restaurants		190–191
Shopping	Antiques and markets	150
	Fashion	135–136, 139

Union Square including Flatiron District at a glance: restaurants and the Flatiron Building

Accommodation	Medium-priced gems	242
	Total bargains	249
Museums and galleries	Museum of Sex	115–116
Nightlife	Comedy clubs	205
	Nightclubs	214, 216
Restaurants		172, 191–192
Shopping	Beauty	139
	Books	152
	Fashion	139
	Food and drink	154
Sights	Flatiron Building	76
	Grace Church	81

UNION SQUARE
including Flatiron District

Take the L, N, Q, R, W, 4, 5, 6 to Union Square at 14th Street (Map 2). This area was once pretty run down and overrun with drug pushers and muggers, but now it's one of the trendiest neighbourhoods in New York. The stretch of Park Avenue South between 14th and 23rd Streets is filled with some truly 'hip' eateries and is known as **Restaurant Row**.

BRITTIP
The West Hotel Union Square on Park Avenue South at 17th Street is home to Underbar (page 216), one of the most stylish nightclubs in New York.

Along here you'll find **Tammany Hall**, the most corrupt City Hall in New York's history. It was home to Jimmy Walker, ostensibly a popular mayor, but a man who had been elected by the gangsters in the 1920s, which is effectively how organised crime was born in America. The gangsters were impossible to prosecute because they knew all the judges, cops and politicians in New York and virtually lived at Tammany Hall. Walker even had showers installed for them. Eventually, in the face of mounting financial problems in the city, Walker was forced to resign and his successor, Fiorello LaGuardia, decided to go after the gangs.

In the middle of Union Square is **Luna Park** (page 276), a great casual place for a bite to eat in the summer, with outdoor seating. Further north on Broadway to Madison Square Park, you'll find **Theodore Roosevelt's birthplace** at 28 East 20th Street. It's not the original building, but it does house some great memorabilia from

the former president's life (open Wed–Sun 9am–5pm; $3). Just around the corner is the wonderful, triangular **Flatiron Building** (page 76), at the end of what was once known as **Ladies Mile**, the city's most fashionable shopping district along Broadway and 6th Avenue from 14th Street.

BRITTIP
Create an instant picnic by buying farm-fresh produce, home-made breads, cheeses and drinks from the Union Square Farmers' Market every Mon, Wed, Fri and Sat.

UPPER EAST SIDE

One of the most conservative areas of New York, the **Upper East Side** (Map 4) stretches from Central Park South to 98th Street and is centred on 5th, Madison, Park and Lexington Avenues. It came into being after Central Park was finally completed in 1876 and the rich and famous of the Gilded Era – the Whitneys, Carnegies, Fricks, Vanderbilts and Astors – decided to build their mansions alongside. It was a time when Neo-Classicism was the favourite architectural design, but many of the houses left standing are not the originals as the grandiose properties were built and rebuilt in an ever-more opulent style or replaced with apartment blocks.

BRITTIP
Get your shoes shined at Jim's Shoe Repair (jimsshoerepair. com) on East 59th Street between Madison and Park Avenues – it's a real institution that has existed since the 1930s.

WHICH MET'S THE MET?

Traditionally, the Metropolitan Opera House, with its crystal chandeliers and red-carpeted staircases, has been known as the Met. Increasingly, though, the Metropolitan Museum of Art is being referred to by the same moniker, which is causing a certain amount of confusion. It probably depends which establishment you stumble across first. For us, the museum will always be the Met!

Two things have always remained the same, though. The neighbourhood is known as the Silk Stocking District because of the vast family fortunes represented in the area, and the grand old apartment houses are known as 'white glove' buildings because of the uniforms of the doormen. People still pay a fortune to live here. For instance, Jackie Onassis's former 14-room apartment at 1040 5th Avenue near East 86th Street sold some years ago for a whopping $9m. The mansion on the corner of East 86th is one of 9 once owned by the Vanderbilts. Nearby residents include Michael J Fox and Bette Midler.

If you're serious about designer clothes, then you'll be visiting the designer stores that line **Madison Avenue**. If you're clever you won't buy, just gather information on what's new for when you go rummaging through the designer selections at **Daffy's** or the sample sales (page 126).

This area is also full of museums, with a staggering array to choose from. They range from the world's largest and, arguably, most magnificent – the **Metropolitan Museum of Art** (pages 109–110) – to the jewel of the **Frick Collection** (pages 106–107), housed in the magnate's former mansion. Near to the Frick is the joyous **Whitney Museum of American Art** (page 122), with its emphasis on contemporary art.

Further north is the beautiful-looking **Guggenheim** (page 120), as well as the **Cooper-Hewitt** (page 105), the **Jewish Museum** (page 108) and the **International Center of Photography** (page 107). Finally, up on the borders of East Harlem, populated by Latin Americans, are the **Museum of the City of New York** (page 114) and **El Museo del Barrio** (page 105).

UPPER WEST SIDE

Central Park divides the Upper East and West Sides not only geographically, but also in terms of attitude. If the East Side is upper

Upper East Side at a glance: museums and shopping

Accommodation	Excellent value	248
	Landmark hotels	228
	Medium-priced gems	246
	Traditional luxury	234–235
Museums and galleries	Cooper-Hewitt Museum	105
	International Center of Photography	107
	Jewish Museum	108
	Metropolitan Museum of Art	109–111
	Mount Vernon Hotel Museum and Garden	112
	Museo del Barrio	105
	Museum of the City of New York	114
	Neue Galerie Museum for German and Austrian Art	116–117
	Solomon R Guggenheim Museum	120
	Whitney Museum of American Art	122
Nightlife	Comedy clubs	206
	Live music	211
Restaurants		192–193
Shopping	Antiques and markets	151
	Beauty	142, 144
	Department stores	125–126
	Fashion	136–137, 139
	Food and drink	154, 156
	Homeware	156–157
	Speciality	157
Sights	Gracie Mansion	76
Tours	Metro Bicycles	84
	Screen Tours	89

crust, conservative old money, then the West Side (Map 5) is more artistic. It's a vibrant neighbourhood filled with bars, restaurants, shops, museums and, of course, the culture of the Lincoln Center.

The area is now anchored by the amazing new **AOL Time Warner Center**'s twin towers at Columbus Circle, which house a mixture of offices, hotel, shopping and cultural centres. The $1.7-billion complex includes the **Mandarin Oriental Hotel and Spa**, the new home of jazz at the Lincoln Center (pages 212 and 233), broadcast facilities for live transmission of CNN, apartments and **The Palladium**, a massive space for shops, restaurants and entertainment venues (nearest subway is the A, B, C, D, 1, 9 to 59th Street/Columbus Circle). As you navigate the traffic lights to cross the roads at Columbus Circle, you can ponder on the fact that this is where Joe Colombo, the boss of one of the 5 Mafia families of New York, was shot.

BRITTIP
Take a break at Whole Foods, a huge market selling a dazzling array of prepared organic foods, on the basement level of AOL Time Warner Center. Either dine at one of the tables there or eat in Central Park across the street.

Up Broadway and left down West 63rd Street you'll find the **Lincoln Center**. This was once filled with the slums that housed poor Puerto Ricans (the setting for the 1961 movie *West Side Story*) until Robert Moses proposed the building of various cultural centres that include the **Metropolitan Opera House**, the **New York State Theater** and **Avery Fisher Hall**. To see more, join one of the popular backstage tours or enjoy the free lunchtime music supplied by visiting jazz and folk bands during the summer.

BUILT TO LAST
The Upper West Side is well known for its beautiful buildings, including the Beaux Arts **Ansonia Hotel** on Broadway between 73rd and 74th Streets, which has been called home by both Babe Ruth and Igor Stravinsky in its time. Starting on the southern tip of Central Park West, which runs all the way up Central Park, is the Art Deco stunner at No 55, which was used as the setting for the film *Ghostbusters*.

On 67th Street near Central Park West is the **Hotel des Artistes** that, as the name suggests, was built for the artistic types who used its studios. Over the years it has been home to such celebrities as Noel Coward and

Isadora Duncan. Today you can dine at the elegant **Café des Artistes** there. Back on Central Park West between 71st and 72nd Streets is the yellow façade of the Art Deco **Majestik** apartment house, which was built in 1930.

BRITTIP
Once you cross West 59th Street going north, 8th, 9th, 10th and 11th Avenues become Central Park West, Columbus, Amsterdam and West End Avenues respectively.

This neighbourhood is particularly favoured by stars of stage and screen who prefer the Big Apple to Hollywood. Many have apartments along Central Park West, where one of the most coveted addresses is the city's first luxury apartment building, the famous **Dakota Building**, which was the first apartment block ever to be built on the Upper West Side in 1884, and was named after the distant territory to indicate its remoteness from anything else on the West Side. Of course, since then it has had a long line of famous inhabitants, including Leonard Bernstein, Judy Garland and Boris Karloff. Its most famous resident of all, **John Lennon**, was gunned down outside the building by a crazed fan in 1980. His widow Yoko Ono still lives here – she owns several apartments – and she donated money to build the Strawberry Fields memorial to the star in Central Park, just across the road.

BRITTIP
For the ingredients for a picnic in Central Park while you're on the Upper West Side, nip to Pioneer Supermarket, 289 Columbus Avenue, 212–874 9506, Mon–Sat 8am–9.45pm.

A couple of blocks north between 73rd and 74th is the Neo-Renaissance style **Langham**, which was built in 1905, and between 74th and 75th is the **San Remo**, built in 1930, where Rita Hayworth died of Alzheimer's in 1987. Residents have included Dustin Hoffman and Paul Simon, and rumour has it that the resident committee turned down Madonna! The **Eldorado**, which Roth designed on Central Park West, has been home to Marilyn Monroe and Groucho Marx.

Several blocks north, on the corner of 81st Street and Central Park West, stands the elegant **Beresford**. Between them, these grand apartment blocks have housed a huge number of celebrities, including such names as Lauren Bacall, Dustin Hoffman, Steve Martin and Jerry Seinfeld, who bought Isaac Stern's sprawling apartment home.

MUSEUM HALF MILE

On Central Park West at 77th Street is the **New York Historical Society** (page 118), which was formed in 1804 and was the only art museum in the city until the opening of the Metropolitan Museum of Art in 1872. It was founded to chronicle New York's history, but still houses the world's largest collection of Tiffany stained-glass shades and lamps and 2 million manuscripts, including letters sent by George Washington during the War of Independence.

Next door is the real big boy of museums, the **American Museum of Natural History** (pages 100–102), which was the brainchild of scientist Albert Smith Bickmore. It first opened at the New York Arsenal in Central Park in 1869, but by 1874 had moved to these bigger premises. Architect Calvert Vaux, who was also responsible for the Met Museum and largely responsible for Central Park, created the bulk of the building, which has since had a Romanesque-style façade added to its 77th Street side and a Beaux Arts-style frontage on the Central Park West side. This is a favourite museum of ours. It's crammed with well laid-out exhibitions that really bring the world of science, scientific discovery and expeditions to life, while the **Rose Center** and **Big Bang Theater** attract major crowds to see the 13-billion-year history of the universe.

The Upper West Side's Museum Half Mile also includes the **Children's Museum of Manhattan** (page 104) on 83rd Street between Broadway and Amsterdam Avenue, where interactive exhibits keep the young ones happy.

West 106th Street, at the top end of the neighbourhood, is now known as **Duke Ellington Broadway**. This is where the great musician lived, premiered many of his songs and was buried in 1974. Over 10,000 people came to his funeral and there is a memorial to him on 5th Avenue at West 110th by Central Park's Harlem Meer.

WEST VILLAGE

The West Village, on the other side of 7th Avenue, has an amazingly pretty collection of cobbled streets lined with picturesque homes and trees. These are among some of the oldest remaining houses in New York, many being built in the 1820s and 1850s, and quite a few have the one thing that is so rare in Manhattan – a back garden, albeit tiny. To get here take the 1, 9 to Christopher Street or the A, C, E to 14th Street or the L subway to 8th Avenue.

FAMOUS SPEAKEASY

On the corner of Bedford Street, number 86 was one of the most famous former speakeasies in New York. Known as **Chumley's**, the front entrance merely had an old grille used for checking over potential customers during Prohibition. In the old days, a dumb waiter took two people at a time to the gambling den upstairs, and the best table in the house was right by the entrance to the cellar, where people could hide if there was a raid. Unfortunately it's now closed, but there are rumours of a reopening.

Upper West Side at a glance: the arts, museums and culture

Accommodation	Excellent value	248
	Modern luxury	233
Museums and galleries	American Museum of Natural History	100, 102
	Children's Museum of Manhattan	104
	New York Historical Society	118
Nightlife	Bars, lounges and pubs	204
	Comedy clubs	206
	Live music	211
	Nightclubs	216
Restaurants		194–195
Shopping	Antiques and markets	151
	Beauty	145
	Food and drink	154
	Homeware	157
Sights	Cathedral of St John the Divine	80–81
Tours	AOL Time Warner Center	211
	Metro Bicycles	84

BRITTIP

Crossing Bedford is Barrow Street, where you'll find One If By Land, Two If By Sea. It's in the oldest building housing a restaurant in Manhattan, a former carriage house built in 1726. Great food, service and decor. If you're in the mood for a romantic splurge, this is the place. Tel 212-228 0822, oneifbyland.com.

At the corner of **Grove Street** is the oldest wooden house in the West Village. Built in 1822, it's the most exclusive cottage in the area and costs $6,000 a month to rent, but it does have its own little garden: what a bargain! All around Grove Street the houses are covered in a network of vines, which blossom in May and have grown in the area for 150 years.

A MATTER OF RIGHTS

Christopher Street, the main drag of the West Village, is the heart of the gay community and a shopping paradise for antique lovers. **Sheridan Square**, one of the Village's busiest junctions, has been the scene of two major riots. First were the New York Draft Riots of 1863, sparked off by the requirement to join the army for the Civil War. The rich could buy their way out, but the poor had no choice and were fearful they would lose their jobs to the newly freed black slaves.

The second riot is the more famous and is known as the Stonewall Riot. This was sparked in 1969 by the police raiding the Stonewall gay bar and arresting its occupants – an event that frequently occurred at the many gay watering holes in the area. This time the community decided to fight back and, over a period of three nights, the gay community held its ground in the Stonewall as it was surrounded by police. It was the crucial first step made by gay people in standing up for their rights.

Christopher Street is still filled with bars, restaurants and bookstores that are used by gays – though not exclusively – but many members of the gay community have moved on to Chelsea.

YORKVILLE

Between Lexington Avenue and the East River from East 77th to 96th Streets is the working to middle class enclave of Yorkville (Map 5) (subway 4, 5, 6 to 86th Street), which has an interesting mix of cultures, singles and families.

BRITTIP

Stop off at The Vinegar Factory in 91st Street (page 156), where you'll find an extensive selection of cheeses, meats, breads and salads, and head for the nearby Carl Schurz Park for a picnic by the river (elizabar.com).

It was originally populated by German-Hungarians, who moved northwards from their first stopping point in the East Village's Thompkins Square with the arrival of Italian and Slavic immigrants. Now, though, you'd be hard-pressed to find the few remnants of German culture, as most left the neighbourhood during the Second World War to avoid anti-German feelings.

BRITTIP

For some of the world's finest coffees and teas, pop in to McNulty's Tea & Coffee Company, 109 Christopher Street, between Bleecker and Hudson streets.

The most famous resident in the area is the mayor, who lives in the official residence at Gracie Mansion (page 76) overlooking the East River and the lovely Carl Schurz Park at East 89th Street.

West Village at a glance: pretty streets

Gay		255, 258–259, 259–60, 262
Nightlife	Bars, lounges and pubs	204
	Comedy clubs	206
	Nightclubs	216
Restaurants		167–169
Shopping	Beauty	142, 144
	Books	152
	Fashion	137
	Speciality	157–158
Tours	Literary Pub Crawl	92

CHAPTER 3

Getting Around

When most people talk about New York, they actually mean Manhattan, which is the long, thin sliver of an island in the middle of the four outer boroughs of Staten Island, Queens, the Bronx and Brooklyn.

You'll find diagrammatic maps, such as the one below, dotted throughout the book to help you focus on the basic geography of the area. Once you get the hang of roughly where everything is, you'll find it easier to use the subway and bus maps on the inside front cover, and the street maps at the back.

ORIENTATION

Manhattan is 21km/13mls long and 3.2km/2mls wide for the most part and almost all of it above 14th Street is on the grid system that was introduced quite early on in New York's history. The main exceptions are Chinatown and Greenwich Village, which, like Downtown, had already established its eccentric random arrangement of streets (like ours in the UK) before urban planning and refused to get on the grid system. The other exception is Broadway, which follows an old Indian trail that runs largely north to south on the west side of the island, then cuts across to the east side as it runs down towards Downtown.

BRITTIP

To New Yorkers, 'downtown' does not mean the city centre, but means south, while 'uptown' means north. You will need to get used to these terms if you are planning to use the subway – which is simpler to use than it looks at first!

Here are a few basic rules about the geography of Manhattan; it is useful to acquaint yourself with them as soon as possible, then you'll be able to walk around with confidence.
▶ Manhattan is divided into three main areas: Downtown, which includes neighbourhoods south of 14th Street; Midtown, the area between 14th and 59th Streets; and Uptown, areas north of 59th Street.
▶ All the roads going across Manhattan east to west are streets and all the roads going north to south are avenues.
▶ The city is divided between east and west by 5th Avenue and all the street numbers begin there. This means that 2 West 57th Street is just a few steps to the west of 5th Avenue while 2 East 57th Street is just a few steps to the east of 5th Avenue.
▶ Most streets in Manhattan are one way. With a few exceptions, traffic on even-numbered streets travels east and traffic on odd-numbered streets travels west. Traffic on major 'crosstown' streets – so-called because they are horizontal on the street maps of Manhattan – travels in both directions. From south to north, these include Canal, Houston, 14th, 23rd, 34th, 42nd, 57th, 72nd, 79th, 86th and 96th Streets.
▶ When travelling north to south or vice versa, remember that traffic on York Avenue goes both ways, 1st Avenue goes from south to north, 2nd Avenue goes south and 3rd goes north mostly, though there is a small two-way section. Lexington goes south, Park

Areas of New York

THE BRONX

QUEENS

EAST RIVER

LAGUARDIA AIRPORT

MANHATTAN

CENTRAL PARK

HUDSON RIVER

JFK AIRPORT

UPPER NEW YORK BAY

BROOKLYN

JAMAICA BAY

LOWER NEW YORK BAY

STATEN ISLAND

AIRPORT SECURITY

Since the terrorist attacks of 11 September 2001, the relaxed security systems that operated in most American airports have been seriously tightened up. Expect longer queues and subsequent waiting times getting through immigration and baggage checks. Remember that it is prohibited to carry any sharp items in your hand luggage, so make sure you put scissors, tweezers and nail files in your main check-in luggage. There's also a restriction on liquids; items such as bottled water, shampoos and conditioners aren't allowed through. You should also be prepared to be asked to open your bags for inspection, remove your shoes and to be frisked by a security guard with a hand-held scanner.

goes in both directions, Madison goes north and 5th Avenue goes south. Central Park West goes both ways, Columbus Avenue goes south, Amsterdam Avenue north, Broadway goes in both directions until Columbus Circle, after which it continues southbound only to the tip of Manhattan. West End Avenue and Riverside Drive go in both directions.

BRITTIP

To calculate the distance from one place to another, 20 north-south blocks or 10 east-west blocks equal about 1.6km/1 mile. This rule does not apply to the Financial District or Greenwich Village.

▶ Numbered avenue addresses increase from south to north.

JFK AirTrain

ENTERING THE US

As of January 2009, all Visa Waiver Programme travellers (if you're entering the US from the UK then you are a VWP traveller) have to get official authorisation before going to America. To do this, go on to the internet-based Electronic System for Travel Authorisation (ESTA) to apply, https://esta.cbp.dhs.gov. Fill in the online application form, submit it and record your application number. Within 72 hours you can check to see if you've been approved, held or rejected (you can ask for the results to be forwarded to your email). If you're not successful, you may still be able to obtain a visa through the US embassy.

BRITTIP

Do not use any sites that charge a fee to provide information or submit ESTA applications.

ARRIVING BY AIR

JOHN F KENNEDY INTERNATIONAL AIRPORT (JFK)
718-244 4444
jfk-airport.net
JFK is in the borough of Queens and is the best place to enter or leave New York by air. It is 24km/15mls from Midtown Manhattan, a journey that will take you 50–60 minutes.

Taxi
New York is unusual because you can't pre-arrange a pickup by a New York taxi; you'll need a car or livery service for that. The cost of a yellow medallion taxi into Manhattan centre is a fixed rate of $45 (per taxi) as set by the New York Taxi and Limousine Commission (nyc.gov/taxi). Bridge and tunnel tolls are extra (around $6 and you can pay at the end of the journey) as is the 15% tip, so think around $50.

Train
The AirTrain JFK: (212-435 7000, jfk-airport. net/airtrain.html) is a flat $5 enter/exit fare. They run every 4–8 minutes 24 hours a day and will take you to the Howard Beach or Jamaica stations from where you connect to the A subway, bus or Long Island Rail Road trains to head into town.

Bus
New York Airport Service Express
Bus: Westside & Eastside, 718-875 8200, nyairportservice.com. Catch one from the Airport Bus Center. They run 6.15am-11.10pm daily every 15–30 minutes, cost $15 (or $27 round trip) and will drop you off Midtown

west or east (serving midtown hotels between 31st and 60th Streets ONLY. Midtown hotels $15 one way, round trip $33).

◀▶ BRITTIP

A great website has been launched covering the main New York airports, airportinfo alerts. com, which notifies you of important information such as delays caused by weather, parking space capacity and AirTrain service charges. You can even have free alerts sent direct to your mobile phone or email account before you travel.

Trans-Bridge Lines: 1-800 962 9135 or 610-868 6001, transbridgebus.com. $17 (one way) $32.30 (round trip) leaving at 3.30 and 7pm daily (from terminal 4 to Port Authority Bus Terminal).
A MetroCard is accepted on all MTA New York City Transit trains and local buses (see page 60).

Private hire car and Super Shuttle
Classic Limousine: 1-800-666 4949 or 631-567 5100, classictrans.com.

Supersaver by Carmel: 1-800-924 9954 or 212-666 6666, carmellimo.com. To Manhattan it costs $40 5am–8pm or $45 8pm–5am.

SuperShuttle: 212-209 7000 (reservations 212-258 3826), supershuttle.com. A door-to-door minibus service from the airport to your hotel operating 24 hours a day year round. Look for the blue van! Costs $15–19.

NEWARK LIBERTY INTERNATIONAL AIRPORT
973-961 6000
newarkairport.com

Taxi
The journey from Newark to central Manhattan takes around 40 minutes, but add at least 30 minutes in the rush hour. Set taxi fares range from $50 to the Battery Park area to $70 and above to 185th Street. There's a $5 extra charge for all destinations to the east side of Manhattan. For more information contact the Newark Taxi Commission, 973-733 8912, nyc.gov/taxi.

Train
AirTrain: 1-888-397 4636, airtrainnewark. com. This $415m link connecting the airport terminals with Newark Liberty International Airport Train Station opened in 2003. You can get to Manhattan from the station by taking an NJ Transit or Amtrak train to New York

Penn Station, from where you can connect to the city's subways and buses with ease, $15 for a 30-minute journey.

Bus
Newark Liberty Airport Express: coachusa. com/olympia/ss.newarkairport.asp. A convenient service to Manhattan that leaves every 15 minutes, 24 hours a day, and 365 days of the year. One-way $15, round trip $25. Three pick-up and drop-off locations in Manhattan – Port Authority Bus Terminal, Bryant Park and Grand Central Station – and terminals A, B and C at the airport.

Private hire car and SuperShuttle services: As from John F Kennedy International airport (see left).

LAGUARDIA AIRPORT (LGA)
718-533 3400
panynj.gov/airports/laguardia.html
This is the airport you'll probably arrive at if you've taken an internal domestic flight from another state. TWIA, United Airlines and Continental Airlines all operate here. It's situated about 13km/8mls from the centre of Manhattan, between Queens and the Bronx.

Areas of Manhattan

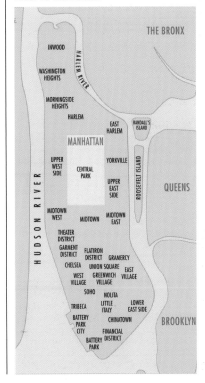

BRITTIP

Brit Guide New York **user** Margy Wooding wrote to us after a visit to Manhattan to pass on the following luggage tip: 'Neither the airports nor the train stations have left luggage facilities (baggage storage). I needed this when I had an extra day in NYC recently after arriving from elsewhere in the US at LaGuardia International Airport at lunchtime, and was leaving for London the same night from JFK. I'd hoped to leave my suitcase at Grand Central Station but was told it wasn't possible. The lady at the information desk there told me the only place for left luggage in Manhattan is Schwartz Travel Services 355 West 36th Street, between 8th and 9th Avenues near Penn Station (0800-2300) or 34 West 46th Street, between 5th and 6th Avenues near Times Square and Grand Central Station (0900-1800), 212-290-2626. I only needed it for one hour and it cost me $10 (but the nice woman there said I could've left it overnight). A bargain I thought.'

Taxi

You'll find a clearly marked taxi rank outside the main terminals. Unlike JFK, you pay by the meter rather than a flat rate, and you will also be charged tolls. A basic guide is $25–30 plus tolls ($4-6) and tip, and the journey should take about 20–25 minutes.

BRITTIP

Ignore offers of transport from people hanging around the terminals. If you're tired and wanting to save some cash it's tempting, but it's not safe so stick to the modes of transport above and you can't go wrong. Also, seek out uniformed porters or airline employees if you need baggage assistance.

Bus

New York Airport Express Bus: 718-875 8200, nyairportservice.com. A far cheaper option into town than taxi, taking around 40–50 minutes. The fare costs only $12 (or $21 round trip) and buses run daily 7.20am-11pm, leaving every 30 minutes. To catch your ride into town, follow the Ground Transportation signs out of the terminal and

METROCARD

The flat fare to travel on the subway or bus is $2.25. For value for money, however, it's wise to buy a MetroCard. You have 2 choices when purchasing: a pay-per-ride (regular) MetroCard or an Unlimited Ride MetroCard. The former allows you to buy as many rides as you want from $4.50 to $80. If you put $8 or more on your card, you'll receive a 15% bonus: for example, a $20 purchase gives you $23 on your card. The second option, Unlimited Ride MetroCard, allows you to buy an unlimited number of subway or bus rides for a fixed price. You can choose from a 1-Day Fun Pass, $8.25, which lasts until 3am the following day; 7-Day Pass, $27; 14-Day, $51.50; 30-Day, $89 or 7-Day Express Bus Plus, $45.

You can purchase the cards from subway ticket offices (cash only), vending machines in most subways, from drugstores such as Rite Aid and Hudson News or from the Times Square Visitors' Center at 1560 Broadway between 46th and 47th Streets. Some hotels also sell them at the reception desk.

For more details, contact the MTA on 1-800-638 7622 or mta.info.

wait at the M60 or Q33 bus stop sign by the curb (serving midtown hotels between 31st and 60th Streets ONLY). Midtown hotels $12 one way, round trip $27).

GETTING AROUND

There are lots of options for getting around Manhattan and the outer boroughs. The yellow cabs that you'll see in abundance are the fastest and most efficient way of getting to a destination, but they're not the cheapest. The subway in New York is easy to use and perfect for people with a limited budget, as well as being under cover when it's raining. If you'd rather see the sights, then jump on a bus, though progress can be slow in rush hour. Then there's the oldest mode of transport: your feet. Walking around Manhattan is a joyful experience and thoroughly recommended; just don't forget to pack some comfy shoes.

TAXI

No trip to Manhattan would be complete without a ride in a yellow Medallion cab. There are more than 10,000 in operation in the city, so you're not going to have trouble spotting one! It's the preferred means of transport for many visitors, largely because there are so many about and the fares are reasonable. However, be warned: even though the fares are much cheaper than in London, the cost still mounts up pretty quickly. Fares start at $2.50 and increase 40c every 0.32km/1/5ml or 20c per minute in stopped or slow traffic, with a 50c surcharge at night (8pm–6am) and $1 in peak hour (Mon–Fri 4–8pm). It's not just the cost of the ride that you have to take into consideration, but the $1 tip to the hotel doorman and the 15% tip to the driver. It can work out to be an expensive option if used too often.

In any case, you will need to have a good idea of where you are going and how to get there, as most of the cab drivers in New York are the latest immigrants to have arrived and have very little clue about how to get around the city. The best way to ensure you don't get into any difficulties is to always carry the full address of where you're going, preferably with a map reference too. Fortunately, thanks to the grid system, it is relatively easy to educate yourself about where you are going and so you can give them directions!

BRITTIP
For more information on taxis, log on to ny.com/transportation/taxis, which has the lowdown on prices, tips on hailing a cab and other useful hints and tips.

▶ First off, never expect the driver to be the chatty character you're used to. Some speak little English and are not interested in making conversation.
▶ Secondly, make sure you get into a taxi heading in the direction that you want to be going. If you are travelling uptown but you're on a road heading downtown, walk a block east or west so you'll be pointing in the right direction. It saves time and money, and if you don't, the taxi driver will know immediately that you're a tourist.
▶ To hail a taxi, look at the lights on the top of the yellow Medallion taxis. If the central light is on, the driver is working and available. If all the lights are out, the driver is working but has a fare. If the outer 2 lights or all 3 lights are on, the driver is off-duty – you'll see the words. The best method for hailing a cab is to hold out your arm while standing at the kerb.
▶ When you get to a toll, expect the taxi driver to turn around and demand the cash to pay for it, but you are quite within your rights to ask him to add it to your final fare.
▶ Beware of trying to get a cab at around 4pm. Not only is it the approach of rush hour, but it is also when most drivers change shifts,

so getting a taxi is well nigh impossible as they don't want to go anywhere but home! If you really need a taxi at this time, call a car service company.

BRITTIP
In 2008, the Taxi and Limousine Commission approved a scheme to install credit and debit card payment systems in the rear of yellow Medallion cabs, so if you don't have cash with you, you can still hail a taxi if you have plastic.

▶ Cabs take cash and credit/debit cards, but if you're paying in cash it's best to have some small bills because cabbies don't usually break anything higher than $20.
▶ In addition to the medallion on the roof, a legitimate taxi will have an automatic receipt machine mounted on the dashboard.
▶ If you find yourself below Canal Street after business hours or at the weekend, you might have difficulty finding a yellow cab. Your best bet is to phone one of the many companies listed under Taxicab Service in the *Yellow Pages*. Fares are slightly higher than for the metered cabs, but they are a safer option.
▶ There is no extra charge per person or for luggage, but a licensed taxi won't be able to take more than four people.
▶ Fasten your seatbelt once in the cab. All taxis are now required by law to provide them and passengers in the front seat have to wear them.
▶ Avoid unregulated cars at all costs. Known as gypsy cabs, these vehicles aren't registered, so are less safe, plus, unlike the UK, they usually cost more than cabs. Basically, if it's not a yellow Medallion taxi, don't get in!

New York cabs

BRITTIP

If you want to know roughly how much you're going to pay for a ride, log on to yellowcabnyc. com/fareestimator, which allows you to key in where you're travelling to and from and whether you're travelling at peak or off-peak times, and will then calculate an average fare.

CAR SERVICE COMPANIES

When you need to be certain you have a taxi ride to the airport or some other destination, here are the companies you can phone, all of which provide a 24-hour service:

Carmel: 212-666-6666, carmelcarservice.com.

Dial 7: 212-777 7777/1-800-777 8888, dial7.com.

Tel-Aviv: 212-777 7777/1-800-222 9888, telavivlimo.com.

Tri-State Limousine: 516-9334759, toll-free (866) NY-LIMO2, tristatelimony.com.

ON THE SUBWAY

The first time you take a look at a subway map of New York, you can be forgiven for thinking you need a degree in the whole system to get anywhere. Plus the signposts – both outside and inside the stations – can easily be missed.

In addition, the Metropolitan Transportation Authority (MTA) is undergoing a billion-dollar rejuvenation programme of many subway stops and has introduced new, clean trains on to the network, though New Yorkers aren't convinced that will last! On the old subway trains, the conductor would always announce stops and interchanges. These, for the large part, were unintelligible, but the new trains have pre-recorded announcements in a non-New York accent that can be understood.

BRITTIP

Generally, if you're going downtown, use subway entrances on the west side of the road and if you're going uptown, use subway entrances on the east side. This way you should be heading in the right direction, but do always check before entering.

SUBWAY MAP

There are subway maps on the inside front cover of this book. You can also get hold of free MTA maps in most subways stations, hotel lobbies and information centres.
▶ The subway lines are all indicated on the map by a colour but, unlike the London Underground, the colours are not used in the stations and on the trains. The important bit is the number or letter. Below the name of every stop you will find the letters and numbers of lines that stop there, such as 7, S Grand Central/42nd Street.

BRITTIP

Changes to subway schedules often occur at the last minute, so pay attention to posters on subway station walls and any announcements you hear on the platforms.

Mosaic art on the MTA subway

▶ When examining a subway map, a number or letter in a diamond means rush-hour service, in a circle it denotes normal service and a square indicates the end of a line. Black and white lines connecting white and black circles indicate a free subway transfer. White circles on coloured lines indicate express stops (express trains skip about three stops for every one that they make).

▶ If the numbers against your destination on the subway map are printed in a lighter tone, they are peak-time only.

◀▶ BRITTIP

The subway's traditional high entrance turnstiles, known by locals as Iron Maidens, are being replaced by high entrance exit turnstiles (HEETs). HEETS only take MetroCard rather than tokens, so if you're going to be travelling a lot by subway, a MetroCard is essential.

RIDING THE SUBWAY

The good news is that New York's subway system is one of the cheapest to ride in the world. Before you can start getting around on the subway you'll need to buy a MetroCard (which also works on buses, see page 60). You can buy these from a booth inside the entrance to the station or from a MetroCard vending machine, which you'll easily spot as they're brightly coloured. The machines accept cash, debit and credit cards. There are 2 types of ticket, pay-per-use and unlimited-ride.

▶ Don't look for obvious signs indicating a subway; instead look for either the very discreet 'M' signs in blue or the signature red and green glass globes – red means the entrance is not always open and green means it's staffed 24 hours a day.

▶ Before going down a subway entrance, check it is going in the right direction for you – many entrances take you to either 'downtown' or 'uptown' destinations, not both. It means that if you make the mistake of going in and swiping your ticket before you realise you're going in the wrong direction, you will have to swipe your card again to get in on the right side, so you'll end up paying double. The alternative is to travel in the wrong direction until you get to one of the larger subway stations (such as 42nd Street) and then change.

▶ The same rules apply if you're in one of the outer boroughs, but instead of looking for a Downtown or Uptown sign, look for one that says Manhattan.

▶ Some trains are express, meaning they stop only at selected stations. At some stations you have to go down 2 flights to get to the platforms for express trains, while at others you don't, and it is easy to get on an express train by mistake.

▶ There are conflicting opinions (hotly debated by the locals) as to whether it is worth waiting for an express. On the plus side, they move quickly, but on the down side you could end up waiting 10 minutes for one, so you won't have saved any time in the end.

▶ There are many different lines going to the same destinations, but they don't all exit at the same place. For example, if you arrive at Fulton Street on the New York subway and head for the exit you can come out at four completely different locations. The Red Line exits at Fulton and William Streets, the Brown Line exits at John and Nassau Streets, the Blue Line exits at Fulton and Nassau Streets, and the Green Line exits at Broadway and John Street – all of which are quite a long way from each other.

▶ The locals consider that the subway is safe to travel on until around 11pm. After that opinions vary, but when making up your mind to travel do be aware that the subway service after 11pm is generally incredibly slow.

New York subway

▶ The subway does have one very good point: because the island of Manhattan is largely made up of granite, they did not have to dig as deep as we have to in London to find the really strong foundation level. This means you generally only have to go down one flight of steps to find the line.

▶ If you've been to New York before but not for a few years, bear in mind there have been a few changes to the subway network – and all for the better – thanks to a $17-billion expansion and renovation programme.

▶ The L line runs almost the full width of Manhattan along 14th Street from 8th Avenue in the west to 1st Avenue in the east on its way to Queens. Other stops in Manhattan include 6th Avenue, Union Square and 3rd Avenue.

▶ The S line should not be confused with the shuttle between Times Square and Grand Central Station. It is another good east–west train linking West and East Villages in Greenwich and runs from West 4th Street to Grand Street.

BRITTIP

If you're worried about getting lost in New York, click on to hopstop.com for online subway and walking directions around the city.

▶ In Manhattan, the new peak-time V line largely runs in conjunction with the F line and includes new stops at 5th Avenue and 53rd Street, as well as Lexington Avenue and 53rd Street.

ON THE BUSES

Travelling by bus is always a little more nerve-wracking because you can never be sure whether you've arrived at your destination, but most people are pretty helpful if asked a direct question.

FINDING A BUS

Our Manhattan bus map inside the front cover will come in handy as often there are no route maps at the bus stops. However, as a general rule buses run north to south, south to north, east to west or west to east.

You can recognise bus stops by a yellow-painted kerb. They are usually located at street corners and have a tall, round blue and white sign with a bus emblem and route number. Some stops have bus shelters and most stops have Guide-a-Ride information, a rectangular box attached to the bus sign pole that displays a route map and service schedule.

RIDING THE BUSES

▶ Get on the bus at the front and click in your MetroCard or feed in $2.25. Exact change is essential – and it must be all in coins as no dollar bills are accepted.

▶ If you're over 65 years old or have a disability, you're eligible for a discount if you have a proper form of ID, like your passport.

MTA bus

FINDING A WC

It is wise to know that public lavatories are thin on the ground in New York. In addition, subway loos – if they are actually open – are dangerous and unhygienic. It is considered impolite to use the word 'toilet'; in America a public toilet is always the 'restroom'. So if you're in need, we have it on good authority from those New Yorkers in the know that you can go to the following places:

Barnes & Noble: The bookstore chain wants people to treat the stores as public meeting places.

Bryant Park: Free toilets and surely the city's, if not the country's, finest; neo-Grecian with pillars, giant marble urn full of flowers, real soap and uniformed attendant!

Department stores: You'll need to ask where they are; they are hidden away to deter street people from using them.

Hotels: The restrooms are usually on the ground floor or you can ask.

Lincoln Center: There are 10 'stalls' open to the public, close to the entrance.

McDonald's and Burger King: Unisex toilets that are usually clean and modern.

Public libraries: They all have public loos.

Restaurants: Some have signs saying 'For customers only', but if you ask authoritatively enough and look okay, they'll probably let you use them.

Statue of Liberty: In the gift shop.

▶ Although there are bus exits at the back, you can also get off at the front.

▶ Requesting a stop may be a little confusing. There are no clearly marked red buttons to press; instead there are black strips that run the full length of the bus between the windows or at the back along the tops of the handles. Simply press one of these to request the next stop.

▶ If the bus says 'Limited Stopping' it means it stops only at major stops, such as the cross-town streets of 14, 23, 34, 42, 50, 57, 68, 72, 79 and 86.

▶ The main bus routes used by tourists are: M1, which travels from 5th Avenue and Central Park to Madison Avenue; and M7, which runs from Union Square to Broadway through the Theater District. There's also M6, which takes in SoHo, Chelsea, Herald Square and 6th Avenue Midtown.

NYINTHEKNOW

'A car is useless in New York, essential everywhere else. The same with good manners.'
American journalist and author, Mignon McLaughlin

TOURIST ROUTES

Certain bus routes link key attractions, so if your feet are killing you, jump on the M1 bus to continue your trawl of Manhattan sights shown here in brackets:

M1: 5th Avenue (Central Park), 5th Avenue/84th Street (Metropolitan Museum of Art), 5th Avenue/49th–50th Streets

(Rockefeller Centre), Madison Avenue/East 43rd Street (Grand Central Terminal/Chrysler Building).

BY WATER TAXI

For a completely different way of getting around, you can go by water taxi. A commuter service runs around the lower part of Manhattan, but the most useful is a hop on/hop off service. The three bright yellow catamarans with black and white check are easy to spot and there are 10 stops from DUMBO to West 44th Street, all easily accessible from the subway and bus stops. The service runs 11am–3pm on weekdays, stopping en route at South Street Seaport, Battery Park, World Financial Center, West Village and Chelsea Piers. At weekends, it runs each hour 11.02am–7.02pm from Hunters Point, stopping at East 34th Street, Schaeffer Landing, Fulton Ferry Landing, South Street Seaport, Red Hook, Battery Park, World Financial Center, Pier 45, West 23rd Street and West 44th Street. The other direction, from West 44th Street, it runs each hour 11.32am–6.32pm.

New York Water Taxi

The Hop on/Hop off pass (212-742 1969, nywatertaxi.com) runs every weekend, on the hour April–Oct, 12pm–4pm taking in 10 stops at the city's top neighbourhoods and attractions, including the Statue of Liberty, the Brooklyn Bridge and Manhattan Skyline. A one-day Hop on/Hop off pass costs $20 for adults, $18 for seniors and $15 for children 12 and under. If you're on a budget or here in winter, check out the commuter route and times.

DRIVING IN NEW YORK

A word of advice: don't even think about it. Most of the streets will be jam-packed, while parking is extremely scarce and astronomically expensive at $8–10 an hour. You can park on the street, but watch out for what is known as alternate-side-of-the-street parking. This means you have to know which day of the week the cleaning truck comes past so you move the car over at the right time. Double parking is common, so it is easy to get boxed in, and frustrated drivers simply get in their cars and honk the horn until the guilty owner moves their car. As one New Yorker told us: 'People do not know how to park here. New Yorkers are not good drivers and are the wildest parkers.'

BRITTIP

Overtaking is permitted on the inside and outside lanes of interstate highways, so if you're driving to Manhattan from one of the airports, be sure to use both of your wing mirrors to look for passing cars.

If you plan to take a trip upstate and wish to do so by car, then there are some dos and don'ts about car hire. Firstly, never hire a car in Manhattan unless you want to pay around $160 a day. Take a ferry to the state of New Jersey and hire a car from there for around $85 for a medium-sized car with unlimited mileage. Secondly, don't consider hiring a car in the summer or at weekends because that's what most New Yorkers will be doing and they'll be difficult to come by. Cars are also snapped up in the autumn when New Yorkers like to go to see the autumn foliage.

Driving is not for the faint-hearted

DRIVING TIPS

▶ Most streets in New York are one way, so be sure to look out for signs before you head down a street.

▶ Drivers have to wear seatbelts by law, as do front-seat passengers and children aged 4–10 in the back.

▶ Check for red signs with street cleaning symbols, which indicate that you will have to move your car to give street sweepers a chance to clean the streets. Failure may result in it being towed away or a fine.

▶ Don't leave anything of value on show in your car or you're liable to have your vehicle broken into. After all, you wouldn't do this at home.

▶ New York is a safe city, but don't let your guard down when you're in a car. If someone approaches your vehicle at traffic lights to ask for money or to wash your windows, it's best to ignore them and keep your doors locked.

▶ Speed limits are 30mph around town, 55mph on highways and freeways.

▶ Private parking facilities are available in the city but they cost $25–40 per day.

▶ Illegally parked cars will be towed away and there's a $150 fine plus $15 per day to be paid. Collect your car from Pier 76, West 38th Street at 12th Avenue (Midtown West). Tel 212-971 0772. It's open 24 hours a day Mon–Sat.

CAR HIRE

If you do decide to drive, there are a number of car hire companies. Most are based at the major airports, so you can simply pick them up when you arrive. Prices vary enormously, from a one-day rental costing from $90 to a week rate of $225–300. Remember that you'll need to be over 25, have a valid driving licence, have your own insurance and some photo ID. You'll also need to have a credit card (or very large cash deposit) and most rental companies add sales tax of around 8.6%.

Car hire companies
Alamo: 1-800-462 5266, alamo.com.

Argus Rentals: 212-372 7266, argusrentals.com.

Avis: 1-800-331 1212, avis.com.

Dollar: 1-800-800 3665, dollar.com.

Hertz: 800-654 3131, hertz.com.

Independent (and often cheaper) car rental companies: carrentalexpress.com.

CHAPTER 4

What to See
and Do

here is so much to see and do in the city that never sleeps that it can all feel a bit daunting when you first step out of your hotel, guidebook in hand. Therefore it's a good idea to make a plan of what you'd really like to see before you're back on the plane and heading home. The major sights are often the number one priority – especially for the first-time visitor – so, to make your life a little easier, we have indicated the location of each of the following sights. It would be advisable to read Chapter 2 first so you get a good feel for each of the neighbourhoods and that way you can make the most of your time by planning your days in specific areas of the city. For instance, if you plan to see the Empire State Building, bear in mind it is deep in the heart of the 34th Street shopping district. The section entitled Orientation (page 57) will also help you make sense of the streets of New York and get to know the intricacies of the grid system and the distances involved. Having said all of that,

do make sure you leave a little time in your schedule for simply wandering. Even if it's only for a couple of hours, the feeling of walking along the streets of New York like a local and discovering a charming café or cool local shop as yet unearthed by a guidebook is marvellous.

PART ONE – SIGHTSEEING

This section gives you our Top 5 must-see sights, plus all the major sights in New York. You can either visit them under your own steam or take advantage of the many and varied tours that are listed in the second part of this chapter.

◀◢▶ BRITTIP
Security at many sights and buildings has been tightened following the tragic events of 11 September, so allow extra time for this when planning your schedules.

67

A–Z of SIGHTSEEING

CENTRAL PARK
Think of New York and Central Park is likely to spring to mind. It's the New Yorkers' playground and a wonderful place to spend time during your stay. For a complete description of the park and all its facilities, see pages 273–275.

ELLIS ISLAND IMMIGRATION MUSEUM AND THE STATUE OF LIBERTY
Battery Park
☎ 877-523 9849
🖱 statuecruises.com
🚗 Statue of Liberty and Ellis Island Ferry, which leaves every 20–30 minutes from Gangway 5 in Battery Park 9.30am–4.30pm. Subway 1 to South Ferry, 4, 5 to Bowling Green
🕐 9am–5pm
$ $12 adults, $10 seniors, $5 children (4–12), under 3s free. Credit cards accepted.

The Statue of Liberty (nps.gov/stli) is reached

The Statue of Liberty

by a ferry, which also takes you to the Ellis Island Museum where you learn the immigration story of America. Ferry tickets are sold at Castle Clinton, the low, circular brownstone building in Battery Park (open 8.30am–4.30pm). Luggage, including backpacks, is not permitted and the security checks can take up to an hour.

BRITTIP
If you depart after 2pm there won't be enough time to visit both Liberty and Ellis Islands as so go early.

The Statue of Liberty originally came to New York in 1886, as a gift from France. You can enjoy the panoramic views from the observation deck, about 16 storeys above ground, and tour the museum in the pedestal. The lift at Liberty Island is in service and if you purchase a Crown Access Ticket you have access to the statue's interior spiral staircase. However, you must be able to walk up the 354 steps to reach the crown at the top. If you can't make the climb you can always stroll along the promenade above the star-shaped former fort on which the statue and its pedestal rise some 30 storeys above the harbour.

BRITTIP
The last boat leaves from Liberty Island at 6.15pm and Ellis Island at 6.30pm in summer and the museum closes at 5pm.

The Statue of Liberty café is small and there are not enough loos. There is space to eat outside, but not much. At Ellis Island, however, you'll find plenty of WCs on all levels, a large café and a huge amount of outdoor seating that looks out over to the Statue of Liberty and Lower Manhattan.

Ellis Island Immigration Museum

TOP 5 SIGHTS
There are plenty of exciting things to see and do in New York, but some are simply unmissable, particularly if you're visiting for the first time. Below is our definitive guide to the top sights, and whatever else you do when you are in the city, these are the ones you mustn't miss:

Central Park: Pages 273–275.

Ellis Island Immigration Museum: With the Statue of Liberty (page 67).

Empire State Building: 34th Street (page 69).

Statue of Liberty: Ferry from Battery Park (page 67).

Times Square: Midtown West (page 73).

BRITTIP
Statue Cruises has started a digital audio library with information about visiting the Statue of Liberty and Ellis Island, for free, and an audio tour for $6. View them at statuecruises.com.

The Ellis Island Immigration Museum (ellisisland.org) is the most visited museum in New York, particularly beloved by crowds of Americans who want to see where their immigrant ancestors arrived. In use 1892–1954, it 'processed' up to 10,000 immigrants a day. Each person was examined and interviewed to find out if they could speak English. An unfortunate 2% were turned away.

Visitors follow the immigrants' route as they entered the baggage room and went up to the Registry and the Staircase of Separation. Poignant exhibits include photos, videos, jewellery, clothing, baggage and the stark dormitories. The Immigrant Wall of Fame lists half a million names, including those of the grandfathers of Presidents Washington and Kennedy.

BRITTIP
When leaving the Statue of Liberty to go on to Ellis Island DO NOT get on the ferry that takes you to New Jersey. That is on the left. It is clearly signposted, but it is very easy to get disorientated!

This is a great museum and well worth allocating a good portion of your day to. Films and guided tour are free. The Ranger Tours last 45 minutes and leave at regular times throughout the day (times in the information booth). At 2pm there is a re-enactment of a board of inquiry, which decides an immigrant's fate. Immigrants tell their stories in the movie *Island of Hope, Island of Tears*, which runs frequently in 2 theatres. Free tickets are available at the desk. Audio tours are available for $6.

BRITTIP
The tour, film and play on Ellis Island are free, but you need to get tickets for each of them from the information desk (just to the left on your way in). Busiest times are obviously just after a boat has arrived, so try to be the first off the ferry and head straight for the desk.

The museum is very well laid out, has lots of benches everywhere and is so big it never feels too crowded. There is a cashpoint (ATM) in the corridor on the way to the café, which is on your right as you enter the building. The café is a little pricey but you could bring your own picnic and sit outside and enjoy the fabulous views.

EMPIRE STATE BUILDING
34th Street
- ✉ 350 5th Avenue between 33rd and 34th Street
- ☎ 212-736 3100
- 🖱 esbnyc.com
- 🚇 Subway B, D, F, Q, N, R, V, W to 34th Street
- ⏰ 8am–2am, last lifts go up at 1.15am, 7 days a week; be sure to bring ID
- $ $20 adults, $18 seniors and youth (12–17), $14 children (6–11), under 5s free. Tickets can be bought online.

BRITTIP
Fancy a coffee when you're in the Empire State Building? To avoid the pricey snack bars, get back down to ground level and visit Starbucks next door.

It is hard to believe that the Empire State, which was for almost 40 years the world's tallest building, was nearly not built at all. Just weeks after its building contract was signed in 1929, the Wall Street Crash brought the financial world to its knees. Fortunately, the project went ahead and was even completed 45 days ahead of schedule, rising to 443m/1,454ft in 1931. The lobby interior features Art Deco design incorporating rare marble imported from Italy, France, Belgium and Germany. It is, once again, New York's

TICKET TO RIDE
The CityPass is an excellent way to avoid long queues and save money if you visit at least 3 of the participating attractions: the American Museum of Natural History, the Empire State Building and New York Skyride, the Metropolitan Museum of Art and the Cloisters, the Guggenheim Museum, the Museum of Modern Art and a harbour tour with the Circle Line or Statue of Liberty and Ellis Island. You can buy a CityPass from any of the attractions, which will save you queuing again. Prices are $79 (a $60 saving on normal admission) for adults and $59 for 6–17s. Call 208-787 4300 or buy online at citypass.com.

tallest building, and one of the world's most recognisable from movies, most recently, the remake of *King Kong*.

BRITTIP
If you've a CityPass booklet (see above), you can avoid the ticket queues at the Empire State Building. Walk straight past the crowds on the ground floor and turn right to go up one flight.

There are two observation decks, one on the 86th floor and another on the 102nd floor, which costs an extra $15 to visit but gives the most fabulous, if dizzying, views. Your best bet is to arrive as early in the morning as possible to avoid long waits for tickets. Weekends, of course, get really crowded. Once you reach the glass-walled

FREE SIGHTS AND ATTRACTIONS
Cathedral of St John the Divine: Upper West Side/Morningside Heights (page 80).

Central Park: Pages 273–275.

Federal Reserve Bank: Financial District (page 76).

Gracie Mansion: Upper East Side (page 76).

Grand Central Station: Midtown East (pages 76–77).

New York Public Library: Midtown (page 78).

Rockefeller Center: Midtown (page 71).

South Street Seaport: Financial District (page 72).

Staten Island Ferry: Battery Park (pages 72–73).

Times Square: Midtown West (page 73).

viewing deck on the 86th floor you can enjoy some fabulous views of Manhattan and the outer boroughs and really get your bearings. Those who lack the stomach for heights can catch the view live through ESB TowerCams on the concourse. If you like you can hire the ESB Audio Tour for $8. You buy your tickets on the concourse level below the main lobby, but don't have to use them on the same day.

The **New York SkyRide** is on the 2nd floor and is open 7 days a week 10am–10pm. It simulates a thrilling flight around the skyscrapers and bridges of New York. Entrance $25.50 adults, $18.50 youth (12–17), $18.50 seniors, $17.50 children (5–11). A combined Skyride and Empire State Building ticket costs $47 adults, $39 seniors and $22 for children (212-279 9777, skyride.com). Save money by buying tickets online.

GROUND ZERO – TRIBUTE TO THE WORLD TRADE CENTER
Financial District
- ✉ 120 Liberty Street, between Greenwich and Church Streets
- ☎ 866-737 1184
- ⌂ tributewtc.org
- 🚇 Subway A, C to Chambers Street/E to World Trade Center/R, W to Rector Street
- ⊙ Mon, Wed–Sat 10am–6pm; Tues 12–6pm; Sun 12–5pm
- $ $10 suggested donation

After a lengthy public consultation, in 2002 the Lower Manhattan Development Corporation (LMDC) began a worldwide search for a suitable design concept for the 6.5ha/16acre former World Trade Center site. There were 400 submissions from around the globe, which were whittled down to 7 and exhibited at the Winter Garden. More than 100,000 visitors saw the exhibition – generating 8,000 comments – and another 8 million looked at the plans on the internet. Finally, after 3 public meetings, Studio Daniel

Radio City

Libeskind's Memory Foundations design was chosen in early 2003.

Originally, Libeskind planned to divide the 'superblock' formed by the World Trade Center into 4 parts. His plan included a sunken memorial site on the spot where the Twin Towers had stood, and around the memorial he envisioned 5 irregularly shaped towers, of which the tallest would be a 541m/1,776ft towering spire of glass called the Freedom Tower.

Eventually, Libeskind redesigned the towers to be slimmer, taller and squarer, in order to provide more office space. Then, the site developer brought in architect David Childs, who changed Libeskind's glass Freedom Tower into a larger, heavier building but retained the spire. Wind turbines will harness the wind and generate the building's energy. The occupied portion will be 60 storeys high. The Freedom Tower is expected to open in 2010.

In January 2004, a jury chose Michel Arad's memorial design, Reflecting Absence, which differed from Libeskind's. It includes a forest of trees planted throughout a plaza around the footprints of the Twin Towers; reflecting pools deep within the footprints, with constantly falling water to mark the voids; exposure of the bedrock-and-slurry wall to reveal the scale of the site and the disaster; and chambers for unidentified remains of the dead, as well as relics of the disaster. Peter Walker, a Californian landscape architect, is designing a park on the broad, open street-level plaza.

Santiago Calatrava, designer of the transportation hub, has incorporated Libeskind's Wedge of Light feature. His steel-and-glass train station will allow a shaft of light to fall between its wings without a shadow each year on 11 September between 8.46am, when the first plane hit, and 10.28am, when the second tower collapsed, in perpetual tribute to altruism and courage.

BRITTIP
No matter what the weather, it is incredibly easy to get dehydrated. Take a small bottle of water and refill along the way.

The design concept is being built in several phases, and includes better street and pedestrian layouts, better connections between subway and PATH train systems, easily accessible shops and restaurants at street level, particularly along Fulton and Church Streets, plus better bus and car parking. There will be a mix of office space, shops and other amenities including

a Performing Arts Center. As part of the
first phase of development, the Tribute
WTC Visitor Center opened in 2006 with
exhibits, programmes and unique personal
walking tours with survivors or those who
were involved in the rescue mission. The
tours begin at 120 Liberty Street and last
approximately 1 hour 15 minutes. Tickets,
$10, can be purchased at the Tribute Center.

MADAME TUSSAUD'S
Times Square
- ✉ 234 West 42nd Street between 7th and
  8th Avenues
- ☎ 212-512 9600
- ⤴ nycwax.com
- 🚇 Subway A, C, E, S to Port Authority or 1,
  2, 3, N, B, D, F, Q, R to Times Square/42nd
  Street
- ⊙ Open daily throughout the year. Sun–
  Thurs 10am-8pm; Fri-Sat 10am-10pm
- $ $35.50 adults, $32.50 senior, $28
  children, under 4s free. If you book
  online, there's a 20% discount and tickets
  are valid for a year

London's famous waxworks has been
spreading around the globe and has opened
attractions in Las Vegas, Hong Kong,
Amsterdam and this one in New York. If
wax models (extremely well done) are your
thing or you have the kids in tow, it is worth
visiting this sight in the heart of Times Square
as the celebs portrayed reflect personalities
associated with the city, such as Woody
Allen, Leonard Bernstein, Jacqueline Kennedy
Onassis, John D Rockefeller, Yoko Ono, Donald
Trump, Andy Warhol and former mayor
Rudolph Giuliani among others. Kids and
teenagers will get to see all their favourite
stars, from Michael Jordan to Zac Efron.
Barack Obama has recently been added.

NBC TOURS
Rockefeller Center/Midtown
- ✉ Lobby level of 30 Rockefeller Plaza
  at 49th Street between 5th and 6th
  Avenues
- ☎ 212-664 7174 tickets, 212-664 3700
  information
- ⤴ nbc.com/tickets
- 🚇 Subway B, D, F, V to 47th–50th Streets/
  Rockefeller Center
- ⊙ Mon–Thurs 8.30am-4.30pm every 30
  minutes, Fri and Sat 9.30am-5.30pm
  every 15 mins, Sun 9.30am-4.30pm
  every 15 mins
- $ $19.25 adults, $16.25 seniors and
  children (6–12), no children under 6.
  For a small extra fee, combine with
  Rockefeller Center Tour (page 72)

You get a 1 hour 10 minute look behind the
scenes at NBC, the major television network
headquartered in New York, including a peek
at some of its most famous studios such
as 1A – home of the *Today Show*. You'll be
shown around by an NBC Page – some of
these characters have gone on to become
famous entertainment personalities.

RADIO CITY MUSIC HALL
Midtown
- ✉ 1260 6th Avenue at 50th Street
- ☎ 212-247 4777/212-307 7171 to order
  tickets
- ⤴ radiocity.com
- 🚇 Subway B, D, F to 50th Streets/
  Rockefeller Center
- ⊙ Tours daily 11am-3pm
- $ $18.50 adults, $15 seniors, $10 under 12s

While you're at the Rockefeller Center you
won't want to miss out on this fabulous
building, which has been fully restored to
its original Art Deco movie palace glory and
is utterly beautiful. This is where great films
such as *Gone With The Wind* were given
their premieres and it has the largest screen
in America. Make a point of visiting the loos
– they have a different theme on each floor,
from palm trees to Chinese and floral. There
are even cigar-theme loos for the boys. The
1-hour Stage Door Tour takes you around the
building and you meet a Rockette.

BRITTIP
Tickets for the live shows are
very hard to come by. However,
you can try for stand-by tickets
by going to the 49th Street side
of 30 Rockefeller Plaza. Tickets
are distributed from 7am. You can
choose a stand-by ticket for either
an 8pm dress rehearsal or the
11.30pm taping. Tickets are limited
to one per person and are issued on a
first-come, first-served basis.

ROCKEFELLER CENTER
Midtown
- ✉ Midtown at 5th Avenue – West 48th to
  West 50th Streets between 5th and 6th
  Avenues
- ☎ 212-698 2000
- ⤴ RockefellerCenter.com
- 🚇 Subway B, D, N, F, V, W, R, 1 to 47th–50th
  Streets/Rockefeller Center
- ⊙ Tours Mon–Sat 11am–5pm, Sun
  10pm–3pm every 2 hours, departing
  from the NBC experience store (opposite)
- $ Tour $12 adults, $10 seniors, and children
  (6–12), no children under 6. Reservations
  are necessary on 212-664 7174

BRITTIP

Buy your ticket for the Radio City Music Hall in the morning and plan your day around that. Alternatively, you can see it as part of the Rockefeller Center Tour.

Built in Art Deco style in the 1930s, this was named after the New York benefactor whose fortune paid for its construction. As well as Radio City Music Hall, it houses opulent office space, restaurants, bars, shopping on several levels and even gardens. To help you find your way round the 19 buildings, collect a map at the lobby of the main building (30 Rockefeller Center). The central plaza, a restaurant in summer, is turned into an ice rink in winter, and a massive Christmas tree with 8km/5mls of fairy lights draws huge crowds.

BRITTIP

Lovers of the Metropolitan Museum shops can get their fix at one of its branches in the heart of the Rockefeller Center. It's just off the main plaza by the ice rink.

You can either wander around the plaza or take the 1-hour Rockefeller Center Tour. This takes in The Channel Gardens, Radio City, the ice rink, NBC and more, while giving an insight into the Center's history, architecture and more than 100 pieces of artwork that create the world's most amazing public collection of Art Deco.

BRITTIP

If you want to combine the Rockefeller Center Tour with Top of the Rock Tour, then buy an Art & Observation Tour, $30, which combines the art and architecture of the centre with the breathtaking view 70 storeys up. Call 212-698 2000, topoftherocknyc.com to book.

South Street Seaport

The Top of the Rock observation deck is now fully open on the 70th floor at 30 Rockefeller Plaza, offering visitors spectacular 360-degree views of the city. The observation deck, first opened in 1933, has been redeveloped into a 5,110sq m/55,000sq ft, multi-level complex with state-of-the-art features such as new transparent safety glass panels that allow completely unobstructed views of the city's landmarks. It's open 365 days of the year 8am–midnight and costs $21 adults, $19 seniors, $14 children, £1.99 for a podcast, $30 for a sunrise/sunset ticket that allows you to visit twice in a day. Ticket reservations 212-698 2000 or topoftherocknyc.com, or take it in as part of the 1½-hour Art and Observation tour that departs every 2 hours from 10am Mon–Sun (212-698 2000). All tours depart from the NBC Experience Store at 30 Rockefeller Plaza across from the *Today Show* studio.

SOUTH STREET SEAPORT
Financial District
- ✉ Water Street to the East River between John Street and Peck Slip
- ☎ (212) SEA-PORT/ (212) 748-8600 museum
- ⌂ southstreetseaport.com
- 🚇 Subway A, C, J, M, Z, 2, 3, 4, 5 to Fulton Street/Broadway Nassau
- ◷ Museum Apr–Sept Tues–Sun 10am-5pm, Nov–Mar Fri–Mon 10am-5pm
- $ Free. Museum $12 adults, $10 seniors and students, $8 children (5–12)

You don't have to go into the South Street Seaport Museum (pages 120–121) to get a feeling of the maritime history of the city – the ships are all around you. So are the shops.

The Seaport is a rare New York approximation of a typical American shopping mall. Most shops are open Mon–Sat 10am–7pm, Sun 11am–6pm, and there are dining options at all prices, indoors and out, some with a view of the Brooklyn Bridge. The port was previously home to the 150-year-old Fulton Fish Market, but this has now been moved to the Bronx.

STATEN ISLAND FERRY
Battery Park
- ✉ Ferry Terminal, 1 Whitehall Street at South Street
- ☎ 718-815 2628
- ⌂ siferry.com
- 🚇 Subway 4, 5 to Bowling Green; R, W to Whitehall Street, 1 to South Ferry, J, M, Z to Broad Street
- $ Free

Probably the best sightseeing bargain in the world, this free ferry between Whitehall

Street in Lower Manhattan and St George on Staten Island transports 20 million people a year. It passes close to the Statue of Liberty and gives dramatic views of Downtown and the bridges and skyscrapers of Lower Manhattan. Runs regularly 24 hours a day and takes 25 minutes for the crossing. Since 2004, 3 new ferries have been designed to capture the feel of the old-style ferries.

BRITTIP
Foods of New York Tours, foodsofny.com, has suggestions of mouthwatering pit stops in the 5 neighbourhoods near key sights.

TIMES SQUARE AND THE THEATER DISTRICT

Another iconic area of New York and a must-see place. Full details of what to see and do are in Chapter 9 Theatre and Film.

THE OUTER BOROUGHS

BRONX ZOO

A wonderful zoo that combines conservation and ecological awareness with Disney-style rides and a children's zoo. Further details are given on page 288.

HISTORIC RICHMOND TOWN AND ST MARK'S PLACE, STATEN ISLAND

The two top historical sites on Staten Island, both give a unique insight into the New York of yesteryear. Further details are given on page 288.

NEW YORK BOTANICAL GARDEN

Home to the Bronx River Gorge, it not only gives a fascinating insight into the geological history of New York, but also has acres and acres of beautiful gardens. Further details are given on page 289.

AMAZING ARCHITECTURE

Whether you have an interest in architecture or not, you won't fail to appreciate just how beautiful many of the buildings in New York are. The fact that Manhattan is an island has been key to so many of the designs over the last 200 years: when space is at a premium the only way to go is up. New York gave the world skyscrapers and it's these soaring buildings that have given the city its sensational skyline.

BROOKLYN BRIDGE

This Gothic creation was considered one of the modern engineering feats of the world when it was completed in 1883 after 16 years

TOP ZOOS FOR THE FAMILY

Like many sights in New York, the zoos here are larger-than-life affairs and a great choice for families – visit newyorkcityzoos.com for an idea. Bronx Zoo is famous worldwide, but those below are also ideal entertainment for children if you happen to be in the neighbourhood:

Bronx Zoo and Wildlife Conservation Society (see page 288)

Central Park Zoo and Tisch Children's Zoo, Central Park (see page 275)

Prospect Park Zoo, Brooklyn (see page 285)

New York Aquarium, Coney Island, Brooklyn (see page 287)

of construction, and at the time was both the world's largest suspension bridge and the first to be built of steel. It was also the first bridge to link the 2 separate cities of New York and Brooklyn, making it now only a 10-minute taxi ride between them.

BRITTIP
To hear the dramatic story of how the bridge was built while walking over it, take Big Onion's Brooklyn Bridge & Brooklyn Heights tour (bigonion.com).

The original engineer, John A Roebling, died even before the project began and his son, who took over, had to oversee the building from his Brooklyn apartment after being struck down by the bends. In all, 20 people died during the construction of the bridge. Take the A or C train to High Street station and stroll back along the walkway to see some incredible views of the Downtown skyscrapers or the 4, 5 or 6 to Brooklyn Bridge/City Hall station. It's a 1.6km/1ml walk across and the most magical walk is from Brooklyn to Manhattan as the sun goes down over the stunning city skyline.

Brooklyn Bridge

CLOWNING AROUND NEW YORK

Circuses lay on their death-defying extravaganzas and even backstage activities for children in the city, mostly arriving in spring. Some of those most popular with families are:

BIG APPLE CIRCUS
Midtown West

✉ 505 8th Avenue, 19th floor; venues vary
☎ 212-268 2500 or 800-899 2775 toll free
🖰 bigapplecircus.org
$ $15 and upwards

A not-for-profit, totally family-friendly circus that celebrated its 30th anniversary in 2008. It appears at Cunningham Park in Queens each spring.

CIRQUE DU SOLEIL
Randall's Island Park

✉ Randall's Island Park
☎ 212-307 7171 (ticketmaster)
🖰 cirquedusoleil.com
🚢 New York Water Taxi daily ferry service, departures from East 35th Street Pier, Midtown
🕐 1-800-450 1480
$ From $60 adult, $42 children (2–12)

This magical, world-famous animal-free circus is perhaps the most popular with parents. *Kooza*, its fantastical new show lasting 2½ hours, sees 50 performers weave circus acts, breathtaking theatrical effects and memorable songs. The show tours, so check the website for details.

RINGLING BROS AND BARNUM & BAILEY CIRCUS
Midtown West

✉ Madison Square Garden, 7th Avenue at 32nd Street
☎ 212-507 8900
🖰 ringling.com
🚇 Subway A, C, E, 1, 2, 3, 9 to 34th Street/Penn Station
$ $12 upwards from TicketMaster 212-307 7171 or go through ticketmaster.com for a 10% saving for weekday matinees

An extremely popular circus, America's original and most famous company keeps children and adults glued to their seats with a triple extravaganza of thrilling high-energy acts taking place in Madison Square Garden. There's a special all-access tour an hour before the performance to learn circus skills, become circusfit™ and meet the animal stars.

UNIVERSOUL CIRCUS
Midtown West

✉ Venues vary (see website)
☎ 800-316 7439 or book through TicketMaster on 212-307 7171, ticketmaster.com
🖰 universoulcircus.com
$ $10 upwards

For thrills with a difference, try this African-American troupe, which provides death-defying circus acts to hip-hop, R&B and salsa music. Catch them at The Wollman Rink in Brooklyn's Prospect Park in spring or playing at the Bronx and Queens.

CHRYSLER BUILDING
Midtown East

✉ 405 Lexington Avenue at 42nd Street
☎ 212-682 3070
🖰 nyc-architecture.com
🚇 Subway S, 4, 5, 6, 7 to Grand Central/42nd Street
🕐 7am–6pm, lobby only
$ Free

Opened in 1930, this was William van Alen's homage to the motor car. At the foot of the Art Deco skyscraper are brickwork cars with enlarged chrome hubcaps and radiator caps. Inside see its marble and chrome lobby and

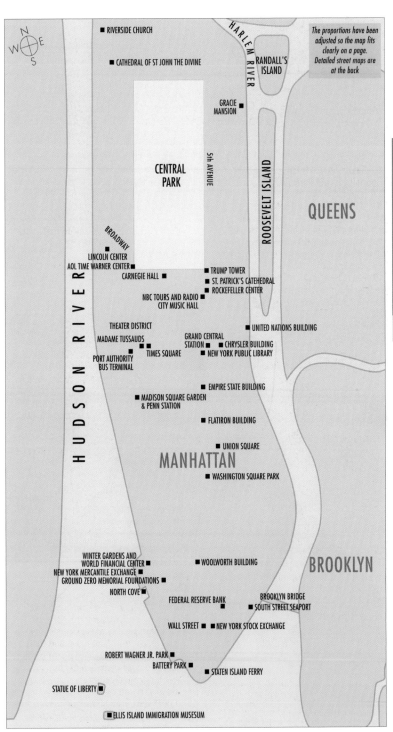

The proportions have been adjusted so the map fits clearly on a page. Detailed street maps are at the back

RIVERSIDE CHURCH

CATHEDRAL OF ST JOHN THE DIVINE

HARLEM RIVER

RANDALL'S ISLAND

GRACIE MANSION

CENTRAL PARK

5th AVENUE

ROOSEVELT ISLAND

QUEENS

BROADWAY

LINCOLN CENTER

AOL TIME WARNER CENTER

CARNEGIE HALL

TRUMP TOWER

ST. PATRICK'S CATHEDRAL

ROCKEFELLER CENTER

NBC TOURS AND RADIO CITY MUSIC HALL

THEATER DISTRICT

MADAME TUSSAUDS

PORT AUTHORITY BUS TERMINAL

TIMES SQUARE

GRAND CENTRAL STATION

CHRYSLER BUILDING

NEW YORK PUBLIC LIBRARY

UNITED NATIONS BUILDING

EMPIRE STATE BUILDING

MADISON SQUARE GARDEN & PENN STATION

FLATIRON BUILDING

HUDSON RIVER

UNION SQUARE

MANHATTAN

WASHINGTON SQUARE PARK

WINTER GARDENS AND WORLD FINANCIAL CENTER

NEW YORK MERCANTILE EXCHANGE

GROUND ZERO MEMORIAL FOUNDATIONS

NORTH COVE

WOOLWORTH BUILDING

BROOKLYN

FEDERAL RESERVE BANK

BROOKLYN BRIDGE

SOUTH STREET SEAPORT

WALL STREET

NEW YORK STOCK EXCHANGE

ROBERT WAGNER JR. PARK

BATTERY PARK

STATEN ISLAND FERRY

STATUE OF LIBERTY

ELLIS ISLAND IMMIGRATION MUSESUM

Major sights in Manhattan

inlaid-wood elevators. Its needle-like spire is illuminated at night and the building vies with the Empire State for the most stunning.

FEDERAL RESERVE BANK
Financial District
- ✉ 33 Liberty Street between William and Nassau Streets
- ☎ 212-720 6130
- ⌖ newyorkfed.org/
- 🚍 Subway 2, 3, 4, 5, A, C, J, M, Z to Fulton Street/Broadway-Nassau Street
- ◷ Mon–Fri 9.30am–3.30pm, by tour only
- $ Free

🇬🇧 **BRITTIP**

Just across the way from the Federal Reserve Bank is probably the poshest McDonald's in the world at 160 Broadway. It has doormen, a chandelier and a grand piano upstairs.

Yes, this really is the place where billions of dollars' worth of gold bars are stashed (as stolen by Jeremy Irons in *Die Hard 3*) on behalf of half the countries of the world, and where money is printed. Security, as you can imagine, is tight, but you can still do a free one-hour Gold Vault Tour that takes you deep into the underground vaults, Mon–Fri at 9.30am, 10.30am, 11.30am 1.30pm, 2.30pm and 3.30pm providing you book at least 5 days in advance. Your name will be placed on a computer list, but the minimum age is 16. Passport or picture identification is essential and you can't use your camera or camera phone, for obvious reasons!

Flatiron Building

FLATIRON BUILDING
Flatiron District
- ✉ 175 5th Avenue between 22nd and 23rd Streets
- ☎ 212-477 0947
- ⌖ nyc-architecture.com
- 🚍 Subway F, V, N, R, 6 to 23rd Street
- ◷ Lobby open office hours
- $ Free

The Renaissance palazzo building was the first-ever skyscraper when it was completed in 1902 and is held up by a steel skeleton covered in white terracotta. Its name refers to its unusual triangular shape. It is set at the windiest crossroads of the city where 5th Avenue crosses Broadway and in the 19th century had to be policed as local New York men hung around here to catch a glimpse up ladies' skirts as they blew up around their ears!

GRACIE MANSION
Yorkville
- ✉ Carl Schurz Park, 88th Street at East End Avenue
- ☎ 212-570 4773
- ⌖ historichousetrust.org
- 🚍 Subway 4, 5, 6 to 86th Street
- ◷ Tours phone ahead to reserve
- $ $7 adults, $4 seniors, under 12s free

Built by the shipping tycoon Archibald Gracie in 1799, this mansion is the last of the elegant country homes that once lined Manhattan's East River shore. Dinner guests here were the likes of Alexander Hamilton and Joseph Bonaparte. It later became the first home of the Museum of the City of New York and then official residence of the mayor. Now, the 'People's House', once visited by Nelson Mandela, offers 45-minute tours on Wednesdays at 10am, 11am, 1pm and 2pm by reservation only (212-570 4773) that take you through the mayor's living room, a guest suite and smaller bedrooms. The best part, though; is the view down the river.

GRAND CENTRAL STATION
Midtown East
- ✉ East 42nd Street and Park Avenue
- ☎ 212-340 2345
- ⌖ grandcentralterminal.com
- 🚍 Subway S, 4, 5, 6, 7 to Grand Central/42nd Street
- ◷ Daily 5.30am–1.30am
- $ Free

Even if you're not going anywhere by train, this huge, vaulted station, which was opened in 1913, is worth a visit. A $196m, 2-year renovation programme completed in the 1990s saw the ceiling once again twinkle with the stars and astrological symbols of the night skies, while the marble balusters and clerestory windows gleam in the main concourse.

🇬🇧 BRITTIP

The Municipal Arts Society sponsors a tour every Wed at 12.30pm. Meet their guide at the centre's information booth on the main concourse. There is a suggested donation of $10 per person for this tour (212-935 3960). Alternatively, the Grand Central Partnership sponsors a free 90-minute walking tour of Grand Central Terminal and the surrounding neighbourhood, with the generous support of Altria Group. The tour meets in the Sculpture Court of the Whitney Museum at Altria on East 42nd Street across from Grand Central. For more information call 212-883 2420, grandcentralpartnership.org.

The Grand Central Map, picked up from the information booth on the main concourse will lead you to a Mediterranean restaurant, Michael Jordan's The Steakhouse NYC and a cocktail lounge, Cipriani Dolci, modelled on a Florentine palazzo. The lower level dining concourse offers inexpensive meals and takeaways, while main floor shopping outlets include Banana Republic and Aveda. Among eating and shopping opportunities, take in a visit to the New York Transit Museum Gallery and Store, with exhibitions of transit memorabilia, and to The Vanderbilt Hall, the former main waiting room, which stages entertainment. Complete your trip to this elegant edifice by tucking in at the Oyster Bar & Restaurant.

MADISON SQUARE GARDEN'S ALL ACCESS TOUR

34th Street

✉ 4 Pennsylvania Plaza at 33rd Street and 7th Avenue

☎ 212-465 MSG1/6741 (information); 212-307 7171 (ticketmaster)

🖰 thegarden.com

🚇 Subway A, C, E, 1, 2, 3, 9, D, F, B, V, N, Q, R, W to 34th Street/Penn station

$ $18.50 adults, $12 children (12 and under), $15 senior, 1-hour tours operate every day, every 30 minutes, 11am–3pm

This is the round building that sits right on top of Penn station and the entrance is on 7th Avenue at 33rd Street. It occupies the site of the original Pennsylvania station, an architectural masterpiece that was even more beautiful than Grand Central Station, but which was razed in the 1960s. (One good thing came out of its destruction, though: the creation of the Landmarks Preservation Commission, which has helped to protect many buildings and areas in New York from developers.)

Madison Square Garden's arena is 10 storeys tall, covers 3.24ha/8 acres and is famous for its circular ceiling, which is suspended by 48 bridge-like cables. Every year it hosts 600 events from concerts to boxing, wrestling, basketball and hockey, bringing in 5 million people. Its most famous residents are the New York Knickerbockers basketball team (known as the Knicks), the New York Rangers ice-hockey team and the New York Liberty women's pro basketball team.

Below the arena are the theatre, exhibition centre, box office and 2 club restaurants. Incidentally, this is actually the fourth Madison Square Garden building. The first two were built at Madison Square on the site of the current New York Life Building; the third was built on 8th Avenue between 49th and 50th Streets, where the Worldwide Plaza stands. This building opened in 1968 with a gala featuring Bob Hope and Bing Crosby.

During the 1-hour behind-the-scenes tour, you will hear about its 125-year history, see the inner workings and the Walk of Fame, and gain access to the locker rooms of both the Knicks and the Rangers.

Excitingly, the world's most famous arena is to undergo renovation. Plans are afoot to transform it into a state-of-the-art building to enhance the experience for fans and performers. Highlights will include a dramatically redesigned 7th Avenue entrance, more comfortable seating with better sightlines and restoration of the famous ceiling. Check the website for more details.

Grand Central Station

MORRIS–JUMEL MANSION
Harlem

- ✉ Roger Morris Park, 65 Jumel Terrace at 160th Street
- ☎ 212-923 8008
- 🖰 morrisjumel.org
- 🚌 Subway C to 163rd Street
- ⏲ Wed–Sun 10am–4pm, closed Mon and Tues
- $ $5 adults, $4 seniors, students and children, free for children under 12; various tours offered (for groups over 12) $6 adults, $4.50 seniors, students and children

Built by British colonel Roger Morris in 1765, this is the oldest house in Manhattan. It was confiscated by George Washington in 1776 and briefly used as his war headquarters until the Brits kicked him out of New York. Charles Dickens visited it, too. Tours are offered every Saturday at noon (register in advance), and family programmes include free art workshops during school holiday times.

NEW YORK PUBLIC LIBRARY
Midtown

- ✉ 5th Avenue at 42nd Street
- ☎ 212-930 0830
- 🖰 nypl.org
- 🚌 Subway B, D, F, V, 7 to 42nd Street
- ⏲ Mon, Thurs–Sat 10–6pm, Tues–Wed 10–9pm, Sun 1–5pm
- $ Free

Opened in 1911, this is one of the best examples of the city's Beaux Arts architecture and the largest branch public library in the world. Inside you'll find more than 8.5 million volumes on 140km/88mls of shelving guarded by the twin marble lions of Patience and Fortitude. Despite this mammoth collection, members can tap what they're looking for into a computer and get it in just 10 minutes. Take a tour, which meet at the reception deck in Astor Hall, at 11am or 2pm Tues–Sat and 2pm Sun to check out the murals by Richard Haas in the Periodicals Room, the fabulous white marble Astor Hall and the cathedral-like main reading room where Leon Trotsky once read under the same brass lamps. The steps up to the library are a suntrap during the day and serve as a meeting place. Alternatively, they make a great place for a sandwich or drink stop.

NEW YORK STOCK EXCHANGE
Financial District

- ✉ 20 Broad Street at Wall Street
- ☎ 212-656 3000
- 🖰 nyse.com
- 🚌 Subway 6, 4, 5 to Wall Street; J, M, Z to Broad Street
- ⏲ Not open to the public at present

Amazing fact: the stock exchange was founded by 24 brokers meeting beneath a tree; now more than 1,300 members crowd on to the building's trading floor where over 2 billion shares change hands on busy days. This Neo-Classical building that represents the heart of capitalism is an interesting place to visit, although for the foreseeable future, due to security concerns, it is closed to the public. For now, a taste of the frenetic activity within can be seen from watching the traders scurrying around the crowded pedestrian-only streets. For the inside story, such as tickertape from the morning of the big crash, head to The Museum of American Finance a few blocks away (page 112).

SEAGRAM BUILDING
Midtown

- ✉ 375 Park Avenue at 53rd Street
- ☎ 212-572 7000
- 🚌 Subway 6 to 51st Street
- ⏲ Open weekdays 9–5pm, tours Tues 3pm

The New York City mile's only Mies Van Der Rohe building, and widely recognised as one of the finest architectural skyscrapers in the world. It ignited a passion for plazas that you can still see in New York today. If you want to splash out, have dinner there in the much praised The Four Seasons restaurant (fourseasonsrestaurant.com) designed by Philip Johnson.

TRUMP TOWER
Midtown

- ✉ 725 5th Avenue between 56th and 57th Streets
- ☎ 212-247 7000
- 🖰 trumpworldtower.com
- 🚌 Subway F, N, R, Q, W to 57th Street
- ⏲ Building daily 8am–10pm; shops Mon–Sat 10am–6pm, Sun noon–5pm
- $ Free

Donald Trump's monument to opulence includes an extravagant pink marbled atrium with waterfalls, cafés, restaurants and

New York Public Library

upmarket shops. The glitzy residences at the top can't be visited, but a glimpse of them could be seen in Trump's reality TV show *The Apprentice*, filmed in the tower. This is not to be confused with Trump International Hotel and Tower at Columbus Circle.

UNITED NATIONS BUILDING
Midtown East
- ✉ 1st Avenue between 42nd and 48th Street
- ☎ 212-963 8687 for tour reservations
- ⌖ un.org/tours
- 🚇 Subway 4, 5, 6, 7 to Grand Central/42nd Street
- 🕐 Mon–Fri 9.45am–4.45pm, Sat and Sun 10am–4.30pm (not at weekends Jan and Feb)
- $ $16 adults, $11 seniors and students, $9 children (5–12). No children under 5

You can't miss this building; the epicentre of global peace, where world leaders meet and international issues are discussed, is heralded by a colourful array of flags from 192 member states. Tours of the General Assembly, the Economic and Social Council and other areas every half hour last around 45 minutes. Despite its fame, this is not the most exciting tour in the world! The lovely Reclining Figure by Henry Moore and the Peace Bell from Japan, among the objects on display around the building may be more tantalising. If you send a postcard from here it will be with its own stamp, being in an international zone.

WINTER GARDEN AT THE WORLD FINANCIAL CENTER
Battery Park City
- ✉ 200 Vesey Street at West Street
- ☎ 212-417 7000
- ⌖ worldfinancialcenter.com
- 🚇 Subway E or PATH to World Trade Center, 2, 3, 4, 5, A, C, J, M, Z to Chambers Street; R, W to City Hall, 1 to Rector Street

The World Financial Center is actually the main focal point for the northern end of Battery Park City, a strip of land running down the west side of Lower Manhattan from Chambers Street to South Park. It was created by landfill from the digging work required to build the foundations for the World Trade Center. The World Financial Center has a complex of 4 office towers, but is most famous for the beautiful glass-roofed Winter Garden that looks over the boats moored in

🇬🇧 **BRITTIP**
The Winter Garden is not just a pretty place to enjoy a drink or two; it also holds a series of free concerts and fairs.

FRIENDS
Although most of the filming was actually done in California, the many *Friends* series, starring Jennifer Aniston and co, were set in New York. There are some locations you may recognise: the place where Ross and Rachel consummated their relationship was filmed in one of the old-school dioramas in The American Museum of Natural History (pages 100–102).

North Cove. Filled with palm trees, it houses upscale shops including Ann Taylor, Godiva Chocolates and Banana Republic and holds free events outdoors in summer. Check the website for schedules.

WOOLWORTH BUILDING
Civic Center/Financial District
- ✉ 233 Broadway at Park Place
- 🚇 Subway 2, 3 4 to Park Place; N, R to City Hall
- 🕐 Weekdays 9–5pm
- $ Free

There is no official tour of the city's second skyscraper, soaring 55 storeys above Broadway and now referred to as the 'Mozart of skyscrapers'. It was built in 1913 at a cost of $13.5 million and it's worth sneaking a look inside the lobby of one of New York's most magical and flamboyant interiors, with extravagant marble walls, bronze filigree and glass-tiled ceiling. The outside is pretty wild, too, with gargoyles and flying buttresses under a pyramid-shaped roof. Incidentally, one-time shop assistant F W Woolworth's building was derided as a 'cathedral of commerce' when it opened, but the 'five and dime' store millionaire took this as a compliment. Just to prove a point, he can be spotted as a sculpture in the lobby, counting out his money.

Woolworth Building

FILM LOCATIONS

New York is one of the most filmed and photographed cities in the world, which is one reason why we feel we know it so well. Here's a taster of locations to visit, ranging from the famous to the plain weird. For an organised tour of Manhattan's locations, turn to pages 89–90.

Annie Hall: The roller coaster next to where Alvy Singer (Woody Allen) grows up is the one on Coney Island (coneyisland.com). Lots of other scenes from this classic 1977 movie starring Allen and Diane Keating were shot all over the city.

Borat: The Wellington Hotel (page 244) is where Borat checks in. He feels like 'da king of the castle', because he's never stayed anywhere so luxurious before!

Breakfast at Tiffany's: Audrey Hepburn immortalised 5th Avenue's most famous jewellery store in this 1961 film (727 5th Avenue at 57th Street, 212-755 8000, tiffany.com).

Ghostbusters: From a fire station at 14 North Moore Street to the New York City Library where the marble lions in the opening shots flanked the steps between 40th and 42nd Streets, this film was set all over the city.

Home Alone 2: Lost in New York: The hotel where Macaulay Culkin fights off the baddies is The Plaza (page 226). Recently renovated (at a cost of $400m!), it's been transformed since Culkin ran through the corridors, but its beautiful façade has remained untouched.

Love Story: Ali MacGraw and Ryan O'Neal's ice-skating scenes were filmed in Central Park.

Maid in Manhattan: Jennifer Lopez and Ralph Fiennes filmed scenes in the Roosevelt Hotel (East 45th Street at Madison Avenue, 212-661 1200, theroosevelthotel.com).

Men in Black II: A scene from the Will Smith blockbuster was filmed in the Art Deco eatery Empire Diner (210 10th Avenue at 22nd Street, 212-243 2736, empire-diner.com).

Serendipity: You can reconstruct Kate Beckinsale and John Cusack's elevator race at the Waldorf-Astoria Hotel (301 Park Avenue at 50th Street, 212-355 3000, waldorfastoria.com) where the film's couple meet, split and reunite.

Sex And The City: For the legions of fans with original DVDs or who have fallen in love with the girls all over again thanks to the 2008 and 2010 films, New York is one big set. Take an organised tour around the girls' haunts, from Jimmy Choos, to The Monkey Bar to The Little Church Around the Corner and the Magnolia Bakery or take some of the girls' shopping trips (page 90).

Sleepless in Seattle: Meg Ryan and Tom Hanks fall for each other at the top of the Empire State Building (350 5th Avenue between 33rd and 34th Street, 212-736 3100, esbnyc.com).

Spider-Man II: The amazing roof-top scenes were filmed at 225 Park Avenue between 18th and 19th streets; 260 5th Avenue at 28th Street. The subway shots were caught at Chambers Street and Park Row.

Wall Street: This 80s classic starring Michael Douglas included shoots at 21 Club, Grand Ballroom of the Roosevelt Hotel at 45 East 45th Street and, of course, the New York Stock Exchange. A sequel was released in 2010.

When Harry Met Sally: The canteen scene where Meg Ryan fakes an orgasm in front of Billy Crystal was filmed at Katz's Delicatessen (205 East Houston Street at Ludlow Street, 212-254 2246, katzdeli.com).

Cathedral of St John the Divine

RELIGIOUS BUILDINGS

CATHEDRAL OF ST JOHN THE DIVINE

Upper West Side/Morningside Heights

✉ 1047 Amsterdam Avenue at 112th Street and Amsterdam Avenue

☎ 212-316 7540 (info); tours 212-932 7347

🖰 stjohndivine.org

🚇 Subway 1 to 110th Street

🕐 Mon-Sat 7am-6pm, Sun 7am-7pm (July and Aug closes at 6pm). Public tours Tues-Sat 11am, Sun 1pm. Special group tours (10 or more) Tues–Sat 10am and 4pm, Sun 2pm. Vertical tours Sat noon and 2pm

$ Entrance free. Tours $5 per person; Vertical tours $15 adult, $10 student or senior

The world's largest Gothic cathedral has one of the world's biggest rose windows with 10,000 pieces of glass. Even more amazing are the main bronze doors, which weigh 3,000 tonnes each and are opened only for an official visit by the bishop. An Episcopal church built in 1892, its grounds cover 4.9ha/12 acres of land and include a school and accommodation for the clergy. It has a capacity to seat 3,000 people, but because it holds so many art and performing art events it has chairs rather than pews. At the back of the cathedral behind the main altar are 7 different chapels, which represent different countries in Europe and are used for weddings, christenings and the services. It's well worth taking the Vertical Tour on a Sat, where you'll get to climb 38m/124ft up a spiral stone staircase to the top of the Cathedral where you'll get a glimpse of the nave restorations and study the grand architecture. The tour culminates on the roof with a wonderful view of the Morningside Heights area of Manhattan. Space is limited so reservations are recommended. All vertical tours meet for registration at the visitor centre inside the cathedral entrance.

One of the highlights of the cathedral's calendar is the Feast of Assisi when real animals, including an elephant and a llama, are ceremonially taken up to the altar to be blessed by the cathedral clergy. Inspired by St Francis of Assisi, whose life exemplified living in harmony with the natural world, the feast usually takes place on the first Sun in Oct. On selected Sat 10am–noon, families can join a Medieval Arts Workshop, which includes stone carving, weaving and sculpting.

 BRITTIP
The Cathedral of St John the Divine is blessed with plenty of loos if you get caught short!

GRACE CHURCH
Union Square
✉ 802 Broadway at 10th Street
☎ 212-254 2000
🖰 gracechurchnyc.org
🚇 Subway N, R, L, 4, 5, 6 to Union Square
🕐 Winter services Sun 9am, 11am, 6pm, Wed 6pm; summer services Sun 1pm, 6pm, Wed 6pm
$ Free

A beautiful example of the Gothic Revival period that was occurring in the city when this was built by James Renwick in 1846, when he was only 23 years old! Grace Church was something of a society church and is still known for its Choir of Men and Boys established in the late 1800s. It is as pretty inside as out with Pre-Raphaelite stained-glass windows and a marvellous mosaic floor. The original wood steeple was replaced by marble in 1888, and it is a landmark on the skyline if you gaze along Broadway from Downtown. Tours take place on the first Sun of the month after the 11am service.

BRITTIP
It is appropriate to tip your guide around 10–15% of the cost of the ticket, if you are happy with the service you received.

RIVERSIDE CHURCH
Morningside Heights
✉ 490 Riverside Drive at 120th Street
☎ 212-870 6700
🖰 theriversidechurchny.org
🚇 Subway 1 to 116th Street

Famous for having the world's largest tuned bell and its Carillon Concerts on Sun at 10.30am, 12.30pm and 3pm. After the Sunday morning service there's a free tour of the church which includes a brief history plus visits to the Christ Chapel, Nave and Chancel, which begins at 12.15pm in the First Balcony.

BRITTIP
If you're peckish on a Sunday lunchtime but don't want to blow the budget you can get a bargain bite to eat in the dining room at the Riverside Church until 3pm.

ST PATRICK'S CATHEDRAL
Midtown
✉ 14 East 51st Street between 50th and 51st Street (entrance 5th Avenue)
☎ 212-753 2261
🖰 saintpatrickscathedral.org
🚇 Subway 6 to 51st Street; E, V to 5th Avenue/53rd Street
🕐 Daily 7.30am–8.30pm
$ Free

BRITTIP
The steps leading up to St Patrick's create a perfect picnic spot for a lunch or snack stop.

The seat of New York's Roman Catholic Archdiocese, the cathedral was begun in 1857 and the stained-glass windows weren't completed until l930. However, the magnificent results have definitely been worth the wait. Check out the Great Bronze doors, The Rose Window and the Pieta statue in the Lady Chapel. It's probably the place of worship you'll most recognise in New York. It's been in the news for decades, from Robert F. Kennedy's funeral to the place where Spider-Man Tobey Maguire swung by in the 2002 film.

PART 2 – TOUR NEW YORK

Time is a precious commodity here, so you need to make sure that any tour you take pays for itself both financially and in terms of time. Your choice will depend on whether it is your first or second visit or you are a regular. Newcomers need to get their bearings and good ways to do this are to take a boat trip and a bus tour. The boat trip goes in a semi-circle around Manhattan from Midtown on one side to Midtown on the other; the bus tour, such as Gray Line's Manhattan Essential New York tour, is known as New York 101 (101 being slang for a first-year university course) because it covers so much of the city in one day. An alternative is the New York Visions tour, which takes less time, is cheaper and is generally more fact filled.

Bus tours are useful when you want to visit an area such as Harlem or the Bronx, but are unsure of your personal safety, in which case the Harlem Spirituals/New York Visions tours are your best bet. Then there are helicopter tours, which will certainly give you breathtaking views, but won't show you the full ins and outs of each area.

The reality is that the best way to see New York, get to know the city and find those interesting nooks and crannies is on foot, which possibly explains why the Big Onion Walking Tours are so popular – or it could be that they are just so darned good – and why so many people take advantage of the Big Apple Greeters, who can show you any area or sight you wish to visit. There is also a wide choice from bike tours to gangland tours and a reasonable selection of food tours.

AIR TOURS

LIBERTY HELICOPTER TOURS
Chelsea
- ✉ VIP Heliport, West 30th Street and Hudson River
- ☎ 212-967 6464 or 800-542 9933 toll free
- ⌨ libertyhelicopter.com
- 🚇 Subway A, C, E to 34th Street/Penn Station
- ⊙ Daily 9am–9pm

This is a fantastic, if pricey, way to see New York, and perfect if you're looking for a once-in-a-lifetime experience. There are lots

Washington Bridge from a helicopter tour

of tours to choose from, such as The Big Apple, around $135 for 15 minutes, if you really want to push the boat out there's the Romance Over Manhattan tour that lasts for 20 minutes and costs $995 for private hire of the whole helicopter, maximum 4 people.

NEW YORK HELICOPTER TOURS
South Street
- ✉ Downtown Heliport, 6 East River
- ☎ 212-361 6060
- ⌂ newyorkhelicoptertours.com
- 🚇 Subway A, C, E to 34th Street/Penn Station
- ⏰ Call for times

You can choose from several tours with this company, which has been offering helicopter rides for more than 20 years. The 10-12-minute Liberty Tour allows you a glimpse of the Statue of Liberty, Ellis and Governors Islands, South Street Seaport, Brooklyn and Manhattan bridges and Wall Street Financial Center, $139 per person. The 15-17-minute Central Park Tour includes The Empire State Building, Central Park and the Intrepid Sea-Air-Space Museum, $206 per person, and the 20-25-minute Grand Tour takes in all the above sights plus the Yankee Stadium, United Nations Building, Queensboro and Brooklyn bridges and Battery Park, $295 per person.

BIKE TOURS

BIKE THE BIG APPLE
- ☎ 201-837 1133 or 877-865 0078 toll free
- ⌂ bikethebigapple.com
- $ $90 includes bike rental for tours and helmet rental. Half-length 3-hour tours $65

Licensed guides take you through a variety of neighbourhoods, to see both historic and hip sides of the city. The 5 main tours include The Ethnic Apple Tour through Queens, Bike and Bite Brooklyn Tour, The Sensational Park and Soul tour travelling from Central Park to Harlem, Secret Streets – from High Finance to Chinatown, and The Brooklyn Bridge and Skyline at Twilight Bike Tour. Tours can be customised to your interests and are taken at a gentle pace.

CENTRAL PARK BICYCLE TOURS AND RENTALS
Columbus Circle
- ✉ 59th Street and Broadway
- ☎ 212-541 8759
- ⌂ centralparkbiketour.com
- 🚇 Subway A, B, C, D, 1, 2 to Columbus Circle/59th Street
- $ $49 adults, $40 children (15 and under) includes bike rental for tours; bike rental

only is $20 for 2 hours, $25 for 3 hours and $40 all day.

🇬🇧 BRITTIP
Ride round the almost deserted Financial District on a Sunday on a bike hired from Canal Street Bicycle Shop.

A 2-hour bike tour of Central Park April-Nov starting at 10am, 1pm and 4pm daily and 9am and 11am on summer weekends, which includes stops at the Shakespeare Garden, Strawberry Fields, Belvedere Castle and other sights, plus bike rentals for your own use. Other tours on offer include a Central Park Picnic Tour, $69, and at weekends the Central Park Movie Scenes Tour, $49, and Architecture Bike Tour, $49.

🇬🇧 BRITTIP
Once you have your bike, don't feel you have to cycle everywhere you go because you can take bikes on the subway. A list of bike rental shops and cycle events can be found on bikenewyork.org.

HUB STATION/PONY PEDICAB
SoHo
- ✉ 517 Broome Street at Thompson Street
- ☎ 212-254 8844/965 9334
- 🚇 Subway C, E to Spring Street; N, R to Prince Street
- ⏰ Open Tues-Sun 11am-7pm
- $ $15 for 30 minutes, $30 for 1 hour

Actually three-man tricycles or 'pedicabs' (one 'driver' and two passengers), these are so amazing-looking that even seen-it-all-before New Yorkers stare! I found them an excellent way to see SoHo without breaking into a sweat or breaking the bank. You may even be able to hail one of these after the theatre in the Times Square area. Don't forget to tip – 'drivers'

Aerial view of New York from a helicopter tour

earn their money! In good weather only. You can either reserve in advance and arrange a meeting point or turn up at the hub.

METRO BICYCLES
Upper West Side and Upper East Side
- ✉ 231 West 96th Street at Broadway and 87th Street at Lexington
- ☎ 212-663 7531
- ⌂ metrobicycles.com
- 🚇 Subway 1, 2, 3, A, C, B, D to West 96th Street; 4, 5, 6 to East 87th Street
- ⏱ Daily 9.30am–6.30pm
- $ $9 hour, $45 same-day return, $55 24 hours, helmets $2.50

If you want to check out Central Park and the Upper West Side along the river or the Upper East Side, rent from here. Metro have 7 shops in convenient locations such as Eastside Bicycles, 1311 Lexington Avenue at 88th Street (212-427 4450), Central Park and Canal Street Bicycle Shop at 417 Canal Street between 6th Avenue and Grand Street in Chinatown (212-334 8000). Check the website links for hours, bikes for hire and other locations.

PEDAL PUSHER BIKE SHOP
Central Park
- ✉ 1306 2nd Avenue at East 69th Street
- ☎ 212-228 5592 or 877-257 9437 toll free
- ⌂ http://pedalpusherbikeshop.com
- 🚇 Subway 6 to Hunter College/E 68th Street
- ⏱ Fri–Mon 10am–6pm, Wed 10am–7pm, Thurs 10am–8pm, closed Tues
- $ $5.99 hour, $24.99 for a day, $29.99 for 24 hours, helmet and lock $3.99 each

This is perhaps the cheapest bike hire in New York City and comes highly recommended by Bike The Big Apple for those who want to go it alone. Just 5 blocks away from Central Park, it is handily located for a whirl around New

THE SOPRANOS
Most of the locations for this ultra-popular series were shot in New Jersey, a short bus ride from main Manhattan. For a more comprehensive tour, see page 90.

Pizzaland: 260 Belleville Turnpike, North Arlington, NJ (pizzalandpizza.com), can be seen in the opening sequence of every episode as Tony Soprano drives past it on his way home.

Satin Dolls: 230 State Route 17 South, Lodi, NJ. (tel 201-845 6494, satindollsnj.com), is a real-life dancing club where scenes for the Bada Bing Club are filmed.

York's backyard. Types of rentals include road, hybrid, mountain and 3-speed.

BOAT TOURS

ADIRONDACK, CLASSIC HARBOR LINE
Chelsea Pier
- ✉ Pier 59, 18th Street at Hudson River
- ☎ 646-336 5270 or 212-209 3370 to book
- ⌂ sail-nyc.com
- 🚇 Subway A, C, E to 8th Avenue/14th Street
- ⏱ End April–end Oct
- $ Tickets $40–$50 for 2-hour sails, $75 for Sun brunch sails

A sail on this three-mast replica of a 19th-century schooner is unforgettable. It sails from Chelsea Pier to Battery Park, allowing you the chance to catch a glimpse of Ellis Island and the Statue of Liberty, Governor's Island and Brooklyn Bridge, while sipping your complimentary glass of wine. Otherwise, you can opt for a brunch cruise on the 80ft 1920s-style yacht *Manhattan* from March to end Dec. Both offer sunset and city lights cruises, too.

Pony cab

Long Island pier from the Circle Line ferry

BATEAUX NEW YORK
Chelsea

✉ Pier 61 at Chelsea Piers on West 23rd Street

☎ 212-727 2789 or 866-817 3463 (toll free)

🖰 bateauxnewyork.com

🚗 Subway C, E, 1, 9 to 23rd Street, transfer to B23 cross-town bus heading west

$ Brunch ticket around $60 without alcoholic drinks, dinner around $120, $5 tax excluded

Indulge in a dinner (7.30–10.30pm daily) or brunch (noon–2pm) while cruising around Lower Manhattan (note: boarding an hour earlier).

BRITTIP
Special value packages combining cruises and even sights such as Top of the Rock or the Empire State Building with a cruise are only available from the Circle Line Box Office at Pier 83. Check circleline42.com for combos and savings.

CIRCLE LINE
West Midtown

✉ Pier 83, West 42nd Street at Hudson River

☎ 212-563 3200

🖰 circleline42.com

🚗 Any subway to 42nd Street, then transfer to an M42 bus heading west

$ From $24 adults, $21 seniors, $16 children; combo packages available

Choose from a 3-hour full island cruise, $35 adults, $22 children, $30 seniors or a 2-hour semi-circle or sunset/harbour lights cruise, $31 adults, $20 children, $27 seniors. Or you can take a Live Music cruise, or a 75-minute Liberty Island cruise ($26 adults, $23 seniors and $18 children) May–Oct.

Alternatively, you can go for a spin on *The Beast*, a speedboat that takes you on a quick and memorable 30-minute tour. Sights fly by as you reach a speed of 64kph/45mph and stop at the Statue of Liberty for photos. May–Oct daily on the hour noon–dusk, $23 adults and seniors, $17 children. If you are lucky enough to be in the city on 4 July, then there's a special fireworks cruise, though booking way in advance is advisable.

NY WATERWAY
Financial District

✉ Pier 78 at West 38 Street and 12th Avenue or Pier A at West St and Battery Place

☎ 800-533 3779

🖰 nywaterway.com

🚗 Any subway to 42nd Street, transfer to M42 bus heading west

☺ A few cruises operate year round, most April–Dec

$ Harbour cruise prices from $26 adults, $21 seniors and $15 children, without service charge.

Offers a wide variety of sightseeing options all year round, including 90-Minute Skyline Cruises to Downtown and Midtown. There is also a Gateway to America Harbor Tour, 90-Minute Twilight Cruise and 90-Minute NY History Cruise, as well as evening cruises with on-board entertainment. Also available in the summer are day trips to Sandy Hook Beach and, for baseball fans, cruise packages that include a round-trip sail on the Yankee Clipper, tickets, souvenirs and the ubiquitous hot dog.

BRITTIP
The harbour cruises are very informative and give a great insight into Manhattan and beyond, but it can sometimes be hard to hear the commentary from the upper deck. If you want to hear everything, it's probably best to stay inside.

BRITTIP

This is the city's only land and water sightseeing tour, The NYC Ducks Tour (grayline.com), aboard a special amphibian aquabus. The hour-long tour, from 10am-4.30pm every 20 mins, splashes out of Times Square and gives views of the city skyline from the Hudson River. Don't worry, you won't get wet!

WORLD YACHT DINNER CRUISES
Midtown West

✉ Pier 81 at West 41st Street and Hudson River
☎ 212-630 8100
🖰 worldyacht.com
🚗 Any subway to 42nd Street, then transfer to M42 bus heading west
🕐 April Thurs–Mon, May–Dec daily for dinner; board at 6pm, sail 7–10pm
$ From around $100, depending on the season/day of the week

With 4-course menus created by a selection of New York's best chefs, linen tablecloths, live music, a dance floor and world-class videos, this is an upmarket experience you are sure to enjoy. The cruise lasts 3 hours and also provides spectacular views of the harbour. Note that the dress code is smart and that jackets are required, so make sure you allow yourself plenty of time to put on your glad rags.

GRAY LINE NEW YORK SIGHTSEEING
West Midtown

✉ 777 8th Avenue between 47th and 48th Streets
☎ 212-445 0848/800-669 0051 toll free
🖰 graylinenewyork.com
🚗 Subway C, E to 50th Street
🕐 Daily 8.30am–5pm
$ Varies, see below; prices are with $5 online booking discount

The oldest sightseeing bus company in New York, it has much to offer, although the average tour guide gives very little information in comparison with the New York Visions tours. Still, if you don't want to be overwhelmed by information on your first visit to New York, then try the **Classic New York Tour** ($88 adults, $65 children (5–11).

A double-decker bus tour with hop-on, hop-off stops, it includes the ferry to the Statue of Liberty and Ellis Island, a ticket to the Empire State Building and a ticket to South Street Seaport Museum. It comes with the 48-hour **All Loops Tour**, which runs around Downtown, Midtown, uptown and Brooklyn and at night with 50 stops. You can do as few or as many as you like, so you can spend as long as you want in each area, giving you plenty of flexibility. A 3-day Super Saver Combo, combines the NYC Official Heritage Tour with the All Loops Tour

Midtown Manhattan skyline

for $112/$88. The newest hottest tours include **The Essential New York**, which takes you to the Top of the Rock, the UN Headquarters and the Statue of Liberty/Ellis Island for $99/$69, a 2-hour **In a New York Minute Package**, which includes a ticket to the Empire State Building, and a Lady Liberty harbour cruise for $70/$50. If you just want to hop on and off, The All Loops Tour gives you 48 hours for $46/$36 if you book online.

The **Night on the Town Tour**, $89, is around 5 hours and includes dinner, a 1-hour cruise, glass of champagne, Top of the Rock entrance, and all the night sights such as SoHo, Battery Park and Rockefeller Center.

HARLEM SPIRITUALS/ NEW YORK VISIONS
Midtown
- ✉ 690 8th Avenue between West 43rd and West 44th Streets
- ☎ 212-391 0900 or 800-660 2166 toll free
- ⌖ harlemspirituals.com or harlemheritagetours.com
- 🚗 Subway A, C, E, 1, 2, 3, 7, 9, S, N, Q, R, S, W, B, F, D, V to 42nd Street/Times Square
- $ Varies

One of the most reputable tour companies in New York, the guides are highly qualified, great founts of knowledge and very friendly, while the buses are modern and comfortable with the all-important air-conditioning. Tours by the Harlem Spirituals include:

Harlem Gospel Tour: A combined walking (though not too far!) and riding tour of Harlem (Sun and Wed), during which you attend a church service, hear a gospel choir and have the option of having lunch or brunch at a soul food restaurant. Prices are $55 adults/$99 with brunch, $39 children (5–11) $75 with brunch. Tours Sun 9.30am–1.30pm, Wed 9am–1pm.

🇬🇧 BRITTIP
In case you're wondering what you'll be served as soul food, this traditional African-American cuisine consists of spicy ribs, fried fish and chicken, cornbread and sides such as okra and black-eyed peas.

Soul Food and Jazz: A chance to relive the heyday of Harlem, thanks to the return of jazz to the area. This combines a walking and riding tour through Harlem's historical sites with a soul food meal and the chance to see a jam session at a local jazz club. Tours are available Mon, Thurs and Sat 7pm–midnight and cost $135 for adults and children (5–11). **The New York Visions Manhattan Sightseeing Tour New York New York:**

An excellent 4-hour introduction to the sights including Times Square, Central Park, Rockefeller Center, Greenwich Village, SoHo, Little Italy, Chinatown and the Wall Street area. Tours Mon, Thurs and Sat 9.30am. $55 adults, $39 children. Pay extra $65/45 (adults/children) and you also get tickets for the ferry to the Statue of Liberty and Ellis Island Immigration Museum (drop off at Battery Park), plus an MTA Fun Pass for 24-hour use on the subways and buses (page 60).

FOOD TOURS

ENTHUSIASTIC GOURMET
Chinatown
- ✉ 245 East 63rd Street
- ☎ 646-209 4724
- ⌖ enthusiasticgourmet.com
- ⏰ 10am and 2pm. Different days for different tours; check website for times and availability
- $ $50 per person, reservations necessary

The Chinatown Discovered Tour explores the neighbourhood's grocery stores, meat and fish markets and produce stands for 3 hours. If you're still hungry, head for Jing Fong Restaurant (20 Elizabeth Street, 212-964 5256) for some of the best dim sum in NYC. There are lots of other gourmet tours, such as the kosher NY Nosh, and a taste of Hispanic, Jewish, Chinese and Italian on The Melting Pot. TMaximum of 8 people.

FOODS OF NEW YORK
Greenwich Village
- ✉ 4th Floor, 9 Barrow Street, meet near 6th and Bleecker Street
- ☎ 212-209 3370/917-408 9539
- ⌖ foodsofny.com
- ⏰ Daily, year round 11am–2pm (but varies so check website)
- $ $44 per person

Rocco's pastry shop

A great-value 3-hour tour, considering the amount of food you eat, and with a friendly atmosphere as they take up to 16.

◀▶ BRITTIP

In the unlikely event you still feel peckish after the Foods of New York tour, head back to Fish at 280 Bleecker Street where you can have 6 oysters and a glass of wine or beer at the bar for just $8.

In Greenwich Village you'll stop to sample the wares of Rocco's pastry shop and Murray's famous cheese shop. You'll also learn about the food of New York, especially of the Italian community, you'll gain hints about architecture and properties in the Village and visit a real speakeasy. Alternatively, you can choose to go on a tour of the Chelsea Gourmet Market and the West Village Meatpacking area (Thurs–Sun) or Central Greenwich Village and SoHo tour (Fri and Sat). Not surprising that it won Citysearch's Best City Tour 2007.

SAVORY SOJOURNS
Chelsea
- ✉ 155 West 13th Street
- ☎ 212-691 7314 or 888-9SAVORY toll free
- ◷ savorysojourns.com
- $ $120–230

For a unique insight into the fine foods and culinary skills of some of New York's finest restaurants, Savory Sojourns promises to give you an insider's guide to New York's best culinary and cultural destinations followed by a great slap-up meal. Some even include a cookery lesson and can last around 4 hours. Areas covered include Upper East Side, Chinatown, Little Italy, SoHo, Lower East Side, Greenwich Village, Flatiron and Chelsea Market, Financial District, Hell's Kitchen, The Bronx, Brooklyn and Harlem. They also offer a whole range of other tours from exclusive customised shopping trips with fashion

---

Chassidic Discovery Welcome Center

industry experts to unique behind-the-scenes tours of New York's art scene and evenings of jazz and gourmet dining. If you don't like the sound of any of these, you can request your own.

INSIDER TOURS

Some of the most interesting New York tours are led by residents who have unique inside perspectives that they are willing to share on everything from shopping to a haircut. Here is a fascinating selection:

KRAMER'S REALITY TOUR
West Midtown
- ✉ The Producer's Club, 358 West 44th Street between 8th and 9th Avenues
- ☎ 212-268 5525 or toll free 1800 KRAMERS/572 6377
- ◷ kennykramer.com
- 🚇 Subway A, C, E to 42nd Street/Penn Station
- ⊕ Sat noon, Sun (on holiday weekends) noon; check site for winter availability
- $ $37.50 plus $2 service charge

The real Kramer behind the *Seinfeld* character has come out of the woodwork and invented his own 3-hour tour based on all the *Seinfeld* spots in the city. Kenny Kramer will answer questions, share backstage gossip and the real-life incidents behind the show. Book early as this tour sells out weeks in advance. It starts from The Producers Club Theater, 358 West 44th Street between 8th and 9th Avenue, a short walk from Times Square.

MYSTICAL WORLD OF CHASSIDIC JEWS
Brooklyn
- ✉ Chassidic Discovery Welcome Center, 305 Kingston Avenue
- ☎ 718-953 5244
- ◷ jewishtours.com
- 🚇 Subway 3 to Kingston Avenue
- ⊕ Sun 10am–1pm for individuals or Sun–Fri for groups
- $ $42 adults, $22 children (12 and under); 3-hour tour includes a kosher deli lunch

◀▶ BRITTIP

The Kingston Avenue subway stop for the Chassidic tour is just one away from Eastern Parkway, the stop for the Brooklyn Museum (page 283) and the Botanic Garden (page 282) – both great places to visit on a Sunday afternoon.

The Lubavitcher Jews in Crown Heights, Brooklyn, are focused on sharing what they have with the outside world, providing a unique opportunity to get an insight into a Chassidic community. Guided by Rabbi Beryl Epstein, with a charming manner and great sense of humour, you'll hear the history of the Chassidic Jews; visit the synagogue to learn about some customs and traditions; watch a scribe working on a Torah scroll; and see the Rebbe's library, a Matzoh bakery and a Chassidic art gallery. A real insight into a fascinating culture.

BRITTIP

It's easy to get to the Chassidic Discovery Welcome Center by the 3 train (the red line). Allow an hour from Midtown.

ROCK 'N' ROLL WALKING TOUR
East Village
☎ 212-209 3370
⌂ rockjunket.com
⏱ Mon–Fri by appointment; Sat 1pm
$ Tickets $29

Die-hard rockers Bobby Pinn and Ginger Ali lead these fun tours around East Village's legendary punk, rock and glam nightspots. Rock Junket also does tours of Union Square and the West Village and artist-specific tours for the Beatles and Bob Dylan.

BRITTIP

If you're feeling peckish after your Rock Junket tour, rock junket.com's *NYC Guide* has a list of cool joints serving food for $10.

ON LOCATION TOURS

SCREENTOURS
Upper East Side
☎ 212-209 3370
⌂ screentours.com

The best company in New York for fun and informative bus tours around the attractions in some of the city's famous shows, plus a general TV and movie tour and a walking tour of Central Park movie sites.

CENTRAL PARK MOVIE TOUR
✉ Meet at the entrance to Central Park, 59th Street between 5th and 6th Avenues
🚇 Subway N, R to 5th Avenue
⏱ Fri, Sat noon
$ $20 (plus $2 ticket fee)

Take some snaps of the Boathouse Café seen in *When Harry Met Sally* and *Sex And The City*, check out Tavern in the Green that featured in *Ghostbusters* and feed pigeons in the park à la Macaulay Culkin in *Home Alone*

2, The Bandshell from *Breakfast at Tiffany's* plus many more choice spots in the park. This walking tour takes 2 hours and, for the novelty, you could do it by bike (page 83).

GOSSIP GIRL
✉ Meet near the New York Palace Hotel (exact location given on purchase of tickets)
🚇 Subway E, V to 5th Avenue/53rd Street
⏱ Fri, Sat, Sun noon
$ $38 (plus $2 ticket fee)

If you love this hit TV show, this is your chance to experience a day in the life of Manhattan's elite, visiting more than 40 locations that have appeared in the show. This includes the hotel that's home to the Bass and Van der Woodson families, the Constance Billard School for Girls, the lavish 5th Avenue building that Blair calls home, the shop at Henri Bendel where Blair and Serena shop and the restaurant where Dan and Serena had their first date.

BRITTIP

Pace yourself. There's no point in trying to pack so much into your day that you arrive back at your hotel exhausted with your head spinning. Less can often be more!

Who you gonna call?

SEX AND THE CITY

✉ Meet by the Pulitzer Fountain on 5th Avenue at 58th Street

🚇 Subway 4, 5, 6, to 59th Street/Lexington Avenue; N, R, W to 5th Avenue

🕐 Daily 11am and 3pm, Sat 11am, 2pm and 3pm, Sun 10am, 11am, 3pm

$ $40 (plus $2 ticket fee)

During this 3-hour bus tour, which includes over 40 locations, you'll visit D&G in SoHo, where Carrie shopped for shoes, and the New York Sports Club where Miranda worked out, plus bars such as O'Neil's and Tao where Carrie, Samantha, Charlotte and Miranda did their flirting. Most important, you'll get some behind-the-scenes scoop on the show and the actors. This is a really fun experience, which gets into the spirit of the show and gives everyone plenty of browsing and chatting opportunities. You'll also get to eat a cupcake from the famous Magnolia Bakery (watch out – they are incredibly sweet!). By the end, you should be fluent in *Sex And The City*-speak and know your Manhattan Guy (a genetically mutant strain of single man that feeds on Zabar's and midnight shows at Angelika) from your Trysexual (someone who will try everything once). Book at least a week in advance.

THE SOPRANOS

✉ Bus departs from the 'Button' statue on 7th Avenue at 39th Street

🚇 B, D, F, V to 42nd Street; N, Q, R, S, W, 1, 2, 3, 7, 9, S to Times Square

🕐 Sat and Sun 2pm

$ $42 (plus $2 ticket fee)

Get the shakedown on a tour of 40 sites used in *The Sopranos* including Satriale's Pork Store, the cemetery where Livia Soprano is buried, the Bada Bing nightclub and the diner where Chris was shot. The 4-hour tour also includes a guide to New Jersey Mafia-speak, a stop for cannolis (traditional Italian pastries) and 6 other stops along the way. The tours tend to sell out quickly, so reserve your place as far in advance as possible.

Bada Bing

TOUR NEW YORK TV AND MOVIE SITES

✉ Bus departs from Ellen's Stardust Diner, 1650 Broadway at 51st Street

🚇 Subway 1, 9 to 50th Street; N, W, R to 49th Street

🕐 Daily at 11am

$ $36 (plus $2 ticket fee)

Takes you to over 40 different locations from over 60 TV shows and movies such as *Friends*, *You've Got Mail*, *Ghostbusters*, *The Bill Cosby Show*, *Will & Grace* and Woody Allen's *Manhattan* in around 3 hours. This is updated as new movies come out, so it now has sites from *Hitch*, *The Devil Wears Prada*, *The Interpreter*, *The Apprentice*, *Spider-Man* and *Rescue Me*.

WALKING TOURS

ADVENTURE ON A SHOESTRING

✉ 300 West 53rd Street

☎ 212-265 2663

🚇 Varies depending on area

🕐 Sat, Sun

$ $5

Adventure has been going strong for nearly 45 years, offering 2-hour tours led by veteran Howard Goldberg around many Manhattan neighbourhoods, as well as outlying areas that are less familiar to tourists, such as Astoria, the Greek section of Queens, and Hoboken, a new artists' centre in New Jersey. Among the most popular tours are Haunted Greenwich Village and Hell's Kitchen. Theme tours, such as those based on Marilyn Monroe's New York and Jacqueline Kennedy Onassis's New York, are also favourites.

ALLIANCE FOR DOWNTOWN NEW YORK
Financial District

✉ Tours start at the steps of the US Custom House, 1 Bowling Green

☎ 212-606 4064

🖰 downtownny.com/walkingtour/

🚇 Subway 4, 5 to Bowling Green

🕐 Thurs and Sat, noon

Just turn up to take this free 90-minute Wall Street Walking Tour exploring the birthplace of New York, including the Customs House, Trinity Church, Wall Street and the Stock Exchange. The Alliance has been doing much work on sprucing up the entire district and employs red-hatted security staff/cleaners to help you find your way around.

BIG ONION WALKING TOURS
Brooklyn

✉ 476 13th Street, Brooklyn, NY 11215
☎ 212-439 1090
🖰 bigonion.com
🕐 Various tours daily, most start 1pm some 11am or 2pm. Always call after 9.30am on the morning of your tour as the time will change if the weather is bad
$ $15 adults, $12 seniors, $10 students

Amazingly informative ethnic, architectural and historic 2-hour walking tours, which you can just turn up to (but reserve the multi-ethnic eating tour), led by history graduates. Tours are offered on a rotating basis and begin in different spots. Call the main number or check the website to see what's on the schedule. Options include the East Village, Central Park, Gay New York, Financial District, Gramercy Park and Union Square, Greenwich Village, Historic Lower Manhattan, Historic TriBeCa, the Jewish Lower East Side, Presidential New York, Revolutionary New York, Roosevelt Island, SoHo and NoLiTa and the Upper East Side. 'Big Onion' was the nickname given to New York in the 19th century by non-New Yorkers who believed it smelled of the immigrants' heavily spiced cooking!

The Original Multi-ethnic Eating Tour: Meet on the corner of Essex and Delancey Streets in front of Olympic Diner. Subway J, M, Z to Essex Street; F to Delancey Street.

🇬🇧 BRITTIP
Some Big Onion tours can get a little crowded. If so, stand as close to the guide as possible to hear their pearls of wisdom.

This is one of the more popular tours, which covers the Lower East Side, Chinatown and Little Italy, and it is offered frequently. You pay a $5 supplement for nosh, which includes delicious spicy tofu, mozzarella and Italian sausage, chicken and shrimp and vegetarian dim sum, plus other food favourites of the locals, all eaten in the streets. The tour also provides a good way to get a feel for areas you may find confusing on your own. It gives a fascinating insight into the history of the area and what modern-day life is like.

🇬🇧 BRITTIP
If you need to visit the loo before you start this tour, head for the McDonald's diagonally opposite the meeting point.

You'll end the tour deep in the heart of Chinatown outside a vegetarian food centre and the Chinese Gourmet Bakery. It may be good to stop for a drink before you head off to the nearest subway stations at Canal Street, where you have the choice of the A, C, E, J, M, N, Q, R, W, 6 lines to take you just about anywhere in Manhattan.

Historic Harlem Tour: Meet at the Schomburg Center at 135th Street and Lenox Avenue. Subway 2, 3 to 135th Street. A great way to find out about Harlem, its history, politics and modern-day life through the eyes of a history graduate.

🇬🇧 BRITTIP
For a cheap and delicious meal before the Harlem tour, head for Mannas at 486 Lenox Avenue at 134th Street (mannasrestaurants.com). After the tour you'll find yourself outside the Apollo Theater. Just a few metres east is a clean McDonald's with TVs on one wall (and a loo on the opposite side).

You'll hear about Martin Luther King and other African-American activists, local literary salons and gospel churches. You'll learn about the old neighbourhood joints of the Renny and Savoy, how the Apollo Theater and Cotton Clubs were only open to rich white folk looking for an 'authentic black' experience, the campaign to allow black people to work in the shops they frequented, Striver's Row, the architecture and the old black pressure groups, two of whose buildings now house beauty parlours.

2nd Avenue at dawn

GREETINGS FROM THE BIG APPLE

It's certainly a novel idea and it's also a winner – the Big Apple Greeters are ready to take you on a personalised and entirely customised tour of any part of New York any day of the week and it costs absolutely nothing. The idea is simple: New Yorkers who are proud of their neighbourhoods and have some spare time will spend between 2 and 4 hours with you. Since it started in 1992 they've greeted more than 88,000 visitors from 50 countries, so you'll be in good hands. They will take you round any area you like and help you do just what you want to do, be it shopping, sightseeing or eating and drinking, rain or shine. Just make your request at least 10 working days (preferably 3–4 weeks) in advance and confirmation will be awaiting you upon your arrival at your hotel. The service is entirely free and no Big Apple Greeters worth their salt will take a tip, but I found that it was no problem to get them to agree to letting me pay for a spot of brunch or lunch, and they're well worth it (212-669 8159, visitrequest@ bigapplegreeter.org, bigapplegreeter.org).

The 'Official' Gangs of New York Tour:

Meet on the south-east corner of Broadway and Chambers Street at City Hall Park, Sun 1pm. Subway 1, 2, 3, 9, A, C, E to Chambers Street, R, W to City Hall. This popular tour is (like the movie of the same name) inspired by Herbert Asbury's 1927 classic book *The Gangs of New York*, and Martin Scorsese's film, which explores every aspect of the city's brutal gang culture centred on Five Points.

Led in conjunction with Miramax Films,

White Horse Tavern

the tour paints a vivid picture of life for the immigrants in the 1800s and includes stops at Paradise Square, Murderer's Alley and other sites associated with Bill 'The Butcher' Poole, William Tweed and the police and draft riots. Before you get too carried away with any notions of glamour, bear in mind that the area then was so unsafe that the police refused to go near it. There was at least one murder a night and ordinary people were so scared of leaving their tenements they even buried their dead in their buildings.

JOYCE GOLD HISTORY TOURS OF NEW YORK

Chelsea
- ✉ 141 West 17th Street
- ☎ 212-242 5762
- 🖱 nyctours.com
- 🕐 Various starting times for 2–3 hours, no reservations needed
- $ $15

Specialists in unusual, in-depth weekend forays into 30 of the city's distinctive neighbourhoods all led by Joyce herself. Fascinating tours include the East Village, culture and counter-culture, Downtown graveyards, Greenwich Village highlights, Colonial New York and Noshing Manhattan.

LITERARY PUB CRAWL

West Village
- ✉ Meet at the White Horse Tavern, 567 Hudson Street at 11th Street
- ☎ 212-613 5796
- 🖱 bakerloo.org/pubcrawl
- 🚇 Subway 1, 9 to Christopher Street
- 🕐 Sat 2pm
- $ $20 adults, $15 students/seniors

Tour 4 pubs in the Village area that attracted writers, poets and artists, among them Dylan Thomas, Ernest Hemingway, John Steinbeck, e e cummings, Jack Kerouac, Jackson Pollock and Frank McCourt.

MUNICIPAL ART SOCIETY

Midtown
- ✉ 111 West 57th Street between 6th and 7th Avenues
- ☎ 212-935 3960
- 🖱 mas.org
- 🚇 Subway N, R to 57th Street
- $ Suggested $10 donation

Walking tours taking in both historic and architectural sites, focusing on skyscrapers in different neighbourhoods, as well as tours around Staten Island. Weekly tour Downtown: Where New York Began, is a 90-minute tour of Downtown, its history, architecture and art, taking in the Stock Exchange, Trinity Church and Fraunces Tavern. Well-run, informative and very enjoyable.

BRIT'S GUIDE AWARDS FOR SIGHTSEEING TOURS

Best overview of city:

By bus: New York Visions (page 87)

By boat: Circle Line (page 85)

Best walking tours:
The Big Onion (pages 91–92)

Best for thrills:
The Beast speedboat (page 85)
Liberty Helicopter Tours (page 82)

Most eye-opening experiences:
Mystical World of Chassidic Jews (page 88)

Best for foodies:
Foods of New York around Greenwich Village and Chelsea Gourmet Market (pages 87–88)

Best for free:
Big Apple Greeters (see page 92)

Best for romance:
Bateaux New York dinner cruises around Manhattan (page 85)

Best TV show tours:
The Sopranos (page 90)
Kramer's Reality Tour (page 88)

Most offbeat:
Hub Station/Pony Pedicabs (pages 83–84)

Best musical tours:
Harlem Gospel Tour (page 87)
Soul Food and Jazz (page 87)

SUSANSEZ NYC WALKABOUTS

Bronx

☎ 917-509 3111

✆ dbsystemsgroup.com/susansez

🚇 Subway various starting points

$ $30–40

Walking tours off the beaten track in Manhattan and the outer boroughs, the Bronx and Queens led by native New Yorker Susan Birnbaum including curiosities such as the Knitting Crawl Walkabout and Pushcarts to Funky Swank, around the Lower East Side.

WALK AND TALK NEW YORK

✉ Planetarium Station, PO Box 742

☎ 212-873 8534

✆ walkandtalknewyork.com

$ 3-hour tour $150 for 2 people

New York resident Phyllis K takes you around the hot spots, or you can fill in a form online and let her know where you'd like to visit. A sample tour includes Chelsea, Meatpacking district, Greenwich and West villages.

YOUR OWN WALKING TOURS

If you don't want to join a group tour but still appreciate knowing what you are seeing as you stroll around, here are some glorious walks, none of which will take more than a couple of hours maximum (at a very gentle pace). So don your trainers (sorry, sneakers), pack some water and enjoy!

1 LOWER MANHATTAN WALK

Little Italy

▶ Start from Mulberry Street at Grand Street heading south and you'll hit the heart of this vibrant, colourful, café-filled neighbourhood, which as the name suggests is home to some 5,000 immigrant Italians. Sit and watch the world go by at one of the authentic cafés.

▶ Suitably refreshed, continue your walk south, which will take you past Umberto's Clam House, the place where Mafia boss Joey Gallo was shot in the '70s.

▶ When you hit Canal Street, turn left.

Chinatown

▶ You'll immediately notice the change from west to east, and if you turn first right on to Mott Street you'll be in the main thoroughfare of Chinatown.

▶ Head south and be intoxicated by the exotica aromas and noisy street vendors selling everything from fresh dim sum to fake handbags in front of the Eastern States Buddhist Temple, home to over 100 glittering Buddhas.

▶ Head right on Bayard Street until you hit Centre Street.

▶ Turn left and after about 1km/0.6mls the road turns in to Park Row; look right and you'll see City Hall Park and the Woolworth Building on Broadway.

Little Italy

Woolworth Building
▶ Gaze up at what was once the Big Apple's tallest building (it lost the crown in 1930) and set the standard for future skyscrapers. Named after retail tycoon Frank W Woolworth, this Gothic-esque creation was built in 1913 and designed by architect Cass Gilbert. You'll instantly spot it thanks to the gargoyles of bats, pyramid roof and 4 towers.
▶ Carry on south down Broadway for around 7 blocks.
▶ Then turn right on to Liberty Street where you'll find the World Trade Center Memorial Visitors' Centre next to Ground Zero.

World Trade Center Memorial
▶ To see more than Ground Zero, where 2,979 people lost their lives when the World Trade Center buildings collapsed after a terrorist attack on 11 September 2001, then visit the WTC Visitor Center, which has exhibitions, programmes and even personal walking tours with survivors.
▶ When you've paid your respects, retrace your steps along Park Row, turn right at the Municipal Building on to the bridge.

Brooklyn Bridge
▶ This 1.6km/1ml gateway to Brooklyn is a Manhattan landmark. Beautiful by day and night, there's a constant flow of traffic, joggers and pedestrians and it's well worth crossing for the panoramic views of the skyline.
▶ A great way to end the day is with a meal or drink at the River Café on Water Street (page 161), which lies just beneath the bridge in Brooklyn.

Municipal Building

2 DOWNTOWN WALK
Flatiron Building
▶ Start the walk at 5th Avenue at West 23rd Street. Look in up awe at this spectacular skyscraper with an unusual triangle shape, which was once the tallest building in the world when it was completed in 1902.
▶ Head south down 5th Avenue, where if in the mood credit cards can be flexed in the designer boutiques.
▶ After 6 blocks turn right on to West 17th Street.

Rubin Museum of Art
▶ At the corner of West 17th Street at 7th Avenue is the Rubin, the first museum in the western hemisphere dedicated to the art of the Himalayas. Admire the stunning Tibetan wall hangings, bronze busts, masks and sculptures from the 2nd to the 20th centuries.
▶ Return to 5th Avenue and continue south until reaching East 14th Street.

St Mark's in the Bowery
▶ Walk along East 14th Street, past Union Square on the left, then turn right on to 4th Avenue, then after a couple of blocks turn right on to East 10th Street and see the spire of St Mark's. Built in 1799, it's one of New York's oldest churches where poet W H Auden was a parishioner and some of the city's most prominent residents are laid to rest.

Greenwich Village
▶ Head west back along 10th Street and turn left on to University Place, where the shops and tree-lined roads of Greenwich Village emerge. This tranquil bohemian haven is a welcome break from the hustle and bustle of 5th Avenue.
▶ Walk south and see the red brick New York University buildings on the left and Washington Square Park on the right.

Washington Square Park
▶ The heart of Greenwich Village, Washington Square Park is one of the city's most vibrant open spaces. Once a magnet for artists and political activists, it's now home to some of New York's elite. Keep your eyes peeled for the magnificent marble arch on the north side of the square.

3 MIDTOWN WALK
Museum of Modern Art (MoMA)
▶ Start the walk at this inspiring modern art museum on 53rd Street between 5th and 6th Avenues, packed full of 19th- and 20th-century masterpieces. If you haven't already visited, take a stroll around the world-renowned painting and sculpture galleries on the first floor and admire the renovations unveiled in 2004 (pages 113–114).

ONE DAY IN NEW YORK

Need to cram everything into 24 hours? I've broken down one day to include some of the must-see, must-do things I think New York has to offer. Obviously there are lots of wonderful experiences that I've had to leave out, but with this whirlwind tour of the city you'll at least come away with a true taste of the Big Apple!

Breakfast: Rise as early as possible (there's a lot to do today!) and, if you haven't already done so, buy a MetroCard to save money getting around (page 60). The best breakfast in town is at **Norma's** at Le Parker Meridien Hotel, Midtown. The only difficulty is choosing from the vast selection of delights on offer, from chocolate French toast to poached eggs and corn beef hash. For something cheaper, tuck into some bagels, one of the city's signature breakfasts. There are dozens of great bagel places throughout New York. I'd recommend **H and H Bagels** at 80th Street and Broadway (212-595 8003). Chow down on a salmon and cheese bagel and great coffee to prepare you for your day.

Morning: It would be a shame to visit the city and not check out at least one of the incredible museums. It's hard to beat the **American Museum of Natural History** (page 100), next to Central Park and an easy stroll from H and H Bagels. Choose a Museum Highlights Tour, free with admission, at 10.15am. After you've had a glimpse of at least some of the museum's wonders, cross Central Park West to access **Central Park** for a walk, past landmarks such as the Obelisk, or Cleopatra's Needle, the oldest public monument in North America, and end at the **BoatHouse Central Park** (page 161) at the northeast tip of the lake, the perfect place for a spot of lunch. It's busy so best to book ahead, but well worth it as this is one of the loveliest restaurants in the city. If it's summer, ask for a table on the outdoor terrace.

Afternoon: Now that you're full, it's time to walk off the calories New York style. Hop on the Metro (B, D at 72nd Street) down to **SoHo** (B, D to Spring Street) and wander around the unique boutiques, like Flying A (page 133) and Anthropologie (page 156) for clothes, and Coconut Company (page 150) for chic antiques, set amid the cobbled streets and cool buildings. If you're feeling peckish or just need to take a load off (New York speak!), pop into **Fanelli's Café** (page 186) on Prince Street for a drink and a snack and maybe even a celeb spot; it's a former speakeasy and one of the oldest watering holes in the area.

Early evening: When it's time for a tipple after all that sightseeing, either take the Metro (V to 5th Avenue/53rd Street) or walk up 5th Avenue to the **Four Seasons Hotel** (page 232), where The Bar offers the city's widest choice of martini and great people-watching. From here, catch a cab or Metro (N, Q, R, W to 14th Street, Union Square) to the **Union Square Café** (page 182). Restaurants come and go but Danny Meyer's top eatery (it's always *Zagat* rated) continues to deliver the best American cuisine you could wish for in really beautiful surroundings – fail safe if you've only got time for one posh dinner in the city.

Night: While you're in the Union Square area, walk up Broadway (only a short distance) to **Gotham Comedy Club** (page 205), which has some of the best line-ups in the land, including comedians who have appeared on *Saturday Night Live* and *The Tonight Show*. If you want late night drinks, head west from here to Chelsea (in a cab, it's close so won't cost a lot) to **APT** (page 202) on West 13th Street. Kitted out like someone's apartment, complete with bed, sofa, table and chairs, it's a great place to enjoy the late-night New York vibe.

▶ Walk west until reaching Avenue of the Americas, then head south to the Rockefeller Center between 49th and 50th streets.

Rockefeller Center

▶ Home to Radio City Music Hall, this New York Art Deco landmark was built in the 1930s and named after the benefactor who paid for its construction. Take a trip to the Top of the Rock observation tower for unmissable views of the city (page 72).

▶ Continue down the Avenue of the Americas, then head west down 42nd Street, the Big Apple's famous theatre district, until reaching Times Square.

Rockefeller Center

ONE FREE DAY IN NEW YORK

If you're short of cash, packing in expensive sightseeing and the best restaurants and bars in town isn't an option, but there's still lots of ways to enjoy Manhattan without spending a dime.

Morning: Kick off your day in the Big Apple with a free **tai chi class in Bryant Park** (bryantpark.org, page 276) 7.30–8.30am Tues and Thurs) or **Birding Tour** (8–9am Mon). While there, check out the free toilets, surely the city's, if not the country's, finest; neo-Grecian with pillars, giant marble urn full of flowers, real soap and uniformed attendant! From here head down to the southernmost tip of the island to catch the **Staten Island Ferry** (siferry.com, page 72), which transports around 20 million people a year to and from Staten Island. You'll see the stunning New York skyline for free plus the Statue of Liberty – sure beats a pricey harbour cruise!

Afternoon: Time for some culture, so hit the museums. **Carnegie Hall** and the **Rose Museum** (page 103) and the **National Museum of the American Indian** (page 116) are both free, and many others don't charge on a Friday evening. If you've still got time on your hands you could arrange a meet-up with a **Big Apple Greeter** (bigapplegreeter.org page 92), a local volunteer who will show you around the city for free (they're also likely to have some good tips on bargain places to go!). Or, take a stroll through **Central Park** (pages 273–275), it doesn't cost a thing and there's lots to see and do.

Evening: If you're hungry after all that sightseeing and culture, then it's time to hit the **Crocodile Lounge** (page 211) which, amazingly, gives out free pizza for every beer you buy. It's a really cool little bar with croc heads poking out from the ceiling and they don't fleece you with the price of the beer, it's around $3. If you're looking for entertainment visit **KGB Bar** (kgbbar.com page 200), which has poetry, book readings or live music most nights of the week without charge. There are also lots of free concerts and screenings in the parks during the summer months, check out what's on before you go at nycgovparks.org.

Times Square
▶ Flashing neon signs and crowds of people mark an arrival at this lively spot, which is buzzing 24 hours a day. It's a great place for people watching and a magnet for New York's weird and wonderful characters, plus it's home to some of the city's top theatres.

▶ Retracing your steps, head east down 42nd Street, catching a glimpse of the Garment District on the way, before arriving at the dramatic Chrysler Building where 42nd Street meets Lexington Avenue.

Chrysler Building
▶ This iconic 77-storey skyscraper, instantly recognisable by its stainless steel Art Deco spire that resembles a car radiator grill, is one of the city's best-loved landmarks. Pop inside to marvel at the lavish marble and granite lobby with a chrome steel trim.

▶ Head west back along 42nd Street and at Grand Central Station turn left and head south down Park Avenue.

▶ Turn right on to 34th Street and see the Empire State Building on the left when reaching 5th Avenue.

Empire State Building

▶ Recognised the world over, the city's tallest skyscraper is synonymous with New York. It opened its doors to the public in 1931 and people have flocked there ever since to view the Art Deco marble lobby and to ride the lifts up to the observatories, where the views of the city are unparalleled.

4 UPPER EAST SIDE WALK
Solomon R Guggenheim Museum
▶ Starting on a section of 5th Avenue nicknamed The Museum Mile, Frank Lloyd Wright's spiral masterpiece houses one of the world's best collections of modern art including 19th- to 21st-century artists such as Picasso and Kandinsky. Worth returning to at night to see the rainbow lit windows which bring the building to life.
▶ Head south on 5th Avenue to reach the Metropolitan Museum of Art in 5 blocks.

Metropolitan Museum of Art
▶ Overlooking Central Park, this beautiful 1880 gothic-style building houses the western world's most comprehensive art collection, with works dating from ancient times to the 21st century, including a vast collection of American masterpieces.
▶ Take the 86th Street Transverse, the road across the Park, which starts behind the Met.

Central Park
▶ Once inside the park, it's a short stroll to East Drive, which heads south through the park taking you past Cleopatra's Needle and the Boating Lake. Stop here for a drink and bite to eat at Park View at the Boat House, one of New York's prettiest eateries.
▶ It's easiest to exit the park at Bethseday Fountain on East 72nd Street, continue on this road, cross over 5th Avenue and head a few blocks south to reach the Frick Collection on the left.

Frick Collection
▶ This priceless art collection housed in the former mansion of steel magnate Henry Clay Frick, provides an insight into New York's gilded age. The opulent furnishings that surround the collection are equally as jaw-dropping as the old master paintings; French antique furniture, oriental rugs and rare Limoge enamels.
▶ Heading north up 5th Avenue, turn right after 5 blocks along East 57th Street to the Whitney Museum on Madison Avenue.

Whitney Museum of American Art
▶ Look up to see the grey granite cube designed by Marcel Breuer, which has an unusual cantilevered façade. Founded in 1930 by sculptor Gertrude Vanderbilt, the museum has the most comprehensive permanent collection of 20th- and 21st-century American art under one roof.

5 Upper West Side Walk
Riverside Park
▶ Start on 96th Street to catch a glimpse of the Cliff Dwellers Apartment at 243 Riverside Drive, where the façade is decorated with buffalo skulls, rattlesnakes and mountain lions. The park is a green oasis, which runs 70km/112mls along the banks of the Hudson river and was designed by Frederick Law Olmsted, who was also the brain behind Central Park.
▶ Enjoy a walk south along Riverside Drive, one of the most beautiful streets in the city, to West 79th Street and head west until hitting Central Park West, where you'll find the American Museum of Natural History.

American Museum of Natural History
▶ With more than 30 million specimens and artefacts, this is one of the world's largest natural history museums spanning 4 city blocks. Previously people headed straight for the dinosaurs, but don't miss the new glass Rose Center for earth and space.

The Rose Center at the American Museum of Natural History

▶ Carry on south down Central Park West for a couple of blocks where you'll find the New York Historical Society.

New York Historical Society

▶ New York's oldest museum, built in 1804, is notable for the world's largest collection of Tiffany lamps; plus more than 40,000 artefacts, including furniture, silver, sculptures and a research library.

▶ Enter Central Park from West 77th Street and turn south down West Park Drive.

Central Park

▶ Known as the lungs of New York, Central Park was created in 1858 on former swampland. It's green and wooded 341ha/843acres make a welcome break for tourists and residents alike. In the summer, the park is alive with children's playgrounds and the boating lake; in winter, the ice skating rink is the main attraction. Watch the cyclists, skaters and joggers whiz by and pass Strawberry Fields, a meadow memorial to John Lennon filled with flowers from all over the world.

▶ On the left heading south is Sheep Meadow, where residents and tourists can be spotted playing ball games and kite flying.

▶ Exit the park at 65th Street and continue east until reaching the Lincoln Center on Columbus Avenue.

Lincoln Center

▶ The sight of dramatic arches signifies your arrival at this centre for the arts. Take a rest by the reflecting fountain in the courtyard of this contemporary building, home to a mix of dance, music and theatre that draws audiences of around 5 million people a year. In the summer, keep a lookout for free concerts, which are held in the adjacent park.

Lincoln Center

CHAPTER 5

Museums and Galleries

New York has some of the best-known museums and galleries in the world, so it's little wonder that some tourists come to the Big Apple just to visit these major attractions. Among the names that you are most likely to be familiar with are the Metropolitan Museum of Art (the Met), the Solomon R Guggenheim Museum, Whitney Museum of Modern Art and the Museum of Modern Art (MoMA). Most of the major museums are located around a specific area of the city called the Museum Mile, which stretches along 5th Avenue on the Upper East Side north to 89th Street.

As befits a city that is famed for regenerating itself, none of the museums sits on its laurels. There is a constant wave of refurbishment and renewal, as well as cutting-edge exhibitions that inspire people to keep returning. The American Museum of Natural History spent $25m updating its Milstein Hall of Ocean Life and then more recently $37 million renovating the Grand Gallery, and MoMA reopened in 2004 after a multi-million-dollar refurbishment and expansion, in a much-praised new building designed by architect Yoshio Taniguchi. The Museum of Jewish Heritage and the Morgan Library have both reopened after extensive refurbishment. Highlights of the recent cultural calendar have included Annie Leibovitz: A Photographer's Life, 1990–2005 at the Brooklyn Museum; an examination of Gold at the American Museum of Natural History from pre-Colombian jewellery to Olympic medals and Doug Aitken's 'sleepwalkers' was projected on the façades of the Museum of Modern Art.

On top of this, a raft of museums has opened in the last decade, including the American Folk Art Museum, the Chelsea Art Museum, the Annette Green Museum dedicated to the history of perfumes, the Jewish Children's Museum in Brooklyn and the National Cartoon Museum (formerly the International Museum of Cartoon Art), which opened in 2007 in the Empire State Building as the largest museum of cartoon art in the world. Also in 2007, Greek and Roman Galleries opened in an entire wing of The Metropolitan Museum of Art and the Elizabeth A Sackler Center for Feminist Art opened at The Brooklyn Museum. The National Sports Museum, the first ever museum dedicated to sports, opened in 2008.

Of course, it does mean there is a lot to choose from and, especially if you're on your first visit to New York, you'll want to ensure you don't waste any time. It should also be noted that many cultural institutions in New York go to great lengths to make themselves family friendly, so don't let having youngsters in tow put you off visiting.

A–Z OF MUSEUMS

ALICE AUSTEN HOUSE MUSEUM & GARDEN
Staten Island
- ✉ 2 Hylan Blvd, Staten Island
- ☎ 718-816 4506
- 🖰 aliceausten.org
- 🚢 Ferry from Battery Park
- 🕐 Thurs–Sun 12–5pm, March–Dec. Closed Jan–Feb
- $ A suggested donation $2 adults, under 12s free

This museum on Staten Island offers a glimpse into the world of photographer Alice Austen. Her former home, a quaint, Victorian cottage,

Alice Austen House

TOP 5 MUSEUMS

Here are the *Brit Guide* favourites. They cover a broad spectrum, from the history of New York City to art and the world's amazing natural history, and each is a true delight in itself.

is one of the key reasons to visit as it offers a magnificent view of New York Harbour and displays prints from the large glass negative collection of her work depicting turn-of-the-century American life. The City bought the Austen house in 1975 and restored it and the grounds in 1984–85. The Victorian garden was replanted according to Austen photographs, complete with shrubs such as weeping mulberry and flowering quince.

AMERICAN FOLK ART MUSEUM
Midtown

✉ 45 West 53rd Street between 5th and 6th Avenues
☎ 212-265 1040
🖰 folkartmuseum.org
🚇 Subway E, V to 5th Avenue/53rd Street; B, D, F, V to 47th–50th Streets, Rockefeller Center
🕐 Tues–Sun 10.30am–5.30pm, except Fri 10.30am–7.30pm, closed Mon
$ $9 adults, $7 students and seniors, under 12s and members free; free Fri after 5.30pm

Originally called the Museum of Early American Folk Arts when it was founded in 1961, it focused on vernacular arts of 18th- and 19th-century America, particularly the north-east. A name change to the more inclusive Folk Art Museum coincided with the museum's $18m new structure, designed by award-winning architects Tod Williams and Billy Tsien. This museum provides an excellent opportunity to get to grips with American folk art and gives an insight into America's history and cultural heritage from the perspective of these arts. It holds more than 5,000 permanent artworks spanning 3 centuries, from textiles to 21st-century photographs, plus has new exhibitions.

AMERICAN MUSEUM OF NATURAL HISTORY
Upper West Side

✉ Central Park West at 79th Street
☎ 212-769 5100
🖰 amnh.org
🚇 Subway B, C to 81st Street/Museum of Natural History; 1, 9 to 79th Street
🕐 10am–5.45pm daily
$ Suggested price $16 adults, $12 students and seniors, $9 under-13s. The most comprehensive package, which includes the space shows, IMAX films and special exhibitions, is the All-Inclusive SuperSaver which costs $32 adults, $24.50 seniors and students and $20 children

Like the Metropolitan, this is an epic of a museum, best seen in parts rather than attempting the whole (although you'll save money if you do!). It provides an entertaining and amazingly detailed yet comprehensive overview of life on Earth and beyond, and has undergone an enormous amount of growth and redevelopment.

One of its most famous permanent exhibitions is the **Milstein Hall of Ocean Life**, given a $25m redesign using the latest marine technology and a $15m donation by museum trustee Irma Milstein and her husband Paul. Using the hall's massive blue whale as its centrepiece, lights, video and sound effects create the breathtaking illusion of being immersed in the ocean.

Other permanent exhibits include the **Anne and Bernard Spitzer Hall of Human Origins,** which has the most amazing collection of up-to-date discoveries to chart humankind; **The Grand Gallery,** which has recently had a $37m renovation involving the famous castle facade on 77th Street, is where you can check out the Grand Canoe, the longest of its type in existence. The **Fossil Halls** are where you'll find more than 600 specimens, including dinosaurs. Much fun is to be had using the many interactive computer exhibits, for instance, to travel back in time in order to trace the roots of evolution.

In addition, there is the **Rose Center for Earth and Space** – a spectacular museum within a museum housed in glass, which incorporates the **Hayden Planetarium** as its centrepiece. This is the place to come to learn about the inner workings of Earth and the outer reaches of the universe. The **Big Bang Theater** gives a dramatic re-creation of the first minutes of the origins of the universe and is found inside a 26.5m/87ft wide sphere that appears to float in a glass-walled ceiling.

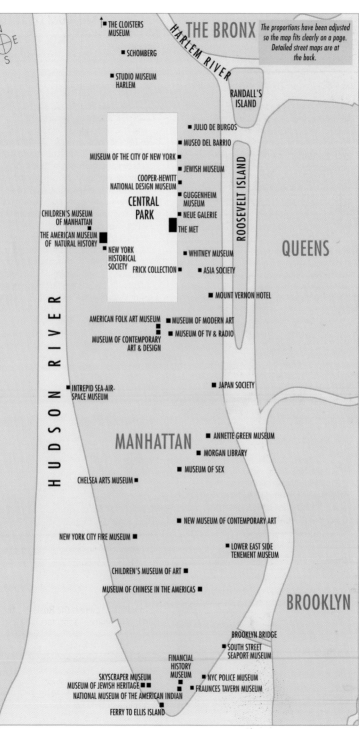

Museums in Manhattan

BRITTIP

Some museums offer free or half price entry late afternoon/evenings on Fri (see page 105).

Here you will also find the **Space Theater**, billed as the most technologically advanced in the world, which shows incredibly realistic views of outer space. There's a spectacular new film, *Journey to the Stars*, narrated by Whoopi Goldberg, which features images from telescopes on earth and in space and never-seen-before footage. The film is shown every half-hour from 10.30am–4.30pm.

BRITTIP

If you're more into stars of the human variety, every Fri and Sat evening at 7.30pm and 8.30pm the Space Theater shows Sonicvision, a collaboration with MTV2. Digital animation is accompanied by some of the most popular music in the world from the likes of Coldplay, U2, Moby, Brian Eno and Radiohead. $15.

There are also mammal halls, the incredible **Biodiversity Hall**, complete with imitation rainforest and **Birds Halls**. The fantastic **Butterfly Conservatory**, which reopened in May 2010, is like being in a Disney film as thousands of butterflies flit around. Entrance $24 adults, $14 children and $18 seniors/students.

BRITTIP

To avoid crowds, heat or cold, take the B or C train to 81st Street and go straight into the American Museum of Natural History from the subway. Follow the tiled signs in the mosaic wall.

Check out the website first to see which activities will be available during your visit. The museum also runs field trips, such as bird watching, bug (insect) hunts or flower inspections in the adjacent Central Park.

Asia Society

AMERICAN MUSEUM OF THE MOVING IMAGE
Queens

It's only a short trip to Queens and worth a visit here if you are into films (page 291).

NYINTHEKNOW

Gilmar Scantamburlo has his ear firmly to the ground for secret and cost-effective gems in the city as concierge of W Times Square hotel. 'No matter how familiar you become with New York's daedal subway system or its hip village eateries, the city will never run out of new things to show you. Head to the Cloisters (metmuseum.org/cloisters), an unexpected but unmissable branch of the Metropolitan Museum of Art located in north Manhattan's Fort Tryon Park. This tranquil hideaway, often overlooked by many, offers fantastic views of the Hudson and Medieval gardens.'

ARTISTS' SPACE
SoHo

- ✉ 3rd Floor, 38 Greene Street
- ☎ 212-226 3970
- 🖱 artistsspace.org
- 🚇 Subway C, E to Spring Street
- 🕐 Tues–Sat 11am–6pm
- $ Free

Situated down a small cobblestone street in SoHo, it's hard to find but worth hunting out if you love to discover new art, as this small gallery is a launching pad for unknown artists. It's a single-floor loft space and there are friendly staff to help explain the works and contemporary styles. Well worth the hour or so it will need.

ASIA SOCIETY
Midtown East

- ✉ 725 Park Avenue at 70th Street
- ☎ 212-288 6400
- 🖱 asiasociety.org
- 🚇 Subway 6 to 68th Street/Hunter College, F to 63rd Street/Lexington Avenue
- 🕐 Tues–Sun 11am–6pm, Fri 11am–9pm, closed Mon
- $ $10 adults, $7 seniors, $5 students, under 16s free; free Fri 6–9pm

Founded in 1956 by John D Rockefeller III with his collection of Asian art, it aims to build an awareness of the 30 Pan-Asian countries, which include Japan, New Zealand, Australia and the Pacific Islands. To this end, it runs films, lectures and seminars in conjunction with its exhibitions and even has a regular schedule of Asian musicians who play at the museum. Daily guided tours of exhibitions are Tues–Sun 2pm, Fri also 6.30pm.

BROOKLYN CHILDREN'S MUSEUM
New York's first children's museum, it has a great programme of events and workshops and is particularly worth the trip if you are on a family holiday (page 282).

BROOKLYN MUSEUM
One of the largest museums in the world and the oldest art museum in the country, it underwent a facelift in 2004 to become the most visitor-friendly museum in the Big Apple. It is easy to reach in Brooklyn, if you have the time to plan it into your schedule. See page 283.

CARNEGIE HALL/ROSE MUSEUM
Midtown
- ✉ 2nd Floor, 154 West 57th Street
- ☎ 212-247 7800
- ⌂ carnegiehall.org
- 🚗 Subway A B, C, D, 1 to Columbus Circle, N, Q, R, W to 57th Street/7th Avenue, E to 7th Avenue
- ☉ Daily 11am–4.30pm, closed 1 July–14 Sept
- $ Free

In 1991, the Rose Museum opened as part of Carnegie Hall's 100th anniversary celebrations. On the First Tier level of Carnegie Hall, the museum houses special temporary exhibitions, as well as a permanent collection of over a century's worth of photographs, letters, musical quotes and Carnegie Hall archival material, from programmes to unique memorabilia, including items from the famous names that have walked through 'the house that music built'.

CHELSEA ART MUSEUM
Chelsea
- ✉ 556 West 22nd Street at 11th Avenue
- ☎ 212-255 0719
- ⌂ chelseaartmuseum.org
- 🚗 Subway C, E to West 23rd Street
- ☉ Tues–Sat 11am–6pm, except Thurs 11–8pm, closed Sun and Mon
- $ $8 adults, $4 seniors and students, free for children under 16

In the heart of Chelsea's new gallery district, this new medium-sized, 3-storey museum provides a venue for abstract work by artists who have not been exhibited in New York before and for mid-size travelling shows from Europe and smaller American museums. It is also the new home of the Miotte Foundation, which is dedicated to the conservation of Informal Art (abstract) works by Jean Miotte, who has had a studio in SoHo since 1978.

BRILLIANT MUSEUMS FOR ALL THE FAMILY
New York is fantastic when it comes to providing exciting and engaging museums and museum activities for children. They not only have plenty of dedicated children's museums, but also many of the major New York museums put their wealth of resources to great use by offering fabulous events and activities that both entertain and educate children from as young as four right up to teens. Below are some of the best:

CHILDREN'S MUSEUMS:
Children's Museum of the Arts (page 103)
Children's Museum of Manhattan (page 104)
Jewish Children's Museum (page 108)

ADULT MUSEUMS:
Intrepid Sea-Air-Space Museum (page 107)
Lower East Side Tenement Museum (page 108)
Museum of Comic and Cartoon Art (page 113)
New York City Fire Museum (page 117)
New York City Police Museum (page 117)
New York City Transit Museum, Brooklyn (page 118)

And a brilliant site: Historic Richmond Town, Staten Island (page 295)

BRITTIP
Be prepared to prove you're a student if you want to make the most of discounted admissions to the museums.

CHILDREN'S MUSEUM OF THE ARTS
Little Italy
- ✉ 182 Lafayette Street between Broome and Grand Streets
- ☎ 212-274 0986
- ⌂ cmany.org
- 🚗 Subway N, R to Prince Street, B, D, F, Q to Broadway/Lafayette Street; 6 to Spring Street
- ☉ Wed, Fri and Sun noon–5pm, Thurs noon–6pm, closed Mon and Tues
- $ $10 adults, free for infants under 1 and seniors. Pay as you wish on Thurs

Under 7s can have an artistic ball with art computers, an art playground and a giant floor-to-ceiling chalkboard in this place, which is more like a giant playroom than a museum. There are also regular performing arts workshops led by local artists. A visit here is the perfect way to combine a shopping trip to SoHo for you with fun for the kids!

CHILDREN'S MUSEUM OF MANHATTAN
Upper West Side

- ✉ The Tisch Building, 212 West 83rd Street between Broadway and Amsterdam Avenue
- ☎ 212-721 1234
- 🖰 cmom.org
- 🚇 Subway 1 to 79th or 86th Street, B, C to 81st Street
- 🕐 Tues–Sun 10am–5pm, closed Mon; call or check the website for summer and school holiday hours
- $ $10 adults and children, $7 seniors, infants under 1 free

> ### ✠ BRITTIP
> After you've explored CMOM, cross the street for a light snack and drinks at Café Lalo (212-496 6031, cafelalo.com), which serves up great cakes and is featured in the Meg Ryan and Tom Hanks movie *You've Got Mail.*

The CMOM is entirely dedicated to children under the age of 10. This is a fabulous place and almost worth a visit even if you don't have kids. Its mission statement is to inspire children and their families to learn about themselves and our culturally diverse world through a unique environment of interactive exhibits and programmes.

They certainly achieve it with their inspiring exhibits, such as Adventures with Dora & Diego, which includes adventures in a rainforest, with kids (aged 2–6) getting the chance to join Diego in a series of animal rescue missions and get ready for a party at Dora's house!

> ### ✠ BRITTIP
> Many museums are closed on national holidays, such as Thanksgiving Day on the fourth Thursday of November. Be sure to check first before you make your trip.

Weather-permitting, in the spring and summer City Splash allows all ages to play with water, whether it be racing boats down a zigzag stream or painting a masterpiece with water.

THE CLOISTERS
Washington Heights

- ✉ 99 Margaret Corbin Drive, Fort Tyron Park
- ☎ 212-923 3700
- 🖰 metmuseum.org
- 🚇 Subway 1, 6 to 86th Street
- 🕐 Mar–Oct Tues–Sun 9.30am–5.15pm, Nov–Feb Tues–Sun 9.30am–4.45pm. Mon closed
- $ Suggested donation $20 adults (includes free same-day admission to the Metropolitan Museum of Art (page 109), $15 seniors and $10 students, under 12s free with an adult

Rockefeller cash allowed the Metropolitan Museum to buy this beautiful red-tiled Romanesque-style building 70 years ago. Now it is purely devoted to medieval art and architecture, including five cloisters – hence the name – some from ruined French monasteries, dating from the 12th to the 15th centuries. It is stunning to look at and houses some really exciting exhibits, probably the most famous being the Unicorn Tapestries, woven in Brussels in the 1500s. Tours Tues–Fri 3pm, Sun noon are included in the price of admission and an audio guide or podcast is available. There are also gallery talks, films and medieval concerts in the wonderful 12th-century chapel from Spain.

The Cloisters has a series of free workshops for children 4–12, on the 1st and 3rd Sat of the month 1–2pm. Subjects include medieval

The Cloisters Arcade

feasts and celebrations and stories from the Middle Ages.

BRITTIP

It's a long way north to The Cloisters, so make the most of your time by combining it with a walking tour of Harlem (page 91).

COOPER–HEWITT NATIONAL DESIGN MUSEUM

Upper East Side

✉ 2 East 91st Street at 5th Avenue
☎ 212-849 8400
🖰 cooperhewitt.org
🚇 Subway 4, 5, 6 to 86th or 96th Street
🕐 Tues–Fri 10am–5pm, Sat 10am–6pm, Sun 11–6pm
$ $15 adults, $10 students and seniors, under 12s free

The only American museum devoted entirely to historic and contemporary design, the Cooper-Hewitt's international collection covers everything from applied arts and industrial design to drawings, prints, textiles and wall coverings. Take time to look at the exterior of the building itself, which was designed in a Georgian style for tycoon Andrew Carnegie and at the time was a triumph of modern engineering.

BRITTIP

Don't forget to visit the shop at the Cooper-Hewitt Museum to check out the quirky bits and pieces on offer, parrot corkscrew anyone? And covetable design books.

EDWYNN HOUK GALLERY

Lower East Side

✉ 4th Floor, 745 5th Avenue between 57th and 58th Streets
☎ 212-750 7070
🖰 houkgallery.com
🚇 Subway N, R, W to 5th Avenue/59th Street
🕐 Tues–Sat 11am–6pm
$ Free admission

A delightful gallery for photography enthusiasts with both vintage and contemporary prints on display and for sale from the likes of Man Ray, Henri Cartier-Bresson and Annie Leibovitz.

EL MUSEO DEL BARRIO

Spanish Harlem

✉ Heckscher Building, 1230 5th Avenue at 104th Street
☎ 212-831 7272
🖰 elmuseo.org

GETTING IN FREE

No charge is made for admission to the following museums, so they make a great addition to your itinerary:

Carnegie Hall/Rose Museum: (page 103)

Forbes Magazine Galleries: (page 106)

National Museum of the American Indian: (page 116)

Schomburg Center for Research In Black Culture: (page 119)

In addition to this, many museums offer times – usually on a Fri – when you can get in free or pay a voluntary donation of whatever you wish:

American Folk Art Museum: 5.30–9pm Fri (page 100)

Asia Society: 6–9pm Fri (page 102)

Frick Collection: after 6pm on certain Fri (page 106)

International Center of Photography: 5–8pm Fri (page 107)

Jewish Museum: 11am–5.45pm Sat (page 108)

🚇 Subway 6 to 103rd Street, 2, 3 to 110th Street/Lenox Avenue
🕐 Tues–Sun 11am–5pm, closed Mon
$ Suggested donation $6 adults, $4 students and seniors, under 12s free with an adult

Opened in 1969 by a group of Puerto Rican parents, teachers and artists, it houses 8,000 objects of Caribbean and Latin American art from pre-Colombian times to date. Exhibits include musical instruments, miniature houses, dolls and masks, as well as posters, paintings and sculptures. Every Jan it stages the Three Kings' Day Parade with lively music, colourful costumes and a theatre programme. Some renovation is underway, so check the website.

Cooper-Hewitt National Design Museum

ELLIS ISLAND IMMIGRATION MUSEUM
Battery Park
The most visited museum in New York, this is worth dedicating a good portion of the day to, combining it with the Statue of Liberty nearby (page 67).

FORBES MAGAZINE GALLERIES
Financial District
- ✉ 62 5th Avenue at 12th Street
- ☎ 212-206 5548
- ⌂ forbesgalleries.com
- 🚋 Subway A, B, C, D, E, 1, 9 from West to 14th Street, or 4, 5, 6, N, R from East to 14th Street
- ⏲ Tues–Sat 10am–4pm, except Thurs (group tours only), closed Sun and Mon
- $ Free

The Forbes Magazine Galleries at the magazine's headquarters showcase The Forbes Collection of home and business furnishings, decorative accessories, gifts, jewellery, books, toy boats, miniature soldiers, the Monopoly game, presidential manuscripts and fine art.

FRAUNCES TAVERN MUSEUM
Financial District
- ✉ 54 Pearl Street at Broad Street, 1st and 2nd floors
- ☎ 212-425 1778
- ⌂ fraruncestavernmuseum.org
- 🚋 Subway J, M, Z to Broad Street; 4, 5 to Bowling Green; 1, 9 to South Ferry

Fraunces Tavern Museum

- ⏲ Mon–Sat noon–5pm, closed Sun
- $ $10 adults, $5 children and seniors, under 6s free

When New York was (briefly) capital of America, the Fraunces Tavern housed the Departments of Foreign Affairs, Treasury and War and was where George Washington delivered his famous farewell speech to his officers. Now, nestled among the skyscrapers of the Financial District, this 18th-century Georgian building, along with four adjacent

BRITTIP
Don't miss the cosy restaurant at the Fraunces Tavern Museum. It serves lovely food in a stately, if a little touristy, environment.

19th-century buildings, houses a fine museum dedicated to the study of early American history and culture. Among the collection of artefacts, paintings, drawings and documents from the revolutionary era is a lock of Washington's hair and one of his false teeth. Although well preserved, it is New York's oldest surviving building and an awful lot of restoration work has been done to keep its 1783 façade. Guided tours need to be booked in advance.

FRICK COLLECTION
Midtown East
- ✉ 1 East 70th Street at 5th Avenue
- ☎ 212-288 0700
- ⌂ frick.org
- 🚋 Subway 4, 5, 6 to 68th Street
- ⏲ Tues–Sat 10am–6pm, Sun 11am–5pm, closed Mon
- $ $18 adults, $12 seniors, $5 students; pay what you wish 11am–1pm on Sun; admission includes ArtPhone audio guide

Henry Clay Frick (1849–1919) was a fascinating man who, obsessed with making money, built up a massive fortune with the Carnegie Steel Company. His sole interest outside the business was art and, as his wealth grew, so did his fabulous collection of European art, which he hung in his palatial mansion on 5th Avenue. Despite having a reputation as an ungenerous man, he bequeathed both the pictures and his mock-18th-century European mansion to the public when he died.

There are 16 galleries displaying this priceless collection of masterpieces from the 14th–19th centuries, including some of the best-known paintings by the European masters. Unusually, the pictures aren't displayed by period or style, but in the way that Frick would have hung them in his home, giving an insight into the lives of New York's rich in the Gilded Age. The Fragonard Room shows the large Fragonard paintings, as well as 18th-century furniture and porcelain. Paintings by Holbein, El Greco, Titian and Bellini are in the Living Room, while in the sky-lit West Gallery you'll find landscapes by Constable and portraits by Rembrandt, as well as a collection of rare Limoges enamels.

BRITTIP

The Frick Collection is well known for its Weds evening lectures, from artists to scholars, which are free and no ticket required, simply first come, first served. Check out frick.org to find out if there's something on while you're in town.

INTERNATIONAL CENTER OF PHOTOGRAPHY
Midtown
- ✉ 1133 Avenue of the Americas at 43rd Street
- ☎ 212-857 0000
- ⌂ icp.org
- 🚇 Subway B, D, F, V to 42nd Street
- ◷ Tues–Thurs 10am–6pm, Fri 10am–8pm, Sat and Sun 10am–6pm, closed Mon
- $ $12 adults, $8 students and seniors, under 12s free; voluntary contribution Fri 5–8pm

The ICP is a school and a museum. It houses some excellent exhibitions, such as legendary photographer Larry Clark's work, as well as a permanent collection that consists of more than 100,000 photographs from famous photographers spanning decades. It has a large body of work by Henri Cartier-Bresson and some original prints by Weegee, who photographed crime scenes and New York nightlife in the 1930s and 1940s. Film screenings, artists' talks and lectures are on offer, as well as a store selling some stunning prints.

BRITTIP

The Catherine K Café on the lower floor of the International Center of Photography is a quick and convenient place for lunch or a snack.

INTREPID SEA-AIR-SPACE MUSEUM
Clinton
- ✉ USS Intrepid, Pier 86, west end of 46th Street at the Hudson River
- ☎ 212-245 0072
- ⌂ intrepidmuseum.org
- 🚇 Subway A, C, E, N, Q, R, S, W, 1, 2, 3, 7, 9 to 42nd Street, then the M42 bus to 12th Avenue

- ◷ Mon–Sun 10am–5pm, Oct–March, closed Mon
- $ $22 adults, $18 students and seniors, $17 children (3–17), children under 3 free

A thoroughly enjoyable museum around a ship berthed on the Hudson River, which appeals to all ages. All the staff are very friendly and there are former members of the crew around the ship who are happy to give an insight into its history and life on board. *Intrepid* was one of 24 Second World War US aircraft carriers and, despite incidents of serious damage to these ships, none of them was ever sunk. *Intrepid's* worst moment came on 25 November 1944, when two kamikaze pilots hit the ship 5 minutes apart, killing 69 and seriously injuring 85.

BRITTIP

The only way to see the submarine at *Intrepid* is on a tour and long queues build up very quickly, so get there early.

The second plane exploded on the hangar deck and the ship burned for about 6 hours, but *Intrepid* made it back to America for repairs and returned to the war. Stories of life on board are told by veterans at film screenings throughout the ship and there are also plenty of hands-on exhibits to keep kids and adults happy, from G-Force, where you get to test your flying skills for $10 to the XD Theater where you put on 3D glasses and whizz through time and space, $8. The museum also exhibits the British Airways Concorde.

JAPAN SOCIETY
Midtown East
- ✉ 333 East 47th Street between 1st and 2nd Avenues
- ☎ 212-832 1155
- ⌂ japansociety.org
- 🚇 Subway E, V to Lexington Avenue/53rd Street; 6 to 51st or 42nd Street
- ◷ Tues–Thurs 11am–6pm, Fri 11am–9pm, Sat and Sun 11am–5pm, closed Mon
- $ $12 adults, $10 students and seniors, under 16s free

All things Japanese, from textiles and modern photography to historical ceramics, paintings, glass and metalworks. The ideal combination of Zen and now, away from the Samurai swords and kimonos, its traditional Japanese garden is a Zen-like space with calming waterfall, reflecting pool and bamboo garden. The Society, which celebrated its centenary in 2007, also has Japanese traditional and contemporary arts performances, films and lectures.

JEWISH MUSEUM
Upper East Side
- ✉ 1109 5th Avenue at 92nd Street
- ☎ 212-423 3200
- 🖱 thejewishmuseum.org
- 🚇 Subway 4, 5, 6 to 86th Street
- 🕐 Sat–Tues and Thurs 11am–5.45pm, Fri 11am–4pm, 5.45pm in summer, closed Wed and Fri. Free on Sat
- $ $12 adults, $10 seniors, $7.50 students, children under 12 free. Free on Sat, 11am–5.45pm

The largest Jewish museum in the Western hemisphere, the Jewish Museum, set in a château-style residence, lays on impressive annual exhibitions. The core exhibit is called **Culture and Continuity: The Jewish Journey** and sets out how the Jewish people have survived through the centuries and explores the essence of Jewish identity. Many of the objects were actually rescued from European synagogues before the Second World War. It covers 4,000 years of history with an emphasis on art and culture. Audio guides, including a family gallery guide, are free with admission. As well as talks, performances and films, there's a free drop-in arts and crafts session for children aged 3 and upwards monthly on Sun or Mon (check website for details).

BRITTIP

Try delicious kosher cuisine at the Jewish Museum's trendy Café Weissman (closed on Fri).

JEWISH CHILDREN'S MUSEUM
This specialist museum has its home in child-friendly Brooklyn (page 282).

JULIA DE BURGOS LATINO CULTURAL CENTER
Spanish Harlem
- ✉ 1680 Lexington Avenue between 105th and 106th Street
- ☎ 212-831 4333
- 🚇 Subway 6 to 110th Street
- 🕐 Tues–Sat noon–6pm, Thurs 1–7pm
- $ Free

Another excellent location to see works by Latino artists, named in honour of the woman considered to have been the greatest poet in Puerto Rico. Around the museum, look out for pavement artwork by James de la Vega, a young local artist.

LOWER EAST SIDE TENEMENT MUSEUM
Lower East Side
- ✉ 108 Orchard Street between Broome and Delancey Streets
- ☎ 212-431 0233
- 🖱 tenement.org
- 🚇 Subway F to Delancey Street; B, D to Grand Street; J, M, Z to Essex Street
- 🕐 Visitor Center open Mon 11am–5.30pm, Tues–Fri 11am–6pm, Sat and Sun 10.45am–6pm; the museum can only be visited via a tour, first tour 10.30am, last tour 5pm 7 days a week – best to book in advance
- $ $20 adults, $15 students and seniors for 1-hour tour; 2-ticket Combo: $25 adults, $18 students and seniors; 3-ticket combo: $34 adults, $24 students and seniors. Under 5s free

After they had gone through Ellis Island, what happened to many of those millions of immigrants? They ended up in tenements on

The Jewish Museum

the Lower East Side of New York, and this is the museum that tells their poignant stories. You'll get the chance to see 4 re-created apartments in a typical, 5-storey tenement, giving a good insight into the living conditions of the seekers of the American Dream.

BRITTIP

Before you take one of the walking tours at the Lower East Side Tenement Museum, it is worth watching the slide show and film.

The museum consists of several tenement houses – essentially America's first public housing, predating almost every housing law in the US – that are accessible only via the tours. These houses contain several apartments, faithfully restored and complete with furniture and clothes. It's a must-see in order to understand not only this neighbourhood, which continues to function as a launching pad for fresh generations of artists and retailers, but also the American success story.

The tour **Piecing It Together** examines the life of the Polish Levine family, who ran a garment shop in their apartment in the early 1900s, plus the stories of other immigrants involved in the garment industry from the 1930s to the present day. The tour **Getting By: Weathering the Great Depressions of 1873 and 1929** focuses on the German-Jewish Gumpertz family in the 1870s and the Sicilian-Catholic Baldizzi family in the 1930s and how they forged new lives for themselves in America.

BRITTIP

Holiday-time tours at the Lower East Side Tenement Museum sell out quickly, so book as far in advance as possible on the internet.

The best tour for children is the 45-minute **Confino Apartment Program**, which aims to bring history to life. The apartment re-creates the life of the Sephardic-Jewish Confino family from Kastoria in Greece in 1916. Teenager Victoria Confino welcomes visitors as if they were newly arrived immigrants and she were teaching them how to adapt to life in America. Along the way you can touch any items in the apartment, try on period clothing and foxtrot to music played on an authentic wind-up Victrola.

Kitchen conversations after selected tours are where participants get a chance to share thoughts and explore thoughts arising from the tours over a drink and a snack. If you have time, the Lower East Side Stories walking tour operated by the museum is an eye-opening look at past and present in this fascinating neighbourhood.

MERCHANT'S HOUSE MUSEUM
East Village

- ✉ 29 East 4th Street between Lafayette and Bowery Streets
- ☎ 212-777 1089
- ⌨ merchantshouse.com
- 🚇 Subway 6 to Astor Place
- ⏰ Thurs–Mon 12pm–5pm, closed Tues and Wed
- $ $10 adults, $5 students and seniors, children under 12 free

Built in 1832, this was home to prosperous merchant Seabury Tredwell and his family for over 100 years and is the city's only preserved 19th-century home, complete with original furnishings and decor, and a resident ghost!

METROPOLITAN MUSEUM OF ART
Upper East Side

- ✉ 1000 5th Avenue at 82nd Street
- ☎ 212-535 7710
- ⌨ metmuseum.org
- 🚇 Subway 1, 6 to 86th Street
- ⏰ Tues–Thurs, Sun 9.30am–5.30pm, Fri and Sat 9.30am–9pm, closed Mon
- $ $20 adults, $10 students and $15 seniors, under 12s free with an adult, same-day entrance to The Cloisters (page 104) is included in the price

New York is filled with fine museums, yet this really is the mother of them all and you could easily spend a well-paced day here. But with 5,000 years of art – around 2 million pieces – from all Continents spread over 186,000sq m/2 million sq ft, it's best to admit that you won't be able to see it all in one visit: and therein lies your perfect excuse to return to the city! If you can, visit the

Lower East Side Tenement Museum

website in advance to get a good feel for the layout. Think about what you really want to see and write out a list of priorities, allowing a reasonable amount of time to absorb what each gallery has to offer. Make sure you visit the Greek and Roman Galleries, with 5,400 objects taking up an entire wing, the talk of the town.

BRITTIP

Don't miss the Metropolitan's fabulous Zagat-rated Roof Garden Café & Martini Bar filled with sculptures on the 5th floor for stunning views of Central Park, open May–early Sept or take some air in the Ming-style meditative Chinese garden in Astor Court, built with handmade tools by Chinese craftspeople.

A good place to start is with an aspect of American culture, which you will find in the **American Wing**, where there is a wonderful collection of Tiffany's along with US arts and crafts and glorious Neo-Classical sculptures in the garden court. It's one of the Met's most popular areas, with 3 floors and 25 rooms filled with more than 1,000 paintings by American artists, 600 sculptures and 2,500 drawings. The 2 real musts are the **Egyptian Art** exhibits and the **Temple of Dendur,** which was built by Egypt to thank the American people after the US helped rescue monuments threatened by the Aswan Dam. Other greats include the **Greek** and **Roman** displays, the **Japanese** and **Chinese** exhibits and the **medieval art**.

Metropolitan Museum of Art

BRITTIP

If visiting the Met on Fri or Sat, you can chill out over cocktails to free live classical music in the Balcony Bar in the afternoon.

Exhibitions here change constantly, but confirmed for 2011 are Steiglitz, Steichen, Strand, the three photography legends of the 18th century, and Katrin Sigurdardottir at the Met, an Icelandic artist who will create an installation for the museum's series of solo exhibitions of contemporary artists. Check the website for loads more.

The wonderful thing about this museum is that you can wander around by yourself, hire an audio guide for the day ($7 adults, $5 under 12s), which you can use in any order you choose, or bag a free podcast, and take advantage of a plethora of free tours, talks, and films.

The hour-long Museum Highlights tour leaves from the Great Hall at 2.30pm. Check the calendar on the website in advance for information on the one-hour gallery talks or lectures, which focus on either a special exhibition or one of the permanent collections and films. You do not need to make reservations except for

THE MET FOR FAMILIES

This magnificent museum uses various means to make its resources as accessible to children as possible – for free – and provides printed gallery guides and museum hunts at the **Uris Information Desk** on the ground floor near the 81st Street entrance. A whole series of workshops and programmes is available both through the week and at weekends. For exact times and dates, check out the calendar section of the website or call 212-570 3961. Programmes include:

Hello Met!: Children 5–12 and their families are given a stimulating introduction to the Met's encyclopaedic collection through sketching its masterpieces. Sun 2–3.30pm.

Look Again!: The history, meaning and cultural aspects of art in the museum are explored through chats, drawing and, from time to time, performances for children 5–12 (plus an adult) on Sat, Sun, 11am–12.30pm, 2–3.30pm.

Start With Art at the Met: Children 3–7 (plus an adult) meet at the Uris tiered seating area to explore art at the Met through storytelling, sketching and games.

TOP 5 GALLERIES FOR MODERN ART

New York is a hotbed of artistic talent so if you want to pick up some original work while you are there, or just look at some, here are 5 places to head for.

Andrew Kreps Gallery: Chelsea
- ✉ 525 West 22nd Street
- ☎ 212-741 8849
- ⌂ andrewkreps.com
- 🚇 Subway 23rd Street
- ⏱ Tues–Sat 10am–6pm

An innovative band of work on display from artists including Ruth Root and Roe Ethridge.

Deitch Projects: SoHo
- ✉ 18 Wooster Street between Canal and Grand Streets
- ☎ 212-343 7300
- ⌂ deitch.com
- 🚇 Subway N, R, W to Prince Street; B, D, F, V to Broadway/Lafayette Street
- ⏱ Tues–Sat noon–6pm
- $ Free

Jeffrey Deitch's gallery is worth a peep if you are in SoHo – a second gallery has opened at 76 Grand Street. Focusing on large-scale installations, and sometimes live spectacles, by contemporary artists (including Yoko Ono) working in all kinds of media, it's not as scary as it sounds.

Gagosian Gallery: Chelsea
- ✉ 555 West 24th Street between 10th and 11th Avenues
- ☎ 212-741 1111
- ⌂ gagosian.com
- ⏱ Tues–Sat 10am–6pm
- $ Free

An excellent, vast gallery that opened in 1999, it has featured exhibitions of work by the likes of Damien Hirst.

Maccarone Inc: Lower East Side
- ✉ 630 Greenwich Street
- ☎ 212-431 4977
- ⌂ maccarone.net
- 🚇 Subway 1, R, W to Rector Street
- ⏱ Wed–Sun noon–6pm
- $ Free

Spread over 4 floors, this cool gallery run by Michele Maccarone features work by up-and-coming local and European artists.

Projectile Gallery: 57th Street
- ✉ 3rd floor, 37 West 57th Street between 5th and 6th Avenues
- ☎ 212-688 4673
- 🚇 Subway F to 57th Street. N, R, W to 5th Avenue/59th Street
- ⏱ Mon–Sat noon–6pm
- $ Free

A darling of the art world since it opened in 1998, it features work by hotter than hot young artists.

the Sat afternoon film. The highlight of the programme is **Sunday at the Met** at 3pm, a combination of lectures, film, performances and discussion.

◀🇬🇧▶ BRITTIP

You can't take luggage, including carry-on bags and big backpacks, into the Met and they can't be checked into the museum's cloakroom either, so if necessary you'll need to leave these in the hotel or in a security locker Downtown (see page 60 for details).

MORGAN LIBRARY & MUSEUM
Midtown East
- ✉ 225 Madison Avenue at 36th Street
- ☎ 212-685-0008
- ⌂ themorgan.org
- 🚇 Subway 6 to 33rd Street, 4, 5, 6, 7 to Grand Central
- ⏱ Tues–Thurs 10.30am–5pm, Fri 10.30am–9pm, Sat 10am–6pm, Sun 11am–6pm
- $ $12 adults, $8 students, seniors and children under 16, under 12s free. Free on Fri 7–9pm

The Morgan reopened in spring 2006 after a 3-year, $102m major expansion and renovation to its already fabulous palazzo-style 1902 building. The glass and steel pavilions designed by Renzo Piano doubled the exhibition space for its fabulous collection which, having started as the private collection of banker Pierpont Morgan, includes medieval and Renaissance manuscripts;

The Morgan Library

drawings and prints from the 14th century on, including: works by Rubens, Degas, Blake and Pollock; ancient Middle Eastern seals and tablets; and original handwritten music manuscripts by Bach, Beethoven, Brahms and Schubert. It also has a reading room and a central court in the style of an Italian Piazza and offers daily tours, concerts, lectures and films.

MOUNT VERNON HOTEL MUSEUM AND GARDEN
Upper East Side

- ✉ 421 East 61st Street between 1st and York Avenues
- ☎ 212-838 6878
- 🖱 mvhm.org
- 🚇 Subway 4, 5, 6, N, R to 59th Street/ Lexington Avenue
- 🕐 Tues–Sun 11am–4pm, arrive 3.30pm for the last tour
- $ $8 adults, $7 students and seniors, under 12s free

An amazing structure that dates back to the colonial era, this was once the coach house of the daughter of America's second president, John Adams. Dating back to the early 18th century, it is one of the 7 oldest buildings in Manhattan and has been lovingly restored by the Colonial Dames of America who will sometimes be on hand to talk about the furnishings in the house and the park at the back.

MUSEUM OF AMERICAN FINANCE
Lower Manhattan

- ✉ 48 Wall Street
- ☎ 212-908 4110
- 🖱 moaf.org
- 🚇 Subway 2, 3, 4, 5 to Wall Street; J, M, to Broad Street, 1, R, W to Rector Street
- $ $8 adults, $5 students and seniors

Founded in 1998, this museum moved into the former headquarters of the Bank of New York on Wall Street in Jan 2008, with the banking hall as its new exhibition space, and traces the growth of the world's largest financial superpower. It has the largest public museum archive of financial documents in the world and exhibits include rare $100,000 bills.

Museum of American Finance

MUSEUM OF ART AND DESIGN
Midtown

- ✉ 2 Columbus Circle
- ☎ 212-299 7777
- 🖱 madmuseum.org
- 🚇 Subway A, C, D Columbus Circle/59th Street
- 🕐 Tues–Sun 11am–6pm, Thurs 11am–9pm, closed Mon
- $ $15 adults, $12 students and seniors, under 12s free; pay what you wish Thurs 6–9pm

Along with the American Folk Art Museum, this museum, formerly known as the American Craft Museum, gives an insight into American arts and crafts. It has everything from wood and metal to clay, glass and fibre. It has just reopened at 2 Columbus Circle (it was previously at 40 West 53rd Street) after a $60m renovation of the building. The new design comes complete with floor-to-ceiling windows on the ground floor and zigzagged windows on the upper floors. There are free (with admission) guided gallery tours daily at 11.30am and 3pm and Thurs evenings at 6.30pm.

MUSEUM OF CHINESE IN THE AMERICAS
Chinatown

- ✉ 215 Center Street
- ☎ 212-619 4785
- 🖱 mocanyc.org
- 🚇 Subway N, R, Q, W, J, M, Z and 6 to Canal Street
- 🕐 Mon 11am–5pm, Thurs 11am–9pm, Fri 11am–5pm, Sat–Sun 10am–5pm, closed Tues, Wed
- $ $7 adults, $4 seniors, students and children, under 12s free; Fri free

A fascinating little museum that was previously tucked away on the tiny 1st floor of the community centre in Mulberry Street. The new larger site contains photographs and personal belongings, and talks are given on the history of Chinese immigrants to both North and South America.

MUSEUM OF COMIC AND CARTOON ART
Midtown
- ✉ 594 Broadway, Suite 401
- ☎ 212-254 3511
- ⌂ mocany.org
- 🚗 Subway L, N, Q, R, W, 4, 5, 6 to Union Square
- ◷ Tues–Sun noon–5pm
- $ $5 adults, under 12s free

A fun little museum which is great for kids and adult cartoon lovers alike. It represents every genre of the art, including comic books, graphic novels, cartoons, humorous illustrations, editorial doodles, caricature and computer-generated art. There are lots of events on here, so be sure to check the website to see what's on when you're in town.

MUSEUM OF JEWISH HERITAGE: A LIVING MEMORIAL TO THE HOLOCAUST
Battery Park City
- ✉ 36 Battery Place, Battery Park City
- ☎ 646-437 4200 info; 646-437 4202 tickets
- ⌂ mjhnyc.org
- 🚗 Subway 1 to South Ferry; R, W to Whitehall Street; 4, 5 to Bowling Green, J, M, Z to Broad Street
- ◷ Sun–Tues, Thurs 10am–5.45pm, Wed 10am–8pm, Fri 10am–5pm, and eve of Jewish holidays 10am–3pm, closed Sat and Jewish holidays
- $ $12 adults, $10 seniors, $7 students, under 12s free; free for all Wed 4–8pm

BRITTIP
Before entering the Museum of Jewish Heritage, take a look at the 6-sided shape of the tiered roof, a symbolic reminder of the 6 million who died in the Holocaust and of the Star of David.

Joy, tradition, tragedy and unspeakable horror are the powerful themes of this museum, which tells the moving story of 20th-century Jewish life from the perspective of those who lived it. Created as a living memorial to the Holocaust, it puts the tragedy into the larger context of modern Jewish history and includes 24 original films that feature testimonies from Steven Spielberg's Survivors of the Shoah Visual History Foundation, as well as the museum's own video archive. Nature sculptor Andy Goldsworthy's living memorial garden, Garden of Stones, is worth a look too, with beautiful views of the river, and the trees, which sprout from stones. The garden was planted by Holocaust survivors and their families as well as the artist. A family guide to the museum is available and a programme of family events, concerts, lectures and performances is on offer.

BRITTIP
It is worth renting an audio guide at the Museum of Jewish heritage, narrated by Meryl Streep and Itzhak Perlman, cost $5.

Museum of Jewish Heritage

MUSEUM OF MODERN ART (MoMA)
Midtown

✉ 11 West 53rd Street between 5th and 6th Avenues

☎ 212-708 9400

🖰 moma.org

🚗 Subway E, V to 5th Avenue/53rd Street

🕐 Sat, Sun, Mon, Weds, Thurs 10.30am–5.30pm (open until 8.45pm on selected Thurs), Fri 10.30am–8pm, closed Tues

$ $20 adults, $16 seniors, $12 students, under 16s free with an adult; Fri 4pm–8pm, pay what you wish

Founded in 1929 by 3 private citizens including Abby Rockefeller, this was the first museum to devote its entire collection to the modern movement. Since then it has retained its pioneering sense of the new, and was the first museum to see architecture, design, photography and film as art forms. The museum's collection started with a gift of 8 prints and 1 drawing, and dates from the 1880s to the present day and now encompasses more than 150,000 works.

MoMA reopened in November 2004 after a much-praised redesign by Yoshio Taniguchi in time to celebrate its 75th anniversary. The new building, with a stunning atrium and high-ceilinged galleries, is a work of art itself and occupies over 58,000sq m/630,000sq ft.

✚ BRITTIP
For a treat, dine in The Modern, a gorgeous restaurant serving French-American cuisine, which has in the past been awarded 3 stars by The New York Times.

If you only have a day, head off with your free audio guide to the 2 fabulous floors of Paintings and Sculpture galleries. Many of the icons of modern art are housed here, including Van Gogh's 'The Starry Night', Monet's 'Water Lilies', Picasso's 'Les Demoiselles' and Andy Warhol's 'Gold Marilyn Monroe'. The photographic galleries are also popular, with exhibits from famous names such as Henri Cartier-Bresson and Man Ray. Films are screened every evening in the 2 cinemas (cost included in the entrance fee, but you need to get a ticket to reserve your place) and afternoons and evenings at weekends. Free gallery talks Wed–Mon 11.30am and 1.30pm, plus 6.30pm Fri. If you need a breath of fresh air during your MoMA day, nip down to the Abby Aldrich Rockefeller Sculpture Garden.

✚ BRITTIP
Pick up a copy of glossy book MoMA Highlights, $20, when you buy an admission ticket, which is not only a great guide but a lovely memento too.

The Family Programs introduce children and their parents to the world of modern art through guided walks, workshops, artist talks and film screenings. Grab a free Family Activity Guide at the entrance and call 212-708 9805 or email familyprograms@moma.org for a list of activities. MoMA has dedicated websites for children to familiarise themselves with the art before coming: 5–8-year-olds can click on moma.org/destination and older children can visit http://red studio.moma.org.

Museum of Modern Art

Museum of the City of New York

MUSEUM OF THE CITY OF NEW YORK

Spanish Harlem

✉ 1220 5th Avenue at 103rd Street

☎ 212-534 1672

🖰 mcny.org

🚌 Subway 6 to 103rd Street

🕐 Tues–Sun 10am–5pm, closed Mon

$ Suggested donation $20 families, $10 adults, $6 seniors, students and children; under 12s free

The breadth of New York's history and those who played parts in its development are celebrated in this fascinating museum, which received The Hundred Year Association of New York's Gold Medal Award in 1982 in recognition of its outstanding contribution to the city. Prints, photographs, paintings, sculptures and even clothing and decorative household objects are used to tell the story of New York City. Particularly noted for its Broadway memorabilia, it has period rooms from famous homes such as the bedroom of philanthropist John D Rockefeller, as well as gritty photographs showing the harsh realities of the Depression. The multimedia presentation that opened in its major renovation and extension in 2006, making the span of history accessible, is a good place to start.

◀🇬🇧▶ **BRITTIP**

At the Museum of the City of New York, groups can buy a family ticket even if they are not related.

MUSEUM OF SEX

Madison Square Park

✉ 233 5th Avenue at 27th Street

☎ 212-689 6337

🖰 museumofsex.org

🚌 Subway 6, N, R to 28th Street

🕐 Sun–Fri 11am–6.30pm (last ticket sold 5.45pm), Sat 11am–8pm

$ $16.25 adults, $15 students and seniors Minimum age 18 and IDs will be checked

Times Square may have been cleaned up, but the prostitutes are back in Manhattan in force at New York's most audacious museum. Not for the fainthearted, the inaugural exhibition examined how New York City transformed sex in America by exploring the histories of prostitution, burlesque, birth control, obscenity and fetish. This and other exhibitions use selections such as blow-up dolls and bawdy house coins from private and public collections never shown before and if you're in any doubt as to whether this is the museum for you, just bear in mind that some of the material was once confiscated as obscene.

The main collections include serious works of art by contemporary artists and a massive collection of films, videos, magazines, books and artefacts acquired over 20 years by Ralph Whittington, the former curator of the Library of Congress. Clearly the entrance fee is designed to put off casual thrill-seekers and the museum strictly enforces the minimum age requirement. Despite the subject matter, it is a serious institution with an important message about past and present sexual subcultures and our modern attitudes to sex and sexuality.

NATIONAL ACADEMY OF DESIGN
Midtown

✉ 1083 5th Avenue at 89th Street
☎ 212-369 4880
🖱 nationalacademy.org
🚇 Subway 4, 5, 6 to 86th Street
🕐 Wed, Thurs noon–5pm, Fri 1–9pm, Sat–Sun 11am–6pm, closed Mon and Tues
$ $10 adults, $5 students and seniors, children free

Both a museum and a design school of fine art, it has the largest collection of 19th- and 20th-century American art in the country, comprising more than 5,000 works. Free museum tours on Fri and Sat at 2pm, no reservations required.

NATIONAL MUSEUM OF THE AMERICAN INDIAN
Bowling Green/Financial District

✉ George Gustav Heye Center, US Custom House, 1 Bowling Green between State and Whitehall Streets
☎ 212-514 3700
🖱 americanindian.si.edu
🚇 Subway 4, 5 to Bowling Green; 1, 9 to South Ferry
🕐 Daily 10am–5pm, Thurs 10am–8pm
$ Free

The first museum dedicated entirely to Native American history, art, performing art and culture housed in one of America's finest Beaux Arts buildings, designed by Cass Gilbert. The collection includes fabulous leather clothing, intricately beaded headdresses, sashes, hats and shoes, explaining the white man's influence on Indian culture, as well as their own centuries-old traditions. Despite the size and grandness of the beautiful building, it has only 500 pieces on display and thus seems quite small. However, it is very well laid out and the explanations of each piece have usually been given by Native Americans. It also has a lively programme of events such as plays, music and dance performances, lectures and crafts workshops and daily film screenings on contemporary Native American life, one especially designed for families.

✠ BRITTIP
Small lockers are provided free of charge on the 2nd floor of the National Museum of the America Indian, so you can travel light around the various floors.

NEUE GALERIE MUSEUM FOR GERMAN AND AUSTRIAN ART
Upper East Side

✉ 1048 5th Avenue at 86th Street
☎ 212-628 6200
🖱 neuegalerie.org
🚇 Subway 4, 5, 6 to 86th Street at Lexington Avenue; B, C to 86th Street at Central Park West
🕐 Sat, Sun, Mon, Thurs, Fri 11am–6pm, closed Tues and Wed
$ $15 adults, $10 students and seniors. Under 12s not permitted, under 16s only with an adult

Founded by the late German Expressionist art dealer Serge Sabarsky and chairman of

National Museum of the American Indian

the MoMA board Ronald S Lauder, the 'New Gallery' exhibits fine and decorative arts of Germany and Austria from the first half of the 20th century, on 2 floors. Think Klimt, Klee and Kandinsky. A real bonus is the building itself – a Louis XIII-style Beaux Art landmark once the home of Mrs Grace Vanderbilt. Check out the Klimt painting that, when purchased in 2006 for $135m, was the most expensive painting ever sold.

BRITTIP
While you're on the Museum Mile, take a pit stop at the fabulous Sabarsky Café in the Neue Galerie, which is open every day except Tues. Catch a classical music performance on Wed and Thurs afternoons or Fri evenings.

NEW MUSEUM OF CONTEMPORARY ART
Chelsea

- ✉ 235 The Bowery, Lower East Side
- ☎ 212-219 1222
- ⌨ newmuseum.org
- 🚇 Subway 6 to Spring Street, N, R to Prince Street
- 🕐 Thurs–Fri 12–9pm, Wed, Sat, Sun 12–6pm, Mon–Tues closed
- $ $12 adults, $10 seniors, $8 students, 18 and under free

When they say 'contemporary', they really mean it. All the works exhibited are by living artists, often looking at social issues through modern media and machinery. Designed by cutting-edge Japanese architects, SANAA, its stunning 7-storey white tower – a stack of

rectangular boxes shifted off axis in different directions dressed in silvery metal and punctuated by skylights – was named one of the top architectural projects of the year in 2003 and is the first museum constructed in Downtown Manhattan in over a century. It houses a theatre, library, learning centre and café, as well as rooftop terraces.

BRITTIP
At the beginning of June, don't miss the wonderful Museum Mile Festival (212-606 2296, museummilefestival.org). On the first Tues of the month all 9 museums along 5th Avenue are free. The road is closed and the traffic is replaced by live bands, street entertainers and outdoor art activities for children.

NEW YORK CITY FIRE MUSEUM
West SoHo

- ✉ 278 Spring Street between Varick and Hudson Streets
- ☎ 212-691 1303
- ⌨ nycfiremuseum.org
- 🚇 Subway 1, 9 to Houston Street; C, E to Spring Street
- 🕐 Tues–Sat 10am–5pm, Sun 10am–4pm, closed Mon
- $ $5 adults, $2 students and seniors, $1 under 12s

Technically not a children's museum, though the bright shiny engines are an undoubted hit with youngsters and the young at heart. Housed in the old quarters of Engine 30, here you will find artefacts and fire engines depicting 200 years of city fire-fighting.

New Museum of Contemporary Art

NEW YORK CITY POLICE MUSEUM
Bowling Green/Financial District
- ✉ 100 Old Slip between South and Water Streets
- ☎ 212-480 3100
- ⌖ nycpolicemuseum.org
- 🚇 Subway 4, 5 to Bowling Green; 2, 3 to Wall Street; 1, 9 to South Ferry/Whitehall
- ⊘ Mon–Sat 10am–5pm, closed Sun
- $ Suggested donation $7 adults, $5 seniors and children 6–18, under 6s free

Opened in January 2000, this museum portraying the 160-year history of the NYPD in the Downtown area is a little corker. It is now permanently housed in the former 1st Precinct building, the oldest cop shop in New York. Highlights include the Mounted Unit – one of the oldest and most prestigious within the NYPD – and the K-9 dog unit. In addition to over 10,000 items of police memorabilia – a line-up of guns, uniforms and badges – there's even the Tommy gun with its original violin case that was used to kill mobster Frankie Yale. Plus, you can have a go at playing detective yourself in the interactive crime scene area. View the NYPD Hall of Heroes, which now has a memorial to the 23 policemen and women who lost their lives in the attack on the World Trade Center in 2001. The museum has just opened a new exhibition, The Life and Legacy of Lieutenant

Petrosino, who was one of the most famous officers of the NYPD. It reveals all, from his arrival in the city in 1872 to his murder in 1909; fascinating stuff.

NEW YORK CITY TRANSIT MUSEUM
Brooklyn Heights
A great little museum that is particularly popular with children (page 286).

NEW YORK HALL OF SCIENCE
Queens
A great science museum with demonstrations (page 292).

NEW YORK HISTORICAL SOCIETY
Upper West Side
- ✉ 170 Central Park West at 77th Street
- ☎ 212-873 3400
- ⌖ nyhistory.org
- 🚇 Subway B, C to 81st Street; 1 to 79th Street
- ⊘ Tues–Fri noon–8pm, Sat 10am–6pm, Sun 11am–5.45pm, closed Mon
- $ $12 adults, $9 students, $9 seniors, under-12s free

When this jewel was formed in 1804 it was the only art museum in the city until the opening of the Metropolitan Museum of Art in 1872. The Historical Society was founded to chronicle New York's history and is home to the world's largest collection of Tiffany stained-glass shades and lamps, 2 million manuscripts, including letters sent by George Washington during the War of Independence, a lock of his hair and his camp bed. Recent additions include The *History Responds* exhibition, which contains artefacts and evidence collected from the 11 September attacks. Presently, the Historical Society is working on the construction of its new Central Park West facade and permanent galleries, set to open in November 2011. Changes will include permanent installations, galleries for all ages, a new 'destination' film on New York by Donna Lawrence and a new restaurant. During this time the Society's 2nd Floor galleries will be closed, the West 77th Street Rotunda Gallery will have exhibitions until the end of 2010 and the library will remain open throughout this period. For more details check the website.

THE NOGUCHI MUSEUM
The Japanese sculptor's art can be seen at this museum in Queens (page 292).

P.S. 1 CONTEMPORARY ART CENTER
Long Island City, Queens
A ground-breaking modern art museum (page 293).

New York Hall of Science

THE PAYLEY CENTER FOR MEDIA
Midtown

- ✉ 25 West 52nd Street between 5th and 6th Avenues
- ☎ 212-621 6600
- 🖱 payleycenter.org
- 🚇 Subway E, V to 5th Avenue/53rd Street; B, D, F, V to 47th–50th Streets/ Rockefeller Center
- ◷ Weds–Sun noon–6pm, Thurs noon–8pm, closed Mon–Tues
- $ $10 adults, $8 students and seniors, $5 under 14s

In addition to the exhibits, the museum also has a daily programme of screenings in 2 cinemas and 2 presentation rooms, as well as guided tours. Pick up a copy of the schedules in the lobby on your way in. You can also make an appointment with the library to check out the museum's collection of over 120,000 radio and TV programmes covering more than 85 years before accessing them on the custom-designed database. You won't miss the building – it looks like a giant antique radio set!

QUEENS COUNTY FARM MUSEUM
Floral Park, Queens

A fun, working historical farm with hayrides (page 293).

SCHOMBURG CENTER FOR RESEARCH IN BLACK CULTURE
Harlem

- ✉ 515 Malcolm X Boulevard at 135th Street
- ☎ 212-491 2200
- 🖱 nypl.org/research/sc/sc.html
- 🚇 Subway 2, 3 to 135th Street
- ◷ Mon–Wed noon–8pm, Thurs–Fri 11am–6pm, Sat 10am–5pm, closed Sun, tours by appointment
- $ Free

THE INSIDE STORY
If you haven't much time, try a 1-hour tour of museums. From Jan to Mar and July to Sept, the **Insider's Hour** gives you a quick peek around the most diverse art collections and interactive exhibits. Participating institutions include the Metropolitan Museum of Art (page 109), Lower East Side Tenement Museum (page 108), Intrepid Sea-Air-Space Museum (page 107), American Museum of Natural History (page 100), Museum of Modern Art (page 113), Museum of Jewish Heritage (page 114) and National Museum of the American Indian (page 116).

Established in 1926 by Arthur Schomburg, this museum under the umbrella of the New York Public Library has more than 5 million items including books, photographs, manuscripts, art works, films, videos and sound recordings that document the historical and cultural development of black people in the United States, the Caribbean, the Americas, Africa, Europe and Asia over 400 years of migration.

BRITTIP
To see the Schomburg Center at its best, phone or check the website in advance to find out about film screenings and jazz concerts.

The research unit is open to anyone, while there are exhibitions on art dating back to the 17th century that include masks, paintings and sculptures. Incidentally, the corner of Malcolm X Boulevard, where the Schomburg sits, was once home to Harlem's Speaker's

Schomburg Center

Corner where people used to come and talk about their political beliefs and organisations.

SKYSCRAPER MUSEUM
Battery Park
- ✉ 39 Battery Place
- ☎ 212-968 1961
- ⌂ skyscraper.org
- 🚇 Subway 4, 5 to Bowling Green; 1, R, W to South Ferry/Whitehall Street
- ⏱ Wed–Sun 12–6pm
- $ $5 adults, $2.50 seniors and students

One of New York's most apt museums, celebrating as it does the city's rich architectural heritage and examining what historic forces and which individuals shaped the different skylines of its past. Through exhibitions, programmes, publications and walking tours, the museum offers a fascinating insight into how individual buildings were created, complete with detailed information about how the contractors bid for the work, what was involved and how the building work was executed, all with comprehensive photographic illustrations. Check out the Manhattan Mini Models permanent exhibition, where you can gaze at an intricate Big Apple, and the Maps and Photographs of Lower Manhattan, to get a perspective of how the city has changed since the 60s, plus find out about the world's tallest building.

SOLOMON R GUGGENHEIM MUSEUM
Upper East Side
- ✉ 1071 5th Avenue at 89th Street
- ☎ 212-423 3500
- ⌂ guggenheim.org
- 🚇 Subway 4, 5, 6 to 86th Street
- ⏱ Sun–Wed, Fri 10am–5.45pm, Sat 10–7.45pm, closed Thurs
- $ $18 adults, $15 students and senior citizens, under 12s free, Fri 5.45pm–7.45pm by donation

The Guggenheim Museum in New York is probably best known for its beautiful spiral-shaped, space age building, designed by 'organic' architect Frank Lloyd Wright. Considered one of the greatest architectural achievements of the 20th century, it is one of the youngest buildings in the city to be designated a New York City landmark. Walk by it at night if you get the chance, to see the glass layers in its shell-like façade lit up like a rainbow. The exterior and infrastructure was under $29m restoration since 2005 but scaffolding finally came down in spring 2008, in time for its 50th Anniversary in 2009.

It houses one of the world's largest collections of Kandinsky, as well as works by Chagall, Klee, Picasso, Cézanne, Degas, Gauguin and Manet. It also has Peggy Guggenheim's entire collection of cubist, surrealist and abstract expressionist art and impressive temporary exhibitions.

BRITTIP
It's best to take the elevator to the skylight at the top of The Guggenheim and wind down the central spiral ramp that passes works by major artists from the mid-19th to the 21st century.

Audio tours and free tours by the museum staff, gallery talks and screenings are included in the price of admission. Educator's Eye tours with trained staff who show you around current exhibitions take place daily at 11am and 1pm and are free.

BRITTIP
Check out the Guggenheim's sculpture gallery for some of the best views of Central Park.

SONY WONDER TECHNOLOGY LAB
- ✉ Sony Plaza, 56th Street and Madison Avenue
- ☎ 212-833 8100
- ⌂ sonywondertechlab.com
- 🚇 Subway E, V to 5th Avenue, F to 57th Street, 4, 5, 6, N, R to 59th Street
- ⏱ Tues–Sat 10am–5pm, Sun noon–5pm, closed Mon
- $ Free, but we recommend you book in advance as there are only a certain number of tickets allocated for walk-in visitors

A technology museum with 4 floors of interactive exhibits with robots and lots of hi-tech entertainment, adults will love playing here as much as kids. Reservations only though, so book well in advance. The 3rd and 4th floors were closed for extensive transformation in 2008, so even if you've been before it's worth popping in again to see what new technological wonders have been installed.

SOUTH STREET SEAPORT MUSEUM
Financial District
- ✉ 12 Fulton Street at South Street
- ☎ 212-748 8600
- ⌂ southstreetseaportmuseum.org
- 🚇 Subway A, C to Broadway/Nassau Street; 2, 3, 4, 5, J, Z, M to Fulton Street
- ⏱ (Apr–Dec) Tues–Sun 10am–6pm, closed Mon; (Jan–March) Thurs–Sun 10am–

Sony Wonder Technology Lab

5pm, noon–4pm ships. Mon 10am–5pm galleries only

$ $12 adults, $10 seniors and students, $8 children (5–12) including all tours, films, galleries and museum-owned ships. Discounted entrance on winter Mon

A sprawling mass of galleries, 19th-century buildings, a visitors' centre and a selection of ships in imposing warehouses built in 1813, gives an insight into life in the olden days of New York. This world-class museum along the East River offers walking tours around this historic area, so full of sailors and their ships in the 19th century, it was called the 'street of sails'. It is also the venue for a series of free outdoor summer concerts held almost nightly.

SPORTS MUSEUM OF AMERICA
Lower Manhattan

✉ 26 Broadway at the base of the Canyon of Heroes, at the starting point for the ferry to the Statue of Liberty and Ellis Island

☎ 212-274 0900

🖱 thesportsmuseum.com

🚇 Subway 1 to South Ferry, 4, 5 to Bowling Green

🕐 Open year-round, Mon–Fri 9am–7pm (last ticket sold 5.30pm), Sat–Sun, 9am–9pm (last ticket sold 7.30pm)

$ $27 adults, $24 seniors, $20 children (4–14), under 4s free

This first ever dedicated sports museum, with interactive exhibitions and multimedia displays on sports across the ages and throughout the world opened in May 2008, delayed from its original opening date of November 2006. It was developed at a cost of $93m in the former Cunard Passenger Ship Line building, and brings together exhibits and memorabilia from over 50 single sports halls of fame, museums and organisations across the US. Sports buffs will enjoy seeing the prestigious Heisman Trophy, awarded

to some of the most notable athletes of the 20th century and it includes a progressive Women's Hall of Fame, initiated by Billie Jean King and a sports-themed eatery.

STUDIO MUSEUM IN HARLEM
Harlem

✉ 144 West 125th Street between 7th and Lenox Avenues

☎ 212-864 4500

🖱 studiomuseum.org

🚇 Subway A, B, C, D, 2, 3, 4, 5, 6 to 125th Street

🕐 Wed–Fri noon–6pm, Sat 10am–6pm, Sun noon–6pm, closed Mon–Tues

$ $7 adults, $3 students and seniors, under 12s free

Works of art by African-American artists in a beautiful space. The photographic archive gives a fascinating glimpse into Harlem history and lectures, children's programmes and a film festival combine to fulfil its mission to be the major centre for African-American art. Target Free Sundays are, as the name implies, free for individuals and families from noon–6pm.

VAN CORTLANDT HOUSE MUSEUM
The Bronx

Fascinating former family plantation estate-turned museum (page 289).

Studio Museum in Harlem

WHITNEY MUSEUM OF AMERICAN ART
Upper East Side

✉ 945 Madison Avenue at 75th Street
☎ 212-570 3600 or 1-800 WHITNEY
🖱 whitney.org
🚇 Subway 6 to 77th Street
🕐 Wed, Thurs 11am–6pm; Fri 1–9pm; Sat, Sun 11am–6pm, closed Mon and Tues
$ $18 adults, $12 students, under 12s free; first Fri of every month 6–9pm pay what you wish, plus musical performances

The Whitney may be housed in ghastly looking buildings – a series of grey, granite cubes designed by Marcel Breuer – but it has the world's leading collection of 20th-century American art. Yet it all came about almost by accident. Gertrude Vanderbilt Whitney offered her entire collection to the Metropolitan but was turned down, so she decided to set up her own museum. As a result, in 1931, the Whitney was founded with a core group of 700 art objects.

Subsequently, the museum's holdings have been greatly enriched by other purchases and the gifts of other major collectors. It now has a permanent collection of 15,000 works including paintings, sculptures, drawings, prints, photographs and multimedia installations and is still growing.

As well as the wide range of artists in its collection, the Whitney is known for its cutting-edge exhibitions and has huge bodies of works by artists such as Alexander Calder, Edward Hopper, Georgia O'Keefe, Gaston Lachaise and Agnes Martin. To make the most of your visit, take an audio tour or join one of the free tours by museum staff.

Whitney Museum of American Art

⚡ BRITTIP
If arriving in even-numbered years, check out the Whitney Biennial, the most significant showcase for contemporary art in America.

The Museum Store in the basement, next to Sarabeth's restaurant, is filled with funky and colourful gifts. There's some great stuff for kids including soap crayons that will wash off baths and tiles, and colourful soap that can be moulded into sculptures.

The Whitney has worked hard to make itself accessible to young children. Free activity guides are provided for families to introduce children and adults to selected works of art and encourage new ways of learning about art together through interactive gallery tours and hands-on activities. People, Places and Spaces is the Whitney's family audio guide to works from the Whitney's permanent collection and is included with the admission fee.

Family Fun! Workshops 10.30am–12.30pm and 1–3pm on selected Saturdays, feature gallery tours and art projects for children aged 6–10 and their families. Registration is necessary. **Whitney Wees** for families with children aged 4–5 are an interactive experience of looking and sharing. 10.30–11.30am, plus some Wed 3pm–4pm.

CHAPTER 6

Shopping and Beauty

For many people, New York is synonymous with shopping. Yes, there are jaw-dropping buildings, amazing museums and exciting nightlife, but when it comes down to it, New York City is one of the best places in the world to indulge in a spot of retail therapy. You can get a taste of fantastic American service at the fabulous and famous department stores, and shop until you drop for cheaper CDs, clothes, shoes and cameras. Although the city does have some real American malls, like the one at the South Street Seaport, it is better known for its many boutiques.

The distinct atmosphere of each New York neighbourhood is reflected in the type of shopping available there. The upper section of 5th Avenue in the Midtown area is where you will find all the best department stores and other posh shops. Even posher – exclusive, actually – is Madison Avenue, which is where the top American and European designers are based, such as Prada, Valentino and Versace.

The Villages are excellent for boutique shops that tend to open late but stay open late, too. In **Greenwich Village** you'll find jazz records, rare books and vintage clothing and the **West Village**'s tree-lined streets are full of fine and funky boutiques and popular restaurants that cater to a young, trendy crowd. On the major shopping streets of Bleecker, Broadway and 8th, you'll find everything from antiques to fashion and T-shirt emporiums. There are plenty of up-and-coming designers and second-hand shops in the **East Village**. Try 9th Street for clothes and 7th for young designers.

The **Flatiron District** around 5th Avenue from 14th to 23rd Streets is full of wonderful old buildings that are brimming with one-of-

a-kind shops and designer boutiques. SoHo has lots of boutiques selling avant-garde fashion and art, plus restaurants and art galleries, all housed in handsome cast-iron 1850s buildings. West Broadway is the main drag, but other important shop-lined streets include Spring, Prince, Green, Mercer and Wooster. High-profile recent openings include Prada and Earl Jeans.

In **TriBeCa** you will find trendsetting boutiques such as the fantastic Issey Miyake flagship store, art galleries and restaurants in an area that combines loft living with commercial activity.

Last but not least is the **Lower East Side**, which is to bargains what Madison Avenue is to high-class acts. Many of the boutiques offer fashion by young designers – some of whom go on to open outlets in the posher areas – and famous-name gear at huge discounts. This whole area reflects the immigrant roots of New York and stands out as a bargain hunter's paradise particularly when the market is open on Sundays. Orchard Street from Houston to Delancey Streets is well known for leather goods, luggage, designer clothes, belts, shoes and fabrics. Ludlow Street is famous for trendy bars, and boutiques filled with clothes by flourishing new designers.

Shopping in SoHo

BRITTIP

If you like to be ahead of the pack fashion-wise then make a beeline for 30 Vandam (212-929 6454), a boutique store in SoHo that showcases 50 handpicked designers that you may not have heard of now, but you will in the future.

DEPARTMENT STORES

The big department stores in New York City are reliable places to buy good quality, brand-named merchandise at fair prices. These stores usually sell a variety of men's, women's and children's clothing, including designer label items. You can also expect to find cosmetics, small appliances, electronics and household goods. Department stores usually hold end-of-season clearance sales with significant price reductions. Most of the following are in the Midtown area either in or near 5th Avenue. Standard opening times are Mon–Fri 10am–8pm, Sat 10am–7pm, Sun noon–6pm.

◀╪▶ BRITTIP

The voltage system is different in America, so any plug-in electrical goods will not work properly in the UK without an adaptor.

5TH AVENUE

Bergdorf Goodman: 754 5th Avenue at 57th Street, 212-753 7300, bergdorf goodman. com. Subway N, R, W to 5th Avenue/59th Street; F to 57th Street.
An air of understated elegance pervades every department – not surprising, given that it has been around for generations. This department store is not only still going strong, but it is also positively booming and has even opened a Bergdorf Goodman Men on the opposite side of the street. Well-known for its classic, high-end, high-priced fashion, homewares and accessories, the store has recently expanded its offer to include items for a younger (although still affluent!) clientele; think Stella McCartney, Antik Batik, H. Stern. There are personal shoppers available for men and women if you need a helping hand, plus a great bridal department.

◀╪▶ BRITTIP

Bergdorf Goodman does now open on Sundays (it was the only large department store that didn't) but only from noon until 6pm.

Henri Bendel: 712 5th Avenue at 55th Street., 212-247 1100, henribendel.com. Subway E, V to 53rd/5th Avenue.
This very small department store, which opened in 1895, is perfect for fashionistas as there are lots of very cool clothes on four compact, easy-to-get-around floors. Bendels, as the style set call it, has Missoni, Matthew Williamson, Michael Kors and Colette Dinigan, but also Street of Shops, which is a set of

TOP 5 SHOPPING TIPS

If you're on a really tight schedule, call ahead and book appointments with the **personal shoppers** at major stores. They're very helpful and their service is absolutely free. Bargain! Call Macy's on 212-560 3618, Bloomingdale's on 212-705 2000 and Saks on 212-940 4650.

You have a right to a **full refund** on goods you return within 20 days with a valid receipt unless the shop has signs saying otherwise. Always check, though, especially if the item is in a sale.

Call in advance for **opening hours**. Smaller shops downtown – in SoHo, the Villages, Financial District and Lower East Side – tend not to open until noon or 1pm, but are often open as late as 8pm. Many are also closed on Mon.

You can **avoid sales tax** if you arrange to have your purchases shipped outside of New York State – a facility that is available at larger stores and those that are more tourist orientated.

Watch out for 'Sale' signs on the Midtown section of 5th Avenue in the streets 30s and 40s. Here most of the shop windows are filled with signs that say 'Great Sales!', 'Going Out Of Business!' – yet they have been around for years and are still going strong. In fact, most of what is on sale there can be bought cheaper elsewhere and with a guarantee.

exclusive in-store boutiques for the likes of Diane Von Furstenberg, and Femmegems Design-Your-Own Gemstone jewellery. There are also accessories, such as hats, hosiery, casual wear lingerie and to top it all Frederic Fekkai – one of NY's top hair stylists – has a salon on the 4th floor.

Lord and Taylor: 424 5th Avenue at 39th Street, 212-391 3344, lordandtaylor.com. Subway B, D, F, V to 42nd Street; 7 to 5th Avenue.
A New York shopping institution that started in 1826, with good service and prices far cheaper than Saks, it's great for highlighting American designers. Plus, if you can't fit all your buys into your suitcase (!), it offers free shipping on purchases over $150. If you're visiting in December check out the store's famous Christmas window displays.

Saks 5th Avenue: 611 5th Avenue at 50th Street, 212-753 4000, saksfifthavenue.com. Subway E, V to 5th Avenue/53rd Street.
One of the finest shopping experiences in New York, it also has fabulous views of the

Rockefeller Center and is right next door to St Patrick's Cathedral. Saks is a classic and has all of the big names. There's also a fabulous beauty area on the ground floor where you can have a personal consultation and makeover and it now also boasts an Elizabeth Arden Red Door Salon and Spa. There are lots of extras here that make for a truly A-list shopping trip, from wardrobe consultations for men and women, a complimentary package delivery to local hotels and even a taxi and limo service, not to mention the serious fashion-lovers labels like Alexander Wang and 7 For All Mankind.

BRITTIP
Go for brunch, lunch or afternoon tea at Cafe SFA at Saks for impressive views of the city while you dine. Open Mon–Sat, 11am–5pm, Sun 12–5pm.

MEATPACKING DISTRICT

Jeffrey: 449 West 14th Street between 9th and 10th Avenues, 212-206 1272, jeffreynewyork.com. Subway N, R to 5th Avenue/59th Street.

A boutique department store sounds like an oxymoron, but this little gem, on the edge of the gritty up-and-coming Meatpacking District is packed full of tremendously hip clothes and accessories. It attracts A-list celebrities – note the limousines waiting at the front – and great labels like Dries Van Noten and Balenciaga. The women's shoe department is one of the best in New York.

MIDTOWN–34TH STREET

Macy's: Herald Square at 151 West 34th Street, 6th Avenue and Broadway, 212-695 4400, macys.com. Subway B, D, F, N, Q, R, V, W to 34th Street.

BRITTIP
Macy's is the venue for the Thanksgiving Day Parade, Fourth of July Fireworks and a Spring Flower Week in April.

You can get pretty much anything you require, provided you are prepared to hunt, as this is a beast of a gigantic store, filling as it does an entire city block and soaring up 10 floors. There are lots of entrances and it's easy to get lost in here, so it's best to select a time and place to meet in the store if you're with a group. If you enter from the Herald Square side, you'll find the Visitors' Center on the mezzanine level up to your left. Here you can pick up a discount card

for international shoppers that entitles you to 10% off most goods, plus there's a cloakroom for small bags and jackets if you want to shop light. A favourite area with Brits is the jeans department and, of course, the beauty counters that throng the ground floor. If you're with children, head for the 7th floor where all their needs are catered for, along with the only McDonald's inside a department store in New York. Don't miss the coffee shops, restaurant and food store run by Cucina & Co (page 156).

UPPER EAST SIDE

Barneys: 660 Madison Avenue at 61st Street, 212-826 8900, barneys.com. Subway N, R, W to 5th Avenue; 4, 5, 6 to Lexington. Open 10am–8pm every weekday.

A truly up-to-the-minute fashion outlet, this store is filled with all the top designers and a good selection of newer ones. There isn't really a Brit equivalent; the nearest would be Harvey Nichols, but it doesn't come close. It has 8 floors of fashion where there's everything from big-name designers to more obscure, but very hip, small labels. There is a branch called Coop on 18th Street in Chelsea, and another one at the World Financial Center in Downtown, but this is the $100-million megastore. Treat yourself to a trip to the Image Studio if you've got the time and money to get a whole new look before heading home. Don't miss it!

BRITTIP
If you plan to be in New York in Aug or Mar, go to the Barneys Warehouse Sale – call ahead for locations or check barneys.com.

Macy's

Bloomingdale's

Bloomingdale's: 1000 3rd Avenue between 59th and 60th Streets, 212-705 2000, bloomingdales.com. Subway 4, 5, 6 to 59th Street; N, R to Lexington Avenue.
Bloomies is probably the most famous of all 5th Avenue's department stores. You can have a signature gift, collected from the state-of-the-art visitors centre if you can show a $200 or more same-day receipt, you can also have a hotel package delivery with every $250 purchase, there's currency exchange and you can even buy theatre and Metro Cards here! A truly glitzy shop filled with all the right designers, you can now also sample its delights at the new SoHo branch (page 133).

🇬🇧 **BRITTIP**
Weekdays before lunchtime are the least crowded time to visit Bloomingdale's and the upper floors tend to be less crowded.

DISCOUNT STORES

Burlington Coat Factory: 707 6th Avenue at 23rd Street, 212-229 1300, burlington coatfactory.com. Subway F, V at 23rd Street. Area: Flatiron.
A retail dream for the fashion-conscious and a proper New Yorker's secret. It's a continual designer overstock sale and it does carry more than just coats, though you have to be prepared to trawl through some less gorgeous pieces. There's lots of casual womenswear and menswear, plus formal apparel from names like Calvin Klein, Ralph Lauren, Michael by Michael Kors and DKNY. There are some golden periods, such as the arrival of AG Jeans selling for around one-third of their original price, but you won't know what's in until you hit the rails.

Century 21: 22 Cortlandt Street between Church Street and Broadway, 212-227

9092, c21stores.com. Subway 1, 2, 4, 5, A, C to Fulton Street/Broadway Nassau. Area: Financial District.
Excellent discounts on everything from adults' and children's clothing to goods for the home. Arrive early or mid-afternoon to avoid the lunchtime rush.

Daffy's: 462 Broadway (corner Grand), 212-334 7444, daffys.com. Subway J, M, Q, W, 2, 6 to Canal Street. Area: SoHo.
335 Madison Avenue at 44th Street, 212-557 4422. Subway S, 4, 5, 6, 7 to 42nd Street/ Grand Central. Area: Midtown East.
1311 Broadway at West 34th Street, 212-736 4477. Subway B, D, F, N, Q, R to 34th Street. Area: 34th Street.
125 East 57th Street between Lexington and Park Avenues, 212-376 4477. Subway 4, 5, 6 to 59th Street; N, R, W to Lexington Avenue. Area: Midtown East.
You'll find an amazing range of designer stock from all over the world at all 7 outlets of this famous discount store, and a hunt could result in a real bargain.

Filene's Basement: 4 Union Square South at 40 East 14th Street, 212-358 0169, filenesbasement.com. Subway F, V, L to 6th Avenue/14th Street. Area: Union Square.
Part of the Boston-based bargain-basement company, which is one of the country's oldest off-price chains, Filene's offers 30-60% off department store prices. There's also an outlet on Broadway (2222 Broadway, 212-873 8000).

Gabay's Outlet: 225 1st Avenue between 13th and 14th Streets, 212-254 3180, gabaysoutlet.com. Subway F, V, L to Ave 1.
An East Village gem offering high-end designer fashion at seriously discounted prices. Its shoes and bags are coveted by the fashion pack and often include Manolo, Christian Louboutin and Tod's.

INA: 21 Prince Street between Thompson and Spring Streets, 212-334 9048, inanyc. com. Subway C, E to Spring Street; N, R, W to Prince Street. Area: NoLiTa.
Women's designer resale stock that changes daily and offers discounts of 30–50% per item. You'll be able to get your hands on plenty of model cast-offs, from Manolo shoes to Prada. There's also a men's branch at 19 Prince Street, plus a men's and women's store at 15 Bleecker Street.

Loehmann's: 101 7th Avenue between 16th and 17th Streets, 212-352 0856, loehmanns. com. Subway 1, 9 to 18th Street. Area: Chelsea.
A 5-storey building filled with bargains – typically 30–65% off – for men and women.

TAXES AND ALLOWANCES

US taxes: Be aware that local taxes will be added to the cost of your purchases when you pay at the till, so don't get too carried away by the often seemingly very low price tags. New York sales tax is around 4%, though it has now been dropped on clothes and shoes costing under $110, while New York state tax is 4%.

UK allowances: Your UK duty-free allowance was raised from £340 to £390 on 1 January 2010; as of 1 September 2007, New York State eliminated sales tax on all clothing and shoes if the single item is priced under $110. Given the wealth of shopping opportunities, you're likely to exceed this, but don't be tempted to change receipts to show a lesser value, because, if you are rumbled, the goods will be confiscated and you'll face a massive fine. In any case, the prices for some goods in America are so cheap that, even once you've paid the duty and VAT on top, they will still work out cheaper than buying the same item in Britain.

Duty can range from 3.5 to 19% depending on the item: for example, computers are charged at 3.5%, golf clubs at 4%, cameras at 5.4% and mountain bikes at a massive 15.8%. You pay this on goods above £145 and then VAT on top of that. Keep your eye on the newspapers though, as the UK government has been pushing for a higher allowance for some time and wants the EU to raise the figure to a more reasonable £1,000 – enough for more than a couple of iPods!

Duty free: Buy your booze from US liquor stores – they're better value than the airports – and the amount allowed is now 4 litres of wine and 16 litres of beer, 1 litre for spirits and liqueurs. If you're a smoker or buying for someone who is, you're allowed 200 cigarettes, 100 cigarillos or 50 cigars, the equivalent to 250g of tobacco.

Go to the top floor for designer labels such as Donna Karan, Calvin Klein and Versace; other floors feature accessories, bags, clothing and shoes all at great prices.

Pearl River Mart: 477 Broadway between Broome and Grand Streets, 212-431 4770, pearlriver.com. Subway R, W at Prince Street. Area: SoHo.
Once in Chinatown, now more fashion-conscious SoHo, its Asian-inspired clothes and homewares are still at bargain prices. Pick up paper lanterns, bamboo blinds, satin slippers, chopstick and rice bowl sets and mandarin-collared jackets for low, low prices.

Syms: 400 Park Avenue, 212-317 8200, syms. com. Subway E, V to 53rd/Lexington, 6 to 51st Street. Area: Midtown.
Lots of top designers such as Oscar De La Renta, Tommy Hilfiger, Kenneth Cole. The tags are different shapes for men, women and children and different colours for each size to make it easier to hunt down clothing to suit you. Register on the website for a further 10% off your first purchase.

BRITTIP
Most of the department and discount stores featured also have fantastic online offers, so you can shop in the UK too!

SHOPPING TOURS
Rebecca Merritt of **Shop Gotham** will help you get under the city's skin with shopping trips around areas like SoHo and NoLiTa, speed shop the big department stores and get huge discounts in the Garment Center. Call 212-209 3370, shopgotham.com. Tours cost from $38, Fri–Sat 11am, Sun at noon.

BRITTIP
If you don't want to go on an organised shopping tour, create your own using the Shopping Walking Tour Map at http://gonyc. about.com/library/maps/bl_shopping. htm.

Pearl River Mart

FASHION

You can find everything in New York from top designers to up-and-coming newcomers. The main shopping areas for fashion are the Upper East Side (for posh), SoHo (for designer), the East Village and Lower East Side (for cheap designer). Call ahead for opening times as many shops do not open until late but do stay open in the evening.

BROOKLYN

A Cheng: 152 5th Avenue, Brooklyn, 718-783 2826, achengshop.com.
A mix of smart and street styles from this trendy designer.

E Lingerie by Enelra: 140 5th Avenue, St John's Place, 718-399 3252. Subway Nostrand Avenue.
Forget Victoria's Secret, this has some of the best lingerie in town, transferred to Brooklyn from the East Village, where Madonna used to visit. Now worth checking out at Halloween when the window displays feature items like full-length latex devil outfits!

CHELSEA

Balenciaga: 542 West 22nd Street at 11th Avenue, 212-206 0872, balenciaga.com. Subway C, E to 23rd Street.
The New York flagship store of this popular womenswear label often spotted on the backs of supermodels such as Kate Moss.

Barney's Co-op Store: 236 West 18th Street between 7th and 8th Avenues, 212-593 7800, barneys.com. Subway 1, 2 to 18th Street.
An abundance of edgy, funky styles and accessories for men and women, it's one of the best stores in New York.

Camouflage: 139–141 8th Avenue at 17th Street, 212-691 1750. Subway A, C, E to 14th Street.
Designer menswear store that offers the highlights of the season from labels like Michael Kors, Etro and Marc Jacobs.

Saks 5th Avenue

BEST FOR BRIDES

If you're a bride-to-be on the look-out for your dream dress, make a beeline for **Kleinfeld** (110 West 20th Street, 646-633 4300, kleinfeldbridal.com). This venerable institution features the world's largest selection of wedding dresses from American and European designers, call first to make an appointment. There's also **Kleinfeld Bridesmaids Loft** (270 West 38th Street, 212-398 5255) to check out if you're travelling with friends. You'll find almost 400 samples in every style, size and fabric imaginable.

If you've got money to burn then you'll also want to make a trip to the Upper East side to visit the **Vera Wang Bridal Salon** (991 Madison Avenue, 212-628 3400, verawang.com). The queen of wedding gowns is world-renowned for her amazing creations and boasts customers such as Sharon Stone. **Saks 5th Avenue** (page 124) has an exclusive bridal salon while you'll find less pricey gowns at **RK Bridal** (318 West 39th Street between 8th and 9th Avenues, rkbridal.com).

Comme des Garcons: 540 West 22nd Street between 10th and 11th Avenues, 212-604 0013. Subway C, E to 23rd Street.
Japanese designer Rei Kawakubo's stark designs are worn by fashion's elite, and the high prices reflect that.

Keiko: 128 West 23rd Street between 6th and 7th Avenues, 212-647 7075, keikonewyork.com. Subway 23rd Street.
Designer swimwear for all tastes – and you may recognise the odd supermodel here.

EAST VILLAGE

Himalayan Vision: 127 2nd Avenue at 7th Street, 212-254 1952. Subway 6 to Astor Place.
Tibetan-style dresses, silk skirts, trousers, tops and hand-knit hats from around $40 can be found in this serene shop.

Jill Anderson: 331 East 9th Street at 1st Avenue, 212-253 1747, jillanderson.com. Subway 6 to Astor Place.
The sweeping coat-dresses and girly slips are in keeping with the bohemian vibe of the artsy East Village.

Mark Montano: 434 East 9th Street between 1st Avenue and Avenue A, 212-505 0325. Subway 6 to Astor Place.
Set up by TV star and artist Mark Montano, it's now run by his protégé Deidra Mongan, who designs in-store line Punkin NYC. Expect eye-catching pretty dresses and coats and a nice selection of handbags and jewellery too.

Pas de Deux: 328 East 11th Street nr 2nd Avenue, 212-475 0075. Subway L to 1st Station.

The fash world went into a bit of a frenzy when this store opened, as the duo behind it were also responsible for hugely popular menswear store Odin next door! This is like a Parisian boutique – chandeliers, chequered floor – and the offering is sublime. Check out the Phillip Lim knit dresses not to mention accessories like Karen Walker eyewear. A must-visit for fashionistas.

Trash and Vaudeville: 4 St Mark's Place between 2nd and 3rd Avenues, 212-982 3590, nygoth.com. Subway 6 to Astor Place.
Fitting out rock stars like Iggy Pop since the early 1980s, you'll get the East Village look in no time in this punk/grunge paradise: outrageous rubber dresses and shirts, black leather outfits and plenty of studded gear and footwear to match.

GREENWICH VILLAGE

Nom de Guerre: 640 Broadway at Bleecker Street, 212-253 2891, nomdeguerre.net. Subway 6, Bleecker St/Lafayette St.
Bit of an underground menswear store, selling great jeans and casual collections from the likes of Ervell, Band of Outsiders and an in-house line.

Untitled: 26 West 8th Street between 5th and 6th Avenues, 212-505 9725. Subway A, C, E, F, V, S to West 4th Street.
Contemporary clothing and accessories from exclusive New York designers as well as the likes of Vivienne Westwood.

LOWER EAST SIDE

Rivington Club: 158 Rivington Street at Clinton Street, 212-3758128, rivington club. com. Subway J, M, Z to Essex Street.
A very cool menswear shoe store specialising in trainers with the air of a gentlemen's club; think dark red carpets and low, black leather sofas against the wood-panelled walls. The shoes are displayed in individually lit cubbyholes and there are more behind locked glass cupboards. This is where to shop if you want the very latest designs, way before your friends are likely to even hear about them. Be warned: they get new arrivals each week and don't restock here, so if you see something you like, buy it!

BRITTIP
For info on sample sales in the Lower East Side area, go to racked.com.

HOW TO FIND A REAL BARGAIN

Goods at normal prices in New York are cheaper than in the UK, but it is possible to find whatever you are looking for at an even better price.

▶ If **shopping bargains** are your main reason for visiting New York, then bear in mind that the major sales are held in March and August. The winter sales seem to start earlier and earlier and may even begin before Christmas.

▶ Visit **http://nymag.com/shopping/ articles/sb/** for all the vital information on when the latest designer and sample sales are about to take place. Hot sale action is also listed on dailycandy.com, citylaunch. com and thebudgetfashionista.com.

▶ Check out the **Sales and Bargains** section of *New York Magazine*, the ads in *The New York Times* and the Check Out section of *Time Out*.

▶ Get the **S&B Report** on lazarshopping. com.

▶ Bear in mind that many of the **vintage clothing outlets** are excellent for barely worn designer clothes and some even specialise in never-worn-before sample sales.

Edith Machinist: 104 Rivington Street at Ludlow Street, 212-979 9992. Subway F to Delancey Street.
Sara Daha used to co-own Edith and Daha, but has since struck out on her own. Lovely vintage style with endorsements from stars like Sienna Miller.

Trash and Vaudeville

MEATPACKING DISTRICT

Alexander McQueen: 417 West 14th Street between 9th Avenue and Washington Street, 212-645 1797, alexandermcqueen.com. Subway A, C, E to 14th Street, L to 8th Avenue.

Despite the British fashion designer's sad death in 2010, the store continued to operate that year. The clothes are way out and very expensive and it's not yet clear if the label will continue – watch this space.

An Earnest Cut & Sew: 821 Washington Street at Gansevoort Street, 212-242 3414, earnestsewn.com. Subway A, C, E to 8th Avenue.

High-end denim label Earnest Sewn's opened its first stand-alone store in 2005 and it has been a major hit with trendy young New Yorkers. The major hook here is its customising – you can have pockets, buttons or zips tweaked and fabric added to ensure you get a genuine one-off garment. The service takes 2 hours and costs $300–350.

Diane von Furstenberg: 874 Washington Street, 646-486 4800, dvf.com. Subway A, C, E to 8th Avenue.

Flagship store of the queen of the classically sexy silk jersey wrap dress. The dramatic shop, with its draped changing rooms, is worth a visit in its own right.

Armani Exchange 5th Avenue

FAMOUS AMERICAN LABELS
SoHo

Marc Jacobs: 163 Mercer Street between Houston and Prince Streets, 212-343 1490, marcjacobs.com. Subway N, R to Prince Street.

The darling of supermodels and superwomen, such as movie director Sophia Coppella, Jacobs' style is minimalist and luxurious.

3.1 Phillip Lim: 115 Mercer Street, 212-334 1160, 31philliplim.com. Subway N, R to Prince Street.

New Yorker whose drapey dresses and cool separates are spotted on the likes of Kate Bosworth, Lauren Conrad, Leighton Meester and Alexa Chung.

Upper East Side

Calvin Klein: 654 Madison Avenue at 60th Street, 212-292 9000, calvinklein.com. Subway N, R to Lexington Avenue; 4, 5, 6 to 59th Street.

CK's leading outlet seems to have enjoyed as much attention from the designers as the clothes themselves!

Donna Karan: 819 Madison Avenue between East 68th and 69th Streets, 212-861 1001, donnakaran.com. Subway 6 to 68th Street.

A leading American designer who is best known for her elegant, simple outfits for women. The floating staircase is worth popping in for.

Helmut Lang: 819 Washington Street, 212-242 3240, helmutlang.com. Subway A, C, E, L to 8th Avenue/14th Street.

A stark, white gallery-like space that contrasts well with the designer's dark creations for men and women. It's pricey, think $500 upwards, but items like tuxedo jackets and shoes are exquisite.

Stella McCartney: 429 West 14th Street, 212-255 1556, stellamccartney.com. Subway A, C, E to West 14th Street.

The famous daughter of a Beatle moved on from shaking up fashion at Chloe to designing under her own label to great acclaim. Her first store in this cool district sees the likes of Liv Tyler and Gwyneth Paltrow when they are shopping in town.

TOP 5 MIDTOWN SHOPS FOR ACCESSORIES

Bottega Veneta: 699 5th Avenue between 54th and 55th Streets, 212-371 5511, bottegaveneta.com. Subway E, V to 5th Avenue/53rd Street.
Who wouldn't covet the gorgeous soft leather, logo-free handbags offered at this Italian designer store.

Ferragamo on Madison: 655 Madison Avenue at 52nd Street, 212-759 3822, ferragamo. com. Subway V to 5th Avenue.
The largest Ferragamo store in the world has an amazing 23,000-plus shoes as well as handbags, scarves and ties.

Jimmy Choo: Olympic Tower 645 5th Avenue at 51st Street (entrance on East 51st Street), 212-593 0800, jimmychoo.com. Subway E, V to 5th Avenue/53rd Street.
Originally part of Jimmy's upscale ready-to-wear 'chain' of stores – think London, Paris, Los Angeles and New York – the designer has sold up most of his shares and gone back to his couture clients. Now the thongs (flip-flops), slingbacks and skinny high-heeled shoes are designed by his niece Sandra Choi, but still remain the favourites of celebs like Madonna and Sarah Jessica Parker. A pair of women's shoes are upwards of $450. Men's loafers, sneakers and thongs start at around $300.

Manolo Blahnik: 31 West 54th Street between 5th and 6th Avenues, 212-582 3007, manoloblahnik.com. Subway E, V to 5th Avenue/53rd Street.
Anyone serious about their shoe collection wouldn't miss this Mecca for celebs. In fact, Manolo has even designed the SJP – an ankle-strapped stiletto named after Sarah Jessica Parker.

Roger Vivier: 750 Madison Avenue at 65th Street, 212-861 5371, rogervivier.com. Subway F at Lexington Avenue/63rd Street.
The designer who gave the world chrome-buckle, square-toe flats in the 1960s, worn by Catherine Deneuve in cult film *Belle de Jour*, has finally opened a store. Marlene Dietrich and our very own Queen Elizabeth II have all stepped out in Vivier's creations, which until now have been available in Saks 5th Avenue. Pop in to marvel at the salon, even if you can't afford the shoes, as the furniture was designed to complement the footwear and the interior decoration is modelled on Vivier's luxurious home, complete with a Picasso sketch.

MIDTOWN

Alice + Olivia: 80 West 40th Street at 6th Avenue, 212-840 0887, aliceandolivia.com. Subway B, D, F, V to 42nd Street.
Situated in Midtown West around Bryant Park, this is the place to stock up on the latest trends, such as shift dresses and 1960s-inspired minidresses. Has some cute handbags, too.

Baby Phat: 151 Herald Square, 212-533 7428, babyphat.com. Subway B, D, F, N, Q, R, W, V to Herald Square/34th Street.
Zebra print walls, crystal chandeliers – it's worth visiting this high-end hip-hop lifestyle store for the decor alone. You'll also find racks heavy with leather mini-skirts and decorated denim, not to mention animal-patterned velour lingerie!

BOSS Hugo Boss: Saks 5th Avenue, 611 5th Avenue at 56th Street, 212-940 2600, hugoboss.com. Subway N, R to 5th Avenue.
Outlet of this fashionable menswear label. It has a wide range of the brand's goodies, from sharp suits to coveted watches.

Burberry: 444 Madison Avenue, 212-707 6700, burberry.com. Subway N, R, W to 5th Avenue.
This great British classic has been a trendsetting force in recent years. There's something for everyone here – men, women, teenagers and even children since the introduction of the tots' clothing line.

Chanel: 15 East 57th Street between 5th and Madison Avenues, 212-385 5050, chanel.com. Subway E, V to 5th Avenue.
The enduring French label offers you the chance to buy all the classics from $1,000 suits to quilted handbags and, of course, the famous No 5 perfume.

Earl Jeans

SoHo street scene

Gianni Versace: 647 5th Avenue between 51st and 52nd Streets, 212-317 0224, versace.com. Subway E, V to 5th Avenue/53rd Street.
A beautiful shop, housed in the former Vanderbilt mansion, selling beautiful clothes for the rich and famous.

Gucci: 685 5th Avenue at 54th Street, 212-826 2600, gucci.com. Subway E, V to 5th Avenue/53rd Street.
You may not be able to afford anything on display, but it's essential to know what 'look' you are trying to achieve when you browse the copy-cat shops downtown.

Lacoste: 575 Madison Avenue near 56th Street, 212-750 8115, lacoste.com. Subway 6 to 51st Street. Also at 608 5th Avenue and 134 Prince Street.
The alligator-logo polo shirts are a classic item to snap up while you're in the Big Apple.

Levi's: 536 Broadway, between Prince and Spring Streets. Area: SoHo, 646-613 1847, levi.com. Also at 750 Lexington Avenue. Area: Upper East Side.
If you've ever had trouble finding a pair of jeans that fit you perfectly, come here to be measured and have your jeans custom-made and sent to you.

Lingerie & Company: 1217 3rd Avenue at 70th Street, 212-737 7700, lingerieandcompany.com. Subway 6 to 68th Street.
A user-friendly shop for a wide choice of gorgeous undies, including Hanro, Wolford, Simone Perele and Chantelle.

NOHO
Cockpit Store: 652 Broadway between Bleecker and Bond Streets, 212-925 5456, cockpitusa.com.
Great for flight and varsity jackets.

Urban Outfitters: 628 Broadway between Houston and Bleecker Streets, 212-475 0009, urbanoutfitters.com. Subway F, V, S to Broadway/Lafayette Street; 6 to Bleecker Street.
The last word in trendy, inexpensive clothes and vintage urban wear. There's quite a few in London now so it's not as special as it used to be, but still worth a visit for its mix of hip clothes, accessories and toys.

NOLITA
Calypso Christiane Celle: 280 Mott Street between East Houston and Prince Street, 212-965 0990, calypso-celle.com. Subway 6 to Spring Street.
A French boutique with a Caribbean influence, this shop is filled with designs from Christiane Celle. There's a riot of sexy silk slip dresses, tie-dye tops and cute beaded cardigans. Her newest store is at 654 Hudson Street in the trendy Meatpacking District and there are 7 others in the city – check the website for locations.

Maverick: 262 Mott Street near Prince Street, 212-965 1150. Subway 6 to Spring Street.
Rebecca Romero's store is full of feminine pieces for an uptown look. Think floral-print pencil skirts and pinstripe shirt dresses.

Selvedge: 250 Mulberry Street near Prince Street, 212-219 0994. Subway 6 to Spring Street.
Known as a laboratory for denim, it sells everything from funky reproductions of cult classics like 501s through to the Levi's Red collection.

Sigerson Morrison: 26 Prince Street, 212-219 3893, sigersonmorrison.com. Subway B, D, F, V Broadway/Lafayette Street.
Gorgeous shoes and bags designed by New York shoe connoisseurs Kari Sigerson and Miranda Morrison, who met while studying at the Fashion Institute of Technology in New York. In 2003 they introduced the sister line BELLE by Sigerson Morrison and the irresistible flats, heels and boots have since been snapped up by fans including Gisele Bundchen and Gwyneth Paltrow. Another store at 19 East 71st Street.

SOHO

Adidas Originals Store: 136 Wooster Street near Prince Street, 212-673 0398, adidas.com. Subway C, E to Prince Street.
If you have a penchant for old-school trainers and sportswear, then this is the place.

Anna Sui: 113 Greene Street between Prince and Spring Streets, 212-941 8406, annasui.com. Subway N, R to Prince Street.
Get the glamour-with-a-hint-of-grunge look with dresses, skirts, blouses, boots and scarves. The small collection for men includes trousers, shirts and jackets from the outrageously loud to the positively restrained.

A.P.C.: 131 Mercer Street near Prince Street, 212-966 9685, apc.fr. Subway N, R to Prince Street.
Men's and women's functional city clothes, such as shirt dresses, crisp shirts and jackets and trench coats, sold in a trendy loft.

A Uno: 198 Spring near Thompson Street, 212-343 2040. Subway C, E to Prince Street.
Edgy sportswear and versatile women's clothing.

Banana Republic: 552 Broadway between Spring and Prince Streets, 212-925 0308, bananarepublic.com. Subway N, R to Prince Street.
A classy chain, famous for classic clothing in feel-good fabrics such as cashmere, suede, velvet and soft cotton at affordable prices. The best buys are in the frequent sales.

Betsey Johnson: 138 Wooster Street between Houston and Prince Streets, 212-995 5048, betseyjohnson.com. Subway C, E to Spring Street; N, R to Prince Street.
A wonderful presentation of a combination of party and working clothes that are thrilling to wear. There are several other stores in the city, see website for details.

Bloomingdale's: 504 Broadway between Spring and Broome Streets, 212-729 5900, bloomingdales.com. Subway N, R to Prince Street.
Aimed at Lower Manhattan's trendy set, this 6-level SoHo branch of the world-famous store offers something for everyone, with plenty of different designer lines.

Burberry: 131 Spring Street between Greene and Wooster Streets, 212-925 9300, burberry.com. Subway C, E to Spring Street.
Don't miss this younger outlet of the trendy British company for rainwear, leather, trench dresses, bags, shoes and casual wear.

Catherine Malandrino's: 468 Broome Street at Greene Street, 212-925 6765, catherinemalandrino.com. Subway 6 to Spring Street.
The designer's own sexy French knitwear in block colours stands alongside more tailored knitted skirts and jackets.

Club Monaco: 520 Broadway at Spring Street, 212-941 1511, clubmonaco.com. Subway 6 to Spring Street.
Once a Canadian company offering high fashion at high street prices, Ralph Lauren loved it so much he bought it.

Street traders

D&G

Curve: 83 Mercer Street at Spring Street, 212-966 3626, shopcurve.com. Subway 6 to Spring Street.
This womenswear boutique is a great place to head for wardrobe classics, such as the little black dress, albeit with a designer label price tag. There's also top quality bags, jewellery and shoes and a same-day-delivery service if you're going for a big shop and don't want to cart bags around.

D&G: 434 West Broadway between Prince and Spring Streets, 212-965 8000, dolcegabbana.it. Subway N, R to Prince Street. Shop for jeans, suits, bags and dresses to a background of (loud) pop music. *Sex And The City's* Carrie's favourite shop!

Eileen Fisher: 397 West Broadway between Spring and Broome Streets, 212-431 4567, eileenfisher.com. Subway A, C, E to Canal Street.
Casual, maintenance-free clothing that travels anywhere. Lots to choose from, such as T-shirts, jackets, skirts and the co-ordinating colour palettes make matching up items a dream. Lots of other outlets around the city, including Upper East Side and Midtown.

J Crew: 99 Prince Street between Mercer and Greene Streets, 212-966 2739, jcrew.com. Subway N, R to Prince Street.
American-style men's and women's clothes plus shoes and accessories.

Le Sportsac: 118 Greene Street, 212-625 2626, lesportsac.com. Subway C, E to Spring Street.
Beloved of Japanese trendoids and US out-of-towners, not to mention Brit hipsters, this Le Sportsac flagship store offers great nylon bags in every style, size, colour and pattern and they're reasonably priced, too. Worth a visit as the range isn't available in the UK.

Marc Jacobs: Page 130.

Operations: 60 Mercer Street at Broome Street, 212-334 4950, operationsny.com. Subway N, R to Prince Street.
The quirky work-style clothing, like red trucker jackets with black elbow patches, hang off meat hooks, while the changing rooms are industrial-sized freezers. Also in the Meatpacking District at 50 9th Avenue.

Patricia Field: 302 Bowery at East Houston Street, 212-925 2741, patriciafield.com. Subway A, 6 to Bleecker Street.
Once only famous for her outrageous club clobber, Patricia now creates much of the fashion for the *Sex And The City* girls. So if you want to emulate Carrie, Samantha or Miranda, then come here to stock up on cool bags and jewellery worn by the cast.

NYINTHEKNOW
Kate Maxwell, a Brit living in NYC who is senior editor at luxe US travel magazine *Condé Nast Traveler*, says her favourite store is 3.1 Phillip Lim (115 Mercer Street, 212-334 1160, 31philliplim.com, subway N, R to Prince Street). 'I go to New York designer Phillip Lim's SoHo store whenever I have a fashion emergency, and I always walk out with the perfect outfit. It's particularly good for understated but flattering day-to-date frocks, in drapey washed silks, jerseys and linens.'

Phat Farm: 129 Prince Street between West Broadway and Wooster Street, 212-533 7428, phatfarmstore.com. Subway C, E to Spring Street.
If you're into hip-hop baggies, you'll find everything you need here.

Philosophy di Alberta Ferretti: 452 West Broadway near Prince Street, 212-460 5500, philosophy.it. Subway C, E to Spring Street.
The younger, more affordable line from top designer Alberta Ferretti.

BRITTIP
A great place for a pit stop is the Universal News and Café Corp (212-965 9042, universalnews usa.com) at 484 Broadway between Broome and Grand Streets, where you'll not only be able to find a snack, but also to check out their range of 7,000 magazine titles!

Pleats Please: 128 Wooster Street at Prince Street, 212-226 3600, pleatsplease.com. Subway N, R to Prince Street.

TOP 5 STORES FOR MENSWEAR

Ascot Chang: 110 Central Park South, 212-759 3333, ascotchang.com. Subway F to 57th Street.
Known as New York's finest shirt-maker, the store also makes suits and overcoats, too. It's a real investment buy as Ascot Chang items don't date and last for ever – but they are pricey. If you're not feeling flush, there are off-the-rack pieces, too, from shirts to pyjamas.

Brooks Brothers: 346 Madison Avenue at 44th Street, 212-682 8800, brooksbrothers.com. Subway E, V at 5th Avenue.
Something for every man at this all-American flagship store. There are hundreds of outfits, plus accessories to check out and a made-to-measure service. A very famous American label known for its preppy and Ivy League type customers, it offers a great range of luxurious suits, shirts and jackets along with cashmere sweaters, polo shirts and blazers. This is the place to come if you're looking for sophisticated menswear with a unique American style.

Duncan Quinn: 8 Spring Street between Bowery and Elizabeth Streets, 212-226 7030, duncanquinn.com. Subway C, E to Spring Street.
For those that believe exciting clothes shopping isn't just for women, this menswear treasure is packed full of brightly patterned suits, ties and shirts all expertly crafted. There are also some excellent shoes on offer.

Sean John: 475 5th Avenue at East 41st Street, 212-220 2633, seanjohn.com. Subway B, D, F, V to 42nd Street.
Lots of sportswear for the hip-hop look, but plenty of other bits to ensure you look cool even at special occasions, such as white linen suits and pink polo shirts. There's also toiletries, ties, watches and belts for a complete bling style.

Tom Ford: 845 Madison Avenue at 70th Street, 212-359 0300. Subway 6 at 66th Street/Hunter College.
A one-stop shop for stylish men everywhere, the man who made Gucci sexy again has made this store a big hit. The ground floor stocks 3-piece suits, colognes and dress shirts in 350 colours. Upstairs, via a velvet-lined lift, there's a made-to-measure service and 3 private rooms where you can have items customised, from shirts and ties to tennis shorts and even pyjamas. Lots of lovely accessories, too, such as sunglasses and cufflinks.

Issey Miyake's tightly pleated skirts, tops, scarves and trousers can be found here.

Prada New York Epicenter: 575 Broadway at Prince Street, 212-334 8888, prada.com. Subway N, R, W to Prince Street.
Art is the byword of this incredible $40m flagship store for Prada. Once the Guggenheim's SoHo museum, the 2-level space has been designed by architect Rem Koolhaas and includes a zebrawood 'wave' in the entry hall and shoe display steps that can be converted into auditorium seating. Other neat design elements include dressing rooms behind a wall that switches from translucent to transparent (be warned!) and clothes suspended from the ceiling in metal cages. And therein lies one of the main drawbacks of the store from a punter's point of view. Prada's entire collection is to be found here, yet all the empty areas make people feel as if there isn't that much to buy. On top of that, the store has taken being cool so seriously that the staff are positively frosty. Deal with them by either telling yourself that you earn a lot more than they do, or as one woman put it: 'You can have fun by asking the sales people for things from the storage rooms and keep them running!'

Sean: 199 Prince Street, 212-598 5980, seanstore.com. Subway 1, 9 to Houston.
A superb range of menswear for work and play at low prices, from colourful shirts to wool sports jackets.

Topshop: 478 Broadway at Broome Street, 212-966 9555, topshop.com. Subway N, R, W to Prince Street.
At the celebrity-packed opening party in spring 2009, Kate Moss dropped by in her capacity as one of the store's key designers. The store is as big as the flagship store in London and houses just as many exciting young designers at excellent prices. You can also get your nails done here, get a bite to eat and see a style advisor.

TRIBECA

Rival: 225 Hudson Street near Canal Street, 212-929 7222, rivalnyc.com. Subway 1, 9 to Canal Street.
Skatewear for grown-ups best describes this store, which is packed full of great labels such as Burton and Oliver Spence. Best of all, you don't have to be under 18 to get the attention of staff; customer service here is

excellent, even if your days of whizzing along on a snow or skateboard are well behind you.

Steven Alan: 103 Franklin Street between Church Street and West Broadway, 212-343 0692, stevenalan.com. Subway 1 to Franklin Street.
A small but perfectly formed boutique filled to the rafters with up-and-coming designers such as Kayatone Adeli's cute disco top and Daryl K's hipster trousers. Also A.P.C and Isabel Marant.

Tribeca Issey Miyake: 119 Hudson Street at North Moore Street, 212-226 0100, tribecaisseymiyake.com. Subway 1, 2 to Franklin Street.
The new Prada store got the old Guggenheim Museum space in SoHo: Issey Miyake got Frank Gehry, the architect of the amazing Guggenheim Museum in Bilbao. Now serious shoppers mingle with art buffs who come to see the titanium tornado that swirls through this 2-storey, 279sq m/ 3,000sq ft boutique, plus art by Gehry's son Alejandro. Fortunately, the purpose of the shop has not been forgotten and the entire Issey collection is here, including the Pleats Please, Haat, A/POC and fragrance lines. What's more, the staff are actually helpful. A truly wonderful experience – especially if you can afford $1,600 for a shirt. Otherwise, wait for the sales!

UPPER EAST SIDE

agnès b: 1063 Madison Avenue, 212-570 9333, agnesb.com. Subway 6 at 77th Street.
Superb designs for women and children here – simple but stunning and beautifully cut. Also look at 13 East 16th Street where there's another store.

Agnès b

Allegra Hicks: 1007 Madison Avenue at 78th Street, 212-249 4241, allegrahicks.com. Subway 6 at 77th Street.
Loved by the jet-set, Bahamas-based Hicks has injected some of her summer style into this brand-new store. As well as her signature beachwear, think brightly coloured bikinis and one-pieces, as well as lots of bold, printed kaftans, high-waisted trousers, knits and floaty empire-line dresses.

American Apparel: 1090 3rd Avenue between 64th and 65th Streets (and 12 other outlets in New York), 212-772 7462, americanapparel.net. Subway N, R, W, 4, 5, 6, Lexington Av/63rd Street.
Stocks a huge selection of cool casual wear, from T-shirts to bikinis and jersey dresses.

Anne Fontaine: 677 Madison Avenue near 62nd Street, 212-421 0947, annefontaine. com. Subway 4, 5, 6 to 59th Street.
The place in New York to snap up the perfect white shirt.

Betsey Johnson: 1060 Madison Avenue, 212-734 1257, betseyjohnson.com. Subway 6 to 77th Street.
Eclectic mix of rock chick chic and artsy boudoir designs.

Billy Martin's Western Wear: 220 East 60th Street, 212-861 3100, billymartin.com. Subway 6 to 68th Street.
Everything for the posh cowboy.

Calvin Klein: page 130.

Cantaloup: 1036 Lexington Avenue at 74th Street, 212-249 3566. Subway 6 to 77th Street.
This candy-coloured boutique is a magnet for trendspotters, thanks to its display rails filled with edgy designers such as True Religion. Has excellent sales.

D&G: 825 Madison Avenue between 68th and 69th Streets, 212-249 4100, dolcegabbana.it. Subway 6 to 68th Street.
Shop for jeans, suits, bags and dresses to a background of (loud) pop music.

Diesel: 770 Lexington Avenue at 60th Street, 212-308 0055, diesel.com. Subway N, R to Lexington Avenue 4, 5, 6 to 59th Street.
A massive store in which you'll find everything from denim to vinyl clothing, shoes and accessories.

Donna Karan: page 130.

Giorgio Armani: 760 Madison Avenue at 65th Street, 212-988 9191, giorgioarmani. com. Subway 6 to 68th Street.
A huge boutique that sells all three of Armani's lines. Come here to find well-tailored classics.

TOP PLACES TO GET YOUR CLOTHES MADE-TO-MEASURE

LS Men's Clothing: 49 West 45th Street, 212-575 0933, lsmensclothing.com. Subway C to 50th Street.
Made-to-measure services on classic suits, sports jackets, overcoats and tuxedos.

Mary Adams: 31 East 32nd Street, 212-473 0237, maryadamsthedress.com. Subway F, J, M, Z at Delancey Street/Essex Street.
A fascinating shop bursting with dresses full of lace, ruffles, satin and feathers. You'll feel like you've stepped into the Moulin Rouge wardrobe and you can even get your own custom-made creation to wow your friends back home.

Ripplu: 66 Madison Avenue, 212-599 2223, ripplu.com. Subway S, 4, 5, 6, 7 to 42nd Street/5th Avenue.
Nip and tuck too scary and expensive? Never fear, your prayers for a better bod have been answered courtesy of Ripplu, the New York women's secret lingerie store. Their custom-made bras and pants lift and reshape those wobbly bits; they even offer free alterations.

Nicole Farhi: 10 East 60th Street near Madison Avenue, 212-223 8811, nicolefarhi.com. Subway 4, 5, 6 to 59th Street.
Elegant, simple designs for men and women. It also sells homeware.

Prada: 841 Madison Avenue at 70th Street, 212-327 4200, prada.com. Subway 6 to 68th Street.
Check out the season's look before you head for the bargain basement stores.

Ralph Lauren: 867 Madison Avenue at East 72nd Street, 212-606 2100, ralphlauren.com. Subway 6 to 68th Street.
Worth a visit just to see the store – it's in an old Rhinelander mansion and is decorated with everything from Oriental rugs to riding whips, leather chairs and English paintings. The clothes are of excellent quality, too.

WEST VILLAGE

Claudine: 19 Christopher Street at Waverly Place, 212-414 4234. Subway 1 to Christopher Street.
Website handbag.com named this the top store in NY to spot new trends. It's a delightful boutique run by fashionista Kyung Lee, with welcoming scented candles, soft music and pretty prints on the wall. The stock's pretty good too, with a mix of casual and formal collections from up-and-coming New York and LA designers. Many of the items are handmade one-offs, so there's lots of potential for bagging outfits no one else has. A good shoe selection, too.

Darling: 1 Horatio Street at 8th Avenue, 212-367 3750, darlingnyc.com. Subway A, C, E to 14th Street.
Ann French Emonts fills this small boutique with her own designs plus choice pieces from other top-notch womenswear designers. Thurs nights are popular as the store stays open until 10pm and customers are offered champagne while they browse.

Lulu Guinness: 394 Bleecker Street between 11th and Perry Streets, 212-367 2120, luluguinness.com. Subway A, C, E to 14th Street; L to 8th Avenue; 1, 2 to Christopher Street.
Lulu started out in Notting Hill, West London, and has established herself in the Big Apple. Her vintage-inspired accessories include embroidered and appliquéd bags and purses, many only available in New York.

Prada

VINTAGE FASHION

BROOKLYN

Guvnors: 178 5th Avenue, Brooklyn, 718-230 4887, guvnorsnyc.com. Subway L to 1st Avenue.
Vintage and secondhand goodies at affordable prices, which you can snap up to a soundtrack of rock and roll. They'll buy as well as sell plus there's a tailoring service.

CHELSEA

Cherry: Showplace Antiques Center 40 West 25th Street, 212-924 1410, cherryboutique. com. Subway A, C, 23rd Street.
A cool vintage shop that was at 8th Avenue but moved in spring 2010 to new premises (call number to check it's now open). Stocks all manner of goodies and shoes dating back as far as the 1940s. It's popular for its one-of-a-kind pieces such as a cute Pucci top or Versace gown. You'll also find lots of fab accessories, from sunglasses to headscarves. Be sure to leave at least a couple of hours, for serious shoppers have been known to disappear for an afternoon in this vintage Mecca.

EAST VILLAGE

Tokio 7: 83 East 7th Street between 1st and 2nd Avenues, 212-353 8443,. Subway 6 to Astor Place; N, R to 8th Street
Plenty of vintage and downtown designer gear to choose from here. Particularly good collection of Japanese designers.

Tokyo Joe: 334 East 11th Street between 1st and 2nd Avenues, 212-473 0724. Subway 6 to Astor Place.
The pre-worn designer offerings are advertised on a blackboard outside the shop every day.

Lulu Guinness

Village Scandal: 19 East 7th Street between 2nd and 3rd Avenues, 212-460 9358. theVillagescandal.com. Subway 6 to Astor Place.
A must-visit for vintage addicts as this retro store is packed full of cool hats and accessories from floppy Bianca Jagger-esque designs to trendy bucket caps. It's open until midnight.

> **BRITTIP**
>
> For the complete lowdown on what New York has to offer shoppers, log on to newyorkmetro.com/shopping, which gives comprehensive listings by neighbourhood or store type.

GREENWICH VILLAGE

Stella Dallas: 218 Thompson Street between Bleecker and West 3rd Streets, 212-674 0447. Subway A, C, E, F, V, S to West 4th Street.
An amazing vintage shop full of girly chiffon and other items.

LOWER EAST SIDE

Foley + Corinna: 114 Stanton Street at Essex Street, 212-529 2338, foleyandcorinna. com. Subway F, V to Lower East Side/Second Avenue.
Sexy, edgy, girly clothing tucked away in a spacious boutique that has become a magnet for uptown girls and celebs looking for something different. There's a great range of vintage shoes that line the floors under the racks of silk tops and Harlowe dresses. It's a wide mix of vintage and new clothing, plus accessories like handbags and jewellery, and it's all exceptional.

> **BRITTIP**
>
> If you need shoe repairs while you're in NY, go to Angelo Shoe Repair at 666 5th Avenue (lower level) at 53rd Street. Tel 212-757 6364, open 7am–6.30pm.

NOLITA

Screaming Mimi: 382 Lafayette Street between 4th and Great Jones Streets, 212-677 6464, screamingmimis.com. Subway N, R to NYU 8th Street.
Everything from polyester dresses to denim shirts and tropical prints from the 1960s. There are also jewellery, sunglasses and other accessories, plus a home department upstairs in which to browse.

SOHO

Transfer International: 594 Broadway, Suite 1002, between Prince and Houston Streets, 212-941 5472, transferny.com. Subway N, R to Prince Street.

Specialises in Gucci, Prada, Chanel and Hermès – one of the best places to buy post-worn designer clothes and accessories. They also carry agnès b and Betsey Johnson.

TRIBECA

Geminola: 41 Perry Street near 7th Avenue, 212-675 1994, geminola.com. Subway 1, 9 to Christopher Street.

Owner Lorraine Kirke travels the world for vintage fabrics, then reworks and dyes them to create gorgeous and unique clothing. Skirts from $165 and accessories and belts from Afghanistan and handbags from India at around $295.

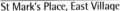

BRITTIP

Americans still measure in feet and inches – good news for older Brits.

UPPER EAST SIDE

BIS Designer Resale: 1134 Madison Avenue between 84th and 85th Streets, 212-396 2760, bisbiz.com. Subway 4, 5, 6 to 86th Street.

For those that like a designer label but don't have the cash to splash, there is a shopping God. BIS is jammed with pieces that have only been worn once or sometimes never, from barely worn Manolos to Chanel quilted jackets. Stock is stored by items, such as

Macy's Christmas lights

shoes or skirts, but if you're after a specific label, such as Gucci, the staff will show you what's available. You may be beaten to some of the best bits by die hard fans who log on to the store's eBay site to snap up bargains. Prices are around 50% of the original value, but while you're saving, don't forget that still means many 3-figure price tags.

UNION SQUARE

Cheap Jack's: 303 5th Avenue at East 31st Street, 212-777 9564, cheapjacks.com. Subway N, R, W to 28th/34th Streets.
A huge selection, but on the pricey side, despite the name!

UPPER EAST SIDE

Gentlemen's Resale: 322 East 81st Street between 1st and 2nd Avenues, 212-734 2739, gentlemensresaleclothing.com. Subway 6 to 77th Street.
Top-notch designer suits at a fraction of the original price.

SHOPPING AND BEAUTY

139

St Mark's Place, East Village

BEAUTY STORES AND SPAS

Everyone knows New York is the place to find fabulous fashion bargains, but not so well known are the great beauty buys to be had. In the first instance, most make-up – particularly the gorgeous American brands such as Philosophy, Hard Candy, Benefit and Laura Mercier – is a lot cheaper in the Big Apple. The exceptions are the 'prestige' French brands such as Décleor, Christian Dior and Chanel, which are generally cheaper in the UK (they are imported to America).

Most brands have dedicated stores in Manhattan, the majority around SoHo and its environs of NoLiTa, north SoHo and West Village.

BEAUTY STORES

FLATIRON

M.A.C Pro: 7 West 22nd Street at 5th Avenue, 212-229 4830, macpro.com. Subway N, Q, R, W to 23rd Street.
A haven for beauty make-up artists and pros, MAC finally opened in 2008 in a 557sq m/6,000sq ft space with mixing studios, photography studio, reference materials and master classes!

MIDTOWN

Sephora: 597 5th Avenue between East 48th and 49th Streets, 212-980 6534, sephora.com. Subway B, D F, V to 47th–50th Streets/Rockefeller Center.
The Rockefeller Center is home to the flagship Manhattan Sephora store packed with aromatic beauty products.

Kiehl's

Shu Uemura: 660 Madison Avenue at 61st Street (in Barneys), 212-833 2007, shuuemura-usa.com. Subway N, R, W to 5th Avenue/59th Street.
Like MAC, Shu Uemura is another make-up range much loved by industry professionals, thanks to its quality and texture. The Japanese cosmetics company, based on Eastern philosophies, is famous for its colour and tools – this is the place to come for everything to do with make-up from brushes to eyelash curlers.

SOHO

To get to SoHo use either the N, R subway lines to Prince Street or the 6, C, E to Spring Street.

> 🇬🇧 **BRITTIP**
> Stores in SoHo tend to open some time between 10am and noon and stay open until 7pm Mon–Sat, while most open from noon to 6pm on Sun.

Aveda: 233 Spring Street between 6th Avenue and Varick Street, 212-807 1492, aveda.com.
This is an appropriately tranquil setting in which to choose your favourite hair and skincare products. Aveda's holistic approach, using natural plant and flower extracts, is carried through all its products, including the make-up ranges and massage oils.

Face Stockholm: 110 Prince Street at Greene Street, 212-966 9110, facestockholm.com.
A glittery emporium filled with the full range of colours and brushes. You can have your make-up done here or take a lesson. Phone for an appointment or just drop in.

> 🇬🇧 **BRITTIP**
> Tracie Martyn is considered by many to be the best facialist in New York, using a massage technique that some – including Liv Tyler and Kate Winslet – say can leave you looking 10 years younger. 59 5th Avenue, 212-206 9333, traciemartyn.com.

Fresh: 57 Spring Street between Lafayette and Mulberry, 212-925 0099, fresh.com.
Soaps, lotions and potions with lovely fragrances based on natural ingredients from the Boston company. It has a *Memoirs of a Geisha* collection, inspired by the film.

Kiehl's: 109 3rd Avenue between 13th and 14th Streets, 212-677 3171, kiehls.com.
One of New York's most famous

JEWELLERY

The 47th Street Diamond District is where the little gems are traded, cut and set. More than 2,600 independent businesses are in a single block between 5th and 6th Avenues. Many have booths in jewellery exchanges such as the World's Largest Jewellery Exchange at 55 West 47th Street (212-719 5235, 55w47.com).

Chelsea

DVVS: 263A 19th Street near 8th, 212-366 4888, dvvs.com. Subway C, E to 23rd Street. Modern, unusual jewellery from contemporary designers. Price range $1,000–2,000.

Midtown

Asprey: 853 Madison Avenue, 212-688 1811, asprey.com. Subway N, R to 5th Avenue. Pricey bling beloved of stars, not least because Jade Jagger has a hand in its designs.

Graff: 710 Madison Avenue near 64th Street, 212-355 9292, graffdiamonds.com. Subway 6 to 68th Street.
Some of the best diamonds that you're ever likely to come across are here, to suit every type of price range, from tiny 1-carat to 100-carat yellow diamonds.

H Stern: 645 5th Avenue near 51st Avenue, 212-688 0300, hstern.net. Subway E, V to 5th Avenue. One of New York's most prestigious jewellers.

Tiffany & Co: 727 5th Avenue, 212-755 8000, tiffany.com. Subway N, R to 5th Avenue. Few can resist popping in to sneak a look at the store that featured so highly in the classic film *Breakfast at Tiffany's* starring Audrey Hepburn. If you can't afford the $2,000-plus diamond necklaces and bracelets, you can always fork out for a $100 keyring.

SoHo

Fragments: 116 Prince Street between Greene and Wooster Streets, 212-334 9588, fragments. com. Subway A, C, E to Spring Street.
A hit with the fashion crowd keen to snap up the works of between 60 and 100 designers.

establishments, the crowds still flock to this emporium in the Union Square area for its luxurious moisturisers and lip balms.

MAC: 113 Spring Street between Greene and Mercer Streets, 212-334 4641, maccosmetics. com.
The wonder of this flagship store for MAC is as much in the architecture, lighting and displays as in the products. In fact, it's such a wonderful place, it has become a big favourite with celebs such as Britney Spears, Gwyneth Paltrow, kd lang and Alanis Morissette.

It sells all MAC products including the MAC Pro range used by make-up artists on fashion shows and movie shoots, which are only available in a few of their outlets.

During your visit, you can either plump for a 45-minute makeover for $40, complete with useful tips, or turn up with nothing but foundation on your face and let the artists finish off your make-up for free.

Make-Up Forever: 409 West Broadway between Prince and Spring Streets, 212-941 9337, makeupforever.com.
A French line specialising in ultra-bright colours, thanks to the triple pigment formula used in all its lipsticks and eyeshadows. This is a funky little shop decked out to look like the make-up area of a film set. The well-trained staff are happy to advise on colours and products, while a $50 makeover is redeemable against purchases, including the company's best-selling silicon-based foundation.

Tiffany & Co

SCO: 5th Floor, 584 Broadway near Prince Street, 212-966 3011, scocare.com. Subway N, R to Prince Street.
Stands for Skin-Care Options, of which there are many. Lots of custom-blended concoctions including face products and sun blocks.

Sephora: 555 Broadway between Prince and Spring Streets, 212-625 1309, sephora.com. One of many New York outlets of this pristine, clean French beauty chain, which has become a sure-fire hit, thanks to its incredibly broad range, sparkling presentations and low-key staff who can provide plenty of help and advice when requested. This is the best place to get your favourite American brands, such as Benefit, Hard Candy, Nars and Philosophy.

UPPER EAST SIDE
Face Stockholm: 687 Madison Avenue at 62nd Street, 212-207 8833, face stockholm. com. Subway 4, 5, 6 to 68th Street.
Another outlet of the fab beauty company. You'll also find another one of these boutiques on the Upper West Side at 226 Columbus Avenue between 70th and 71st Streets (212-769 1420).

L'Occitane: 1046 Madison Avenue at 80th Street, 212-639 9185, loccitane.com. Subway 6 to 77th Street.
Ultra-luxurious bath and beauty products

from the famous French company. Also branches at 510 Madison at 52nd Street and 1288 Madison at 92nd Street.

WEST VILLAGE
Aedes de Venustas: 9 Christopher Street near 6th Avenue, 212-206 8674, aedes.com. Subway 1, 9 to Christopher Street.
Sublime emporium where you can pick up almost impossible-to-find skincare products.

Fresh: 388 Bleecker Street between Perry and West 11th Streets, 917-408 1850, fresh.com. Subway 6 to 68th Street.
A Boston-based company specialising in beauty products made from natural ingredients such as honey, milk, soy, sugar and even Umbrian clay. Other branches can be found at 1367 3rd Avenue (212-585 3400) and 872 Broadway (212-477 1100).

BRITTIP
For the best shave a man can have in New York, take a seat and join the queue in one of three The Art of Shaving barber shops (305-593 0667, theartofshaving. com/locations) located around the city. You can get every type of shave imaginable, including a hot, straight-edged Royal Shave, at these Victorian-style outlets.

Sephora

Relaxing in SoHo

HAIR

MIDTOWN
The Ouidad Salon: 4th Floor, 37 West 57th Street between 5th and 6th Avenues, 212-888 3288, ouidad.com.
Named after the owner, this hair salon specialises in cutting and styling curly hair. In fact, they take curly hair so seriously you won't be allowed in without it! The dedicated team spends up to 4 hours styling and taming your locks and the salon has its own range of products. This new premises has the feel of a SoHo loft, with faux snakeskin couches to boot.

SOHO
To get to SoHo use either the N, R subway lines to Prince Street or the 6, C, E to Spring Street.

Devachan: 425 Broome Street at Crosby Street, 212-274 8686, devachansalon.com. Small salon where celebs come to get perfect locks and an amazing scalp massage. It also doubles as a spa.

Frédéric Fekkai: 394 West Broadway at Broadway, 212-888 2600, fekkai.com. Subway B, D, F, V to Broadway/Lafayette Streets; 6 to Spring Street.
A more relaxed vibe to the uptown salon,

this latest branch to open in SoHo is already proving a big hit, particularly as you can get your make-up done here, too. Open until 9pm Thurs and Fri.

Prive: The Soho Grand, 310 West Broadway between Canal and Grand Streets, 212-274 8888, sohogrand.com.
Home of Laurent D, who looks after Gwyneth's hair when she's in town. His haircuts start at around $200.

WEST VILLAGE
Avalon Salon & Day Spa: 112 Christopher Street between Bleecker and Hudson Streets, 212-337 1966, avalonsalondayspa.com. Subway 1 to Christopher Street/Sheridan Square.
A popular local salon that is a world away from snooty 5th Avenue. Friendly staff, lots of cutting stations and excellent products, such as Keratase and Aveda, guarantee you'll walk away happy.

Gemini Salon & Spa: 547 Hudson Street between Perry and Charles Street, 212-675 4546, geminisalonnyc.com. Subway 1, 9 to Christopher Street.
If you have wild, untameable hair or you just want your locks to be sleeker, then book an appointment to test out this salon's patented Opti-smooth straightening treatment for yourself.

Park Avenue, Upper East Side

NAILS

EAST VILLAGE
Jin Soon Natural Hand & Foot Spa: 56 East 4th Street between Bowery and 2nd Avenue, 212-473 2047, jinsoon.com. Subway F, V to Lower East Side/2nd Avenue.
When in town, actress Julianne Moore always books a full foot treatment with Jin Soon Choi. Expect rose petals and botanicals with the ultra pampering $30 pedicure – a basic manicure costs just $15. The tiny spa became such a Mecca for celebs and those wanting perfect hands and feet that a second, larger Jin Soon Spa has been established in the West Village at 23 Jones Street between Bleecker and West 4th Streets, 212-229 1070, plus a joint on the Upper East Side too, 421 East 7th Street, 212-249 3144. Check out the 'floating room' where gorgeous orange silk hangs over a small pond.

BRITTIP
For excellent manicures with no frills for just $10, head to the East Village where a plethora of salons dot the streets of Marks Place and 2nd Avenue. Generally New Yorkers pay around $25 for a manicure or a pedicure.

MEATPACKING DISTRICT
Rescue Beauty Lounge: 34 Gansevoort Street 2nd floor, 212-206 6409, rescuebeauty. com. Subway A, C, E, L to 8th Avenue/14th Street.
Famous for intensive treatments, this is a complete nail specialist.

MIDTOWN
50th Street Madison Nail: 44 East 50th Street at Madison Avenue, 212-754 2277. Second-floor salon that isn't going to break the bank, with prices far lower than its neighbours. Look for Panini Totz Deli at street level; the sign for the nail salon is above it.

Pinky Nail Fifty Six Corp: 240 East 56th Street, 212-446 9553.
A fab chain of nail salons where manicures start at $10 and pedicures at $20. This location is particularly well known for its cleanliness and friendliness.

UPPER EAST SIDE
Charming Nails: 212 East 87th Street at 3rd Avenue, 212-987 7239.
A fashionista's secret, who knows that you get spa-quality results for budget prices here.

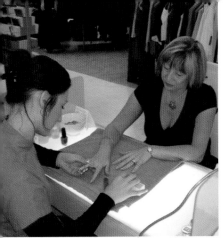

Treat yourself to a manicure

UPPER WEST SIDE

Fashion 74 Nails: 303 Amsterdam Avenue at 74th Street, 212-799 5252.
Where those in the know get their nails done – even, it's rumoured, other spa owners!

PERFUMES

MIDTOWN

Bond No 9 New York: 680 Madison Avenue at 61st Street, 212-838 2780, bondno9.com. Subway 4, 5, 6 to 59th Street.
Delicious scents with witty names like Chelsea Flowers, Gramercy Park and Madison Soirée. Or you can have your own custom blended. Branches also at 897 Madison Avenue (212-794 4480) and 9 Bond Street (212-228 1940).

UPPER EAST SIDE

Caron: 715 Lexington Avenue, 877-882 2766, parfumscaron.com. Subway 4, 5, 6 to 59th Street.
The complete range of glitzy, crystal-bottled Caron fragrances, from $80 upwards.

SPAS

CHELSEA

Nickel: 77 8th Avenue at 14th Street, 212-242 3203, heavensspa.com. Subway A, C, E, 9 to 19th Street.
One of the only men-only spas in the city – in a chic, 2-storey haven – offering a wide range of treatments from massages (from $60) to facials and waxing. Book at least 4 weeks in advance.

Sam-C Spa and Margolin Wellness Center: 2nd Floor, 166 5th Avenue at 21st Street, 212-675 9355.
A doctor-meets-spa centre in Chelsea, owned and run by chiropractor Dr Margolin and celebrated masseur Sam-C. Famous treatments include the hydrotherapy tub in which you are immersed in a large, very hot tub of pulsating water while a therapist massages your head and applies cold compresses, and the Sam-C Massage, a unique, intensive body massage. Other treatments include chiropractic, reflexology, acupuncture, body scrubs and steam shower.

MIDTOWN

Affinia Wellness Spa: 125 East 50th Street at Lexington Avenue (The Benjamin Hotel), 212-715 2517, affinia.com. Subway 6, 5 to 51st Street.
A tiny but perfect spa where you can have candlelit massages, hot-salt body scrubs and self-tanning treatments. Also at Oasis Day Spa, Affinia Dumont, 150 East 34th Street, 212-545 5254.

Avon Center Spa: 6th Floor, Trump Tower, 725 5th Avenue between 56th and 57th Streets, 212-755 2866, avoncompany.com.
An incredible space and a wonderful opportunity to enter the spanking Trump Tower for a face and body treatment. Eliza Petrescu is famous for her eyebrow waxings, so book early.

Bliss 57: 3rd floor, 19 East 57th Street between 5th and Madison Avenues, 212-219 8970, blissworld.com. Subway N, R to 59th Street.
Sarah Jessica Parker's favourite spa, which also sells its own skincare range, BlissLabs.

Elizabeth Arden Red Door Salon & Spa: 691 5th Avenue at 54th Street, 212-546 0200, reddoorspas.com. Subway E, V to 5th Avenue/53rd Street.

Elizabeth Arden Red Door Salon & Spa

For the ultimate beautifier, nothing beats the Pomegranate Warm Stone Facial, which promises to firm up skin and deflect damage-inducing free radicals in a trice, with the help of a pomegranate paste.

BRITTIP

For all the latest spa openings and products in the city, log on to spa-nyc.com before you go.

Green Tea Nail & Spa: 141 West 35th Street between Broadway and 7th Avenue, 212-564 6971, greenteanailspa.com. Subway A, C, E to 34th Street/Penn Station.

Nestled in the 34th Street district right next to Macy's is this large Japanese spa in which you are served antioxidant-rich green tea in a clean, minimalist environment. Treatments include waxing, facials, manicures, pedicures and massages. For the perfect pick-me-up-in-an-instant opt for the 10-minute neck massage for $10.

J Sisters International: 35 West 57th Street at 6th Avenue, 212-750 2485, jsisters.com. Subway N, Q, R, W to 57th Street.

Family-run beauty centre famous for its extremely thorough Brazilian waxes. You can also have your make-up, nails and hair done.

Juvenex Spa: 25 West 32nd Street, 5th floor, 646 -733 1330, juvenexspa.com. Subway N, Q, R, W, F, D, B to 34th Street.

An unusual spa with saunas, steam rooms and plunge pools, plus the Jade Igloo made from 20 tonnes of semi-precious stones! It has a big list of treatments, such as hot stone massage, $125 for 60 minutes and reflexology, $65 for 30 minutes.

NYINTHEKNOW

Francisca Ovalle, who works for NYC & Company, has a top tip for partying and preening. 'For cocktails, a favourite is the Beauty Bar (beautybar.com) on 231 East 14th Street. Transformed from a 1950s beauty parlour it offers a martini and manicure for $10 6–11pm Mon–Fri.'

La Prairie Spa: The Ritz Carlton Hotel, 50 Central Park South at 6th Avenue, 212-521 6135, ritzcarlton.com. Subway F, N, R, Q, W to 57th Street.

An extremely high-end spa beloved by celebrities. The Caviar Firming Facial is the signature treatment and rings in at around $260 a go.

Physical Advantage: Penthouse, 139 East 57th Street at Lexington Avenue, 212-460 1879, physical-knead.com. Subway 4, 5, 6 to 59th Street.

This is not the type of spa where you are going to get reiki and reflexology; it's a no-nonsense massage centre often patronised by professional athletes and dancers. The ideal place if you want a treatment without the frills.

SOHO

To get to SoHo, use either the N, R subway lines to Prince Street or the 6, C, E to Spring Street.

Acqua Beauty Bar: 7 East 14th Street between 5th Avenue and Union Square West, 212-620 4329, acquabeautybar.com.

This hip beauty parlour in the ultra trendy

SoHo

TOP 5 NEW SPAS IN NEW YORK

Meatpacking District
G Spa & Lounge: Hotel Gansevoort (page 236).
Situated in the lower level of this chic hotel, which transforms into a VIP hot spot lounge after 9pm. By day you enjoy treatments such as the signature hot stone massage or 45-minute fitness facial in one of 3 red-lit compartments, or you can opt to have your treatment in a cabana on the hotel's wonderful roof top. You can even get your hair chopped at the Hiro Haraguchi satellite salon that lies just past the spa's laser-lit steam room. Très chic.

Midtown
Caudalie Vinotherapie Spa: The Plaza, 5th Avenue at Central Park, 212-265 3182, theplaza. com. Subway 4, 5, 6 to 59th Street.
How to make The Plaza, Manhattan's most famous landmark hotel, even more impressive? Install a multi-million dollar spa with Caudalie, the French beauty house's only US outpost. It mixes wine and spa for the ultimate pampering experience.

Lather Spa: 127 East 57th Street at Lexington Avenue, 212-644 4449, latherspa.com. Subway 4, 5, 6 to 59th Street.
Formerly the Greenhouse Spa, this 3-storey space has now been relaunched as the Lather line's first US store. Check in on the street-level floor where you'll also get your robe and rubber clogs. The relaxation area is great; all white with a skylight and a wall covered with plants and flowers. There are 8 pedi-stations for hands and feet, and a further 15 treatments rooms for facials, massages and body treatments using concoctions of fruits, plants and herbs from around the world. There are men's treatments here, too.

Ohm Spa: 7th floor, 260 5th Avenue at 28th street, 212-481 7892, ohmspa.com. Subway N, R, W to 28th Street.
Aiming to be the antithesis of overly feminine spa design, owners Jonathan Ho and Kathy Yan have come up with clean lines and a gender neutral palette of blue and brown, the message being that men are welcome here, too. As you'd expect, the treatments are similarly straightforward, including massages that target certain muscle groups that give you problems and facials from Dermalogica and Plantogen. You can watch movies on flat-screen TVs while you have a manicure or pedicure.

TriBeCa
Tribeca MedSpa: 114 Hudson Street at Franklin Street, 212-925 9500, tribecamedspa.com. Subway 1 at Franklin Street.
Lots of therapies on the menu dedicated to getting rid of wrinkles. There are 4 treatment rooms, including one for Injectables, such as Botox and Restalyne, which are only given by licensed professionals. If you want something less heavy, there are Medi-Pedis plus Titan skin-tightening and rejuvenation laser treatments. It's rumoured that Robert DeNiro is both the landlord and a customer.

Union Square area offers a full menu of nail, body and face treatments from just $12 for a manicure and $60 for a Bye Bye Eye Bags facial – or splash out on the works for $150!

BRITTIP
The best anti-ageing facial in the Big Apple is the Intense Pulsed Light treatment at Shizuka, a Japanese day spa in Midtown East (7 West 51st Street, 6th Floor, 212-644 7400, shizukany.com).

Amore Pacific: 114 Spring Street between Mercer and Greene Streets, 212-966 0400, amorepacific.com.
A feng shui-influenced spa that uses Korean AP products and where you can have a

Amore Pacific

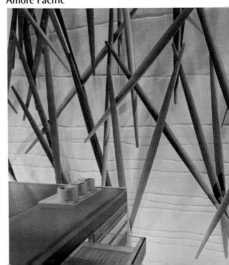

Oasis Day Spa

massage according to your elemental disposition: wood, metal, earth, water or fire.

Bliss Soho: 2nd Floor, 568 Broadway between Houston and Prince Streets, 212-219 8970, blissworld.com.
One of New York's most famous spas, this is the place where you can get it all and in the fastest possible time. You can have a manicure at the same time as your facial and even an underarm wax, too. Therein lies its down side though – for some, it can seem too swift and impersonal.

Inspiration – a Rose Alcido Day Spa: Suite 1005, 1133 Broadway between 25th and 26th Streets, 212-243 0432, rosealcido.com.
A teeny space that's become famous for Rose's signature Golden-Spoon facial. Following a full facial, two hot spoons are used to massage the face, giving an intense, penetrating treatment.

John Masters Organic Spa: 77 Sullivan Street between Spring and Broome Streets, 212-343 9590, johnmasters.com.
Outstanding full-body massages and facials for those who like to ensure all aspects of their life are organic.

Ling Skin Care: 191 Prince Street at Sullivan Street, 212-982 8833, lingskincare.com.
Not big on pampering, so don't expect scented candles, white fluffy robes and feng shui, but extremely good facials from $115 that are considered the best in town by some New Yorkers, including the salon's celebrity clientele.

Maximus Soho: 15 Mercer Street between Grand and Canal Streets, 516-333 4083, maximusspasalon.com. Subway A, C, E, N, Q, R, W to Canal Street.
Treatment rooms that change colour every few seconds for mood enhancement is just one of the reason's to visit this lovely, water-centric spa.

The Mezzanine Spa at Soho Integrative Health Centre: 62 Crosby Street between Broome and Spring Streets, 212-431 1600, mezzaninespa.com.
Dr Laurie Polis founded this tiny spa at her office. Body treatments include volcanic mud therapy, while the Diamond Peel involves suction and microcrystals to exfoliate the face.

Monique K Skin Care: 345 East 9th Street between Avenues A and B, 212-673 2041, moniquek.com/facials.
For an excellent deal on superb facials, head to this East Village hideaway. Owned by Monique K, once head facialist at the famous Georgette Klinger Salon, you get the same quality facials at much better prices.

Oasis Day Spa: 150 East 34th Street between Lexington and 3rd Avenues, 212-254 7722, oasisdayspanyc.com. Subway 6 to 33rd Street.
Get off the beaten track for a truly relaxing experience at one of New York's best-kept secrets. Here you'll escape all elements of hustle and bustle in a sweet-smelling space where you are given your own massage slippers and a comfy robe. Fab therapies include a deep-penetrating Lava Stone Massage for $100, or an exquisite facial with customised face mask and warm hand mitts for $95.

Prema Nolita: 252 Elizabeth Street between Houston and Prince Streets, 212-226 3972. Subway 6 to Spring Street.
Thought to be the smallest spa in town, Celeste Induddi and her two partners have just one treatment room, but sell their own Prema line plus celeb faves Jurlique and Anne Semonin.

SoHo Sanctuary: 3rd Floor, 119 Mercer Street at Princes Street, 212-334 5550, sohosanctuary.com.

TOP 5 SPAS FOR MINOR COSMETIC SURGERY

You're visiting one of the leading cities in the world for beauty treatments, including minor cosmetic surgeries such as laser eye treatment or Botox. Many tourists even combine a long weekend of shopping with a trip to a clinic so that they can return to the UK looking 10 years younger!

If you're considering a minor treatment, make sure that the spa or beauty centre is registered, book well in advance as they tend to get booked up quickly, and be sure to have a consultation prior to any treatment so that you understand exactly what you're getting. Below are 5 highly rated spas regularly used by New Yorkers, from celebrities to Upper East Side ladies who lunch.

Midtown

Sleek New York: 800B 5th Avenue at 61st Street, 212-521 3100, sleekmedspa.com. Subway 4, 5, 6 to 59th Street.
Nurses, practitioners and dermatologists are on hand at this no-nonsense clinic to treat a wide variety of skin issues, from wrinkles to spots. Treatments include glycolic peels, Botox, microdermabrasion, beta for acne, and laser hair removal.

Smooth Synergy: 686 Lexington Avenue at East 57th Street, 212-397 0111, smoothsynergy. com. Subway 4, 5, 6 to 59th Street.
Laser hair and tattoo removal, microdermabrasion, Botox, vein therapy and glycolic peels are just some of the many treatments on offer at this highly regarded spa.

Upper East Side

Ajune: 1294 3rd Avenue at 74th Street, 212-628 0044, ajune.com. Subway 6 to 77th Street.
Experts in laser wrinkle reduction, collagen implants and Botox, all administered in a tranquil setting with slate floors and wooden features.

Dr Ronald Sherman/Trish McEvoy Skincare Centre: 4th Floor, 800A 5th Avenue at 61st Street, trishmcevoy.com, 212-758 7790. Subway N, R to 5th Avenue.
Laser hair removal, Botox and skin cancer examinations can be had at the make-up guru and top dermatologist's skincare Mecca.

Howard Sobel Skin & Spa: 960 Park Avenue at 82nd Street, 212-288 0060, drsobel.com. Subway 4, 5, 6 to 86th Street.
Award-winning specialists in Botox treatments.

Fabulous massages in this mellow favourite of the fashion pack. There are also yoga and Pilates classes, plus a steam room.

ANTIQUES AND FLEA MARKETS

In balmy weather, nothing beats strolling through the treasure trove of antiques, collectables and one-off pieces at any of New York's outdoor markets or in some of the unusual individual shops.

CHELSEA

Chelsea Antiques Building: 110 West 25th Street between 6th and 7th Avenues, 212-929 0909. Subway F, V to 23rd Street.
This 12-storey building houses 90 galleries of antiques and collectables with merchandise ranging from Japanese textiles to vintage phonographs and radios.

The Garage: 112 West 25th Street between 6th and 7th Avenues, 212-647 0707. Subway F, V to 23rd Street.

The Garage is exactly that – a 2-storey parking garage that transforms into another bustling venue at the weekend.

The Showplace: 40 West 25th Street, 212-741 8520, nyshowplace.com. Subway F, V to 23rd Street.
An indoor extension of the outdoor market (open at weekends only), with a small café downstairs.

Upper West Side

EAST VILLAGE

Irreplaceable Artifacts & Demolition Depot: 216 East 125th Street between 2nd and 3rd Avenues, 212-860 1138, demolitiondepot.com.
An excellent selection of architectural bits and bobs, from religious objects to vintage shutters.

GREENWICH VILLAGE

Alan Moss: 436 Lafayette Street near Astor Place, 212-473 1310, alanmossny.com. Subway 6 to Astor Place.
Glass gems and interesting lighting from the mid-20th century.

HELL'S KITCHEN

Annex/Hell's Kitchen Flea Market: 39th Street between 9th and 10th Avenues, 212-243 5343, hellskitchenfleamarket.com. Subway A, C, E or 1, 2, 3, 9 to 34th/42nd Streets.
Now includes The Annex, America's most famous outdoor market, where celebrities browse through vintage clothing, furniture, pottery, glassware, jewellery and art. Get there early for the best finds. Weekends only.

MADISON SQUARE

Old Print Shop: 150 Lexington Avenue between East 29th and East 30th Streets, 212-683 3950, oldprintshop.com. Subway 6 to 33rd Street.
This is the place to search out Americana up to the 1950s.

MIDTOWN EAST

Lillian Nassau: 220 East 57th Street between 2nd and 3rd Avenues, 212-759 6062, lilliannassau.com. Subway 4, 5, 6 to 59th Street.
Come here for art nouveau lamps and glassware, especially original Tiffany.

Manhattan Arts & Antiques Center: 1050 2nd Avenue between East 55th and East 56th Streets, 212-355 4400, the-maac.com. Subway 4, 5, 6, to 59th Street; F, N, R, W to Lexington Avenue.

SOHO

Coconut Company: 131 Greene Street near Prince Street, 212-539 1940. Subway N, R to Prince Street.
A fascinating, eclectic mix of 19th- and 20th-century antiques, from photographs and books to coffee tables.

The SoHo Antiques Fair: Broadway and Grand Street.
Antiques and collectables all year round.

BRITTIP

If you're in the Big Apple on a Wed, check out the Fulton Street Plaza Flea Market at Cliff Street between Fulton and Beekham Streets near South Street Seaport. There's an outdoor market with around 25 dealers. 212-809 5000, keysfleamarket.com.

TRIBECA

Antiqueria Tribeca: 129 Duane Street near Broadway, 212-227 7500, antiqueria.com. Subway 1, 2, 3, 9, A, C to Chambers Street.
Filled with French Art Deco pieces, from furniture to accessories. Often some lovely Lalique and Murano glass items to be found.

Burden & Izett Ltd: 180 Duane Street near Houston Street, 212-941 8247, burdenandizett.net. Subway 1, 2, 3, 9, A, C to Chambers Street.
Extremely pricey, high-end, one-of-a-kind pieces of furniture to gaze at in awe.

SoHo street market

UPPER EAST and WEST SIDES

Green Flea Market: Greenwich Avenue at Charles Street between West 10th and 11th Streets on Sat 10am–5.30pm and Columbus Avenue between West 76th and 77th Streets on Sun 10am–5.30pm, 212-239 3025, greenfleamarkets.com. Subway 1, 9 to 79th Street; B, C to 77th/81st Street.
Antiques, collectables, bric-a-brac, handmade pottery and discount clothing in this indoor and outdoor market.

BOOKS

Books are big business in New York and book readings are a popular form of entertainment. For a real slice of the New York lifestyle, there are a number of places that specialise in readings: **The Drawing Center** (35 Wooster Street between Grand and Broome Streets, 212-694 0910, drawingcenter.org) gives readings related to the exhibitions; **The Poetry Project** at St Mark's Church (131 East 10th Street, 212-674 0910, poetryproject.org) has 3 evening readings a week, Mon and Wed 8pm, Fri 10.30pm.

The **92nd Street Y** (1395 Lexington Avenue, 212-414 5500, 92y.org) has a great series of lectures and readings, as does **The Dia Center for the Arts** (548 West 22nd Street, 212-989 5566, diacenter.org). Also check out **Barnes & Noble** (page 152) and **192 Books** (below) for more.

CHELSEA

192 Books: 912 10th Avenue between 21st and 22nd Streets, 212-255 4022, 192books. com. Subway C, E to 23rd Street.
A good range of art and literature titles as well as a large children's section. The atmosphere in this bright, airy shop is very comfortable, with reading tables and comfy chairs to help you relax. There are weekly readings here.

EAST VILLAGE

Alabaster Bookshop: 122 4th Avenue at 12th Street, 212-982 3550, alabaster bookshop.visualnetcom. Subway 4, 5, 6, L, N, Q, R, W at 14th Street, Union Square.
Only one used bookstore remains on what was once book row. Owner Steve Crowley is still there with a great array of paperbacks that are around half the cover price, to rare photography books by the likes of Lou Reed, locked in ornate wood cabinets. There are carts to trawl through on the sidewalk, too.

St Mark's Bookshop: 31 3rd Avenue on the corner of 9th Street, 212-260 7853, stmarksbookshop.com. Subway 6 to Astor Place.
An excellent bookstore established in 1977 with a broad range of books. The bulletin board in the front gives details of local literary events.

GREENWICH VILLAGE

Shakespeare & Co: 716 Broadway at Washington Place, 212-529 1330, shakeandco.com. Subway N, R to 8th Street; 6 to Astor Place.
This is an excellent bookstore. Unlike many a Barnes & Noble, where the staff sometimes don't appear to recognise joined-up writing, all the assistants here are graduates and will be genuinely helpful.

MIDTOWN

Rizzoli: 31 West 57th Street between 5th and 6th Avenues, 212-759 2424, rizzoliusa.com. Subway N, R, W to 5th Avenue/59th Street; F to 57th Street.
This trendy store has a good stock of art, fashion and design publications and is popular with those in the media and with design students.

MIDTOWN EAST

Argosy: 116 East 59th between Park and Lexington Avenues, 212-753 4455, argosybooks.com. Subway 4, 5, 6, F, N, R to 59th Street.
The best bookshop in New York if you're looking for rare, hard-to-find books. There are 7 storeys of out-of-print publications, antiques, maps, autographs and letters to browse through. Beware, though: you can easily lose an afternoon engrossed in here.

News stand

Borders Books & Music: 461 Park Avenue at 57th Street, 212-980 6785, borders.com. Subway N, R to Lexington Avenue; 4, 5, 6 to 59th Street.
Excellent outlet for books, CDs, DVDs and more obscure books, too. A few other megastores throughout the city.

Urban Centre Books: 457 Madison Avenue, between East 50th and East 51st Streets, 212-935 3595, urbancenterbooks.org. Subway 6 to 51st Street; E, F to 5th Avenue.
Housed in the pretty Villard Houses, this bookstore is a treasure trove for anyone interested in architecture and buildings.

NOLITA

Tower Books: 383 Lafayette Street at 4th Street, 212-228 5100, tower.com. Subway B, D, F, Q to Broadway/Lafayette; 6 to Bleecker Street.
A wide range of contemporary fiction and a huge magazine section.

WEST VILLAGE

Biography Bookshop: 400 Bleecker Street at West 11th Street, 212-807 8655. Subway 1, 2, 3 to 14th Street.
A massive selection of biographies covering all genres.

Bookleaves: 304 West 4th Street near Bank Street, 212-924 5638. Subway 1, 2, 3 or A, C, E or L to 14th Street.
Just what you imagine a New York bookstore to be like: dusty, quiet and tucked away in a neighbourhood and offering a fabulous selection of everything from paperbacks to out-of-print pricey tomes.

Three Lives Bookstore: 154 West 10th Street off 7th Avenue, 212-741 2069, threelives.com.
A delightful shop with a charming ambience,

known for attentive staff with encyclopaedic knowledge. Specialises in literary fiction, poetry and design books, as well as memoirs.

UNION SQUARE

Barnes & Noble: 105 5th Avenue at 18th Street, 212-675 5500, bnnewyork.com. Subway L, N, R, 4, 5, 6 to 14th Street/Union Square.
This is the original store of one of the largest chains of bookstores in America and offers a massive selection of books, CDs and DVDs. Barnes & Noble is responsible for putting many independent bookstores out of business, but is well worth a visit. Many branches have coffee shops and seating areas for you to browse before buying. You'll see branches everywhere.

Books of Wonder: 18 West 18th Street at 5th Avenue, 212-989 3270, booksof wonder. net. Subway 1 at 18th Street.
Top place in New York to go for children's books, limited editions and art from children's literature. There are rare collector's editions through to picture pop-ups, and as many adults flock here as kids. There's a storytelling time to 3- to 6-year-olds every Sun at noon.

BRITTIP
If shopping's sapping your energy and you're feeling in need of a sugar rush, tuck into some of the delicious desserts and pastries at the Cupcake Cafe in Books of Wonder.

Strand Book Store: 828 Broadway at 12th Street, 212-473 1452, strandbooks.com. Subway L, N, R, Q, W, 4, 5, 6 to 14th Street/ Union Square.
This whole area used to be famous for antiquarian bookshops, but the Strand is the only one left. The store has over 2 million second-hand and new books on any subject you'd care to name – all at around half the published price.

CHILDREN

MIDTOWN

The Disney Store: 711 5th Avenue between 55th and 5th Streets, 212-702 0702, worldofdisney.com. Subway E, F to 5th Avenue. Also at 218 West 42nd Street, 212-302 0595. Subway 1, 2, 3, 9, N, R to Times Square/42nd Street.
If it comes with a pair of ears, then you'll find it here!

FAO Schwarz: 767 5th Avenue at 58th Street, 212-644 9400 ext. 4242, fao.com. Subway N, R to 5th Avenue.

Biography Bookshop

Toys R Us

The most famous children's store in the world, it's not only huge but is also an entertainment centre in its own right, with oversized displays that take your breath away, plus every conceivable toy your child could want.

BRITTIP
If you stay at the Ritz-Carlton Hotel in Battery Park City, you'll be entitled to a 10% discount at FAO Schwarz.

Hershey's Times Square: 48th Street and Broadway, 212-581 9100, hersheys.com. Subway N, R, S, 1, 2, 3, 7, 9, A, C, E to 42nd Street/Times Square.
The Cadbury's of America now has a massive chocolate haven in Times Square. Enter (at your peril) under the 65m/215ft tall, 18m/60ft wide giant Hershey bar to find every kind of Hershey sweet under the sun, as well as clothing, toys and giant chocolate greetings cards.

Toys R Us: 1514 Broadway between 44th and 45th Streets, 212-225 8392, toysrus. com. Subway N, Q, R, S, W, 1, 2, 3, 7 to Times Square.
In the heart of the rejuvenated Times Square

district, this 3-storey, glass-enclosed building is home to an 18m/60ft Ferris wheel, a giant roaring dinosaur and a life-size Barbie townhouse. If you are here with kids, it's a must-see.

DRINK

CHELSEA
Chelsea Wine Vault: 75 9th Avenue at Chelsea Market, 212-462 4244, chelseawinevault.com. Subway A, C, E to 14th Street.
More than 3,000 labels to choose from. Take advantage of the fun free tastings – mainly at weekends (see website).

BRITTIP
Don't be fooled by the bottles of wine you may see in food shops in New York. They are either non-alcoholic or low alcohol as it is illegal for food stores to sell wine. However, this doesn't apply to beer.

EAST VILLAGE
Astor Wines & Spirits: 399 Lafayette Street at 4th Street at the corner of Astor Place, 212-674 7500, astorwines.com. Subway 6 to

Union Square Wines and Spirits

Astor Place; R, W to 8th Street.
Stocks a wide range of wines and spirits.

MIDTOWN EAST

Park Avenue Liquor Shop: 292 Madison Avenue between 40th and 41st Streets, 212-685 2442, parkaveliquor.com. Subway 4, 5, 6, 7 to Grand Central/42nd Street.
Specialises in Californian wines and European bottles. Discounts are given with bulk purchases.

Schumer's Wine & Liquor: 59 East 54th Street between Park and Madison Avenues, 212-355 0940, schumerswines.com. Subway E, F to Lexington Avenue; 6 to 51st Street.
With a great range of American and European wines, it also stocks a good selection of spirits and champagne.

UNION SQUARE

Union Square Wine and Spirits: 33 Union Square West between 16th and 17th Streets, 212-675 8100, unionsquarewines.com. Subway 4, 5, 6, L, N, Q, R, W to Union Square.
More than 4,000 wines, good prices and the staff know their wines.

UPPER EAST SIDE/YORKVILLE

Best Cellars: 1291 Lexington Avenue at 87th Street, 212-426 4200, bestcellars.com. Subway 4, 5, 6 to 86th Street.
One of the best-value stores in the city for fine wines under $10. Free tastings every weekday 5–8pm, Sat 2–4pm paired with food from top new chefs are even better value!

Sherry-Lehmann: 679 Madison Avenue between 61st and 62nd Streets, 212-838 7500, sherry-lehmann.com. Subway 4, 5, 6 to 59th Street.
The most famous wine shop in New York, established in 1934. A huge selection and well situated for that Central Park picnic.

UPPER WEST SIDE

Acker, Merrall & Condit Wine Merchants: 160 West 72nd Street between Broadway and Columbus, 212-787 1700, ackerstore.com.

Subway 1, 2, 3, 9 to 72nd Street.
America's oldest wine store – it opened in 1820 – is well worth a visit for its vast selection of wines from around the world that range in price from a couple of dollars to more than $20,000. In-store tastings.

ELECTRONICS

Have a clear idea of what you're looking for before buying – pick up a copy of Tues' *New York Times* to check out prices in the science section first. Of course, you can always find electrical items at really cheap prices in the Chinatown stretch of Canal Street, but you won't get a guarantee.

CHELSEA

Adorama: 42 West 18th Street near 6th Avenue, 212-741 0052, adorama.com. Subway 1, 9 to 18th Street.
Six floors that cover all your photographic needs, from disposable cameras through to $10,000 professional snappers. In addition, it offers a range of other services including creating digital prints for 20c each.

MADISON SQUARE MIDTOWN

Datavision Computer Video: 445 5th Avenue near 39th Street, 212-689 1111, datavis.com. Subway 7, B, D, F, V to 42nd Street/5th Avenue.
You'll find whatever techie treat you desire, from laptops to iPod accessories, in this cramped but comprehensive store.

Harvey Electronics: 2 West 45th Street at 5th Avenue, 212-575 5000, harveyonline.com. Subway B, D, F, V to 42nd Street/Bryant Park.
Not bargain basement prices, but specialists where you are guaranteed great products and deals. Stocks a good selection of top brands such as Fujitsu and Pioneer.

34TH STREET–PENN STATION

B&H Photo & Video: 420 9th Avenue between West 33rd and West 34th Streets, 212-444 6615, bhphotovideo.com. Subway A, C, E to 34th Street/Penn Station.
A massive 3-storey, block-long store that stocks every conceivable piece of electronic imaging, audio, video and photo equipment you've ever heard of. All the staff are professionals in their own right and really know their onions. They're helpful, too, which is why this emporium is an excellent place to go for everyone from novices to professionals.

Willoughby's: 136 West 32nd Street between 6th and 7th Avenues, 212-564 1600, willoughbys.com. Subway B, D, F, Q, N, R, V, W, 1, 2, 3 to 34th Street.
Reputedly the world's largest collection of cameras and all things audio, but the service isn't brilliant so make sure you know what you want before you go.

FOOD

CHELSEA

Chelsea Market: 75 9th Avenue between 15th and 16th Streets, 212-243 6005, chelseamarket.com. Subway A, C, E, L to 14th Street and 8th Avenue.
You'll find everything you need here for a gourmet feast, from fishmongers and bakers to wine merchants, and even florists for table decorations. Check out Buon Italia for great cheeses, sauces and all manner of Italian fodder and Amy's for breads you never dreamed of. An instant picnic!

CHINATOWN

Asia Market: 71 Mulberry Street between Canal and Bayar Streets, 212-962 2020. Subway 6, J, M, N, Q, R, W, Z to Canal Street. The tightly packed Asia Market is loved by chefs and residents alike. There's everything here from canned curries to dried cuttlefish and dozens of varieties of noodles; every staple of Thai, Malaysian and Indonesian cuisine under one roof.

GREENWICH VILLAGE

Take the subway A, C, E, F, V, S to West 4th Street for a whole area of foodie shops.

Aphrodisia: 264 Bleecker Street between 6th and 7th Avenues, 212-989 6440, aphrodisiaherbshoppe.com.
A huge selection of bulk herbs, spices, teas and potpourri.

Balducci's: 155A West 66th Street, near the Lincoln Center just west of Broadway, 212-653 8320, balduccis.com.
One of the most famous gourmet food emporiums in New York. You can find everything from fresh vegetables and fruit to edible flowers and hung game.

BRITTIP

If you'd like a taste of the foods sold in some of the shops in Greenwich Village, go on the Foods of New York tour, which also introduces you to great restaurants in the area (page 87).

Faicco's Pork Store: 260 Bleecker Street between 6th and 7th Avenues, 212-243 1974. A landmark Italian speciality food shop established in 1900, it is known for its own sausages that are made daily (and sold to many of the neighbouring restaurants), its home-made mozzarella cheese, again made daily, plus rice balls made with three cheeses and rolled in breadcrumbs. Other specialities include prosciutto balls, potato croquettes, fried ravioli and stuffed breads.

Murray's Cheese Shop: 254 Bleecker Street between 6th and 7th Avenues, 212-243 3289, murrayscheese.com.
The owner travels all over the world to bring back a fascinating selection of more than 350 cheeses with amazing names such as Wabash Cannonball, Crocodile Tears, Mutton Buttons and Cardinal Sin, a British cow's milk cheese. They also sell olives, chorizos, pâtés and breads and you may even catch a cookery class.

Pasticceria Bruno: 506 Laguardia Place, 212-982 5854, pasticceriabruno.com.
An Italian-French bakery run by one of the top 10 pastry chefs in New York. It does miniature and large fruit tarts, mousses, cookies, sorbets, ice-cream cakes and home-made chocolates, and you can sit down to try any of them with a nice cup of tea or coffee.

Rocco's: 243 Bleecker Street between 6th and 7th Avenues, 212-242 6031, roccospastry.com.

Chelsea Market

Famous for its fresh cannolis (an Italian pastry filled with cream), it sells large and small sizes of everything from Italian cheesecakes to chocolate, hazelnut and lemon cakes. You can eat in, too, with a cup of delicious coffee.

LITTLE ITALY

Di Palo's: 200 Grand Street at Mott Street, 212-226 1033, dipaloselects.com. Subway J, M, N, Q, R, W, Z, 6 to Canal Street.
One of the last remaining Italian speciality food stores in Little Italy, it was founded 80 years ago and is particularly famous for its mozzarella and Italian sausages and salami. It even has its own ageing room for cheeses.

LOWER EAST SIDE

Russ & Daughters: 179 East Houston Street between Allen and Orchard Streets, 212-475 4880, russanddaughters.com. Subway F to 2nd Avenue.
Along with Katz's Deli (page 171), this is one of the most famous outlets in the Lower East Side. Established in 1914, it sells every possible kind of fish, caviar, pickled vegetables and bagels.

SOHO

Dean & Deluca: 560 Broadway at Prince Street, 212-226 6800, deandeluca.com. Subway N, R, Q, W to Prince Street.
Gourmets love the fresh bread, cheese, coffee beans and other delicious foods on sale at this SoHo secret.

34TH STREET

Cucina & Co: In the Cellar at Macy's (page 125), 151 West 34th Street, 6th Avenue and Broadway, 212-868 2388, patina.com. Subway B, D, F, N, Q, R, V, W to 34th Street.
One of the most fabulous grocer's markets in New York, now famous for its supplies of lobster and caviar.

Taxis are a great way to get around

UPPER EAST SIDE/YORKVILLE

Martine's Chocolates: 400 82nd Street off 1st Avenue, 212-744 6289, martineschocolates.com. Subway 6 to 86th Street.
If you're not on a diet, drool over the rich Belgian choccies, which take up to 3 days to make. Chocolate heaven!

The Vinegar Factory: 431 East 91st Street between York and 1st Avenues, 212-987 0885, elizabar.com/zabar/. Subway 4, 5, 6 to 86th Street.
One of the most famous markets in the city. Here you'll find stacks of cheeses, meats, breads, salads and cakes – in fact, everything you need to create a perfect picnic.

HOMEWARE

CHELSEA

Authentiques Past & Present: 255 West 18th Street at 8th Avenue, 212-675 2179, fab-stuff.com. Subway 1 to 18th Street.
A must-visit for lovers of interiors from the 1950s and 60s. The long attic-style room is like a time capsule stocking fab American glass, barware, kitchen items, lamps and lots of cool kitsch items.

GREENWICH VILLAGE

Broadway Panhandler: 65 East 8th Street, between Broadway and University, 212-966 3434, broadwaypanhandler.com. Subway N, R, W to 8th Street.
All things for the kitchen, from the latest gadgets to classic pieces such as steel saucepans and Alessi toasters. There are hundreds of items to choose from and it's a must-visit for any domestic gods or goddesses when in town. Famous chefs often give in-store demonstrations.

MIDTOWN

Crate & Barrel: 650 Madison Avenue at 59th Street, 212-308 0011, crateandbarrel.com. Subway 4, 5, 6 to 59th Street.
Fashionable, funky furniture, accessories, kitchen and tableware for incredibly low prices. There's also another branch in SoHo at 611 Broadway at Houston Street.

SOHO

Anthropologie: 375 West Broadway at Spring Street, 212-343 7070, anthropologie.com. Subway C, E to Spring Street.
One of my favourite shops selling gorgeous boudoir items, such as silk quilts, Venetian-style mirrors and night stands, in an airy loft-like space. There's also a collection of stylish women's clothes on sale with the same thrift-store, trendy feel.

UPPER EAST SIDE

Charlotte Moss: 20 East 63rd Street at Madison Avenue, 212-308 3888, charlottemoss.com. Subway 4, 5, 6 at 59th Street.
Newly opened gorgeous townhouse filled with expensive items you'll want to snap up for your own home, from doorknobs to stools and even the bedroom floor.

Laytner's Linen and Home: 237 East 86th Street at 2nd Avenue, 212-996 4439, laytners.com. Subway 4, 5, 6 to 86th Street.
Come here to buy some luxurious high thread-count linen to take home.

UPPER WEST SIDE

Avventura: 463 Amsterdam Avenue at 82nd Street, 212-769 2510, forthatspecialgift.com. Subway A, 9 to 79th Street.
Contemporary tableware, from cocktail and champagne glasses to Deruta dishes.

MUSIC STORES

EAST VILLAGE

A-1 Records: 439 East 6th Street at Avenues A, 212-473 2870. Subway F, V at Lower East Side, Second Avenue.
Geared towards those still interested in vinyl, with a focus on soul, jazz, hip-hop and an ever-changing assortment of house and dance. You can listen to records in store before you buy and A-1 has just joined dailysession.com, so you can tune in to live broadcasts before you even visit the store!

Downtown Music Gallery: 342 Bowery between East 2nd and East 3rd Streets, 212-473 0043, downtownmusicgallery.com. Subway 6 to Astor Place.
Jazz aficionados love this specialist shop with its wide selection of records and CDs to search through. Live performances take place Sun 6pm.

FINANCIAL DISTRICT

J&R Music World: 23 Park Row between Ann and Beekman Streets, 212-238 9000, jr.com. Subway A or C to Broadway/Nassau Street.
The weekly ads in the *New York Post* and *Village Voice* give an idea of what's on offer. They sell jazz, Latin and pop as well as loads of cheap electronic gear like cameras and iPods.

GREENWICH VILLAGE

Bleecker Bob's Golden Oldies Record Shop: 118 West 3rd Street at MacDougal Street, 212-475 9677, bleeckerbobs.com. Subway A, B, C, D, E, F, V to West 4th Street.
Whatever sounds you're into, you'll find something to satisfy your tastes. Choose from thousands of jazz, rock, punk and R&B vinyls and now CDs and DVDs, too.

Tower Records: 692 Broadway at 4th Street, 212-505 1500, towerrecords.com. Subway N, R, W to 8th Street.
An excellent range of CDs and tapes. Around the block on Lafayette Street is the knockdown Tower Clearance shop.

SPECIALITY AND GIFT SHOPS

CHELSEA

Chelsea Merit Florist: 237 8th Avenue, 800-488 3577, chelseamerit.net. Subway 1, 2, 3, 7, N, Q, R, S, W to Times Square/42nd Street.
Just in case you need to grab some flowers while you're away – a birthday or anniversary! – this is a great florist to visit with competitive prices with bouquets starting at around $50.

MIDTOWN

Midtown Comics: 2nd floor, 200 West 40th Street at 7th Avenue, 212-302 8192, midtowncomics.com. Subway 1, 2, 3, 7, N, Q, R, S, W to Times Square/42nd Street.
A 2-storey comic emporium with bags of back issues running up and down the length of the store. 500,000 volumes are available, from Japanese manga to Spider-Man.

UPPER EAST SIDE

E.A.T. Gifts: 1062 Madison Avenue at 80th Street, 212-861 2544, elizabar.com. Subway 6 to 77th Street.
You can hardly move for the shelves that are tightly packed with every conceivable gift, from gadgets to trinkets, a lot of it fun stuff for kids.

WEST VILLAGE

Alphaville: 226 West Houston Street at Varwick Street, 212-675 6850, alphaville.com. Subway 1 to Houston Street.
Nostalgia-lovers and design geeks need to make a stop at this unique store and gallery, which offers an excellent range of mid-century vintage toys and posters. Original Mr Potato Heads sit in their original packaging next to 1950s rocket-shaped water pistols. Movie buffs will want to part with their cash for the vintage film posters and covet the iconic action figures from film and TV.

Flight 001: 96 Greenwich Avenue between Jane and West 12th Streets, 212-691 1001, flight001.com. Subway 1, 2, 3, 9 to 14th Street.

A travel accessories shop that looks like a sleek 1960s airport lounge, it stocks fabulously cool carry-on items such as digital cameras, spray-on vitamins and WAP-activated global travel guides. It also has practical but funky luggage.

MXYPLYZYK: 125 Greenwich Avenue at West 13th Street, 212-989 4300, mxyplyzyk.com. Subway 1, 2, 3, 9 to 14th Street.
Kitschy-cool gifts and whatnots including Devil Ducks (with horns – glow-in-the-dark or plain red) and tractor-seat stools for when you're tired of serious shopping.

Tea and Sympathy: 110 Greenwich Avenue between 12th and 13th Streets, 212-989 9735, teaandsympathynewyork.com. Subway 1, 2, 3, 9 to 14th Street.
Filled with all things the Brit abroad loves, this is a combination of a shop and café offering sausage rolls, fish and chips and 'proper' tea. Liz Hurley orders food for her fashion shoots, David Bowie had his 50th birthday bash here, and Kate Moss and Rupert Everett are regulars.

WOODBURY COMMON PREMIUM OUTLETS

It's no exaggeration to say that shopaholics from around the world call in at this American colonial-style village that's just a 1½-hour bus ride away from Manhattan. With more than 220 discount shops, it's the equivalent of paradise. For ordinary folk, it's still a wonderful place to make useful and fun purchases. Midweek is the quietest time to visit.

WOODBURY COMMON SHOPPING

- ✉ 498 Red Apple Court, Central Valley
- ☎ 1-845 928 4000
- ⌂ premiumoutlets.com/woodburycommon
- ⊙ Mon–Sat 10am–9pm, Sun 10am–8pm (check the website for seasonal and holiday hours)

Upon arrival by Gray Line (800-669 0051), you'll be dropped off close to the tower entrance where you'll also find the information office, pushchairs (essential with a young child on a hot day), lockers, telephones, cashpoints and WCs.

Pick up a copy of the full-colour Shopping Guide (or download one from the website before you go) and in the centre you'll find a map with the 5 different sections in different colours. The colour coding is carried throughout the village, so as you walk around

you can work out which area you are in by the colour of the apple above each shop sign.

The information tower is in the main red section, called Red Apple Court, which is largely dedicated to designer boutiques; to its south is Evergreen Court, home to many lifestyle stores; to the north of Red Apple Court is the Food Court and then Bluebird Court. To the left from the main entrance is the purple Grapevine Court.

Filled with the most upscale designer shops, Grapevine Court is serious droolsville territory and the first port of call for Japanese shoppers, who tend to be known as Goochers thanks to their love of Gucci. Here you'll find Betsey Johnson, Chanel, Christian Dior, Fendi, Giorgio Armani General Store, Hugo Boss, Missoni, Nieman Marcus Last Call, Off 5th – Saks 5th Avenue, La Perla, Valentino and the Thyme To Eat Restaurant. The Cosmetics Company Store here has great deals on many brands including Clinique, Estée Lauder, Bobbi Brown, MAC, Prescriptives and Origins.

Big names in Red Apple Court include A/X Armani Exchange, Burberry, Brooks Brothers, Carolina Herrera, Donna Karan/DKNY, Escada, Giorgio Armani, Gucci, Liz Claiborne, Polo Ralph Lauren, Salvatore Ferragamo and Versace.

Good shops that you should make a beeline for in the Bluebird Court are Claire's Accessories, Bombay Outlet, OshKosh B'Gosh, Perfumania, Puma, LeSportsac, Bebe and Nike Factory Store.

In the Evergreen Court you will discover other great stores such as Lancôme – The Company Outlet, Timberland, the Zegna Outlet Store, Benetton, Banana Republic, Reebok and Claiborne Menswear.

SALES TIMES

You can save even more money on your favourite labels by heading to Woodbury at sales times. Before you go, visit premiumoutlets.com/woodburycommon to check out the next sales date – there's usually one a month. However, the big sales times coincide with all the American holidays including 4 July, Memorial Day, President's Day, Labor Day Weekend, Columbus Day and the day after Thanksgiving (page 272).

Best time of all, though, is around Christmas, when some of the biggest savings are to be had – along with the biggest crowds, so arrive early!

STAYING NEAR WOODBURY COMMON

The Orange County Bed & Breakfast Association offers shop-and-stay packages, 800-210 5565, new-york-inns.com.

CHAPTER 7
Restaurants

New York is a city of extremes when it comes to dining out. There are nearly 18,000 restaurants to choose from. At one end are the classics, such as Union Square Café, that seem to transcend fashion and continually turn out delicious cuisine to cross the Atlantic for; at the other end of the spectrum are eateries that are so hip they're practically going out of fashion before they've even served up their first plate of fusion food.

Brit Guide aims to help you to experience the must-eat-at places that have been around for years and those achingly hip joints that are as much about who you're going to spot air kissing as the food. We also include a smattering of restaurants that sit between the established and the new that are just plain good value – or unusual.

BRITTIP

New Yorkers swear by the *Zagat Survey* as the best guide for foodies. It lists hundreds of top restaurants reviewed by members of the public, and you can buy it in most UK bookshops, or visit zagat.com.

One of the great things about New York restaurants is that they're usually excellent value for money when compared with eating out in the UK, particularly London. You can get a first class breakfast for under $10 and a slap-up dinner for less than $40. It's well worth heading off the beaten track to find some of your own delectable diners in the city's coolest neighbourhoods, but we have plenty of suggestions for you if you don't fancy chancing it. The chapter starts with a selection of our favourite restaurants for fine dining, romance and views, categories that cover the majority of enquiries we receive from Brits keen to sample the culinary delights of Manhattan in a wonderful environment.

DINING PRICE GUIDE

It's clear from the outset what price categories many Big Apple eateries fall into. Crisp white tablecloths, wine glasses the size of goldfish bowls and waiters in designer garb indicate a blow-the-budget $100-plus bill. Dark, dingy diners with Formica tabletops and a waitress with a nametag suggest that you're going to be paying cash, and not much of it. However, there are some restaurants where the tariff doesn't match the decor or the standard of food the façade, so we have compiled a price guide to help you make your dining decisions with confidence.

$	Cheap and cheerful
$$	Good value
$$$	Posh meal out
$$$$	Blow the budget

Restaurant Row, 46th Street and 9th

BRITTIP

If you're a foodie, visit New York during Restaurant Week (see website for exact dates, there's more than one), when more than 100 of the city's best restaurants offer 3-course prix fixe meals for bargain prices around $24 for lunch and $35 for dinner. (212-484 1222, nycgo. com/restaurantweek).

A–Z AREA-BY-AREA GUIDE TO RESTAURANTS

BATTERY PARK AND BATTERY PARK CITY

2 WEST $$–$$$
American fusion
- ✉ 2 West Street between Battery Place and West End
- ☎ 212-344 0800
- 🖰 ritzcarlton.com
- 🚇 Subway 1, 9 to Rector Street

The lobby-level restaurant of the Ritz-Carlton has fabulous views of the Hudson River and Statue of Liberty, plus outdoor seating for al fresco dining in the warmer months. Menu is full of classic comfort food, such as lobster bisque, croque monsieur, organically fed salmon and oven-roasted free-range chicken. There's a vast wine list and the lunch menu also offers quick and easy Bento Boxes with Italian and Spanish themes.

BATTERY GARDENS $$$$
Gourmet American
- ✉ South-west corner of Battery Park (State Street) by the river
- ☎ 212-809 5508
- 🖰 batterygardens.com
- 🚇 Subway 1, 9 to South Ferry

A superb American restaurant in an elegant, glass building that shows off the spectacular views of the Hudson and East rivers and

Battery Gardens

the Statue of Liberty from every table. In good weather you can eat outside on the terrace. Sumptuous American dishes with an Asian inflection may include miso-glazed Chilean sea bass with jasmine rice, shiitake mushrooms and haricots verts or Amish chicken breast with roasted chestnuts, broccoli flan and sherry mushroom sauce. If you can't get in at night, book the excellent Sunday brunch, 11am–3pm.

GIGINO AT WAGNER PARK $$
Italian
- ✉ 20 Battery Place at Hudson River
- ☎ 212-528 2228
- 🖰 gigino-wagnerpark.com
- 🚇 Subway 1, 9 to South Ferry

Great little café/diner with outside dining near the Museum of Jewish Heritage in the relatively new Robert Wagner Junior Park. Great views of the harbour and Statue of Liberty while you tuck into delicious dishes like bruschetta ($9.50), caprese ($12) or penne al pesto ($16.50).

BRITTIP

If you want an even cheaper pit stop than Gigino while in Battery Park City, opt for items from the snack cart in Wagner Park.

BROOKLYN

GRIMALDI'S $
Italian
- ✉ 19 Old Fulton Street between Front and Water Streets
- ☎ 718-858 4300
- 🖰 grimaldis.com
- 🚇 Subway A, C to High Street/Brooklyn Bridge

Their pizza has been rated number one in the city in the Zagat Survey and it truly is considered the best place in New York to get a delicious pizza at a great price.

NOODLE PUDDING $$
Italian
- ✉ 38 Henry Street between Cranberry and Middagh Streets
- ☎ 218-625 3737
- 🚇 Subway A, C to High Street/Brooklyn Bridge

Despite its name, this is a dedicated Italian rather than an Asian eatery, and it's very good. Traditional dishes such as osso buco (veal knuckle) and penne arrabiata ensure that it attracts an Italian-American crowd and is constantly packed. It is also praised for its fine pizza.

RIVER CAFE $$$

Gourmet American

- ✉ 1 Water Street under the Brooklyn Bridge
- ☎ 718-522 5200
- 🖰 rivercafe.com
- 🚇 Subway A, C to High Street/Brooklyn Bridge

If a panoramic view of the Manhattan skyline makes you feel romantic, and it does the majority of us, then the River Café on Brooklyn's waterfront is for you. Even better, the food matches up to the location – in fact it's worth leaving Manhattan for. It celebrated its 30th anniversary in 2009, and still serves up superb dishes such as wild rock lobster, River Café oysters, Wagyu steak and sautéed Hudson Valley foie gras.

CENTRAL PARK

THE BOATHOUSE CENTRAL PARK $$–$$$

American–seafood

- ✉ Central Park Lake, Park Drive North at East 72nd Street
- ☎ 212-517 2233
- 🖰 thecentralparkboathouse.com
- 🚇 Subway 6 to 68th Street/Hunter College

This picture-book restaurant boasts one of the most wonderfully romantic locations in New York. Set right by a lake dotted with blue rowing boats in the heart of Central Park, circled by the famous high-rise skyline, the outside terrace provides a particularly gorgeous place to bag a seat at sunset. After dark, the restaurant's sparkling lights add to the romantic atmosphere. The mainly seafood menu isn't what you'd call adventurous, but it's delicious and well cooked, and *Zagat* recommends the tasting menu. There is also a roaring open fireplace in the bar for those wintry days, when you can almost feel as if you really were deep in the countryside. Be sure to book well in advance in the summer.

TAVERN ON THE GREEN $$$

Gourmet American

- ✉ Central Park at West 67th Street
- ☎ 212-873 3200
- 🖰 tavernonthegreen.com
- 🚇 Subway B, C to 72nd Street

At the time of going to print, the restaurant was being sold. Check out the website to find out the latest news before you travel. Looking at the glitzy razzmatazz that is the Tavern, it's hard to imagine this building started life in 1870 as a house for the sheep that roamed Central Park. By the early 1930s, Parks Commissioner Robert Moses had spotted its potential as a restaurant. He banished the sheep to Brooklyn's Prospect Park and,

TOP 5 NEW OPENINGS

The last 12 months has proved an exciting time for the dining capital of the world, with openings of new eateries adding around 5,000 more restaurant seats to a city that already boasts over a million.

TriBeCa
Terrior Tribeca (page 191)

SoHo
Quattro Gastronomia Italiana (page 187)

Midtown
Må Pêche (page 176)
Zengo (page 185)

Little Italy
Kenmare (page 170)

in 1934, opened what was known as The Restaurant with a coachman in full regalia at the door and the blessing of Mayor Fiorello LaGuardia.

✠ BRITTIP

You don't have to eat at the Tavern to enjoy its fabulous garden. May–Oct you can sip a cocktail in the garden bar.

In the 1970s, famous restaurateur Warner LeRoy spent $10 million turning it into a spectacle in its own right, creating the Crystal and Terrace Rooms with his lavish use of brass, stained glass, etched mirrors, antique paintings and prints and chandeliers – including genuine Baccarat crystal and stained-glass Tiffanys. The Tavern on the Green took the city by storm when it opened in 1976. Celebrities, politicians and anyone who was anyone flocked to see and to be seen here.

Now the Tavern pulls in out-of-towners, who've all been told by their friends to visit this unique site, and the restaurant has a

Tavern on the Green

staggering turnover of around $34 million a year! And what a riot of colours and textures its clients are greeted with. The food is classic gourmet American with typical main courses including cedar-planked salmon, herb-roasted chicken and prime rib.

CHELSEA

202 $$
British–Mediterranean
- ✉ 75 9th Avenue at 16th Street
- ☎ 646 638 1115
- 🖰 nicolefarhi.com
- 🚇 Subway A, C, E to 14th Street

The line between fashionable food and, well, fashion blurs here as this is a hot little restaurant tucked away in the Nicole Farhi store. It makes the perfect place for a spot of lunch or dinner, where you can watch the waistline by tucking into dishes such as warm goat's cheese salad and smoked salmon with blini-thin scallion pancakes, or add to the waistline with fish and chips.

BONGO $$$–$$$$
Seafood
- ✉ 299 10th Avenue between 27th and 28th Streets
- ☎ 212-947 3654
- 🖰 bongonyc.com
- 🚇 Subway C, E to 23rd Street; 1, 9 to 28th Street

A swish oyster bar where Chelsea gallery types sip champagne and slip down half a dozen oysters for $18. If you're not a fan, there are other delicacies, including smoked trout salad, lobster roll and cod cakes.

BOTTINO $$
Italian
- ✉ 246 10th Avenue between 24th and 25th Streets
- ☎ 212-206 6766
- 🖰 bottinonyc.com
- 🚇 Subway C, E to 23rd Street

This is the place to go if you want to see the chic art dealers in recreational mode. You can tuck into the delicious Tuscan cuisine, such as roast rack of lamb with rosemary, in either the minimalist dining room or the back garden. If you don't have time to stop and eat, grab a sarnie to take away from the next-door Bottino to Go.

✠ BRITTIP

Bottles of water can cost $10 at some of the pricier restaurants. Save your money! New York has access to the finest and cleanest tap water, direct from the Catskill Mountains upstate.

ZAGAT'S TOP RESTAURANTS 2010

Best food: Le Bernardin (le-bernardin.com)

Most popular: Gramercy Tavern (gramercytavern.com)

Best decor: Asiate (mandarinoriental.com)

Best service: Per Se (perseny.com)

Best burger: Burger Joint at Le Parker Meridien (parkermeridien.com)

Best Japanese/sushi: Sushi Yasuda (sushiyasuda.com)

Best pizza: Di Fara (Brooklyn, 718-258 1367)

Most romantic: Daniel (danielnyc.com)

BUDDAKAN $$$–$$$$
Pan-Asian
- ✉ 75 9th Avenue at 16th Street
- ☎ 212-989 6699
- 🖰 buddakannyc.com
- 🚇 Subway 1, 2, 3, 9 to 14th Street

A Pan-Asian import from the successful restaurant in Philadelphia. It was introduced to New York by Stephen Starr and is watched over by consultant Angelo Sosa, formerly of Yumcha. The awe factor isn't just the food (delicacies like Cantonese spring rolls and steamed pork buns in bamboo containers), but the great hall, which has oak-covered walls 2 storeys high, huge chandeliers and a banquet table to seat 30. Expect seriously beautiful people and food.

CAFETERIA $$
American diner
- ✉ 119 7th Avenue at 17th Street
- ☎ 212-414 1717
- 🖰 cafeteriagroup.com
- 🚇 Subway 1, 9 to 18th Street

Another diner comfort-food experience, only this time filled with the hipsters who use the 24-hour joint before and after hitting the local clubs.

MARKT $$
Belgian
- ✉ 676 6th Avenue
- ☎ 212-727 3314
- 🖰 marktrestaurant.com
- 🚇 A, C, E at 23rd Street

A stylish Belgian brasserie with a popular bar. Great mussels and good beer selection.

THE PARK $$$
Mediterranean
- ✉ 118 10th Avenue at 18th Street
- ☎ 212-352 3313
- 🖰 theparknyc.com
- 🚇 Subway C, E to 23rd Street

Once a mechanic's garage, this is one of the

'in' spots for film-industry executives. It's a huge industrial bar-cum-restaurant space with a kind of African safari camp interior serving Mediterranean food. There's a huge garden at the back full of Japanese maple trees and wisteria vines that seats 400 and is a great place to dine in the summer.

THE RED CAT $$
Mediterranean–American
- ✉ 227 10th Avenue between 23rd and 24th Streets
- ☎ 212-242 1122
- ⌂ redcatrestaurants.com
- 🚇 Subway C, E to 23rd Street

One of the earlier arrivals in Chelsea, along with the original galleries, this is a real staple with the art pack. It serves up Mediterranean-influenced American food, but you can just go for a cocktail.

CHINATOWN

Hundreds of tiny restaurants line the Chinatown streets, mostly serving good-value food from various regions in China. Here is our top 5 to get you started.

BIG WONG KING $
Cantonese
- ✉ 67 Mott Street between Bayard and Canal Streets
- ☎ 212-964 0540
- 🚇 Subway J, M, N, Q, R, W, A, Z, 6 to Canal Street

Cheap, tasty food – particularly the duck, shrimp and chicken noodles, and congee. Don't expect much of the decor but the service is good and lots of Chinese eat here, which is always a good sign. The wonton noodle soup is a bargain.

BRITTIP

Well-priced, steaming-hot food is the trademark of the restaurants in Chinatown. But don't expect elegance in the decor or any politeness from the waiters!

DIM SUM GO GO $$
Chinese–vegetarian
- ✉ 5 East Broadway between Catherine Street and Chatham Square
- ☎ 212-732 0797
- 🚇 Subway J, M, Z, 6 to Canal Street; F to East Broadway

Zagat-rated and one of the more popular restaurants in the area, thanks to its delicious dim sum, and fantastically priced: dim sum platter, $10.95 for 10 pieces; roast chicken with fried garlic stems, $13.95; hamburger in a steamed bun with ginger sauce, $9.95.

TOP 5 FOR FINE DINING

Considering how many thousands of eating establishments there are in New York and how many of them serve up wonderful food in delightful environments, it's difficult to narrow them down to a top 5. Yet all the restaurants listed below have earned their stripes for getting all the elements of fine dining and hospitality right: consistently excellent and innovative cuisine, attentive service and an enjoyable ambience in a wonderful setting. They obviously have prices to match, but for a once-in-a-holiday treat they won't disappoint.

Le Cirque: French–American, Midtown East (page 180)

Union Square Café: Gourmet American, Midtown East (page 182)

Le Bernardin: Seafood, Midtown West (page 184)

Babbo: Italian, Greenwich (page 167)

Nobu: Japanese, TriBeCa (page 190)

JOE'S SHANGHAI $$
Chinese–Shanghai
- ✉ 9 Pell St between Bowery and Mott Street
- ☎ 212-233 8888
- ⌂ joesshanghairestaurants.com
- 🚇 Subway J, M, N, R, Z, 6 to Canal Street

A Chinese restaurant known for creating the most fabulous soup dumplings in New York. 'Lots of food for little money' says the *Zagat Survey*. No reservations. Cash only.

NICE GREEN BO $–$$
Chinese–Shanghai
- ✉ 66 Bayard Street between Elizabeth and Mott Streets
- ☎ 212-625 2359
- 🚇 Subway J, M, Z, N, Q, R, W, 6 to Canal Street

Joe's Shanghai had little in the way of competition for delicious dim sum and dumplings at great prices, then along came

The Red Cat

GARDEN DINING

Aureole: French, Upper East Side, $$$$ (page 174)

Barbetta: Northern Italian, Midtown West, $$$$ (page 183)

Bottino: Italian, Chelsea, $$$ (page 162)

Remi: Italian, Midtown, $$$$ (page 177)

Tavern on the Green: Gourmet American, Central Park West, $$$ (page 161)

The Park: Mediterranean, Chelsea $$$ (page 162)

this place, giving New Yorkers another place to rave about. There is a famous teahouse of the same name in Shanghai, and it feels like you could be there. The dumplings are extremely fresh, hot and succulent and their fish fillet in wine sauce is excellent.

EAST VILLAGE

There are dozens of great places to dine in the East Village. It's a very safe part of town so, if you have the time, it's well worth taking a wander around at night and having a look at all of the various options before you make your choice.

ANGELICA KITCHEN $$
Vegetarian–vegan
- ✉ 300 East 12th Street between 1st and 2nd Avenues
- ☎ 212-228 2909
- ⌂ angelicakitchen.com
- 🚐 Subway L, N, Q, R, W, 4, 5, 6 to 14th Street/Union Square

A surprise for anyone who thinks veggie food

is boring. This cool spot, open since 1976, serves up organic, very tasty soups, chilli and noodle dishes like butternut squash and tempeh made from soya beans, and seasonal dishes. Macrobiotic heaven? No alcohol.

FRANK $
Italian
- ✉ 88 2nd Avenue between 5th and 6th Streets
- ☎ 212-420 0202
- ⌂ frankrestaurant.com
- 🚐 Subway 6 to Astor Place

A tiny Italian restaurant with a real parlour feel. No matter the hour, Frank is full of hungry hipsters looking to fill up on Grandma Carmela's slow-cooked ragu.

✈ BRITTIP
If you want to walk and eat rather than sit down and dine, Frank also has a great takeaway or delivery menu!

GNOCCO CUCINA & TRADIZIONE $$
Italian
- ✉ 337 East 10th Street between Avenues A and B
- ☎ 212-677 1913
- ⌂ gnocco.com
- 🚐 Subway 6 to Astor Place

Named after an Italian snack of crispy, puffy fried dough, you know you're in for some good Italian food at this eatery owned by Pierluigi Palazzo. Lovely dishes such as pork tenderloin sprinkled with Parmigiano shavings.

Momofuku Ko

LA PALAPA $$
Mexican

- ✉ 77 St Mark's Place between 1st and 2nd Avenues
- ☎ 212-777 2537
- 🖱 lapalapa.com
- 🚇 Subway E, V to Lexington Avenue/ 53rd Street

Superb Mexican cuisine with shrimp dishes and barbecued cod with Chile guajillo and achiote rub. Rices are flavoured with tomato, saffron and tomatillo; sauces concocted from sesame seeds, pumpkin seeds and guajillo chillies. The restaurant is dark and sultry and serves refreshing fresh fruit margaritas. Check out the calendar on the website to find out about events such as a cocktail and small bites masterclass. The cocktails here are seriously good – try the white hibiscus sangria!

MOMOFUKU $$
Noodles

- ✉ 171 1st Avenue, between 10th and 11th streets
- 🖱 momofuku.com
- 🚇 Subway L to 1st Avenue

The menu changes daily at this cool noodle bar. Expect to pick up pieces of wild striped bass with pickled pearl onion or chilled somen noodles, kimchi, sesame and fried egg with your chopsticks. It's interior is quite stark, with wooden benches and chairs, but it's open noon–2am on weekends and well worth a visit if you're in the area.

BRITTIP
Sometimes the only way to get into a very popular restaurant is to go very early or very late in the evening. Ask what times are available when you book.

THE ELEPHANT $$
French–Thai fusion

- ✉ 58 East 1st Street between 1st and 2nd Avenues
- ☎ 212-505 7739
- 🖱 theelephantrestaurant.com
- 🚇 Subway F, V to 2nd Avenue

The food is tasty Thai with a dash of French, but the dark, loud, crowded red and gold interior is most definitely more of a French scene. A fun place to enjoy a cocktail or two; the cool crowd often end up spilling out on to the sidewalk.

TOP 5 RESTAURANTS WITH A VIEW

2 West: America fusion, Battery Park (page 160)

Battery Gardens: Gourmet American, Battery Park (page 160)

The View: Continental, Theater District (page 189)

Water Club: Seafood, Midtown East (page 182)

World Yacht Dinner Cruises: Gourmet American, Midtown West (page 184)

YAFFA CAFE $
American diner

- ✉ 97 St Mark's Place between 1st and Avenue A
- ☎ 212-674 9302
- 🖱 yaffacafe.com
- 🚇 Subway 6 to Astor Place

A classic American diner with a grungy East Village twist. Open 24 hours.

FINANCIAL DISTRICT AND SOUTH STREET SEAPORT

ADRIENNE'S PIZZA BAR $-$$
Italian

- ✉ 54 Stone Street near Hanover Square
- ☎ 212-248 3838
- 🖱 adriennespizzabar.com
- 🚇 Subway 2, 3 to Wall Street

If you're sightseeing Downtown and start to feel peckish, pop into this stylish place for some truly delicious thin-crust square, the restaurant's latest take on the pizza. There's also salads, antipasti and pastas to enjoy.

Yaffa Café

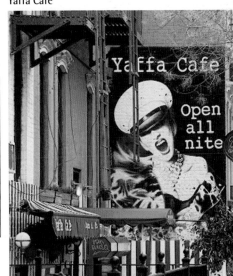

Babbo

KOODO SUSHI $-$$
Japanese
- ✉ 55 Liberty Street
- ☎ 212-425 2890
- ⌂ koodosushi.com
- 🚇 Subway 1, 2, 4, 5 to Wall Street

This place doesn't look like much, but it has one of the best sushi chefs in town. The fish is impeccable, but the chef really shines in his daily specials.

MARKJOSEPH STEAKHOUSE $$
Steakhouse
- ✉ 261 Water Street between Peck Slip and Dover Street
- ☎ 212-277 0020
- ⌂ markjosephsteakhouse.com
- 🚇 Subway 1, 2, 4, 5, A, C, J, M, Z to Fulton Street/Broadway Nassau

This restaurant has made its mark as one of the best steakhouses in the city. The porterhouse steak is so tender some people have said it 'could be eaten through a straw'. Team it with the delicious hash browns. Wearing a jacket is advisable.

GRAMERCY PARK

ELEVEN MADISON PARK $$$$
French–American
- ✉ 11 Madison Avenue (the corner) at 24th Street
- ☎ 212-889 0905
- ⌂ elevenmadisonpark.com
- 🚇 Subway 6, N, R to 23rd Street

With a soaring ceiling, marble floors and French-influenced dishes, this is one of New York's hottest restaurants. It's expensive but not

Eleven Madison Park

snooty and the service is attentive, as seen in *Sex And The City*, and you would be advised to go dressy as shorts, T-shirts and trainers aren't allowed. If you want to blow the budget the 11-course taster menu is $175.

GRAMERCY TAVERN $$$
Gourmet American
- ✉ 42 East 20th Street between Broadway and Park Avenue South
- ☎ 212-477 0777
- ⌂ gramercytavern.com
- 🚇 Subway N, R to 23rd Street

Another real winner, serving tasty, traditional dishes like venison loin and sausage, always highly ranked by the *Zagat Survey* – an excellent American restaurant.

TAMARIND $$
Indian
- ✉ 41-43 East 22nd Street between Broadway and Park Avenue South
- ☎ 212-674 7400
- ⌂ tamarinde22.com
- 🚇 Subway N, R to 23rd Street

Lovely modern decor that defies the normal Indian dining room cliché of flock wallpaper. The cuisine is equally contemporary, with lots of fruit-infused dishes such as fritters with spinach, banana and homemade cheese. If you want a cheaper, lighter snack try their tea room next door.

VERITAS $$$$
Gourmet American
- ✉ 43 East 20th Street between Broadway and Park Avenue South
- ☎ 212-353 3700
- ⌂ veritas-nyc.com
- 🚇 Subway N, R to 23rd Street

BRITTIP
If you're a true wine connoisseur you can download the most up-to-date list of Veritas's wine cellar before you go from veritas-nyc.com.

The city's largest wine list can be found here – an impressive 2,700-plus bottles to choose from. The cuisine is as impressive, think tender braised ribs with parsnip purée and porcini mushrooms or scallops with a black truffle vinaigrette. The prix fixe dinner is $85.

RESTAURANTS

Cornelia Street Cafe

GREENWICH & WEST VILLAGE

BABBO $$$$
Italian
- ✉ 110 Waverly Place between MacDougal and 6th Avenues
- ☎ 212-777 0303
- 🖰 babbonyc.com
- 🚇 Subway A, B, C, D, E, F, Q to Washington Square

BRITTIP

Order one of the fabulous tasting menus at Babbo for a really great choice of dishes. The pasta tasting menu is particularly mouth-watering, including black tagliatelle with parsnips and pancetta, garganelli with funghi trifolatia and pappardelle Bolognese. It's also a cheaper option than choosing individual dishes, as the menus ring in at around $69 per person.

The crown jewel of Greenwich Village restaurants is unmatched for the quality and quantity of its Italian dishes; forewarned is forearmed, so make sure you wear a skirt or trousers with an elasticated waist, because we're talking large, rich portions here. Everything in Mario Batali's restaurant is delightful, from the simple split-level dining room that seats 90 to the stunning bar area. However, it's the imaginative food that pushes this restaurant into the top 5 fine dining experiences. How about black tagliatelle with parsnips and pancetta? Or chocolate polenta cake with espresso gelato? Yum!

COMMERCE $$-$$$
New American
- ✉ 50 Commerce Street at Barrow Street
- ☎ 212-524 2301
- 🖰 commercerestaurant.com
- 🚇 Subway 1, 9 to Christopher Street

Commerce opened its doors in West Village at the beginning of 2008, but the original building started life as a Prohibition speakeasy! The new place has gone down a storm as lots of New Yorkers are reminiscing about this restaurant when it was Grange Hall, a hip 90s stomping ground for locals propping up the massive bar beneath the Art Deco mural and enjoying intimate chats in the booths. Luckily, the new owners recognised that these were important features to keep. The menu is bang up to date and inventive, however. Think beef tataki and boar ragu.

CORNELIA STREET CAFE $$
Eclectic
- ✉ 29 Cornelia Street between Bleecker and West 4th Streets
- ☎ 212-989 9319
- 🖰 corneliastreetcafe.com
- 🚇 Subway A, C, E, B, D, F, V to West 4th Street

A fabulous neighbourhood restaurant with good service that serves lunch and dinner 7 days a week. Specials include butternut squash risotto, sesame-crusted salmon, lobster ravioli and Thai bouillabaisse, or choose from the prix fixe menu for $25. Local artists' work hangs on the walls, and there is a small downstairs performance space for readings, acoustic performances and, in particular the jazz club, which begins at 9pm and costs from $6 for the whole evening plus a house drink (page 212).

GARAGE RESTAURANT & CAFÉ $
American
- ✉ 99 7th Avenue South between Barrow and Grove Streets
- ☎ 212-645 0600
- 🖱 garagerest.com
- 🚗 Subway 1, 2, 3, 9 to Christopher Street
A friendly spot for contemporary American food in a great location; it also has live jazz and some cool people-watching.

GOTHAM BAR AND GRILL $$$
Gourmet American
- ✉ 12 East 12th Street between 5th Avenue and University Place
- ☎ 212-620 4020
- 🖱 gothambarandgrill.com
- 🚗 Subway L, N, R, 4, 5, 6 to Union Square/14th Street
Always highly rated by *Zagat*, the excellent American cuisine is served up in a superb environment to a stylish crowd. It costs $25 for the lunch prix fixe.

PHILIP MARIE $$-$$$
American
- ✉ 569 Hudson Street at West 11th Street
- ☎ 212-242 6200
- 🖱 philipmarie.com
- 🚗 Subway 1, 9 to Christopher Street
Hearty American fare. Try the prix fixe lunch for a bargain $10.95, which includes dishes like grilled breaded country chicken served over tossed field greens salad with a glass of soda or iced tea.

SOTO $$$-$$$$
Japanese
- ✉ 357 6th Avenue at Washington Place
- ☎ 212-414 3088
- 🚗 Subway A, B, C, E, F, V to West 4th Street/ Washington Square
Opened in May 2007 by third generation sushi chef Sotohiro Kosugi, this is a very sleek restaurant where you can savour Eastern delights such as sea urchin wrapped in squid, sweet shrimp tartare with yuzu tobiko and soy foam.

RESTAURANTS

Gotham Bar and Grill

TOMOE SUSHI $$
Japanese
- ✉ 172 Thompson Street between Bleecker and West Houston Streets
- ☎ 212-777 9346
- 🚇 Subway 6 to Bleecker Street

This place looks pretty grotty but there is usually a queue outside and not without reason. You can get the best sushi in New York here for about a tenth of the price it would cost you at Nobu.

HARLEM

AMY RUTH'S HOME STYLE SOUTHERN CUISINE $$
Southern soul food
- ✉ 113 West 116th street at Lenox Avenue
- ☎ 212-280 8779
- 🖰 amyruthsharlem.com
- 🚇 Subway 2, 3 to 116th Street

Absolutely delicious southern-style food, BBQ spare ribs, chicken and waffles, catfish and ham hocks.

BRITTIP
If you need a break around 110th Street, drop in for a cuppa and a delicious cake at Make My Cake, 121 St Nicholas Avenue at 116th Street, 212-932 0833, makemycake.com.

RAO'S $
Italian
- ✉ 455 East 114th Street at Pleasant Avenue
- ☎ 212-722 6709
- 🖰 raos.com
- 🚇 Subway 6 to 116th Street

This 10-table Italian restaurant is an institution and notoriously hard to get a reservation for, so if you fancy it, book now! Famous for its sauces, which Sinatra used to have flown to him around the world. Now the jukebox plays all the crooner's favourites.

BEST OF LITTLE ITALY
It's hard to go wrong with any of the restaurants in Little Italy, but here is a round-up of the best, moving northwards along Mulberry from Hester to Grand Street: **Pellegrino's** (138 Mulberry, 212-226 3177); **Angelo's** (146 Mulberry, 212-966 1277, angelomulberry.com); **Lombardi's** (32 Spring St between Mulberry and Mott Streets, 212-941 7994, firstpizza.com); **Il Palazzo** (151 Mulberry, 212-343 7000). To get to Little Italy, take subway 6 to Spring or Bleecker Streets.

BRITTIP
If you can't get in to Rao's, you can still taste their fabulous sauces, by buying them either direct from the restaurant or from Faicco's Pork Store in Bleecker Street, Greenwich Village (page 155).

SYLVIA'S $
Southern soul food
- ✉ 328 Lenox Avenue between 126th and 127th Streets
- ☎ 212-996 0660
- 🖰 sylviassoulfood.com
- 🚇 Subway 2, 3 to 125th Street

Southern home-style cooking – aka soul food. Sylvia's place is a New York institution and famous for its Sun gospel brunch, but you need to book a few weeks ahead as it's always very busy.

HELL'S KITCHEN

TERRAZZA TOSCANA $$
Italian
- ✉ 742 9th Avenue at 50th Street
- ☎ 212-315 9191
- 🖰 terrazzatoscana.com
- 🚇 Subway 1, C, E trains to 50th Street

Ignazio Pietra, owner of Strata 57, has opened the flashy Terrazza Toscana. The pièce de résistance here is an outdoor terrace, located on the 1-storey building's roof, seating 70 people. The dining room seats about 100. Downstairs, there's a wine vault holding about 1,500 bottles.

LITTLE ITALY
Mulberry Street from Hester to Kenmare Street and along Grand Street to Mott Street is all that remains of a once thriving Italian community. Thankfully, though – especially for anyone who feels relieved to have escaped the madness and mayhem of Chinatown – the tiny area is incredibly vibrant and filled with ambient pizzerias and trattorias, many with pavement tables and some even having gardens at the back.

Of course, the area gets packed with tourists, but locals also eat here so the food is 100% authentic. The restaurants all have plenty in common – fading decor, if any, large portions of piping hot Italian classics, friendly service and great value for money. If you're really on a budget, stick to the excellent fixed-price menus, then just sit back and watch the world go by.

Bar Martignetti

BAR MARTIGNETTI
$$-$$$
Italian
- ✉ 406 Broome Street at Centre Street
- ☎ 212-680 5600
- ⌂ barmartignetti.com
- 🚇 Subway 6 to Spring Street

The Martignetti brothers have opened up this bustling bar and restaurant that has proved a real hit with locals. They've hired a top brasserie chef and you can order food all day and into the small hours.

BREAD
$$
Italian
- ✉ 20 Spring Street between Elizabeth and Mott Streets
- ☎ 212-334 1015
- 🚇 Subway 6 to Spring Street

A lovely little café serving up delicious panini, soup and various salads and great fresh bread. There's also a good choice of wine, many of which are sold by the glass. There's an equally good Bread in TriBeCa (breadtribeca.com).

CAFE GITANE
$$
French–North African
- ✉ 242 Mott Street at Prince Street
- ☎ 212-334 9552
- 🚇 Subway 6 to Spring Street

Great value Moroccan-style dining; think couscous and tajines. Tables and chairs are put out on the sidewalk in the summer, but they are in a hot spot so you're more likely to end up in the noisy but nice dining room.

FERRARA
$
Italian café
- ✉ 195 Grand Street between Mulberry and Mott Streets
- ☎ 212-226 6150
- ⌂ ferraracafe.com
- 🚇 Subway S to Grand Street

This is the oldest surviving pastry joint (it opened in 1892) in an area that was once teeming with cannoli caverns. A spacious area, it serves up delicious drinks and cakes and provides plenty of entertaining people-watching.

BRITTIP

If you've been wandering around Chinatown for a while and don't want a meal but do need a WC, Ferrara's has a lovely clean one on the 1st floor (up the stairs at the back). Keep the owners happy, though, by at least buying something to take away.

KENMARE
$$-$$$
New American
- ✉ 98 Kenmare Street between Lafayette and Mulberry Streets
- ☎ 212-274 9898
- ⌂ kenmarenyc.com
- 🚇 Subway S to Grand Street

Classy new eatery with inventive menu; scallops with spinach and strawberry salad, and swordfish and caramelised fennel.

SAL ANTHONY'S SPQR
$$-$$$
Italian
- ✉ 133 Mulberry Street between Hester and Grand Streets
- ☎ 212-925 3120
- ⌂ spqrnyc.com
- 🚇 Subway 6 to Spring Street

An authentic Italian that's big on fresh ingredients – the mozzarella is made twice a day on the premises to ensure it's perfect. There are lots of regional dishes such as trout with garlic and rosemary and fusilli pasta with prosciutto and tomato, all served in elegant, wood-panelled surroundings at prices far below what you'd expect to pay uptown for similar fare. There's a 'La Famiglia', family-style menu, which has extra large portions if you want to share dishes.

LOWER EAST SIDE

ALIAS $$
American
✉ 76 Clinton Street at Rivington Street
☎ 212-505 5011
🖰 aliasrestaurant.com
🚇 Subway F to Lower East Side/2nd Avenue
This cool bodega has lower lighting, tablecloths and a small but serious wine list, yet remains funky with laid-back clients and staff. The chef turns out some pretty big tastes from his mini kitchen but at far less than Midtown pricing. Open for lunch, dinner and brunch on a Sat and Sun.

BEREKET $
Turkish
✉ 187 East Houston Street at Orchard Street
☎ 212-475 7700
🚇 Subway F to 2nd Avenue
A good place to pop into if you've got the munchies after a big night out as it's open 24/7 and the food is filling but fresh. The hummus, stuffed vine leaves and lamb shawarma sandwich are recommended.

BONDI ROAD $$
Seafood
✉ 153 Rivington Street at Suffolk Street
☎ 212-253 5311
🖰 thesunburntcow.com
🚇 Subway J, M, Z to Suffolk Street
Photomontages of Australia's Bondi Beach run down both sides of this laid-back eatery. The menu's simple: pick a fish, such as sea bass, barramunda or grouper, and then select a cooking method – grilled, breaded or fried.

THE CLERKENWELL $-$$
English/Gastro pub
✉ 49 Clinton Street between Stanton and Rivington Streets
☎ 212-614 3234
🖰 clerkenwellny.com
🚇 Subway F at Delancy St; J, M, Z at Essex Street
If you're pining for some English pub grub while you're in the Big Apple, then head to The Clerkenwell, where Shay Kelly is serving up chunky chips and toad in the hole.

KATZ'S DELICATESSEN $
American–Jewish
✉ 205 East Houston Street at Ludlow Street
☎ 212-254 2246
🖰 katzdeli.com
🚇 Subway F to 2nd Avenue
A real institution, this deli has been here since 1888. The sandwiches may sound pricey at around $9, but I defy you to finish one. Luckily, there are plenty of brown paper bags around to take your leftovers away with you (as everybody else does). Stick to the sandwiches though – the soups are a bit disappointing. You take a ticket on the way in, order your food at the counter and have your ticket filled out, then you pay for it all as you leave.

✚ BRITTIP
If the canteen-style seating at Katz's seems familiar to you, it's because that fake orgasm scene with Meg Ryan and Billy Crystal in *When Harry Met Sally* was filmed here.

WHITE SLAB PALACE $$
Scandinavian
✉ 77 Delancy Street at Allen Street
☎ 212-334 0913
🚇 Subway J, M, Z at Bowery
This new bar and restaurant has a sparse industrial decor, with a long granite bar where you can enjoy the extensive cocktail list. Interesting cuisine and space.

Katz's Delicatessen

A VOCE
$$$–$$$$

Italian

✉ 41 Madison Avenue near 26th Street
☎ 212-545 8555
🖱 avocerestaurant.com
🚇 Subway 6 to 26th Street

Has a great Italian menu, think chicken cacciatora, lamb shanks, veal chops and even wild boar and the modern decor is very calming and sophisticated. The prix fixe lunch menu is $29. There's a 100-seat outside dining piazza adorned with lemon trees, flowers and herbs.

ALDEA
$$$–$$$$

Mediterranean

✉ 31 West 17th Street
☎ 212-675 7223
🖱 aldearestaurant.com
🚇 Subway L, N, Q, R, W, 4, 5, 6 to 14th Street–Union Square

Opened in May 2009 by George Mendes, formerly chef de cuisine at Tocqueville and Wallse. Mendes returns to his roots with a menu of Mediterranean dishes influenced by the flavours of Spain and Portugal. Evoking a relaxed, coastal vibe, the restaurant offers a selection of petiscos, all $9 and under, plus a variety of seasonal appetisers and entrées, such as sardines with Madeira raisins and bitter almond milk, and arroz de pato with black olives. Designed by Stephanie Goto, the bi-level restaurant reflects the colour palate of azulejos, the blue and white ceramic tiles common in Portugal. Open 5.30pm Mon–Sat.

TABLA
$$$$

American Indian

✉ 11 Madison Avenue at 25th Street
☎ 212-889 0667
🖱 tablany.com
🚇 Subway N, R, W, 6 to 23rd Street

Bi-level restaurant serving American Indian cuisine (dishes like shiitake and oyster mushroom korma and grilled calamari if you're wondering how that combination works!) is a big hit and attracts a trendy crowd. Downstairs is cheaper, you'll be pleased to know, and there's a $31 lunch menu.

MEATPACKING DISTRICT

Manhattan's Meatpacking District, between Chelsea and the West Village on the lower west side of Manhattan, used to be a no-go area for diners. Now it has become a style magnet for the kind of restaurants that you want to brag to your friends about. If you don't want to splash out in the chic venues, however, there are some groovy little coffee and cake shops that will take the weight off your feet but not your wallet.

5 NINTH
$$$

American nouveau

✉ 5 9th Avenue at Gansevoort Street
☎ 212-929 9460
🖱 5ninth.com
🚇 Subway A, C, E to 14th Street; L to 8th Avenue

Discreet setting but buzzing on the inside, serving up expensive but delicious dishes such as pork chop with potato gratin, that are infused with ingredients from far-off destinations, particularly the East.

A Voce

5 Ninth

DEL POSTO $$$
Italian
- ✉ 85 10th Avenue at 16th Street
- ☎ 212-497 8090
- 🔗 delposto.com
- 🚇 Subway A, C, E to 14th Street

This restaurant from Mario Batali and the Bastianich family is posh Italian nosh that has left the New York restaurant critics split. The surroundings are super-plush – think old-style gentleman's club – with a live pianist, and the food fancy and grand tasting.

OLD HOMESTEAD
STEAK HOUSE $$
American
- ✉ 56 9th Avenue between 14th and 15th Streets
- ☎ 212-242 9040
- 🔗 theoldhomesteadsteakhouse.com
- 🚇 Subway L, A, C, E to 14th Street/8th Avenue

An original chophouse joint, complete with tacky cow sculpture outside, that opened in 1868 and is still serving massive portions of good ol' steak and chips.

PASTIS $$$
French
- ✉ 9 9th Avenue at Little West 12th Street
- ☎ 212-929 4844
- 🔗 pastisny.com
- 🚇 Subway A, C, E to 14th Street; L to 8th Avenue

One of the names that made the Meatpacking neighbourhood hip was Keith McNally, who set up this Parisian-style brasserie. It's always full and the atmosphere's buzzy, the food is good, not great, such as steak frites and sautéed prawns. Open for breakfast, brunch, lunch and dinner.

MIDTOWN

21 CLUB $–$$$
Gourmet American
- ✉ 21 West 52nd Street between 5th and 6th Avenues
- ☎ 212-582 7200
- 🔗 21club.com
- 🚇 Subway F to 5th Avenue

Despite its name, this landmark restaurant has never been a club, but during Prohibition it was a speakeasy, starting life in Greenwich Village before moving to its Midtown location in 1929. West 52nd Street between 5th and 6th Avenues was known then as the 'wettest block in Manhattan' because there were at least 38 speakeasies.

173

21 Club

One of the most discreet was the 21 Club, which purposefully remained a tiny, clandestine retreat behind the iron gate of its townhouse façade, to avoid both the gangsters and police raids. Its success depended on an employee who was assigned to spot gangsters, policemen and revenue agents through the peephole – and who was so skilful that 21 escaped most raids and troubles except for one in 1930. After that the owners had a new security system designed to create false stairways and walls to hide its 2,000 cases of fine wines. It involved the building of a 2-tonne door to the secret cellar, made out of the original bricks to look like a wall. The cellar is still going strong and now houses $1.5 million-worth of wine, much of which is owned by the celebrities and power brokers who call the 21 Club their own. Former US President Gerald Ford kept his bottles here, as does actress Elizabeth Taylor.

Once Prohibition ended in 1932, many of the former speakeasies went out of business, but the 21 turned itself into a fine dining establishment that has been attracting celebrities and movers and shakers ever since. Patrons have included Joe DiMaggio, Aristotle Onassis, Franklin D Roosevelt, Humphrey Bogart, Ernest Hemingway and Jackie Gleason.

AJ MAXWELL'S $$-$$$
American
✉ 57 West 58th Street, Rockefeller Centre
☎ 212-262 6200
⌂ ajmaxwells.com
🚇 Subway B, D, F, V to Rockefeller Centre
The steak house that hits the spot if you're looking to satisfy hunger pangs with big portions in pleasant surroundings. Good

Aquavit

wine list and there's also an excellent range of seafood dishes if you don't want the filet mignon et al.

AQUAVIT $$$$
Scandinavian
✉ 65 East 55th Street between Madison and Park Avenues
☎ 212-307 7311
⌂ aquavit.org
🚇 Subway E, V to 53rd Street/5th Avenue
Swedish chef Marcus Samuelsson won the Best Chef in New York City award in 2003, but the menu, which has some innovative Scandinavian influences, is still as varied and imaginative today. Seafood stew and brioche-wrapped salmon are mouth-watering, while the tasting menus, including a vegetarian one, are a great idea and comprise 7-course Aqua Bite meals.

BRITTIP
If you don't want to pay out the big prices demanded in Aquavit's smart dining room, there's also a lively, cheaper café to try with an eclectic menu featuring fish, game and pickled and preserved dishes.

AUREOLE $$$$
American
✉ 1 Bryant Park, 135 West 42nd Street
☎ 212-319 1660
⌂ charliepalmer.com
🚇 Subway B, D, F, Q to 42nd Street
Once situated in a brownstone on the Upper East Side, now relocated in the spectacular Bank of America Tower. Celebrity chef Charlie Palmer – considered the king of New York chefs – frequently changes the menu, but delicious concoctions have included sesame-seared Atlantic salmon with orange-miso vinaigrette and sticky rice croquettes, and foie gras with port-glazed Bing cherries and young onions. Expensive, but worth it to experience dining in one of the best restaurants in town. Closed on Sun.

BG $$$-$$$$
American nouveau
✉ 754 5th Avenue at 58th Street
☎ 212-872 8977
⌂ bergdorfgoodman.com
🚇 Subway N, R, W to 5th Avenue/59th Street
The restaurant at Bergdorf Goodman department store makes a posh place to stop for a long lunch during a shopping spree. Or head here for an early dinner, as the restaurant shuts at 8pm. You can also go for the afternoon tea option – which is fabulous, darling.

db Bistro Moderne

BRASSERIE 44 $$$
Gourmet American
- ✉ Royalton Hotel, 44 West 44th Street between 5th and 6th Avenues
- ☎ 212-944 8844
- 🖥 royaltonhotel.com
- 🚇 Subway B, D, F, Q to 42nd Street

A très trendy joint in the Philippe Starck-designed Royalton Hotel, serving new American cuisine. A favourite with the media set.

CHINA GRILL $$$
Chinese
- ✉ CBS Building, 60 West 53rd Street between 5th and 6th Avenues
- ☎ 212-333 7788
- 🖥 chinagrillmgt.com
- 🚇 Subway B, D, F, V to 47th–50th Streets/ Rockefeller Center

Classy establishment, with soaring 8m/30ft ceiling, multilevel dining platforms and limestone floor. Serves eclectic food in a fairly noisy setting and has a bar that gets pretty crowded.

db BISTRO MODERNE $$$-$$$$
French–American
- ✉ City Club Hotel, 55 West 44th Street between 5th and 6th Avenues
- ☎ 212-391 2400
- 🖥 danielnyc.com/dbbistro.html
- 🚇 Subway B, D, F, V, S, 4, 5, 6, 7 to 42nd Street

The latest showcase for one of New York's superstar chefs, Daniel Boulud. It got lots of press for its $29 hamburger (now $32!), and became an instant scene. Located in the very star-chic City Club Hotel, this is one of the few really good places to eat close to the Theater District.

GORDON RAMSAY AT LONDON NYC HOTEL $$$$
British fusion
- ✉ 151 West 54th Street at 7th Avenue
- ☎ 212-307 5000
- 🖥 thelondonnyc.com
- 🚇 Subway B, D, E to 7th Avenue

London's most notorious Michelin three-star chef hit the Big Apple in style early 2007 at the former Righa Royal Hotel, which, after a $50 million refurbishment and name change, is now the new darling of the dining and bar scene. His food didn't go down too well with NY food critics initially, but we love it.

HARD ROCK CAFE $
American
- ✉ 1501 Broadway at 43rd Street
- ☎ 212-343 3355
- 🖥 hardrock.com
- 🚇 Subway N, Q, R, S, W, 1, 2, 3, 7, 9 to Times Square/42nd Street

Classic burger and chips 'cuisine' in a noisy, rock 'n' roll environment. It's now open for breakfast every Fri-Sun, 8–10am if you fancy eating your eggs over easy while checking out rock memorabilia, such as stage costumes worn by Madonna.

Gordon Ramsay at London NYC Hotel

INAKAYA
$$–$$$

Japanese

✉ 231 West 40th Street at 6th Avenue

☎ 212-354 2195

🖱 inakayany.com

🚗 Subway 1, 2, 3, 7, N, Q, R, S, W at Times Square/42nd Street

Newly opened buzzing Japanese, with a vast menu including sushi, sashimi and maki rolls, which come in 18 varieties, including spicy shrimp tempura, soft-shell crab and a yummy dragon roll.

◀🇬🇧▶ BRITTIP

Inakaya's lunchtime bento boxes are a good deal, particularly the $25 *take* option, which includes sashimi salad, pork belly and a grilled fish of the day.

JOHN'S PIZZERIA
$

Italian

✉ 260 West 44th Street between 7th and 8th Avenues

☎ 212-391 7560

🖱 johnspizzerianyc.com

🚗 Subway 1, 2, 3, 7, N, Q, R, S, W at Times Square/42nd Street

A grand setting with sweeping staircase and giant mural which happily still serves its brick-oven pizzas, such as the simple but tasty tomato and cheese, from just $12.50.

L'ATELIER DE JOEL ROBUCHON
$$$$

French

✉ 57 East 57th Street

☎ 212-758 5700

🖱 joel-robuchon.com

🚗 Subway 4, 5, 6 to 59th Street

L'Atelier de Joel Robuchon

With famous restaurants in Paris, Tokyo and Las Vegas, super chef Joel Robuchon finally opened a place in New York at the Four Seasons Hotel a couple of years ago. It's a very sophisticated and elegant dining experience, from the open kitchen in the centre of the restaurant so you can see the team in action to the red lacquer and light wood finishes on the furnishings. The best seats are the ones at the pearwood counter so you can see the kitchen, but there are only 20 so you are best to book well in advance. There are 26 other tables. Specialities include truffled mash potatoes and free-range quail stuffed with foie gras.

🇺🇸 NYINTHEKNOW

Head concierge Josephine Danielson at the Four Season Hotel recommends L'Atelier. 'New Yorkers are very jaded when it comes to dining out because they really have seen it all. However, when L'Atelier opened, even the most seasoned gourmet had to admit they had really experienced something unique. The counter seating and Asian-influenced French cuisine offered in Chef Robuchon's L'Atelier is truly unlike anything found in the city ... and this is no easy claim to make!'

MÅ PÊCHE
$$–$$$

French–Vietnamese

✉ 15 West 56th Street between 5th and 6th Avenues

☎ 212-757 5878

🖱 chambershotel.com

🚗 Subway F to 57th Street

Part of David Chang's empire, this is upscale dining courtesy of chef Tien Ho. It's all very minimalist, with blank walls and wooden tables laid out in an X formation. The food, such as pork sausage with rice noodles, is good value.

◀🇬🇧▶ BRITTIP

For the best cookies in town, pop into Momofuku Milk Bar, a takeout place at the front of Må Pêche.

NOBU FIFTY SEVEN
$$$$

Japanese–Peruvian

✉ 40th West 57 Street between 5th and 6th Avenues

☎ 212-757 3000

🖱 noburestaurants.com

🚗 Subway F to 57th Street

Opened in 2005, Nobu Fifty Seven is every bit as glam as the original Nobu New York and the food every bit as delicious served up in must-be-seen-to-be-believed surroundings according to *Zagat*, who describe it as a 'triumph of theatrical feng shui'. It is also said to be as hot for celeb-watching as the original.

NORMA'S $–$$
American
✉ Le Parker Meridien Hotel, 118 West 57th Street between 6th and 7th Avenues
☎ 212-708 7460
🖱 parkermeridien.com
🚇 Subway B, D, E to 7th Avenue

This award-winning all-day breakfast joint is très chi-chi, beautifully decorated and serves some of the most inventive 'breakfast' food going! Specialities include molten chocolate French toast with pineapple chutney, caramelised onion corned beef hash with poached eggs, and a serious stack of strawberry and rhubarb pancakes. Also desserts and fruit smoothies.

OPIA $$–$$$
French
✉ 130 East 57th Street at Lexington Avenue
☎ 212-688 3939
🖱 opiarestaurant.com
🚇 Subway 4, 5, 6, N, R, W to 59th Street/ Lexington Avenue

Recently renovated and with a new menu by chef Ted Pryor, Opia is an elegant restaurant that's also a hideaway, with lounge, bar and den too. The French-inspired cuisine is absolutely delicious and the expanded terraces outside are ideal for summer dining, though you need to book in advance.

REMI $$$
Italian
✉ 145 West 53rd Street between 6th and 7th Avenues
☎ 212-581 4242
🖱 remi.ypguides.net
🚇 Subway N, R to 49th Street; B, D east to 7th Avenue

To New Yorkers, this special restaurant is like a taste of Venice with its enchanting Atrium Garden that offers foreign films and live music to accompany dinner al fresco. It also has rotating art exhibitions all year long in the Rialto Room. The food, like roasted sardines or grilled octopus, is delicious and you can even get Remi takeaways.

ROCK CENTER CAFE $$
American
✉ Rockefeller Center, 20 West 50th Street between 5th and 6th Avenues
☎ 212-332 7620
🖱 rapatina.com/rockcentercafe/
🚇 Subway B, D, F, Q to 47th–50th Streets/ Rockefeller Plaza

Norma's at Le Parker Meridien

TOP 5 ROMANTIC RESTAURANTS

There are many restaurants in New York that can deliver on the food front, but don't quite get it right with the ambience. The venues listed below are the top places in town if you really want to inject a bit of romance into your dining experience, from tactile furnishings and soft lighting to sensuous food, they're a must-visit for lovers who are also food lovers.

Aureole: French, Upper East Side (page 174)

Daniel: French, Upper East Side (page 193)

The View: Continental, Theater District (page 189)

The Boathouse at Central Park: American–seafood, Central Park (page 161)

River Café: Gourmet American, Brooklyn (page 161)

A Mecca for tourists, thanks to the scenic setting on the north side of the Rockefeller's skating rink. Some original Warhol prints on the wall and open for breakfast, lunch and dinner.

SEAGRILL $$$$
Seafood
✉ Rockefeller Center, 19 West 49th Street between 5th and 6th Avenues
☎ 212-332 7610
🖰 theseagrillnyc.com
🚆 Subway B, D, F, Q to 47th–50th Streets/ Rockefeller Center

Surrounded by lush greenery, the outdoor tables topped with striped umbrellas in summer are replaced in winter by the famous

The Russian Tea Room

skating rink. The seafood specialities include Australian barramundi with wilted arugula, poached lobster with truffled potato and herb-crusted skate. Note that the refurbished restaurant's dress code has changed to exclude jeans, shorts and trainers.

SEPPI'S $$
French–Italian–Turkish
✉ 123 West 56th Street between 6th and 7th Avenues
☎ 212-708 7444
🖰 seppisny.com
🚆 Subway B, D, E to 7th Street

Perfect for Carnegie Hall-goers and open until 2am. A French bistro, eclectic dishes range from escargots in garlic butter to beef carpaccio with baby arugula and Parmesan and crawfish ravioli with lobster bisque, which are served in an informal, laid-back environment.

THE RUSSIAN TEA ROOM $$$$
Russian
✉ 150 West 57th Street at 7th Avenue
☎ 212-581 7100
🖰 russiantearoomnyc.com
🚆 Subway B, D, E to 7th Aveue

You're in luck! The legendary tea room was shut for some time and reopened in 2008 after a group of investors stepped in to resurrect this New York institution. Opened in the 1920s, it was bought by Warner LeRoy in 1995 and he poured $30 million into it and it reopened in 1999. However, the starry clientele that adored the tea room weren't so impressed with LeRoy's theatrical furnishings and it sadly closed its doors. Thankfully, the public can now be let loose again in this over-the-top playground, which has swooping eagles on the walls, red leather banquettes and fake Picassos on the walls. As for the dining, it's caviar all the way here, the most expensive being the Iranian special reserve that costs $300 for 30g/1oz, brought to the table on silver trays. Lots of other dishes too, but not as memorable, though the pre-theatre dinner menu of 3 courses for $55 is good value.

UPSTAIRS AT 21 $$
Gourmet American
✉ 21 West 52nd Street between 5th and 6th Avenues
☎ 212-582 7200
🖰 21club.com
🚆 Subway F to 5th Avenue

Here you can get many of the 21 Club's classic dishes in a less formal but equally well-serviced restaurant – and see out of windows into the bargain! It has quickly become a favourite with the trendy jet set.

ADOUR $$$-$$$$
French

✉ St Regis Hotel, 2 East 55th Street, between 5th and Madison Avenues
☎ 212-710 2277
🖰 adour-stregis.com
🚇 Subway E, V to 5th Avenue/53rd Street

Named after the river in south west France near which acclaimed chef Alain Ducasse was born, this restaurant is in the St Regis Hotel. Ducasse chose Tony Esnault as his executive chef to interpret traditional French cooking techniques with local flavours. The sumptuous dining room seats 70, with interior design by David Rockwell. There's a prix fixe and a tasting menu, featuring delicious French fusion dishes like venison saddle and olive oil-poached cod.

ASIA DE CUBA $$$-$$$$
Asian–Cuban

✉ Morgan's Hotel, 237 Madison Avenue between 37th and 38th Streets
☎ 212-726 7755
🖰 chinagrillmanagement.com
🚇 Subway 6 to 33rd Street; 4, 5, 6, 7 to Grand Central/42nd Street

The Philippe Starck interior guarantees a trendy crowd for the fusion Asian and Cuban food.

BULL & BEAR $$$-$$$$
Steakhouse

✉ The Waldorf Hotel entrance on Lexington Avenue at 49th Street
☎ 212-872 4900
🖰 waldorfastoria.com
🚇 Subway 6 to 51st Street

A landmark restaurant renowned for its excellent hospitality and unashamedly masculine decor that pays homage to the stock market bull and bear symbols. This is the number one restaurant in New York for delicious, melt-in-the-mouth, prime, aged Black Angus beef dishes, yet has plenty to offer the less carnivorously inclined.

If you want something a little lighter, there are mouth-watering dishes that include yellowfin tuna mignon and shrimp Creole with Andouille sausage and rice. For something lighter opt for one of the salads, such as lobster salad with mango, avocado and corn. Note, there's a no jeans or trainers policy here and a happy hour on drinks 5-6pm in the week.

CAVIAR RUSSE $$$$
Caviar

✉ 2nd floor, 538 Madison Avenue, between 54th and 55th Streets
☎ 212-980 5908
🖰 caviarrusse.com
🚇 Subway F to 5th Avenue

Posh caviar and cigar lounge where you can see how the other half lives, dining on caviar costing up to $300 for 25g. A spoon of the cheapest caviar is from $7 though, so it's possible to indulge without going bankrupt.

CHIN CHIN $$
Chinese

✉ 216 East 49th Street between 2nd and 3rd Avenues
☎ 212-888 4555
🖰 chinchinny.com
🚇 Subway 6 to 51st Street

One of New York's finest Chinese restaurants, it frequently plays host to the power crowd.

DOCKS OYSTER BAR $$$
Seafood

✉ 633 3rd Avenue at 40th Street
☎ 212-986 8080
🖰 docksoysterbar.com
🚇 Subway 4, 5, 6, 7 to Grand Central/42nd Street

This fish and seafood speciality restaurant also has a popular bar. Main dishes, such as red snapper, from $26.

EUROPA CAFE $
Mediterranean

✉ 599 Lexington Avenue at 53rd Street
☎ 212-755 6622
🖰 europacafe.com
🚇 Subway E, F to Lexington/3rd Avenue

A welcoming restaurant that has been designed in natural elements of wood, stone and earth tones to create a soothing environment. There are lots of branches dotted around the city (check the website) and you can pick up breakfast, lunch and snacks here, including creating your own sandwiches, wraps and salads. This one isn't open on Sat and Sun.

RESTAURANTS

179

Adour

FOUR SEASONS $$$$
Continental

✉ 99 East 52nd Street between Lexington
and Park Avenues

☎ 212-754 9494

🖰 fourseasonsrestaurant.com

🚗 Subway 6 to 51st Street; E, F to
Lexington/3rd Avenue

You have a choice between the Grill Room or
the Pool Room at this landmark restaurant,
and whichever you opt for will make you
feel like one of New York's movers and
shakers – this is where they come for their
power lunches. The Continental dishes are
exquisite, the setting elegant and the service
impeccable. Pricey? You bet.

ISTANA $$
American

✉ NY Palace Hotel, 455 Madison Avenue at
51st Street

☎ 212-303 6032

🖰 newyorkpalace.com

🚗 Subway 6 to 51st Street

A little-known but excellent restaurant
serving American cuisine for breakfast
– including favourites such as blueberry
pancakes, and lunch – a popular choice
is New York strip steak, in the incredibly
beautiful environs of the former Villard
Houses that are also home to Le Cirque.

LA GRENOUILLE $$$
French

✉ 3 East 52nd Street between 5th and
Madison Avenues

☎ 212-752 1495

🖰 la-grenouille.com

🚗 Subway 6 to 51st Street

A sophisticated temple for Francophiles that
first opened its doors in 1962, the exquisite

Four Seasons

French food is well worth its price. If money's
no object, go for dinner; otherwise go for a
more economical lunch.

LE CIRQUE $$$-$$$$
French–American

✉ One Beacon Court, The Bloomberg
Building, 151 58th Street at Lexington
Avenue

☎ 212-644 0202

🖰 lecirque.com

🚗 Subway 4, 5, 6 to 59th Street

Sirio Maccioni's family-run restaurant has been
the toast of the city for 30 years. After shutting
the doors on Le Cirque 2000 at the New York
Palace Hotel, it took over a year for the master
restaurateur to find a suitable place to reopen.
One Beacon Court, as it's officially known, is
attracting the same regular patrons it used
to, from the political, financial, music and
film worlds, including Robert De Niro, Oprah
Winfrey, Bill Clinton and The Rolling Stones.
The 1,486sq m/16,000sq ft restaurant features
a main dining room, separate bar area and
private mezzanine for those who want to see
but not be seen. Expect lots of jaw-dropping
sights such as a soaring wine tower that
connects the mezzanine to the first floor, an
all-glass bar and giant abstract Big Top light
shade. There's a prix fixe 3-course lunch menu
for $45.

MAMA MEXICO $$
Mexican

✉ 214 East 49th Street between 2nd and
3rd Avenues

☎ 212-935 1316

🖰 mamamexico.com

🚗 Subway 6 to 51st Street

A proper Mexican restaurant with bright
colours, pulsating mariachi music and a
festive crowd enjoying the extensive menu,
which includes 20-plus appetisers and great

Le Cirque

Oyster Bar

main courses like grilled rack of lamb with chilli and pineapple sauce. The margaritas and over 40 types of tequila will help put you in the party mood.

OYSTER BAR $$–$$$
Seafood

✉ Grand Central Station, lower level, between 42nd Street and Vanderbilt Avenue

☎ 212-490 6650

🖰 oysterbarny.com

🚗 Subway 4, 5, 6, 7 to Grand Central/42nd Street

It seems only appropriate to have a landmark restaurant like this in the landmark that is Grand Central Station. Its fame stems from the generations of connoisseurs who have consumed 1,000 dozen oysters every day at the counters of this atmospheric saloon since 1913. There's lots of other types of seafood available too.

PALM $$
Seafood–steakhouse

✉ 837 2nd Avenue between 44th and 45th Streets

☎ 212-687 2953

🖰 thepalm.com

🚗 Subway 4, 5, 6, 7 to Grand Central/ 42nd Street

A family-run business and now the heart of a multi-million-pound empire of Palm restaurants the length and breadth of North America, this establishment celebrated its 80th anniversary in 2006. Thanks to the double steak speciality, it had earned its reputation as one of New York's greatest steakhouses by the 1930s. In the 1940s, lobster was introduced, setting the seal on the surf-and-turf trend.

Palm continues to be a Mecca for celebrities and the wheelers and dealers of Manhattan, who come not only for the giant steaks and jumbo Maine lobsters but also for the Italian classics and wide choice of dishes. Palm Too across the road (840 2nd Avenue, 212-697 5198) was opened to take the overspill and now has its own loyal customers.

Mama Mexico

UNION SQUARE CAFE $$–$$$
American–Italian

✉ 21 East 16th Street between 5th Avenue and Union Square

☎ 212-243 4020

⌂ unionsquarecafe.com

🚇 Subway 4, 5, 6, L, N, R to Union Square.

One of America's most popular restaurants, Danny Meyer's Union Square Cafe serves robustly flavoured, seasonal American cuisine in a relaxed setting of casual elegance. It's worth noting that, despite the proliferation of fashionable eateries that regularly open in New York, it's this restaurant that the city's movers and shakers still flock to, to flex the company credit card. There are 3 dining areas: balcony seating and a cluster of tables on the lower level, both offshoots of the long mahogany bar, and an adjacent main dining room. The decor is simple but effective – think polished cherrywood floors, oversized pussy willows and colourful artwork on the walls. There's a full lunch and dinner menu with daily specials in the dining room and the bar.

BRITTIP
Restaurant mogul Danny Meyer, the brains behind the Union Square Cafe, has also opened The Modern at the Museum of Modern Art (212-333 1220, themodernnyc.com).

Union Square Cafe is as famous for its impeccable, friendly service as it is for its unusual but fabulous food. Top chef Carmen Quagliata's Italian-influenced menu includes delicacies such as housemade fettuccine pasta with roasted artichokes and pan-seared rainbow trout with local warm vegetables. Weekly specials include a lobster and pork chop.

WATER CLUB $–$$$
Seafood

✉ 500 East 30th Street at East River – entrance on East 23rd Street

☎ 212-683 3333

⌂ thewaterclub.com

🚇 Subway 6 to 28th Street, near Madison Square

Another delightful and special venue from the owner of the River Café (page 161), this nautical restaurant, set on an East River barge, also specialises in seafood. The Crow's Nest, a seasonal outdoor patio, sits atop the main dining room and features a moderately priced menu and fun drinks mid-May–late Sept and offers fab views of the East River. Although on the pricey side, it's well worth splashing out for the fine cuisine and, if you're counting the pennies, the weekend brunch option at a prix fixe is an excellent way to sample some delicious dishes while gazing at that view.

RESTAURANTS

Union Square Cafe

Barbetta

MIDTOWN WEST

BARBETTA $$$

Italian

✉ 321 West 46th Street between 8th and
9th Avenues

☎ 212-246 9171

🖱 barbettarestaurant.com

🚇 Subway A, C east to 42nd Street

During the summer, the rather special
Barbetta garden is one of the city's most
sought-after sites for dining, with its
century-old trees and the scented blooms
of magnolia, wisteria, jasmine and gardenia.
Having celebrated its 100th birthday in 2006,
Barbetta is the oldest Italian restaurant in
New York and features cuisine from Piedmont
in north-west Italy. Inside it's incredibly
ornate and luxurious, with drapes, candles
and chandeliers.

BOMBAY PALACE $$

Indian

✉ 30 West 52nd Street between 5th and
6th Avenues

☎ 212-541 7777

🖱 bombay-palace.com

🚇 Subway B, D, F, V, to 47th Street.

This upmarket Indian has a regal air, thanks
to the dark wood panelling and crystal
chandelier. It opened in 1979 and has been
feeding the city masses every since with very
good dishes, primarily Punjabi, which include
seekh kebab, chicken tikka and tandoori
shrimp and achar gosht, a chilli lamb stew.

JEAN GEORGES $$$$

French

✉ Trump International Hotel, 1 Central Park
West between 60th and 61st Streets

☎ 212-299 3900

🖱 jean-georges.com

🚇 Subway A, B, C, D, 1, 9 to 59th Street/
Columbus Circle

Celebrity chef Jean-Georges Vongerichten's
exquisite French dishes are served in an
elegant and visually stunning landmark
restaurant that is both romantic and relaxed.
'Prepare to sit open mouthed – when you're
not eating, that is' declares a *New York
Metro* review of this Adam Tihany-designed
contemporary Art Deco-style restaurant. The
upscale crowd also gets to enjoy superb views
of Central Park, while in good weather it's
possible to sit outside. An advantage of this
is the bargain $29, 2-plate, prix fixe lunches
on the terrace, also served in the Nougatine
Room. Dish highlights on a continually
changing menu have included asparagus
with rich morel mushrooms, Arctic char baked
with wood sorrel, and Muscovy duck steaks
with sweet and sour jus. It's an unbeatable
combination, so book your table in advance.

Jean Georges Restaurant

World Yacht Dinner Cruises

LE BERNARDIN $$$$
Seafood

✉ 155 West 51st Street between 6th and 7th Avenues
☎ 212-554 1515
🖱 le-bernardin.com
🚗 Subway V, F, B, D to Rockefeller Center

This is a marvellous restaurant. It's very pricey, the prix fixe lunch alone is $69, with dinner from $110 each, but it's more than worth it as the mouth-watering dishes are sublime. Chef Eric Ripert's cuisine is regarded by NY gourmets as very inventive. He provides an almost raw menu, which has featured

Le Bernadin

delicacies such as lemon-splashed scallops with olive oil and chives. From the cooked menu, tasty treats include celeriac open ravioli with lobster and shrimp with foie gras truffle sauce, or baked snapper in spicy sour broth. The dining room itself is also a pleasure to experience, featuring crisp white linen, rich furnishings and a wood-panelled bar with smart blue-and-gold striped chairs for lounging in pre- and post-dinner.

✚ BRITTIP
If you want to experience Le Bernardin but aren't keen on seafood, you can put in a request with a waiter for pasta or lamb dishes.

WORLD YACHT DINNER CRUISES $$$
Gourmet American

✉ Pier 81, West 41st Street at Hudson River
☎ 212-630 8100
🖱 worldyacht.com
🚗 Subway A, C, East to 42nd Street

If there's one thing that you do before you leave the city, it's to book a 4-course dining experience with World Yacht. This seasonal cruise down the river and around the bay offers, without a doubt, the best views of Midtown and Lower Manhattan plus the Statue of Liberty. You can chow down on delicacies like steak and lobster skewer, filet mignon, sevruga caviar and mustard-marinated organic chicken cooked while gazing at the city spread out before you. The chefs are some of the finest in New York, yet the prix fixe meals are pretty reasonable – including a 3-hour cruise and live music for dancing – $99 Sun–Thurs, $108.25 Fri and Sat. Smart dress; jackets required.

FIVE POINTS $$
American
- ✉ 31 Great Jones Street between Lafayette Street and Bowery
- ☎ 212-253 5700
- 🖱 fivepointsrestaurant.com
- 🚇 Subway B, V, S to Broadway/Lafayette; 6 to Bleecker Street

Named after the once infamous gangland area, this is a popular neighbourhood restaurant with a friendly bar, so now there's no need to worry. For a good, tasty meal, try out the Maine scallop with apple cider sauce or the home-made sweet potato ravioli.

INDOCHINE $$$
Vietnamese–French
- ✉ 430 Lafayette Street between Astor Place and East 4th Street
- ☎ 212-505 5111
- 🖱 indochinenyc.com
- 🚇 Subway 6 to Astor Place

This celebrity haunt serves delicious Vietnamese–French dishes, such as spring rolls and sole fish wrapped in banana leaf, in tiny portions.

BRITTIP
Indochine serves great cocktails. Try the Indochine Martini: pineapple and ginger infused Imperia vodka with fresh lime juice – delicious!

CAFE HABANA $
Cuban
- ✉ 17 Prince Street at Elizabeth Street
- ☎ 212-625 2001
- 🖱 ecoeatery.com
- 🚇 Subway N, R to Prince Street; 6 to Spring Street

It claims to be NYC's first eco eatery; a restaurant that uses earth friendly practices in its design, construction and day-to-day operations, plus it aims to reduce wasteful consumption and promote sustainability. So, you can chow down on home-style Latin food – think chicken tacos with coriander and tomato salsa – with a clear conscience in this hot and hip little joint.

EIGHT MILE CREEK $$$
Australian
- ✉ 240 Mulberry Street between Prince and Spring Streets
- ☎ 212-431 4635
- 🖱 eightmilecreek.com
- 🚇 Subway N, R to Prince Street; 6 to Spring Street

Just a few steps north of Little Italy, the laid-back Aussies have arrived serving up cuisine from Down Under. Good Aussie food is both deliciously exotic and pricey – and this tiny restaurant is no exception. There's now an OuT-the-bAck beer garden, which is home to weekly 'You bring meat, we'll supply the barbie' parties in the summer.

HOOMOOS ASLI $–$$
Middle Eastern
- ✉ 100 Kenmare Street between Mulberry and Center Streets
- ☎ 212-966 0022
- 🚇 Subway 6 to Spring Street

This is a great find if you're on a budget, small but not a dive and offering tasty Israeli cuisine – falafel, pittas, pan-fried chicken in bread crumb and spices, beef with caramelised onions and rice, with prices starting at around $8.

BRITTIP
If you want refreshments but are too busy shopping or sightseeing for a lengthy stop at a restaurant, then pop into the fantastically named Mud Spot (themudtruck.com), 307 East 9th Street, where you can buy a warming espresso to perk you up.

ZENGO $$–$$$
Mexican–Asian
- ✉ 622 3rd Avenue at 40th Street
- ☎ 212-808 8110
- 🖱 modernmexican.com
- 🚇 Subway 1, 2, 3 Grand Central Station

Just opened, this three-level restaurant includes a mezzanine with a sake lounge and

RESTAURANTS

185

Cafe Habana

the lower floor houses La Bibliotheca, which serves 400 tequilas in a library setting. The main dining room has a dark wood interior and leather banquettes. The food is excellent: Wagyu beef with miso mustard, $16, roasted chicken salad wtih mandarin oranges, cabbage and ginger vinaigrette, $11. Don't miss the Mexican chocolate tart for pudding.

SOHO

SoHo is a great place to head for when eating out, day or night. Its diverse range of restaurants, at all different price points, means that you're pretty much guaranteed to find something to appeal to even the most picky of dining partners.

BALTHAZAR $$
Bistro
- ✉ 80 Spring Street between Broadway and Crosby Streets
- ☎ 212-965 1414
- ⌖ balthazarny.com
- 🚇 Subway N, R to Prince Street

A classy French brasserie, with a genuinely French ambience, serving up good food to a trendy crowd. Great oysters.

BLUE RIBBON BRASSERIE $$$
American
- ✉ 97 Sullivan Street between Prince and Spring Streets
- ☎ 212-274 0404
- ⌖ blueribbonrestaurants.com
- 🚇 Subway C east to Spring Street

This restaurant gets packed at any time of the day or night so don't decide to come here if you are on a tight schedule. If you're not, the eclectic seafood dishes, like fried oysters and sautéed skate, are definitely worth the wait.

DOS CAMINOS SOHO $$–$$$
Mexican
- ✉ 475 West Broadway at Houston Street
- ☎ 212-277 4300
- ⌖ brguestrestaurants.com
- 🚇 Subway C, E to Spring Street

Excellent margaritas here while you're gazing at the fab menu that includes salad with calamari and chorizo, red snapper scallop with spicy mango and passion fruit and lime cilantro marinated gulf shrimp.

FANELLI'S CAFE $
American
- ✉ 94 Prince Street at Mercer Street
- ☎ 212-226 9412
- 🚇 Subway N, R to Prince Street

Contemporary crowds pack this former speakeasy, now an old saloon-style bar and dining room serving American food. It does excellent sandwiches for lunch.

KITTICHAI $$
American
- ✉ 60 Thompson Street between Spring and Broome Streets
- ☎ 212-219 2000
- ⌖ kittichairestaurant.com
- 🚇 Subway C, E to Spring Street

Based in trendy SoHo hotel 60 Thompson, this is a fashionable restaurant in its own right and serves up delicious American cuisine at reasonable prices.

L'ECOLE $$
French
- ✉ 462 Broadway
- ☎ 212-219 3300
- ⌖ frenchculinary.com/lecole
- 🚇 Subway 6, J, M, Z, N, Q, W to Canal Street; 6 to Spring Street.

This is the place to come if you want haute cuisine for café prices, as the chefs of this bright, airy restaurant are students of the French Culinary Institute who try out their cooking skills on willing customers. Just think, you could be eating poached sole with shrimp and mussels for just $28 from the prix fixe lunch menu made by a star chef of the future.

Dining al fresco in SoHo

RESTAURANTS

NEW YORK FOODS AND FOOD TERMS

Arugula: The American name for rocket, used in salads.

Bagels: As opposed to bialys, these are the delicious Jewish creations, which are at their very best when filled with smoked salmon and cream cheese.

Bialy: A cousin of the bagel, it originates from Bialystock in Eastern Europe and is kosher Jewish food. The dough is not as chewy as a bagel and there is no hole in the middle, just a depression in which garlic and onions are put. Without any tasty extras such as cream cheese, this is truly boring food.

Cannoli: Tubular-shaped biscuit bells with fresh cream on the inside, these come from Italy and are truly delicious.

Cilantro: American name for the fresh leaves of coriander.

Cobbler: A fruit pie topped with a biscuit-style crust.

Grits: Corn kernels.

Halva: Sweetened, crushed sesame paste. It originates from the Mediterranean, Turkey and Arabia.

Konja: A Chinese dessert that you can buy in bags – they are individual mouth-size pots of lychee jelly.

Lox: Thinly sliced pieces of smoked salmon, generally sold with a 'schmear' of cream cheese. It tastes the same as a smoked salmon and cream cheese bagel but works out much cheaper.

Morels: Deliciously meaty mushrooms from Oregon.

Pie: Used to refer to an entire pizza. Most are much larger than the ones we eat in the UK, so people tend to buy by the slice or share a whole 'pie'.

Scallion: Spring onion.

Schmear: A spreading of cream cheese on a bagel.

Sub: An extra large, long roll, named for its submarine-like shape.

You can find a list of more general US foods and food terms on pages 20–21.

LUCKY STRIKE $$
French
- ✉ 59 Grand Street between West Broadway and Wooster Street
- ☎ 212-941 0772
- ⌂ luckystrikeny.com
- 🚇 Subway A, C, E, 1, 9, N, A, 6 to Canal Street

Restaurateur Keith McNally's hot spot has become a watering hole for models, celebrities and club kids, as well as SoHo's art crowd. Ask for the cocktail list and marvel at the many martinis, including chocolate and espresso.

MERCER KITCHEN $$$
French–eclectic
- ✉ Mercer Hotel, 99 Prince Street at Mercer Street
- ☎ 212-966 5454
- ⌂ jean-georges.com
- 🚇 Subway N, R, W to Prince Street

Jean-Georges Vongerichten (he of Jean-Georges fame) oversees the eclectic French-inspired cuisine that is served to a trendy crowd in a chic environment.

QUATTRO GASTRONOMIA $$$
Italian
- ✉ Trump SoHo Hotel 246 Spring Street
- ☎ 212-842 4500
- ⌂ quattronewyork.com
- 🚇 Subway N, R, W to Prince Street

Traditional north Italian fare served in a plush setting of leather banquettes and chandeliers. You may even spot Donald and family as you tuck into dishes like porcini ravioli with porcini truffle sauce ($15).

Lucky Strike

THEATER DISTRICT (BROADWAY)

From 6th Avenue in the east to 9th Avenue in the west and from West 40th Street to West 53rd Street, the Theater District is as good a place as any to get a pre-theatre meal. As well as the many theatres, there are hundreds of restaurants and you'd be hard-pressed to go wrong.

BRITTIP

The main drag for eating in the Theater District is between 8th and 9th Avenues on West 46th Street and is known as Restaurant Row.

BLUE FIN $$
Seafood
- ✉ W Times Square Hotel, 1567 Broadway at 47th Street
- ☎ 212-918 1400
- ⌂ brguestrestaurants.com
- 🚇 Subway N, R, W to 49th Street

Serves up fresh fish in theatrical surroundings. Sushi is available on the first floor and there's a raw bar.

CAFE UN-DEUX-TROIS $$
French
- ✉ 123 44th Street between 6th and 7th Streets
- ☎ 212-918 1400
- ⌂ cafeundeuxtrois.biz
- 🚇 Subway all lines to 42nd Street

A tip from a reader, this beautiful bistro serves up mouthwatering favourites like steak frites ($31) and poulet cordon bleu ($24.50) in a lovely space, complete with long wooden bar, chandeliers, black and white pictures on the wall and leather and wood seating. A little bit of Paris in NYC.

Hudson Cafeteria

COLORS $$-$$$
International
- ✉ 417 Lafayette Street at Astor Place
- ☎ 212-777 8443
- ⌂ colors-newyork.com
- 🚇 Subway 6 to Astor Place

Colors made the headlines in 2006 as the restaurant where dozens of surviving workers from Windows on the World, the restaurant that was atop the World Trade Center, have regrouped; and they not only work there, but also have a financial say and stake in it. It's a co-operative venture, owned and run by its waiters and waitresses, bus boys and cooks. The menu is as global as you can get, from Eastern spring rolls with shellfish to Caribbean goat stew, or American rib-eye steak and seared scallops.

FIREBIRD $$-$$$
Caviar–Russian
- ✉ 365 West 46th Street between 8th and 9th Avenues
- ☎ 212-586 0244
- ⌂ firebirdrestaurant.com
- 🚇 Subway A, C east to 42nd Street

The opulent Russian decor creates a fabulous setting for tucking into the caviar and blinis. The prix fixe pre-theatre dinner is pretty good value at $49.99, but prices have crept up.

FRANKIE & JOHNNIE'S STEAKHOUSE $$
Steakhouse
- ✉ 269 West 45th Street between Broadway and 8th Avenue
- ☎ 212-997 9494
- ⌂ frankieandjohnnies.com
- 🚇 Subway A, C, E, N, R to 42nd Street

This is considered to be one of the longest-running shows on Broadway, having first opened as a speakeasy in 1926. Now it still retains its intimate hideaway aura and archetypal New York reputation as a classic steakhouse that has become renowned for its generous portions.

HUDSON CAFETERIA $$
Asian
- ✉ The Hudson Hotel, 356 West 58th Street between 8th and 9th Avenues
- ☎ 212-554 6500
- ⌂ chinagrillmgt.com
- 🚇 Subway A, B, C, D, 1, 2 to 59th Street/Columbus Circle

Described as the Ivy League meet Alice in Wonderland, the restaurant at Ian Schrager's hotel is a haven for people- and celeb-watching. Currently being refurbished, watch this space.

MARS 2112 $

American

✉ 1633 Broadway at 51st Street

☎ 212-582 2112

🖱 mars2112.com

🚇 Subway 1, 9 to 51st Street

This theme restaurant offering will take you out of this world to Mars via the space shuttle. Fortunately, the food is pretty American Earthbound so you won't be eating little green men. Of course, it comes with the ubiquitous shop where you can buy your own Martian doll. Be sure to have drinks first in the Mars Bar.

BRITTIP

Due to the law that bans smoking in all indoor public spaces, it is no longer possible to smoke even at a restaurant's bar. Some restaurants with outdoor seating are able to set aside tables for smoking, though.

PALM NEW YORK WEST SIDE $$–$$$

Seafood–steakhouse

✉ 250 West 50th Street between Broadway and 8th Avenue

☎ 212-333 7256

🖱 thepalm.com

🚇 Subway 1, 9 to 50th Street

A sister restaurant to the incredibly successful Palm restaurant (page 181), this has very quickly become a hot spot for celebrities, theatre-goers and tourists.

PETROSSIAN $$$

Caviar–Russian

✉ 182 West 58th Street at 7th Avenue

☎ 212-245 2214

🖱 petrossian.com

🚇 Subway N, R to 57th Street

TOP 5 RESTAURANTS TO SPOT A CELEBRITY

Blue Water Grill: Union Square (page 191)

Lucky Strike: SoHo (page 187)

Mercer Kitchen: SoHo (page 187)

Nobu: TriBeCa (page 190)

TriBeCa Grill: TriBeCa (page 191)

Take advantage of the $35 prix fixe theatre menu to enjoy caviar, foie gras and smoked salmon.

PLANET HOLLYWOOD $

American

✉ 1540 Broadway at West 45th Street

☎ 212-333 7827

🖱 planethollywood.com

🚇 Subway N, Q, R, S, W, 1, 2, 3, 7 to Times Square

Hollywood memorabilia with the standard American burger fare.

RUBY FOO'S $$

Asian

✉ 1626 Broadway at 49th Street

☎ 212-489 5600

🖱 brguestrestaurants.com

🚇 Subway A, C, E, 1, N R to Times Square

Beautiful Asian decor combined with delicious Asian food. Dim sum is a speciality of the house.

THE VIEW $$$–$$$$

Continental

✉ Top floor, Marriott Marquis Hotel, 1535 Broadway at 45th Street

☎ 212-398 1900

🖱 nymarriottmarquis.com

🚇 Subway N, R, S, 1, 2, 3, 7, 9 to Times Square/42nd Street

New York's recently spruced-up revolving restaurant attracts lovebirds and tourists

Mars 2112

in droves, and serves up a high standard of Continental cuisine. As expected, the views over Manhattan are spectacular, particularly at sunset.

◀ ▶ BRITTIP
Don't be too put off by the prices of landmark restaurants – many offer fixed price menus and the cheapest is for lunch, when it's also easier to get a table. Go on, treat yourself!

TRIBECA

ACAPPELLA $$$–$$$$
Italian
- ✉ 1 Hudson Street at Chambers Street
- ☎ 212-240 0163
- ⌂ acappella-restaurant.com
- 🚇 Subway 1, 9 to Franklin Street

You can chow down on wild boar, quail and venison at this lovely restaurant specialising in northern Italian cuisine. The decor is as impressive as the menu, with 5m/16ft high beamed ceilings and Italian tapestries on the walls, plus huge windows offering views over TriBeCa.

AGO $$–$$$
Tuscan
- ✉ 377 Greenwich Street, at Moore Street
- ☎ 212-925 3797
- ⌂ agorestaurant.com
- 🚇 Subway 1, 9 to Franklin Street

Opened in 2008 in Robert De Niro's hip Greenwich Hotel, this bustling restaurant offers exceptionally good traditional Tuscan

dishes such as a starter of steamed octopus with potatoes and string beans, $15, and main courses like hand-rolled pasta with fresh ahi tuna, diced tomato and black olives, $24.

BOULEY $$$–$$$$
New French
- ✉ 163 Duane Street
- ☎ 212-964 2525
- ⌂ davidbouley.com
- 🚇 Subway A, C, 1, 2, 3, 9 to Chambers Street

Latest eatery from creative chef David Bouley, offering incredible food like Maine day boat lobster, rhubarb, peas and parsnip cloud, in a fabulous setting of red, vaulted ceilings. Has gone down a storm with critics and locals alike.

HARRISON $$–$$$
Continental
- ✉ 355 Greenwich Street at Harrison Street
- ☎ 212-274 9310
- ⌂ theharrison.com
- 🚇 Subway 1, 2 to Franklin Street

Created by the owners of the hip Red Cat in Chelsea (page 163), this chic restaurant serves up delicious Continental cuisine in an elegant setting.

NOBU $$$$
Japanese-Peruvian
- ✉ 105 Hudson Street at Franklin Street
- ☎ 212-219 0500
- ⌂ noburestaurants.com
- 🚇 Subway 1, 9 to Hudson Street

It's been around for 13 years now (ancient for a fashionable New York restaurant), but this TriBeCa Mecca is still without a doubt the best Japanese restaurant in the US, serving excellent fresh cuisine that will find 'tastebuds you never knew you had' according to the restaurant researchers at *Zagat*. The decor, by architect David Rockwell, is east meets west, with birch trees, wood floors, seaweed mats and subdued lighting. The multi-award-winning menu includes lots of cooked and raw delicacies, the black cod with miso continues to be a favourite and the new-style sashimi lightly cooked with garlic is also amazing.

◀ ▶ BRITTIP
If you can't get into the celeb-jammed Nobu, try Nobu Next Door (212-334 4445), which only takes walk-ins and is, unsurprisingly, located next door to the main restaurant. It is a more reasonably priced outlet for mere mortals who would rather wait for an hour than a month to sample some of the food everyone is raving about.

RESTAURANTS

Acappella

ODEON $$
American–French
- ✉ 145 West Broadway between Duane and Thomas Streets
- ☎ 212-233 0507
- ⌂ theodeonrestaurant.com
- 🚕 Subway 1, 9 to Chambers Street

A très hip hangout that still attracts celebrities for its cool atmosphere and American–French cuisine. You'll need to book ahead. A great late night stop as it stays open until 2am.

TERROIR TRIBECA $$
American
- ✉ 24 Harrison Street
- ☎ 212-625 9463
- ⌂ wineisterroir.com
- 🚕 Subway A, B, C to Franklin Street

Technically a wine bar, but the fodder here is so good and reasonable we're putting it in the restaurant section. You can order lots of dishes or a large main, like funky meatballs, sage leaves with lamb sausage or beet gorgonzola risotto balls, all $7 each. Simple, tasty and with a great selection of wines too.

TRIBECA GRILL $$$
American
- ✉ 375 Greenwich Street at Franklin Street
- ☎ 212-941 3900
- ⌂ tribecagrill.com
- 🚕 Subway 1, 9 to Franklin Street

Robert De Niro and Drew Nieporent's popular American restaurant opened in 1990 and is one of the main reasons why TriBeCa has become such a hip hangout in recent years. It's located on the first 2 floors of the TriBeCa Film Center where De Niro has his film production company, so it's a good place to try to spot a celeb or two. Dishes like braised short ribs with foie gras ravioli are rich and filling. The lunch menu attracts major crowds, with dishes like rare seared tuna and citrus marinated shrimp cocktail.

UNION SQUARE

BLUE WATER GRILL $$$$
Seafood
- ✉ 31 Union Square West at 16th Street
- ☎ 212-675 9500
- ⌂ brguestrestaurants.com
- 🚕 Subway L, N, Q, R, W, 4, 5, 6 to Union Square

Rated highly by *Zagat*, this place is not only brilliant for people- and celeb-watching, it is also a Mecca for all those who love their seafood. Dishes include almond-crusted mahi mahi and blackened swordfish. It also has an oyster bar and a 150-seat jazz club for nightly entertainment and dining.

CHAT 'N' CHEW $
American diner
- ✉ 10 East 16th Street between 5th Avenue and Union Square West
- ☎ 212-243 1616
- 🚕 Subway L, N, R, 4, 5, 6 to Union Square/14th Street

Classic 1950s American diner with huge servings of meatloaf, etc. Regulars know to order the crispy-topped macaroni and cheese, with chicken or bacon added.

🇬🇧 BRITTIP
Wine is incredibly expensive in New York. Do as New Yorkers do – have a glass of wine or cocktail before you go out and drink beer with your meal or just stick to the one glass of wine.

MESA GRILL $$
South-western
- ✉ 102 5th Avenue between 15th and 16th Streets near Union Square
- ☎ 212-807 7400
- ⌂ mesagrill.com
- 🚕 Subway L, N, R, 4, 5, 6 to Union Square/14th Street

Delicious and inventive south-western cuisine, think spice-crusted tuna steak or southwestern spice duck, from chef Bobby Flay. A real winner, so give it a try if you are in the area.

Blue Water Grill

THE AMERICAN DINER

We don't have a real equivalent of an American diner in the UK, but the closest is probably a cross between a transport café and a Garfunkel's. In a nutshell, diners are relatively cheap, have a homey feel to them, but are a lot smarter than your average café. They specialise in American comfort food – pancakes, waffles, crispy bacon, eggs, grill foods, meatloaf – the kind of things that we would choose for a brunch. Go to just about any American city or town and you'll find a good smattering of diners. The one exception is Manhattan, where they are very thin on the ground. Some of the few diners in New York include:

Midtown West

Market Diner: 572 11th Avenue at West 43rd Street, 212-695 0415, marketdinernyc.com. One of the most famous diners in Manhattan, this is where clubbers go to get breakfast or to fill up before the evening run.

Morningside Heights

Tom's Restaurant: 2880 Broadway at 112th Street, 212-864 6137. The exterior was made famous by its use in *Seinfeld*. If you come here you'll be sharing the space with Columbia University students, who enjoy the cheap comfort food.

NoHo

Great Jones Cafe: 54 Great Jones Street between Bowery and Lafayette Streets, 212-674 9304, greatjones.com. Set up in 1983, it's a cheap and cheerful place with weekend brunch from 11.30am–4pm.

Theater District

Ellen's Stardust Diner: 1650 Broadway at 51st Street, 212-956 5151, ellensstardustdiner. com. Tourists and children love this 1950s-style diner thanks to its kitsch-retro decor and the singing waitresses. It's great fun, but you wouldn't want to eat here too often – think burgers, chips and anything else that's greasy!

Upper West Side

EJ's Luncheonette: 447 Amsterdam Avenue between 81st and 82nd streets, 212-873 3444. A traditional American diner that serves a mean cup of coffee.

REPUBLIC $
Asian
- ✉ 37 Union Square West between 16th and 17th Streets
- ☎ 212-627 7172
- ⌂ thinknoodles.com
- 🚇 Subway L, N, R, 4, 5, 6 to Union Square/14th Street

Specialists in excellent, quick, noodle-based pan-Asian dishes in a canteen-style environment that seats 150. There is also a branch in Upper West Side.

STRIP HOUSE $$
American
- ✉ 13 East 12th Street between 5th Avenue and University Place
- ☎ 212-328 0000
- ⌂ theglaziergroup.com
- 🚇 Subway L, N, Q, R, W, 4, 5, 6 to 14th Street/Union Square

You can eat succulent beef here, especially, of course, the New York 'strip'. Lots of other cuts are available as well as some fish, all served in the glorious surroundings of leather banquettes and velvet.

UPPER EAST SIDE

ATLANTIC GRILL $$–$$$
Seafood
- ✉ 1341 3rd Avenue between 76th and 77th Streets
- ☎ 212-988 9200
- ⌂ brguestrestaurants.com
- 🚇 Subway 77th Street

A long-standing popular restaurant with the fussy Upper East Side set. It's all very chic, from the polished wood floors and artwork to the well-prepared, very fresh fish. There's also an excellent wine list.

CAFE SABARSKY $$
Bistro
- ✉ 1048 5th Avenue at 86th Street
- ☎ 212-288 0665
- ⌂ wallse.com
- 🚇 Subway 4, 5, 6 to 86th Street

This is not just in a fabulous location – all but opposite the Metropolitan Museum of Art, yet quietly tucked away in the new Neue Galerie Museum for German and Austrian Art (page 116) – but is a wonderful pit stop for light breakfasts, lunches and afternoon tea;

crêpes with smoked trout and scallops with asparagus. You'll also love its elegant decor to match the Austrian-German art theme of the museum itself.

CANDLE 79 $-$$

Vegetarian

- ✉ 154 East 79th Street at Lexington Street
- ☎ 212-472 0970
- 🖐 candle79.com
- 🚇 Subway 6 to 77th Street

An unusual place in this swish neighbourhood as it's veggie – though undoubtedly upscale. It was voted the Best Vegetarian Restaurant by *Zagat* in 2007, and you can see why when you glance at the menu, which is well thought out and attracts plenty of meat-eaters because it's so tasty. There's organic wine on offer, along with fresh juices and smoothies.

CARLYLE $$$

French

- ✉ Carlyle Hotel, 35 East 76th Street at Madison Avenue
- ☎ 212-744 1600
- 🖐 thecarlyle.com
- 🚇 Subway 6 to 77th Street

An old establishment that attracts an older clientele, but if you want to see how NY socialites mix, try the divine French cuisine for breakfast or brunch.

DANIEL $$$$

French

- ✉ 60 East 65th Street between Park and Madison Avenues
- ☎ 212-288 0033
- 🖐 danielnyc.com
- 🚇 Subway 6 to 68th Street; F to Lexington Avenue/63rd Street

This is the place to 'dazzle a date' according to hip website gonyc.about.com. It's a grand, elegant place with soaring ceilings, gilded columns, plush wall hangings and upholstery, plus fine art and mosaics. Daniel Boulud's haute cuisine is sumptuous, the best of which are the amazing, award-winning desserts; the chocolate bombe is indeed the bomb. It's fine dining with excellent service that will transport you as close to heaven as a mortal can get! A jacket is required to start the journey.

◀⊞▶ BRITTIP

Café Boulud at 20 East 76th Street (212-772 2600) also offers the Daniel's creativity at more accessible prices in a casual setting.

ITHAKA $$

Greek

- ✉ 308 East 86th Street between 1st and 2nd Avenues
- ☎ 212-628 9100
- 🖐 ithakarestaurant.com
- 🚇 Subway 4, 5, 6 to 86th Street

A superb Greek restaurant with exposed brick walls painted white, stone floor and recessed lighting filtered through white fabric. It's known for its large portions, a real locals' favourite with the added benefit of a guitar player Wed–Sat.

ROSA MEXICANO $$

Mexican

- ✉ 1063 1st Avenue at 58th Street
- ☎ 212-753 7407
- 🖐 rosamexicano.com
- 🚇 Subway 4, 5, 6 to 59th Street

Extremely popular Mexican eatery that is known as much for its margaritas as for its delicious food. Its signature dish is its guacamole mashed right beside your table.

SERAFINA FABULOUS GRILL $$$

Italian

- ✉ 29 East 61st Street
- ☎ 212-702 9898
- 🖐 serafinarestaurant.com
- 🚇 Subway 4, 5, 6 to 59th Street

Famous for thin-crust pizzas that have been voted the best in the world by gourmets, this is a haunt of both Prince Albert of Monaco and Ivana Trump. Toppings include Al Porcini with porcini mushrooms, fontina cheese, and mozzarella and Al Caviar with salmon caviar, potatoes and crème fraîche. The signature focaccias – 2 layers of stuffed dough with delicious fillings – range from a delicious Scottish smoked salmon, asparagus and Italian robiola cheese, to truffle oil and robiola.

Serafina

ALOUETTE $$$
French bistro
✉ 2588 Broadway between 97th and 98th Streets
☎ 212-222 6808
🖱 http://alouettenyc.com
🚗 Subway 1, 2, 3, 9 to 96th Street

This French bistro attracts the crowds despite having a very simple menu.

BENOIT $$
French Bistro
✉ 60 West 55th Street between 5th and 6th Avenues
☎ 646 943 7373
🖱 benoitny.com
🚗 Subway N, Q, R, W to 57th Street

This upscale casual French Bistro from Alain Ducasse opened in 2008 to great acclaim. Booking is wise.

NYINTHEKNOW

'For a great outdoor venue – and one of our best kept secrets – try the Boat Basin (boatbasincafe. com) under the West Side Highway at West 79th Street. It's hard to find even for New Yorkers but the views of the Hudson perched above the water's edge are amazing. Don't expect gourmet, it's fun food (burgers, hot dogs, nachos) and drinks – basically beer and coke,' says Mike Ricci, director of communications Hilton Hotels Corporation north-east US and Canada.

El Malecon II

EL MALECON II $
Dominican Caribbean
✉ 764 Amsterdam Avenue between 97th and 98th Streets
☎ 212-864 5648
🖱 maleconrestaurants.com
🚗 Subway 1, 9 to 66th Street

Great value for money. Locals pop in for the fried chicken, plantain, rice, peas and steak. The dining room is pretty mediocre, but who cares when the food is this tasty and $6 for the best roasted chicken outside the Caribbean. You can eat in or take out.

FATTY CRAB $$
Malaysian
✉ 2170 Broadway at 77th Street
☎ 212-496 2722
🖱 fattycrab.com
🚗 Subway 1, 2, 3 to 72nd Street

US celeb chef Zak Pecaccio's *Zagat*-rated place (it opened in 2009) has a really eclectic menu just perfect for foodies who like to try something new, like Malay fish fry, quail egg shooters and chilli crab. There's also a branch in West Village.

BRITTIP

The Fatty Crab has introduced a brunch menu, so pop here if you're feeling peckish and you've missed your hotel brekkie!

GABRIEL'S $$$
North Italian
✉ 11 West 60th Street
☎ 212-256 4600
🖱 gabrielsbarandrest.com
🚗 Subway A, B, C, D, 1 West 59th Street/ Time Warner Center

Recommended to us by a reader, this is a classy little joint with crisp, white tablecloths, wooden chairs and leather banquettes. It's where people from the entertainment industry like to congregate and sip blueberry bellinis and dine on delicious dishes like tortelloni filled with lamb and sea scallops sautéed with tarragon aioli and roast potatoes.

OUEST $$-$$$
French–American
✉ 2315 Broadway between 83rd and 84th Streets
☎ 212-580 8700
🖱 ouestny.com
🚗 Subway 1, 2 to 86th Street

Once you can get your tongue around the restaurant's name – it's simply pronounced 'West'! – you'll be ready to enjoy the French–American cuisine created by Valenti.

Fatty Crab

PASHA $$
Turkish

- ✉ 70 West 71st Street between Columbus Avenue and Central Park West
- ☎ 212-579 8751
- 🖰 pashanewyork.com
- 🚇 Subway 1, 2 to 86th Street

A delightfully sumptuous restaurant; think deep reds and yellows, luxurious fabrics and tapestries hanging on the walls. You can order Turkish delights, from stuffed vine leaves to kebabs and there are some outside tables.

PICHOLINE $$$
Mediterranean

- ✉ 35 West 64th Street between Broadway and Central Park West
- ☎ 212-724 8585
- 🖰 picholinenyc.com
- 🚇 Subway 1, 9 to 66th Street/Lincoln Center

A beautiful restaurant serving exquisite Mediterranean dishes in a refined and elegant setting. Opt to make it one of your 'special' treats while in the city so you can sample the amazing cheese trolley – yes trolley, not board. Each day more than 50 different cheeses, out of a total of 70 varieties, are on offer and, if you don't know which to choose, all the waiters are well versed in what cheeses go well with what wines and for what kind of palates. Take advantage of their considerable knowledge. A tradition to be savoured.

PIZZERIA UNO $
Italian

- ✉ 432 Columbus Avenue at 81st Street
- ☎ 212-595 4700
- 🖰 unos.com
- 🚇 Subway B, C to 81st Street

OK, so this is a chain restaurant, but it actually provides good-quality food for those wanting a simple, but tasty, meal at a very good price. This one is a great little neighbourhood joint offering an excellent range of family-friendly dishes just around the corner from the American Museum of Natural History (page 100). There is an excellently priced children's menu, plus crayons. What more could you ask after tramping round dinosaur exhibits?

SPAZZIA $$
Mediterranean

- ✉ 366 Columbus Avenue at West 77th Street
- ☎ 212-799 0150
- 🚇 Subway 1, 9 to 79th Street

This restaurant serves delicious Mediterranean food just a stone's throw away from the American Museum of Natural History (page 100).

Picholine

RESTAURANT REFERENCE GUIDE

Name	Area	Style	Price range	Page
2 West	Battery Park	American fusion	$$–$$$	160
5 Ninth	Meatpacking District	American nouveau	$$$	172
21 Club	Midtown	Gourmet American	$–$$$	173
202	Chelsea	British–Mediterranean	$$	162
A Voce	Madison Square/Flatiron	Italian	$$$–$$$$	172
Acappella	TriBeCa	Italian	$$$–$$$$	190
Adour	Midtown East	French	$$$–$$$$	179
Ago	TriBeCa	Italian	$$–$$$	190
Adrienne's Pizza Bar	Financial District	Italian	$–$$	165
Aldea	Flatiron District	Mediterranean	$$$–$$$$	172
Alias	Lower East Side	American	$$	171
AJ Maxwell's	Midtown	American	$$–$$$	174
Alouette	Upper West Side	French bistro	$$$	194
Amy Ruth's Home Style Southern Soul Food	Harlem	Southern Cuisine	$$	169
Angelica Kitchen	East Village	Vegetarian–vegan	$$	164
Angelo's	Little Italy	Italian	$	169
Aquavit	Midtown	Scandinavian	$$$$	174
Asia de Cuba	Midtown East	Asian–Cuban	$$$–$$$$	179
Atlantic Grill	Upper East Side	Seafood	$$–$$$	192
Aureole	Midtown	American	$$$$	174
Babbo	Greenwich Village	Italian	$$$$	167
Balthazar	SoHo	Bistro	$$	186
Bar Martignetti	Little Italy	Italian	$$–$$$	170
Barbetta	Midtown West	Italian	$$$	183
Battery Gardens	Battery Park	Gourmet American	$$$$	160
Benoit	Upper West Side	French Bistro	$$	194
Bereket	Lower East Side	Turkish	$	171
BG	Midtown	American nouveau	$$$–$$$$	174
Big Wong King	Chinatown	Cantonese	$	163
Blue Fin	Theater District	Seafood	$$	188
Blue Ribbon Brasserie	SoHo	American	$$$	186
Blue Water Grill	Union Square	Seafood	$$$$	191
Boathouse, The	Central Park	American–Seafood	$$–$$$	161
Bombay Palace	Midtown West	Indian	$$	183
Bondi Road	Lower East Side	Seafood	$$	171
Bongo	Chelsea	Seafood	$$$–$$$$	162
Bottino	Chelsea	Italian	$$	162
Bouley	TriBeCa	New French	$$$–$$$$	190
Brasserie 44	Midtown	Gourmet American	$$$	175
Bread	Little Italy	Italian	$$	170
Buddakan	Chelsea	Pan–Asian	$$$–$$$$	162
Bull & Bear	Midtown East	Steakhouse	$$$–$$$$	179
Café Gitane	Little Italy	French–North African	$$	170
Café Habana	NoLiTa	Cuban	$	185
Café Sabarsky	Upper East Side	Bistro	$$	192
Cafeteria	Chelsea	American diner	$$	162
Café Un-Deux-Trois	Theater District	French	$$	188
Candle 79	Upper East Side	Vegetarian	$–$$	193
Carlyle	Upper East Side	French	$$$	193
Caviar Russe	Midtown East	Caviar	$$$$	180
Chat 'n' Chew	Union Square	American diner	$	191
Chin Chin	Midtown East	Chinese	$$	180
China Grill	Midtown	Chinese	$$$	175
Clerkenwell, The	Lower East Side	English/Gastro pub	$–$$	171
Colors	Theater District	International	$$–$$$	188
Commerce	Greenwich	New American	$$–$$$	167
Cornelia Street Café	Greenwich Village	Eclectic	$$	167
Daniel	Upper East Side	French	$$$$	193
db Bistro Moderne	Midtown	French–American	$$$–$$$$	175
Del Posto	Meatpacking District	Italian	$$$	173
Dim Sum Go Go	Chinatown	Chinese–vegetarian	$$	163
Dock's Oyster Bar	Midtown East	Seafood	$$$	180
Dos Caminos Soho	SoHo	Mexican	$$–$$$	186
Eight Mile Creek	NoLiTa	Australian	$$$	185

Name	Area	Style	Price range	Page
EJ's Luncheonette	Upper West Side	Diner	$	192
El Malecon II	Upper West Side	Dominican Caribbean	$	194
Elephant, The	East Village	French–Thai fusion	$$	165
Eleven Madison Park	Gramercy Park	French–American	$$$$	166
Ellen's Stardust Diner	Theater District	Diner	$	192
Europa Café	Midtown East	Mediterranean	$	180
Fanelli Café	SoHo	American	$	186
Fatty Crab	Upper West Side	Malaysian	$$	194
Ferrara	Little Italy	Italian café	$	170
Firebird	Theater District	Caviar–Russian	$$–$$$	188
Five Points	NoHo	American	$$	185
Four Seasons	Midtown East	Continental	$$$$	180
Frank	East Village	Italian	$	164
Frankie & Johnnie's	Theater District	Steakhouse	$$	188
Gabriel's	Upper West Side	North Italian	$$$	194
Garage Restaurant & Café	West Village	American	$	168
Gigino at Wagner Park	Battery Park	Italian	$$	160
Gnocco Cucina & Tradizione	East Village	Italian	$$	164
Gotham Bar and Grill	Greenwich Village	Gourmet American	$$$	168
Gordon Ramsay	Midtown	British fusion	$$$$	175
Gramercy Tavern	Gramercy Park	Gourmet American	$$$	166
Great Jones Cafe	NoHo	Diner	$	192
Grimaldi's	Brooklyn	Italian	$	160
Hard Rock Café	Midtown	American	$	175
Harrison	TriBeCa	Continental	$$–$$$	190
Hoomoos Asli	NoLiTa	Middle Eastern	$–$$	185
Hudson Cafeteria	Theater District	Asian	$$	188
Il Palazzo	Little Italy	Italian	$	169
Inakaya	Midtown	Japanese	$$–$$$	176
Indochine	NoHo	Vietnamese–French	$$$	185
Istana	Midtown East	American	$$	180
Ithaka	Upper East Side	Greek	$$	193
Jean Georges	Midtown West	French	$$$$	183
Joe's Shanghai	Chinatown	Chinese–Shanghai	$$	163
John's Pizzeria	Midtown	Italian	$	176
Katz's Delicatessen	Lower East Side	American–Jewish	$	171
Kenmare	Little Italy	New American	$$–$$$	170
Kittichai	SoHo	American	$$	186
Koodo Sushi	Financial District	Japanese	$–$$	166
La Grenouille	Midtown East	French	$$$	180
La Palapa	East Village	Mexican	$$	165
L'Atelier de Joel Robuchon	Midtown	French	$$$$	176
Le Bernardin	Midtown West	Seafood	$$$$	184
L'Ecole	SoHo	French	$$	186
Le Cirque	Midtown East	French–American	$$$–$$$$	180
Lombardi's	Little Italy	Italian	$$	169
Lucky Strike	SoHo	French	$$	187
Mama Mexico	Midtown East	Mexican	$$	181
Mã Pêche	Midtown	French–Vietnamese	$$–$$$	176
Market Diner	Midtown West	Diner	$	192
MarkJoseph Steakhouse	South Street Seaport	Steakhouse	$$	166
Markt	Chelsea	Belgian	$$	162
Mars 2112	Theater District	American	$	189
Mercer Kitchen	SoHo	French–eclectic	$$$	187
Mesa Grill	Union Square	South-western	$$	191
Momofuku	East Village	Noodles	$$	165
Nice Green Bo	Chinatown	Chinese–Shanghai	$–$$	163
Nobu	TriBeCa	Japanese–Peruvian	$$$$	190
Nobu Fifty Seven	Midtown	Japanese–Peruvian	$$$$	176
Noodle Pudding	Brooklyn	Italian	$$	160
Norma's	Midtown	American	$–$$	177
Odeon	TriBeCa	American–French	$$	191
Old Homestead Steakhouse	Meatpacking District	American	$$	173
Opia	Midtown	French	$$–$$$$	177
Ouest	Upper West Side	French–American	$$–$$$	194
Oyster Bar	Midtown East	Seafood	$$–$$$	181
Palm	Midtown East	Seafood–steakhouse	$$	181

Name	Area	Style	Price range	Page
Palm New York West Side	Theater District	Seafood-steakhouse	$$-$$$	189
Park, The	Chelsea	Mediterranean	$$$	162
Pasha	Upper West Side	Turkish	$$	195
Pastis	Meatpacking District	French	$$$	173
Pellegrino's	Little Italy	Italian	$	169
Petrossian	Theater District	Caviar-Russian	$$$	189
Philip Marie	West Village	American	$$-$$$	168
Picholine	Upper West Side	Mediterranean	$$$	195
Pizzeria Uno	Upper West Side	Italian	$	195
Planet Hollywood	Theater District	American	$	189
Quattro Gastronomia	SoHo	Italian	$$$	187
Rao's	Harlem	Italian	$	169
Red Cat, The	Chelsea	Mediterranean-American	$$	163
Remi	Midtown	Italian	$$$	177
Republic	Union Square	Asian	$	192
River Café	Brooklyn	Gourmet American	$$$	161
Rock Center Café	Midtown	American	$$	177
Rosa Mexicano	Upper East Side	Mexican	$$	193
Ruby Foo's	Theater District	Asian	$$	189
Russian Tea Room	Midtown	Russian	$$$$	178
Sal Anthony's SPQR	Little Italy	Italian	$$-$$$	170
Seagrill	Midtown	Seafood	$$$$	178
Seppi's	Midtown	French-Italian-Turkish	$$	178
Serafina Fabulous Grill	Upper East Side	Italian	$$$	193
Soto	Greenwich & West Village	Japanese	$$$-$$$$	168
Spazzia	Upper West Side	Mediterranean	$$	195
Strip House	Union Square	American	$$	192
Sylvia's	Harlem	Southern soul food	$	169
Tabla	Madison Square	American Indian	$$$$	172
Tamarind	Gramercy Park	Indian	$$	166
Tavern on the Green	Central Park	Gourmet American	$$$	161
Terrazza Toscana	Hell's Kitchen	Italian	$$	169
Terroir Tribeca	TriBeCa	American	$$	191
Tomoe Sushi	Greenwich Village	Japanese	$$	169
Tom's Restaurant	Morningside Heights	Diner	$	192
TriBeCa Grill	TriBeCa	American	$$$	191
Union Square Cafe	Midtown East	American-Italian	$$-$$$	182
Upstairs at 21	Midtown	Gourmet American	$$	178
Veritas	Gramercy Park	Gourmet American	$$$$	166
View, The	Theater District	Continental	$$$-$$$$	189
Water Club	Midtown East	Seafood	$-$$$	182
White Slab Palace	Lower East Side	Scandinavian	$$	171
World Yacht Dinner Cruises	Midtown West	Gourmet American	$$$	184
Yaffa Café	East Village	American diner	$	165
Zengo	NoLiTa	Mexican-Asian	$$-$$$	185

Petrossian

CHAPTER 8

Nightlife

New York is known for its shopping and exciting nightlife. After a hard day hitting the shops and sightseeing, it's time to take to the streets at night to discover exactly what makes the Big Apple one of the top cities in the world for partying.

A glance at any of the listings pages in the press will confirm that there is an amazing amount of evening entertainment to choose from. Any night of the week you'll find comedy shows with stand-up routines from some of the best in the business and live music from the hottest bands. The bar scene in NYC is particularly exciting: whether it's soaking up some cool jazz in the West Village, partying into the small hours in the hip Meatpacking District or sipping apple martinis in a sophisticated Upper East Side joint, there's a bar or lounge to suit every type of person.

BARS, LOUNGES & PUBS

Here's a selection of bars to drop into while you are out and about in the city, including some that are super swish, some more grungy and some lounges that stay open into the early hours. Lounges are very much an integral part of the New York nightlife scene. Placed somewhere between a plush bar and a club, they're somewhere for you to stay late, listen to DJs and sip cocktails, but most don't have dance floors. Pubs may not be quite the same as the Brit equivalent, but there are some great neighbourhood joints where you can get a pint of Guinness or beer.

CHELSEA

Bungalow 8: 515 West 27th Street at 10th Avenue. 212-629 3333, bungalow8.com. Closed for refurbishment at time of going to press. One of the snobbiest door policies in Manhattan may prevent you from actually getting into this notorious lounge and blowing all your money on mega-priced drinks. If you do manage to wheedle your way in, you may well spot a celeb or three, not to mention lots of Park Avenue princesses. If you don't have a car waiting for you outside, the concierge can arrange a helicopter!

Chelsea Brewing Company: Chelsea Pier, Pier 59, West Side Highway at 20th Street. 212-336 6440, chelseabrewingco.com. A venue that caters for all types of night-time needs, it's Manhattan's largest micro-brewery, with more than 20 brews on tap. Downstairs there's a sports bar atmosphere, while upstairs in the mezzanine lounge it's more romantic, with a fireplace and 2-storey glass windows overlooking the river. Outside a rowdy crowd gathers post-work. From all angles, the view of New Jersey at sunset makes it worth a visit. The fact that you can also eat here – light bites like salads and pizzas – means it is even more appealing. It also has a cigar lounge.

NIGHTLIFE

199

7th Avenue after dark

BRITTIP

Get yourself in the Manhattan mood before you even arrive by whipping up one of Bungalow 8's most popular cocktails, The Valentini. Mix 30ml/1oz of passion fruit purée, 30ml/1oz Stoli strawberry vodka, 15ml/½oz grenadine and a dash of sugar. Pour into a champagne flute, top with Moet & Chandon and garnish with a strawberry – good enough for Lindsay Lohan.

Suzie Wong: 547 West 27th Street between 10th and 11th Avenues, 212-268 5105, suziewongnyc.com.

Sip exotic sake 'cocktails' while nibbling on dim sum in this sumptuous red Chinese-style lounge, with red lanterns, red-stained floors, red banquettes and staff floating round in red cocktail dresses. Geisha is a blend of Asian pear, vodka and plum sake, and Madame Butterfly is plum sake and muddled apricot with a sake float.

EAST VILLAGE

11th Street Bar: 510 East 11th Street between Avenue A and B. 212-982 3929, 11thstbar.com.

Marked only by an illuminated Guinness sign, this Irish pub is the place to enjoy a decent pint without having to look like you walked out of the pages of a lifestyle magazine. Sometimes has live music and is open until 4am.

Angel's Share: 8 Stuyvesant Street between East 9th Street and 3rd Avenue. 212-777 5415. Dedicated to the art of mixology, this little gem of a bar will rustle up any cocktail you desire. Part of its charm is the fact that it's so hard to find, you'll feel as if you've stumbled across a city secret. Take the stairs to the 2nd floor and veer left past the restaurant to the door at the rear. Inside you'll find a dark, intimate bar where classy city dwellers take their first dates.

Bar on A: 170 Avenue A near 11th Street. 212-353 8231.

Stitch

This bar's been popular with villagers for more than a decade and it's easy to understand why. It's got a lovely laid-back vibe, snakeskin bar stools, lots of cooling ceiling fans and an excellent selection of beers.

Beauty Bar: 231 East 14th Street between 2nd and 3rd Avenues. 212-539 1389, beautybar.com.

Deb Parker's theme bar is equipped with 1960s-style hairdryers and chairs, real manicurists, great drinks and a heavy dose of the hip and beautiful.

NYINTHEKNOW

Kate Maxwell, a Brit living in NYC who is senior editor at luxe US travel magazine *Condé Nast Traveler* says, 'I love Mayahuel (304 East 6th Street, 212-253-8888, mayahuelny.com, subway 2nd Avenue). This Mexican cocktail joint behind an unmarked door in the East Village serves incredible drinks made from tequila and its smokier cousin mescal. I always order the Smoked Palomino and great stomach-lining snacks like tamales. And its door policy is much less fierce than at many of Downtown's cocktails dens.'

Buddha Lounge: 29 East 3rd Street between 2nd Avenue and Bowery. 212-505 7344. Exposed brick walls, pricey cocktails and popular all week. Some say it's pretentious, others love it; you decide.

KGB: 85 East 4th Street between 2nd and 3rd Avenues. 212-505 3360, kgbbar.com. Decorated with deep-red walls, portraits of Lenin and Brezhnev, propaganda posters and an oak bar from when it was a front for the Communist party. The crowd is a mix of actors, writers and drunks who love the private-parlour feel. Up-and-coming writers and successful authors often do free readings, so call to see who's on.

Sutra: 16 1st Avenue between 1st and 2nd Street. 212-677 9477, sutranyc.com. Red velvet and lots and lots of candles create an intimate atmosphere in this sumptuous new lounge bar serving exotic cocktails and known for its music.

GARMENT DISTRICT

Stitch: 247 West 37th Street between 7th and 8th Avenues. 212-852 4826, stitchnyc.com. A good name for this bar in the heart of the clothing district. Cocktails, such as the Stiletto, are just as well named. Voted best after work bar in New York by Citysearch.com in 2007, it's a place to meet the locals.

TOP 5 BARS FOR ALFRESCO DRINKING

Brooklyn

Gowanus Yacht Club: 323 Smith Street, 718-246 1321. You'll feel you've really got off the tourist trail at this small outdoor beer garden close to the lovely Carroll Gardens. It attracts a chilled crowd of locals who sip beer and wine beneath the fairylight-bedecked trees before and after sunset. Bar food is also available.

Chelsea

Glass: 287 10th Avenue, 212-904 1580, glassloungenyc.com. 'Cool' is usually the reaction staff get when people see the bamboo-filled patio in this hip bar for the first time. It's a place to see and be seen in, so if you don't mind rubber-necking alongside models and aspiring actors, you'll fit right in.

Lower East Side

Barramundi: 67 Clinton Street between Rivington and Stanton Streets, 212-529 6999, barramundiny.com. A gorgeous walled garden covered with twinkling fairylights is romantic or cool depending on who you are with. Attracts a mixed crowd of internationals.

Upper East Side

Rooftop at the Met: 1000 5th Avenue at 82nd Street, 212-879 5500, moma.org. The terrace (open in the summer) at the Metropolitan Museum of Art (page 109) offers stunning views of the city, particularly at sunset. It's also known as a great singles pick-up joint.

West Village

B-Bar & Grill: 40 East 4th Street, 212-475 2220, bbarandgrill.com. The large outside patio, with bar, chic furniture and trees, is a magnet for fashionable West and East Villagers and is enclosed and fully heated in winter.

GREENWICH VILLAGE

Madame X: 94 West Houston Street between Thompson Street and La Guardia Place. 212-539 0808, madamexnyc.com.
There's a real London Soho den-of-iniquity feel to this joint, bathed as it is in red and lit by the glow of lanterns. Known for serving pretty potent cocktails and rare imported beers. In summer, head for the black door at the rear and you'll find the new outdoor alcove, where red lights above the benches bring the boudoir theme outside. Best of all, you'll probably be able to find a free corner.

BRITTIP

If you're looking for a romantic bar go to Rise (14th floor of the Ritz-Carlton hotel, 2 West Street, Battery Park City, 917 790 2626, ritzcarlton.com) where sweeping views of the New York Harbor and the outside balcony is the perfect spot to sip a drink together at sunset.

HELL'S KITCHEN

Rudy's Bar and Grill: 627 9th Avenue near 44th, rudysbarnyc.com.
Opened in 1933 and still with the same front door, when you walk through it the feel of the old neighbourhood saloon is still there with cheap beer, free hot dogs, and great people!

NYINTHEKNOW

Mike Ricci, director of communications Hilton Hotels Corporation, north-east US and Canada, says, 'Any bar on 9th Avenue in Hell's Kitchen will make a good night out, particularly Rudy's Bar and Grill (rudysbarnyc.com), a real dive with a real Hell's Kitchen atmosphere. It features circular booths with electrical and duct tape holding the ripped vinyl upholstery together. It offers patrons free hot dogs all year round (given the current economy, this is a great value add!) and there are big burly bouncers outside the door.'

LITTLE ITALY

GoldBar: 389 Broome Street at Mulberry Street. 212-274 1568, goldbarnewyork.com.
This hot bar from the owners of Cain and former GM of Lotus is lavished in gold, from the skulls in the wall to the chains separating the rooms. The drinks tables are golden love bracelets engraved with Latin sayings and the theme of the cocktails is golden honey.

BLVD: 199 Bowery near Rivington Street. 212-982 7767, blvdnyc.com.
An expensive club where you have to buy a bottle to secure a table and mix with the B and C-listers. It is worth trying to get in,

though, if you are looking for a big night out in a big NY club, as there are several rooms to wander around and a large dance floor where you can join good-looking NY scenesters dancing to hip-hop and rock.

Boss Tweed's: 115 Essex Street between Rivington and Delancey Streets. 212-475 9997, bosstweeds.com.
This is the closest you'll get to a local in Manhattan. The glass-bricked bar offers everything from pints of Guinness to vodka shots, each served up with a great story by bartender and co-owner Stuart Delves. Very entertaining. Has an outdoor beer garden.

Good World: 3 Orchard Street between Canal and Hester Streets. 212-925 9975, goodworldbar.com.
A mellow bar with a semi-regular DJ and an attractive young crowd. Stars that have been spotted here include Keanu Reeves, Bjork, Courtney Love and Matt Dillon. Best time to go is Sun–Thurs and order the Scandinavian-style Good World, an elderberry-infused caipirinha.

Hogs & Heifers

Inoteca: 98 Rivington Street at Ludlow Street. 212 614-0473, inotecanyc.com.
The staff at this wine bar and restaurant are ingratiating and knowledgeable. The crowd is a mixture of neighbourhood denizens and drop-ins from uptown, creating a good atmosphere. Serves food, too.

Kush: 191 Chrystie Street between Rivington and Stanton Streets. 212-677 7328, kushlounge.com.
Get a taste of the exotic by sipping a few cocktails and nibbling on tasty bar snacks such as mixed olives and salted almonds in this Moroccan oasis. The decor is fab, with wonderful tiling and whitewashed walls lit by candles. Open 7pm–4am Wed-Sat.

MEATPACKING DISTRICT

APT: 419 West 13th Street between 9th Avenue and Washington Street. 212-414 4245, aptnyc.com.
A real hit with trendy New Yorkers since the day it opened, this intimate bar/club makes you feel you are somewhere extra special. The dark, candlelit first floor is furnished like an apartment, complete with bed, dining table and chairs and sofas, offering comfortable lounging. Charming staff serve up tasty cocktails, such as Moscow Mules and Appletinis, for around $10. The wood-walled room downstairs has a more modern vibe, and punters propping up the long bar often end up strutting their stuff to the DJ's hip tunes. Book in advance for the weekend.

Hogs & Heifers: 859 Washington Street at West 13th Street. 212-929 0655, hogsandheifers.com.
The hogs are the motorcyclists and the heifers are the dames, who are known for hanging their bras on the ceiling. There's no longer bar dancing here, though!

Hudson Bar & Books

MIDTOWN

Campbell Apartment Bar: Gallery Level, Grand Central Station, 15 Vanderbilt Avenue between 42nd and 43rd Streets. 212-953 0409, hospitalityholdings.com.
This apartment used to be the office/salon of the 1920s tycoon John W Campbell. The beamed ceiling, huge leaded-glass window and the massive stone fireplace make a unique, almost castle-like space. But the dark wood couches and club armchairs create an intimate place for a drink

D'Or: 204 West 55th Street between Broadway and 7th Avenue. 212-245 1234, amalia-nyc.com.
Fairly new lounge in the basement of the Amalia restaurant, where you reach the bar via an illuminated stained-glass staircase. Once down there it's hard not to gawp at the crystal chandeliers, gilded mirrors and beautiful people sprawled on leather banquettes.

Langans: 150 West 47th Street near 7th Avenue. 212-869 5482, langans.com.
This Irish bar and restaurant is a hangout for journalists from the newspaper world, in particular the *New York Post*. Good place to pick up some brunch or an early-evening pint and listen to the gossip. Rupert Murdoch has been known to pop in from time to time.

Russian Vodka Room: 265 West 52nd Street between Broadway and 8th Avenue. 212-307 5835, russianvodkaroom.com.
A brilliant vodka bar that doesn't require you to take out a second mortgage. There are 53 different vodkas, plus cheap smoked fish platters, delicious cocktails and marvellous vodka infusions. It tends to attract the publishing crowd.

MIDTOWN EAST

Nikki Midtown: 151 East 50th Street between Lexington and 3rd Avenues. 212-753 1144, nikkibeach.com. Subway 6 to 51st Street.
Part of the glitzy Nikki Beach chain (other bars/lounges are in Miami and the Caribbean), this stylish lounge is part heaven, part harem. It brings some of that beach-club style to Manhattan, with all-white interiors, bamboo posts, rustic wood tables, large pillows for lounging on and an after-work happy hour for cocktails like Nikki's Delight. You can also order food here, such as sushi and tapas. Late in the evening, the long community table becomes a dance floor and top Manahttan DJs play tunes throughout the night. The downside is it's pretty pricey.

SOHO AND TRIBECA

Antarctica: 287 Hudson Street at Spring Street. 212-352 1666, antarcticabar.com.
This is one of the best places in the city to enjoy a beer and a game of pool, as it's rarely packed so you can actually get a table. There's also a good jukebox and a friendly crowd once you've finished your game.

Blind Tiger: 281 Bleecker Street at Jones Street. 212-462 4682, blindtigeralehouse.com.
Recently opened micro-brewery offering more than 30 beers, with great names like Sly Fox Irish stout. It's got a garden for summer, a fireplace for winter and is popular with the locals. Open 7 days a week.

Botanica: 47 East Houston Street between Mott and Mulberry Streets. 212-343 7251.
Serving drinks at decent prices in très chic SoHo, this dark and rather grungy basement bar is a watering hole for artists and college students.

Brandy Library: 25 North Moore Street at Varwick Street. 212-226 5545, brandylibrary.com.

As its name suggests, this new bar is dedicated to the finest brandies, plus there are more than 100 cocktails on the menu. Waitresses climb ladders to pick out your chosen tipple from the brandy-lined shelves. A lovely place to end a sophisticated evening, as it stays open until 4am.

NYINTHEKNOW

Head concierge Josephine Danielson at the Four Seasons Hotel says of the Brandy Library bar: 'Old-world charm meets downtown chic at this fabulous New York bar. It's one of those places that leaves you saying "only in New York". The people you'll find include a wonderful mix of throw-backs to a bygone era and trendy Manhattanites. And they are known for offering tastings of any spirit imaginable, which is great fun and very sophisticated.'

Café Noir: 32 Grand Street at Thompson Street. 212-431 7910, cafenoirny.com.

An extensive wine list at this cute urban oasis that also serves Moroccan comfort food meets Spanish tapas. Think tagines, stews and pitchers of sangria. There's also the occasional live jazz session.

Merc Bar: 151 Mercer Street between Prince and Houston Streets. 212-966 2727, mercbar.com.

A long-time fixture on the SoHo scene, this cool bar draws an attractive crowd to its luxuriously deep sofas. It's at its best in summer when worn leather chairs get an airing on the sidewalk – a great place to sit and people-watch. Be warned: the drinks are pricey at $10-plus.

Milady's: 160 Prince Street at Thompson Street. 212-226 9340.

If you want a beer and not a ridiculously priced cocktail, and a down-to-earth atmosphere then pop in here. It's tiny, plays rock music during later hours and the people-watching is great, from pensioners who have lived in SoHo for decades to young city slickers.

UPPER WEST SIDE

Ding Dong Lounge: 929 Columbus Avenue at 106th Street. 212-663 2600, dingdonglounge.com.

Feel like a local at this hip, laid back hangout; think battered old chairs, large wooden tables lit by chandeliers, pool table, live music, daily happy hour 4–7pm. Open every day until 4am.

WEST VILLAGE

Peculiar Pub: 145 Bleecker Street between La Guardia Place and Thompson Street. 212-353 1327, peculiarpub.com.

A truly impressive selection of beers, with 2 separate menus – one listing domestic brews, the other international. It's a bit like a museum to beer once you're inside, from the art of brewing to the evolution of the aluminium can on the walls. It gets packed with students during peak times, so it's best to visit early on week nights so you can chat to the bartender about the various brews.

Brandy Library

TOP 5 BARS TO SPOT STARS

Alphabet City – East Village

2A: 25 Avenue A. 212-505 2466. A real musos hangout - 'grungily fab'. The Strokes is just one of the combos that you may find enjoying the New Wave and punk 1970s music in this supercool bar and lounge.

Meatpacking District

Lotus: 409 West 14th Street between 9th and 10th Avenues. 212-243 4420, lotusnewyork. com. Three storeys devoted to nightlife, including a bar, restaurant and club. Jennifer Lopez, Bruce Willis and Britney Spears have been seen here, but the celeb scene has cooled off since it opened in 2000. There are still star DJs, though, plus C-listers and their model girlfriends to gaze at. Avoid the weekend crush by going midweek. Try their Tartini – a Cosmo with Chambord.

Midtown East

Wet Bar at W New York, The Court Hotel: 130 East 39th Street at Lexington Avenue. 212-592 8844, starwoodhotels.com. George Clooney, Whoopi Goldberg and D'Angelo Marc Anthony have all been spotted in this sleek and uncluttered setting, which plays host to professionals and hotel guests. Try their apple martini.

NoHo

Joe's Pub: 425 Lafayette Street between 4th Street and Astor Place. 212-539 8778, joespub. com. This cabaret continues to be a real hot spot. An extension of the Public Theater, Joe's brings you live music, spoken-word performances and a crowd jam-packed with trendy types. Stars spotted here include Ethan Hawke, Minnie Driver, Janeane Garofalo and Camryn Manheim. The drink to order is the Lady Macbeth – 115ml/4fl oz of champagne and 115ml/ 4fl oz of ruby port. Strong stuff!

SoHo

The Anchor: 310 Spring Street. 212-463 7406, theanchornyc.com. This bar, which opened in 07, encouraged celebrity clientele to conceive a drink which they'd be named after, so you can sip on a Murricane, by film star Bill Murray, a John Mayer (singer who dated Jennifer Aniston and Cameron Diaz), Drea de Matteo, Bijou Phillips and Adriana Lima (model). Lindsay Lohan has also been seen propping up the bar, as have Kirsten Dunst and Natalie Portman in 2010.

COMEDY CLUBS

While comedy clubs have started to spring up in cities all over the UK, they've been firmly cemented in New York nightlife since the 1970s. It's a real experience and always worth the money to visit one of these Manhattan institutions, which have produced some of the world's top comedians.

CHELSEA

Comix: 353 West 14th Street between 8th and 9th Avenues. 212-524 2500, comixny. com.
Large 320-seat club in a renovated supermarket attracting big names. Don't expect a dive – there are marble floors and plasma TVs. Cover charges vary from show to show, but expect to pay around $25.

FLATIRON DISTRICT

Gotham Comedy Club: 34 West 22nd Street between 5th and 6th Avenues. 212-367 9000, gothamcomedyclub.com.
This club opened in 1996 and was an instant success. It's elegant and sophisticated, with a solid oak bar and a chandelier. The line-ups are equally dazzling, from surprise guests to comedians who have appeared on *Saturday Night Live* and *The Tonight Show.*

MIDTOWN

Caroline's Comedy Club: 1626 Broadway between 49th and 50th Streets. 212-757 4100, carolines.com.
It opened in 1981 as a small club in Chelsea

Caroline's Comedy Club

but proved such a hit it moved uptown, where it offers live comedy every night of the year, including big names such as Jerry Seinfeld and Rosie O'Donnell.

UPPER EAST SIDE

Comic Strip Live: 1568 Second Avenue at 81st Street. 212-861 9386, comicstriplive.com. Founded in 1975, this is still one of the best comedy clubs in the city with some of the biggest names in the business appearing, such as Chris Rock and Adam Sandler. If you can't get in for one of the big nights or you fancy yourself as a bit of a comedian, then go to Monday's Talent Spotlight where up-and-coming comics get a chance to shine.

Dangerfield's: 118 First Avenue at 61st Street. 212-593 1650, dangerfields.com. Allegedly the oldest comedy club in the country, it was established in 1969 by actor and comedian Roger Dangerfield. It's a magnet for tourists because of its reputation, but locals still frequent it too, drawn by the decent line-ups both new and regulars.

UPPER WEST SIDE

Stand-Up NYC: 236 West 78th Street near Broadway. 212-595 0850, standupny.com. This club has been hosting huge names in comedy – Robin Williams, Roseanne Barr, Jerry Seinfeld – since it opened in 1986. It's not a flashy venue and there's seating for just 175 punters, but it really pulls in the best on the circuit. From $15 cover charge.

WEST VILLAGE

The Comedy Cellar: 117 MacDougal Street between West 3rd Street and Minetta Lane. 212-254 3480, comedycellar.com.

This club has been a starting ground for many famous faces for more than 20 years. It's basic, with brick walls and cramped seating, and in a basement so it's not a glam night out in New York, but it will certainly be a funny one. The cover charge is $12 Sun–Thurs, $18 Fri and Sat.

HOTEL BARS

Hotel bars have always been a popular place to meet for New Yorkers. From sinking into leather sofas in legendary hangouts, to propping up the bars in some of Midtown's trendy hotels where the fashionable crowds gather, they make an ideal place to start or end a big night out.

BRITTIP

If you can, visit Plunge (see box on page 208) on a Mon night when it's much quieter so you are guaranteed a space and you'll be able to hear what the person next to you is saying.

GREENWICH VILLAGE

North Square at the Washington Square Hotel: 103 Waverly Place at MacDougal Street. 212-254 1200, northsquareny.com. Subway A, B, C, D, E, F, V to West 4th Street/ Washington Square.
The small, cosy basement space's classic bar and luxurious leather chairs are a reminder of another era, while beautifully stencilled windows offer a glimpse of the current street scene. It attracts a large European crowd, who find it the perfect spot to pore over a

North Square

Cellar Bar

map and a martini, but locals – as well as the occasional celeb – can also be found enjoying the laid-back atmosphere. There is a jazz brunch every Sunday afternoon.

MIDTOWN

Cellar Bar at the Bryant Park Hotel: 40 West 40th Street between 5th and 6th Avenues. 212-869 0100, bryantparkhotel.com. Subway B, D, F, V, 7 to 42nd Street/Bryant Park.

A must-do for any fashionista, because this new boutique hotel on the block has been adopted by the fashion pack. Expect to see models, designers and magazine editors propping up the bar, but don't even think about dropping in during Fashion Week – you won't be able to move for the wafer-thin clientele.

The Bar at the Four Seasons Hotel: 57 East 57th Street between 5th and Park Avenues. 212-758 5700, fourseasons.com/newyork. Subway N, R, Q, W to 5th Avenue.

The Four Seasons is dynamic in early evening when celebs rub shoulders with power-broking businessmen and hip hotel guests, while a pianist provides the background music. Be sure to sample some of the 15 types of martini on offer.

Mé Bar at La Quinta Manhattan: 17 West 32nd Street between Broadway and 5th Avenue. 212-736 1600, applecorehotels.com. Subway N, R, W to 28th Street.

A cross between a backyard deck and a funky beach bar, this partially enclosed rooftop watering hole is packed year-round with international visitors who appreciate the casual atmosphere and towering views of the Empire State Building.

MIDTOWN EAST

Gilt at the New York Palace Hotel: 455 Madison Avenue between 50th and 51st Streets. 212-888 7000, newyorkpalace.com. Subway E, V to 5th Avenue; 6 to 51st Street. Located inside the Madison Avenue courtyard gates of the Palace Hotel's historic Villard Mansion, this new restaurant and bar has been pulling in the city's most glamorous movers and shakers since it opened. You'll be wowed by the gilded walls, cathedral ceilings, funky lighting and amazing food whipped up by super chef Paul Liebrandt (that's if you can get a table).

Oasis at W New York: 541 Lexington Avenue at 49th Street. 212-755 1200, starwoodhotels.com. Subway 6 to 51st Street. An oasis of tranquillity, the bar heats up when the fashion, art and music crowd descends for cocktails before dinner at the hotel's Heartbeat restaurant. The ambience is Californian and casual with clever touches that include a waterfall and backgammon tables disguised as tree stumps. Also at the hotel is the Whiskey Blue, overseen by Randy Gerber, otherwise known as Cindy Crawford's husband. The hip clientele enjoy cosy sofas that are great for people-watching and a top-notch sound system that plays until the wee small hours.

Upstairs at the Kimberly: 145 East 60th Street, 212-702 1600, kimberlyhotel.com. Subway 4, 5, 6 to 59th Street. This hot new bar is on the rooftop of the luxe Kimberly Hotel and offers 360-degree views of the city. It is open all year round thanks to a retractable glass ceiling and heated floor. You can access the bar from a lift in the

TOP 5 HOTTEST HOTEL BARS

Chelsea

Cabana at the Maritime Hotel: 88 9th Avenue between 16th and 17th Streets. 212-242 4300, themaritimehotel.com. Subway A, C, E to 14th Street.
So hot it's practically on fire, this plant-filled rooftop retreat is the perfect place to sip a martini in winter as it has patio heaters. Sean Penn and Paris Hilton are recent celeb visitors.

Plunge at Hotel Gansevoort: 18 9th Avenue at 13th Street. 877-426 7386/212-206 6700, hotelgansevoort.com. Subway A, C, E to 14th Street.
Take the lift to the penthouse on the 15th floor and you'll arrive at one of NYC's most happening bars of the moment. On a dry day it's open-air: if it's rainy or cold there's a glass cover, so you still get the views. The only downside of Plunge is that, despite its name, you're not allowed in the rooftop swimming pool unless you're a guest and it's absolutely packed for most of the week.

Lower East Side

Thor Bar & Restaurant at Hotel On Rivington: 107 Rivington Street. 212-475 2600, hotelonrivington.com. Subway F to Delancey Street.
One of New York's trendiest hotels has an equally hip bar. Thor is housed in a lofty glass atrium designed by Marcel Wanders and closes at 3am.

Midtown

Thom Bar at the 60 Thompson Hotel: 60 Thompson Street between Broome and Spring Streets. 212-219 2000, 60thompson.com. Subway 6, C, E to Spring Street.
A sophisticated decor of dark wood, soft violet seats, brown leather club chairs and polished wood floor make for pleasant surroundings. The entertainment is provided by the chic crowd who know that this boutique hotel is the only place to be seen in midweek. Drinks are surprisingly cheap, like flavoured vodka for $7.50.

street. There are living green walls to marvel at and the iconic Chrysler Building is in full view. Simply stunning.

MIDTOWN WEST

Bar 44 at the New York Royalton: 44 West 44th Street between 5th and 6th Avenues. 212-869 4400, royaltonhotel.com. Subway B, D, F, V to 42nd Street; 7 to 5th Avenue.
The first of the Philippe Starck-designed hotels is still holding its own against all newcomers. Bar 44 is a reincarnation of the Royalton's legendary Round Bar. Furnished by John McDonald, creator of the acclaimed Lever House and Lure Fishbar, wood-panelled Bar 44 is a real hit with Manhattan's movers and shakers.

Hotel Metro Rooftop Bar: 45 West 35th Street between 5th and 6th Avenues. 212-279 3535, hotelmetronyc.com. Subway B, D, F, N, Q, R, V, W to 34th Street.
The views of the Empire State Building from this compact rooftop retreat is 1 reason why this is well worth a visit. The cheap beer and laid-back vibe created by the DJ are 2 others.

Hudson Hotel Bar at the Hudson Hotel: 356 West 58th Street between 8th and 9th Avenues. 212-554 6000, hudsonhotel.com. Subway A, B, C, D, 1, 9 to 59th Street/Columbus Circle.
This Ian Schrager and Philippe Starck-designed Mecca for the in crowd provides wonderful theatre. There's a glowing glass floor, flashy DJ and dark and enticing Games Room. In the summer, the after-work crowd heads to the Private Park – the hotel garden – and sip cocktails next to giant watering cans. Pure, surreal magic.

MObar

King Cole Bar at the St Regis Hotel: 2 East 55th Street. 212-339 6721, starwoodhotels.com/stregis. Subway E, V to 5th Avenue at 53rd Street.
The specialities of the (very upscale) house are the Bloody Mary and the mural behind the bar, by noted American illustrator Maxfield Parrish.

Living Room at the W Times Square Hotel: 1567 Broadway at 47th Street. 212-930 7444, starwoodhotels.com. Subway 4, 5, 6, L, N, Q, R, W to 14th Street.
Another of the cool W Hotel bar scenes, a magnet for fashion models (many agencies are in the area) and other pretty people.

MObar at the Mandarin Oriental: 59th Street at Columbus Circle. 212-805 8800, mandarinoriental.com. Subway A, B, C, D, 1, 9 to Columbus Circle.
In the dazzling AOL Time Warner Center, the sleek lobby lounge is drawing the crowds. The cocktails are $15 but the spectacular view of Central Park from the 35th floor (not to mention celebrity sightings) is free.

Salon de Ning at the Peninsula Hotel: 700 5th Avenue, 23rd Floor. 212-956 2888, newyork.peninsula.com. Subway E, V to 5th Avenue/53rd Street; N, R, W to 5th Avenue/59th Street.
Formerly the Pen-Top Bar, this rooftop terrace opened in May 2008 and is a fusion of east meets west; think 1930s Shanghai, says the blurb. Whatever the decor, the views of Manhattan's glittering skyline are breathtaking and the prices can be, too, but in beautiful weather you'll feel you're at the centre of the universe – like the power brokers who surround you.

The Blue Bar at the Algonquin: 59 West 44th Street between 5th and 6th Avenues. 212-840 6800, algonquinhotel.com. Subway B, D, F, V to 42nd Street; 7 to 5th Avenue.
Once world-famous as the New York literary set's salon of choice, this handsome room provides an intimate and civilised setting for some of the country's leading jazz and cabaret artists, who are usually booked for extended runs. The clientele is clubby and patrician, but anyone can buy drinks here or dinner in the Oak Room.

TRIBECA
Church Lounge at TriBeCa Grand Hotel: 2 6th Avenue at White Street. 212-519 6600, tribecagrand.com. Subway A, C, E to Canal Street.
The Wall Street crowd has made this upscale bar an after-work hangout. It's meant to look like a living room – if your living room was full of amazing furniture. Sanctum Lounge with DJs, open Thurs–Sun only, is the even more exclusive adjunct.

LIVE MUSIC
There are some fantastic live music venues in the city, from dingy rock clubs to vast stadiums where legends have played. As many of the venues get booked up quickly, do check websites for listings well before you visit the city so that you'll be able to book tickets in advance.

34TH STREET
Madison Square Garden: 4 Pennsylvania Plaza at 33rd Street and 7th Avenue. 212-465 MSG1 info, thegarden.com. Subway A, C, E, 1, 2, 3, 9, B, D, F, N, Q, R, V, W to 34th Street/Penn Street Station.
New York's biggest and most famous rock venue, which doubles up as a sports stadium. Also the Theater at Madison Square Garden, which is underneath, plays host to big-name stars who want to share some intimacy with their audience.

BROOKLYN
Knitting Factory: 361 Metropolitan Avenue, 347-529 6696, knittingfactory.com. Subway L to Bedford Avenue.
A funky performance venue run by the Knitting Factory record label, which is well known for avant-garde live bands spanning all types of music, from heavy rock to choral music. There are sometimes poetry readings and film screenings as well as music. Check out the website to see who'll be playing when you're in town. Open until 4am.

GARMENT DISTRICT
Hammerstein Ballroom: 311 West 34th Street between 8th and 9th Avenues. 212-279 7740, mcstudios.com.
Elegant pre-war ballroom that holds up to 2,500 people for rock music gigs from the likes of Jay-Z and Alicia Keys to top DJs.

GREENWICH
Cafe Wha?: 115 MacDougal Street between West 3rd and Bleecker Streets. 212-254 3706, cafewha.com.

Cafe Wha?

Village hangout since the beginning of time. There is something fun and exciting on every night of the week here, including live Brazilian dance parties with the Brazooka band on Mon and the Cafe Wha? disFUNKtion night on Tues – live funk from the likes of Inaya Day and Mike Davis.

HARLEM

Apollo Theater: 253 West 125th Street between Adam Clayton Powell Jr and Frederick Douglas Boulevards. 212-531 5300 info; 212-531 5301 events hotline, apollotheater.com. Subway A, B, C, D, 2, 3 to 125th Street.

This venue started life as a burlesque house for whites only when Harlem was actually a white neighbourhood, but it very quickly changed and became a theatre for blacks with live entertainment. The Amateur Night has been a launching-pad for Stevie Wonder and James Brown. When Ella Fitzgerald came here she planned to dance, but at the last moment decided to sing and, as the saying goes, a star was born. Wed's Amateur Night is still going strong and is shown on NBC at 1am on Saturday night/Sunday morning.

LOWER EAST SIDE

Bowery Ballroom: 6 Delancey Street near Bowery. 212-533 2111, boweryballroom.com. Consistently voted one of New York's best live rock venues, it's been packing in the punters since it opened its doors in 1998. Great acoustics, a well-stocked bar and lots of great acts. Log on to the website to see who's playing and for advance tickets.

Apollo Theater

BRITTIP

For old-school, glamorous cabaret, try the Metropolitan Room at Gotham, 34 West 22nd Street between 5th and 6th Avenues, 212-206 044, metropolitanroom. com. It's only been open a couple of years, but it was a hit from the start, with fabulous acts.

MIDTOWN

B B King Blues Club & Grill: 237 West 42nd Street near 7th Avenue. 212-997 4144, bbkingblues.com. Subway 1, 2, 3, 7, N, Q, R, S Times Square/42nd Street.

An intimate supper club that's played host to some of the greats – James Brown, Peter Frampton and Chic. There's a souvenir stall upstairs so you can wear the T-shirt.

Carnegie Hall: 154 West 57th Street at 7th Avenue. 212-247 7800, carnegiehall.org. Subway B, D, E, N, R, Q, W to 57th Street. Built in the Beaux Arts style under the patronage of Andrew Carnegie, this is perhaps one of the most famous classical concert venues in New York and a real landmark. Check the listings sections of newspapers or *Time Out* for details of visiting artists or take a guided tour Mon–Fri 11.30am, 2pm and 3pm.

Radio City Music Hall: 1260 6th Avenue at 50th Street. 212-247 4777, radiocity. com. Subway B, D, F, V to 47th–50th Street/ Rockefeller Centre.

Recently renovated, this home to the

Rockettes in its Art Deco splendour also plays host to some big-name stars.

UPPER EAST SIDE

Café Carlyle at The Carlyle Hotel: 35 East 76th Street at Madison and Park Avenues. 212-744 1600, thecarlyle.com. Subway 6 to 77th Street.
A highly glamorous bar and restaurant that specialises in cabaret. Woody Allen still plays clarinet with The Eddie Davis New Orleans Jazz Band on Monday nights and Bobby Short, a New York favourite, plays piano during spring and autumn. $75 per person cover charge.

✠ BRITTIP

If want to go to a cabaret club, visit Don't Tell Mama (343 West 46th Street near 9th Avenue, Hell's Kitchen, 212-757 0788, donttellmama nyc.com). There's a piano bar and 2 side rooms for excellent shows, with up to 3 performances nightly.

UPPER WEST SIDE

Lincoln Center: 65th Street at Columbus Avenue. 212-875 5400, lincolncenter.org. Subway 1, 9 to 66th Street/Lincoln Center. The major venue for classical music in New York, the Lincoln Center, a collection of buildings that includes the home of the Metropolitan Opera, was built on slums that were featured in the film *West Side Story*. The Alice Tully Hall (212-875 5050) houses the Chamber Music Society of Lincoln Center; the Avery Fisher Hall (212-875 5030) is home to the New York Philharmonic; the Metropolitan Opera House (212-362 6000); the New York State Theater (212-870 5570) is the base of New York City Opera; and the Walter Reade Theater (212-875 5600) is home to the Film Society of Lincoln Center. Jazz at Lincoln Center is at the AOL Time Warner Center (page 212).
You can take a behind-the-scenes tour of the Lincoln Center, which is really the only way to see beyond the ornate lobbies of the buildings, unless you're paying big bucks for a performance. The tours are fabulous and give a really good insight into the workings of the various venues. Options include a 1-hour Lincoln Center tour, Tours with a Bite – at Café Vienna, the Sea and Symphony tour that includes a tour of the Lincoln Center plus a private performance and backstage conversation with a leading Broadway opera artist, and Starry Nights, the full treatment including a performance and, if in a group,

meeting the artists. The tours are very popular so it's best to book in advance on 212-875 5350.

✠ BRITTIP

Standing room tickets to the Met go on sale on the day of the performance for $20.

In addition to the tours, you can enjoy the Lincoln Center environment with a series of jazz and folk bands that entertain the crowds for free during the summer. The Autumn Crafts Fair is held in the 1st week of Sept.

✠ BRITTIP

If you're on a budget, get down to the new Crocodile Lounge (325 East 14th Street between 2nd and 3rd Avenues, tel 212-477 7747), a funky bar covered in, you've guessed it, crocodiles – even the door handles are crocs – that gives out free pizza from its ovens for every beer you buy.

NIGHTCLUBS

The club scene in New York literally changes by the week. Venues are constantly opening, closing and relaunching so we've picked out the best of the well-established clubs, plus a scattering of new or smaller places that are currently creating a stir. By the way, while many of the clubs stay open until 4am, hours do vary so check out the listings in the *Village Voice, Paper, New York Press* and *New Yorker* and on websites such as nymag.com and nyclubs.com.

New York has a vibrant jazz scene

ALL THAT JAZZ

A visit to New York City wouldn't be complete without an evening at one of the various jazz venues, but it can get very expensive, so it's good to know your way around. At all the main venues it'll cost you around $25 to hear one set, which lasts only 1-1½ hours. It's worth it if you're happy with the music, but the idea of having to move on after only one set is a bit strange to us Brits, so be warned!

The most important relatively new venue is **Jazz at Lincoln Center**'s recent $128-million home at the AOL Time Warner Center at Columbus Circle, with 3 performance spaces - 2 large and 1 intimate. Visit jalc.org to find out about events or call the JazzTix hotline, 212-258 9800.

THE MAIN CLUBS

One of the best jazz clubs is the **Iridium** (1650 Broadway at 51st Street, 212-582 2121, iridiumjazzclub.com). It's not too touristy, is smaller than many clubs and has a nice intimate feel. Try it for Sunday brunch! The entrance fee varies but there's a $10 minimum. The **Village Vanguard** (178 7th Avenue South at Perry Street, 212-255 4037, villagevanguard.com), probably the most famous club of all, always hosts great talent and sets last the full 1½ hours. Another famous Greenwich Village venue is the **Blue Note** (131 West 3rd Street between MacDougal and 6th Avenue, 212-475 8592, bluenote.net), but this is more touristy, very expensive and has a Las Vegas-style interior. **Swing 46 Jazz & Supper Club** (349 West 46th Street between 8th and 9th Avenues, 212-262 9554, swing46.com) offers big bands and small combos to suit hip downtown loungers and traditional uptown swingers - it's rapidly becoming an institution.

Other good venues include **Birdland** (315 West 44th Street between 8th and 9th Avenues, 212-581 3080, birdlandjazz.com) in Midtown West; the **Jazz Standard** (116 East 27th Street between Park and Lexington Avenues, 212-576 2232, jazzstandard.com) near Madison Square; **Bubble Lounge** (228 West Broadway at White Street, 212-431 3433, bubblelounge.com) in TriBeCa, which has live music Mon and Tues, closed Sun. **55 Bar** (55 Christopher Street, 212-929 9883, 55bar.com) has been a West Village institution since 1919 and has shows all week from 6/7pm and late shows 9.30/10pm; open until 4am. **Smoke** (2751 Broadway, 212-864 6662, smokejazz.com) is an intimate club with low-hanging chandeliers, red velvet curtains and seating for 70. Open until 4am. Finally, book early for Monday nights at **Café Carlyle** (page 211) where Woody Allen and friends play a set.

CHEAP AND CHEERFUL

One of the best off-the-beaten-track jazz venues is in the heart of Greenwich Village at the **Cornelia Street Café** (29 Cornelia Street, 212-989 9319, corneliastreetcafe.com). You'll get to see some great musicians play and feel like you're part of the village scene. **Zinc Bar** (90 West Houston Street between Thompson Street and LaGuardia Place, 212-477 8337, zincbar.com) is one of the most intimate places in town to enjoy live jazz, open until 4am weekends and it's only $10 to get in. **Arthur's Tavern** (57 Grove Street near 7th Avenue, 212-675 6879, arthurstavernnyc.com) is a West Village jazz joint that's been going since the 1930s. Some say it's lost its sparkle, but most still love it's scruffy, old-world charm and enjoy a night free of pricey cover charges listening to great jazz. **Fat Cat** (75 Christopher Street at 7th Avenue, 212-675 6065, fatcatjazz.com), is a novelty as it features jazz and billiards. For a $10 admission you get 6 hours of music 10pm-4am.

The cheapest jazz clubs tend to be in Harlem, Queens and Brooklyn, but because they can't afford to advertise you really don't hear about them. Furthermore, most don't even have names on the door. Good places to look for venues are the *New York Times* weekend edition and the *Village Voice*. The latter is a lot better and it's free; visit villagevoice.com.

BROOKLYN

Legacy Night Club: 437 88th Street between 4th and 5th Avenues. 718-749 1002. Subway N, R to 86th Street.
Located in Bay Ridge, this ultra-flashy club is like a set from *Saturday Night Fever*. It dates back to the 1950s and sharply dressed New Yorkers are still dancing today on the sunken dance floor beneath the spinning disco balls and strobe lights. Cool tunes from '70s disco to hip-hop.

CHELSEA

Bungalow 8: (page 199). Currently closed for refurbishment.

Home: 532 West 27th Street near 10th Avenue. 212-273 3700, homeguesthouse.com. Subway, C, E to 23rd Street.
Wants to be the hippest place in town, Home has kicked up a bit of a storm, attracting the likes of Lindsay Lohan. The 2nd floor has chandeliers and a leather ceiling and a very

swish party crowd dancing the night away. There are black day beds to lounge on and DJs such as Stretch Armstrong spin hip-hop, rock and pop.

Marquee: 289 10th Avenue at 26th Street. 645-473 0202, marqueeny.com. Subway C, E to 23rd Street.

One of the coolest clubs in the city, or so the hype would have you believe, so there's always a massive queue. We can confirm that once inside it's worth the wait; intimate banquettes around the edge of the room with chandeliers overhead and ice buckets on every table.

BRITTIP

For the lowdown on what's happening on the jazz scene in New York, from shopping to tours to clubs, click on to bigapplejazz.com.

CHINATOWN

Happy Endings: 302 Broome Street at Forsyth Street. 212-334 9676, happyendinglounge.com, Subway 6, N, R to Canal Street.

A brothel-turned-bar with a DJ in the basement dance room and a mixed lounge scene that attracts hip young things.

EAST VILLAGE

Lit: 93 2nd Avenue between 5th and 6th Streets. 212-777 7987, litloungenyc.com. Subway 6 to Astor Place; F, V to Lower East Side/2nd Avenue.

If you've always wanted to see a hot bartender in action, this art-meets-celebs joint is the place to come. A haven for indie filmsters, it has an art gallery – The Fuse – a

TOP 5 CLUBBING TIPS

▷ On Fri and Sat nights, the clubs are packed with crowds from boroughs outside Manhattan. For a quieter night, go on Thurs. Sun is the big night for Manhattanites, so you'll get the real vibe then, along with the crowds.

▷ Call ahead early in the evening to find out if there's a cover charge, when to arrive and how to dress. Also find out if there's a party theme on the night that you plan to go. Clubs can change nightly – for example, catering for straights one night, gays the next.

▷ The real nightlife doesn't get going until after midnight, so get some zeds in before you go out.

▷ Carry some ID with you just in case – it would be very annoying if you couldn't get a drink when you're over 21.

▷ Large groups of men don't stand much hope of getting into straight clubs – they'll have more chance if they are with a woman.

cellar-like dance room downstairs plus live music too.

Webster Hall: 125 East 11th Street between 3rd and 4th Avenues. 212-353 1600, webster-hall.com. Subway L, N,Q, R, W, 4, 5, 6 to 14th Street/Union Square.

There are lots of different rooms with different sounds, so you're bound to find something you enjoy. The best area is the main dance floor in the huge, ornate ballroom. It attracts a fairly straight crowd from the suburbs, but is a fun night out.

Webster Hall

TOP HOT CLUBS

Chelsea

Cain: 544 West 27th Street between 10th and 11th Avenues. 212-947 8000, cainnyc.com. Based around a safari theme– elephant-trunk door handles, zebra-hide bar and game lodge-style wood pillars – it's caught the imagination of young Manhattanites.

Lower East Side

Libation: 137 Ludlow Street between Stanton and Rivington Streets. 212-529 2153, libationnyc.com. Subway F to Delancey Street. DJs play Wed-Sat at this sleek club that attracts a good mix of people. It also boasts a seasonal cocktail and tapas menu to help keep you going through the night.

Union Square

Aura: 5 East 19th Street at 5th Avenue. 212-671 1981, aurathenightclub.com. Subway 4, 5, 6, I, N, Q, R to West 14th Street/Union Square. Newly opened club with posh cocktails, light box bar that glows, small hardwood dance floor to move to thumping house and a VIP balcony that combined equal a fun night out.

FLATIRON

40/40 Club: 6 West 25th Street between Broadway and 6th Avenue. 212-832 4040, the4040club.com.

If you want some serious bling, and a possible celebrity sighting, then look no further than rapper Jay-Z's lavish 2-level club. It's like being on an MTV set; 7 cream-coloured leather swing chairs are suspended from the ceiling; floors are sleek Italian marble, and a collection of LCD flat-screen televisions (including 3 60in plasmas) display the ESPN sports channel. There's also a Rémy Lounge, named after Rémy Martin (Jay's cognac of choice), a cigar lounge and 2 VIP rooms tucked away on the 2nd level. After you've watched the game on the screens, the DJ blasts R&B and hip-hop until 4am.

BRITTIP

As clubs and club nights change so frequently, log on to papermag.com and clubplanet.com to find out what's on where.

GARMENT DISTRICT

Arena: 135 West 41st Street near Broadway. 212-278 0988, arenanyc.net.

New club that's proving to be a hit with New Yorkers. Matt silver walls and a cool dome ceiling above the dance floor make it visually pleasing, while the 4 bars, giant digital screens and excellent nights, such as Susanne Bartsch's Thursday Freakfest, keep clubbers happy until 4am. Can be hired for private events. Cover charge $20.

GREENWICH VILLAGE

SOBs: 204 Varick Street at Houston Street. 212-243 4940, sobs.com. Subway 1, 9 to Houston Street.

The name stands for Sounds Of Brazil, so it's the place to come for the last word in Latin music from salsa to samba and even reggae. DJ Rekha's new monthly Bhangra Basement party has got New Yorkers in a spin and it celebrated 25 years in 2009 in style.

Greenhouse: 150 Varick Street, 215-807 7000, greenhouseusa.com.

Eco-friendly materials, a huge glittering space and great atmosphere – the place to be.

NYINTHEKNOW

Mike Ricci, director of communications Hilton Hotels Corporation, north-east US and Canada, says, 'For clubbing, I'd recommend Greenhouse (greenhouseusa.com) on Varick Street. It claims to be the first eco-friendly club, is made from recycled or recyclable materials and it's a very cool space featuring garden- and flower-style lighting on the ceiling. There are also great DJs; I'd say it's currently the hottest nightspot in Manhattan.'

HELL'S KITCHEN

PACHA: 618 West 46th Street. 212-209 7500, pachanyc.com. Subway C, E to 50th Street. The Mediterranean–style club that's massive in Europe has finally hit New York and it's attracting a massive crowd. It's a 2,787sq m/ 30,000 sq foot building split into 4 levels, each with its own vibe and top-flight DJ.

LOWER EAST SIDE

Pianos: 158 Ludlow Street between Rivington and Stanton Streets. 212-505 3733, pianosnyc.com. Subway F, J, M, Z to Delancey Street/Essex Street.

A former piano shop turned clean, whitewashed bar space that attracts trendy fashionistas plus the NYU students from the area. Local and national up-and-coming rock bands play in the somewhat dingy back room, while there's also a more intimate lounge upstairs.

Sapphire Lounge: 249 Eldridge Street between Houston and Stanton Streets. 212-777 5153, sapphirenyc.com. Subway F to 2nd Avenue.
Pretension and attitude are left at the door in this tiny dance club that plays a great mix of hip-hop, reggae, acid jazz, R&B and disco classics. Opens at 7pm.

Slipper Room: 167 Orchard Street between Rivington and Stanton Streets. 212-253 7246, slipperroom.com. Subway F, M, J, Z to Delancey Street/Essex Street.
Adding some real showbiz panache to the Lower East Side, this glitzy retro lounge is the venue for genuinely good cabaret as well as some far out, gender-bending burlesque. A great evening out.

MEATPACKING DISTRICT

Cielo: 18 Little West 12th Street between 9th Avenue and Washington Street. 212-645 5700, cieloclub.com. Subway A, C, E to 14th Street; L to 8th Avenue.
The dance floor is sunken but the fabulous sound system hits the heights. Deep Space on a Monday is award winning. This is one of the hottest spots in the city, and the good news (and bad news) is that it draws the big crowds.

MIDTOWN EAST

Vue: 151 East 59th Street between Lexington and 3rd Avenues. 212-753 1144. Subway 6 –to 51st street
Is it the visuals projected on to a planetarium-type dome or is it the great sound and big club feeling? Whatever, this is still one of the most popular clubs in the city.

SOHO

Don Hill's: 511 Greenwich Street at Spring Street. 212-219 2850, donhills.com. Subway 6, C, E to Spring Street; N, R to Prince Street. Open nightly 9pm–4am.
One of the top rock venues in the city, Don Hill's is a live venue, club and bar all rolled into one, with great effect. It used to attract lots of celebs and the in-crowd; now it's not so showy, there's very little attitude and it's a fun place for a top night out.

Naked Lunch: 17 Thompson Street. 212-343 0828, nakedlunchnyc.com. Subway 1, 9, A, C, E to Canal Street.
A smart-looking bar that's a good place to

spot the occasional celeb. It's one of SoHo-ites favourite places to salsa, plus dance to great '80s tunes at the weekend. After work hours, you may see a few business types here, but in general it's more easy-going crowd who just want to shake their booty.

THEATER DISTRICT

China Club: 268 West 47th Street between Broadway and 8th Avenue. 212-398 3800, chinaclubnyc.com. Subway C, E to 50th Street.
Drinks are expensive at this hip club, which holds hundreds and plays '80s, disco, Euro and house. It's loud and proud and Stevie Wonder, Elton John and David Bowie have been spotted here in the past. There's an indoor/outdoor terrace that can hold up to 500 people.

✠▷ BRITTIP

Get dressed up if you are going clubbing. Check the website. If there's an entrance fee don't wear trainers or jeans – you probably won't get in.

Sapphire Lounge

Show: 135 West 41st Street between 6th Street and Broadway. 212-278 0988. Subway N, Q, R, S, 1, 2, 3, 9 to 42nd Street/Times Square.

A Moulin Rouge-inspired hot spot with scantily-clad burlesque dancers, swinging trapeze artists, go-go girls aplenty and a gilded stage for dancing to the mainstream music. Edgier hip-hop is played in the small upstairs lounge.

TRIBECA

Santos Party House: 96 Lafayette Street. 212-714 4646, santospartyhouse.com. Subway J, M, Z, N, Q, R, W, 6 to Canal Street. Hosts clubland legends and innovators on a regular basis – definitely one to check out if you're really into your clubbing. There are two levels, and the main floor has a live music system so check the website to see what's on when you're in town.

UNION SQUARE

Underbar at the W Hotel Union Square: 201 Park Avenue South at 17th Street. 212-253 9119, starwoodhotels.com/whotels. Subway 4, 5, 6, L, N, Q, R, W to 14th Street/Union Square.

The plush velvet couches, the insistent throb of the music and the curtained-off private nooks all help send a seductive message in a way that some find amusing, others find a touch unsubtle. Still, the crowds – especially Europeans – keep coming.

UPPER WEST SIDE

Shalel Lounge: 65 West 70th Street between Central Park West and Columbus Avenues. 212-799 9030. Subway B, C to 72nd Street. Dark and dangerous – in the nicest kind of way. The exotic North African atmosphere transports aficionados directly to Morocco or a similar locale.

WEST VILLAGE

Love: 179 Macdougal Street at 8th Street. 212-477 5683, musicislove.net. Subway A, B, C, D, E, F, V to West 4th Street/Washington Square.

If you like your clubbing to have an underground vibe, then go to this below-the-radar set-up. It takes place in an unmarked basement beneath a barber shop. You'll start in the cave-like bar, complete with faux stone walls, then move into the main room where they play house and electronic. Sometimes goes on until 8am, so ideal if you want an all-nighter.

Sullivan Room: 218 Sullivan Street between Bleecker and West 3rd Streets. 212-252 2151, sullivanroom.com. Subway A, B, C, D, E, F, V to West 4th Street.

An absolutely brilliant, intimate club with no attitude, which is rare in New York. You can dance to soulful house with other friendly types, or just lounge around, chat and sip relatively cheap drinks. Has served as a launch pad for young local DJs.

Night skyline

CHAPTER 9

Theatre and Film

Think about theatre in New York and just one word comes to mind: Broadway, and all the glamour and clamour that goes with it. One of the first things you discover about Broadway, as we Brits think of it, is that it is just one tiny stretch of almost the longest thoroughfare on Manhattan. The Theater District, as it is known, is a congregation of theatres between Broadway and 8th Avenue from about 44th to 52nd Streets (take the N, R, Q, W, 1, 2, 3, 7, 9, S lines to 42nd Street/Times Square). This is Broadway. You'll also see and hear the terms 'Off Broadway' and 'Off-Off-Broadway' (yes, really), which refer to uptown and downtown theatres, particularly in Greenwich Village, East Village and SoHo. These theatres are well worth a visit, as they may be offering rarely seen revivals, the innovative work of new playwrights, or productions featuring hilarious, off-the-wall humour. But they do change frequently, so we have included only a sample selection.

Of course, Broadway productions are changing all the time, but many of the big shows – the ones that many Brits want to see – do stay around a little longer. We have included reviews of those shows we believe will be available for the next couple of years, but for a completely up-to-date guide to what's on at the theatre, look in *The New York Times*, which has comprehensive listings of dance, classical music, opera, Broadway, Off-Broadway and Off-Off-Broadway every day. Other papers and magazines that you can check out include the *New Yorker*, *Village Voice*, *New York Metro* and *New York Press*. If you want to find out what's on before you go, visit the Keith Prowse or Theatre Direct websites given below.

BOOKING YOUR TICKETS

You can book tickets in advance in the UK through either your travel agent or Keith Prowse (UK 0870 840 1111 or US 800-669 8687 toll free, keithprowse.com). An alternative is to use TicketMaster (212-307 7171, ticketmaster.com).

If booking in New York, try Theater Mania (212-352 3101, or 866-811 4111

toll free, theatermania.com); Prime Tickets and Tours (800-480 8499, primetickets.com); Continental Guest Services (800-BWY TKTS/299 8587, continentalguest services.com); Telecharge.com (212-239 6200, telecharge.com) and All Tickets Inc. (800-922 0716, allticketsinc.com).

BRITTIP
Look for discount coupons for Broadway shows at neighbourhood information stands and barrows throughout Manhattan as well as picking up coupons from NYC's Visitor Information Centre at 810 Seventh Avenue at 53rd Street (212-484 1222, nycvisit.com).

For cheaper tickets, go to one of the **Theater Development Fund**'s TKTS three booths (212-221 0013, tdf.org). The less crowded (but less convenient) downtown booth is in South Street Seaport at 199 Water Street at the corner of Front Street, and John Street, subway J, M, Z, 2, 3, 4, 5 to Fulton Street. For same-day evening performances open Mon–Sat 11am–6pm, Sun 11am–4pm;

Times Square

matinee tickets bought here are for the following day's performance. A booth is also located under the red steps in Father Duffy Square on Broadway at 47th Street, subway 1, 2, 3, 4, 5, 6, N, R, W, A, C to Times Square. It's open Mon-Sat 3–8pm for evening performance tickets, Sun 3pm until half an hour before the latest curtain time being sold. For matinees, Wed-Sat 10am–2pm, Sun 11am–3pm. It gets very busy so arrive early for the best selection, then spend the day in Midtown (Chapter 2 New York Neighbourhoods, page 44). The third booth is in downtown Brooklyn and 1 MetroTech Center at the corner of Jay Street and Myrtle Avenue Promenade, subway A, C, F to Jay Street. Open Tues-Sat 11am–6pm, closed for lunch 3–3.30pm. Discounts range from 25–50% for same-day tickets to Broadway, Off-Broadway shows and other arts events, and there's a $4 per ticket fee that helps fund the TDF. They accept credit cards, cash, travellers' cheques and gift certificates. If you are flexible about what you would like to see, you can decide to go to a show at the very last minute, since TKTS Midtown is open right until show time.

For Off-Broadway shows, the Alliance of Resident Theaters (offbroadwayonline. com) has dozens of performances for all budgets daily across New York. Bookings for all the shows and performances below can be made with Theater Direct International (800-BROADWAY, broadway.com) or for the best seats in the house, via the official information and ticket resource, the Broadway Ticket Center, in the Times Square Information Center at 1560 Broadway, bang in the heart of Times Square (next to the Palace Theatre at 226 West 47th Street between 46th and 47th Street).

ON BROADWAY

All the Broadway and Off-Broadway shows listed here have one interval (unless stated). The suggested ages are for guidance only.

AMERICAN IDIOT

✉ St James Theatre, 246 West 44th Street
🖱 stjames-theater.com
🕐 Tues 7pm; Wed, Sat 2pm and 8pm; Thurs, Fri 8pm; Sun 2pm and 7pm

US rock group Green Day won two Grammys for their album *American Idiot* and now those tunes have been made into a musical that has so far earned 8 Tony Awards. It follows characters from working-class backgrounds from the suburbs, city and Middle East as they seek redemption in a world full of frustration

Times Square TKTS stand

– sounds heavy but the excellent tunes lift it.
Awards: 8 Tony Awards
Length of show: Around 2 hours
Age: 12 and over

BILLY ELLIOT

- ✉ Imperial Theatre 249 West 45th Street
- 🖱 billyelliottbroadway.com
- 🕐 Tues 7pm; Wed 2pm; Thurs, Fri 7.30pm; Sat and Sun 2pm and 7.30pm

The smash hit in London has come across the pond and hit Broadway in Oct 2008. This heart-warming story of one young boy's dream to be a ballet dancer despite problems all around him, is magical.
Length of show: Around 2 hours 45 minutes
Age: 12 and over

CHICAGO

- ✉ Ambassador Theater, 219 West 49th Street between Broadway and 8th Avenue
- 🖱 chicagothemusical.com
- 🕐 Mon, Thurs, Fri, Sat 8pm; Tues, Sun 7pm; matinees Sat 2.30pm; Sun 2.30pm and 7pm

This great musical with wonderful dancing is the winner of 6 Tony Awards and has other productions throughout the world, but many still consider this one to be the best. In fact, on 14 November 2007, it celebrated its 10th Anniversary. *Chicago* tells the story of a chorus girl who kills her lover and then escapes the noose and prison with the help of a conniving lawyer. If greed, corruption, murder and treachery are your bag, then this is the musical for you.
Awards: 6 Tony Awards in 1997
Length of show: 2 hours 30 minutes
Age: 12 and over (parental guidance)

HAIR

- ✉ Al Hirschfeld Theater, 302 West 45th Street
- 🖱 alhirschfeldtheater.com
- 🕐 Wed–Sat 8pm, Tues 7pm, matinees Wed and Sat 2pm, Sun 3pm

The story of young Americans searching for love and peace during the Vietnam War era. Popular songs such as the 'Age of Aquarius' are a hit with young and old and the message of embracing change and other people is as relevant today as it was 30 years ago when it was created. A high feelgood factor.
Awards: Tony for Best Musical in 2006
Length of show: 2 hours 25 minutes
Age: 12 and over

JERSEY BOYS

- ✉ August Wilson Theater, 245 West 52nd Street
- 🖱 jerseyboysbroadway.com
- 🕐 Wed–Sat 8pm, Tues 7pm; matinees Wed, Sat 2pm, Sun 3pm

This musical chronicles the rags-to-riches story of the group Frankie Valli and The Four Seasons, four blue-collar boys who became one of the biggest American pop music sensations of all time. Sing along to classics such as 'Sherry', 'Big Girls Don't Cry' and 'Can't Take My Eyes off You'.
Awards: Tony for Best Musical in 2006
Length of show: 2 hours 30 minutes
Age: 12 and over

Chicago

Mamma Mia!

THE LION KING

✉ Minskoff Theater, 200 West 45th Street between Broadway and 8th Avenue

🖱 disneyonbroadway.com

🕐 Tues 7pm; Sat 8pm, Sun 6.30pm; matinees Wed, Sat 2pm, Sun 1pm

With the original music from Elton John and Tim Rice (which won them Oscar and Grammy awards) combined with new music from Hans Zimmer and Lebo M. Disney tells the story of Simba, a lion cub who struggles to accept the responsibilities of adulthood and his destined role as king. Ten years on Broadway in 2008.

Awards: 6 Tony Awards in 1998
Length of show: 2 hours 45 minutes
Age: From the very young to the very old

MAMMA MIA!

✉ Cadillac Winter Garden Theater, 1634 Broadway at 50th Street

🖱 mamma-mia.com

🕐 Mon 8pm; Wed–Sat 8pm; 2pm matinee Sat, Sun; Sun 7pm

If you haven't had a chance to see this fabulously uplifting musical in London, then why not try it in New York? Set on a mythical Greek island, it tells the story of a single mum and her daughter on the eve of her daughter's wedding – and comes with 22 cracking ABBA songs.

Length of show: 2 hours 30 minutes
Age: 5 and over

MARY POPPINS

✉ New Amsterdam Theater, 214 West 42nd Street

🖱 http://disney.go.com/theatre/marypoppins

🕐 Tues–Sat 8pm; matinees Wed, Sat 2pm, Sun 3pm

Mary Poppins flew into Broadway with her carpetbag packed and her umbrella unfurled in Nov 2006 high on the success of her hit debut in the West End of London. Based on the Oscar-winning 1964 Walt Disney film, the world's most famous nanny is bringing 'Supercalifragilisticexpialidocious' to a new generation of children under the directorship of legendary producer Cameron Mackintosh.

Length of show: 2 hours 45 minutes
Age: 6 and over

MEMPHIS

✉ Shubert Theater, 225 West 44th Street between Broadway and 8th Avenue

🖱 schubert-theater.com

🕐 Tues–Sat 8pm, matinee Wed and Sat 2pm, Sun 3pm

A music-loving mixed-race couple struggle to survive during the early Civil Rights era in Memphis. Part of the bigger picture, a 50s DJ in the city starts to play African-American music to white listeners. The story was inspired by legendary DJ Dewey Philips and the tunes and dancing are terrific.

Length of show: 2 hours 30 minutes
Age: 12 and over

MILLION DOLLAR QUARTET

✉ Nederlander Theater, 208 West 41st Street

🖱 nederlandtheater.com

🕐 Tues–Thurs 7.30pm, Fri–Sat 8pm, Sun 6.30pm, matinee Wed 2pm and Sat 5pm

The story of music legends Johnny Cash, Jerry Lee Lewis, Carl Perkins and Elvis Presley brought together in 1956 at Sun Records' studio in Memphis. It was the only time they were united during their careers and the impromptu recording session embodied the birth of rock 'n' roll. More popular songs than

Memphis

Times Square

The longest-running show in Broadway history, Andrew Lloyd Webber's famous musical of Gaston Leroux's novel set in 19th-century Paris tells the timeless story of a mysterious spectre who haunts the Paris opera house, spooking the owners and falling in love with a beautiful singer.
Awards: 7 Tony Awards in 1998, including Best Musical
Length of show: 2 hours 30 minutes
Age: 5 and over, depending on whether your child may be scared of the mask

BRITTIP
Queues for the Times Square TKTS booth start long before it opens, so arrive early to get a good choice. But even if you arrive at the last minute, you may catch a show, because the booth stays open right until show time.

you've ever heard before under one roof.
Length of show: 2 hours 30 minutes
Age: 8 and over

BRITTIP
For fantastic views of Times Square, treat yourself to a drink at the Broadway Lounge on the 8th floor lobby level of the Marriott Marquis Hotel at 1535 Broadway (nymarriottmarquis.com).

ROCK OF AGES
✉ Brooks Atkinson Theater, 265 West 47th Street
🏛 brooksatkinsontheater.com
🕐 Mon 8pm, Tues 7pm, Wed no performance, Thurs & Fri 8pm, Sat 2pm & 8pm, Sun 3pm
Set in 1987 on Sunset Strip, this is one for anyone who loves a bit of '80s soft rock. Small town girl meets a famous band in an LA rock club and they fall in love to the hits of the '80s. Think Twisted Sister, Poison, Whitesnake and Night Ranger. Party on!
Length of show: Around 2 hours 30 minutes
Age: 10 and over

THE PHANTOM OF THE OPERA
✉ Majestic Theater, 247 West 44th Street between Broadway and 8th Avenue
🏛 thephantomoftheopera.com
🕐 Tues 7pm, Mon, Wed–Sat 8pm; matinees Wed, Sat 2pm

WEST SIDE STORY
✉ Palace Theater, 1564 Broadway
🏛 broadwaywestsidestory.com
🕐 Tues 7pm, Wed–Sat 8pm, Wed & Sat 2pm, Sun 3pm
One of the finest musicals ever written hit Broadway in 2009. Based on two rival gangs, the Jets and the Sharks, in the '50s, it's ultimately a classic love story. The score, by Leonard Bernstein and Stephen Sondheim, is one of the most memorable ever, including 'Tonight', 'America', 'Maria' and 'I Feel Pretty'.
Length of show: 2 hours 40 minutes
Age: 13 and over

The Lion King

WICKED

- ✉ Gershwin Theater, 222 West 51st Street
- ⌐ wickedthemusical.com
- ⏱ Tues 7pm, Wed 2pm & 8pm, Thurs & Fri 8pm, Sat 2pm & 8pm, Sun 3pm

Long before Dorothy drops in, two other girls meet in the Land of Oz. One, born with emerald-green skin, is smart, fiery and misunderstood. The other is beautiful, ambitious and very popular. Based on the 1995 novel by Gregory Maguire, this musical tells the story of their remarkable odyssey, how these two unlikely friends grow to become the Wicked Witch of the West and Glinda the Good Witch.

Awards: 3 Tonys
Length of show: 2 hours 45 minutes
Age: From the young to the very old

Wicked

Avenue Q

OFF BROADWAY

AVENUE Q

- ✉ New World Stages, 340 West 50th Street between 8th and 9th Avenues
- ⌐ avenueq.com
- ⏱ Mon, Wed, Thurs, Fri 8pm; Sat 2pm and 8pm; Sun 3pm and 7.30pm

A bright and entertaining show with people and puppets about the struggles with life when you're straight out of college. Funny and urbane. Has been called a mix of *Sesame Street*, *The Simpsons* and *Sex And The City*. Now playing in London, too.

Awards: Several Tony Awards, including Best Musical
Length of show: 2 hours 15 minutes
Age: 18 and over (even with puppets!)

BLUE MAN GROUP: TUBES

- ✉ Astor Place Theater, 434 Lafayette Street at Astor Place
- ⌐ blueman.com
- ⏱ Mon–Thurs, Sun 8pm, Fri, Sat 7pm, 10pm; matinees Sat 4pm, Sun 2pm, 5pm

One of the most successful Off-Broadway shows. Take a trio of post-modern clowns, cover them in blue rubber and allow them to be outrageous with sound and art and you have this wonderful avant-garde extravaganza that is both hilarious and challenging to watch.

Length of show: 2 hours
Age: 15 and over

MY BIG GAY ITALIAN WEDDING

- ✉ St Luke's Theater, 308 West 46th Street
- ⌐ stlukestheatre.com
- ⏱ Wed–Sat 8pm

Launched on 22 May 2010 with an open run.

CINEMAS

Catch some great blockbuster movies! For complete listings of movies and cinemas near your hotel, check *Time Out* or the free *Village Voice* and *New York Press*.

AMC Empire 25: 234 West 42nd Street between 7th and 8th Avenues, 212-398 3939, amctheatres.com. This has 25 screens on 5 levels and has devoted 7 screens on the top floor, known as the Top of the Empire, to repertory classics and independent films. You can catch a pre-show snack – pizza to ribs – in the 42nd Street Food Court.

Film Forum: 209 West Houston Street between 6th and 7th Avenues, 212-727 8110, filmforum.org. A 3-theatre venue showing independent and vintage films. There are seasons, such as a run of films dedicated to Audrey Hepburn, and talks given by directors plus film merchandise on sale.

Quad: 34 West 13th Street; quadcinema.com. A New York institution for 25 years, showing the best of foreign and independent films. It's family owned and in the heart of Greenwich Village, so near to lots of greats shops and restaurants if you're making a night of it.

Regal E-Walk Stadium 13: 247 West 42nd Street between 7th and 8th Avenues, 212-840 7761, regmovies.com. This mega-plex cinema with 13 screens and all-stadium seating is a modern-day movie palace. A single-storey, hand-painted mural honours the local landmarks of Broadway and Times Square.

The Angelika Film Center: 18 West Houston Street, 212-995 2000, http://angelikafilmcenter. com. A good selection of the latest art films is shown here, as well as at the Lincoln Plaza Cinemas, 1886 Broadway at 62nd Street, 212-757 2280, http://lincolnplaza.moviefone.com. The Angelika has a café and the Lincoln Plaza Cinemas sell sandwiches and pastries.

Sunshine Cinema: 143 East Houston Street on the Lower East Side, 212-330 8182, landmarktheatres.com. This cinema has 5 comfortable screening rooms, state-of-the-art sound systems and plays excellent art house movies. It has been voted New York's hippest cinema in days gone by.

Hopefully this funny play about planning a wedding and planning to ruin a wedding makes it well into 2011. From bickering relatives to jealous ex-boyfriends, this has sparkle.
Length of show: 2 hours
Age: 15 and over

✚ BRITTIP
If you're mad about movies and movie stars, head to New York at the beginning of April when the TriBeCa Film Festival takes place. More than 100 films are featured from 31 countries around the world, including world premieres. Tickets for the festival are $15 for evening and weekend screenings and $8 for daytime and late screenings (tribecafilmfestival.org).

THE 39 STEPS
✉ New World Stages, 340 West 50th Street between 8th and 9th Avenues
🖰 39stepsonbroadway.com
🕐 Mon–Sat 8pm, Sun 7pm, matinee Sat and Sun 3pm
Apparently Broadway's longest running comedy, Hitchcock's 1935 movie classic

thriller is brought to life by four actors and contains every single scene from the award-winning film, including the chase on the Flying Scotsman and the stockings and suspenders scene!
Length of show: 1 hour 50 minutes
Age: 12 and over

✚ BRITTIP
AMCinema and AMC Theatres offers its cheapest deal on all shows before noon Fri, Sat, Sun and holidays. Check show times for prices and availability at amcentertainment.com.

THE FANTASTICKS
✉ Snapple Theater Center, 210 West 50th Street
🖰 thefantasticks.com
🕐 Mon, Tue, Fri, Sat 8pm; Sun 7.15pm; matinee Wed and Sat 2pm, Sun 3pm
The world's longest musical returned to New York in 2006. A young couple fall in love in the hands of their meddling fathers, but soon grow restless and stray. Can they return to the love they once shared?
Length of show: 2 hours and 10 minutes
Age: Adult

COOL SCREENINGS

Cool screenings in New York City can be found at the American Museum of the Moving Image Astoria, Queens (page 291) and where early each year the Annual New York Film Critics: Great Documentaries series featuring more than 20 of the nation's top film critics introduce their favourite documentaries. Also check out the BAMcinématek programme at the Brooklyn Academy of Music (718-636 4100, bam. org), which holds The African Diaspora Film Festival in February. Perhaps one of the coolest film festivals of them all is The Tribeca Film Festival (tribecafilmfestival. org) in different locations around the city in spring, which has a great line-up of actors and filmmakers for Q&A sessions with the audiences.

STOMP

✉ Orpheum Theater, 126 2nd Avenue at 8th Street
🖱 http://stomponline.com
🕐 Mon–Sat 8pm, matinee Sat and Sun 3pm

A very unusual show now in its 14th year. Dancers make their own music by using everyday objects such as dustbin lids, brooms and sticks. The rhythmic beats are infectious and the performers' stamina amazing.

Length of show: 1 hour 45 minutes
Age: All ages (although noisy)

BRITTIP

Phone 212-777 FILM or visit moviefone.com for accurate movie show times and, to make sure you don't miss out, buy tickets in advance. You can also book online at movietickets.com.

Times Square

CHAPTER 10

Where to Stay

The beauty of a city as diverse and cosmopolitan as New York is that you can find pretty much any kind of accommodation that you desire. From über-romantic suites in super swish hotels to quirky little downtown boutique retreats, you're guaranteed to find something that meets your taste and budget.

By early 2010, there were 80,899 hotel rooms in Manhattan. Fewer than half of these hotels belong to national or international chains and some of them are also springing up in outer boroughs like Brooklyn and Queens, so the Big Apple is bursting with hotels of character and charm that you're unlikely to find anywhere else.

You may be surprised at the size of some of the rooms in the city, which are on the small side, but remember that Manhattan is a small island where space is at a premium. What rooms lack in size they usually make up for in decor and views, as architects had to design vertically rather than horizontally; many of the high-rise hotels, such as the Four Seasons, offer breathtaking panoramic vistas.

If you're visiting the city for the first time, be sure to do some research before you book so that you can decide which area you would like to be based in. This will save you much time and money on getting around. For example, if your prime reason for visiting the city is for theatres and shopping, you're going to want to be staying in Midtown where everything is on your doorstep. It may be that if you intend to stay for a week it would work out best to stay at 2 hotels – 1 in Lower Manhattan and 1 in Midtown, helping you save on travelling time and expensive cab fares.

The most upmarket hotels have always been clustered on the east side of Manhattan from Midtown up to 96th Street. However, in recent years first class hotels have been popping up all over the place and there are now several in SoHo, Greenwich Village and the Financial District. The best deals tend to be around Herald Square and on the Upper West Side, but if you go for these options check you won't be spending more than you need to on transport. The average rate for a room that can accommodate 2 people is around $238 a night – so if you get something for less (and there are plenty of ways to do this), you will be doing well.

BRITTIP

If you are planning to take in the sights of Lower Manhattan, Chinatown, Lower East Side, SoHo and the Village, choose a downtown hotel. It'll save you loads of time on travel and money on cab fares.

The Plaza Hotel

HOTEL TIPS

▶ Demand for hotel rooms at peak times of the year is high, so your best bet for both ensuring a bed and getting the best price is to go in the off-peak times of Jan–Mar and July–Aug.

▶ Most hotels reduce their rates at weekends – including some of the poshest. If you're staying for more than a weekend, negotiate the best rate you can for the rest of your time or switch to a cheaper hotel.

▶ If noise is a particular problem for you, bear in mind that hotels downtown and uptown tend to be quieter than those in Midtown. Also, hotels on streets tend to be quieter than those on avenues, except those nearer the river.

▶ For longer stays, try to choose a hotel room or apartment with a kitchenette, then you won't have to eat out all the time.

▶ Smaller hotels tend not to book large groups, so they often have rooms available even during peak periods.

▶ When booking your room, check there isn't going to be a major convention on at the same time. If there is, ask to be put on a different floor.

▶ Ask for a corner room – they are usually bigger and have more windows and, therefore, more light than other rooms and don't always cost more.

▶ Renovation work is often going on in New York hotels so, when making a reservation, ask if any is being done there and, if it is, ask for a room as far away as possible from the work.

Below is the *Brit Guide* pick of the best hotels in Manhattan, priced by room per night, covering all price brackets. They range from romantic hideaways to the latest hip openings to grand hotels that have been on the map for nearly a century.

The Oak Bar at the Plaza

$	Less than $100
$$	$100–200
$$$	$200–300
$$$$	$300–400
$$$$$	$400 and over

LANDMARK HOTELS

These hotels aren't simply hotels, they are institutions. Brimming with history, which most hotel staff will be only too willing to tell you about, these grand dames of the New York hotel scene are in a class of their own, and we're not just talking about the high prices.

MIDTOWN

THE PLAZA $$$$$

✉ 768 5th Avenue at 59th Street
☎ 212-759 3000
🖰 fairmont.com/theplaza
🚇 Subway 6 to 51st Street

A true New York landmark built in the style of a French Renaissance chateau. Built by Henry Janeway Hardenbergh and opened to the public on 1 October 1907, its position next to Central Park and 5th Avenue is unbeatable as a base in NYC. After recent renovations, it now offers 282 guest rooms, including 102 suites, which the hotel claims boast the largest square footage of any luxury hotel in NY. Other developments include exclusive boutiques, which opened in autumn 2008, and sell food as well as clothing and accessories, a Caudalie Spa, Warren Tricom Salon and fitness centre by Radu. While those who adored The Plaza may be sceptical of the changes, enough has been preserved of its glamorous traditions to keep even the most die-hard patron happy. The Palm Court has been fully resorted and once again offers afternoon tea, for which it was famous. Likewise, the opulent Grand Ballroom (where Catherine Zeta Jones and Michael Douglas had their wedding celebrations) and Terrace Room have been restored to their former glory. The legendary Oak Room and Oak Bar are still intact, but there's also a new Champagne Bar and stylish Rose Club, both located in the 5th Avenue lobby and bound to be an instant hit with New York's stylish crowd. You're likely to recognise the building from the string of films and TV shows that have been shot in and around it, such as *North by Northwest*, *Funny Girl*, *The Way We Were*, *Cotton Club*, *Crocodile Dundee*, *Home Alone 2* and *The Sopranos*, as well pictures from celebrity events.

WALDORF-ASTORIA $$$-$$$$$

✉ 301 Park Avenue at 50th Street
☎ 212-355 3000
🖰 waldorfastoria.com
🚇 Subway 6 to 51st Street

A colossus of a hotel in more than one sense, it's an Art Deco marvel with a wonderful history and has been designated a New York City landmark since 1993. Now is a great time to visit as it has had a $50 million makeover, which includes a $5.5 million revamp of Peacock Alley, the hotel's top restaurant headed by chef Cedric Tovar, and a Guerlain Spa.

It all started in 1893 when millionaire William Waldorf Astor opened the 13-storey Waldorf Hotel at 33rd Street. It was the embodiment of Astor's vision of a grand hotel and came with 2 innovations – electricity throughout and private bathrooms in every guest chamber – and immediately became the place to go for the upper classes. Four years later, the Waldorf was joined by the 17-storey Astoria Hotel, built next door by Waldorf Astor's cousin, John Jacob Astor IV. The corridor between the 2 became an enduring symbol of the combined Waldorf and Astoria Hotels.

In 1929 it closed, and on its original site now stands another icon of the New York skyline, the Empire State Building. In the meantime, the Waldorf Astoria was rebuilt in Midtown, opening its doors in 1931 and immediately dubbed New York's first skyscraper hotel. It rose 42 storeys high, stretched from Park Avenue to Lexington and contained an astonishing 2,200 rooms. It was

such an amazing event, opening as it did in the middle of the Depression, that President Herbert Hoover broadcast a message of congratulations. Ever since, the Waldorf-Astoria has had a long association with presidents of countries and corporations.

The Art Deco aspects of the hotel were brought back into view during a restoration in the 1980s when architects found a huge cache of long-lost treasures, including a magnificent 148,000-piece mosaic depicting the Wheel of Life, by French artist Louis Regal, in the Park Avenue lobby, 13 allegorical murals by the same artist and ornate mouldings on the ceilings. The legendary Starlight Roof nightclub with its retractable roof, which had epitomised glamour and sophistication in the 1930s and 1940s, was restored during the same period.

⚡ BRITTIP

If you're not happy with the quality of your room, change it. Americans wouldn't tolerate anything but the best, so why should you?

Another $60-million upgrade in 1998 saw the Park Avenue Cocktail Terrace and Sir Harry's Bar being restored to their full Art Deco glory. Oscar's, named after the Waldorf Astoria's famous style-setting maître d' Oscar Tschirky, was redesigned by Adam Tihany, the hottest restaurant designer in town.

Of course, you'll want to know about the service – excellent – and the standard of the rooms – large, for New York, beautifully decorated and with marble-encased en-suite bathrooms. What more could you ask for?

Waldorf-Astoria

WALDORF TOWERS $$$$$

✉ 301 Park Avenue at 50th Street
☎ 212-355 3100
🖰 waldorfastoria.hilton.com
🚇 Subway 6 to 51st Street

A boutique hotel occupying the 28th to the 42nd floors of the Waldorf-Astoria, this is one of the most exclusive addresses in New York, filled as it is with presidents of countries and global corporations. Thanks to the hotel's security arrangements (it has its own private car parking facilities underground), this is the place where treaties and mergers have been negotiated and signed, momentous peace initiatives have begun and unforgettable music has been made.

The hotel has its own dedicated entrance, lobby, concierge desk, reception and private lifts operated by white-gloved attendants. Guests have included the Duke and Duchess of Windsor, who maintained their New York residence here, Jack and Jackie Kennedy, Frank Sinatra and Cole Porter, who wrote many of his most famous compositions in a room here.

The rooms are not so much rooms or suites, but rather more like apartments. Many come with dining rooms, full kitchens and maids' quarters. Four-footed guests are greeted with a biscuit!

UPPER EAST SIDE

THE CARLYLE $$$$–$$$$$

✉ 35 East 76th Street between Madison and Park Avenues
☎ 212-744 1600
🖰 thecarlyle.com
🚇 Subway 6 to 77th Street

Established in the 1930s, The Carlyle is a timeless classic, patronised by a wide range of people from world leaders and top businessmen to It girls and leading lights

The Carlyle, a Rosewood Hotel

in entertainment and the arts. Brilliantly positioned on Madison Avenue, it is a true New York landmark. The 180 apartment-style rooms and suites are elegant and very plush – some even have grand pianos and all have whirlpools in the bathrooms. In fact, it feels as though you're staying in your elegant Upper East Side pied-à-terre rather than renting a hotel room. If you really want to push the boat out, there's a new, breathtaking Royal Suite on the 22nd floor. It's famous for its impeccable and discreet service but also for its live music in Café Carlyle where Woody Allen regularly plays jazz on Mon nights (page 211).

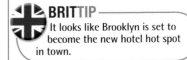

BRITTIP
It looks like Brooklyn is set to become the new hotel hot spot in town.

Premier suite at the Waldorf Towers

Gansevoort Park

TALK OF THE TOWN

New Yorkers love the buzz of a new hotel, and you can be guaranteed they'll be queuing up to see whether a recent opening's restaurant, bar and rooms live up to the hype. If you want to join in the mêlée and be at the heart of what's new and happening, book yourself in for a night at one of these hotels.

THE CHATWAL NEW YORK $$$$$

✉ 130 West 44th Street
☎ 212-764 6200
🖰 thechatwal.ny.com
🚇 Subway N, Q, R, W to Times Square/ 42nd Street

This polished Art Deco-inspired modern gem restored by architect Thierry Despont is very slick. It evokes the glamour of the 30s and opened spring 2010 in the former home of the Lambs Club in the Theater District. Its 88 bedrooms incorporate retro touches, hi-tech sound systems and big TVs.

DISTRIKT HOTEL $$$-$$$$

✉ 342 West 40th Street between 8th and 9th Avenues
☎ 212-706 6100
🖰 distrikthotel.com
🚇 Subway A, C, E to 42nd Street

Opened spring 2010, steps away from the New York Times Building and Times Square. Part of the Ascend Collection, Distrikt Hotel New York offers a dedication to detail with impeccable service, cutting-edge technology, comfortable yet luxurious guestrooms, 4-star amenities and fresh cuisine using locally grown ingredients. Each of the 155 guestrooms are designed for the comfort and needs of the guest to include relaxing Simmons Beauty Rest pillow-top mattresses, decadent Frette bed and bath linen, a 37-in LG flatscreen television, a business desk with ergonomic chair, Ecru New York soaps and amenities and wireless internet in every room.

GANSEVOORT PARK $$$$

✉ Corner of Park Avenue and 29th Street
☎ 877-426-7386
🖰 gansevoorthotelgroup.com
🚇 Subway 6 to 28th Street

A 249-room hotel that opened summer 2010 and promises an uptown experience with a downtown vibe. The dramatic 3-storey lobby and rooms are designed by Manhattan-based architect Stephen B. Jacobs and interior designer Andi Pepper, as is the chic Infusion bar. Unusually for NYC, some of the rooms have balconies and floor-to-ceiling windows. There's also an amazing heated indoor–outdoor rooftop pool, 6 distinctive event spaces, unobstructed views of the Empire State Building, Exhale spa including a yoga and core studio, Cutler Salon, fitness room, sauna and Asellina, an Italian trattoria.

HYATT ANDAZ $$$$

✉ 275 Wall Street
☎ 877-875 5036
🖰 andaz.com
🚇 Subway 2, 3 to Wall Street

Andaz is the latest boutique brand from international chain Hyatt, and it's been a hit in London. The Wall Street hotel, which opened last year, has 250 suites and 350 residential units. Expect chic, masculine interiors perfect for upscale businessmen.

TRUMP SOHO NEW YORK $$$$

✉ 246 Spring Street
☎ 212-965 0008
🖰 trumpsohohotel.com
🚇 Subway C, E to Spring Street

This 46-storey silver and glass tower opened in spring 2010 and boasts spectacular views of the city's skyline, Hudson River, Statue of Liberty and Empire State Building, so ideal for those who want to feel in the heart of the city. There are 391 rooms and suites with floor-to-ceiling windows, furnishings by Fendi

Casa and custom bedding by Bellino. With just 12 rooms per floor, they're actually a decent size, which is unusual for NYC. Its aim is high-end luxury, and with amenities like restaurant Quattro Gastronomia Italiana, The Spa at Trump (with New York's only authentic luxury hammam), Bazaar lounge, seasonal Bar d'Eau on the lush 6,000-sq-ft pool deck and The Library, outfitted with TASCHEN books, it certainly achieves it.

🇬🇧 BRITTIP

Our favourite find of 2010 is the ACE Hotel (20 West 29th Street, 212-679 222, acehotel.com). Just 3 blocks from the Empire State Building, it's a new 12-storey 260-room gem of a Midtown hotel. It's edgy without being intimidating – DJs play in the lobby bar, the Breslin dining room serves up organic and seasonal English-style grub and No 7 Sub Shop is a great place to pick up a sarnie for a picnic in Central Park. There are funky bedrooms with murals on the walls, with words like 'Play Safe'. From around $299, through to bunk rooms with bathrooms from $209, it's a cheap way to see NYC in style.

MODERN LUXURY

A rash of large, new super-stylish hotels have opened in Manhattan in the last couple of years, which have set new standards worldwide for architecture and interiors. We also include a couple of hotels that have been around for a decade that were so ahead of their time they're still attracting a modern crowd. These are the places to check into if you want contemporary rooms with all the trimmings; think fluffy white bathrobes, designer toiletries in the bathroom, plasma screen TVs and a hip cocktail bar or restaurant to spend some time in.

BATTERY PARK CITY

RITZ–CARLTON NEW YORK $$$$$

- ✉ 2 West Street between Battery Place and West End
- ☎ 212-344 0800
- 🖱 ritzcarlton.com
- 🚇 Subway 4, 5 to Bowling Green

A world-class, award-winning hotel with Art Deco-inspired interiors, incredible views of the Hudson River and Statue of Liberty, state-of-the-art business support services and unparalleled service. A 39-storey glass-and-brick edifice in Lower Manhattan, it has 298 sumptuous guest rooms, an outdoor waterfront deck and even the Skyscraper Museum (page 120).

The rooms come with the very finest Frette linens, feather beds and goose-down pillows, cotton bathrobes, Ritz-Carlton pyjamas, marble bathtubs and separate marble shower stalls, silk curtains, in-room safe, working desk with 2 chairs, dual-line cordless phones with voicemail and high-speed internet access. The extensive guest services include a fully equipped health club and spa, massage treatments, limo, complimentary shuttle service in Lower Manhattan and a bath butler! Sheer luxury!

Ritz-Carlton

GRAMERCY PARK

GRAMERCY PARK HOTEL $$$–$$$$
- ✉ 2 Lexington Avenue at Gramercy Park North
- ☎ 212-201 2161
- ⌂ gramercyparkhotel.com
- 🚗 Subway L, N, R, 4, 5, 6 to 14th Street/ Union Square

Once a famous hotel where the likes of JFK and Humphrey Bogart liked to spend time, now it's back on the style radar once again, thanks to a multi-million dollar refurbishment by über-hotelier Ian Schrager. It's got all the flair that you usually find in a Schrager creation; think jaw-dropping reception area, quirky bar and super-sexy bedrooms. It has a much coveted roof club and garden, and the penthouse is incredible, too, with wonderful views of Gramercy Park and a massive bedroom, dining room, multi-media centre and kitchen.

LOWER EAST SIDE

THE COOPER SQUARE HOTEL $$$$
- ✉ 25 Cooper Square, between East 5th and 6th Streets, Bowery
- ☎ 212-475 5700
- ⌂ thecoopersquarehotel.com
- 🚗 Subway F to Delancey Street

This 21-storey hip hotel opened in 2009. Developers Gregory Peck and Matthew Moss have created a hotel worth checking out. In the heart of the Bowery area, which is fast becoming one of NY's hotspots, it's close to SoHo for shopping and nightlife. Its innovative in a good way; there's no check-in desk (guests are greeted by a host informed electronically of their arrival at the front door), a tree-canopied back garden, signature scent and a range of indie films in the minibar. If you've money to burn, the penthouse has incredible views.

MEATPACKING DISTRICT

THE STANDARD $$$
- ✉ 848 Washington at 13th Street
- ☎ 212-645 4646
- ⌂ standardhotels.com
- 🚗 Subway A, C, E, L to 8th Avenue/ 14th Street

Andre Balazs's third foray into New York City hospitality is this super-chic 337-room, 18-storey high, $200m new build in the Meatpacking District. It opened spring 2009, has a rooftop lounge, 18th-floor bar and ground-level restaurant and beer garden. Lifts have video installations!

MIDTOWN

FLATOTEL $$$–$$$$
- ✉ 135 West 52nd Street
- ☎ 212-887 9400
- ⌂ flatotel.com
- 🚗 Subway B, D, F, Q to 42nd Street

A towering glass complex just around the corner from Radio City Music Hall (page 71) that's home-from-home for rock stars thanks to the 288 large, light rooms that have fab marble bathrooms, flatscreen TVs, CD players and huge beds. The view from the floor-to-ceiling windows is awesome.

THE LONDON NYC $$$–$$$$$
- ✉ 151 West 54th Street
- ☎ 212-307 5000
- ⌂ thelondonnyc.com

The former Rihga Royal New York Hotel has been transformed into an über hip destination; out with the tired furnishings and in with deluxe rooms with high-speed internet access. London chef Gordon Ramsey's first restaurant in the city is here (though it didn't go down well with New York food critics) and a concierge service by Camilla Parker Bowles's son Tom's upper crust do-it-all company. This is the hot hotel for grown-ups. Lots of offers, such as The London Suite from $299 per night, so check the website.

ROYALTON $$$–$$$$
- ✉ 44 West 44th Street between 5th and 6th Avenues
- ☎ 212-869 4400
- ⌂ royaltonhotel.com
- 🚗 Subway B, D, F, Q to 42nd Street

Still an in place with the magazine and showbiz crowd, despite the fact that this

The Royalton

SoHo Grand

hotel, originally designed by Philippe Starck, first opened in the 1980s. Its theatre-style lobby, recently re-created by New York design firm Roman and Willian, runs the length of an entire block and is worth a visit alone. The 168 rooms have been refurnished by Charlotte Macaux and include neutral shades, built-in banquettes running the entire width of the room, mahogany furniture and crisp white linens. Starck's sumptuous bathrooms now have slate and mirrored tiles and 1.5m/5ft Roman soaking tubs. It's also a honeypot for gourmets, as it boasts Brasserie 44 (page 175) and Bar 44 (page 208). Check out the special offers section on the website before you book.

MIDTOWN EAST

FOUR SEASONS $$$$-$$$$$

✉ 57 East 57th Street between Madison and Park Avenues
☎ 212-758 5700
⌂ fourseasons.com
🚇 Subway 4, 5, 6 to 59th Street

This soaring hotel has access to some of the best views of the city. It's expensive and the rooms are a touch on the small side, but you get electronically controlled curtains, marble-clad bathrooms and the best service in the world.

SOHO

SOHO GRAND $$$$

✉ 310 West Broadway between Grand and Canal Streets
☎ 212-965 3000
⌂ sohogrand.com
🚇 Subway C east to Canal Street

Famous for its style, this was the first real top-notch hotel to open in the SoHo area in 1996. Cocktails and light meals are served in the Grand Bar, an intimate, wood-panelled club room, as well as the fashionable Salon,

a lively lounge that is excellent for people-watching and pet-friendly, so perhaps dog-watching, too.

TRIBECA

THE GREENWICH HOTEL $$$$-$$$$$

✉ 377–383 Greenwich Street at Northmoore Street, TriBeCa
☎ 212-941 8600
⌂ thegreenwichhotel.com
🚇 Subway 1 to Franklin Street Station

This fabulous hotel opened it doors in 08 and has made lots of headlines because it's been developed by actor Robert DeNiro, with his partner Ira Drukier. They allegedly poured $43 million into the 6-storey luxury hotel, which sits nicely alongside his existing portfolio, which includes the TriBeCa Film Institute. It's instantly recognisable as the terracotta brick building at the corner of Northmoore and Greenwich Streets. It has 88 rooms all of which are individually furnished, from Tibetan silk rugs to oak floors and small libraries. It's very luxurious, with toiletries developed specially for the hotel, iPod docking stations, mini-bars stocked in advance with guests' preferences and you can even have a newspaper from your home town delivered (though that's within the US rather than the UK!). There's also an inner courtyard that is incredibly serene, Ago Restaurant and Shibui Spa.

DIAMOND DISCOUNTS

You can cut your room rates significantly by taking advantage of the New York Travel Advisory Bureau's (NYTAB) tie-up with Express Reservations – call 303-440 8481 or visit quikbook.com. It offers major discounts on more than 25 hotels across most price categories.

The lobby at the Greenwich Hotel

Tribeca Grand

SMYTH TRIBECA $$$–$$$$
✉ 85 West Broadway, TriBeCa
☎ 212-587 7000
⌂ smythhotel.com
🚇 Subway A, C, 1, 2, 3 to Chambers Street
Part of the chic Thompson hotels portfolio, this super-cool hotel opened in 2009. Designed by Yabu Pushelberg, it has modern interiors, a 24-hour concierge, Kiehls toiletries, Jour et Nuit restaurant, bar and lounge.

TRIBECA GRAND $$$$–$$$$$
✉ 2 Avenue of the Americas (6th Avenue) at Church Street
☎ 212-519 6600, UK freephone 0800-028 9824
⌂ tribecagrand.com
🚇 Subway 1, 9 to Franklin Street
Sister property to the extremely stylish Soho Grand, this was the first major hotel to open in the TriBeCa area. It's popular with the film crowd, thanks to its 98-seat private screening room and the annual TriBeCa Film Festival that it hosts. Amenities in the 203 rooms, including studio 'digital lifestyle' rooms and a Grand Suite with rooftop terrace, include iPods, complimentary local phone calls and faxes, digital cable TV with movies-on-demand, Bose sound dock, and radio/CD player with library, wireless internet access, and complimentary pet goldfish on request.

UPPER WEST SIDE

MANDARIN ORIENTAL $$$$–$$$$$
✉ 80 Columbus Circle at 60th Street
☎ 212-805 8800
⌂ mandarinoriental.com
🚇 Subway A, B, C, D, 9 to 59th Street/ Columbus Circle
On the top floors of the AOL Time Warner Center on the north-west arc of Columbus Circle, the 248 rooms and suites are steps away from Central Park and just a stroll from

TOP 5 HOTEL SPAS
The Cowshed Spa at SoHo House (page 238)

The Peninsula Spa at The Peninsula New York (page 241)

Plus One Spa at Trump International Hotel & Tower (page 239)

Spa at Four Seasons Hotel (page 232)

Spa at Mandarin Oriental (page 233)

5th Avenue. Inside, the luxurious rooms are simply breathtaking, with floor-to-ceiling windows offering spectacular views of the Manhattan skyline. Hang out at the trendy MO bar, or enjoy dinner in Asiate on the 35th floor, which offers a fusion of French and Japanese cuisine. If you're tired after your journey, try a massage at the hotel spa.

TRADITIONAL LUXURY
The following hotels are all about plush furnishings, impeccable service and the right location. They are often very discreet, which is why celebrities love them, and most have extremely good gourmet restaurants.

GRAMERCY PARK

INN AT IRVING PLACE $$$$–$$$$$
✉ 56 Irving Place between East 17th and East 18th Streets
☎ 212-533 4600
⌂ innatirving.com
🚇 Subway L, N, R, 4, 5, 6 to 14th Street/ Union Square
Delightful, tiny Victorian boutique hotel (there's no sign outside). Each of the 12 rooms has a romantic fireplace and 4-poster bed, Frette linen, Penhaligon's toiletries and a desk. There is also Lady Mendl's Tea Salon, and Cibar. Exquisite.

Inn at Irving Place

MIDTOWN EAST

ELYSÉE $$$$–$$$$$
- ✉ 60 East 54th Street between Park and Madison Avenues
- ☎ 212-753 1066
- ⌂ elyseehotel.com
- 🚗 Subway 6 to 51st Street

A small hotel dating from the 1920s whose decor includes antique furnishings and Italian marble bathrooms. Once a home-from-home to movie stars, it's still filled with discerning guests, who have use of a nearby sports club as the hotel has no gym.

BRITTIP
Most hotels are now predominantly non-smoking.

NEW YORK PALACE $$$$–$$$$$
- ✉ 455 Madison Avenue between 50th and 51st Streets
- ☎ 212-888 7000
- ⌂ newyorkpalace.com
- 🚗 Subway 6 to 51st Street

Built in 1882, the opulent Palace rises 55 floors from its prime spot in Midtown and is a favourite stopover for celebs visiting New York. The main hotel is in the atmospheric Villard Houses, but the adjacent Towers has the advantage of more luxurious rooms. Its fêted restaurant, Gilt, serves modern European cuisine and the new Palace Gate, an outdoor lounge situated inside the courtyard of the palace's Villard Mansion, serves up cocktails and fine dining.

UPPER EAST SIDE

HOTEL PLAZA-ATHENEE $$$$–$$$$$
- ✉ 37 East 64th Street between Madison and Park Avenues
- ☎ 212-734 9100
- ⌂ plaza-athenee.com
- 🚗 Subway 6 to 68th Street

New York Palace

Upmarket, uptown discreet getaway loved by in-the-know tourists and locals alike. What the 114 rooms lack in size they make up for in elegant antique French furnishings; the 35 suites are bigger. The hotel has introduced a great range of packages for tourists, including a shopping package with discounts at lots of stores including Bloomingdales and private car pick-up. The Arabelle Restaurant is also the place to brunch.

THE LOWELL $$$$$
- ✉ 28 East 63rd Street at Madison Avenue
- ☎ 212-838 1400
- ⌂ lowellhotel.com
- 🚗 Subway N, R, W to Lexington Avenue/ 59th Street

Classic Upper East Side retreat, far from the hustle and bustle of Midtown. Everything here looks and feels very expensive, from the marble floors to the mahogany desk lobby. The 47 suites and 23 deluxe rooms are decorated like the interiors of an ageing Park Lane princess's home; think rich fabrics and plush sofas. Some even have a working fireplace, although there are hi-tech touches, such as a flat-screen TV at the foot of the bath, Bulgari toiletries and Fiji water at turndown.

THE MARK $$$$–$$$$$
- ✉ 25 East 77th Street between 5th and Madison Avenues
- ☎ 212-744 4300
- ⌂ themarkhotel.com
- 🚗 Subway 6 to 77th Street

A recent refurbishment has breathed new life into this super-smart hotel, where the likes of Kate Moss and Johnny Depp used to hang out in the 90s. It was the city's first really beautiful upmarket boutique hotel and the mix of swanky rooms and suites full of the latest Bang Olufsen equipment and marble bathrooms combined with the most discreet service in town will ensure it stays at the top.

BRITTIP
Pay for your first night deposit only if you're booking in advance. That way, if you don't like your room, you're free to leave and try somewhere else.

UPPER WEST SIDE LUXURY
Want more of a home than a hotel vibe? Try Wyman House at 36 Riverside Drive at 76th Street (212 799-8281). Pam and Ronald Wyman have created 6 unique and luxurious suites in their c.1888 home on the Upper West Side. Take a look at their website at wymanhouse.com.

SHERRY-NETHERLAND $$$$–$$$$$

✉ 781 5th Avenue at East 59th Street
☎ 212-355 2800
🖰 sherrynetherland.com
🚇 Subway 4, 5, 6 to 59th Street

A true New York secret, this is one of the grand hotels with real charm and is also the permanent home of many a celebrity. It's just undergone a multi-million-dollar renovation of all its suites, with internet access in all rooms now included. It also boasts the Cipriani Restaurant, popular with ladies who like to lunch.

🇬🇧 BRITTIP

When making a booking directly with a hotel, make sure they send you confirmation of your reservation (by email is simplest).

BOUTIQUE CHIC

These hotels are stylish and small. If you love modern design and crave the latest looks, then check them out. If you can't stay, most have great bars where you can soak up the ambience for an evening.

FINANCIAL DISTRICT

GILD HALL $$$$

✉ 15 Gold Street, Financial District
☎ 212-232 7700
🖰 60thompson.com
🚇 Subway 2, 3 to Fulton Street

The latest opening from the 60 Thompson gang (see page 237) is causing hearts to flutter downtown. Just minutes from Wall Street, this gorgeous boutique retreat is not just for city slickers, it's for anyone who loves their hotels to be stylish and laid-back. Attractions include bi-level library, champagne bar, English tavern restaurant by Todd English, 126 rooms, 24-hour concierge, Frette robes and mini-bars stocked by Dean & Deluca.

LOWER EAST SIDE

BLUE MOON $$$

✉ 100 Orchard Street, Lower East Side
☎ 212-533 9080
🖰 bluemoon-nyc.com
🚇 Subway F to East Broadway

This 22-room boutique retreat in the trendy Lower East Side gets its inspiration from another era, with each room individually styled and named after screen celebrities. Situated around a quaint cobbled street, it's a little gem if you don't want to break the bank. The complimentary continental breakfast served in the lobby includes delicious bagels.

BOWERY $$$$–$$$$$

✉ 335 Bowery at 3rd Street
☎ 212-505 9100
🖰 theboweryhotel.com
🚇 Subway F to Delancey Street

Super cool and discreet. Celebs love it and so do we thanks to its 400-thread count cotton, valet parking, complimentary DVD library and *New York Times*, iPod docking stations, marble bathrooms and Gemma Restaurant.

🇺🇸 NYINTHEKNOW

If you want to rub shoulders with the stars where you're staying, check in to the Bowery. On her website, goop.com, film star Gwyneth Paltrow says, 'The Bowery has been one of my homes-away-from-home in the last year. It is a very cool spot, with the people to match. As it is located on Bowery I wouldn't recommend it to the Park Avenue set, but my English rock star friends can't get enough of it.'

HOTEL ON RIVINGTON $$$$–$$$$$

✉ 107 Rivington Street between Ludlow
and Essex Streets
☎ 212-475 2600
🖰 hotelonrivington.com
🚇 Subway F to Delancey Street

Another hip hotel to open up in the Lower East Side, this glass and aluminium 20-storey building is very slick. The entrance of deep red carpet and velvet curtains isn't the same tone as the rest of the hotel. On the ground floor is a hip restaurant, Thor; above this is the sleek concierge desk with low-lying sofas and tables with arty books; and above this lie the rooms, all very minimalist and tasteful with cloud-like duvets, boxy armchairs in slate grey and flat-screen TVs. If you can afford it, go for one of the upper level rooms with great views of the East River from floor-to-ceiling windows.

Hotel on Rivington

MEATPACKING DISTRICT

HOTEL GANSEVOORT $$$–$$$$$
- ✉ 18 9th Avenue at 13th Street
- ☎ 212-206 6700
- ⌂ hotelgansevoort.com
- 🚇 Subway N, R to 5th Avenue

In the heart of the Meatpacking District, the Gansevoort is a much-feted 187-room, 23-suite hang-out that's just a stroll away from the Stella McCartney store and some great restaurants. The feature that really makes it a place to head for is the 14m/45ft long rooftop pool with underwater music. The new spa, with salon and infinity-edge hydro pools, is great, too.

MIDTOWN

BRYANT PARK $$$$–$$$$$
- ✉ 40 West 40th Street
- ☎ 212-869 0100
- ⌂ bryantparkhotel.com
- 🚇 Subway D, B, V, F to 42nd Street

This hide-out for the fashion pack since 2001 overlooks the park that gives the hotel its name. It's just off 5th Avenue, so ideal if you are on a shopping trip and convenient for visiting all of the major sights. Inside, the rooms resemble New York lofts; think white walls, sleek Italian furniture in warm orange and ochre and cool bathrooms with giant porcelain sinks and stainless steel shelves.

CHAMBERS $$$–$$$$$
- ✉ 15 West 56th Street between 5th and 6th Avenues
- ☎ 212-974 5656
- ⌂ chambershotel.com
- 🚇 Subway B, Q to 57th Street

Owned by the same team behind the Mercer Hotel in SoHo, it attracts the likes of Jennifer Love Hewitt and Kid Rock to its gorgeous rooms. The ultra-modern decor is comfortable and luxurious and the hotel displays over 500 pieces of original art. The bath tubs are deep, cashmere throws adorn the beds and flat-screen TVs with DVD and CD players grace every room. Its new restaurant Má Pêche (page 176) is a great spot for lunch.

CITY CLUB HOTEL $$$–$$$$
- ✉ 55 West 44th Street between 5th and 6th Avenues
- ☎ 212-921 5500
- ⌂ cityclubhotel.com
- 🚇 Subway 7 to 5th Avenue; B, D, F, V to 42nd Street

The owner-manager Jeffrey Klein is one of the most socially visible hoteliers in the city and some of his very famous friends cocoon themselves in his hotel. Based in an old gentlemen's club building, it is one of the smartest but least showy boutique hotels in New York. There's no queuing in the lobby as check-in happens in your room, which has a big TV hidden in the wall, a day bed and vintage books. These rooms are designed to spend time in!

BRITTIP
If you hire a car, bear in mind that most hotels charge a parking fee of around $30 a night.

MORGANS $$$–$$$$
- ✉ 237 Madison Avenue
- ☎ 212-686 0300
- ⌂ morganshotel.com
- 🚇 Subway 4, 5, 6 to 6th Avenue and 34th Street

This Ian Schrager hotel started the boutique phenomenon and is still going strong today

Hotel Gansevoort pool

thanks to its unique sense of style and effortless cool. The bedrooms are apartment-style havens, all ivory, camel and taupe soft furnishings plus it has one of Manhattan's most popular restaurants, Asia de Cuba (page 179).

THE MODERNE $$$–$$$$
✉ 243 West 55th Street between Broadway and 8th Avenue
☎ 212-397 6767
🖰 modernehotelnyc.com
🚇 Subway C, E, 1, 9 to 50th Street

There are only 34 rooms, 5 on each floor, in this smart boutique getaway that lies close to Carnegie Hall and The Museum of Modern Art. You can lie in soft Belgian linen beneath a Warhol print of Marilyn Monroe or pamper yourself with the Gilchrist & Soames goodies in the very plush bathrooms.

MIDTOWN EAST

DYLAN $$$–$$$$
✉ 52 East 41st Street between Madison and Park Avenues
☎ 212-338 0500
🖰 dylanhotel.com
🚇 Subway S, 4, 5, 6, 7 to Grand Central/42nd Street

Located in the former Chemist's Club building, this small hotel was developed to preserve the 1903 Beaux Arts structure. A mezzanine lounge and bar overlooks the dramatic, high-ceilinged restaurant, Benjamin Steakhouse. In-room amenities include a state-of-the-art digital entertainment system with large cable TV, DVD and CD players that can access a library of thousands of video and CD titles, 2-line telephones with voicemail and data port, complimentary high-speed and wireless internet, large safes and complimentary newspaper.

BRITTIP
For sleek New York style without too hefty a price tag, check into one of the W New York hotels, a small chain of hotels that continue to spring up around the city. W New York The Court (212-685 1100), W New York The Tuscany (212-686 1600), W New York Union Square (212-253 9119), W New York Times Square (212-930 7400) and W New York on Lexington Avenue (212-755 1200) each offer exceptional standards of minimalist-style accommodation. View them all at whotels.com.

SOHO

6 COLUMBUS CIRCLE $$$
✉ 6 Columbus Circle between West 58th and 60th Streets
☎ 212-204 3000
🖰 60thompson.com
🚇 Subway 1, B, C, D to 59th Street/Columbus Circle

Overlooking Columbus Circle and Central Park, this 88-room and suite inspired urban retreat with a 1960s modernist feel opened in summer 2006. The renovation was masterminded by Jason Pomerac, who opened 60 Thompson 3 years ago.

60 THOMPSON $$$–$$$$$
✉ 60 Thompson Street between Broome and Spring Streets
☎ 877-431 0400
🖰 60thompson.com
🚇 Subway C, E to Spring Street

A sleek, 14-storey, 100-bedroom hotel that is a great retreat from the bustling streets of SoHo. Rooms are designed for relaxing in – the best are on the top floor and have breathtaking panoramic views of landmarks such as the Empire State Building. The front patio, sheltered by stands of black bamboo, is a wonderful place to just sit and people-watch and restaurant Kittichai is a favourite of New Yorkers. Outstanding!

MERCER $$$–$$$$
✉ 147 Mercer Street at Prince Street
☎ 212-966 6060
🖰 mercerhotel.com
🚇 Subway N, R to Prince Street

A bijou 75-room boutique hotel in a Romanesque revival building slap-bang in the middle of SoHo. Offering a taste of New York loft living, it quickly gets packed with the fashionable and young corporate sets. Rooms

Loft at the 60 Thompson

even provide condoms in the bathroom and video games to play on the TV, and The Kitchen re-creates the casual feeling of a meal at home.

SOHO HOUSE NEW YORK
$$$$–$$$$$

✉ 29–35 9th Avenue between West 13th and 14th Streets
☎ 212-627 9800
🖰 sohohouseny.com
🚇 Subway 1, 9 to 14th Street

Soho House is the baby sister of London's Soho House and has already proved a similar magnet for celebrities and media bigwigs with its chandeliers-meets-Corbusier decor, 24 bedrooms, Cowshed Spa and cinema. It's actually a private members' club, but if you're lucky enough to book one of the rooms you can use the members' facilities, which includes the fabulous rooftop pool that has already gained iconic status as the set for one of the classic *Sex And The City* episodes.

THEME HOTELS

CHELSEA

MARITIME HOTEL
$$$–$$$$

✉ 363 West 16th Street at 9th Avenue
☎ 212-242 4300
🖰 themaritimehotel.com
🚇 Subway 1, 9 to 14th Street

A fun, stylish hotel where all rooms have a maritime theme; think porthole windows overlooking the Hudson River, teak panelling and blue and white nautical stripes. The 24-hour room service can be enjoyed with the latest on-demand movies plus computer games. There's a sizeable roof terrace and it's in a great location for exploring Chelsea and the Meatpacking District.

MIDTOWN

THE LIBRARY
$$$$–$$$$$

✉ 299 Madison Avenue at 41st Street
☎ 212-983 4500
🖰 libraryhotel.com
🚇 Subway 4, 5, 6, 7, S to 41st Street/Grand Central

A fabulous hotel that, you've guessed it, has the theme of a city library. It has the feel of a cosy gentlemen's club when you first walk in, all mahogany panelling, fancy artwork and bookcases. The rooms are a revelation. Each of the 10 floors is dedicated to a category that you'd find in a real library, such as philosophy or art and literature, and there are books and artworks in rooms to match the theme of each level. Original and luxurious, but pricey.

Amalia portrait gallery at the Dream

MIDTOWN WEST

DREAM
$$–$$$

✉ 210 West 55th Street
☎ 212-247 2000
🖰 dreamny.com
🚇 Subway N, R to 5th Avenue

If you're seeking peace, tranquillity and possibly even a spiritual experience, then this hotel promises to deliver. It's the unique vision of hotelier Vikram Chatwal and is all about promoting spiritual well-being, from the mind-enhancing lobby with its Subconscious Lounge to the Ayurvedic healing centre created by spiritualist Deepak Chopra. But you needn't forego the hi-tech; its modern, eclectic-style rooms have 94cm/37in plasma TVs and iPod digital audio players.

THE NIGHT HOTEL
$$$–$$$$$

✉ 132 West 45th Street between 6th and 7th Avenues
☎ 212-835 9600
🖰 nighthotelny.com
🚇 Subway B, D, F, V to 47th Street/Rockefeller Center

This stylish, petite 72-room hotel is Vikram Chatwal's latest offering. It's black and white, modern Gothic décor is refreshingly cool in a city full of beige neutral hotel rooms. It's sexy and stylish Nightlife bar and restaurant is a great place to unwind after a day's sightseeing or work.

TOP 5 CELEBRITY HOTELS

Check out where the stars check in – spotted in 2010:

Gramercy Park Hotel: Janet Jackson, Chace Crawford, Kid Rock (page 231)

The Bowery: Ashley Olsen, Blake Lively, Rachel Bilson (page 235)

60 Thompson: Kirsten Dunst, Jessica Simpson, Christina Aguilera, Matt Damon (page 237)

The Greenwich Hotel: Robert De Niro, Mel Gibson, Spike Lee, Uma Thurman (page 232)

The Carlyle: Tom Cruise and Katie Holmes hosted a tea party for daughter Suri here (page 228)

THEATER DISTRICT

TIME $$–$$$

✉ 224 West 49th Street between Broadway and 8th Avenue
☎ 212-246 5252
🕐 thetimeny.com
🚇 Subway C, E, 1, 9 to 50th Street

Themed around Alexander Theroux's book *The Primary Colours* (not Times Square as you might think), this brightly coloured bolthole is the perfect place if you want to stay in a touristy area in style. Primary colours are used throughout, of course: red rooms are for lovers, blue if you're feeling sad and yellow if you're a bit lacklustre. The colours continue through to the finishing touches, such as bowls of jellybeans in matching shades. There's a buzzing bar downstairs, where guests have included the likes of Liza Minnelli.

Also home to the highly rated Serafina restaurant (page 193).

UPMARKET

If you want your hotel to be smart and sophisticated rather than ultra-trendy or traditional, these are for you.

CENTRAL PARK

TRUMP INTERNATIONAL
HOTEL & TOWER $$$$–$$$$$

✉ 1 Central Park West between 60th and 61st Streets
☎ 212-299 1000
🕐 trumpintl.com
🚇 Subway N, R to 5th Avenue

Billionaire Donald Trump's first foray into hotels is a shimmering tower that houses 167 rooms and suites, as well as various shops and restaurants. The best thing about the hotel is the views of Central Park and 5th Avenue through floor-to-ceiling windows – simply spectacular. The spa is a must-visit for those in need of pampering. The staff are charming and helpful, from booking theatre tickets to handing you an umbrella if it's raining. Check out the company's latest hotel in SoHo too (page 229).

🇬🇧 BRITTIP

There aren't many hotels with car parks. If you're driving in New York, our tip is the Ramada Inn Eastside (212-545 1800, the.ramada.com), which is a clean, pleasant hotel on 30th Street at Lexington Avenue where rates start from $110.

Trump International Hotel & Tower

BOOKING IT YOURSELF

You may want to use a travel agent to make room reservations for you, but you can also do it yourself either directly with the hotel by phone or internet, or through companies that specialise in offering excellent rates at off-peak and low-peak times or can even just guarantee finding you a room during busy periods. These include:

Hotel America Ltd: 08700 464010, hotelanywhere.co.uk/america. A British company providing hotel discounts anywhere in the world.

Hotel Conxions: 212-840 8686, hotelconxions.com. You can find out about availability and price and book a room on their website.

Last Minute: lastminute.com. A great website for booking cheap through to more expensive hotels in New York, complete with description. Also has lots of hotel deals.

Quikbook: 212-779 7666, quikbook.com. A service providing discounts on hotels all over America. They promise there are no hidden cancellation or change penalties, and pre-payment is not required.

A great internet discount reservation service can be found at hotres.com and hoteldiscount. com, or you can look for cheaper rates through the hotel discount service on usacitylink.com.

When discussing room rates with any of these organisations, always check that the prices you are quoted include the New York City hotel tax of 13.25% and the $2 per night occupancy tax or 4% for a 1-bedroom suite.

MIDTOWN

GIRAFFE $$–$$$

✉ 365 Park Avenue South between 26th and 27th Streets
☎ 212-685 7700
🖰 hotelgiraffe.com
🚇 Subway 6 to 23rd Street

Small boutique hotel, in lavish colours and textures. Each floor has 7 rooms, many with their own balconies adorned with fresh flowers. There's also an on-premises restaurant and access to a nearby health club for guests.

Salon de Ning at the Peninsula

LE PARKER MERIDIEN $$$$–$$$$$

✉ 118 West 57th Street between 6th and 7th Avenues
☎ 212-245 5000
🖰 parkermeridien.com
🚇 Subway B, D, E to 7th Avenue

A classic New York hotel in the design sense, yet with a traditional French feel, this hotel is not only in an excellent location just minutes from Central Park and Carnegie Hall, but also offers great service and amenities. The recently refurbished rooms have a Zen-like calmness, thanks to the minimalist and cherrywood decor. Great touches include a revolving unit that allows you to watch the massive TV screen either in the sitting area or in the bedroom. It also has a useful desk unit, CD and DVD players.

🇬🇧 BRITTIP

Make sure you look upwards when you enter the lifts of Le Parker Meridien – all 3 have a TV screen offering classic film clips of *Abbott and Costello* or *Tom and Jerry*.

Even if you don't plan to use the swimming pool, you must visit its penthouse location to see the fab views of Central Park. Down in the basement is the massive Gravity gymnasium, which covers everything from Cybex training to aerobics, sauna, massage rooms, spa services and squash courts.

Other facilities include the much-raved-about Norma's restaurant in the lobby, which serves creative breakfast dishes throughout the day (page 177).

Kitano Hotel

THE PENINSULA $$$$$
✉ 700 5th Avenue at 55th Street
☎ 212-956 2888
🖰 peninsula.com
🚇 Subway F to 53rd Street; 6 to 51st Street

A beautiful hotel that has undergone a massive $45-million renovation in the public areas, restaurants and 239 guestrooms and suites. These are of classic contemporary style with touches of Art Nouveau, and oversized marble bathrooms where you can watch TV from the bath. The state-of-the-art technology allows you touch-button control of your environment, and a water bar is on hand for hangover recovery. The views from rooftop bar Salon de Ning are fabulous and afternoon tea in the Gotham Lounge is ideal if you need a break from shopping.

MIDTOWN EAST

KITANO HOTEL $$$–$$$$$
✉ 66 Park Avenue at East 38th Street
☎ 212-885 7000
🖰 kitano.com
🚇 Subway S, 4, 5, 6, 7 to Grand Central/ 42nd Street

A first-class, Japanese-run hotel with top-notch service and a deliciously decadent, deep-soaking tub in each room. In the Murray Hill area, it has Manhattan's only authentic Japanese tatami suite. From Wed–Sat there's live jazz in the Bar Lounge.

MIDTOWN WEST

HILTON NEW YORK $$$$$
✉ 1335 6th Avenue at 53rd Street
☎ 212-586 7000
🖰 hilton.com
🚇 Subway B, D, F, Q to 47th–50th Streets/ Rockefeller Center

After a recent $100-million renovation, the city's largest hotel now has a beautiful new façade and entrance lobby, plus 2 new restaurants and lounges.

JUMEIRAH ESSEX HOUSE
$$$$–$$$$$
✉ 160 Central Parade at 7th Avenue
☎ 212-247 0300
🖰 jumeirah.com
🚇 Subway 1, A, B, C, D at 59th Street/ Columbus Circle

An Art Deco hotel formerly known as the Westin Essex House & St Regis Club is now a plush hotel loved by well-heeled travellers. As well as the usual upmarket hotel touches, such as heated towel rails and cosy white fluffy robes, there are some cool extras, such as tub phones in the bathroom and an on-site health spa. The rooms are also fabulously quiet, so make a welcome retreat from the noisy city.

SOFITEL $$$-$$$$

- ✉ 45 West 44th Street at 5th Avenue
- ☎ 212-354 8844
- ⌂ sofitel.com
- 🚇 Subway 7 to 5th Avenue/Bryant Park

French-run outfit that soars 30 storeys in a curved limestone tower. The 398 rooms are tightly packed and on the small side, but the decor is tasteful. The top floors, added in 2000, have private balconies and wonderful views and Gaby, the hotel's Art Deco French restaurant, is a great place to dine.

MEDIUM-PRICED GEMS

CHELSEA

HOTEL INDIGO CHELSEA-NEW YORK $$$-$$$$

- ✉ 127 West 28th Street between 6th and 7th Avenues
- ☎ 212-973 9000
- ⌂ ichotelsgroup.com
- 🚇 Subway 1 to 28th Street Station

Intercontinental's new baby, which lies between its budget Holiday Inns and swish Intercontinental properties, opened in August 09. It's urban modern; think 24-hour fitness centre, duvets rather than sheets, complimentary wireless access and a Starbucks.

FINANCIAL DISTRICT

MILLENIUM HILTON $$-$$$$$

- ✉ 55 Church Street between Fulton and Dey Streets
- ☎ 212-693 2001
- ⌂ newyorkmillenium.hilton.com

A black skyscraper geared to business, with 471 rooms and 98 suites, a fitness centre and pool. For a stunning view of the harbour, ask for a high-floor room.

🇬🇧 BRIT TIP

Hotels in the Financial District can be especially good value at weekends when many business people leave the city.

WALL STREET INN $$$

- ✉ 9 South William Street opposite 85 Broad Street
- ☎ 212-747 1500
- ⌂ thewallstreetinn.com
- 🚇 Subway 2, 3 to Wall Street; J, M, Z to Broad Street

An elegant boutique hotel in an old office building in the heart of the financial and historic district. Original features include mahogany wall panels and granite floors.

🇬🇧 BRIT TIP

Confusingly, American hotel lifts use 'L' for lobby or '1' to indicate the ground floor.

FLATIRON DISTRICT

CARLTON $$-$$$

- ✉ 22 East 29th Street between 5th and Madison Avenues
- ☎ 212-532 4100
- ⌂ carltonhotelny.com
- 🚇 Subway 4, 5, 6 to 28th Street

Revamped rooms by renowned architect David Rockwell have seen this hotel go from standard tourist class to top class. There are tall leather headboards, walnut trimmings and plush duvets. The view of the Empire State Building and its excellent location for 5th Avenue and Garment District shopping also make it a great place to check-in.

Sofitel restaurant

GRAMERCY PARK

THE MARCEL AT GRAMERCY $$$

- ✉ 201 East 24th Street at 3rd Avenue
- ☎ 212-696 3800
- 🖰 themarcelatgramercy.com
- 🚇 Subway 6 to 23rd Street

Catering to a clientele of international crowds from the arts, film and fashion worlds, you'd expect this hotel to be pricier than it is. You can get a standard room from around $268 upwards, which are average size for New York and pleasantly decorated. Its great location for Midtown and Downtown makes it a winner.

MIDTOWN

CASABLANCA $$$-$$$$

- ✉ 147 West 43rd Street off Times Square
- ☎ 212-869 1212,
- 🖰 casablancahotel.com
- 🚇 Subway 1, 2, 3, 7, 9, N, R, S to Times Square/42nd Street

Calling itself 'an oasis in the heart of Times Square', its elegant Moroccan theme includes ceiling fans, palm trees and mosaic tiles. Small, with just 48 newly renovated luxury rooms, the service is good and it also offers complimentary use of the New York Sports Club, with pool, just steps away. Some specials from $240 per night.

MANSFIELD $$$-$$$$$

- ✉ 12 West 44th Street between 5th and 6th Avenues
- ☎ 212-944 6050
- 🖰 mansfieldhotel.com
- 🚇 Subway B, D, F, Q to 47th–50th Street/Rockefeller Center

A beautiful lobby with vaulted ceiling and white marble marks the Mansfield out as an elegant hotel for those also wanting the charm of a boutique establishment. The rooms have plush robes and Aveda toiletries and its M Bar, with its domed skylight and mahogany bookshelves, has been described by *Zagat* as 'an off the beaten path, classy, romantic sweet spot'.

SHOREHAM $$$-$$$$$

- ✉ 33 West 55th Street at 5th Avenue
- ☎ 212-247 6700
- 🖰 shorehamhotel.com
- 🚇 Subway F to 5th Avenue

This hotel has won awards for its ultra-modern decor following its renovation. It now has a new bar, restaurant, fitness centre and some more good-sized rooms. Has some great packages to consider, including Sexy Weekend (which amongst other things includes two tickets to the Museum of Sex, see page 115),

see page 115

> ## ALL WIRED UP!
> America has different plugs and works on 115 volts, not 240, so you'll need a travel appliance that works on both voltages, or bring an adaptor with you.

I Love NYC package which includes a two-day city pass to see more than 40 attactions.

WARWICK $$$-$$$$

- ✉ 65 West 54th Street at 6th Avenue
- ☎ 212-247 2700
- 🖰 warwickhotelny.com
- 🚇 Subway B, D, F, Q to 47th–50th Streets/Rockefeller Center

A medium-sized hotel built in 1927 with good-quality rooms and excellent service in an excellent location. In its heyday many a Hollywood celeb stayed here, including Cary Grant. Randolph's Bar remains a favoured meeting place and a great spot for lunch or a light dinner in its recently opened restaurant, Murals on 54, which offers innovative Continental cuisine.

MIDTOWN EAST

70 PARK AVENUE $$$-$$$$

- ✉ 70 Park Avenue at 38th Street
- ☎ 212-973 2400
- 🖰 70parkave.com
- 🚇 Subway 4, 5, 6 to 42nd Street

A beautiful boutique hotel with a home-from-home atmosphere whose motto is 'Live Life Well'. It has a bar, restaurant and excellent room facilities, as well as services like a hosted evening wine tour in the hotel's living room, morning newspaper, valet parking for $2, 'Forgot it? We've Got It' essential travel items you may have forgotten, and access to the nearby spa and fitness centre.

FITZPATRICK $$$-$$$$

- ✉ 687 Lexington Avenue between East 56th and East 57th Streets
- ☎ 212-355 0100
- 🖰 fitzpatrickhotels.com/manhattan
- 🚇 Subway 4, 5, 6 to 59th Street

The 91 rooms and suites are equipped with everything from trouser presses to towelling

---

Millenium Hilton

THE MILLENIUM HILTON

robes, useful after indulging in the whirlpool bath you'll find in many of the rooms. Irish celebs and dignitaries often make this their home when in town and The Fitz is a friendly bar and restaurant that locals use too.

FITZPATRICK GRAND CENTRAL $$$

- ✉ 141 East 44th Street between Lexington and 3rd Avenues
- ☎ 212-351 6800
- ⌖ fitzpatrickhotels.com/grandcentral
- 🚗 Subway S, 4, 5, 6, 7 to Grand Central/ 42nd Street

The Fitzpatrick Family Group of hotels continues its Irish theme at this hotel just across from Grand Central station. It includes an Irish pub and you can order a traditional Irish breakfast here. Check out the shopper's package, to help you get the best of shopping in New York.

KIMBERLY $$$

- ✉ 145 East 60th Street
- ☎ 212-702 1600
- ⌖ kimberlyhotel.com
- 🚗 Subway 4, 5, 6 to 59th Street

Nestled in the fashionable East Side and a short walk from Times Square, Rockefeller Center and the Theater District, this is a very comfortable and convenient place to base yourself while in town. The rooms are sumptuous with fluffy white pillows and lots of polished wood and the service is excellent, including helpful extras such as travel confirmations, reservations at restaurants and tickets to Broadway shows. There isn't a fitness centre, but you get complimentary access to the New York Health and Racquet Club. However, the best thing about the hotel we've discovered is the new rooftop lounge, which is 4,000 sq ft of fabulousness. Opened in spring 2010, the views at night are truly spectacular.

✠ BRITTIP

If you stay at the Kimberly in the summer (May–Sept), there's the chance to go for a free ride along the scenic East River for a sunset cruise or Sunday brunch on the hotel's yacht.

Wellington

THE ROOSEVELT $$–$$$$

- ✉ East 45th Street at Madison Avenue
- ☎ 212-661 9600
- ⌖ theroosevelthotel.com
- 🚗 Subway S, 4, 5, 6, 7 to Grand Central/ 42nd Street

Built in 1924, this classy hotel was named after President Theodore Roosevelt and completed a $70m renovation in 1998 when the lobby was restored to its original grandeur with crystal chandeliers hanging from the ceiling, columns and lots of marble. The opening of its Rooftop Lounge, Mad 46, has proved a hit.

MIDTOWN WEST

HUDSON $$–$$$$$

- ✉ 356 West 58th Street between 8th and 9th Avenues
- ☎ 212-554 6000
- ⌖ hudsonhotel.com
- 🚗 Subway A, B, C, D, 1, 9 to 59th Street/ Columbus Circle

Built on the site of the former *Sesame Street* studios, this Ian Schrager and Philippe Starck collaboration is heaving with chic guests. It's loud and proud, so don't check in if you are looking for peace and quiet in the city. From the neon entrance escalator to the glowing glass floor of the Hudson Bar, you'll be in the limelight. The rooms are stylish but very small. In a great location for Central Park, the Lincoln Center and Theater District, but definitely on the west side of town so keep this in mind when considering your sightseeing plans.

WELLINGTON $$$–$$$$

- ✉ 871 7th Avenue at 55th Street
- ☎ 212-247 3900
- ⌖ wellingtonhotel.com
- 🚗 Subway N, R to 57th Street

Recent renovations, which include a swish marquee, have moved the Wellington from bargain stay category. The rooms are comfortably furnished, with a mix of king, twin and double rooms plus a scattering of 1-bedroom suites. All have high-speed wireless internet access. The best thing about this hotel is still its location – deep in the heart of Midtown within striking distance of Carnegie Hall, 5th Avenue, the Rockefeller Center and Times Square. If you can get a corner room with a view of 7th Avenue, you'll understand the big deal about the bright lights associated with the Theater District – they're absolutely stunning viewed from this position.

THE PERFECT APPLE

A major hotel chain, Apple Core, runs 5 hotels in excellent Midtown locations with extremely reasonable rates of $139–300 a night. They are: **Red Roof Inn Manhattan** on 32nd Street, west of 5th Avenue; the smoke-free **Comfort Inn Midtown** on 46th Street west of 6th Avenue; **Super 8 Hotel Times Square** on 46th Street between 5th and 6th Avenues near the Rockefeller Center (page 247); **La Quinta Manhattan** on 32nd Street between Broadway and 5th Avenue; and **Ramada Inn Eastside** at 30th Street and Lexington Avenue.

All the hotels offer complimentary continental breakfast, well-equipped fitness centres and business centres. In-room facilities include cable television and pay-per-view movies, free wireless internet, telephones with data port and voicemail, coffee makers, irons and ironing boards. The modern bathrooms all come with marble units and hairdryers.

Occupancy rates are above 90% – so book early through Apple Core's central reservations: 212-790 2710, applecorehotels.com.

THEATER DISTRICT

NEW YORK MARRIOTT
MARQUIS $$-$$$$

✉ 1535 Broadway at 45th Street
☎ 212-398 1900
🖥 marriott.com
🚇 Subway N, R, S, 1, 2, 3, 7, 9 to Times Square/42nd Street

Its location in the heart of Times Square and Broadway make this a popular tourist spot. There are lots of packages here, such as Romance with champagne, truffles and special dinner for 2. Other attractions include sushi bar, Katen, in the atrium lobby, big fitness centre and it's also home of The View, New York's only revolving restaurant.

ON THE AVE $$-$$$$

✉ 2178 77th Street at Broadway
☎ 212-362 1100
🖥 ontheave-nyc.com
🚇 Subway 1, 9 to 79th Avenue

This hotel is a breath of fresh air to the rather jaded Upper West Side hotel scene. It has 16 floors, 266 rooms of gorgeous minimalism, lots of white beds and industrial sinks with walk-in showers big enough for 2. New in spring 2008 were 2 restaurants, The West Branch serving American nosh, and Fatty Crab, peddling Malaysian street-food-inspired cuisine. It also promises a fitness

centre and mini-bar in all rooms. Its location, close to Central Park, is superb. It's also very pet-friendly, so the ideal place to bring your pooch. You can have food treats, water/food bowl, a list of local dog runs and parks and a list of pet stores in the area for an extra $25.

PARAMOUNT HOTEL
TIMES SQUARE $$-$$$$$

✉ 235 West 46th Street between Broadway and 8th Avenue
☎ 212-764 5500
🖥 nycparamount.com
🚇 Subway C, E, 1, 9 to 50th Street

A hip hotel in an amazing location with a glorious sweeping staircase in the lobby. The 597 rooms are small but well equipped. The mezzanine restaurant is good for people-watching.

PREMIER $$$-$$$$

✉ 133 West 44th Street between 6th Avenue and Broadway
☎ 212-768 4400
🖥 milleniumhotels.com
🚇 Subway N, R, S, 1, 2, 3, 7, 9 to Times Square/42nd Street

The Millennium Broadway in Times Square built this 22-storey tower in 1999 to increase its total room count to 752. The Premier has its own private entrance on 44th Street and elegant, modern guest rooms with large bathrooms, 2 phone lines, voicemail and a separate modem and fax machine.

WESTIN NEW YORK
AT TIMES SQUARE $$$$

✉ 270 West 43rd Street at 8th Avenue
☎ 212-201 2700
🖥 westinny.com
🚇 Subway A, C, E, N, R, S, 1, 2, 3, 7, 9 to 42nd Street/Times Square

A large, 863-room hotel, that's got something to suit all types. It is particularly family-friendly; families will love the Kids Club, which

Paramount Hotel

gives children a sports bottle, toys, colouring books and even a bedtime story! Toddlers get a Molton Brown designer amenities box with baby wash, nappy hamper, potty seat and step stool. There's also Nintendo Wii systems to keep older kids happy!

BRITTIP
Got some free time and want to get lots off your hotel rate? Log on to priceline.com and bid for your room! Now a big craze in the US, you make a bid and then wait to see.

UPPER EAST SIDE

FRANKLIN $$$
✉ 164 East 87th Street between 3rd and Lexington Avenues
☎ 212-369 1000
⌂ franklinhotel.com
🚇 Subway 4, 5, 6 to 86th Street
Known for its good service, this pleasant Art Deco boutique hotel has lovely touches in its rooms that include canopies over the beds, fresh flowers and cedar closets.

EXCELLENT VALUE

BROOKLYN

NEW YORK MARRIOTT AT THE BROOKLYN BRIDGE $$–$$$
✉ 333 Adams Street at Tillary Street
☎ 718-246 7000
⌂ brooklynmarriott.com
🚇 Subway A, C, F to Jay Street/Borough Hall; N, R to Court Street; 2, 3, 4, 5 to Borough Hall just 5 minutes' walk away

Hotel Chelsea

This is the only full-service hotel in Brooklyn and 282 more rooms were added in late 2006. Although over the water from Manhattan, you get excellent facilities, such as a large swimming pool, at very good prices.

CHELSEA

HOTEL CHELSEA $$
✉ 222 West 23rd Street between 7th and 8th Avenues
☎ 212-243 3700
⌂ hotelchelsea.com
🚇 Subway A, C, E, 1, 2, 3, 9 to 23rd Street
A true icon of New York City, this hotel has been associated with artistic and literary types since it opened in 1912. Residents have included Dylan Thomas, Jack Kerouac, Mark Twain and Thomas Wolfe and it still pulls in the celebs. On the darker side, Sex Pistols singer Sid Vicious is alleged to have killed his girlfriend Nancy Spungen here. Besides that, Andy Warhol filmed *Chelsea Girls*, the stairwell has starred in Bon Jovi and Mariah Carey videos, and room 822 was used to shoot Madonna's book *Sex*.

Downstairs in the basement is Serena's, a Moroccan den lounge bar that has been attracting a new round of celebs, such as Leonardo DiCaprio and Brazilian supermodel Giselle, and is popular with the trendy Brit-pack crowd. Despite all the star stories, the prices start at $139 for a studio with shared bathroom.

CHINATOWN/LOWER EAST SIDE

HOLIDAY INN DOWNTOWN $$
✉ 138 Lafayette Street at Canal Street
☎ 212-966 8898
⌂ hidowntown-nyc.com
🚇 Subway N, R to Canal Street
Well-equipped, spotless rooms available at excellent prices.

FINANCIAL DISTRICT

HOLIDAY INN WALL STREET $$–$$$$
✉ 15 Gold Street at Platt Street
☎ 212-232 7700
⌂ ichotelsgroups.com
🚇 Subway J, M, Z, 2, 3, 4, 5 to Fulton Street
Opened in 1999, billing itself as the most hi-tech hotel in New York, complete with high-speed internet connectivity. It's not bursting with character, but we think it's a great place to stay if you're not on expenses, and the Lafayette Grill serves up quality American cuisine.

TOP 5 HOTEL POOLS WITH VIEWS

If you like a swim while you're away, check into one of these establishments whose penthouse pools offer some of the best views in Manhattan.

Le Parker Meridien: The penthouse pool provides a perfect retreat for relaxation and a sun deck offers scenic views of Central Park. It's available to hotel guests for free, or you can pay $50 for a day-pass to use it as well as the gym (page 240).

Mandarin Oriental: Floor-to-ceiling windows light up an inviting 23m/75ft indoor lap pool on the 35th floor, with amazing views of the New York skyline (page 233).

Hotel Gansevoort: This trendy hotel has a suitably cool pool. Take the elevator straight to the top floor and you'll be rewarded with a 14m/45ft heated outdoor pool that also has underwater music. There are plenty of people to watch while you have your dip (page 236).

Crowne Plaza Times Square Manhattan: 1605 Broadway, between 48th and 49th Streets, 212-9777 4000, manhattan.crowneplaza.com. The 15th floor of this plush hotel houses a 15m/50ft indoor pool, which costs $10 for hotel guests or $25 for non-residents. It has a glass roof through which you can see the skyscrapers.

Millennium UN Plaza Hotel New York: 1 United Nations Plaza, 44th Street and 1st Avenue, 212-758 1234, millenniumhotels.com. Take a trip up to the 27th floor and you'll be wowed by the wonderful panoramic views through the floor-to-ceiling windows of this 13m/44ft city oasis.

GREENWICH VILLAGE

WASHINGTON SQUARE HOTEL $$

✉ 103 Waverly Place between 5th and 6th Avenues
☎ 212-777 9515
🖱 wshotel.com
🚌 Subway A, B, C, D, E, F, Q to West 4th Street/Washington Square

Over a century old, this hotel is clearly doing something right. It has a bohemian air and overlooks Washington Square. The rooms are quite small but comfortable, the bar small, dark and 1930s-esque and a fab place to end a night and the rates very reasonable and include breakfast. Bob Dylan was known to stay here in the 1960s, though he may not approve of the smoke-free rule introduced.

MIDTOWN

ALGONQUIN $$–$$$

✉ 59 West 44th Street between 5th and 6th Avenues
☎ 212-840 6800
🖱 algonquinhotel.com
🚌 Subway B, D, F, Q to 47th–50th Streets/Rockefeller Center

◀ ▶ BRITTIP

If you're an author or an aspiring one, take advantage of the Algonquin's Writer's Block offer, which gives you 25% off the best possible room rate if you can show a work in progress or published work.

Famous for the literary meetings held here by Dorothy Parker and her cohorts,

the Algonquin underwent a $45 million refurbishment some years ago in its 174 rooms and 24 suites. The Round Table Room is a favourite spot for a pre-theatre dinner, while Blue Bar is good for a cocktail or two.

METRO $$–$$$

✉ 45 West 35th Street between 5th and 6th Avenues
☎ 212-947 2500
🖱 hotelmetronyc.com
🚌 Subway B, D, F, N, Q, R to 34th Street

Well located near the Empire State Building, which can be seen from its rooftop garden terrace, this hotel is great value for money, offering plenty of Art Deco style and loads of amenities, like a big gym, beauty salon and rooftop garden terrace.

SUPER 8 $$

✉ 59 West 46th Street between 5th and 6th Avenues
☎ 212-719 2300
🖱 applecorehotels.com
🚌 Subway B, D, F, Q to 47th–50th Streets/Rockefeller Center

A well-priced hotel with excellent amenities that include a fitness centre, coffee makers and irons in the rooms, free local phone calls, wireless internet and continental breakfast (The Perfect Apple, page 245).

MIDTOWN WEST

AMERITANIA $$

✉ 230 Broadway at West 54th Street
☎ 212-247 5000
🖱 ameritaniahotelnewyork.com
🚌 Subway 1, 9 to 50th Street; B, D east to 7th Avenue

Located just outside the Theater District and near Restaurant Row. Well-appointed with modern, comfortable rooms.

THEATER DISTRICT

COURTYARD BY MARRIOTT TIMES SQUARE SOUTH $$–$$$
- ✉ 114 West 40th Street between 6th Avenue and Broadway
- ☎ 212-391 0088
- 🖰 marriott.com
- 🚇 Subway B, D, F, Q to 42nd Street

This hotel, which opened in 1998, is part of the massive redevelopment of Times Square. The spacious rooms all have a sitting area, large work desk, 2 phones and in-room coffee facilities.

RADISSON MARTINIQUE ON BROADWAY $$–$$$$$
- ✉ 49 West 32nd Street at Broadway
- ☎ 212-736 3800
- 🖰 radisson.com
- 🚇 Subway B, D, F, N, Q, R to 34th Street

Opened in 1998 on the site of the former Hotel Martinique, this hotel is good value for money. There are 533 clean, tasteful rooms, a cocktail lounge and KumGangSan, an excellent Korean and Japanese restaurant with 2-storey waterfall and eat-in cave!

TRIBECA

COSMOPOLITAN HOTEL $$–$$$
- ✉ 95 West Broadway at Chambers Street
- ☎ 212-566 1900
- 🖰 cosmohotel.com
- 🚇 Subway 1, 2, 3 to Chambers Street

Finding a pleasant, comfortable Downtown hotel that's not going to cost you hundreds of dollars a night can be tricky. That's where this hotel steps in. It's not exactly the TriBeCa Grand, but most of the 20- and 30-somethings who pay from $169 here are happy with the neutral decor and grateful for added extras like hairdryers and satellite TV.

UPPER EAST SIDE

BENTLEY $$–$$$
- ✉ 500 East 62nd Street at York Avenue
- ☎ 212-644 6000
- 🖰 hotelbentleynewyork.com
- 🚇 Subway 4, 5, 6, N, R to Lexington Avenue/59th Street

This recently renovated hotel is within walking distance of Bloomingdale's. Most of the 197 oversized rooms overlook Upper East Side Manhattan, with fab river and skyline views. Rates include breakfast and start at $179 online.

UPPER WEST SIDE

DAYS HOTEL BROADWAY $$–$$$
- ✉ 215 West 94th Street at Broadway
- ☎ 212-866 6400
- 🖰 dayshotelnyc.com
- 🚇 Subway 4, 5, 6, N, R to Lexington Avenue/59th Street

A 349-room hotel situated in a far from happening part of town, but it's a clean and inexpensive place and you get free wireless hi-speed internet, free coffee in-room, hair dryer and fitness room.

BRITTIP
If you're travelling in a group of 10 or more, the Days Hotel Broadway offers discounts on rooms.

HOTEL BEACON $$–$$$
- ✉ 2130 Broadway at 75th Street
- ☎ 212-787 1100
- 🖰 beaconhotel.com
- 🚇 Subway 1, 2, 3, 9 to 72nd Street

Good-sized rooms and suites, some with a third bed and all with kitchenettes, so ideal if you're travelling in a group. Plus the 25-storey hotel is well located for the American Museum of Natural History, the Lincoln Center and Central Park.

WEST VILLAGE

THE JANE $–$$
- ✉ 113 Jane St
- ☎ 212-924 6700
- 🖰 thejanenyc.com
- 🚇 Subway A, C, E, L to 8th Avenue/14th Street Station

Landmark waterfront property in the Far West Village, originally the American Seaman's Friend Society Sailors' Home and Institute built in 1908, has been reborn as a 200-room micro hotel for young travellers 'with more style than money'. Rates start at $99.

TOTAL BARGAINS

BROOKLYN

GLENWOOD HOSTEL $
- ✉ 339 Broadway between Rodney and Keap Streets
- ☎ 718-387 7858
- 🚇 Subway J, M, Z to Marcy Avenue

The choice of backpackers on a tight budget. The rooms are tiny, there's space for a bed and little else, and the walls are paper thin so you can hear every move your neighbour makes. It's not popular on web forums, but on the plus side, it's VERY cheap, rates are from $30 for a single. Rentals are available on a nightly, weekly or monthly basis.

FLATIRON DISTRICT

GERSHWIN $–$$
✉ 7 East 27th Street between 5th and Madison Avenues
☎ 212-545 8000
🖱 gershwinhotel.com
🚇 Subway 6 to 28th Street
This is such a cool hotel for so little money – rooms with bunk beds start at $40. It's best described as a character-crammed budget boutique with some of the best rates in the city. You can opt for plain doubles or dormitory-style rooms with 10 beds and the hotel has theatre, stand-up comedy, poetry and live music on site.

GRAMERCY PARK HOTEL 17 $–$$
✉ 45 225 East 17th Street at Union Square
☎ 212-475 2845
🖱 hotel17ny.com
🚇 Subway 6, A, C, E to 14th Street
An undiscovered chic hideaway well off the tourist radar. It's where Woody Allen filmed *Manhattan Murder Mystery* and Madonna used to stay and did many photo shoots. Rooms are stark and sleek – a place to lay your head rather than snuggle up for a romantic anniversary, but a total bargain in New York with rooms starting from $99 in low season.

HERALD SQUARE HOTEL $$
✉ 19 West 31st Street between 5th Avenue and Broadway
☎ 212-279 4017
🖱 heraldsquarehotel.com
🚇 Subway N, R to 28th Street
Once the headquarters of *Life* magazine, now a small, quirky extremely well-priced hotel (rooms start from $99) near the Empire State Building and Macy's. Every room is different, from chandeliers to iron bed frames and all-white bathrooms. Very original and at a good price.

THIRTY THIRTY NEW YORK CITY $$
✉ 30 East 30th Street between Park and Madison Avenues
☎ 212-689 1900
🖱 thirtythirty-nyc.com
🚇 Subway 6 to 29th Street
Formerly the Martha Washington Hotel, this was turned into a modern, sophisticated but affordable boutique hotel in 1999. Don't miss the full American breakfast for $10.

GREENWICH VILLAGE

LARCHMONT $–$$
✉ 27 West 11th Street between 5th and 6th Avenues
☎ 212-989 9333
🖱 larchmonthotel.com
🚇 Subway F to 14th Street
Clean, well-sought-after Village boutique hotel. No private baths in any rooms, rates from $90.

LOWER EAST SIDE

HOWARD JOHNSON EXPRESS INN $–$$
✉ 135 Houston Street between Forsyth and Eldridge Streets
☎ 212-358 8844
🖱 hojo.com
🚇 Subway F, V to 2nd Avenue
The Lower East Side celebrated the arrival of its first hotel, a modern, without frills but incredibly well-priced getaway. Right next door is the renovated landmark Sunshine Cinema, which was once a showplace for Yiddish vaudeville and films and is now a multiplex for art films.

OFF SOHO SUITES $$
✉ 11 Rivington Street between Chrystie Street and The Bowery
☎ 212-979 9808
🖱 offsoho.com
🚇 Subway F to Delancey Street
Well positioned alternative to New York's inflated hotel rates, with good-sized, clean suites with fully equipped kitchens.

MADISON SQUARE GARDEN

CHELSEA STAR HOTEL $–$$
✉ 300 West 30th Street at 8th Avenue
☎ 212-244 7827
🖱 starhotelny.com
🚇 Subway 1, 2, 3, 9 to 28th Street
Cool little, low-budget hotel, which has been imaginatively decorated; think Salvador Dali melting clocks and dark blue walls with stars! There are dormitories or private rooms, some of which can sleep up to 4.

MURRAY HILL

HOTEL 31 $–$$$
✉ 120 East 31st Street at Lexington Avenue
☎ 212-685 3060
🖱 hotel31.com
🚇 Subway 6 to 33rd Street
Seventy-two renovated rooms, some shared, some private, packed with young Europeans. Essentials such as air con and cable TV and even a 24-hour concierge service. If you can ignore the flowery bedspreads, it's a good one.

MIDTOWN EAST

POD HOTEL $-$$$
- 230 East 51st Street between 2nd and 3rd Avenues
- 212-355 0300
- thepodhotel.com
- Subway 6 to 51st Street

A massive hit in Japan, the pod-style hotel has now hit Manhattan. Your pod is a tiny space, just big enough to fit a bed and not much else, and consequently prices are lower. It's ideal if you've got a small budget but don't want to end up in an old-fashioned B&B or hostel. Choices vary from a Bunk Pod, which is perfect if you're travelling with a friend as you get 2 bunked twin beds with a reading light, 25cm/10in LCD TV with headphones, iPod docking station, free WiFi. There's even just enough room for a closet and safe. The shared bathrooms, of which there are many, have rain-head showers, designer sinks and marble and granite interiors. Queen Pods are the most spacious rooms and most expensive and have a workspace, 50cm/20in TV and tiny private bathroom.

VANDERBILT YMCA $-$$
- 224 East 47th Street at 2nd Avenue
- 212-756 9600
- ymcanyc.org
- Subway 6 to 51st Street

One of the oldest buildings in Manhattan, though not the plushest, is named after its benefactor Cornelius Vanderbilt. The rooms are tiny and will set you back around $90 for a single; if you want a double with a private bathroom it rises to around $110 per night. It's part of a community centre, so you get access to 2 swimming pools and a gym.

MIDTOWN WEST

PORTLAND SQUARE HOTEL $-$$
- 132 West 47th Street between 6th and 7th Avenues
- portlandsquarehotel.com
- Subway B, D, F, Q to 47th–50th Streets/ Rockefeller Center

This hotel is under new management and they're making positive additions such as queen-sized beds and free WiFi. The rooms are small but neutrally decorated and clean and the hotel is very near the Theater District, so it's convenient if that features on your itinerary.

FURTHER AFIELD

If you're planning on going on a huge shopping spree at the 200-plus discount stores at Woodbury Common Premium Outlets (page 158), you might want to stay overnight to make the most of opening hours.

THE THAYER HOTEL $$-$$$
- 674 Thayer Road, West Point, New York
- 845-446 4731 or freephone 800-247 5047
- thethayerhotel.com

A 3-star hotel at West Point – the scene of a decisive battle in the War of Independence and now home to one of the most famous officer training camps in America, with fabulous views of the Hudson River. The hotel has comfortable en-suite rooms, which have been recently refurbished. There's a restaurant open for breakfast, lunch and dinner and the lounge, which overlooks the river, is open until 1am Fri–Sat. Shop-and-stay packages are available.

FOR SOMETHING DIFFERENT...

Abode Ltd: PO Box 20022, New York, NY 10021, 212-472 2000, abodenyc.com. $-$$$. Unhosted, good-quality studios and apartments all over the city, but you have to book for a minimum of 4 days.

Bed & Breakfast (& Books): 35 West 92nd Street, Apt. 2C, New York, NY 10025, 212-865 8740. $-$$. Hosted and unhosted apartments – and you may end up being the guest of a writer.

Bed and Breakfast: bedandbreakfast.com/. $-$$$. From comfortable to smart and both hosted and unhosted.

Inn New York City: 266 West 71st Street between Broadway and West End Avenue, 212-580 1900, innnewyorkcity.com. $$$-$$$$. This romantic boutique retreat has just 4 suites, each with a kitchen, and is fantastically placed for shopping, theatres and restaurants.

Jazz on the Park Hostel: 36 West 106th Street at Central Park West, 212-932 1600, jazzhostels. com. $. Clean, comfortable rooms for the budget traveller. Double and 'dormitory' rooms, laundry room, rooftop terrace and garden. Price includes breakfast. Sister hostels include **Jazz on the Town** (307 East 14th Street in the midst of the bars, restaurants and clubs of East Village, 212-228 2780) and a new hostel, **Jazz on Harlem** (104 West 128th Street, 212-222 5773).

ACCOMMODATION REFERENCE GUIDE

Hotel	Area	Style	Price range	page
6 Columbus Circle	SoHo	Boutique chic	$$$	237
60 Thompson	SoHo	Boutique chic	$$$–$$$$$	237
70 Park Avenue	Midtown East	Medium-priced gem	$$$–$$$$	243
ACE Hotel	Midtown	Excellent value	$$$	230
Algonquin	Midtown	Excellent value	$$–$$$	247
Ameritania	Midtown West	Excellent value	$$	247
Bentley	Upper East Side	Excellent value	$$–$$$	248
Blue Moon	Lower East Side	Boutique chic	$$$	235
Bowery	Lower East Side	Boutique chic	$$$$–$$$$$	235
Bryant Park	Midtown	Boutique chic	$$$$–$$$$$	236
Carlton	Flatiron District	Medium-priced gem	$$–$$$	242
Carlyle, The	Upper East Side	Landmark	$$$$–$$$$$	228
Casablanca	Midtown	Medium-priced gem	$$$–$$$$	243
Chambers	Midtown	Boutique chic	$$$–$$$$$	236
Chatwal New York, The	Theater District	Modern luxury	$$$$$	229
Chelsea Star Hotel	Madison Square Garden	Total bargain	$–$$	249
City Club Hotel	Midtown	Boutique chic	$$$–$$$$	236
Cooper Square Hotel, The	Lower East Side	Modern luxury	$$$$	231
Cosmopolitan Hotel	TriBeCa	Excellent value	$$–$$$	248
Courtyard by Marriott Times Square South	Theater District	Excellent value	$$–$$$	248
Days Hotel Broadway	Upper West Side	Excellent value	$$–$$$	248
Distrikt Hotel	Theater District	Modern luxury	$$$–$$$$	229
Dream	Midtown West	Theme	$$–$$$	238
Dylan	Midtown East	Boutique chic	$$$–$$$$	237
Elysée	Midtown East	Traditional luxury	$$$$–$$$$$	234
Fitzpatrick	Midtown East	Medium-priced gem	$$$–$$$$	243
Fitzpatrick Grand Central	Midtown East	Medium-priced gem	$$$	243
Flatotel	Midtown	Modern luxury	$$$–$$$$	231
Four Seasons	Midtown East	Modern luxury	$$$$–$$$$$	232
Franklin	Upper East Side	Medium-priced gem	$$$	246
Gansevoort Park	Midtown East	Modern luxury	$$$$	229
Gershwin	Flatiron District	Total bargain	$–$$	249
Gild Hall	Financial District	Boutique chic	$$$$	235
Giraffe	Flatiron District	Excellent value	$$–$$$	240
Glenwood Hostel	Brooklyn	Total bargain	$	248
Gramercy Park Hotel	Gramercy Park	Modern luxury	$$$–$$$$	231
Gramercy Park Hotel 17	Flatiron District	Total bargain	$–$$	249
Greenwich Hotel, The	TriBeCa	Traditional luxury	$$$$–$$$$$	232
Herald Square Hotel	Flatiron District	Total bargain	$$	249
Hilton New York	Midtown West	Upmarket	$$$$$	241
Holiday Inn Downtown	Chinatown/Lower East Side	Excellent value	$$	246
Holiday Inn Wall Street	Financial District	Excellent value	$$–$$$$	246
Hotel 31	Murray Hill	Total bargain	$–$$$	249
Hotel Beacon	Upper West Side	Excellent value	$$–$$$	248
Hotel Chelsea	Chelsea	Excellent value	$$	246
Hotel Gansevoort	Meatpacking District	Boutique chic	$$$–$$$$$	236
Hotel Indigo	Chelsea	Medium-priced gem	$$$–$$$$	242
Hotel on Rivington	Lower East Side	Boutique chic	$$$$–$$$$$	235
Hotel Plaza-Athenee	Upper East Side	Traditional luxury	$$$$–$$$$$	234
Howard Johnson Express Inn	Lower East Side	Total bargain	$–$$	249
Hudson	Midtown West	Medium-priced gem	$$–$$$$$	244
Hyatt Andaz	Financial District	Boutique chic	$$$$	229
Inn at Irving Place	Gramercy Park	Traditional luxury	$$$$–$$$$$	233
Jane, The	West Village	Excellent value	$–$$	248
Jumeirah Essex House	Midtown West	Upmarket	$$$$–$$$$$	241
Kimberly	Midtown East	Medium-priced gem	$$$	244
Kitano	Midtown East	Upmarket	$$$–$$$$$	241
Larchmont	Greenwich Village	Total bargain	$–$$	249
Le Parker Meridien	Midtown	Upmarket	$$$$–$$$$$	240
Library, The	Midtown	Theme	$$$$–$$$$$	238
London NYC, The	Midtown	Modern luxury	$$$–$$$$$	231
Lowell, The	Upper East Side	Traditional luxury	$$$$$	234
Mandarin Oriental	Upper West Side	Modern luxury	$$$$–$$$$$	233
Mansfield	Midtown	Medium-priced gem	$$$–$$$$$	243
Marcel at Gramercy, The	Gramercy Park	Medium-priced gem	$$$	243

Hotel	Area	Style	Price range	page
Maritime Hotel	Chelsea	Theme	$$$–$$$$	238
Mark, The	Upper East Side	Traditional luxury	$$$$–$$$$$	234
Mercer	SoHo	Boutique chic	$$$–$$$$	237
Metro	Midtown	Excellent value	$$–$$$	247
Millenium Hilton	Financial District	Medium-priced gem	$$–$$$$	242
Moderne, The	Midtown West	Boutique chic	$$$–$$$$	237
Morgans	Midtown	Boutique chic	$$$–$$$$	236
New York Marriott at the Brooklyn Bridge	Brooklyn	Excellent value	$$–$$$	246
New York Marriott Marquis	Theater District	Medium-priced gem	$$–$$$$	245
New York Palace	Midtown East	Traditional luxury	$$$$–$$$$$	234
Night Hotel, The	Midtown West	Theme	$$$–$$$$$	238
Off Soho Suites	Lower East Side	Total bargain	$$	249
On The Ave	Theater District	Medium-priced gem	$$–$$$$	244
Paramount Hotel Times Square	Theater District	Medium-priced gem	$$–$$$$$	245
Peninsula, The	Midtown	Upmarket	$$$$$	241
Plaza, The	Midtown	Landmark	$$$$$	226
Pod Hotel	Midtown East	Total bargain	$–$$$	250
Portland Square Hotel	Midtown West	Total bargain	$–$$	250
Premier	Theater District	Medium-priced gem	$$$–$$$$	245
Radisson Martinique	Theater District	Excellent value	$$–$$$$$	248
Ritz-Carlton New York	Battery Park City	Modern luxury	$$$$$	230
Roosevelt, The	Midtown East	Medium-priced gem	$$–$$$$	244
Royalton	Midtown	Modern luxury	$$$–$$$$	231
Sherry-Netherland	Upper East Side	Traditional luxury	$$$$–$$$$$	235
Shoreham	Midtown	Medium-priced gem	$$$–$$$$$	243
Smyth Tribeca	TriBeCa	Modern luxury	$$$–$$$$	233
Sofitel	Midtown West	Upmarket	$$$–$$$$	242
Soho Grand	SoHo	Modern luxury	$$$$	232
Soho House New York	SoHo	Boutique chic	$$$$–$$$$$	238
Standard, The	Meatpacking District	Modern luxury	$$$	231
Super 8	Midtown	Excellent value	$$	247
Thayer Hotel, The	West Point	Further afield	$$–$$$	250
Thirty Thirty New York City	Flatiron District	Total bargain	$$	249
Time	Theater District	Theme	$$–$$$	239
TriBeCa Grand	TriBeCa	Modern luxury	$$$$–$$$$$	233
Trump International Hotel & Tower	Central Park	Upmarket	$$$$–$$$$$	239
Trump SoHo New York	SoHo	Modern luxury	$$$$	229
Vanderbilt YMCA	Midtown East	Total bargain	$–$$	250
Waldorf-Astoria	Midtown East	Landmark	$$$–$$$$$	227
Waldorf Towers	Midtown East	Landmark	$$$$$	228
Wall Street Inn	Financial District	Medium-priced gem	$$$	242
Warwick	Midtown	Medium-priced gem	$$$–$$$$	243
Washington Square	Greenwich Village	Excellent value	$$	247
Wellington	Midtown West	Medium-priced gem	$$$–$$$$	244
Westin New York at Times Square	Theater District	Medium-priced gem	$$$$	245

The Chatwal

CHAPTER 11

Gay New York

New York is home to some of the world's most exciting gay clubs and lounges; a combination of fantastic DJs, incredible lighting, vast or intimate spaces and seriously sexy crowds make it a dream for night owls. The only requirements are an open mind and the ability to stay up late!

The West Village is traditionally the spiritual home of gays and lesbians in New York, but in today's cosmopolitan city a person's sexual persuasion rarely raises an eyebrow. Gay bars, clubs and restaurants have sprung up all over Manhattan, and Chelsea is the predominant 'gaybourhood'. In fact, most restaurants and bars across the Big Apple are open to everyone – whether you're gay or straight.

If you'd like to get to know more about the gay and lesbian culture in New York, Big Onion's Gay and Lesbian History Tour gives a good insight into the historical side, tracing the development of Greenwich Village as a community Mecca (see Big Onion Walking Tours, page 91). For a tour of the modern-day Gay New York, try Limotour's VIP Gay Tour of New York City, which looks at everything from the importance of rent parties to what

led to camp culture. It can be arranged online (limotours.com) and costs $85 per hour for the whole limo. Check out year-round gay art tours around the Chelsea Galleries led by Rafael Risemberg PhD, gay studies professor and art critic for gay newspaper the *New York Blade* (212-946 1548, nygallerytours.com). They run Sat 1pm and cost $20.

INFORMATION

THE LESBIAN, GAY, BISEXUAL & TRANSGENDER COMMUNITY CENTER

✉ 208 West 13th Street between 7th and 8th Avenues
☎ 212-620 7310
🖱 gaycenter.org
🚇 Subway A, C, E, 1, 2, 3 to 14th Street; L to 8th Avenue

By far the best organisation in New York for information, you'll find millions of leaflets and notices about gay life in the city, as well as information on events online. There are now around 400 groups that meet here and it also houses the National Museum and Archive of Lesbian and Gay History.

Heritage of Pride Parade

PUBLICATIONS

The main gay weeklies are *HX* (HomoXtra), *HX for Her* and *Next* (nextmagazine.net), which are available in gay bars, clubs, hotels and cafés. They include listings of bars, dance clubs, sex clubs, restaurants and cultural events. Good newspapers are the *LGNY* (Lesbian and Gay New York), though it's a lot more serious and covers political issues, and *Gay City News* (gaycitynews.com).

BRITTIP

Download a free gay map to Manhattan from funmaps.com to find everything from hot nude yoga to gay-friendly shops.

ACCOMMODATION

Turn to page 226 for some hotel tips and booking info. Prices are per room.

CHELSEA PINES INN
Chelsea

- ✉ 317 West 14th Street between 8th and 9th Avenues
- ☎ 212-929 1023
- ⌂ chelseapinesinn.com
- 🚇 Subway A, C East to 14th Street; L to 8th Avenue
- $ Rooms from $90 single and $125 double

In an excellent location in Chelsea on the border with the Village, this hotel, which is one of the best gay hotels in the city, has recently been given a facelift, and now each room is named after a film star (yes, there is a Judy Garland). In the morning, guests wake to the aroma of homemade bread and doughnuts. Open to both men and women. You need to book at least 6 to 8 weeks in advance.

Chelsea Savoy

CHELSEA SAVOY HOTEL
Chelsea

- ✉ 204 West 23rd Street
- ☎ 212-929 9353/866-929 9353 toll free
- ⌂ chelseasavoynyc.com
- 🚇 Subway 1, 9, 3 to 23rd Street
- $ Rooms $99–425

This hotel is in a superb location, being close to the Theater District, Financial District, great restaurants, museums and galleries, and SoHo just down the road. The rooms are a good size for NY with all essential amenities such as bathroom and television. Great value, too.

COLONIAL HOUSE INN
Chelsea

- ✉ 318 West 22nd Street between 8th and 9th Avenues
- ☎ 212-243 9669
- ⌂ colonialhouseinn.com
- 🚇 Subway C east to 23rd Street
- $ Rooms from $130

A beautiful place to stay and also spotlessly clean. The economy rooms are tiny, but all have cable TV, air con, phone and daily maid service, smoking is allowed in rooms and the price includes breakfast. The hotel was set up by Mel Cheren, the 'Godfather of Disco' and head of production at Paramount, who campaigned about AIDS prevention until he sadly died from the disease himself. The main lobby has been turned into The 24 Hours For Life gallery, a charity fighting the spread of AIDS of which Mel was a member of the board.

BRITTIP

Chelsea is the top 'gaybourhood' in New York City, although Hell's Kitchen is creeping into style. The headquarters for *HX*, Chelsea is one of the best places for gay people to base themselves.

Book as early as you can because this place gets packed with groups coming into town for drag conventions and so on. It's especially popular in the summer months because of its roof deck with a clothing-optional area. The hotel has a 24-hour doorman. Mostly for gay men.

EDISON HOTEL
Theater District

- ✉ 228 West 47th Street between Broadway and 8th Avenue
- ☎ 212-840 5000
- ⌂ edisonhotelnyc.com
- 🚇 Subway N, R to 49th Street
- $ Rooms from $189

One of New York's great hotel bargains. The Art Deco Edison's 700 rooms have been totally refurbished, and it has a new coffee shop, the Café Edison, considered to be the best place to spot lunching theatre luminaries. Book well in advance.

HOTEL WOLCOTT
Midtown

✉ 4 West 31st Street between 5th Avenue and Broadway
☎ 212-268 2900
🖱 wolcott.com
🚇 Subway N, R to 28th Street
$ Rooms $200; suites from $210

Well, darling, it's location, location, location, for this 300-room hotel. Just 3 blocks down from 5th Avenue and the Empire State Building, this is a favourite with the serious tourist and budget-minded business traveller. Complimentary coffee, tea and muffins served in the lobby each morning. Call in advance to find out the bargain seasonal, weekend and holiday rates on offer.

◀▶ **BRITTIP**

The main event of the gay year is the Heritage of Pride Parade (formerly Gay Pride) in June (page 267), where half a million people turn up to parade the streets and party all week. If you're coming then, also catch the NewFest gay film festival in mid-June.

INCENTRA VILLAGE HOUSE
West Village

✉ 32 8th Avenue between West 12th and Jane Streets
☎ 212-206 0007
🖱 incentravillage.com
🚇 Subway A, C east to 14th Street; L to 8th Avenue
$ Rooms from $169 (single occupancy)

A moderately priced guesthouse in 2 redbrick townhouses from the 1840s (that's old by American standards!). The 12 suites all have kitchens, phones and private bathrooms and some can even accommodate groups of 4 or 5. All the rooms are decorated with different themes. The Bishop Suite is a split-level apartment, the Garden Room has

Hotel Wolcott

a private garden filled with flowers and the Maine Room has a 4-poster bed. All rooms are smoker-friendly. A 1939 Steinway piano stands in the parlour and anyone is allowed to play.

THE INN AT IRVING PLACE
Gramercy Park

✉ 56 Irving Place between 17th and 18th Streets
☎ 212-533 4600/800-685 1447
🖱 innatirving.com
🚇 Subway L, N, R, 4, 5, 6 to 14th Street/ Union Square
$ Rooms $445-645

The building is filled with exquisite antique furniture and elegant decor, if you feel like splashing out. All 12 rooms have queen-size beds and come with private facilities; some even have study areas. There is a 24-hour concierge, plus laptops and fax on request, laundry and dry-cleaning, video rentals, a gym within walking distance and 24-hour massage.

THE ROYALTON
Theater District

✉ 44 West 44th Street between 5th and 6th Avenues
☎ 212-869 4400/800 697 1791
🖱 royaltonhotel.com
🚇 Subway 4, 5, 6 to 42nd Street; 7 to 5th Avenue
$ Rooms from $309

Ian Schrager's beautiful hotel, designed by Philippe Starck, is now considered to be the best address for gays and lesbians looking for an upmarket hotel. A chic tone is set by the lively fashion and publishing crowd that frequents the lobby bar and restaurant. The modern rooms all have CD players, VCR, mini bar and 2 phone lines.

Gym Sports Bar

CLUBS AND LOUNGES FOR HIM

CHELSEA

Barracuda: 275 West 22nd Street between 7th and 8th Avenues. 212-645 8613. Subway C, E to 23rd Street.
This club attracts a mellow mix of people. Head to the rear lounge, which has a better atmosphere than the dingy front bar and a decent pool table, and wait for drinks to be brought in by gorgeous young cocktail waiters. Mon night is the hilarious Star Search, where drag queens battle it out between each other to reign supreme. Open 4pm–4am every day and a popular 2-for-1 Happy Hour 4–9pm during the week. Cash only.

XES Lounge: 157 West 24th Street between 6th and 7th Avenues. 212-604 0212, xesnyc. com. Subway F, V, 1 to 23rd Street.
It promises no attitude, sexy bartenders and strong drinks. Love the Starck furniture in here, which goes with the exposed brick walls and patio sporting Japanese maple trees. Drag shows and parties every weekend, very funny week nights, such as karaoke with Miss Tina Burner or *Glee* watching, smoking allowed. Open daily 4pm–2am and happy hour 2-for-1 drinks every weeknight 4–9pm.

Eagle: 554 West 28th Street between 10th and 11th Avenues. 646-473 1866, eaglenyc. com. Subway C, E to 23rd Street.
No-expense-spared renovation of the original Eagle, the new incarnation is a spacious 2-storey watering hole filled with congenial leather-clad S&M New Yorkers. No surprise then that it was voted Best Leather Bar by *New York Magazine*. Open Mon–Sat 10pm–4am, Sun 5pm–4am.

Gym Sports Bar: 167 8th Avenue between 18th and 19th Avenues. 212-337 2439, gymsportsbar.com. Subway 1, 9 to 18th Street.
This first and only gay sports bar serves big drinks at low prices and offers after-work billiards, as well as parties around gay sports leagues and nightly sports events shown on big screens. 2-for-1 Happy Hour Mon–Fri 4pm–9pm and all night Mon.

g Lounge: 225 West 19th Street between 7th and 8th Avenues. 212-929 1085, glounge. com. Subway C, E to 23rd Street; 1 to 18th Street.
A super-popular, sophisticated nightspot for gorgeous hunks to see and be seen. Its centrepiece is its oval bar, which the sexy clientele prop up when they're not shimmying to house music. It gets packed later on when the queues build up outside. Open nightly 4pm–4am; DJ 6pm–1am, G-licious Happy Hour Mon–Fri 4–9pm. Cash only, but a handy ATM on site.

Kurfew: 212-533 1222, kurfew.com. Subway A, C, E, F to 34th Street.
America's youngest all-gay party, with big nights out at different gay clubs around town. Sunday night is college fest at the Avalon. Also holds events at SBNY (see below). Eight beers for $10, anyone?

Rawhide: 212 8th Avenue at 20th Street. 212-242 9332. Subway C, E to 23rd Street.
A darkly lit, leather and Levi's bar in the heart

of Chelsea. Has male go-go dancers and strong drinks. Closes 4am.

SBNY Splash: 50 West 17th Street between 5th and 6th Avenues. 212-691 0073, splashbar.com. Subway L, N, R, W, 4, 5, 6 to 14th Street/Union Square.
This is a popular place to hang out on any night of the week, and not just because the handsome bartenders are shirtless. It's done out South Beach style, with a huge dance floor emporium, a downstairs bar for cruising and an adult store in the basement. It's popular with preppy men and those who enjoy attention. Open daily 4pm–5am with a cover charge of $5–20. Happy Hour 2-4-1 drinks Mon–Sun 4–9pm.

View Bar: 232 8th Avenue at 22nd Street. 212-929 2243, viewbarnyc.com. Subway 1, C, E at 23rd Street.
This trendy new spot delivers what it suggests: a view of the Chelsea boys parading down 8th Avenue through floor to ceiling windows. $5 cosmopolitans 10pm–2am Wed, and Liquid Brunch, $3 bloody Mary's 2–6pm Sat. Open every night. Daily Happy Hour and *Six Feet Under* and *Queer as Folk* reruns.

EAST VILLAGE
B Bar & Grill: 40 East 4th Street between Lafayette Street and the Bowery. 212-475 2220, bbarandgrill.com. Subway B, D, F, V to Broadway/Lafayette Street; 6 to Bleecker Street.
This is a super-trendy lounge filled with models and gorgeous people. Madonna has been known to drop in. Beige, the weekly A-list gay party, is the place to be on Tues night, and it's free. Open Mon 11.30am–2am, Tues, Thurs and Fri 11.30am–4am, Wed 11.30am–3am, Sat and Sun 10.30am–3am.

Boiler Room: 86 East 4th Street at 2nd Avenue, 212-254 7536, boilerroomnyc.com.
A great place to start your evening. No DJ but there's an internet jukebox with hundreds of thousands of tunes, from the Pointer Sisters to Pantera, boys from all neighbourhoods and down-to-earth ambience. Cash only.

Eastern Bloc: 505 East 6th Street. 212-777 2555, easternblocnyc.com.
The old gay haunt, The Wonderbar has been given a Russian refit, with its walls painted a tongue-in-cheek red and black. Surprisingly attitude-free, this dive bar was *New York Magazine*'s Best Gay Bar 2007. This is the place to ditch the vodka-sodas and have a beer with the locals.

Urge: 33 2nd Avenue at 2nd Street. 212-533 5757, theurgenyc.com. Subway F to 2nd Avenue.

Very spacious and friendly East Village lounge with a massive 2-tier centre bar, comfy nooks to frolic in, nightly DJs, cute bartenders, go-go boys and drag queens; what more could you want from a night out? Daily happy hour 4–10, 2-for-1 drinks.

GREENWICH VILLAGE
The Stonewall Inn: 53 Christopher Street between 6th and 7th Avenues. 212-463 0950, thestonewallinnyc.com. Subway 1 at Christopher Street/Sheridan Square.
Restored and reopened, Stonewall is the historic spot where gay activism began and therefore a centre point for the gay community, with multicoloured lights, disco balls and cheesy tunes. Mostly male, there are nightly drag impresarios upstairs. Open daily 3pm–4am; Happy Hour 2–8pm, Sun $3 beer and $5 martinis. Cash only.

Manhattan Monster, Inc: 80 Grove Street at Sheridan Square. 212-924 3558, manhattanmonster.com. Subway 1 to Christopher Street/Sheridan Square.
Probably the most popular bar in Greenwich Village, now in its 29th year. Right on Sheridan Square across from the infamous Stonewall. Happy piano bar draws older crowd; downstairs dance floor draws younger hotties; Mon night has a drag show. Mon, there's a cover charge of $6, Fri & Sat, $7 after 10pm and after 8pm Sun, probably the only club with a cover charge in the Village but you always get a show too. Happy Hour weekdays 4–9pm and Sat 2–9pm, draws the crowds for its free hors d'oeuvres. Open 4pm–4am, party starts at 10pm.

HELL'S KITCHEN
Posh: 405 West 51st Street. 212-957 222, poshbarnyc.com. Subway C, E to 23rd Street.

B Bar & Grill

A laid-back lounge bathed in beauty-enhancing red light. Exposed brick walls, a sound system blaring dance remixes of staples like the Bee Gees and Abba. The back room has a more intimate feel than the packed front bar.

 BRITTIP

Head to Posh Bar if it's your birthday, they promise to give you 5 drinks for free (take your passport as proof!).

MIDTOWN EAST

OW Bar: 221 East 58th Street at 2nd Avenue. 212-355 3395. Subway 4, 5, 6 at 59th Street, N, R, W at 5th Avenue/59th Street.
OW are Oscar Wilde's initials, but this gay bar is lively, too, with drag and cabaret and nightly parties spilling on to an outdoor patio. Open daily 4pm–4am. Happy Hour 4–8pm.

Vlada Lounge: 331 West 51st Street. 212-974 8030, vladabar.com. Subway C, E to 50th Street.
Winner of AOL and *City Guide Magazine's* Best Gay Bar 2007, its worth checking out this sleek Hell's Kitchen bar where the vodka flows, the escargot rolls and drag queens drift. There's no cover charge for the nightly shows. Open Tues–Sun 4pm–4am.

Therapy: 348 West 52nd Street between 8th and 9th Avenues. 212-397 1700, therapy-nyc.com. Subway C, E at 50th Street.
A chic, scene lounge with stylish wood-panelled walls under a vaulted skylight in the heart of 'New Chelsea' district Hell's Kitchen. Try one of the appropriately named house cocktails such as Pavlov's Dog or The Freudian Slip. Nightly entertainment, open Sun–Wed 5pm–2am, Thurs–Sat 5pm–4am. Happy Hour 5pm–8pm daily and there's food, too.

MIDTOWN WEST

La Nueva Escuelita: 301 West 39th Street at 8th Avenue. 212-631 0588, escuelita.com. Subway A, C east to 42nd Street.
A fantastic Latino club famed for its fabulous shows and nights of salsa, merengue and Latin-style drag shows. Lots of different shows, such as Karaoke Sundays.

UPPER EAST SIDE

Townhouse: 236 East 58th Street. 212-754 4649, townhouseny.com. Subway E, V to 53rd Street.
An East Side institution that locals describe as more like an upscale gentleman's club than a bar. Music is more in the background than at some of the larger, louder venues and there are areas for intimate conversations. A classy joint if you're looking for something more relaxed. Note, the dress code here is quite smart so no ripped jeans or lycra.

Lips: 227 East 56th Street. 212-675 7710, lipsnyc.com. Subway E, V, 6 to East 51st Street. Open 6 nights from 5.30pm. Dinner Tues–Thurs 7–7.30pm and 9–9.30pm, open until midnight, open until 11pm Sun. Fri-Sat dinner 7pm and 9.30pm, the Dirty Show 11.30pm Gospel brunch Sun at 12pm and 2pm. $10 cover Thurs–Sat.

WEST VILLAGE

The Dugout: 185 Christopher Street between Washington and West Streets. 212-242 9113, thedugoutny.com. Subway 1 to Christopher Street/Sheridan Square.

Therapy

Cubby Hole

A great neighbourhood bar and club especially popular for its Sunday afternoon beer blast where 600ml/20oz drafts cost just $4. The foremost Chelsea Bear bar, it attracts African-American guys and an older crowd. Open Mon-Sun 12-4am. Happy Hour Mon-Fri 4-9pm. Cash only.

CLUBS AND LOUNGES FOR HER

BROOKLYN

Cattyshack: 249 4th Avenue between Carroll and President Streets, Park Slope. 718-230 5740. cattyshackbklyn.com. Subway M, R at Union Street.

A 2-storey industrial chic oasis in the heart of Brooklyn's hottest district advertising cheap drinks, heated smoking deck, go-go pole and hot bar staff. Open mic Mon and Fri go-go dancers grind around the pole to hip-hop favourites on the dance floor. Open Mon-Fri 2pm-4am, Sat and Sun noon-4am. Daily Happy Hour 4-8pm.

BRITTIP
Visit outaboutbrooklyn.com for loads of info.

Ginger's Bar: 363 5th Avenue between 6th and 7th Streets, Park Slope. 718-788 0924.

Subway M, R to Union Street.
The drinks are generous, the pool table at the back is always full of sexy dykes, and this dark wooden bar is a friendly, neighbourhood place to hang out. Open Mon-Fri 6pm-4am, Sat and Sun 2pm-4am.

LOWER EAST SIDE

Bluestockings: 172 Allen Street between Rivington and Stanton Streets. 212-777 6028, bluestockings.com. Subway F, V to Lower East Side/2nd Avenue.
Not strictly a club or lounge, more a bookstore and café, but it's a great neighbourhood joint that gives women the opportunity to showcase their talents at open-mic sessions. Open daily 11am-11pm.

MIDTOWN WEST

La Nueva Escuelita: 301 West 39th Street at 8th Avenue. 212-631 0588, escuelita.com. Subway A, C east to 42nd Street
As good for women as for guys; mostly filled with Latin women from the über-feminine to the ultra-butch, there are go-go dancers galore on which to feast the eyes, a drag show at 2am and a lap-dancing lounge.

WEST VILLAGE

Cubby Hole: 281 West 12th Street between West 4th and West 12th Streets. 212-243 9041, cubbyholebar.com. Subway 1, 2, 3 to 14th Street.
It looks as though the owners of this lesbian bar have raided a New Orleans thrift store a few days after Mardi Gras: hundreds of illuminated plastic blowfish, goldfish and Chinese lanterns dangle from the ceiling. Old-timers straggle in long before sunset for half-price drinks (Mon-Sat 4-7pm); after 9pm, younger gals (and a fair number of guys) take centre stage. There's no karaoke here anymore, but it almost doesn't matter. Like a pianoless piano bar, Cubby Hole is packed full of regulars who like to belt out

West Village

Benny's Burritos

tunes along with the jukebox. It was voted Best Lesbian Bar by *New York Magazine* in 2007. Open Mon–Fri 4pm–4am, Sat and Sun 2pm–4am. Cash only.

Henrietta Hudson's: 438 Hudson Street at Morton Street. 212-924 3347, henriettahudsons.com. Subway 1, 9 to Christopher Street.
This is probably the most popular lesbian lounge in the city, which has been going for 19 years. Even when there's no specific party, gals come from far and wide to hang out at this great watering hole. Thursday night is girlMEETSgirl night, with R&B, hip-hop and Latin music for $5 after 9pm. If you're into go-go girls, the Fri night extravaganza is the party for you – and hordes of others, too! Open Mon–Fri 4pm–4am and Sat–Sun 2pm–4am.

RESTAURANTS

BROOKLYN

Superfine: 126 Front Street between Jay and Pearl Streets, Dumbo. 718-243 9005.
Cool is moving out of Manhattan, and this hip place proves it. Serves mainly Mediterranean fare, but is best known for its themed brunches.

CHELSEA

Better Burger NYC: 178 8th Avenue at 19th Street. 212-989 6688, betterburger nyc.com. Subway C, E to 23rd Street.
Low-fat, health-conscience, 100% organic,

antibiotic-free and hormone-free fare – ostrich, turkey, chicken, soy and vegetarian burgers (and the classic beef) plus other options. Open 11am–11pm.

Pad Thai: 114 8th Avenue at 16th Street. 212-691 6226, padthaibox.com.
Elegant, mellow and seductive noodle lounge with above-average Thai fare.

EAST VILLAGE

Mannahatta: 310 Bowery at Bleecker Street. 212-477 1979, mannahatta.us/.
Beautiful space with lounge furniture rather than dining tables, tapas dishes like salmon ceviche and duck salad. There's a DJ booth downstairs that attracts stylish night owls.

B Bar & Grill: 40 East 4th Street between Lafayette Street and Bowery. 212-475 2220, bbarandgrill.com.
Home to Beige on a Tues night, this gorgeous bistro serves excellent food.

Benny's Burritos: 93 Avenue A, near 6th Street. 212-254 3286, harrysburritos.com.
This establishment looks as though it has survived from the 1960s: lava lamps, pink walls and Formica tables make up the decor.

TOP RESTAURANTS

B Bar & Grill: East Village (above)

Lips: West Village (page 262).

Townhouse Restaurant: Midtown East (page 261).

Serves super-filling burritos and enchiladas, but watch out for the lethal margaritas. (You'll find a larger and more crowded Benny's at 113 Greenwich Ave in the West Village.)

Lucien: 14 1st Avenue at 1st Street. 212-260 6481, luciennyc.com.
Always packed, this tiny French bistro serves delicious food and is particularly known for its Sunday brunch. Also open until 2am for late night munchies. It's sister restaurant is The Pink Pony (see right).

Pangea: 178 2nd Avenue between 11th and 12th Streets. 212-995 0900, pangeanyc.com.
Known for its wonderful homemade pastas and Mediterranean cuisine. A-list film star siblings Jake Gyllenhaal and Maggie Gyllenhaal have been papped here. Go for cocktails at the large oak bar before a night out too.

Yaffa Café: 97 St Marks Place at 1st Avenue. 212-674 9302, yaffacafe.com.
This 24-hour hipster hangout serves up hummus, sandwiches, pasta and chicken entrées (page 165). Very inexpensive and with a large garden – and they hand out free condoms to the clientele!

HELL'S KITCHEN
Eatery NYC: 798 9th Avenue at 53rd Street. 212-765 7080, eaterynyc.com.
This created a buzz in the gay community when it opened in 2009, thanks to its style and eclectic clientele. There's a large concrete-chic dining area and packed bar plus globe-hopping dishes like seared tuna with tempura noodle rolls, barbecued duck with chili relish on a tostada, and roasted pork loin topped with caramelised sauerkraut.

MIDTOWN EAST
Arriba Arriba!: 762 9th Avenue at 51st Street. 212 489 0810, arribaarribawest.com.
Neighbourhood queens flock to this Mexican-style joint.

BRITTIP
The frozen margaritas at Arriba Arriba! are some of the city's best and come in three sizes – bebe, mama or papa.

Juice Generation: 644 9th Avenue at 45th Street. 212-541 5600, juicegeneration.com.
Delicious fresh juices, smoothies, protein shakes and bakery products served 7 days a week. They have three other joints in the city – West 72nd Street, Broadway and West 4th Street.

Maracas: 317 East 53rd Street at 2nd Avenue. 212-593 6600, maracasnyc.com.
It's always fiesta time at this OTT, fun Mexican bar and grill from the creators of Lips. Frozen margaritas, explosive visuals, electric ambience. Champagne brunch on Sun, happy hour from 4–7pm weekly and all day until closing Sun.

Townhouse Restaurant: 206 East 58th Street between 2nd and 3rd Avenues. 212-826 6241, townhouseny.com.
This is owned by the same people as The Townhouse Bar, one of the oldest, most upscale and gay-safe haunts, especially among the more mature crowd. It serves delicious food at reasonable prices.

NOLITA, SOHO AND TRIBECA
Basset Café: 123 West Broadway at Duane Street. 212-349 1827.
Tuck into a delicious salad or sandwich, or treat yourself to the homemade cakes at this light and airy haven. Smoking is permitted.

The Pink Pony: 176 Ludow Street at Stanton Street. 212-253 1922, pinkponynyc.com.
Young, laid-back, unpretentious crowd enjoying inexpensive comfort food.

THEATER DISTRICT
Coffee Pot: 350 West 49th Street at 9th Avenue. 212-265 3566.
Nice little coffee bar with live music and tarot card readings. Open 7 days a week until 11pm.

44 & X Hell's Kitchen: 622 10th Avenue at 44th Street. 212-977 1170, 44andX.com.
Great post-theatre sleek spot, packed with queens and serving tasty American fare.

Mangia East Bevi: 800 9th Avenue at 53rd Street. 212-956 3976.
An excellent, popular Italian in the middle of Midtown's gay district.

Mexican food at Arriba Arriba!

Garage Restaurant

Vintage: 753 9th Avenue at 51st Street.
212-581 4655.
A hip bar/restaurant that serves dinner until midnight and cocktails until 4am.

WEST VILLAGE

Cowgirl: 519 Hudson Street at West 10th Street. 212-633 1133, cowgirlnyc.com.
This isn't just great for men and women who feel at home surrounded by cowgirl memorabilia, but is also frequented by families. It serves cheap American food – fried onion loaf, huge spare ribs and chicken-fried steak – and is also known for its margaritas. The people-watching outside the restaurant in summer is a treat.

Garage Restaurant: 99 7th Avenue South at Christopher Street. 212-645 0600, garagerest. com.
Serves American cuisine including steaks and a raw bar, with live jazz nightly and a friendly crowd (page 168).

La Ripaille: 605 Hudson Street at West 12th Street. 212-255 4406, laripailleny.com.
Authentic French country dining since 1980. A small, cosy and romantic restaurant with excellent bistro food. Proudly serving the gay community for more than 20 years.

Lips: 2 Bank Street at Greenwich Avenue.
212-675 7710, lipsnyc.com.
Italian menu with dishes named after popular queens like Spanky, a lasagne; all the waitresses are in drag and plenty of entertainment is provided (page 259).

Nadine's: 99 Bank Street at Greenwich Street. 212-924 3165.
Eclectic and good-value food in a funky but glamorous setting.

Sacred Chow: 227 Sullivan Street between Bleecker and West 3rd Streets. 212-337 0863, sacredchow.com.
Healthy bohemian vegan food shop and café.

BRITTIP
For a wide selection of restaurants as well as gay-friendly bars, clubs and lounges, log on to queenofnewyork.com

Stonewall Bistro: 113 7th Avenue at Christopher Street. 917-661 1335.
An elegant and cosy dining experience from the creators of the famous Stonewall; continental cuisine with a French flair. Cabaret every night; dinner and drink specials all week. Thurs networking night.

Sushi Samba 7: 87 7th Avenue at Barrow Street. 212-691 7885, sushisamba.com.
This establishment serves up excellent sushi, ceviches, tiraditos and pratos.

CHAPTER 12

Festivals and Parades

New Yorkers love an excuse to party, from celebrating the changing of the seasons to championing their cultural roots. In fact, judging by the number of parades, open-air concerts and festivals taking place every month, it's a wonder anyone gets any work done. The good news is that you can be sure that whatever time of year you decide to visit the Big Apple, there will be some truly spectacular entertainment going on, and what's more, most of it is free!

ANNUAL AND BIENNIAL EVENTS

JANUARY AND FEBRUARY

Winter Restaurant Week
Citywide. Last 2 weeks in Jan. 212-484 1222, nycgo.com/restaurantweek.
Amazing offers at lots of eateries. In 2010 you could grab a lunch for $24.07 (to reflect the 24/7 New York lifestyle) or dinner for $35 with this great promotion. For daily offers check out twitter.com/nycgo.

Winter Antiques Show
21–30 Jan 2011. 7th Regiment Armory, Park Avenue at 67th Street, 718-292 7392 or 718-665 5250, winterantiquesshow.com.
Admission $20 with catalogue. Open daily noon–8pm; Sun and Thurs noon–6pm.
The Winter Antiques Show kicks off New York's winter season with a glitzy Opening Night Party on 22 Jan, but as tickets for that event start at $1,000 each your best bet is to wait until the next day to see the treasures within. From the simplicity of arts and crafts to ornate baroque clocks, you can be sure there will be fine antiques to suit everyone's taste. Private collections from all over America are also on show.

BRITTIP
A central number for New York events is 212-484 1222; and a website that reports many free events is newyorkled.com. A good events site for planning ahead is new. york.eventguide.com.

Chinese New Year Parade/Lunar New York
Chinese New Year begins on 3 Feb 2011 (it's year of the rabbit if you're interested). Chinatown around Mott Street, 212-484 1216, explorechinatown.com.

Chinese New Year Parade

FESTIVALS AND PARADES

263

TOP 5 FESTIVALS & PARADES

Grammy Awards: February.

St Patrick's Day Parade: March.

Heritage of Pride Parade: June.

Bryant Park Free Summer Season: June–Aug.

Macy's Thanksgiving Day Parade: November.

New York City is known for having some of the most authentic celebrations of the Chinese New Year in the US, and the festivities range from a firecracker ceremony to the magnificent dragon parade in Chinatown to various other performances around the city. The party continues for 10 days.

Black History Month

Throughout Feb. A series of shows is put on to celebrate the African-American experience in New York. See the newspapers and guides for cultural events, concerts and lectures scheduled around the city, or visit http://nymag.com for detailed listings of events.

Grammy Awards

Late Feb. Madison Square Garden, 212-465 6741, grammy.com.

The Grammy Awards are to music what the Oscars are to the movies. Over the years, Los Angeles and New York have played tug-of-war with the Grammy Awards show and New York has won. You may not get to attend the Awards, but you can go stargazing by the red carpet as celebs arrive in their limos.

MARCH AND APRIL

St Patrick's Day Parade

17 Mar 5th Avenue between 44th and 86th Streets. saintpatricksdayparade.com.

One of the bigger parades the city has to offer. If you're in town, you won't be able to miss the sea of green that goes with this annual Irish-American day. The parade starts at 11am up 5th Avenue from 44th to 86th Streets and the festivities go on late into the night. The 2011 parade will be the 249th!

BRITTIP

A good vantage point to watch the St Patrick's Day parade is the steps of St Patrick's Cathedral (page 81), where the Bishop of New York greets the marching bands.

Greek Independence Day Parade

Sun closest to 25 Mar (when Greek Independence Day falls in the Orthodox Lent, the parade is shifted to Apr or even May). Along 5th Avenue to 49th Street, 718-204

St Patrick's Cathedral steps

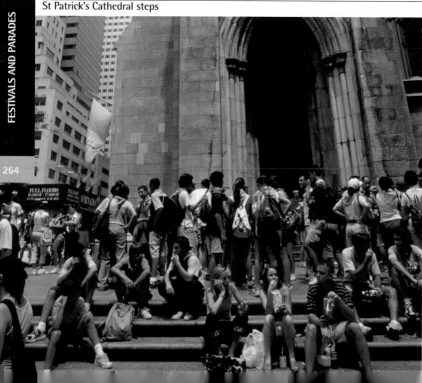

St Patrick's Day Parade

6500, greekparade.org.
This one's a Zorba-style parade with lots of flag waving and national dress, as well as plenty of Greek food, music and dancing.

Easter Parade
Easter Sun. 5th Avenue between 49th and 57th Streets.
This is not an official parade, just a chance to watch strollers flaunting Easter bonnets from gorgeous to outrageous. The steps of St Patrick's Cathedral (page 81) are an advantageous viewing spot. Kick-off is at 10am, so arrive early to bag a space.

Upper West Fest
End Apr–May. Download the brochure and plan your visit at upperwestfest.com.
From 60th Street to 120th Street, the doors of more than 20 world class arts and cultural organisations open their doors and more than 50 performances and exhibitions are laid on. Highlights include Symphony Space's free 12-hour opera marathon, the NY Yiddish Film Festival and jazz at the Lincoln Center.

New York City Ballet Spring Gala
Late Apr–June. New York State Theater, 20 Lincoln Center Plaza, 65th Street at Columbus Avenue, 212-870 5570, nycballet.com.
Student rush tickets (available on day of performance) cost $12 (212-870-7766). Even ordinary tickets start from a bargain $20. The New York City Ballet performs its spring season in New York before touring. Go to see the world-famous dancers, trained in the classic style of ballet masters Balanchine and Robbins.

MAY AND JUNE
See also New York City Ballet (left).

American Ballet Theater
May–July. Metropolitan Opera House at the Lincoln Center, 212-362 6000, abt.org.
Going to see the ABT at the Met is exhilarating. The majesty of the Metropolitan Opera House combines with the passion, power and movement of one of the world's most innovative dance companies to create a magical experience. The Theater also runs an ABTKids programme.

Cuban Day Parade
Usually the first Sun in May. Free.
Lively day-long Cuban carnival with salsa bands and partying into the night along 6th Avenue that ends at the Cuban Independence statue of José Marti on Central Park South.

TriBeCa Film Festival
Late Apr–early May. TriBeCa area, 212-941 2400, tribecafilmfestival.org.
The 12-day TriBeCa Film Festival was founded in 2002 by Robert DeNiro, Jane Rosenthal and Craig Hatkoff as a response to the attacks on the World Trade Center. The now prestigious festival showcases independent movies, runs workshops and has a children's film programme, as well as Q&A sessions with actors and filmmakers. During the week, local restaurants offer cut-price meals. You can buy tickets for the various events online or from the main box office at 15 Laight Street.

9th Avenue International Food Festival
Mid-May (15–16 in 2010). 9th Avenue

New York City Ballet

SUMMER IN THE CITY FOR FAMILIES

Puppet shows, free story-telling, films and workshops in libraries – these form just a part of what's on offer in the city throughout the summer, so you'll be hard pressed to find a moment's peace! To find out what's going on where and when, pick up a copy of *Events For Children* from any branch of the New York Public Library. Most are free or very good value for money.

Here is an outline of some of the many activities available for children in summer. More details can be found by month in this chapter or in Chapter 13 Sports and Leisure.

Central Park
The park is a year-round winner, but summer time is when it really comes into its own. Specific children's events abound, from canoeing to field days, all listed under the Kids to Do section on centralparknyc.org, while the whole family can enjoy offerings put on by the **Central Park SummerStage** (212-360 2756, summerstage.org) and **Shakespeare in the Park** (212-539 8500, publictheater.org).

Bryant Park Summer Film Festival: 212-768 4242, bryantpark.org.
Perfect for adults and children alike, head to Bryant Park on a Mon night and pull up a chair or lay out a rug to enjoy a free outdoor film on the massive screen. Remember to take some snacks and drinks. Children can let off steam before or after at the nearby carousel.

New York Philharmonic Young People's Concerts: Avery Fisher Hall, 10 Lincoln Center Plaza, 212-875 5656, newyorkphilharmonic.org.
A series of summer Sat concerts where children aged 6–12 get to meet the musicians and try out their instruments for an hour before the concert. Book early, however, as they're very popular. You'll also be in the right spot for the Lincoln Center's free Out-of-Doors Festival, with events throughout Aug (see below). The Lincoln Center also offers a family programme of music and dance afternoons for children.

Puppet Theater: 212-680 1400, hensonfoundation.org.
Sign up on the website for puppet happenings that may time with your visit.

Lincoln Center Out-of-Doors: Lincoln Center plazas and Damrosch Park, 212-LIN COLN, lincolncenter.org.
A free festival for all ages running throughout Aug with specific events for families and children.

between 37th and 57th Streets, 212-581 7029, hellskitchen.bz.
This festival, which has been going for 10 years, is a gourmet's delight. Hell's Kitchen cooks up a feast of foods from around the world and hundreds of stalls line the streets selling every type of food imaginable. Go for lunch and then walk it all off by strolling on down to Chelsea's fabulous art galleries nearby.

Fleet Week
Last week in May.
New York City Fleet Week brings thousands of sailors and marines from US naval vessels to the Big Apple and includes dozens of military demonstrations. Unless you're a boat nut, it's normally not worth visiting the huge armada of US Navy – free tours are offered daily – and other ships that visit New York, but this week they'll be very hard to miss.

Central Park

Lower East Side Festival of the Arts
Last weekend in May. Along East 10th Street.
Theater for the New City, 212-254 1109,
theaterforthenewcity.net/les.htm.
Running since 1996, deep in the heart of the
neighbourhood that helped create the East
Coast Beat Movement, method acting and
pop art. It's a free, 3-day indoor and outdoor
annual arts festival and carnival for everyone,
with more than 250 performers and 70
groups, offering everything from drama to
dance, music and poetry, art to food.

Washington Square Outdoor Art Exhibition
Memorial Day weekend in May, the weekend
that follows it and every Labor Day Weekend
in Sept. Washington Square, 212-982 6255,
washingtonsquareoutdoorartexhibit.org.
An old and revered tradition of arty
Greenwich Village (it's been going since
1933), this is a huge outdoor art show with
easels and food trolleys set up in the streets
all around the park.

Puerto Rican Day Parade
Second Sun in June from 11am. 5th Avenue
between 44th and 85th Streets, 718-401
0404, nationalpuertoricandayparade.org.
This is a New York parade on a grand scale
– expect more than 100,000 marchers and
3 million spectators. The largest of several
Puerto Rican celebrations in the city, with 3
hours of colourful floats, music and dancing,
from 2pm at St Patrick's Cathedral on 5th
Avenue.

Museum Mile Festival
Second Tues in June. 5th Avenue between
82nd and 104th Streets, 212-606 2296,
museummilefestival.org.
Museum Mile is neither a museum nor a
mile, but nine museums stretching along 5th
Avenue and Central Park on the Upper East
Side. All are worth a visit. During the festival
you can get into all of them, including the
fabulous Metropolitan, for free from 6–9pm.
An added perk is the fascinating outside
entertainment, including live bands and street
art. This will be the 41st anniversary and more
than 50,000 visitors took part last year.

Theater Under the Stars
The Great Lawn, mid-park, from 79th to
85th Street, Central Park, 212-768 4242,
centralpark.com or nycvisit.com.
Broadway kicks off New York's summer
outdoor concert season in Central Park with a
free showcase of its hottest talent performing
major show songs at 8.30pm. Award-winning
celebs and hot new talent sing and dance for
90 minutes backed by a 35-piece orchestra.

✈ BRITTIP
Check out the many street
fairs from spring to autumn
throughout the city with food, craft
and other stalls. Visit nycstreetfairs.
com and nyctourist.com.

Mermaid Parade
Third or last Sat in June (check website for
2011 date). 8th Street between Steeplechase
Park and Broadway, Coney Island, Brooklyn,
718-372 5159, coneyisland.com.
The Mermaid Parade celebrates the beginning
of summer. Catch the B, D or F trains to
Stillwell Avenue on the Sat following the
first official day of summer to sample a wild
and boisterous scene of carnival floats and
costumes. The parade is followed by the
Mermaid Parade Ball.

Heritage of Pride March and PrideFest
Last Sun in June. From Columbus Circle along
5th Avenue and 52nd Street to Christopher
Street in Greenwich Village, 212-807 7433,
nycpride.org.
Formerly known as the Gay Pride Parade, this
march kicks off every year at 5th Avenue and
ends with PrideFest, a street party and rally in
the traditional heart of the gay community.
There is a packed club schedule, fireworks and
an open-air dance party at Hudson Street
between Abingdon Square and West 14th
Street.

Central Park SummerStage
June–Aug. Rumsey Playfield, Central Park at
72nd Street and Central Park West, 212-307
7171 for tickets to benefit concerts or 212-
360 2756 for information, summerstage.org.
Subway 1, 2, 3, 9, B, C to 72nd Street.
You can experience many kinds of

Bryant Park

MIdsummer Night Swing

entertainment for free in New York and some of the best are the free weekend afternoon concerts put on by the SummerStage, which celebrated its 25th anniversary last year. Featuring over 33 performances from top international artists, on weeknights, dance and spoken-word events are also put on in Central Park.

New York Philharmonic/Metropolitan Opera Parks Concerts

Various sites in summer, nycgovparks.org, 212-875 5656, nyphil.org, 212-362 6000, metopera.org (Met).

These free, open-air events in parks around the city are wildly popular so arrive early to stake out a site.

Shakespeare in the Park

Late June–late Aug. Delacorte Theater, Central Park at 81st Street, 212-539 8500 info, 212-967 7555 to order tickets, publictheater.org. Plays held in the open-air theatre every summer are free. There are 2 each year – 1 Shakespeare and 1 American, with performances almost nightly. Although free, you still have to get tickets to see them, which are available from 1pm on the day of the performance, and the queues are long.

Bryant Park Summer Film Festival

Every Mon June–Aug. 6th Avenue at 42nd Street, 212-768 4242, bryantpark.org. Subway F, V, B, D to 42nd Street/Bryant Park.
Bryant Park is one of the few green spaces

available in the Midtown area, and this is a summer-long series of free classical music, jazz, dance and film showings during the day and evening. Classic films shown in the park on Mon are a great way to unwind after a hard day's shopping or sightseeing. The lawn opens at 5pm for blankets and picnicking. The films begin at dusk.

Midsummer Night Swing

Mid-June to mid-July. Lincoln Center for Performing Arts, Josie Robertson Plaza, Columbus Avenue at 63rd Street, 212-875 5766, lincolncenter.org. Single tickets from $17, the swing passes that admit 2 start from $90 for 6 nights.

Considered the city's hottest outdoor dance party, with dance-filled nights when energetic bands play everything from swing to salsa. Lots of dance instructors are on hand to give lessons in every type of dance, or you can just listen to the live music.

Celebrate Brooklyn! Performing Arts Festival

All summer. Prospect Park Bandshell, 9th Street at Prospect Park West, Park Slope, Brooklyn, 718-855 7882, celebratebrooklyn. org.

Here's a very good reason to break out of Manhattan and visit one of the outer boroughs – for New York's longest running festival of free music, dance, theatre and film events lasting 9 weeks. Last year Norah Jones performed at the free opening gala in June.

OTHER MEMORABLE DAYS in NYC

Super Bowl Sunday (day of National Football League's championship): Usually first Sun in February

Groundhog Day (day on which behaviour of groundhog coming out of its burrow predicts spring): 2 February

Valentine's Day: 14 February

St Patrick's Day (celebration of Irish heritage, lots of New Yorkers wear green, drink and parade!): 17 March

April Fools Day: 1 April

Good Friday/Spring Holiday (holiday to commemorate crucifixion of Jesus or 'Spring Holiday' in schools and universities that want to avoid direct reference): Late March/early April

Earth Day: 22 April

Arbor Day (day for planting trees): Last Friday in April

Cinco de Mayo (celebration of Mexican culture): 5 May

Mother's Day: Second Sunday in May

Flag Day (commemorates the adoption of the US flag): 14 June

Father's Day: Third Sunday in June

Women's Equality Day: 26 August

Patriot Day (in remembrance of victims of 11 September 2001 attacks): 11 September

Citizenship Day (to commemorate the adoption of the constitution): 17 September

Rosh Hashanah (beginning of Jewish high holidays and new year on Hebrew calendar): September or October

Halloween (bigger deal in NY than in the UK): 31 October

Pearl Harbor Remembrance Day: 7 December

Winter solstice: 21 December

Christmas Eve: 24 December

Kwanzaa (African-American holiday celebration created in 1966): 26 December–1 January

JULY AND AUGUST

See also American Ballet Theater at the Met, Thursday Night Concert Series, Central Park SummerStage, New York Philharmonic/Met Opera Concerts, New York Shakespeare Festival, Bryant Park Free Summer Season, Midsummer Night Swing and Celebrate Brooklyn! Performing Arts Festival (left).

Broadway in Bryant Park
Thurs from 12.30–1.30pm, July and August. Bryant Park between 40th Street and 6th Avenue.
Experience the glamour of Broadway in the great outdoors. Each week several of the year's biggest hits come to the park for a dazzling show of song and dance, for free!

Fourth of July
The Americans still celebrate achieving independence from their colonial masters – and they do it in style! Throughout New York there are various celebrations going on, but by far the biggest and most spectacular is Macy's Fireworks Spectacular, which is held on the East River between 14th and 51st Streets, 212-494 4495, macys.com. A good spot to see the $1 million, 30-minute firework extravaganza is from FDR Drive (Franklin D Roosevelt Drive) or from Pier 17 at South Street Seaport. Another popular event is the Travis Fourth of July Parade (718-494

Breakdancers at Columbus Circle

The Lincoln Center

0378) where the town of Travis is decorated in red, white and blue and marching bands and costumed characters take to the streets.

Summer Restaurant Week
Mid-July, 212-484 1222, nycgo.com/restaurantweek.
For 2 weeks, more than 150 of the city's finest restaurants offer 3-course fixed-price lunches and dinners at prices that reflect the year.

Summer Garden Concerts
July–Aug. Flushing Town Hall, 137-35 Northern Boulevard, Queens, 718-463 7700, flushingtownhall.com.
A diverse line-up with many musical styles including country, jazz, soul and oldies.

Concerts in the Abby Aldrich Rockefeller Sculpture Garden
July–Aug. Museum of Modern Art, 11 West 53rd Street between 5th and 6th Avenues, 212-708 9400, moma.org. Subway E, V to 5th Avenue/53rd Street.
An added bonus to visiting the little gem that is MoMA is the series of free classical and jazz concerts that are presented in the museum's sculpture garden every summer.

Lincoln Center Festival
Mid–late July. Lincoln Center for the Performing Arts, 140 West 65th Street, although venues vary. 212-875 5766, lincolncenter.org.
A veritable feast of dance, drama, ballet, children's shows and multimedia and performance art, involving both repertory companies and special guests, at venues inside and outside at the Lincoln Center (page 266).

Lincoln Center Out of Doors
Aug. Lincoln Center plazas and Damrosch Park, 212-LIN COLN, lincolncenter.org.
Over 100 free outdoor performances including an exciting line-up of music, dance events, storytelling, puppetry and other family events.

Harlem Week
Aug. Along 5th Avenue from West 125th to West 135th Streets, 212-862 7200, harlemweek.com.
The largest black and Hispanic festival in the world, its highlight is the street party with R&B, gospel and All That Jazz. In addition to the music, there are films, dance, fashion, sports and exhibitions. What a great way to experience Harlem!

Sounds at Sunset
Aug. Hudson River Park, 212-627 2020, hudsonriverpark.org. 212-416 5328, batteryparkcity.org.
The Battery Park City Authority presents a free summer series of poetry readings, cabaret and classical music in this park.

SEPTEMBER AND OCTOBER
See also Washington Square Outdoor Art Exhibition (May and June); Concert Series in the Rockefeller Sculpture Garden (see left).

West Indian-American Day Parade
First Mon of Sept (Labor Day). 5th Avenue to Christopher Street in Brooklyn, 718-467 1797, wiadca.com.
Fabulous festival celebrating Caribbean culture with food (all along Eastern Parkway) and entertainment from top Caribbean artists. It's attended by more than 3 million people,

including brightly costumed marchers put on a special children's parade on the Sat, with an even bigger event on Labor Day (first Mon in Sept).

Feast of San Gennaro

Mid-Sept for 11 days. Mulberry Street to Worth Street in Little Italy, 212-768 9320, sangennaro.org.

Held in honour of the Neapolitan saint, this festival, now in its 84th year, is the best time to see what is left of the once-bustling Little Italy that is now reduced to just Mulberry Street. There are lots of fairground booths, plenty of food – look out for the cannoli-eating contest – and even more vino.

Broadway on Broadway

Sept (varies, last year Sun 13 Sept) at 11.30am Times Square, 212-768 1560, broadwayonbroadway.com.

Quintessentially New York – a free annual concert when numbers from Broadway shows are performed live on a giant outdoor stage by a galaxy of celebrities surrounded by TV cameras. It all ends in a big finale with loads of confetti.

◀️🇬🇧 BRITTIP

Parades are great fun, but they also provide perfect opportunities for pickpockets, so keep your bags and wallets close to you – and never put your wallet in your back pocket.

Columbus Day Parade

Second Mon in Oct at 11.30am–3pm, 5th Avenue between 44th and 79th Streets, 212-249 9923, columbuscitizensfd.org.

The traditional celebration of the first recorded sighting of America by Europeans is now somewhat controversial in some quarters, but despite its lack of political correctness, Columbus Day still gets the big 5th Avenue parade treatment, which is well worth a view. The parade has nearly 1 million participants plus celebrities – the likes of Frank Sinatra, Sophia Loren and Luciano Pavarotti have all paraded in the past.

New York City Marathon

Last Sun in Oct/first Sun in Nov. Staten Island to Central Park, 212-423 2249, nycmarathon.org.

Starts at the Staten Island side of the Verrazano Narrows Bridge as a mad pack of 35,000 men and women run 42km/26.2mls around all 5 boroughs, to finish at the Tavern on the Green in Central Park at West 67th Street. If you would like to enter the marathon you need to fill out an application form, pay a small fee, and then wait to see if you get picked. You can do this through the website.

DUMBO Art Under the Bridge Festival

Mid-Oct. Brooklyn, between Manhattan and Brooklyn bridges. 718-624 3772, dumboartscenter.org.

The single largest urban forum for experimental art in the USA, where more than 1,500 emerging and professional artists show their work in 250 open galleries. The parade of concepts (robots, remote-controlled vehicles and floats) kicks of the show in the neighbourhood, Down Under the Manhattan Bridge Overpass.

Halloween Parade

31 Oct at 7pm. 6th Avenue from Spring Street, Greenwich Village to 21st Street, 212-475 3333, halloween-nyc.com.

A uniquely Village event, with the outlandishly over-the-top costumes (or lack of them!) on (or off!) many of its participants. The organisers decree a different theme each year and a lot of work goes into the amazing outfits that range from the exotic to

Columbus Day Parade

Fire truck at the Halloween Parade

the nearly non-existent. It attracts between 50,000 ghouls, ghosts and onlookers. So get creative and dress up to join in – only those in fancy dress can march. Or you can watch the fun on screens live on 6th Avenue Spring Street to 21st Street from 7–10pm.

NOVEMBER AND DECEMBER

See also New York City Marathon (page 271).

Macy's Thanksgiving Day Parade

Thanksgiving Day, 9am. From Central Park West at 77th Street to Macy's (page 121) on Broadway at 34th Street, 212-494 4495, macysparade.com.

Definitely one for the family, this is the Big Mama of all New York's parades, with enormous inflated cartoon characters, fabulous floats and the gift-giving Santa

Claus himself. New Yorkers in the know like to come by and watch it being set up the night before between 77th and 81st Streets off Central Park West. The parade is even televised for the rest of America. If you miss it, you can go to see Santa in Santaland in Macy's until Christmas.

Christmas Tree Lighting Ceremony

Late Nov/early Dec. The Rockefeller Center, from 5th–7th Avenue between 47th and 51st Streets, 212-632 3975, rockefellercenter.com. The Rockefeller Center (page 71) in front of the towering RCA building provides the magical setting for the annual switching on of nearly 8km/5mls of dazzling lights on a huge Christmas tree. The plaza leading up to the tree is decked with lights, too!

New Year's Eve Ball Drop

31 Dec, midnight, Times Square, 212-768 1560, timessquarenyc.org.

This event is a real New York classic, though you may prefer to watch safely on TV rather than be packed in with the freezing masses. Remember, Times Square is a misnomer – it's a junction, so there isn't really that much room and all the side streets get packed too. If you do manage to get a good spot, though, you'll see the giant glitterball of 180 bulbs and 12,000 rhinestones being dropped along with 1 tonne (yes, really) of confetti, to bring in the New Year. The revellers kick off at 5pm, so get there early.

New Year's Eve Fireworks in Central Park

31 Dec, midnight, 5th Avenue and 90th Street or Bethsheda Fountain (Central Park at 72nd Street) are the best viewing spots, 212-360 3456, nycgovparks.org. The hot apple cider and spirit of camaraderie begin at 11.30pm.

Macy's Thanksgiving Day Parade

CHAPTER 13

Sports and Leisure

New York is as famous for its parks as it is for the Statue of Liberty – and there's not *only* Central Park. The parks are very busy and remarkably safe, but be prudent about going into the less populated areas and especially cautious about visiting them at night if you are unfamiliar with the neighbourhood. Visit nycgovparks.org for loads of information about every park in New York.

CENTRAL PARK

✉ From Central Park South at 59th Street to 110th Street in Harlem

☎ 212-310 6600

🖰 centralparknyc.org

🚇 Subway A, B, C, D run along the Upper West Side to 59th, 72nd, 81st, 86th, 96th and 103rd Streets; 1, 9 to 59th Street/Columbus Circle; 2, 3 to 110th Street in the North; N, R, W to 57th Street or 5th Avenue on the South side

🕐 Daily 6am–1am; visit the website for weekly scheduled events and tours around the park

$ Free

This is the New Yorkers' playground and meeting place and attracts 25 million visitors every year. Covering 6% of Manhattan, its 341ha/843 acres stretch 96km/6mls from Central Park South at 59th Street to Central Park North at 110th Street, with 5th Avenue and Central Park West forming its eastern and western boundaries. It was created over a 20-year period by architect Calvert Vaux and landscaper Frederick Law Olmsted, was completed in the 1860s and had its 150th Anniversary in 2003.

BRITTIP
Log on to centralparknyc.org for a complete listing of year-round activities.

To enter from the south, cross the street from **Grand Army Plaza** at 5th Avenue and 59th Street. Immediately in front of you is the Pond, and then the **Wollman Memorial Rink** (62nd Street), which hosts a Victorian amusement park in the summer and ice-skating in the winter. Close by is the **Visitor Information Center**, where you can pick up free maps and schedules of events, including the series of free concerts and dramas performed at the **SummerStage** (page 266). Here also are the **Gotham Miniature Golf Course** (a gift from Donald Trump), **The Dairy**, a 19th century-style building with an interactive touchscreen information kiosk and an exhibition on the park's history and design and the antique carousel (65th Street). To the east is the **Central Park Wildlife Center** (63rd–66th Streets) and the **Central Park Zoo** and **Tisch Children's Zoo** (page 275).

The **Sheep Meadow** (66th–69th Streets) to the north of the carousel is much used by New Yorkers for picnics and sunbathing. To its left is the **Tavern on the Green** restaurant (page 161) and to the right is the Mall (69th–72nd Streets), a tree-lined walkway where locals skate and run in summer. Follow the Mall to the top and you will find the **Central Park Bandshell** (70th Street), one of the park's concert venues. Further north is the **Loeb Boathouse** (74th and 75th Streets), which is home to **The Boathouse at Central Park** restaurant (page 161) and where you can hire bikes and boats (page 279). One of the Parks' most visited spots is **Strawberry Fields** (72nd Street). With a mosaic of the word 'Imagine' in the centre, it is a memorial to John Lennon who lived in the Dakota Building nearby.

BRITTIP
Put sturdy shoes on, as this park is big. To get an idea, if you walked all of the paths it would add up to 93km/58mls!

Continuing north, you will come to the **Ramble** (71st Street), a heavily wooded area scattered with paths and streams and a great place for bird-watching, which leads (if you can find the way through) to the Gothic revival **Belvedere Castle** (74th Street) housing another information centre. Also here are the **Delacorte Theater**, where summer productions are presented by Shakespeare in the Park (page 268) and the **Great Lawn** (79th–86th Streets) where the

Central Park

Philharmonic and Metropolitan Opera concerts are held – the only time you can witness tens of thousands of New Yorkers all being quiet at the same time (page 268).

BRITTIP
The Philharmonic/Met Concerts are thrilling, surprisingly tranquil summer experiences. Join tens of thousands of New Yorkers with your picnic on the Great Lawn 2 or 3 hours ahead of concert time. The first concert of the season ends with fireworks.

Further north again is the huge **Jacqueline Kennedy Onassis Reservoir** (86th–96th Streets). A well-kept secret is the formal 2.4-ha/6-acre, 3-part **Conservatory Garden** (104th–106th Streets), where dozens of wedding parties come for photographs on summer weekends. It was bequeathed by the Vanderbilt family, and there are free tours and concerts in the summer.

BRITTIP
Join some of the great volunteer-led tours in Central Park, such as Conservatory Gardens Tour (Sat, April–Oct, 11am and monthly Wed at noon, lasts 75 mins) or Amble Through The Ramble, a stroll through the 38-acre woodland at Belvedere Castle (times and dates vary). More info at centralparknyc.org.

BRITTIP
For a romantic lunch or dinner in the park, book at table at Park View at the Boathouse (page 161).

CENTRAL PARK FOR FAMILIES

Top of the pile for all-round entertainment, Central Park has 21 playgrounds, a small but perfectly formed Wildlife Conservation Center and Children's Petting Zoo, the fun carousel, ice-skating at the Wollman Rink and the Discovery Center at Belvedere Castle, a children's theatre plus a whole host of fun activities. For the schedule of current events, exhibits and workshops visit centralparknyc. org and click: Bring the kids, or on the following attractions.

Entering through the Grand Army Plaza at the southern end of the park at 59th Street, you will find the following family-friendly places to visit:

BELVEDERE CASTLE DISCOVERY CENTER

✉ Mid-park at 97th Street
☎ 212-722 0210
🚇 Subway B, C to 79th Street
🕐 Tues–Sun 10am–5pm; 4pm in winter
$ Free

Sitting on Vista Rock, this is the highest point in the park and gives great views in all directions. The Henry Luce Nature Observatory includes exhibits on flowers, trees and birds in the park. The kids can borrow Discovery Kits, a backpack with binoculars, guidebook, maps and sketching materials for bird-watching in the Ramble and other locations. For children aged 6 and up; those under 12 must be with an adult.

CAROUSEL

✉ Mid-park at 64th Street and 5th Avenue
☎ 212-439 6900
🖱 centralpark.com/pages/attractions/carousel.html
🚇 Subway N, R to 5th Avenue; 6 to 68th Street
🕐 Apr–Nov daily 10am–6pm; Nov–Apr weekends and holidays 10am–4.30pm, weather permitting
$ $2 a ride

A carousel has been on this site since 1871 when the original was powered by a blind mule and a horse that walked a treadmill in an underground pit. Fortunately, no animals have to be put through such torture any more as the current electrical ride was donated by the Michael Friedsam Foundation in 1951. It features some of the largest hand-carved horses in the US.

CHARLES A DANA DISCOVERY CENTER

- ✉ North East Corner at the Harlem Meer/110th Street between 5th and Lenox Avenues
- ☎ 212-860 1370
- 🚇 Subway 2, 3, 6 to 110th Street
- 🕐 Tues–Sun 10am–5pm, closes 4pm in winter
- $ Free

This is the park's only environmental educational centre with children's workshops year-round. Free to all, the centre sponsors workshops, musical performances and park tours and also loans fishing poles for fishing in the well-stocked Meer. Its catch-and-release fishing programme is open to all ages and gives people the chance to fish for large-mouth bass, catfish, golden shiners and bluegills. Open April–Oct.

CENTRAL PARK ZOO AND TISCH CHILDREN'S ZOO

- ✉ Mid-park at 5th Avenue between 63rd Street and 66th Streets
- ☎ 212-439 6500
- 🖱 centralparkzoo.com
- 🚇 Subway N, R to 5th Avenue; 6 to 68th Street
- 🕐 Nov–Mar daily 10am–4.30pm; Mar–Oct Mon–Fri 10am–5pm, weekends and holidays 10am–5.30pm
- $ $10 adults, $7 seniors, $5 3–12, under 3s free

A small but perfectly formed zoo and conservation centre. Exhibits include a polar bear, tamarin monkeys and red pandas, plus other endangered species. Watch the sea lions being fed at 11.30am, 2pm and 4pm. Tisch Children's Zoo is available for toddlers and there is a rainforest journey for older children. Call to register for programmes. The Dancing Crane Cafe is kid-friendly and healthy, or there's a picnic spot if you've bought a snack from elsewhere and the Zootique is a shop full of wild and exciting toys, games and souvenirs.

NORTH MEADOW RECREATION CENTER

- ✉ Mid-park at 97th Street
- ☎ 212-348 4867
- 🚇 Subway B, C, 6 to 96th Street
- 🕐 Sept–Jun Tues–Fri 10am–6pm, Sat–Sun 10am–5pm, closed Mon; July–Aug Mon–Thurs 10am–8pm, Fri 10am–6pm, Sat–Sun 10am–5pm
- $ Free

Open to all ages, the park's largest open space at 9.3ha/23 acres provides free Field Day Kits that include everything you need to equip a family for a day of fun and games in the park, including a basketball, football, Frisbee, skipping rope and hula-hoops. Call in advance to register. The Center also has a 6m/20ft climbing wall with adventure programmes for children and lends equipment for the basketball and handball courts.

SWEDISH COTTAGE MARIONETTE THEATER

- ✉ Mid-park West at 79th Street
- ☎ 212-988 9093
- 🚇 Subway B, C to 79th Street
- 🕐 Oct–Jun Tues–Fri 10.30am and noon, Sat, Sun 1pm
- $ $8 adults, $5 children

Formerly a 19th-century Swedish schoolhouse, this cottage was moved to Central Park in 1876 and now holds various marionette plays for children throughout the year. Book in advance; credit cards are not accepted.

THE WOLLMAN RINK

- ✉ Mid-park East between 62nd and 63rd Streets
- ☎ 212-439 6900
- 🖱 wollmanskatingrink.com
- 🚇 Subway N, R W to 5th Avenue/59th Street
- 🕐 Nov–Mar Mon and Tues 10am–2.30pm, Wed and Thurs 10am–10pm, Fri and Sat 10am–11pm, Sun 10am–9pm
- $ $10 (Mon–Thurs) $14 (Fri–Sun) adults, $5.25 (Mon–Thurs) $5.50 (Fri–Sun) children, $4.75 (Mon–Thurs) $8.25 (Fri–Sun) seniors; skate rental $6 extra, spectators $5

Skating for beginners and ice dancing are offered on this popular rink. An ideal and scenic place to take children and join in the traditional activity of a New York winter.

⚡ BRITTIP

The best way to beat a hot summer in New York City is with a cool lifeguard job earning a minimum $13.57 an hour at the city's pools and beaches. British students are encouraged to apply by April. More information on nycgovparks.org.

Central Park Zoo

THE MAIN PARKS

Battery Park: With a decent yet distant view of the Statue of Liberty, this park is visited by thousands. Situated at the southern tip of Manhattan, it is a beautiful space overlooking New York Harbor and the Hudson River. Here's where you can see Andy Goldsworthy's Garden of Stones (page 115) and The Solaire, the city's first 100% green building (212-417 2000, batteryparkcity.org).

Brooklyn Botanic Garden: Across in the outer borough of Brooklyn, this botanic garden is famous for its cherry trees that bloom from mid-Mar to late May – you can watch their progress on the garden's website. More details are given in Chapter 14 Taste of the Outer Boroughs (page 282) (718-623 7200, bbg.org).

✈ BRITTIP
Go Fish! in the 800km/500mls of shoreline, inland lakes and rivers around New York City. Get the low-down from nycgovparks.org.

Bryant Park: This small park is a great spot for a picnic lunch or you could dine at the fancy restaurant here. It even puts on free films and concerts on Mon nights during the summer (page 266). The Beaux Arts-style Le Carrousel – specially created to complement the park's French classical style – costs $2 a ride and is open 11am–7pm daily. Park open 7am–11pm May–Sept, 7am–7pm winter (212-768 4242, bryantpark.org).

Carl Schurz Park: In the family-friendly Upper East Side, this park sits right next to Gracie Mansion (page 76), once the official residence of the mayor of New York, and has an esplanade along the river. It is a popular destination for families and fitness fanatics, especially at weekends. There are lots of events in the park, including the annual Gracie Square Art Show in the first weekend of Oct where around 100 artists exhibit their work, 10am–5pm, rain or shine (212-459 4455, carlschurzparknyc.org).

City Hall Park: This space near the fabulous Woolworth Building and civic buildings (page 79) is charming. Given a major facelift in 1999, parts of the park have been restored to the way they were in the 18th and 19th centuries, in particular the beautiful lanterns surrounding the gorgeous Jacob Wrey Mould Fountain.

Gramercy Park: East 20th and 21st at Irving Place. One of the prettiest squares in the city, and New York's last private park: visitors can only peek through the railings. The townhouses were designed by some of the city's best architects – think Stanford White and Calvert Vaux – and lived in by some of its most distinguished residents. The brasserie in the Gramercy Park Hotel (page 231) on the square following Ian Schrager's renovations is a great place for lunch.

✈ BRITTIP
Get the low-down on New York park events and activities by category from sports to arts from cityparksfoundation.org.

Luna Park, Union Square: This public park is the gateway to Downtown, a stone's throw from the East Village, SoHo and Greenwich Village, and as close as New York gets to a European piazza. It has an open-air restaurant of the same name and is right by the Union Square green market (grownyc.org/greenmarket), one of the city's largest farmers' markets where regional purveyors sell their products at stalls in the middle of what is now one of the hippest areas of New York. The market opens year round on Mon, Wed, Fri and Sat.

New York Botanical Garden: From antique treasures to family adventures, this extensive, wonderful garden in the Bronx is a must-see. In 2006, it launched the Nolen Greenhouses for Living Collections, considered the most sophisticated behind-the-scenes greenhouses

Castle Clinton Battery Park

in botanic gardens in America. Get there by train from Grand Central station. More details are given in Chapter 14 Taste of the Outer Boroughs (page 289) (718-817 8700, nybg.org).

Prospect Park: A 213-ha/526-acre urban oasis in the heart of Brooklyn, this is an incredible park that was landscaped by the same designers as Central Park. It has a wealth of open spaces, activities, events and museums. More details are given in Chapter 14 Taste of the Outer Boroughs (page 284) (718-965 8951, prospectpark.org).

Riverside Park: Stretching over 6.5km/4mls along the Hudson River from 68th to 155th Streets, this is New York's narrowest park. It is also one of only 5 official scenic landmarks in the city, designed by Frederick Olmstead of Central Park fame. A combination of winding paths and rock outcrops and English country garden, it also has a buzzing marina at 79th Street where you can have a light meal and watch the pleasure craft and houseboats. Make sure you get a glimpse of Riverside Drive, which winds along it as its one of the most attractive streets in the city, with a canopy of American Elms hanging over late 19th-century townhouses. Open 6am–1am daily (212-870 3070, riverside park.org).

Washington Square Park: In the heart of Greenwich Village, this popular park is best known for its bohemian character. It is not so much a park as an area covered in tarmac and filled with a hotchpotch of individuals who flock here to snack and people-watch. The main attraction is the marble Washington

Yankee Stadium

arch designed by Stanford White and built in honour of George Washington's inauguration as the first US president. More details are in Chapter 2 New York Neighbourhoods (page 36) (212-NEW YORK, washingtonsquarepark.org).

BRITTIP

Don't be afraid to wander. New York is one of the safest cities in the US, so do get off the pavements and into the parks. They're easy to navigate and a refreshing break from the midtown madness.

SPECTATOR SPORTS

Ask any New Yorker and they'll tell you that they read their newspapers from back to front. That's just how important sports are to them, and they have plenty to choose from: 2 football teams and 2 baseball teams to support, plus basketball, hockey, tennis and racing. But it can be really tough to get in to watch some of the games, especially to see football's New York Giants and the Mets baseball team in action. Still, it's worth making the effort just to see another side of New York life. If you can't get tickets directly through the box offices listed below, then try TicketMaster on 212-307 7171, ticketmaster. com. They've got most games covered.

An expensive alternative is to try one of the companies that specialises in selling tickets at exorbitant prices – anything from $100 for a football game to $1,000 for a baseball game. They include Prestige Entertainment on 800-243 8849 or 800-2 GET TIX, prestigeentertainment.com; Ticket City on 1-800-SOLD-OUT or 800-765 3688, ticketcity.com.

New York Jets play the New England Patriots

A third alternative is to try a ticket tout – they're known as 'scalpers' in New York – outside Madison Square Garden. However, your best bet is probably to ask the concierge at your hotel. They have an amazing ability to come up with the goods.

MADISON SQUARE GARDEN

This venue on 7th Avenue at 32nd Street (subway A, C, E, 1, 2, 3, 9 to 34th Street/Penn Street) is home to all the following teams. Buy tickets from the Garden Box Office in person at 4 Pennsylvania Plaza, call TicketMaster on 212-307 7171 or visit thegarden.com.

NBA's New York Knicks basketball team: Nov–June

NHL's New York Rangers ice-hockey team: Oct–April

WNBA New York Liberty women's pro basketball team: May–Aug

Madison Square Garden is also famous for its boxing Fight Nights, and it hosts college/high school basketball matches. Since January 2007, the New York Titans of the National Lacrosse Team have also been playing here.

FOOTBALL

The 2 teams are the **New York Giants** (201-935 8111, giants.com) and the **New York Jets** (516-560 8200, newyorkjets.com). Both teams play at the Giants Stadium at Meadowlands (meadowlands.com) in New Jersey (get there on a bus from the Port Authority's 41st Street bus terminal at 42nd Street and 8th Avenue – 0800 772 2222). Meadowlands event information hotline is 201-935 3900 and the box office is 201-507 8900 or TicketMaster at 212-307 7171, ticketmaster.com. You'll have

just as hard a time getting tickets for the Jets as for the Giants. The season runs Sept–Jan.

BASEBALL

The Yankee Stadium (page 290) in the Bronx is the most famous baseball ground, although the original ground at 161st street was demolished in 2009 and the land made into a public park. The new Yankees Stadium, between 161st and 164th Streets, has cost $800m, has capacity for 53,000 and has a grass surface. (Subway 4 (weekdays only), D to 161st Street/Yankee Stadium. Box office 718-293 4300 or yankees.com.

The **New York Mets** play at Shea Stadium (page 294) in Flushing Meadows, Queens (subway 7 to Willetts Point/Shea Stadium). The box office is 718-507 8499/TI000 or visit mets.com. The season for both teams is April–Sept. Post-season games are played in Oct/Nov by the best teams for a gargantuan amount of money. It costs a fortune to get into one of these games, which is why the stands are usually filled with season ticket holders and celebs.

TENNIS

The US Open is held every year at the US Tennis Center in Flushing Meadows, Queens (subway 7 to Willetts Point/Shea Stadium), from late Aug–early Sept. For tickets call TicketMaster on 1-866-OPEN-TIX or the USTA Billie Jean King Tennis Center Ticket office on 718-760 6200 or visit usopen.org. Like Wimbledon, tickets for the finals are impossible to get, but it's worth seeing some of the earlier rounds to watch how it's done American style (page 294 in Chapter 14 Taste of the Outer Boroughs for details on Shea Stadium and Queens).

HORSE RACING

One of the 4 local tracks is **Aqueduct Stadium** in Queens (110-00 Rockaway Blvd, Jamaica) (subway A to Aqueduct Racetrack) Oct–May every Wed–Sun. Free admission 2 Jan–early March, 718-641 4700, nyra.com.

The $1 million **Belmont Stakes** race, on a Saturday in early June, is the major event at the **Belmont Park Racetrack** (2150 Hempstead Turnpike, Elmont, Long Island) (take the Long Island Rail Road's 'Belmont Special' from Penn Station at 7th Avenue and 34th Street) May–July, 516-488 6000, nyra.com/belmont. Tickets from $20 including $5 admission to the clubhouse, gates open 11am.

If you want to take part in some kind of sporting activity while in New York, your best bet is to go to Central Park. Probably the most popular sports here are boating, biking, skating and running.

BIKING

You can rent bikes from the Loeb Boathouse, Central Park, East 72nd Street and Park Drive (212-517 2233, thecentralparkboathouse.com) for $9 per hour for a cruiser, $15/$6 (kids) per hour, for a 21-speed bike including helmet, leaving a credit card deposit or ID and $200 cash; 10am–6pm Apr–Nov. Try tackling the 11km/6ml road loop closed to traffic at weekends. Get to the boathouse with the free trolley shuttle service every 15 minutes from 5th Avenue. For other bike rental information, see Chapter 4 What to See and Do Bike Tours (page 83).

BRITTIP

May is Bike Month in the parks and over 150 bike-related events from rides, races and art shows to a film festival can be found on transalt.org. Keen cyclists may be interested in the Five Boro Bike Tour, a great way to 'do' New York.

BOATING

Also from the Loeb Boathouse (212-517 2233, thecentralparkboathouse.com), you can rent a rowing boat for $12 per hour and $2.50 each additional 15 minutes with a $20 deposit, cash only. Open 10am–dusk.

HORSE RIDING

Riding in Central Park is no longer an option now the Claremont Academy has closed, but pretty riding trails wind through The Ravine, in Prospect Park, which gives you a good excuse to head out to Brooklyn and the Outer Boroughs (page 284). Take a guided trail ride for $37 (book in advance) from Kensington Stables (718-972 4588, kensingtonstables.com).

ICE-SKATING

The Wollman Memorial Rink, mid-Park between 62nd and 63rd Streets (212-439 6900, wollmanskatingrink.com) is open Nov–Mar Mon and Tues 10am–2.30pm, Wed and Thurs 10am–10pm, Fri and Sat 10am–11pm, Sun 10am–9pm. It's $10 (Mon–Thurs) $14 (Fri–Sun) for adults, $5.25 (Mon–Thurs) $5.50 (Fri–Sun) for children and $4.75 (Mon–Thurs) $8.25 (Fri–Sun) seniors; skate rental $6 extra, spectators $5.

The Trump Lasker Rink, north-Park at 106th Street, is a bit rougher but less crowded at $6.25 for adults, $2.25 seniors and $3.50 students and $5.50 for skate rental. Call 914-492 3857 or visit wollmanskatingrink.com for information on lessons.

ROLLER SKATING

On a hot summer's day, Central Park is filled with thousands of in-line skaters. The most popular places to skate are:

The Bandshell: for skate dancers and those who like to watch them.

The Mall: between 69th and 72nd Streets, a tree-lined walkway where locals skate in summer.

West Drive at 67th Street: a slalom course has been set up here for all to try.

Wollman and Lasker Rinks: in summer these rinks are set up for the hot-shot in-line skater; fascinating to watch, too.

If you want to join them, help is at hand from Blades, Board and Skate (888-55 BLADES/888-552 5233, blades.com). It has 15 shops across New York, including 120 West 72nd Street between Columbus and Amsterdam Avenues, and rents skates for $20 a day. You can then join the Tues night skaters who gather at 8pm May–Oct outside Blades Board & Skate at 156 West 72nd Street between Columbus and Amsterdam Streets (empireskate.org). Practise a bit first as they cover up to 11 miles and sometimes more, though the dinner and drinks afterwards is fun.

Central Park Golf Course

BRITTIP
The best time to go skating on the park drives circling Central Park is when they are closed to traffic, Mon–Fri 10am–3pm and 7–10pm and all weekend.

RUNNING

Every day, hundreds of runners encircle Central Park. If you want to run here, it helps to know the distance. The outer loop of the Park is approximately 10km/6mls. The middle loop is about 6km/4mls and the Reservoir loop is about 2km/1¼mls. The Road Runners Club (212-860 4455, nyrrc.org) can provide information on running in New York. Or, for a fun run and a chance to meet some locals join the New York branch of the Hash House Harriers (212-427 4692, hashnyc.com), the 'drinking club with a running problem'.

SWIMMING

Cool off for free in the Lasker Pool (Mid-park from 108th to 109th Streets) – by far one of the favourite kids' activities in Central Park. It is open every day during summer 11am–3pm and 4–7pm. Click on activities on centralparknyc.org or call 212-534 7639. Another free pool can be found at the Asser Levy Recreation Center, East 23rd street at FDR Drive (Subway 6 to 23rd Street). The outdoor pool is free and open from 6.30am–9.30pm Mon–Fri and 8am–4pm Sat–Sun. It's open from July through to Labor Day and is clean and not too packed. (212-447 2020).

TENNIS

There are more tennis courts in Central Park than anywhere else in Manhattan. The Tennis Center can be found between West 94th Street and West 96th Street, near the West Drive (Subway 1, 6, 9, B, C to 96th Street). Courts are open April–Nov and a single play costs $8; lessons are available (212-360-0800, nytennis.net). For tennis courts all around the city, visit nycgovparks.org.

YOGA

Lots of native New Yorkers, from Madonna to Gwyneth Paltrow, when they're visiting home from the UK, love yoga, which is why there are so many studios around the city. If you can't bear not to practise while you're away, or if you just fancy giving it a go, here are some of the best teachers in town. Laughing Lotus Yoga Centre, 59 West 19th Street at 6th Avenue (212-414 2903, laughinglotus. com) teaches a Vinyasa (flow) style of yoga at all levels. Check the website for an ongoing list of classes, which include a groovy Friday Midnight Yoga with live music! Kula Yoga, 28 Warren Street between Church and Broadway (Subway 1, 2, 3, A, C to Chambers Street) also teaches a Vinyasa style of yoga, with classes running throughout the day and evening (212-945 4460, kulayoga.com). If you're staying around SoHo, pop into the SoHo Sanctuary (119 Mercer Street between Prince and Spring streets) for a 1-hour yoga session of SoHo Yoga, $105 (212-334 5550, sohosanctuary.com).

Lasker skating rink, Central Park

CHAPTER 14

Taste of the Outer Boroughs

You may be surprised to learn that it's just a quick 10-minute taxi drive across the Brooklyn Bridge to Brooklyn, a fascinating borough that houses many interesting sights if you have time. Head north-east and you'll hit Queens, just 15 minutes from Manhattan, the largest New York borough and one of its most cosmopolitan, with attractions including the stadium that's home to the Met baseball team. A trip across the East River from Harlem on Manhattan Island takes you to the Bronx, once one of New York's dodgiest areas but now home to some surprisingly good tourist attractions, such as the Bronx Zoo. Of the many islands dotted around Manhattan, Staten Island, south-west of Brooklyn and south of Lower Manhattan is worth a visit for the ferry ride alone, which passes the Statue of Liberty.

A TASTE OF BROOKLYN

Named after the Dutch city Breukelen, Brooklyn, in the very north of Long Island, was once a city in its own right, until it became part of New York City in 1898. Some still refer to the event as its annexation and the borough certainly has its own unique style and language, Brooklynese, which is most obvious in the pronunciation of words such as absoid (absurd), doity (dirty), noive (nerve) and toin (turn). One of the most populous of the city's five boroughs with about 2.5 million residents and accessed by ferries and bridges, Brooklyn houses a melting pot of nationalities that make up its colourful and well-defined neighbourhoods.

Famous Brooklynites include Woody Allen, Barbra Streisand and Mel Brooks, and the John Travolta movie *Saturday Night Fever* was set in Bay Ridge, an Italian neighbourhood in the south. Its architecture has been noticed by celebrities and arty types and a whole host have moved into the neighbourhood, meaning its arts scene gets increasingly cooler.

The two most important 'sightseeing' areas are Brooklyn Heights and Prospect Park, home to the Brooklyn Botanical Gardens and the cutting edge Brooklyn Museum, but there's also fun to be had and a stunning beach at Coney Island, America's original amusement park now enjoying a renaissance.

BROOKLYN HEIGHTS

Whether you've had lunch or dinner, a walk across the stunning Brooklyn Bridge will certainly help the digestion. It's the most famous bridge in New York and was the world's largest suspension bridge when it was completed in 1883. The views are fantastic and strolling along the wooden walkway gives an insight into why it took 16 years to build. If you've walked to Brooklyn from Manhattan via the bridge, you'll find yourself in the heart of Brooklyn Heights.

By the water's edge is the River Café (page 161), a refined and elegant setting to soak up fantastic views of the Manhattan skyline. Night-time is best, when the twinkling lights in the skyscrapers look just like a picture postcard. Have a drink at the bar to enjoy the best views before tucking into a sumptuous supper. It is expensive and you will have to book well in advance, but it's an experience you are never likely to forget. Jackets are essential after 5pm.

The Heights themselves are home to some of the most beautiful and sought-after brownstone townhouses in New York. These were built in the early 18th century when bankers and financiers chose to escape Manhattan, yet could still be close enough to keep an eye on their money. Once again,

Brooklyn Children's Museum

TASTE OF THE OUTER BOROUGHS

281

Tony Muia, who works for A Slice of Brooklyn Bus Tours, was born and bred in Brooklyn and says, 'My favourite summer spot in NYC, which most out-of-towners don't know but which is a true NYC summer hidden gem, is L&B Spumoni Gardens (www.spumonigardens.com) in the Bensonhurst section of Brooklyn. The place has been around since 1939, is a true Brooklyn landmark and is still run by the Barbati family. Sit outside and grab some slices or watch out for cast members of *The Sopranos* who regularly swing by when they're in the neighbourhood.'

Brooklyn Heights is much in demand as an area of tranquillity close to the madness and mayhem of the city. If you walk along the Esplanade, you will see below you the former docks that were the setting for Marlon Brando's movie *On The Waterfront*.

BRITTIP

Williamsburg is fast becoming the hippest place to hang out in Brooklyn, and New York for that matter. It's an ethnic melting pot and there's a thriving arts community. No wonder famous Brits like model Agyness Deyn and TV presenter Alexa Chung have moved there.

BROOKLYN BOTANIC GARDEN

✉ 1000 Washington Avenue between Eastern Parkway and Empire Boulevard
☎ 718-623 7200
🖥 bbg.org
🚇 Subway 2, 3 to Eastern Parkway; Q to Prospect Park
🕐 Tues–Fri 8am–6pm, Sat, Sun 10am–6pm, closed Mon; Nov–mid-Mar closes 4.30pm daily
$ $8 adults, $4 students and seniors, under 12s free

Right next door to Prospect Park and the Brooklyn Museum, the Botanic Garden has 10,000 different kinds of plants from around the world. It includes the world-famous Rose Garden, Japanese Garden, a Shakespeare Garden and the Celebrity Path, which commemorates some of Brooklyn's more famous children. It is most famous, though, for its Japanese cherry trees and huge collection of beautiful bonsai. Relax and enjoy the vibe in its Terrace Café.

KIDS' STUFF IN THE OUTER BOROUGHS

These neighbourhoods are a wonderful place to spend time with children. Brooklyn in particular has a whole host of things on offer to entertain all ages. The massive Prospect Park has its own children's museum, a zoo, a boating lake and wildlife activities including the Wollman Rink, the Audubon Centre at the Boathouse, the Carousel, Prospect Park Zoo and the Lefferts Homestead Children's Museum and America's largest amusement park at Coney Island lies to the south.

Try these for size:

Bronx Zoo: page 288.
Brooklyn Children's Museum: below.
New York Aquarium, Coney Island: page 287.
Prospect Park: page 284.
Queens County Farm Museum: page 293.
WonderWheel, Coney Island: page 287

BRITTIP

Do as the locals do and head out to Brooklyn Botanical Gardens for Sakura Matsuri, the spring 2-day Cherry Blossom festival, and sample Japanese art and food after a stroll under the canopy.

BROOKLYN CHILDREN'S MUSEUM

✉ 145 Brooklyn Avenue at St Mark's Avenue, Crown Heights
☎ 718-735 4400
🖥 bchildmus.org
🚇 Subway 3, C to Kingston Avenue
🕐 Spring, Wed–Fri 12–5pm, Sat–Sun 10am–5pm, Mon & Tues closed; rest of year Wed–Fri 1–6pm, Sat, Sun 11am–6pm, closed Mon, Tues
$ $7.50, under 1s free

A fabulous place for children, this was the first-ever museum for little ones. They can have a ball here playing with synthesisers, operating water wheels to dam a stream, dancing on the keys of a walk-on piano and playing instruments from around the world. The museum reopened above ground in 2007 following a $39 million expansion to double its size and it now has a Kids' Café among other exciting developments such as state-of-the-art technology, making it New York's first Green Museum. Check the website for up-to-date details and information about workshops, performances and events.

BROOKLYN HISTORICAL SOCIETY

- ✉ 128 Pierrepont Street at Clinton Street
- ☎ 718-222 4111
- ⌂ brooklynhistory.org
- 🚇 Subway 2, 3, 4, 5 to Borough Hall, A, C, F to Jay Street/Borough Hall, M, R to Court Street
- ◷ Wed–Sun 12–5pm; closed Mon, Tues; Sat 10am–5pm
- $ $6 adults, $4 students and seniors, under 12s free

It's said that 1 in 7 Americans can trace their roots to Brooklyn and, as many US families originally came from the UK. It's worth popping into this academic retreat to see if you can trace your family tree. Plus there are innovative exhibitions, educational programmes and a wonderful library.

BROOKLYN MUSEUM

- ✉ 200 Eastern Parkway at Washington Avenue
- ☎ 718-638 5000, TTY 718-399 8440
- ⌂ brooklynmuseum.org
- 🚇 Subway 2, 3 to Eastern Parkway/Brooklyn Museum
- ◷ Sun 11am–6pm, Wed–Fri 10am–5pm, first Sat of month 11am–11pm, all other Sat 11am–6pm, closed Mon, Tues
- $ Suggested donation $10 adults; $6 concessions and children; under 12s free

◀🇬🇧▶ BRITTIP

To enjoy some of the delicious Middle Eastern cuisine that centres around Brooklyn's Atlantic Avenue, join a tour with Savory Sojourns (page 88), whose expert guide Addie Tomei will reveal this treasure trove of sights and smells with stops at delicatessens and markets, where you can try treats such as fresh pitta.

The spring of 2004 saw the opening of a magnificent glass entrance pavilion, complementing the beautiful 19th-century Beaux Arts building that has housed this huge and important art museum since 1897. A new central lobby and public plaza have also been constructed, making the building the most visitor-friendly museum in NYC. With one of the best collections of Egyptian art in the world, housed on the 3rd floor, it also has an extraordinary collection of Auguste Rodin sculptures among the million objects in its permanent collection. Well known for its African art, it was the first-ever museum to display what were once considered to be anthropological objects as fine art. The museum has a long tradition of collecting non-Western art and, since 1934, it has

Brooklyn Museum

concentrated on fine art. The collections comprise: Egyptian, Classical and Ancient Middle Eastern Art; Painting and Sculpture; Arts of Africa, the Pacific and the Americas; Asian Art; Decorative Arts; and Prints, Drawings and Photography.

◀🇬🇧▶ BRITTIP

The Brooklyn Art and Garden ticket gives an 8% saving on the cost of separate tickets to the Brooklyn Museum and the Brooklyn Botanic Garden.

The Brooklyn Museum is known for its ground-breaking art exhibitions and has a cinema theatre that screens movies and documentaries coinciding with the exhibitions. In March 2007, it hosted one of the biggest arts events of the year in New York, the opening of the Elizabeth A Sackler Centre for Feminist Art on the 4th floor. Its 8,300sq m/10,000sq yd space includes a gallery exhibiting 'The Dinner Party' by Judy Chicago, an icon of 1970s feminist art, which commemorates important women from history, and 999 other women whose names are inscribed in gold on the whitetile floor.

The Brooklyn Museum also organises gallery talks, films, concerts, tours and performances for children and adults. The 1st Sat of each month is known as Target First Saturdays, when a free programme of events is offered from 5–11pm that includes a hands-on look at art, a film, storytelling and activities for all the family and a live band to dance to. As they're popular, get there early. On the third Wed of every month, 5–9pm, is BrooklyNites, a live jazz evening, for $10. Gallery tours are free with admission Wed–Fri at 1.30pm and weekends at 2pm, 3pm and 4pm. Otherwise, you can pick up an audio tour for $3 or explore the museum with a free printed family guide.

It's useful to know that the museum has its own subway stop at Eastern Parkway, just 1 stop down from Brooklyn's Grand Army Plaza. This stands in a complex of 19th-century parks and gardens that includes Prospect Park, the Brooklyn Botanic Garden and the Wildlife Centre. It takes about 30 minutes to get to the museum from Midtown Manhattan.

GRAND ARMY PLAZA AND PROSPECT PARK

✉ At the intersection of Flatbush Avenue, Eastern Parkway and Prospect Park West
☎ 718-965 8951
🖰 prospectpark.org
🚗 Subway 2, 3 to Grand Army Plaza; B, F, Q, S to Prospect Park
🕐 Open daily 5am–1am
$ Free

This urban oasis with 237ha/585 acres of meadows, waterfalls, fields and forest is one of Brooklyn's most beautiful areas. The enormous Prospect Park and Grand Army Plaza were laid out by Olmsted and Vaux after they'd completed Central Park, and many feel that these creations were even better. It contains the following:

The Arch: New York's answer to the Arc de Triomphe, the elaborately carved, 24m/80ft arch provides a grand gateway to Prospect Park, plus a majestic overview of both the park and Manhattan. It was built as a memorial to the defenders of the Union in the Civil War, and is now the base for a series of bronze sculptures that aregrouped all around the Plaza, includingone of John F Kennedy.

Art in the Arch: Exhibitions are held in the spring and autumn, generally featuring artwork with a distinct Brooklyn theme. The Arch is open to the public during spring and autumn when an exhibition is on. Weekends and holidays 1–5pm, 718-965 8943.

Long Meadow: At nearly 1.6km/1ml in length, the Long Meadow stretches from the Park's northern end at Grand Army Plaza to its western end at Prospect Park Southwest. Once the home of grazing sheep and lawn tennis and croquet players, it is now frequented by strollers, kite-flyers and the Little League Baseball. At the Picnic House you'll find WCs and picnic tables, while the Metropolitan Opera and the New York Philharmonic Orchestra put on summer events here (page 268), 718-965 8951.

The Long Meadow is accessible via the Grand Army Plaza and any entrance along Prospect Park West, such as 3rd Street or 9th Street. It is free to enter and is only closed 1–5am.

The Bandshell: Close to Long Meadow, this is one of the park's main attractions for live outdoor entertainment. With its 3-storey-high acoustic shell, raised stage and large circular plaza, the Bandshell features food and drinks, WCs and first-come, first-served seating in the 2,000-seat plaza or 5,000-seat lawn. In addition to musical performances, the Bandshell hosts film events on its 6.5m/21ft high and 15m/50ft wide movie screen. But it is best known for the Celebrate Brooklyn! Performing Arts Festival – a series of music, dance, film and spoken word performances each June–Aug at 7.30pm for a $3 donation, which attract nearly 250,000 people per season. For further information, 718-855 7882, briconline.org. The nearest subway is the F train to 15th Street/Prospect Park Station or the 2, 3 to Grand Army Plaza.

🇬🇧 BRITTIP

Walking tours to Brooklyn's 'Gold Coast', the celebrity-packed Park Slope and its masterpiece of design, Prospect Park, are offered by Big Onion (212-439 1090, bigonion.com).

The Ravine: One of Prospect Park's most natural features, here you will find a steep narrow gorge lined with the trees and foliage of Brooklyn's only forest. Still recovering from decades of overuse that caused soil erosion, the Ravine and surrounding woodlands have been gradually restored by the Prospect Park Alliance since 1996. You can explore on your own or take one of the weekend guided nature tours.

The Ravine is open daily 5am–1am, with possible tours by arrangement from the Audubon Center at The Boathouse. For

🇬🇧 BRITTIP

The Grand Army Plaza is home to the 2nd largest open-air green market in New York. Held every Sat 8am–4pm, it sells more than 600 varieties of farm-fresh fruits, vegetables, baked goods, dairy products and more.

information on tours, 718-287 3400. Best subways to take are the F to 15th Street/ Prospect Park or 7th Avenue or the Q to 7th Avenue.

PROSPECT PARK FOR FAMILIES

With nature trails, wildlife and activities from boating, skating and baseball to arts and crafts, there is plenty of entertainment for the family in this mini Central Park.

Audubon Center at The Boathouse

- ✉ Lincoln Road/Ocean Avenue entrance to Prospect Park
- ☎ 718-287 3400 Audubon Center; 718-965 8999 events hotline
- 🖱 prospectpark.org
- 🚇 Subway Q, S, B to Prospect Park
- 🕐 April–Nov Thurs–Sun and school holidays noon–5pm; Dec–Mar weekends and school holidays noon–4pm
- $ Free admission. Electric boat tour $8 for those aged 13 and over, $4 for 3–12s, children 2 and under free. Pedal boat rental available from the Wollman Rink for $15 per hour.

The design of this beautiful 1905 Beaux Art boathouse, with its elegant arches, decorative tiles and classical balcony, was based on a 16th-century Venetian library. Now an official Historic New York City Landmark, it is home to the state-of-the-art Audubon Center, which is dedicated to preserving wildlife and natural education. Families can take tours along the new Lullwater Nature Trail or on the Lullwater by the electric boat Independence (April–Oct), as well as one of four nature trails or participate in family activities such as craftwork, music and technology sessions. Regular weekly events include Nature Crafts Sat–Sun 1–3pm, and free birdwatching on Sat noon–1.30pm. Don't miss the annual Macy's Fishing Contest mid July.

The Carousel

- ✉ Children's Corner, Prospect Park, at intersection of Flatbush and Ocean Avenues and Empire Blvd
- ☎ 718-789 2822
- 🖱 prospectpark.org
- 🚇 Subway Q, S, B to Prospect Park
- 🕐 Noon–5pm April–May and Sept–Oct weekends Jun–Aug Thurs–Sun, plus all public holidays.
- $ $2 per ride; 5 tickets for $9

Right next door to the zoo and museum is the magnificently carved carousel, which features 51 horses, a lion, giraffe, a deer and 2 dragon-pulled chariots. It is also one of the few carousels in the world that is wheelchair accessible.

Audubon Center

Lefferts Historic House

- ✉ Children's Corner, Prospect Park, at intersection of Flatbush and Ocean Avenues and Empire Blvd
- ☎ 718-789 2822
- 🖱 prospectpark.org
- 🚇 Subway Q, S, B to Prospect Park
- 🕐 April–Dec Thurs–Sun 12am–5pm; Dec–March 12am–4pm
- $ Free

Right by the main Grand Army Plaza entrance to Prospect Park stands this restored 18th-century farmhouse, built by Dutch settlers in Brooklyn. Children can play with traditional toys, cooking tools, and take part in craft activities such as candle-making, sewing, butter-churning and making fire with a flint and steel. At weekends throughout the summer, stories are told under a tree, there are hoop games to play and gardening to do including planting potatoes and flax which are harvested by the kids in the autumn.

Prospect Park Zoo

- ✉ Prospect Park, 450 Flatbush Avenue
- ☎ 718-399 7339
- 🖱 prospectparkzoo.com
- 🚇 Subway Q, S or B to Prospect Park
- 🕐 Mar–Oct Mon–Fri 10am–5pm; weekends and holidays 10am–5.30pm; Nov–Mar daily 10am–4.30pm
- $ $7 adults, $4 seniors, $3 children 3–12; under 3s free

Again close to the Grand Army Plaza entrance to Prospect Park, this is Brooklyn's only zoo. It features nearly 400 animals and more than 80 species in an environment that gives children close-up views of some of the world's most unusual creatures. They include prairie dogs, wallabies, tamarin monkeys, baboons, a red panda, and a vibrant band of birds, reptiles and amphibians. The interactive Discovery Center is open every weekend 11am–3pm. Other fun family activities include Storytelling Tues and Games Thurs in summer 11am–1pm and 2.30pm–4pm, milking cows mid-May to mid-Oct or catching the daily sea lion feeding at 11.30am, 2pm and 4pm.

The Wollman Rink

Like its namesake in Central Park, it offers ice-skating in winter and pedal boats on the lake May–Oct. It's best accessed through the

Parkside/Ocean Avenues entrance. Ice-skating costs $5 for adults, $3 for children 14 and under, and seniors. Admission is half price on Fridays. Skate rental for $6.50. Pedal boating costs $15 an hour (cash only). Hours vary by day and season; 718-287 6431 or visit prospectpark.org for details.

NEW YORK CITY TRANSIT MUSEUM

- ✉ Schermerhorn Street at Boerum Place
- ☎ 718-694 1600
- ⌖ mta.info
- 🚗 Subway M, R to Court Street; A, C, G to Hoyt-Schermerhorn Street
- ⏰ Tues–Fri 10am–4pm, Sat, Sun noon–5pm, closed Mon
- $ $5 adults, $3 seniors and children 3–17; Wed seniors free

This is a great museum for transport buffs of all ages and is located in an old subway station in Brooklyn Heights. Steel, Stone and Backbone traces the tale of the city's subway and includes old subway cars that you can get on, and you can even hang on to one of the original leather straps (nowadays replaced by metal poles and bars) that created the nickname of 'straphangers' for people who use the subway. The museum has recently undergone a major renovation and now has a new art gallery, a classroom for a children's workshop, a computer lab and a reference library. The main interactive exhibit depicts the history of buses and trolleys in the city, with a display of more than 200 trolleys and buses. There is also a film about the building of the subway, old turnstiles, maps and a gift shop.

JEWISH CHILDREN'S MUSEUM

- ✉ 792 Eastern Parkway at corner of Kingston Avenue, Crown Heights, Brooklyn
- ☎ 718-907 8833
- ⌖ jcmonline.org
- 🚗 Subway 3 to Kingston Avenue
- ⏰ Mon–Thurs 10am–4pm, Sun 10am–6pm; closed Fri, Sat (apart from select evenings)
- $ $10 per person; children under 2 free

The first of its kind in the world, opened in 2005 at a cost of $35 million by Jewish Children International, its interactive multimedia exhibits entertain, educate and engage children of all backgrounds about Jewish heritage.

CONEY ISLAND

At the Southern end of Brooklyn, America's largest amusement park is undoubtedly tacky, and has definitely seen better days, but that doesn't stop children having fun, making it a great family day out.

It has around 35 rides and other attractions along a 6.4km/4mls stretch and the Native American Indians called it 'land without shadows' as its stunning beach was bathed in sunlight all day.

BRITTIP

Visit coneyisland.com for the schedule of quirky shows by the seashore such as the Coney Island Circus Sideshow and the Mermaid Parade.

New York City Transit Museum

New York Aquarium

Gentrification is spilling over from Brooklyn making this an up-and-coming neighbourhood, with a $1.5b renovation and expansion plan that started in 2007 and continues, adding a water park, a manmade canal for boat rides, 21 rides and shopping, hotels and cinemas. In the meantime, MCU Park (718-499 8497, http://brooklyncyclones.com) has been bringing in the crowds to see the popular baseball league team The Brooklyn Cyclones.

✚ BRITTIP

Try one of Nathan's hot dogs (516-338 8500, nathans famous.com) a Coney Island institution and still sold from its original site. Nathan holds an eating contest here every 4 July; the record is 68 hot dogs with buns in 10 minutes!

NEW YORK AQUARIUM

- ✉ 610 Surf Avenue at West 8th Street, Brooklyn
- ☎ 718-265-FISH
- 🖰 nyaquarium.com
- 🚗 Subway F, Q to West 8th Street, NY Aquarium
- ☼ Winter (to April) 10am–4.30pm; 10am–5pm Mon–Fri, 10am–5.30pm weekends.
- $ $13 adults, $9 under 13s, $10 seniors, under 2s free, groups $6

Most famous for its beluga whale family and performing sea lions, this excellent aquarium has another unusual exhibit showing the creatures that live in New York's East River. Sharks, dolphins and a re-creation of the Pacific coast also feature. Penguin feeding 10.50am.

WONDERWHEEL

- ✉ Boardwalk at Denos Vourderis Place (3059 West 12th St),Coney Island
- ☎ 718-372 2592
- 🖰 wonderwheel.com
- 🚗 Subway Q to West 8th Street, B, F, Q, N to Stillwell Avenue
- ☼ April, May, Sept, Oct open weekends and holidays only. Open Mon–Sun from noon–late during summer

✚ BRITTIP

A stroll along the legendary Coney Island boardwalk to Brighton Beach will take you to Little Odessa, a thriving Russian community complete with traditional bathhouses, bookshops and restaurants serving borscht, vodka and caviar.

$ $6 adults or pack of 5 $25; children $3 each or 10 pack $25

A New York landmark, the wheel was built in 1920 by the Eccentric Ferris Wheel Company using 100% Bethlehem Steel forged right on the premises! WonderWheel is part of Coney Island's heritage and part of the Coney Island Renaissance project with the brand new Luna Park opening in late May 2010.

A TASTE OF THE BRONX

Diversity definitely drives the energy of this vibrant destination in the northernmost tip of the city. Nearly 50% of Bronx residents are Latino, including its most famous former resident Jennifer Lopez, with the highest concentration hailing from 'the islands' – Puerto Rico and the Dominican Republic – and Mexico. However, it's also a place where traditions from Italy and Ireland continue to flourish, and a growing number of Asian immigrants are now making this area their home.

The Bronx has a scary reputation, but parts of it are very safe and have attractions that make a visit here well worthwhile. The Bronx history dates back to 1609 when Henry Hudson took refuge from a storm here. It is the northernmost borough of New York and the only one on the mainland. In 1639 Jonas Bronck, a Swedish captain from the Netherlands, settled here with his wife and servants. The story goes that when people left Manhattan to visit the family, they would say they were going to the Broncks' and the name stuck.

The horrible part is the south Bronx, but even here things are improving. In the north lies the beautiful Botanical Garden that includes a huge chunk of the original forests that once covered all of New York, and the Bronx Zoo, one of the world's leading wildlife conservation parks.

BRONX MUSEUM OF THE ARTS

- ✉ 1040 Grand Concourse at 165th Street
- ☎ 718-681 6000
- 🖰 bronxmuseum.org
- 🚗 Subway B, D to 167th Street/Grand Concourse, 4 to 161st Street/Yankee Stadium

Ⓒ Thurs–Sun 11am–6pm; Mon–Wed closed
$ $5 adults, $3 students and seniors, under 12s free; free Fri

Housed in an attractive glass building, the museum's collection consists of more than 700 contemporary works of art in all media by African, Asian and Latin American artists. At the end of 2006, the museum expanded into a $19 million new building that won the Art's Commission's Excellence in Design prize, giving it a major new gallery, events space and an outdoor terrace to sit and absorb the edgy vibe of this vibrant area.

◀⬛▶ BRITTIP
If you're looking to eat in the Bronx, visit the Neighbourhood section of the Bronx Museum of the Arts website bronxmuseum.org for some suggestions.

BRONX ZOO AND WILDLIFE CONSERVATION SOCIETY
✉ Bronx River Parkway at Fordham Road
☎ 718-220 5100
🖰 bronxzoo.org
🚇 Subway 2, 5 to East Tremont Avenue/ West Farms Square
Ⓒ April–Oct Mon–Fri 10am–5pm, Sat, Sun 10am–5.30pm daily; rest of the year 10am–4.30pm
$ $15 adults, $13 seniors, $11 children, under 3s free; suggested donation on Wed; under 17s must be accompanied by an adult; cheaper Nov–Mar; individual attractions/rides $3–5 each, Pay-One-

Price ticket that includes admission and all rides $27 adult, $23 seniors, $21 children

The Bronx Zoo is known as New York's 'wild backyard' and respected worldwide for its tradition of conservation and ecological awareness alongside the naturalistic habitats it provides, such as the African Plains where antelope roam. It is the largest urban zoo in America and houses 4,000 animals and 560 species. The Congo Gorilla Forest is a 2.5ha/6-acre rainforest, inhabited by 2 troops of gorillas. Other highlights include the rare snow leopard in the Himalayan Highlands and meeting Big Bears like Veronica and Betty, two grizzlies and cubs Glacier, Kootz, Denali and Sitka. Don't miss Tiger Mountain, which takes you a whisker away from the largest member of the cat family.

Disney-style rides include a guided monorail tour through Wild Asia, an aerial safari, camel rides and a zoo shuttle. There is also a children's zoo. Some of the exhibits and all the rides, apart from the bug carousel, are open only April/May–Oct. For a tour by Friends of Wildlife Conservation, 718-220 5103.

◀⬛▶ BRITTIP
If you want to discover more of Little Italy and the Irish neighbourhood of Woodlawn, contact Susan Birnbaum, who runs SusanSez NYC Walkabouts (917–509 3111, dbsystems group.com/susansez). She leads tours around Arthur Avenue and beyond on her Bronx Walkabout.

LITTLE ITALY
Technically, this area is known as Belmont or simply Arthur Avenue, but it is tagged the Little Italy of the Bronx. Take the D train to Tremont Avenue and walk east to Arthur Avenue. Treat yourself to a relaxing lunch at one of the many Italian restaurants here. The old-world Belmont District is a charming area filled with shops selling every Italian delicacy you can think of. To catch a movie stop by the Enrico Fermi Cultural Centre in the Belmont Library (610 East 186th Street at Hughes Avenue, 718-933 6410, nypl.org/branch/local/bx/ber.cfm).

◀⬛▶ BRITTIP
If you're feeling peckish, pop into Mike's Deli in the Arthur Avenue Retail Market (718-562 0129, arthuravenue.com) for a taste of Italy.

Bronx Zoo

Afterwards, walk north on Arthur, then east on Fordham Road past Fordham University to the Bronx Park.

NEW YORK BOTANICAL GARDEN

- ✉ Bronx River Parkway and Fordham Road
- ☎ 718-817 8700
- ⌂ nybg.org
- 🚌 B, D or 4 to Bedford Park and then the BX26 bus or Metro-North from Grand Central Terminal.
- 🕐 April–Oct Tues–Sun 10am–6pm; Nov–Mar 10am–5pm, closed Mon
- $ Grounds only ticket $6 adults, $3 seniors/students, $1 children 2–12, under 2s free. Free to all Wed and Sat 10am–12pm.

Originally supported by magnates Cornelius Vanderbilt, Andrew Carnegie and JP Morgan, society folk still support these gardens today. Check out the Peggy Rockefeller Rose Garden, with over 2,700 bushes. This is one of the oldest and largest botanic gardens in the world, and the magnificent Victorian iron and glass conservatory near the main entrance is modelled on the one at Kew Gardens in London. It has been refurbished to perfection and is home to the gardens highlight, A World of Plants, a trip through the world's ecosystems, from dripping rainforest to dry desert. In the grounds, you can see the stunning Bronx River Gorge where the meandering waterway tumbles over a rocky outcrop formed by the retreat of the Wisconsin Ice Sheet. For thousands of years, New York was covered by a hemlock forest and a 16ha/40-acre fragment remains in the gardens. Look out for the rock carving of a turtle drawn by the Weckquasgeek Indians many years ago. The 50 gardens and 100ha/250 acres include The Everett Children's Adventure Garden, which is a great outdoor science experience for kids, and the Family Garden, created by children. There are also puppet shows, dance and music concerts, and other events throughout the year.

✚ BRITTIP

The Botanical Garden is just a road away from the Bronx Zoo – sadly that is an 8-lane highway and the entrances are 1.6km/1ml apart. In the absence of a pedestrian link, take a short taxi ride. Call Miles Taxi Co on **718-884 8888.**

VAN CORTLANDT HOUSE MUSEUM

- ✉ Van Cortlandt Park, Broadway at West 246th Street
- ☎ 718-543 3344
- ⌂ vancortlandthouse.org

New York Botanical Garden

- 🚌 Subway 1 to 242nd Street/Van Cortlandt Park
- 🕐 Tues–Fri 10am–3pm, Sat, Sun 11am–4pm, closed Mon
- $ $5 adults, $3 seniors/students, free on Wed, under 12s free

Once an 18th-century family-run plantation, Van Cortlandt House was turned into a historic house museum at the end of the 19th century by the National Society of Colonial Dames. Now you can walk through the family's public and private rooms, including a slave bedchamber, and see the fascinating decorative art collections from the colonial and federal periods.

WAVE HILL

- ✉ West 249th Street at Independence Avenue
- ☎ 718-549 3200
- ⌂ wavehill.org
- 🚌 Subway A to 207th Street or and then the Bx7/Bx10 bus on Broadway northbound to West 252nd Street or take 1 train to West 242nd Street where a free shuttle runs at 10mns past the hour from 9.10am to 3.10pm
- 🕐 15 April–14 Oct Tues–Sun 9am–5.30pm; June and July until 9pm Wed; 15 Oct–14 April 9am–4.30pm
- $ $8 adults, $4 seniors/students, $2 children over 6; free Tue and Sat 9am–noon year-round

A scenic public garden and cultural centre, Wave Hill holds international events throughout the year, such as the Barefoot Dancing series when you're invited to move to the music from Kotchegna or folk music from Bulgaria. So it's worth checking the website to see what's happening when you visit. Each Sat Irving Yee teaches Tai Chi Chuan to beginners at 10am for $15. There are free garden and conservatory tours on Sundays and Tuesday and sunset tours at 7pm on Wednesdays throughout the summer..

Yankee Stadium

BRITTIP

Sports fans can take a break and enjoy a hot dog and a drink at the Sidewalk Café on the Plaza next to Gates 4 and 6 at the Yankee Stadium.

YANKEE STADIUM

✉ River Avenue at 161st Street
☎ 718-293 4300
🖰 yankees.com
🚇 Subway 4 (east side), (weekdays only), B and D (west side) to 161st Street/Yankee Stadium

After the original Yankees Stadium was demolished in 2009, a new Yankee Stadium, which cost a cool $1.3 billion became the legendary New York Yankees new home in April 2009. As for the old Yankee home, it's to become a green space for the South Bronx featuring soccer and football fields, tennis and basketball courts and even a waterfront esplanade with play and picnic areas.

A TASTE OF QUEENS

The largest of all the New York boroughs at 290sq km/112sq mls, Queens has the highest percentage of first-generation immigrants. Given the borough's suburban look, it is hard to imagine it as the densely forested area it was 4 centuries ago. Then it was inhabited by the Algonquin Indian tribes, who fished in its freshwater streams and creeks, hunted game and gathered shellfish from its bays. It is also difficult to picture 17th-century Queens and the borough's early Dutch and English farmers, along with Quakers fighting for religious freedom.

Yet there remain places where such scenes can easily be reconstructed, such as at the Jamaica Bay Wildlife Refuge (718-318 4340) on open marshland, once the territory of Jameco Indians and now home to many species of birds spotted along the nature walkways, and the Queens County Farm Museum (page 293). This has the largest tract of farmland left in New York and its colonial farmhouse is thought to date back to 1772.

BRITTIP

The Queens Council on the Arts produces an annual Cultural Guide filled with information about the borough. Order from 718-647 5036 or queenscouncilarts.org.

Today, Queens is as much about the ethnic diversity of the borough and in each of the places mentioned in this section you will find many examples of the cultures of people from Asia, the West Indies, Latin America and Greece. In fact, Queens is home to the largest Greek population outside of Greece; Astoria is the Athens of the United States, with authentic restaurants and markets on the main thoroughfare of Ditmars Boulevard. Jackson Heights is a little India, with colourful sari shops, restaurants and video stores with the latest Bollywood offerings.

In fact, so diverse is this sprawling borough that the local subway line number 7 has been

BRITTIP

For shopping, attractions, events, tours and restaurants in Queens, click on to discoverqueens.info or call 718-263 0594.

jokingly renamed the International Express. It's also home to JFK and LaGuardia airports, so Queens is often the first entry point for millions of people to New York and the rest of the United States.

Top things to see in this borough include the American Museum of the Moving Image in Astoria and in Flushing, The New York Hall of Science, with 450 exhibits in a bubble-shaped space-age building, and the Queen's Museum of Art (queensmuseum.org, 718 592 9700), which even has aeroplanes flying over its miniature model of New York City. A stroll through Little Asia en route to the Shea Stadium, home to the Mets baseball team, will give you a taste of the ethnic diversity of this borough. The mouthwatering smells coming from the Vietnamese, Chinese and Korean restaurants may even make you want to stop awhile.

AMERICAN MUSEUM OF THE MOVING IMAGE

✉ 35th Avenue at 36th Street, Astoria
☎ 718-784 0077
⌂ ammi.org
🚇 Subway G, R, V to Steinway Street
🕐 Tues–Fri, 10am–3pm
$ Suggested admission $7 adults, seniors/ students; children under 8 free

Partly closed due to expansion works until early 2011. You can, however, see the museum's interactive exhibition Behind The Screen during construction. The plan is to double the size of the existing building, providing visitors with even more experiences with motion pictures, television and digital media. The 3-storey construction will be clad in pale blue aluminium panels for an eye-catching effect, so you won't miss it when you reach 35th Avenue. When you pass through the doors, you'll walk into a 242-video monitor installation and images will be projected on to the wall. There'll also be a 264-seat film theatre, complete with an orchestra pit for musical accompaniment to silent films, plus a 68-seat screening room for special screenings and lectures. Finally, the grand stairs from the lobby to the second floor will have the capacity to turn into a video screening amphitheatre and will be a space for changing video art. Go and investigate, but check on the website first to make sure the grand unveiling due early 2011 has happened!

 BRITTIP

Astoria is the heart of New York's Greek community and is filled with delis and restaurants. After you've been to the American Museum of the Moving Image, head to 31st Street and Broadway for a spot of lunch.

BOWNE HOUSE

✉ 37-01 Bowne Street, Flushing
☎ 718-359 0528
⌂ bownehouse.org
🚇 Subway 7 to Main Street
🕐 Tues, Sat, Sun 2.30–4.30pm
$ $4 adults, $3 seniors, $2 students and children under 12

Currently closed for renovation until 2012 although group visits to the grounds can be organised by appointment. You can walk to this NYC landmark from Corona Park. Built in 1661 by John Bowne, this is the oldest house in Queens and the second oldest in New York City. It is a rare example of Dutch–English architecture, with an unusual collection of decorative arts, paintings and furniture, all of which belong to 9 generations of the Bowne family. Bowne was a pivotal figure in the fight for religious freedom in the New World.

Bowne House

LITTLE ASIA

✉ Roosevelt Avenue and Main Street

The nearby jumble of Chinese, Korean, Thai and Vietnamese markets and restaurants offers everything from soft-shell turtles and bentwood bows to kimchi and wire baskets. At 45–57 Bowne Street is the beautiful Hindu Temple Society of North America (718-460 8484, nyganeshtemple.org), which is adorned with carvings of Hindu gods and is open Mon–Fri 8am–9pm; 7.30pm–9pm weekends..

Dinner: Choopan Kabab House, 43–27 Main Street, 718-539 3180. A great place to try out Afghan fare. Alternatively, you could sample Korean food at the 24-hour Kum Gang San, 128-38 Northern Boulevard between Bowne and Union Streets, 718-461 0909, kumgangsan.net.

Nightclubs: Try Chibcha (79-05 Roosevelt Avenue, 718-429 9033, elchibcha.com, subway 7 to 82nd Street), a Colombian nightclub and restaurant. Or, if you prefer, Sun night is Irish music night at Taylor Hall (45 Queens Boulevard, subway 7 to 46th Street). For something more exotic, there are operettas, flamenco and tango shows at the Thalia Spanish Theatre (41–17 Greenpoint Avenue, Sunnyside, 718-729 3880, thaliatheatre.org, subway 7 to 40th Street).

⊞▶ BRITTIP

For more information on the arts in Queens, contact the Queens Council on the Arts on 718-647 5036 or visit queenscouncil arts.org.

LITTLE INDIA

Take the International Express – subway 7 from Times Square to the 74th Street/ Broadway station and, at 74th Street between Roosevelt and 37th Avenues at Jackson Heights – to find this Indian haven. Stroll through the cumin-scented streets looking at the intricately embellished gold and silk on display. Two stops you should include are the Menka Beauty Salon (37-56, 74th Street, Jackson Heights, 718-424 6851) where traditional henna designs are drawn on the skin, and the Butala Emporium (37-46 74th Street, Jackson Heights, 718-899 5590), which sells everything from Southern Asian art and children's books in Punjabi to Ayurvedic medicine and religious items.

Lunch: Travel one stop to 82nd Street in Elmhurst for an Argentinian lunch at La Fusta (80-32 Baxter Avenue, 718-429 8222, lafustanewyork.com).

NEW YORK HALL OF SCIENCE

✉ 47-01 111th Street at 47th Avenue, Flushing Meadows/Corona Park at 48th Avenue
☎ 718-699 0005
⌂ nyscience.org
🚗 Subway 7 to 111th Street
🕐 Sept–Mar Tues–Thurs 9.30am–2pm, Fri 9.30am–5pm, Sat, Sun 10am–6pm; April–June Mon–Thurs 9.30am–2pm, Fri 9.30am–5pm, Sat, Sun 10am–6pm; July–Aug Mon–Fri 9.30am–5pm, Sat, Sun 10am–6pm
$ $11 adults, $8 seniors and children 2–17, free Sept–June Fri 2–5pm and Sun 10–11am

The bubble-shaped building features memorable daily science demonstrations and 450 interactive exhibits explaining the mysteries of digital technology, quantum theory, microbes and light and also offers slides, whirligigs, space nets and a giant teeter-totter (seesaw). Rated as the best science museum in the country, all events are free with admission.

THE NOGUCHI MUSEUM

✉ 9-01 33rd Road at Vernon Boulevard, Long Island City
☎ 718-204 7088
⌂ noguchi.org
🚗 Subway N, W to Broadway stop in Queens, F to Queensbridge/21st Street or 7 to 33rd Street/Vernon Boulevard (Wed–Fri), then Q103 bus or take the Sunday Shuttle from Manhattan
🕐 Wed–Fri 10am–5pm; Sat, Sun 11am–6pm; closed Mon, Tues
$ Suggested donation $10 adults, $5 seniors/students, pay what you wish first Fri of the month

If you love your ballet and Balanchine in particular, you'll enjoy seeing some of the sets created by this Japanese artist, who strove to bring art and nature into the urban environment. These were Noguchi's studios and there are now more than 300 of his works on display. A fascinating spot for art and ballet buffs.

⊞▶ BRITTIP

For an active tour of Queens consider Back to the Old Country – The Ethnic Apple Tour offered by Bike The Big Apple (877 865-0078, bikethebigapple.com) a full day tour that leaves every Fri at 10am year round, weather permitting, and costs $90.

TASTE OF THE OUTER BOROUGHS

BRITTIP

Queens Theatre in the Park (718 760 0064, queenstheatre.org) at Flushing Meadows Corona Park hosts some excellent drama, dance and theatre performances, as well as music concerts and cabaret for all ages.

P.S. 1 CONTEMPORARY ART CENTER

- ✉ 22–25 Jackson Avenue at 46th Avenue, Long Island City
- ☎ 718-784 2084
- 🖰 ps1.org
- 🚇 Subway E, V to 23rd Street/Ely Avenue; G to 21st Street/Van Alst; 7 to 45th Road/Court House Square
- ⏱ Thurs–Mon noon–6pm
- $ Suggested donation $5 adults, $2 seniors/students

All forms of artistic expression are found in the oldest and second largest non-profit-making arts centre, affiliated to MoMA and known for its cutting edge exhibitions. Check out paintings and videos of performance art that depict elements of American culture and life in the 20th and 21st centuries.

BRITTIP

Why not travel to Queens by Water Taxi (nywater taxi.com)? Cruise up the East River and get off at Hunter's Point near the P.S. 1 Contemporary Art Center.

Queens County Farm Museum

P.S. 1 Contemporary Art Center

QUEENS BOTANICAL GARDEN

- ✉ 43-50 Main Street, Flushing
- ☎ 718-886 3800
- 🖰 queensbotanical.org
- 🚇 Subway 7 to Main St/Flushing then Q44 or Q20 bus or walk 8 blocks
- ⏱ April–Oct Tues–Fri 8am–6pm, Sat, Sun 8am–6pm; Nov–Mar Tues–Sun 8am–4.30pm, closed Mon
- $ $4 adults, $3 seniors and $2 students/children over 3. April – October. Nov-March Free. Walk back to the north-east corner of Corona Park to see the 16ha/39 acres of plants, shrubs and trees created for the 1939 World Fair.

BRITTIP

If you get thirsty, pop into one of the many fun, friendly and lively Irish pubs in Queens. You're bound to meet locals who'll be able to give you a colourful account of life in the 'burbs. Irish Circle (101–19 Rockaway Boulevard, 718-474 9002, irishcircletavern.com), Mary McGuire's (38–04 Broadway, Astoria, 719-728 3434) and the newer, Woodhaven House (63–98 Woodhaven Boulevard, 718-894 5400, woodhavenhouse.com) in Rego Park are highly recommended.

QUEENS COUNTY FARM MUSEUM

- ✉ 73-50 Little Neck Parkway at Union Turnpike, Floral Park
- ☎ 718-347 3276
- 🖰 queensfarm.org
- 🚇 Subway E, F to Kew Gardens/Union Turnpike, then take the Q46 bus to Little Neck Parkway
- ⏱ Mon–Fri 9am–5pm outdoor visiting only; free tours of the farmhouse are available Sat, Sun only 10am–5pm. Check website for paying special events like wine tasting or dinner on the farm days.

$ Free, $6 farmyard tour and hayride, $6 apple pressing workshops, $6 21 day eggs-periment

This 19-ha/47-acre site is the only working historical farm that still exists in New York and includes the 18th-century Adriance farmhouse, barns, outbuildings, a greenhouse and livestock. Animal feed is on sale to feed the sheep and goats, making it popular with little ones, as are the tractor-drawn hayrides offered on weekends April–Oct.

QUEENS MUSEUM OF ART

✉ New York City Building, Flushing Meadows/Corona Park
☎ 718-592 9700
⌂ queensmuseum.org
🚇 Subway 7 to Willets Point/Shea Stadium
◷ Wed–Sun 12–6pm; closed Mon–Tues
$ Suggested donation $5 adults; $2.50 seniors and children; children under 5 free.

The most famous exhibit here is the miniature scale model of the entire city of New York, complete with miniature lights that turn dark every 15 minutes, and aeroplanes flying into the airports. You can rent binoculars to check out where you're staying. The museum is on the site of the 1964 World Fair, reopened recently after a $15m renovation and which has seen new additions, including a multimedia spotlight on New York attractions. You can now adopt NY property on the Panorama from $50.

Socrates Sculpture Park

BRITTIP

Tours are free with admission every Sunday at 2pm, 3pm and 4pm. Private one-hour tours from noon to 5pm Wed–Sun from $75. Free on Sundays.

SHEA STADIUM

✉ 123-01 Roosevelt Ave, Flushing
☎ 718-507 8499/TIXX
⌂ http://newyork.mets.mlb.com
🚇 Subway 7 to Willets Point/Shea Stadium
◷ Ticket office Mon–Sat 9am–6pm; Sun 9am–5pm

Stroll through Corona Park to the home of the Mets baseball team (page 276). On the way you will see huge remnants of both the 1939 and the 1964 World Fairs, plus a series of weird buildings such as the New York Hall of Science. The park also has barbecue pits and boating on the lake. This is where Flushing Meadows plays host to the US Open tennis championship. As well as being a sports stadium, in the past it also hosted music concerts. Its stage has seen the likes of The Beatles, Jimi Hendrix, The Rolling Stones and Elton John.

SOCRATES SCULPTURE PARK

✉ 32-01 Vernon Boulevard at Broadway, Long Island City
☎ 718-956 1819
⌂ socratessculpturepark.org
🚇 Subway N or W (Mon–Fri only) to Broadway/Long Island City
◷ Daily 10am–sunset
$ Free

A great place to take children as they can climb, romp and run around these massive sculptures laid out in the park. Hard to believe it was once an abandoned riverside landfill and illegal dumpsite! It also has films outdoors in summer.

A TASTE OF STATEN ISLAND

With its picturesque scenery, Staten Island deserves its Indian name Monacnong, which means 'enchanted woods'. It's long been a haven for Italian-American and Irish-American populations and hasn't had a vast melting pot of cultures like the other outer boroughs. But in recent years that has slowly begun to change, with the population growing and diversifying. Hispanics now account for around 12% of the population, while 6% is Asian.

Even if you don't have much time you should try to fit in a trip on the free Staten Island Ferry, which leaves Manhattan Island from Battery Park (page 72) and offers brilliant views of Downtown and the Statue of Liberty.

(page 72)

BRITTIP
Staten Island was one of the communities hardest hit by the 11 September attacks, and has constructed its own uplifting memorial, opened in 2004, that looks like outstretched wings rising from the ground or a flower about to blossom. Pay your respects as you get off the ferry. It is on the adjacent North Shore Waterfront Esplanade.

ALICE AUSTEN HOUSE
A unique museum in the restored Victorian house and garden of Alice Austen, one of America's first female documentary photographers. A great place to gain an insight into life in New York at the turn of the century (see page 99).

(see page 99)

HISTORIC RICHMOND TOWN
- ✉ 441 Clarke Ave between St Patrick's Place and Richmond Road
- ☎ 718-351 1611 ext 280
- 🖱 historicrichmondtown.org
- 🚗 S74 bus from the ferry to Richmond Road and St Patrick's Place
- 🕐 Sept–June Wed–Sun 1–5pm; July–Aug Wed–Fri 11am–5pm, Sat, Sun 1–5pm
- $ Adults $5, seniors $4, children 5-17 $3.50

BRITTIP
Head down to the South Beach Boardwalk to catch a free concert if you're here in summer, or, if the family are in tow, to Midland Beach for sandcastle building and the Sea Turtle Fountain where kids can play under the sprinklers.

Historic Richmond Town

Jacques Marchais Museum

A magnificent 40.5-ha/100-acre village that features buildings from 300 years of life on the island including the oldest schoolhouse still standing, which was built in 1695 (that's really old by American standards!). Guided tours Wed–Fri 2.30pm, Sat and Sun 2pm and 3.30pm, apart from in the summer season when costumed interpreters and craftspeople demonstrate the chores, gardening, crafts and trade of daily life in this rural hamlet.

JACQUES MARCHAIS MUSEUM OF TIBETAN ART
- ✉ 338 Lighthouse Avenue
- ☎ 718-987 3500
- 🖱 tibetanmuseum.org
- 🚗 From Staten Island Ferry take bus S74 to Lighthouse Avenue
- 🕐 Wed–Sun 1pm–5pm
- $ $6 adults, $5 seniors/students; $3 children under 12 galleries and gardens

One of New York's best-kept secrets, which the Dalai Lama visited in 1991. It has terraced gardens and a fishpond. Inside, there are Tibetan, Nepalese and Mongolian arts from the 17th to the 19th century.

BRITTIP
Download a Staten Island map, or order one by mail from statenislandusa.com, that gives the low-down on cultural and other attractions, as well as parks and beaches.

Staten Island Botanical Park

ST SNUG HARBOR CULTURAL CENTER

✉ 1000 Richmond Terrace between Tysen Street and Snug Harbour Road
☎ 718-448 2500
🖰 snug-harbor.org
🚌 Bus S40 from the Staten Island Ferry to Snug Harbor
🕐 Tues–Sun 10am–5pm, closed Mon
$ $3 adults, $2 seniors/children under 12

On this plot of land once stood some rundown retirement homes for fishermen, which were going to be demolished by developers planning various money-making schemes. However, the local residents wanted it to be used for the community's benefit, and the result is a fascinating 33.5-hectare/83-acre park containing 26 buildings modelled on historical architecture, such as Greek revival Victorian and Italian Renaissance. The various buildings are used for events throughout the year, for example the Harmony Fair in June, a celebration of music, dance, food and cultures from around the world.

The Staten Island Botanical Park (718-448 2500), open dawn to dusk daily (free) is also here with the internationally renowned Chinese Scholar's Garden, which has courtyards, pools, a Tea House and pure-flow bridge. Open Tues–Sun 10am–4pm. Admission is $6 for adults, $5 students/seniors/children and guided tours are available for $4 per person.

Also in the grounds is Staten Island Children's Museum (718-273 2060, statenislandkids.org), with entertaining interactive exhibitions such as crawling through an ant hill to watch butterflies emerging from the chrysalis and exploring a pirate ship and becoming a sailor. Open Tues–Sun 12–5pm when school is in session, 10am–5pm during school holidays, and costs $5 for the over 1s. Great Explorations takes children from the rainforest canopy to dog-sledding and building an igloo and there's a chance to be a fireman, learn dog body language, host a radio show or go to sea on an outdoors boat (weather permitting). There's daily Storytime and Feeding the Animals sessions, a range of activities for tots and weekly creative workshops including Science Thursday and crafty kids on Tues, both 1.30–4.30pm.

BRITTIP

After a day of exploration you'll be hungry, so make a reservation at one of the tasty Staten Island restaurants. Angelina's Ristorante (399 Ellis Street, 718-227 2900, angelinasristorante.com) is good.

ST MARK'S PLACE, ST GEORGE

Standing on the hill above the St George Ferry terminal, St Mark's Place is the only landmarked historical district on Staten Island. Here New York's fabulous skyline forms a dramatic backdrop to a wonderful collection of residential buildings in Queen Ann, Greek revival and Italianate styles. Visit preserve.org/stgeorge for a self-guided walking tour.

CHAPTER 15
Essentials

TRAVEL INSURANCE

The one thing you should not forget when travelling to America is insurance. Medical cover is very expensive and if you are involved in an accident you could be sued, which could be very costly indeed. If you do want to make savings in this area, don't buy insurance from tour operators as they are notoriously expensive. We have taken a random selection of premiums offered by tour operators specialising in North America and found that 2 weeks' worth of cover for 1 person varied in price from £20 to a staggering £90. If you're travelling for up to 4 weeks, the premiums go up to nearly £110 per person.

The alternative, particularly if you plan to make more than 1 trip in any given year, is to go for an annual worldwide policy direct from the insurers. These can start at around £60 and go up to £120, and will normally cover all trips taken throughout the year up to a maximum of 31 days per trip. These worldwide annual policies make even more sense if you're travelling as a family. For instance, cover for 4 people bought from your tour operator could easily cost you £160 for a 2-week trip, which is little different from an annual worldwide family policy premium.

Companies offering annual worldwide insurance policies include the **AA** (0800 085 7240, theaa.com), **Barclays** (0800 015 4751, barclays.co.uk), **Bradford & Bingley** (0800 11 3333, bradford-bingley.co.uk/insurance), **Columbus** (0845 222 0020, columbus-insurance.com), **Direct Travel** (0845 605 2700, direct-travel.co.uk), **Norwich Union** (0800 121 007, norwich union.com), **Our Way** (020 8313 3900), **Post Office** (0800 169 9999, postoffice.co.uk), **Premier Direct** (0845 6028002, alliance-leicester.co.uk) and **Travel Insurance Direct** (0870 00 55 622, oinc.com). Many of these companies also offer straightforward holiday cover for a given period, such as 2 or 3 weeks, which again will be cheaper than insurance offered by tour operators.

To compare prices of most of the major insurers, go to moneysupermarket.com.

CHECK YOUR COVER

Policies vary not only in price but also in the cover they provide. In all cases, you need to ensure that the one you choose gives you the following:

▶ Medical cover of at least £2 million in America.
▶ Personal liability cover of at least £2 million in America.
▶ Cancellation and curtailment cover of around £3,000 in case you are forced to call off your holiday.
▶ Cover for lost baggage and belongings of around £1,500. Most premiums only offer cover for individual items worth up to around £250, so you will need additional cover for expensive cameras or camcorders.
▶ Cover for cash (usually around £200) and documents, including your air tickets, passport and currency.
▶ A 24-hour helpline to make it easy for you to get advice and instructions on what to do in an emergency.

THINGS TO WATCH OUT FOR

Sharp practices: In some cases your tour operator may imply that you must buy their travel insurance policy. This is never the case; you can always arrange your own. Alternatively, they may send you an invoice for your tickets that includes travel insurance unless you tick a certain box, so watch out.

Read the policy: Ask for a copy of the policy document before you go and, if you are not happy with the cover, cancel and demand your premium back. You may have only 7 days in which to do this.

Don't double up on cover: If you have an all-risks house insurance policy on your home contents, this will cover your belongings outside the home and may even cover lost money and credit cards. Check if this covers you abroad, and includes your belongings when in transit, before buying insurance for personal possessions.

MORE THINGS TO CHECK

Gold card cover: Some bank gold accounts and cards automatically provide you with travel insurance cover, such as Lloyds TSB

ESSENTIALS

297

(lloydstsb.com), which offers annual travel insurance plus Airmiles travel service.

Dangerous sports cover: In almost all cases, mountaineering, racing and hazardous pursuits such as bungee jumping, skydiving, horse riding, windsurfing, trekking and even cycling are not included in normal policies.

Make sure you qualify for full cover: If you have been treated in hospital during the 6 months prior to travelling or are waiting for hospital treatment, you may need medical evidence that you are fit to travel. If your doctor gives you the all clear (the report may cost £25) and the insurance company still says your condition is not eligible for the insurance you want, shop around to find the right cover.

HEALTH HINTS

Don't allow your dream trip to New York to be spoilt by not taking the right kind of precautions.

MEDICATION

If you are on regular medication, make sure you take sufficient for the duration of your trip. Always carry it in your hand baggage, in case your luggage goes astray, and make sure it is clearly labelled. If you should need more for any reason, remember that many drugs have a different name in the US, so check with your GP before you go.

BRITTIP
While we're on the subject of drugs, Class A drugs such as cocaine and heroin are illegal in the state of New York and, despite its liberal tendencies, so is marijuana. If you're caught with 25g/2oz or less of marijuana you can end up in prison for 5 days or be slapped with a large fine.

IN THE SUN

Although the biggest season for New York is winter, many Brits still travel to America at the hottest time of the year, the summer, and most are unprepared for the sheer intensity of the sun. Before you even think about going out for the day, apply a high-factor sun block (at least factor 15) as it is very easy to get sunburned when you are walking around sightseeing or shopping. It is also a good idea to wear a hat or scarf to protect your head from the sun, especially at the hottest times (11am–3pm), to prevent you from getting sunstroke. If it is windy, you may be lulled into thinking that it's not so hot.

BRITTIP
Always carry plenty of water, even in winter. Air conditioning and heating are incredibly dehydrating and you'll find yourself wanting to keel over very quickly without lots of liquid. It is also best to avoid drinking alcohol during the day.

SECURITY

AT YOUR HOTEL

In America, your hotel room number is your main source of security. It is often your passport to eating and collecting messages so keep the number safe and secure. When checking in, make sure none of the hotel staff mentions your room number out loud. If they do, give them back the key and ask them to give you a new room and to write down the new room number instead of announcing it (most hotels follow this practice in any case). When you need to give someone your room number – for instance, when charging a dinner or any other bill to your room – write it down or show them your room card rather than calling it out.

When in your hotel room, always put on the deadlocks and security chains and use the door peephole before opening the door. If someone knocks and you don't know who it is, or they don't have any identification, phone the reception desk. When you go out, make sure you lock the windows and door properly, even if you just leave your room to go to the ice machine.

CASH AND VALUABLES

Most hotels have safe deposit boxes, so use these to store important documents such as airline tickets and passports. Keep a separate record of your travellers' cheque numbers. When you go out, do not take all your cash and credit cards with you. Always leave at least 1 credit card in the safe as an emergency back-up and only take enough cash with you for the day.

Using a money belt is a good idea and, if your room does not come with its own safe, leave your valuables in the main hotel safe.

BRITTIP
American banknotes are similar in size and colour so familiarise yourself with the bills in the safety of your room before you go out so you don't end up handing over the wrong amount all the time. Keep large denominations separate from small ones.

EMERGENCIES

For the police, fire department or ambulance: Dial 911 (9-911 from a hotel room). This is a free number, even from mobiles.

If it's a medical emergency: Call the front desk of your hotel as many have arrangements with doctors for house calls. If they don't, they may tell you to go to the nearest casualty (emergency) department, but that's really not a good idea (Haven't you seen *ER*?). Instead, you have 3 choices: contact **New York Hotel Urgent Medical Services** on 212-737 1212, travelmd.com, **Dial-a-Doctor** on 212-971 9692, or walk in or make an appointment at a **DOCS Medical Center**. There are 3 in Manhattan: 55 East 34th Street (212-252 6000), 1555 3rd Avenue (212-828 2300) and 202 West 23rd Street (212-352 2600).

If you need a pharmacy: There are several 24-hour pharmacies, mostly run by the Duane Reade chain. The most centrally located 24-hour pharmacy is at 224 West 57th Street at Broadway (212-541 9708, duanereade.com), near Columbus Circle.

If you need a dentist: You can call 212-679 3966 or 212-371 0500. If you need help after hours, try the 24-hour Emergency Dental Associates on 212-972 9299, nysdental.org.

British information services: 845 3rd Avenue, NY, NY 10022, ukinusa.fco.gov.uk. This is the information service of the British embassy in Washington and acts as the political, press and public affairs office of the New York Consulate-General, which covers the states of New York, New Jersey, Connecticut and Pennsylvania.

BRITTIP

From 10 February 2011, a new design of the $100 bill will be issued. The front has an enlarged portrait of Benjamin Franklin, a unique teal background and words from the Declaration of Independence. The back has a picture of the rear of Independence Hall. The new bills contain Crane & Co., a security feature that allows an underlying image to shift when moved to prevent counterfeiting.

SAFETY IN CARS

Unless you have a driver, a car in New York is not a good idea. If you do hire a car, however, be sensible. Never leave your car unlocked or leave any valuable items on the car seats or anywhere else where they can be seen. Always put maps and brochures in the glove compartment as these will be obvious signs that your car belongs to a tourist.

NEW YORK STREET SAVVY

It may surprise you to know that New York City remains the safest big city in the USA, according to the FBI. Although the city is nowhere near as dangerous as it used to be, it is still a large city and there are always people on the lookout for an easy opportunity. To reduce your chances of becoming a victim of street crime, follow these simple guidelines:

▶ Always be aware of what is going on around you and keep an arm free – criminals tend to target people who are preoccupied or have both arms laden down with packages or briefcases.

Trump Tower

▶ Stick to well-populated, well-lit areas and, if possible, don't go out alone.

▶ Don't engage any suspicious people, such as street beggars, in conversation, though you can tip buskers if you wish.

▶ Visible jewellery can attract the wrong kind of attention. If you are a woman wearing rings, turn them round so that the stone or setting side is palm-in.

▶ If you're wearing a coat, put it on over the strap of your shoulder bag.

▶ Men should keep wallets in their front trouser or inside coat pockets or in a shoulder strap.

▶ Pickpockets work in teams, often involving children to create a diversion.

▶ Watch out for pickpockets and scam artists, especially in busy areas, as you would in any big city.

▶ Do not carry your wallet or valuables in a bumbag. Thieves can easily cut the belt and disappear into the crowds before you've worked out what has happened.

BRITTIP

It cannot be stressed enough that you should only ever carry as little cash as possible – and never count your money in public.

A useful trick is to have 2 wallets – a cheap one carried in your hip pocket or bag containing about $20 in cash and some out-of-date credit cards, and another hidden somewhere on your body or in a money belt containing the bulk of your cash and credit cards. If you are approached by someone who demands money from you, your best bet is to get away as quickly as possible. Do this by throwing your fake wallet or purse in one direction, while you run, shouting for help, in the other. The chances are that the mugger will just pick up the wallet and run off rather than chase after you. If you hand over your wallet and just stand still, the mugger is more likely to demand your watch and jewellery, too. This advice is even more important for women, who could be vulnerable to personal attack or rape if they hang around.

Having given you some essential safety advice, however, it is important to remember that this is very much common sense and applies if you are travelling almost anywhere in the world, especially in a major city. New York is a busy, feisty city, but it is a great holiday destination and no doubt you'll have a brilliant time and want to come back soon!

Strawberry Fields, Central Park

INDEX to MAP PAGES

LEGEND

92	Highways/Interstate
3	Throughroutes
	Main Roads
	Other Roads
	Railways
	Places of Interest
	Bus/Rail Stations
	Parks
SOHO	Districts

MAP 8

MAP 7

MAP 6

MAP 5

MAP 4

MAP 3

MAP 2

MAP 1

MAP 11

MAP 9

MAP 10

Queens

New York

Manhattan

Brooklyn

Upper New
York Bay

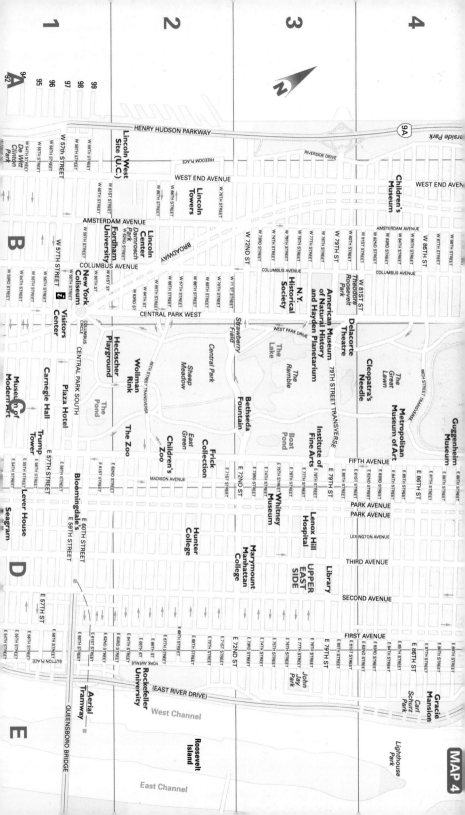

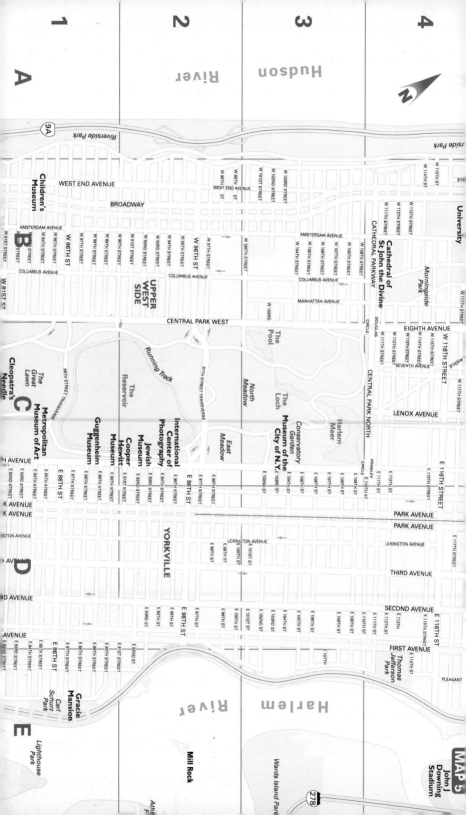

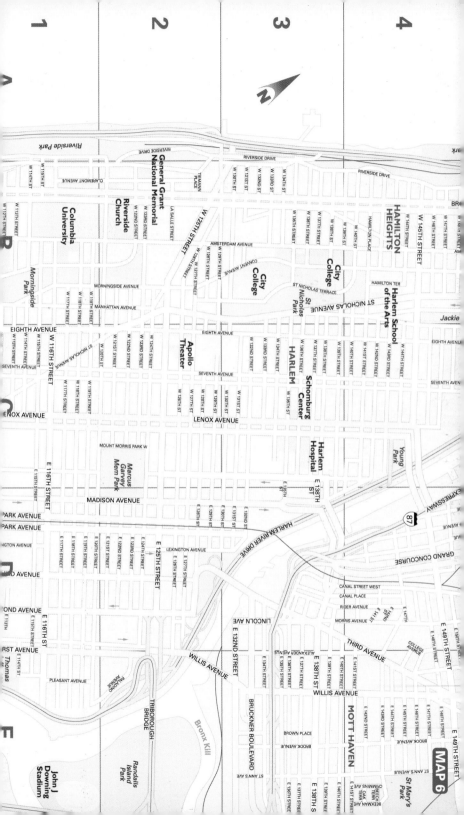

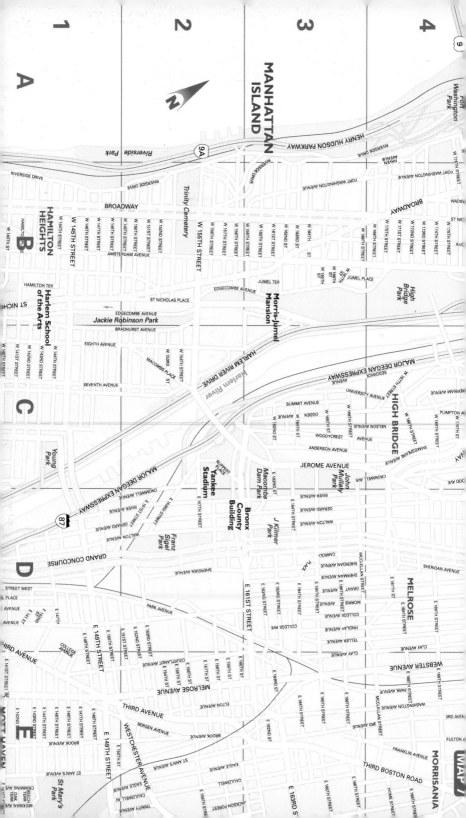

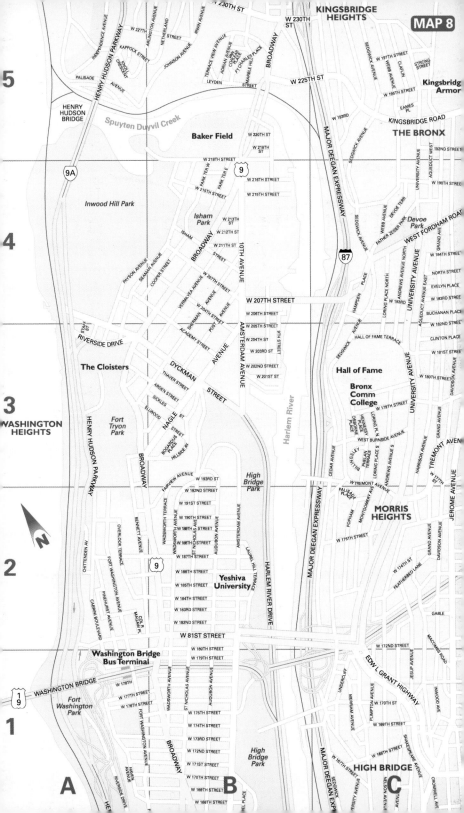

MANHATTAN STREET INDEX

Single bold number refers to map number
Alpha numerics refer to those within specified map

1st Place	**1** B1–C1
1st Street (E)	**2** D2
2nd Street (E)	**2** D2–E2
3rd Avenue	**7** E4–E3
3rd Street (E)	**2** D2–E2
3rd Street (W)	**2** C2
4th Street (E)	**2** C2–E2
4th Street (W)	**2** C2
5th Street (E)	**2** C2–E2
6th Street (E)	**2** C2–E2
7th Street (E)	**2** C2–E2
8th Street (E)	**2** C2, D2–E2
8th Street (W)	**2** C2
9th Street	**8** B4–B3
9th Street (W)	**2** D2–E2
10th Avenue	**8** B4
10th Street (E)	**2** D2–E2
10th Street (W)	**2** B2
11th Street (E)	**2** D3–E2
11th Street (W)	**2** B2
12th Street (E)	**2** D3–E3
12th Street (W)	**2** A2–B2
13th Street (E)	**2** C3–E3
13th Street (W)	**2** A3–C3
14th Street (E)	**2** C3–E3
14th Street (W)	**2** A3–C3
15th Street (E)	**2** C3–D3
15th Street (W)	**2** A3–C3
16th Street (E)	**2** C3–D3
16th Street (W)	**2** A3–C3
17th Street (E)	**2** C3–D3
17th Street (W)	**2** A3–C3
18th Street (E)	**2** C3–D3
18th Street (W)	**2** A3–C3
19th Street (E)	**2** C3–D3
19th Street (W)	**2** A4–C3
20th Street (E)	**2** C4–D3
20th Street (W)	**2** A4–C4
21st Street (E)	**2** C4–D4
21st Street (W)	**2** A4–C4
22nd Street (E)	**2** C4–D4
22nd Street (W)	**2** A4–C4
23rd Street (E)	**2** C4–D4
23rd Street (W)	**2** A4–C4
24th Street (E)	**2** C4–D4
24th Street (W)	**2** A4–C4
25th Street (E)	**2** C4–D4
25th Street (W)	**3** A1–C1
26th Street (E)	**3** C1–D1
26th Street (W)	**3** A1–C1
27th Street (E)	**3** C1–D1
27th Street (W)	**3** A1, B1–C1
28th Street (E)	**3** C1–D1
28th Street (W)	**3** A1–C1
29th Street (E)	**3** C1–D1
29th Street (W)	**3** A1–C1
30th Street (E)	**3** C1–D1
30th Street (W)	**3** A1–C1
31st Street (E)	**3** C1–D1
31st Street (W)	**3** C1
32nd Street (E)	**3** C2–D1
32nd Street (W)	**3** B2
33rd Street (E)	**3** C2–D2
33rd Street (W)	**3** A2–D2
34th Street (E)	**3** C2–D2
34th Street (W)	**3** A2–D2
35th Street (E)	**3** C2–D2
35th Street (W)	**3** B2
36th Street (E)	**3** C2–D2
36th Street (W)	**3** B2–C2
37th Street (E)	**3** C2–D2
37th Street (W)	**3** B2–C2
38th Street (E)	**3** C2–D2
38th Street (W)	**3** B2–C2
39th Street (E)	**3** C2–D2
39th Street (W)	**3** B2–C2
40th Street (E)	**3** C2–D2
40th Street (W)	**3** A2–C2
41st Street (E)	**3** C2–D2
41st Street (W)	**3** A3–C2
42nd Street (E)	**3** C3–D2
42nd Street (W)	**3** A3–C3
43rd Street (E)	**3** C3
43rd Street (W)	**3** A3–C3
44th Street (E)	**3** C3–D3
44th Street (W)	**3** A3–C3
45th Street (E)	**3** C3–D3
45th Street (W)	**3** A3–C3
46th Street (E)	**3** C3–D3
46th Street (W)	**3** A3–C3
47th Street (E)	**3** C3–D3
47th Street (W)	**3** A3–C3
48th Street (E)	**3** C3–D3
48th Street (W)	**3** A3–C3
49th Street (E)	**3** C3–D3
49th Street (W)	**3** A3–B3
50th Street (E)	**3** D3
50th Street (W)	**3** A3–C3
51st Street (E)	**3** C3–D3
51st Street (W)	**3** A4–C3
52nd Street (E)	**3** C4–E3
52nd Street (W)	**3** A4–C4
53rd Street (E)	**3** C4–E4
53rd Street (W)	**3** B4
54th Street (E)	**3** C4–E4
54th Street (W)	**3** A4–C4
55th Street (E)	**3** C4–E4
55th Street (W)	**3** A4–C4
56th Street (E)	**3** C4–E4
56th Street (W)	**3** A4–B4
57th Street (E)	**3** C4–D4
57th Street (W)	**4** A1
58th Street (E)	**4** C1
58th Street (W)	**4** A1–B1
59th Street (E)	**4** D1
59th Street (W)	**4** A1–B1
60th Street (E)	**4** C1–E1
60th Street (W)	**4** B1
61st Street (E)	**4** C1–E1
61st Street (W)	**4** B1
62nd Street (E)	**4** C2–E1
62nd Street (W)	**4** B2
63rd Street (E)	**4** C2–E2
63rd Street (W)	**4** B2
64th Street (E)	**4** C2–E2
64th Street (W)	**4** B2
65th Street (E)	**4** C2–E2
65th Street (W)	**4** B2
66th Street (E)	**4** C2–E2
66th Street (W)	**4** B2
66th Street Transverse	**4** C2
67th Street (E)	**4** C2–E2
67th Street (W)	**4** B2
68th Street (E)	**4** C2–E2
68th Street (W)	**4** B2
69th Street (E)	**4** C2–E2
69th Street (W)	**4** B2
70th Street (E)	**4** D2–E2
70th Street (W)	**4** B2
71st Street (E)	**4** C2–E2
71st Street (W)	**4** B2
72nd Street (E)	**4** B3–E2
72nd Street (W)	**4** A3–B3
73rd Street (E)	**4** C3–E3
73rd Street (W)	**4** B3
74th Street (E)	**4** C3–E3
74th Street (W)	**4** B3
75th Street (E)	**4** C3–E3
75th Street (W)	**4** B3
76th Street (E)	**4** C3–E3
76th Street (W)	**4** B3
77th Street (E)	**4** C3–E3
77th Street (W)	**4** B3
78th Street (E)	**4** C3–E3
78th Street (W)	**4** B3
79th Street (E)	**4** C3–E3
79th Street (W)	**4** B3
79th Street Transverse	**4** C3
80th Street (E)	**4** C3–E3
80th Street (W)	**4** B3
81st Street (E)	**4** C3–E3
81st Street (W)	**4** B4
82nd Street (E)	**4** C4–E4
82nd Street (W)	**4** B4
83rd Street (E)	**4** C4–E4
83rd Street (W)	**4** B4
84th Street (E)	**4** C4–E4
84th Street (W)	**4** B4
85th Street (E)	**4** C4–E4
85th Street (W)	**5** A1–B1
86th Street (E)	**5** C1–E1
86th Street (W)	**5** A1–B1
86th Street Transverse	**5** C1
87th Street (E)	**5** C1–E1
87th Street (W)	**5** A1–B1
88th Street (E)	**5** C1–E1
88th Street (W)	**5** A1–B1
89th Street (E)	**5** C1–E1
89th Street (W)	**5** A1–B1
90th Street (E)	**5** C1–E1
90th Street (W)	**5** B2–B1
91st Street (E)	**5** C2–E1
91st Street (W)	**5** B2
92nd Street (E)	**5** C2–E2
92nd Street (W)	**5** B2
93rd Street (E)	**5** C2–D2
93rd Street (W)	**5** B2
94th Street (E)	**5** C2–E2
94th Street (W)	**5** B2
95th Street (E)	**5** C2–D2
95th Street (W)	**5** B2
96th Street (E)	**5** C2–D2
96th Street (W)	**5** B2
97th Street (E)	**5** C2–D2
97th Street (W)	**5** B2
97th Street Transverse	**5** C2
98th Street (E)	**5** C2–D2
98th Street (W)	**5** B2
99th Street (E)	**5** D2
99th Street (W)	**5** B2
100th Street (E)	**5** D2
100th Street (W)	**5** B3
101st Street (E)	**5** D3
101st Street (W)	**5** B3
102nd Street (E)	**5** C3–D3
102nd Street (W)	**5** B3
103rd Street (E)	**5** C3–D3, D3
103rd Street (W)	**5** B3
104th Street (E)	**5** C3–D3
104th Street (W)	**5** B3
105th Street (E)	**5** C3–D3, D3–E3
105th Street (W)	**5** B3
106th Street (E)	**5** C3–E3
106th Street (W)	**5** B3
107th Street (E)	**5** C3–D3, E3
107th Street (W)	**5** B3
108th Street (E)	**5** C3–D3, D3–E3
108th Street (W)	**5** B3
109th Street (E)	**5** C3–E3
109th Street (W)	**5** B3
110th Street (E)	**5** C4–E3
111th Street (E)	**5** C4–E4
111th Street (W)	**5** B4, C4
112th Street (E)	**5** C4–D4
112th Street (W)	**5** B4–C4
113th Street (E)	**5** D4
113th Street (W)	**5** B4–C4
114th Street (E)	**5** E4
114th Street (W)	**5** B4–C4
115th Street (E)	**5** C4–E4
115th Street (W)	**6** B1–C1
116th Street (E)	**6** C1–E1
116th Street (W)	**6** C1
117th Street (E)	**6** C1–E1
117th Street (W)	**6** B1–C1
118th Street (E)	**6** C1–E1
118th Street (W)	**6** B1–C1
119th Street (E)	**6** C1–E1
119th Street (W)	**6** B1–C1
120th Street (E)	**6** C1–E1
120th Street (W)	**6** B2–C2
121st Street (E)	**6** C2–D2
121st Street (W)	**6** B2–C2
122nd Street (E)	**6** C2–D2
122nd Street (W)	**6** B2–C2
123rd Street (E)	**6** C2–D2
123rd Street (W)	**6** B2–C2
124th Street (E)	**6** C2–D2
124th Street (W)	**6** B2–C2
125th Street (E)	**6** C2–D2
125th Street (W)	**6** B2–C2
126th Street (E)	**6** C2–D2
126th Street (W)	**6** B2–C2
127th Street (E)	**6** B2–C2
127th Street (W)	**6** C2–D2
128th Street (E)	**6** B2, C2
128th Street (W)	**6** C2–D2
129th Street (E)	**6** B2, C2
129th Street (W)	**6** C2–D2
130th Street (E)	**6** C3–D3
130th Street (W)	**6** B3, C3
131st Street (E)	**6** C3–D3
131st Street (W)	**6** B3, C3
132nd Street (E)	**6** D3, D3–E3
132nd Street (W)	**6** B3, C3
133rd Street (W)	**6** B3, C3
134th Street (E)	**6** D3–E3
134th Street (W)	**6** B3, C3
135th Street (E)	**6** C3–D3, E3
135th Street (W)	**6** B3, C3
136th Street (E)	**6** E3
136th Street (W)	**6** B3, C3
137th Street (E)	**6** D3–E3
137th Street (W)	**6** B3, C3
138th Street (E)	**6** C3–D3, D3–E3
138th Street (W)	**6** B3, C3
139th Street (E)	**6** D3–E3
139th Street (W)	**6** B4, C3
140th Street (E)	**6** D3–E3
140th Street (W)	**6** B4, C4
141st Street (E)	**6** D4, E4
141st Street (W)	**6** C4
142nd Street (E)	**6** D4, E4
142nd Street (W)	**6** C4
143rd Street (E)	**6** E4
143rd Street (W)	**6** C4
144th Street (W)	**6** E4
144th Street (E)	**7** B1–C1
145th Street (E)	**7** E1
145th Street (W)	**7** B1–C1
146th Street (E)	**7** E1
146th Street (W)	**7** B1
147th Street (E)	**7** D1, E1
147th Street (W)	**7** B1, C1
148th Street (E)	**7** D1–E1
148th Street (W)	**7** B1
149th Street (E)	**7** D1–E1
149th Street (W)	**7** B2
150th Street (E)	**7** D1–E1, E1
150th Street (W)	**7** B2, C2
151st Street (E)	**7** D2, D2–E2
151st Street (W)	**7** B2

Index